HANDBOOK OF
RACIAL-CULTURAL PSYCHOLOGY AND COUNSELING

HANDBOOK OF

RACIAL-CULTURAL PSYCHOLOGY AND COUNSELING

Training and Practice

Volume Two

Edited by

ROBERT T. CARTER

WILEY

John Wiley & Sons, Inc.

Library of Congress Cataloging-in-Publication Data:

Handbook of racial-cultural psychology and counseling : theory and research, volume 2 / edited by
    Robert T. Carter.
      p. cm.
    Includes bibliographical references.
    ISBN 0-471-38628-6 (cloth : v. 1) — ISBN 0-471-38629-4 (cloth : v. 2) —
    ISBN 0-471-65625-9 (set)
      1. Psychiatry, Transcultural—Handbooks, manuals, etc. 2. Psychology—Cross-cultural
    studies—Handbooks, manuals, etc. 3. Cross-cultural counseling—Handbooks, manuals, etc.
    I. Carter, Robert T., 1948–
    RC455.4E8H368 2004
    616.59—dc22

                                                                        2004042222

Contents

112728

A Cultural-Historical Model for Understanding Racial-Cultural Competence and Confronting Dynamic Cultural Conflicts: An Introduction

As discussed in the Introduction to Volume One, Jennifer Simon, who was at Wiley at the time, was instrumental in convincing me to edit the two-volume reference *Handbook on Racial-Cultural Psychology and Counseling.* I agreed to take the project through her persistence and encouragement. She prompted me to think about what type of material would help advance the field and at the same time build on existing research and scholarship. It was also her belief that conceptual and research issues combined into one volume with training and practice would not be practical. More important, as we discussed the project, it seemed unwise to try to combine what might be a large body of scholarship into one volume. So, reluctantly, I agreed to think in terms of two volumes for the *Handbook,* one that focused on critical and core concepts and research findings and one devoted to practice and training in racial-cultural counseling and psychology. The task of editing a collection of scholarship is demanding. Yet the complexity of putting together a two-volume reference handbook was beyond what I might have imagined. The *Handbook* is a reflection of the patience and commitment of the contributors and the editorial assistants who helped keep things organized.

During my conversation with Jennifer Simon I became convinced that what was needed in the field was a collection of scholarship that met two important goals. One goal was for the material to go beyond the typical emphasis on "minorities" as the focus for cultural knowledge, mental health interventions, and training. The other goal was to use a conceptual framework for the *Handbook* that was distinctive and important.

DEFINING TERMS: WHY A RACIAL-CULTURAL FOCUS?

In the Introduction to Volume One, I explain how I came to think in terms of racial-cultural as a conceptual framework and how come I use that perspective as opposed to the conceptual framework reflected in the popular terms "multicultural" and "cultural diversity." I contend that such broad terms are useful only if one intends to address a range of differing and distinct reference group memberships as equally important (i.e., gender, ethnicity, sexual orientation, region, social class). Because so much is included in such broad concepts and frameworks it is hard to know what the specific cultural reference is; moreover, it becomes possible to argue for greater and greater inclusiveness until the meaning and use of the term become lost and one is unable to guide training or practice. An example offered by Alderfer (2000) stands out in my mind. In a discussion on how language about race relations has been altered in organizations and political discourse, he makes an important observation about the use of the term "diversity." Noting that the term was introduced to affirm group differences, he proceeds:

> As time has passed, however, the practical meaning of [multicultural or cultural] diversity has become increasingly diffuse. It no longer stands for a variety of meaningful group memberships. It has been transformed to include virtually any dimension of human difference that someone might choose to notice. (p. 30)

Alderfer followed—his observation with an illustration of a dialogue that took place between two White men at a corporate diversity training session. One man notes that he thinks of his coworkers differently or not in a negative way now that he has been taught about diversity. In another exchange, a 40-year-old White male states:

> Now take this company. We used to be required to wear only red neckties. Now that we have a corporate policy to value diversity, we can wear blue ties as well. This corporation values diversity (Laughter again). (p. 30)

Clearly, it is important to use terms and concepts that convey more specifically the aspects of race or culture of concern and interest for training and practice. Therefore, I have introduced a typology of assumptions as a way to clarify the meaning of various terms related to racial and cultural differences. In Volume One's Introduction, I describe five assumptions that seem to underlie the various terms people use in scholarship and practice associated with cultural difference (Carter, 2000b, this *Handbook,* Volume One). In brief, the assumptions of cultural difference and their meaning could fall into the following types:

Universal: A focus on the individual and individual difference is the traditional psychological perspective.

Ubiquitous: Social identity groups are treated as equally important aspects of cultural and social group differences, also termed multicultural or culture diversity.

Traditional: One's country as culture perspective—is reflected in globalization, international, intercultural or transcultural perspectives, in psychology and counseling.

Race-based: Race, as socially constructed categories based on skin color, physical features, and language, is the basis of culture, with psychological variations within racial groups.

Pan-national: Oppressed/oppressing groups are the context for culture and differences in culture, reflecting imperial and colonial divisions of countries and the resulting meaning of culture that emerged.

What makes the typology of assumptions necessary is the confusion surrounding the use of language regarding racial-cultural differences and what appears to be a lack of attention to the historical beginning of the field of psychology and other mental health disciplines. It is imperative that we understand that only through the prism of our past can racial-cultural competence be applied effectively in training and practice. The need for racial-cultural training and practice arises because of the central and critical place in our history and current life that race, and through race culture, holds. Each citizen and immigrant learns to understand differences between groups on the basis of race (APA, 2003). In addition, other reference groups (e.g., gender, social class, sexual orientation, ethnicity, age) have meaning in the context of one's race and psychologically identified culture. I believe that a multicultural perspective is too broad, vague, and nonspecific, and that it deemphasizes race and its meaning and ignores Whites as members of racial-cultural groups (Carter, 2000b).

Nevertheless, there is value in using terms or conceptual frameworks that are broad and inclusive. Members of the dominant racial-cultural groups feel less threat and more acceptance. The cost is that historically disenfranchised racial groups and some members of sociodemographic groups are left behind or forgotten (e.g., poor and working-class people). Moreover, the use of the terms diversity and multicultural allow people, regardless of their race or social position, the opportunity to think of themselves as a member of an oppressed "group." Last, the lens and power of the superordinate dominant cultural worldview seems to be obscured when multiculturalism is the focus of cultural competence (see Carter, 2000b; Helms & Cook, 1999).

In my own teaching, consultation, training, and clinical practice, it has become apparent that people struggle more with race than any other group membership. Also, in teaching, consultation and training, when I have not focused on or introduced race as the primary subject of the course or workshop discussion, race is brought in and used as a proxy for culture or it is ignored. Students and participants (regardless of race) often assume that only people of Color are members of racial groups or they ignore race as an aspect of difference. So it seems to me that a race-based approach to cultural understanding and building competency in counseling and psychology is essential and imperative. It is one of the things we think we know about a person on sight, and from that visible marker we make automatic assumptions about qualities, abilities, behaviors, and other reference group memberships (e.g., ethnicity, religion, social class; Carter, 2003).

To be clear about the concepts and core ideas for a racial-cultural approach to counseling and therapy for the handbook I asked contributors to adhere to the following distinctions and definitions of core ideas of race, culture, and ethnicity. My letter inviting contributions to this volume in part stated:

The *Handbook* is intended to be one that focuses on Racial-Cultural Psychology, which in my view is a perspective on cultural difference that uses race as the context for understanding culture. However, it does not mean that one should focus on specific racial groups. Rather, the focus should be on how race and through race culture, effects psychological and social functioning. The conceptual idea of race is defined in terms of skin color, language, and physical features and its sociopolitical use. Ethnicity is defined as one's country of origin and is connected to one's heritage and family background. Culture is defined as patterns of behavior and thought learned through socialization.

I ask that you work with me in an effort to achieve coherence and consistency around these important constructs. In addition, I request that you use the conceptual schema outlined above with regard to race, culture, and ethnicity and that you use the racial-cultural frame for the development of your chapter.

Many contributors applied the distinctions and some did not. It was hard for some to let go of the focus on people of Color or "minorities." I contend that such a focus is victim-oriented and does not capture the reality of how we as Americans understand racial-cultural interactions. I think we are socialized to think of cultural difference as racial difference. We also tend to be less conscious of the patterns of our dominant superordinate American cultural patterns and confuse culture, race, and ethnicity.

THE AMERICAN WORLDVIEW AND CULTURAL LEARNING

One would expect that how mental health professionals are trained and the ideas that they bring to their training and practice are central to the health and well-being of the people they seek to serve. To the extent that the values, attitudes, and beliefs that mental health professionals learn in training are congruent with the people they help, their effectiveness is greatly enhanced. To the extent that there are incongruities between the system of care, the client, and the helper's interventions, the more likely the care will be ineffective.

Training and mental health practices are shaped by several interrelated factors. One significant factor is the worldview or the cultural patterns and beliefs of the dominant group in the society. The dominant group's cultural beliefs shape the norms and structure of institutions and organizations (see Carter & Pieterse, this *Handbook,* Volume One). All institutions and organizations are linked in that they exist to serve the goals and pass on the teachings and values of the society as reflected in the worldview of the dominant racial-cultural groups (Carter, 1995, 2000a).

These institutions and organizations include schools, colleges and universities, hospitals, mental health systems, and families and communities. Families socialize their members to participate in the structure of society and teach the values, communication patterns, behaviors, attitudes, and beliefs that are congruent with the sociocultural context in which they live (see Bowser, this *Handbook,* Volume One; Yeh & Hunter, this *Handbook,* Volume One).

The North American Eurocentric view dominates theory and practice in mental health professions and in society in general. This dominance has not allowed for consideration that other cultural worldviews may exist or should be understood. The prevailing view is that mental health professionals assume that the dominant racial-cultural worldview is universal. Differing worldviews are not taught or used in practice so that mental health professionals can be racially and culturally competent and effective (Helms & Cook, 1999; Sue & Sue, 1999, 2003).

By racial-cultural competency I do not mean being able to work primarily with non-White or immigrant group members. Racial-cultural competence as I define it is broad: It encompasses conscious knowledge of one's own racial-cultural group; it means recognizing the versatility of knowing, feeling, and behaving in particular ways due to one's reference group within one's own racial-cultural worldview (i.e., gender, ethnicity, social class, religion); and it means having knowledge about people who belong to groups other than one's own, including factual information about each group's social-political history and how that history influences the group's current status and participation in the country. To achieve racial-cultural competency, self-knowledge coupled with knowledge of one's racial-cultural group must be enhanced by individual racial-cultural self-exploration and development (Carter, 2001, 2003). One must evolve an identity that is free of bias, or in which the existence of bias is recognized and monitored. Said another way, effective and competent mental health professionals have evolved advanced racial and ethnic group identities such that they are able to facilitate growth and exploration in others as educators, advocates, policymakers, or practitioners.

Yet, unlike other scholars, I contend that the knowledge of one's reference groups comes through the lens of racial group membership and one's racial identity ego status. That is, how one understands one's ethnic or gender group membership is determined by one's racial group and one's corresponding racial identity ego status (Carter & Pieterse, this *Handbook,* Volume One).

The approach that I advocate treats all racial-cultural groups as important to understand and focus on in our teaching and practice. We should avoid the practice of describing the ills of our social system and the outcomes of exploitation and oppression by focusing on the victims of oppression. Emphasis on the victims of oppression, regardless of the group of interest, is a limited and fragmented view. The use of such a victim focus does not help us fully understand the role of racial-cultural worldviews, sociocultural norms, and institutional policies in the development of illness or in notions of abnormality and health. We must make a conscious effort to keep in the foreground the context of our racial-cultural worldview and remember how it sets and shapes our perceptions, thinking, feelings, interaction patterns, communication styles, and beliefs about what is normal and what is not. It is easier to see cultural difference in those who are immigrants to the United States, but somewhat more difficult to see the role of race and culture among people who belong to groups that have been here for many generations. Furthermore, we must always remember that skin color, physical features, and language are the primary sources of difference in our society, culture and communities, and at the same time that there are other sources of difference that also need to be understood.

CULTURE AND COMMUNITY

Many professionals accept that our cultural and social environments shape who we are and how we behave and feel in the world. Often, our culture is reflected in our neighborhoods and communities. Many racial communities have historically been segregated; today many are still subject to external forces that maintain their social separation, while other communities may exist as distinct enclaves by choice. Nevertheless, our experiences as members of racial-cultural groups in society, as well as our personal understanding of that experience (i.e., one's racial-cultural identity), affect our mental health.

Our racial-cultural context (race, ethnic group, gender, religion, language, social class, etc.) influences how we understand health and mental well-being. Our culture also determines what is considered normal and abnormal. The circumstances we encounter in society, such as access to work, shelter, and health care, also influence our understanding of our experience and how we function in our communities and in society.

It is important to acknowledge at the outset the elements of American culture or worldview that characterize our society and dominate our belief systems, behaviors, and expectations. American culture has evolved from White ethnic upper- and middle-class values and beliefs. American cultural systems are superordinate to ethnic group values. According to Carter (1995, 2000a) and Marger (2000), White American cultural patterns include individualism, expressed through personal preferences; self-expression, reflected in a combination of conformity to social expectations and achievement of goals based on external criteria (e.g., good grades, good job); authority and power that is hierarchical; communication patterns that are verbal and normal only if standard English forms are used; a future time orientation; a Judeo-Christian religious system; belief that the nuclear family structure is ideal; and standards of music, beauty, and social traditions (holidays, monuments, etc.) based on European cultures. And a way of knowing that is practical and technical and that reduces ideas to their simplest terms (parsimony) and discusses ideas in terms of common elements (Stewart & Bennett, 1991).

Thus, our way of understanding health, both physical and mental, is based on the worldview that characterizes our culture and is embedded in our professions and institutions. What do we know about cultural influences on mental health? The National Institute of Mental Health's (NIMH, 2003) Web page reports cultural differences from a traditional assumptive perspective and notes. For instance, people with schizophrenia do better in developing countries than in North America; a majority of people in Nigeria and India who are thought to have schizophrenia were better or in remission in about two years. Anthropological and cross-cultural studies have shown that cultural beliefs about mental illness affects its course and treatment. For White Americans, a person with schizophrenia is "crazy," with no hope for recovery, whereas in other countries the same people are seen as having a temporary condition that can be addressed.

Race and culture also influence diagnosis. Researchers find but cannot explain, that Black African/Americans are more often diagnosed with schizophrenia and are less often diagnosed as having affective disorders than White Americans (NIMH, 2003). Researchers argue that this reflects cultural bias on the part of clinicians (irrespective of racial-cultural group membership) who are socialized and taught during professional development to see people of Color and Blacks as more disturbed than Whites.

When participants in research studies are members of the dominant culture group, the studies' conclusions are overwhelmingly believed to apply across racial-cultural groups (i.e., are believed to be universal). Thus, the expressions of normality and illness in the majority race and culture are assumed to be true of all people irrespective of race, culture, or ethnicity. Evidence to the contrary has been mostly ignored or de-emphasized (NIMH, 2003). Yet, decades of research make it quite clear that however universal the categories (e.g., depression) of mental illness may be, the patterns of onset and duration and even the nature and clustering of specific symptoms vary widely across racial and cultural groups.

There is also racial-cultural variation in how people view and understand self and personal identity (Sue & Sue, 2003). For instance, among many Asian cultures, the self is interdependent (Yeh & Hunter, this *Handbook,* Volume One); in dominant North American cultural practices, the self is primarily individual and internal. Because mental health is influenced by notions of self and personal identity, Asians' relationships with others matter a great deal to and affect their mental health. Regardless of culture, we are all humans and therefore share similarities in our physiological and neurochemical systems. Thus, some common expressions of emotion do seem to characterize human experience. However, subjective meaning associated with particular emotions and their expression vary by culture.

Members of racial-cultural groups vary in the level of identification and investment they make in their group culture. Acculturation to the dominant culture and levels of psychological identification with the racial group vary by individual, and the variation influences the meaning and significance of the group and its culture for the individual person. Socioeconomic resources, among other factors, also influence the vulnerability one has to stressors of life events. Fewer resources and lower social status seem to be associated with greater vulnerability to life event stressors. One's community and its organizations can have both positive and negative effects on mental health. Support systems and organizations that seek to reduce the effects of social, personal, and economic problems can protect people from the harm of stressors and reduce the incidence and prevalence of negative mental and physical health outcomes (NIMH, 2003).

It is easy to see differences when people speak another language, wear clothes that are different, or look physically different. It is harder to see and understand cultural differences in perception of the world, in thinking, and in interpersonal relationships when there is more perceived similarity. It is more difficult within the context of American society where many groups of Americans have been in the society for hundreds of years and acculturated but not assimilated into mainstream cultural patterns (Marger, 2000). Under these circumstances, it is difficult to discern less obvious racial-cultural variation among Americans. Moreover, the process of learning about and understanding cultural differences in training and practice conflicts with dominant American cultural patterns; what I call dynamic cultural conflicts arise and need to be acknowledged and addressed (Carter, 2004). *Dynamic cultural conflicts occur when two cultural styles are operating at the same time but in contradiction to one another.*

For example, the American cultural norm is to reduce an issue to its simplest terms. Thus, Americans attempting to understand a different culture reduce that culture to its bare essentials. But cultures are complex, not simple; understanding a different culture requires accounting for that complexity. And therein lies the conflict: We either allow complexity or we strive for simplicity. We must allow complexity to exist to learn about cultural influences, and so we must suspend our style of reducing things to simple terms. That is, we cannot reduce a racial-cultural group to general characteristics or understand a person through statistical information about the group.

We are taught as part of the culture to be professional and leave our personal beliefs out of our professional work and practice, so as individuals we fragment these parts of ourselves (Stewart & Bennett, 1991). For example, as American mental health care professionals we are taught to separate our professional and personal lives. Yet to learn about race and culture we must explore our personal experiences and beliefs; that is a violation of our cultural norms and a dynamic cultural conflict (Carter, 2004).

Usually when we are learning something new we are focused on something other than our personal selves, something that is external to us. As part of our culture, we focus on the practical and technical; that is, we learn what it is and how it works. However, learning about racial-cultural experiences, I believe, requires that we learn about ourselves, a dynamic cultural conflict in itself. We, as Americans are not accustomed to revealing ourselves or being the focal point of learning. Nevertheless, racial-cultural learning is most effective when it is grounded in self-exploration.

The more aware you are of your racial-cultural norms, values, and communication styles, the easier it is for you to grasp another racial-cultural way of seeing and experiencing the world. A fish doesn't know that it is in water and you are not. From the perspective of the fish, there is no other way to be. And it is likely that the fish does not see the world as being in water, but simply as the world. If you believe that the world is as you see it without variation and you use your worldview to understand those who seek your help, then miscommunication will occur (Carter, 2004). It will be impossible to acknowledge that another worldview exists and to see the world through another racial or cultural lens. It will be difficult to learn and understand another cultural worldview, another way to communicate, another way to behave if one is unaware that one's perceptions and ways of knowing and being are bound by one's own unexamined racial-cultural worldview.

It is hard to overcome dynamic cultural conflicts when the prevailing beliefs about the racial-cultural groups in North American society are so negative and demeaning. As part of the dynamic cultural conflict, mental health professionals must overcome the racial-cultural legacies of the past. It is necessary to fight the notion, however framed, that nondominant racial-cultural group members are inferior or culturally deprived or disadvantaged. These notions have been part of the foundation of theories of human development and personality and have dominated the way scholars and researchers have characterized and in many instances continue to characterize people who are not considered members of the mainstream or who are victims of poverty or poor educational systems, or crime and so forth. Thus, psychotherapy has been a tool of the status quo used to control and demand compliance with dominant group behavioral norms and it has not been used to help people on their own racial-cultural terms.

OVERCOMING THE RACIAL LEGACY OF THE PAST

Carter and Pieterse (this *Handbook,* Volume One) describe the historical development of race and how it is distinct from ethnicity and culture. Culture and ethnicity are fluid and flexible; they can change over time, usually over a few generations. Race and the characteristics associated with it are considered not to be flexible but persistent; beliefs about the attributes and characteristics associated with race seldom change over time, even over centuries. Carter and Pieterse show how race has come to be the context for culture in the United States. In developing racial-cultural competency training and mental health practice it is important to understand the historical legacy of race and culture, particularly how they have been treated and taught in psychology, in related disciplines, and in mental health practice. There is a considerable history regarding race and culture that has to be overcome; some beliefs and traditions surrounding race and culture remain prominent in mental health training and practice.

Pedersen (this *Handbook,* Volume One) and Draguns (this *Handbook,* Volume One) describe the relationship between anthropology and cultural psychology. The discipline that studied culture prior to the rise of cultural or cross-cultural psychology was anthropology. Much of the science of anthropology during the late nineteenth and early twentieth centuries was comparative: Western culture was held as the standard for a mature or civilized and socially-morally advanced cultures; other cultures and worldviews were described as immature, underdeveloped and uncivilized. The primary mechanism used to distinguish a mature society was racial classification.

Carter (1995) noted that during the nineteenth century anthropologists developed racial classification systems by using measurements of skin color, hair texture, and lip thickness. Psychology during that era was a science that studied the mind by building on biology and physics. Yet psychology as a discipline adopted the racial systems used by anthropology to explain and justify differences between human groups. Thus, early in the history of the discipline the research associated with race and culture was devoted to psychological investigations that affirmed the prevalent paradigm of the times, which held that Whites were psychologically and genetically superior to non-Whites.

That leading psychological health professionals accepted this paradigm is well documented by Carter (1995). G. Stanley Hall, the first president of the American Psychological Association, wrote in a popular book on adolescence that people of Color were not civilized. Louis Terman, another highly influential psychologist who adapted intelligent tests for use in the United States, proclaimed that non-White Americans were unable to benefit from education, nor could they be productive citizens, because they did not possess normal levels of intellectual ability. Similar sentiments were restated in the mid-1960s by Arthur Jensen and also by Hernstein and

Murray in the 1990s (see Carter, 1995, pp. 31–32). Belief in racial group inferiority has been challenged and rejected by many researchers and scholars (Graves, 2001; Jones, 1997). Yet the ideas and practices based on racial-cultural differences are still present in many spheres of American life. In the mental health professions, some practices that produce disparities in access and treatment reflect to some degree the dominant and traditional belief that the poor, the working class, and people of Color cannot benefit from education, training, or treatment.

In some cases, the inferiority models were replaced by the notion of "disadvantage" or "deprivation." Carter (1995) stated, "The social activism of the 1950s and 1960s brought about a shift from the inferiority paradigm to the oppression or cultural and social deprivation paradigm" (p. 39). The new paradigm became an important mechanism for explaining the differences in people's health and mental health experiences and still is used widely today. Cultural deprivation merges the beliefs and visions of social and biological notions regarding race and, through race, culture. People from non-White racial groups, it was argued, were culturally or socially deprived of the community structures, family systems, and economic and moral-emotional resources typical of White dominant racial group members. Thus, they were "disadvantaged" and Whites were in the language of today "privileged." Many factors contribute to disadvantage, such as poverty, lack of education and learning, discrimination, and social and family disruption; these factors are believed to determine the mental and psychological functioning of non-White racial group members. In that the effects are attributed to the effort, ability, morals, or personality of the person or racial group members who have to cope with the effects of such factors in this way the victim is at fault rather than the effects of the external stressors. Thus, mental health scholars and professionals propose interventions for people of Color to address the significant levels of what is described as dysfunction in the form of low self-esteem, mental disturbance, poor impulse control, violent tendencies, and other deviations from dominant racial-cultural group norms.

Researchers and scholars observed that the norm used to assess or determine "cultural deprivation" was White middle-class society and argued that people of Color—Blacks, Asians, Native Americans, and Hispanics/Latinos—were not deprived of culture, but were culturally different. The claim of cultural difference began what has become the multicultural movement. To me, it seems more accurate to refer to the movement as one that argued for changes in race relations and an end to racial oppression with acceptance of racial-cultural differences. The position in the beginning of the cultural difference movement was essentially that Americans from historically disenfranchised groups identified on the basis of racial characteristics (i.e., skin color) had retained distinct aspects of their culture of origin because they were segregated and isolated from mainstream American society. Due to racial separation, over the course of generations, and for some groups centuries, people were able to retain cultural traditions, values, and behaviors from their respective countries and cultures of origin. As immigrants of Color came to the country, they too were often isolated and segregated, while White immigrants over time were able to overcome the initial resistance to their assimilation in the mainstream society (Carter & Pieterse, this *Handbook,* Volume One).

Racial-cultural difference was slowly being replaced or at least used as an alternative to the inferiority and cultural deprivation paradigms. It is unfortunate that all paradigms (inferiority, deprivation, and difference) continue to exist in the twenty-first century, though perhaps in slightly different forms but with the same message and assumptions. Nevertheless, the focus on racial-cultural differences has also shifted to some extent into multicultural or cultural diversity, an approach that is promoted as inclusive, yet for some is no more than another term for individual differences. I and my colleagues, as well as many contributors to this *Handbook,* contend that race as a socially constructed category is used to establish the sociopolitical-economic structure of our society. Though racial categories have no scientific basis, those in power and those who wish to share power and authority believe that race, based on skin color, determines a person's ability, morality, intelligence, and emotional state, not to mention access and opportunity.

I have pointed out (see Carter, 1995) that race and identity, both personal and social, are intertwined and interrelated. As such, race and racial identity (psychological orientation to race) are central aspects of development and mental health practice and training: "To understand racial influences in psychotherapy, one must first understand how race is integrated into personality" (p. 76). The importance of these ideas for training and practice lies in the reality that our present is shaped by our past and that each person who is training to be a mental health professional or educator is socialized in a society where race is an integral part of our daily lives in substantial ways:

> Because race is an aspect of American culture, it is reasonable to conclude that, in early intellectual and social development, a child will internalize the respective psycho-social meanings assigned to his or her racial group. For instance, racial groups vary in terms of family structure and the values attached to particular activities (e.g., cognitive versus interpersonal skills) and to forms of language (e.g., standard English, Black English, traditional Native American Indian, Korean, Chinese and Japanese language, Spanish and spanglish). These variations are also influenced by social customs and stereotypes regarding members of each racial/ethnic group. (p. 78)

Just as gender identity is learned, so are people socialized to adopt race-appropriate roles and behaviors throughout the life span process of development (Carter, 1995; Thompson & Carter, 1997). So the effort to infuse mental health training, practice, and service delivery with people and systems that are racially-culturally competent requires overcoming the legacy of cultural oppression and racism as well as the messages regarding race and culture communicated through each person's socialization in North American society.

A recently issued report that supplemented *Mental Health: A Report of the Surgeon General* for the U.S. Department of Health and Human Services (2001) titled *Mental Health: Culture, Race, and Ethnicity* addressed the striking disparities in mental health access and care provided to American "minority" groups. The report noted:

> Racial and ethnic minorities (i.e., Blacks, Hispanics, Asians, and Native Americans, historically disenfranchised Americans), have less access to mental health services than do

whites. They are less likely to receive needed care. When they receive care, it is more likely
to be poor in quality. (p. 3)

The authors of the report also observed:

Additional barriers include clinicians' lack of awareness of cultural issues, bias, or inability
to speak the client's language, and the client's fear and mistrust of treatment. More broadly,
disparities also stem from minorities' historical and present day struggles with racism and
discrimination, which affect their mental health and contribute to their lower economic, social, and political status. (p. 4)

Overt discrimination and prejudice is contrary to our legal codes and for some
does not exist in the daily life experiences of people of Color. Yet research shows
that racial-cultural discrimination is still a factor in the lives of people of Color
and that racial discrimination increases their levels of stress and contributes to
psychological symptoms. Discrimination occurs in education, employment opportunities, housing and health care (NIMH, 2003).

So the legacy of the past still is with us; people of Color are treated as if they
have less value as citizens in our nation. To overcome the past we must recognize
the problem of dynamic cultural conflicts in training and practice and we must recognize the variation within each racial-cultural group regarding both psychological
identification and reference group memberships (gender, ethnicity, etc.). We also
must embrace complexity and resist the cultural pattern of wanting to make the issues simple or to focus on how we are similar. As a profession we need to accept the
reality that our lives and society are bounded by our cultural worldviews and that
the tradition of racism and segregation has created distinct racial-cultural worldviews. The contributions to Volume Two of the *Handbook of Racial-Cultural Psychology and Counseling* illustrate many of the points raised here and in many
instances go further. They all provide a way to grasp, understand, and use the complexity of racial-cultural psychology in mental health training and practice.

OVERVIEW AND OUTLINE

The volume is composed of two parts: training and practice. Derald Wing Sue and
Gina C. Torino lay a strong foundation for Volume Two by outlining concrete manifestations of racial-cultural impositions by dominant group members and systems
in their discussion of the mental health profession, training, and service provision.
Moreover, Sue and Torino note the limits of cognitive-based racial-cultural education and how programs isolate the training to one course. They also point to the role
of systemic influences in learning about racial-cultural issues; it is not just the program that teaches racial-cultural competency, but the institution as a whole.

Joseph G. Ponterotto and Richard Austin describe various approaches used to train
for cultural competence. They include training for U.S. groups as well as international initiatives. They describe best practices in various programs across the country
that have been used to teach mental health professionals racial-cultural competence.

Robert T. Carter follows the overview presented by Ponterotto and Austin and provides a description of the racial-cultural counseling laboratory course, identified by the previous authors as an example of a best training practice, and the curriculum context in which it is taught at Teachers College, Columbia University.

Like Carter, Charleen Alderfer describes a course that has a critical and central role in the training of family and marriage therapists. She describes the course in detail and highlights a combination of immersion and group interaction experiences as vehicles for raising awareness of racial-cultural issues. She illustrates the power of race and the cultural context for learning about differences in the family and in her course as well as the experiences that students have in the course that illuminate the importance of not losing sight of race in mental health training programs.

Vivan Ota Wang argues for the use of racial identity theory and its application in helping professionals from many disciplines learn "to be." She proposes that critical race theory, racial identity, and Bronfenbrenner's ecological model be used together to help professionals see the role of power and oppression in the lives of U.S. citizens.

Barbara C. Wallace describes an approach for racial-cultural skill acquisition. She builds on the extant literature by offering a model that seeks to teach professionals and students about the integration of affect, thought, and action. Like Ota Wang, Wallace contends that personal racial-cultural identity must be integrated into the training of mental health professionals to foster skill development. She presents specific and concrete guidelines on how to assess and acquire racial-cultural helping skills.

Marie Faubert and Don C. Locke address an extremely important issue that receives less attention in the racial-cultural literature: language diversity. They describe how American society is not receptive to multiple languages by illustrating the role of language in therapy and training. These authors do a good job of showing the relevance of language for U.S. citizens as well as for immigrants and refugees.

Mary B. McRae and Ellen L. Short discuss the important topic of racial-cultural mental health interventions for work with therapy and support groups. They provide an overview of what is known about group work and how race and culture influence interactions in groups. They propose the use of a group relations model for understanding how race and culture operate in groups and organizational settings.

It is clear that language diversity and group interactions are important components when people seek and receive mental health services. Lack of knowledge and skill with groups and language can limit the therapist's or trainer's grasp of the client's communication and culture. Trainers, educators, and practitioners also need to recognize what William Ming Liu and Donald B. Pope-Davis define as therapy ruptures and impasses. These contributors observe that racial-cultural scholars and practitioners have paid more attention to the therapist and patient matching and descriptions of client culture's and less attention to psychotherapy process issues. In particular, they present research evidence of cultural misapplications by therapists and trainees that can result in a rupture or impasse in therapy interactions. More important, they contend that cultural ruptures and impasses can lead to client termination of therapy, particularly when a therapist introduces racial-cultural issues into treatment at a time or in a manner that does not fit with or is not consistent with the client's presenting issues or level of development. The authors provide guidelines for clinicians as well as for trainers and supervisors in how to recognize and cope with cultural impasses and ruptures in mental health service delivery.

A cornerstone of training in the mental health profession is supervised instruction, observation, and feedback. Almost all mental health disciplines use the model of a supervisor who is established or has acquired the requisite credentials (i.e., degree, license, experience) to observe and provide feedback to a trainee and evaluate his or her interactions with patients/clients. Eric C. Chen's chapter is focused on the clinical supervisor and enhancing the supervisor's understanding and skill in racial-cultural supervision. Of particular importance, Chen focuses on the various roles a clinical supervisor assumes and illustrates the central role of supervision in mental health training. The strength of his unique approach is that it offers a structured, practical, and specific framework that can be used to integrate racial-cultural training into the work of supervisors and educators.

As was noted earlier, supervision is a mechanism we use as mental health professionals to teach, learn, and correct our work. Amy L. Reynolds illustrates issues that arise in racial-cultural supervision dyads. She provides excellent guidance for how supervision can be improved.

Charles R. Ridley and Debra Mollen conclude the training part of the *Handbook* by presenting a model for postdoctoral racial-cultural competence. They propose several features of a postdoctoral program that would build racial-cultural competence beyond predoctoral training, such as regular evaluations, learning objectives, links to practice, leader support, and preevaluation of trainees. The authors call for the development of systematic and standardized postdoctoral training programs and practices.

Part II of Volume Two focuses on practice issues associated with racial-cultural counseling and psychology. Chalmer E. Thompson's chapter on theory and practice discusses how race and culture are interdependent aspects of a person's life. She points out how psychological theory and practice can be elevated to include a more holistic view of people such that aspects of race and culture will no longer be treated as fragments of identity that belong only to nondominant group members. She adeptly integrates racial identity ego status development into a model that promotes racially-culturally effective theory and practice.

Alvin N. Alvarez and Ralph E. Piper's chapter goes a bit further and lays out a framework for how practitioners can use racial-cultural theory in practice. They show how racial-cultural theory (models of racial identity, acculturation, etc.) can be integrated into assessment, diagnosis, and intervention and used for particular outcomes. The authors fill a void in the existing literature by including ways to integrate racial-cultural models effectively into day-to-day practice.

Kevin Cokley provides a brief review of how the constructs of race and ethnicity have typically been used in the psychotherapy literature. He does this by offering an outline of methods to incorporate race, ethnicity, and related constructs in clinical work. He presents transcripts of clients to demonstrate how knowledge of race and ethnicity were incorporated and applied in his clinical work.

The chapter by Cokley is followed by one that deals with career counseling and how racial-cultural factors influence our understanding and practice in helping people move between school and work. Kris Ihle-Helledy, Nadya A. Fouad, Paula W. Gibson, Caroline G. Henry, Elizabeth Harris-Hodge, Matthew D. Jandrisevits, Edgar X. Jordan III, and A. J. Metz analyze current theory and research to illustrate what we know about the career counseling process and they test a model of culturally oriented career counseling. In general, these authors report that culture and race play important roles in the career counseling process.

Tamara Buckley and Deidre Franklin address the complex issue of racial-cultural factors in diagnosis. Diagnosis is a core feature of our mental health service delivery system: It is used to determine client competence, personality, and basic mental health and third-party payments. These authors discuss the absence of consideration of racial-cultural context in mainstream notions of normality and abnormality as well as how racial-cultural factors influence the expression of emotions and behaviors. They call for greater consideration of the role of racial-cultural factors in our understanding of mental health.

The focus on diagnosis sets the stage for three chapters that examine aspects of assessment and testing, also important tools used by mental health professionals to determine a person's psychological and emotion functioning. Lisa A. Suzuki, John F. Kugler, and Lyndon J. Aguiar provide readers with an understanding of the psychometric flaws of many tests and assessment instruments used often with little consideration of their limits. They provide guidance for practitioners in how to determine if a test or assessment procedure is appropriate for particular racial-cultural group members. For the most part, while some measures attend to racial-cultural issues, most tests (cognitive ability, personality) use universal assumptions and do not adequately incorporate racial-cultural variation into their development and construction.

Curtis W. Branch also discusses issues of clinical assessment, yet he reviews unexamined assumptions and the research evidence regarding use of traditional assessment procedures, including interviews. He asks clinicians to examine their assumptions and calls on psychological and mental health professionals to be aware of the limits of trusted assessments. Branch asks clinicians and researchers to use race- and culture-specific measures to accurately assess members of nondominant racial-cultural groups.

Tina Q. Richardson and Eric E. Frey's chapter rounds out the section on assessment. They describe a projective strategy for assessing White racial identity ego statuses and show its utility with a case example.

Donna E. Hurdle presents a chapter on working with groups using a racial-cultural perspective. Of particular value is her guidance on how to integrate traditional healing methods into group work.

Anita Jones Thomas focuses on how family therapists can use racial-cultural factors in treatment with families. She provides valuable conceptual models and case examples for work with families. She describes how racial-cultural factors influence family dynamics, socialization, and child rearing. Of particular value is her guidance on how to assess for racial-cultural factors as well as how such knowledge informs the therapist about appropriate intervention strategies.

Dennis Miehls highlights cultural and racial identity themes that are important to assess when working with couples. It is important for the clinician to be aware of his or her own cultural biases and attitudes, or to be self-aware, to enhance working relationships when conducting racial-cultural therapy.

Patrica Arredondo examines clinical practice with immigrant populations. She offers a psychohistorical framework for effective racial-cultural competent practice that sets the context for how immigrants are treated in the current sociocultural environment. The author discusses the various stressors experienced by the new wave of immigrants, who are primarily people of Color. They face considerable stress due to their race and culture, information vital to mental health service providers.

Shawn O. Utsey, Rheeda L. Walker, Nancy Dessources, and Maria Bartolomeo present Black Americans' unique racial-cultural experiences. Their focus is on a specific racial group because, the authors suggest, Blacks' bicultural experience is distinct from that of other groups. They argue further that current theory about bicultural or acculturative processes does not capture the experience of people of African descent.

James E. Dobbins and Judith H. Skillings offer a clinical diagnosis and treatment model for individual White racism and its manifestations. They argue that there are parallels between being socialized to hold racist attitudes and beliefs and substance abuse or abuse of personal/social power.

Robert T. Carter, Jessica M. Forsyth, Slivia L. Mazzula, and Bryant Williams introduce the topic of race-based stress and offer evidence from an exploratory study of how racism is experienced by people of Color. They call for new legal standards and definitions, organizational policies and clinical standards to adequately address the psychological, physical and emotional effect of the experience of racism.

Elizabeth M. Vera, Larisa Buhin, Gloria Montgomery, and Richard Shin discuss how mental health professionals can expand how they deliver services and conceptualize their roles. They argue that racially-culturally competent mental health service should include outreach, advocacy, and prevention, activities typically outside the boundaries of traditional service delivery and practice.

Arthur C. Evans Jr., Miriam Delphin, Reginald Simmons, Gihan Omar, and Jacob Tebes describe in detail the elements of creating and maintaining a system of care that is racially-culturally competent. The authors share some of the complexity involved in establishing a racially-culturally competent statewide system of mental health care. Yet they also show that it is possible if multilevel and multifaceted policies, procedures, and programs are used to make racial-cultural competency an integral part of mental health care. I think the model described represents an advance, designed to reduce health disparities and at the same time require racially-culturally competent mental health practice and service delivery.

Leon D. Caldwell and Dolores D. Tarver reflect on the impact of the American Psychological Association's Ethical Code on racially-culturally competent practice. They effectively point to contradictions and conflicts in the premises of the

Ethnical Code that limit racial-cultural practice. They extend the thinking of Farah Ibrahim and Susan Chavez Cameron (this *Handbook,* Volume One), who raised similar issues about ethics in research in Volume I of the *Handbook.* The value of Caldwell and Tarver's contribution is the way the authors use case examples to illustrate the cultural limits of the Ethical Code.

ROBERT T. CARTER, PhD
Professor of Psychology and Education
Department of Counseling and Clinical Psychology
Teachers College, Columbia University

REFERENCES

Alderfer, C. P. (2000). National culture and the new corporate language for race *relations.* In R. T. Carter (Ed.), *Addressing cultural issues in organizations: Beyond the corporate context* (pp. 19–34). Thousand Oaks, CA: Sage.

American Psychological Association. (2003). Guidelines on multicultural education, training, research, practice, and organizational change for psychologists. *American Psychologists, 58*(5), 377–402.

Bowser, B. P. (in press). The role of socialization in cultural learning: What does the research say? In R. T. Carter (Ed.), *Handbook of racial-cultural psychology and counseling: Theory and research* (Vol. 1, pp. 184–206). Hoboken, NJ: Wiley.

Carter, R. T. (1995). *The influence of race and racial identity in psychotherapy.* New York: Wiley.

Carter, R. T. (Ed.). (2000a). *Addressing cultural issues in organizations: Beyond the corporate context.* Thousand Oaks, CA: Sage.

Carter, R. T. (2000b). Reimagining race in education: A new paradigm from psychology. *Teachers College Record, 102*(5), 864–896.

Carter, R. T. (2001). Back to the future in cultural competence training. *The Counseling Psychologist, 29,* 787–789.

Carter, R. T. (2003). Becoming racially and culturally competent: The racial-cultural counseling laboratory. *Journal of Multicultural Counseling, 31*(1), 20–30.

Carter, R. T. (2004). *Disaster response to communities of Color: Cultural responsive intervention.* Technical report for the Connecticut Department of Mental Health and Addiction Services (DMHAS). Available from http://www.dmhas.state.ct.us.

Carter, R. T. (in press). Uprooting inequity and disparities in counseling and psychology: An Introduction. In R. T. Carter (Ed.), *Handbook of racial-cultural psychology and counseling: Theory and research* (Vol. 1). Hoboken, NJ: Wiley.

Carter, R. T., & Pieterse, A. (in press). Race: A social and psychological analysis of the terms and its meaning. In R. T. Carter (Ed.), *Handbook of racial-cultural psychology and counseling: Theory and research* (Vol. 1, pp. 41–63). Hoboken, N J: Wiley.

Draguns, J. G. (in press). Cultural psychology: Its early roots and present status. In R. T. Carter (Ed.), *Handbook of racial-cultural psychology and counseling: Theory and research* (Vol. 1, pp. 163–183). Hoboken, NJ: Wiley.

Graves, J. L., Jr. (2001). *The emperor's new clothes: Biological theories of race at the millennium.* New Brunswick, NJ: Rutgers University Press.

Helms, J., & Cook, D. (1999). *Using race and culture in counseling and psychotherapy.* Boston: Allyn & Bacon.

Ibrahim, F. A., & Cameron, S. C. (in press). Racial-cultural ethical issues in research. In R. T. Carter (Ed.), *Handbook of racial-cultural psychology and counseling: Theory and research* (Vol. 1, pp. 391–413). Hoboken, NJ: Wiley.

Jones, J. M. (1997). *Prejudice and racism* (2nd ed.). New York: McGraw-Hill.

Marger, M. (2000). *Race and ethnic relations: American and global perspectives* (5th ed.). Belmont, CA: Wadsworth.

National Institute of Mental Health. (2003). *Sociocultural and environmental process.* Retrieved February 13, 2003 from www.nimh.nih.gov.publicat/basechap7.

Pedersen, P. (in press). The importance of "cultural psychology" theory for multicultural counselors. In R. T. Carter (Ed.), *Handbook of racial-cultural psychology and counseling: Theory and research* (Vol. 1, pp. 3–16). Hoboken, NJ: Wiley.

Stewart, E. C., & Bennett, A. (1991). *American cultural patterns: A cross-cultural perspective* (2nd ed.). Yarthmouth, ME: Intercultural Press.

Sue, D. W., & Sue, D. (1999). *Counseling the culturally different: Theory and practice* (3rd ed.). New York: Wiley.

Sue, D. W., & Sue, D. (2003). *Counseling the culturally diverse: Theory and practice* (4th ed.). New York: Wiley.

Thompson, C. E., & Carter, R. T. (Eds.). (1997). *Racial identity development theory: Applications to individual, group and organizations.* Hillsdale, NJ: Erlbaum.

U.S. Department of Health and Human Services. (2001). *Mental health: Culture, race, and ethnicity—A supplement to Mental health: A report of the surgeon general.* Rockville, MD: U.S Department of Health and Human Services, Substance Abuse and Mental Health Services Administration, Center for Mental Health Services.

Yeh, C. J., & Hunter, C. D. (in press). The socialization of self: Understanding shifting and multiple selves across cultures. In R. T. Carter (Ed.), *Handbook of racial-cultural psychology and counseling: Theory and research* (Vol. 1, pp. 78–93). Hoboken, NJ: Wiley.

Contributors

Lyndon J. Aguiar, MS
New York University
New York, New York

Charleen Alderfer, EdD, NCC, LMFT
The College of New Jersey
Ewing, New Jersey

Alvin N. Alvarez, PhD
San Francisco State University
San Francisco, California

Patrica Arredondo, EdD
Arizona State University
Tempe, Arizona

Richard Austin, MSEd
Fordham University
New York, New York

Maria Bartolomeo, MA
Seton Hall University
South Orange, New Jersey

Curtis W. Branch, PhD
College of Physicians and Surgeons
Columbia University
New York, New York

Tamara R. Buckley, PhD
Hunter College, City University of
   New York
New York, New York

Larisa Buhin, PhD
Loyola University–Chicago
Chicago, Illinois

Leon D. Caldwell, PhD
University of Nebraska
Lincoln, Nebraska

Robert T. Carter, PhD
Teachers College, Columbia University
New York, New York

Eric C. Chen, PhD
Fordham University
New York, New York

Kevin Cokley, PhD
University of Missouri at Columbia
Columbia, Missouri

Miriam Delphin, PhD
Yale University School of Medicine
New Haven, Connecticut

Nancy Dessources, MA
Seton Hall University
South Orange, New Jersey

James E. Dobbins, PhD, ABPP
Wright State University
Dayton, Ohio

Arthur C. Evans Jr., PhD
Connecticut Department of Mental
    Health & Addiction Services
Hartford, Connecticut
Yale University School of Medicine
New Haven, Connecticut

Marie Faubert, CSJ, EdD
University of Saint Thomas
Houston, Texas

Jessica M. Forsyth, EdM
Teachers College, Columbia University
New York, New York

Nadya A. Fouad, PhD
University of Wisconsin–Milwaukee
Milwaukee, Wisconsin

**Deidre Cheryl Franklin-Jackson,
    PhD**
Harlem Educational Activities
    Fund, Inc.
New York, New York

Eric E. Frey
Lehigh University
Bethlehem, Pennsylvania

Paula W. Gibson, PhD
University of Wisconsin–Milwaukee
Milwaukee, Wisconsin

Elizabeth Harris-Hodge, MS
University of Wisconsin–Milwaukee
Milwaukee, Wisconsin

Caroline G. Henry, MS
University of Wisconsin–Milwaukee
Milwaukee, Wisconsin

Kris Ihle-Helledy, PhD
Northwestern University Career
    Services
Evanston, Illinois

Donna E. Hurdle, PhD
University of North
    Carolina–Wilmington
Wilmington, North Carolina

Matthew D. Jandrisevits, MA
University of Wisconsin–Milwaukee
Milwaukee, Wisconsin

Edgar X. Jordan III, MSE
University of Wisconsin–Milwaukee
Milwaukee, Wisconsin

John F. Kugler, PhD
New York University
New York, New York

William Ming Liu, PhD
University of Iowa
Iowa City, Iowa

Don C. Locke, EdD
North Carolina State University
Raleigh, North Carolina

Silvia L. Mazzula, MA
Teachers College, Columbia University
New York, New York

Mary B. McRae, PhD
New York University
New York, New York

A. J. Metz, MS
University of Wisconsin–Milwaukee
Milwaukee, Wisconsin

Dennis Miehls, PhD, LICSW
Smith College School for Social Work
Northampton, Massachusetts

Debra Mollen, PhD
Texas Women's University
Denton, Texas

Gloria Montgomery, MA
Loyola University–Chicago
Chicago, Illinois

Gihan Omar, PhD
Yale University School of Medicine
New Haven, Connecticut

Alex Pieterse, MA
Teachers College, Columbia University
New York, New York

Ralph E. Piper, PhD
Princeton University
Princeton, New Jersey

Joseph G. Ponterotto, PhD
Fordham University
New York, New York

Donald B. Pope-Davis, PhD
University of Iowa
Iowa City, Iowa

Amy L. Reynolds, PhD
Buffalo State College
Buffalo, New York

Tina Q. Richardson, PhD
Lehigh University
Bethlehem, Pennsylvania

Charles R. Ridley, PhD
Indiana University
Bloomington, Indiana

Richard Shin, MA
Loyola University–Chicago
Chicago, Illinois

Ellen L. Short, PhD
New York University
New York, New York

Reginald Simmons, PhD
Connecticut Department of Children
 and Families
Hartford, Connecticut

Judith H. Skillings, PsyD
Private Practice
Amherst, Massachusetts

Derald Wing Sue, PhD
Teachers College, Columbia University
New York, New York

Lisa A. Suzuki, PhD
New York University
New York, New York

Dolores D. Tarver, EdM
University of Nebraska
Lincoln, Nebraska

Jacob Tebes, PhD
Yale School of Medicine
New Haven, Connecticut

Anita Jones Thomas, PhD
Northeastern Illinois University
Chicago, Illinois

Chalmer E. Thompson, PhD
Indiana University
Bloomington, Indiana

Gina C. Torino, EdM
Teachers College, Columbia University
New York, New York

Shawn O. Utsey, PhD
Virginia Commonwealth University
Richmond, Virginia

Elizabeth M. Vera, PhD
Loyola University–Chicago
Chicago, Illinois

Rheeda L. Walker, PhD
University of South Carolina
Columbia, South Carolina

Barbara C. Wallace, PhD
Teachers College, Columbia University
New York, New York

Vivan Ota Wang, PhD
National Human Genome Institute
Bethesda, Maryland

Bryant Williams, MA
Teachers College, Columbia University
New York, New York

PART I

Training for Racial-Cultural Competence

CHAPTER 1

Racial-Cultural Competence: Awareness, Knowledge, and Skills

Derald Wing Sue and Gina C. Torino

In the United States, the population of people of Color has grown dramatically in recent years and is expected to continue to increase (Sue & Sue, 2003). According to the U.S. census (2000), most of the population increase between 1990 and 2000 was composed of visible racial ethnic groups. For example, the Latino population increased by almost 58%, the Asian American/Pacific Islander population by over 50%, the African American population by 16%, and American Indian/Alaska Native population by 15.5%; however, the White population increased by only 7.3% (Sue & Sue, 2003). It is projected that people of Color will become a numerical majority in the United States between 2030 and 2050 (Sue et al., 1998), yet there is no such trend in the field of counseling psychology. Whites still compose the majority of counselors and trainees in the United States (Sue & Sue, 2003). With an increasingly diverse population and a comparatively homogeneous counseling profession, the importance of racial-cultural counseling competence will become crucial.

Thus, many counseling psychology programs and professional organizations, such as the American Psychological Association (APA), have shifted their foci to train counselors to work competently with various racial/ethnic groups. For example, Ponterotto (1997) found that 89% of APA- and non-APA-accredited counseling psychology programs had at least one multicultural training course, and 58% of the respondents stated that multicultural issues are integrated into all course work. In addition, the APA has recently endorsed the *Guidelines on Multicultural Education, Training, Research, Practice, and Organizational Change for Psychologists* (American Psychological Association [APA], 2003). The goals for these guidelines are to provide psychologists with (1) the rationale and need for addressing racial and ethnic issues in education, training, research, practice, and organizational change; (2) basic information, relevant terminology, and current empirical research from psychology and related disciplines; (3) references to enhance ongoing education, training, research, practice, and organizational change methodologies; and (4) paradigms that broaden the purview of psychology as a profession (APA, 2002).

Why do we believe that the aforementioned changes in the field of counseling psychology and in psychology in general are so important? In this chapter, we explore the limitations of the Eurocentric approach to counseling and therapy and demonstrate how this approach can cause harm to individuals from various racial/ethnic groups. Next, we define multicultural therapy and show how it expands on traditional definitions of counseling and therapy in several important ways. We define cultural competence and elaborate on the three components of awareness, knowledge, and skills. We conclude this chapter with a discussion of the implications of racial-cultural competence for education and training.

LIMITATIONS OF EUROCENTRIC APPROACHES TO COUNSELING AND THERAPY

All forms of healing and helping originate from a specific cultural context and, as such, strongly reflect the cultural values and assumptions of the particular society (Carter, 1995; Harner, 1990; Highlen, 1994; Sue, 1999, 2001). The concepts "counseling" and "psychotherapy" are uniquely Euro-American in origin and are based on certain philosophical assumptions and values strongly endorsed by Western civilizations: (1) a belief that the individual is the psychosocial unit of operation, (2) mind-body dualism: the separation of physical and mental functioning, (3) rational cause-effect orientation to understanding the world, (4) mastery and control over people and the environment, (5) a future orientation, and (6) a strong belief in equal access and opportunity (Highlen, 1996; Katz, 1985; Kluckhohn & Strodtbeck, 1961; Stewart, 1971; Sue & Sue, 1999; Wehrly, 1995). These cultural assumptions are not often shared by persons of Color, whose worldviews and life experiences are quite different from those of their White counterparts. As a result, the imposition of these cultural beliefs and values on clients of Color may result in cultural oppression (Sue & Sue, 1999). For example, the belief in equality of opportunity has strong sociopolitical connotations, which have adversely affected the diagnosis and treatment of many marginalized groups in the United States.

As a result, Western forms of psychotherapy operate from a worldview that is individualistic and emphasizes the uniqueness, independence, and self-reliance of people. Success is believed to be due to one's own efforts, and lack of success is attributed to one's shortcomings or inadequacies. The effects of sociopolitical or systemic forces are minimized in favor of the belief that everyone, regardless of race, gender, or social class, has an equal opportunity to succeed in life. Statistics indicating that persons of Color have higher unemployment rates and are more likely to have less education and to live in communities with higher poverty and crime are often seen as evidence of negative personal attributes (laziness, lower intelligence, and poor impulse control) among racial/ethnic groups. The belief that everyone can succeed if they work hard enough may unintentionally blame the victim for his or her current life situation.

The Euro-American worldview, which emphasizes individuality, independence, and self-reliance, assumes universality: All clients are the same, and the goals and techniques of counseling and therapy are equally applicable across all groups. Taken to its extreme, the approach assumes that persons of Color should be like their White counterparts and that race and culture are insignificant variables in counseling and psychotherapy. Statements like "We are all the same under the skin" and "Apart from your racial/cultural background, you are no different from me" are indicative of the tendency to avoid acknowledging how race and culture may influence identity, values, beliefs, behaviors, and the perception of reality (Carter, 1995; Helms, 1990; Sue, 2001, 2003). The failure to recognize the importance of race and culture in counseling may lead to visible racial/ethnic group members underutilizing mental health services and terminating therapy earlier than their White counterparts (Atkinson, Morten, & Sue, 1998), making clients of Color feel that they are at fault because of the failure to consider systemic factors (bias and discrimination) as contributing to their problems (Sue & Sue, 1999), and being denied needed mental health services because these are structured in such a manner as to meet only the needs of White people.

Many psychologists who believe that issues of race and culture affect the lives of our clients and the therapeutic relationship in significant ways have concluded that the theories of counseling and psychotherapy, the standards used to judge normality and abnormality, the definitions of what is appropriate professional therapeutic behavior, and the codes of ethics are not only culture-bound but culturally biased (Highlen, 1996; Katz, 1985; Pedersen, 1994; Ridley, 1995). As such, theories of counseling and psychotherapy may potentially clash with racial/ethnic groups whose worldview may differ from that of their White counterparts. Others have pointed out that clinical practice with African Americans, Asian Americans, Hispanic Americans, and Native Americans may result in cultural oppression (Paniagua, 1998; Parham, White, & Ajamu, 1999; Sue & Sue, 1999), that the profession must begin to develop racial-cultural competencies that recognize the racial diversity of the clientele (Sue, Arredondo, & McDavis, 1992; Sue et al., 1982), and that *cultural competence* must become a defining feature of the mental health profession's standards of practice (Sue, Bingham, Porche-Burke, & Vasquez, 1999). The term "cultural competence" is defined later in this chapter.

As a point of clarification, several psychologists have noted that the term "multicultural" or "multiculturalism" obscures the concept of race by including gender, ability/disability, sexual orientation, social class, and religion in the definition (Carter, 1995, this *Handbook,* Volume One; Carter & Qureshi, 1995; Helms, 1995, 2001; Helms & Richardson, 1997). In this chapter, we use the term "racial-cultural" to emphasize the importance of race but not to the exclusion of other important cultural variables (e.g., gender, social class) in the lives of our clients.

To define racial-cultural counseling competence, we must first define the more general concept of multicultural counseling and therapy (MCT). Understanding the basic premises and concepts of MCT will lay the groundwork for understanding the acquisition of racial-cultural competence by counselors and other mental health professionals.

MULTICULTURAL COUNSELING AND THERAPY

Helms and Richardson (1997) state that MCT

> should refer to the integration of dimensions of client cultures into pertinent counseling theories, techniques, and practices with specific intent of providing clients of all sociodemographic and psychodemographic variations with effective mental health services. (p. 70)

Sue, Ivey, and Pedersen (1996) define MCT on a conceptual level as a "metatheory (i.e., a theory about theories) in that it offers an organizational framework for understanding the numerous helping approaches that humankind has developed" (p. 13). Such a definition includes the importance and legitimacy of non-Western indigenous healing systems. Therefore, MCT can be defined in the following manner:

> Multicultural counseling and therapy is both a helping role and a process that uses modalities and defines goals consistent with the life experiences and cultural values of clients, utilizes universal and culture-specific helping strategies and roles, recognizes client identities to include individual, group, and universal dimensions, and balances the importance of individualism and collectivism in the assessment, diagnosis, and treatment of the client and client systems.

More traditional definitions of counseling and therapy tend to ignore issues of culture in the therapeutic process. For example, counseling and therapy have been described as conversations with a therapeutic purpose (Korchin, 1976); development of a therapeutic alliance for the purpose of catharsis and/or the opportunity to develop or change behaviors, attitudes, insights, or feelings (Grencavage & Norcross, 1990); using techniques based on scientifically grounded psychological principles (Reisman, 1971); and even as "the talking cure" or the "purchase of friendship" (Schofield, 1964). These traditional definitions reveal certain common characteristics related to the process and goal of counseling. First, counseling is seen as centered in the counselor-client relationship primarily on a one-to-one basis. Second, the primary mode of providing help is through talking or verbal behavior. Third, the goal is to change behaviors, feelings, and attitudes and to develop insights. Fourth, mental health professionals emphasize the importance of basing therapeutic interventions on well-grounded scientifically determined psychological principles. In addition, depending on the theoretical orientation, counselors may seek to modify primarily thoughts or behaviors (cognitive-behavioral), social-familial relationships (family systems), or feelings and expectancies (existential); to facilitate the client's self-insight and rational control of his or her own life (psychodynamic); or to enhance mental health or self-actualization (humanistic).

MCT accepts many of these basic premises, but broadens and expands the traditional definitions of counseling and therapy in the following manner (Sue et al., 1996):

1. MCT broadens the perspective of the helping relationship. Rather than a singular focus on the individual, it takes a self-in-relation orientation. The individualistic approach is balanced with the collectivistic reality that we are embedded in our families, significant others, communities, and culture. The client is perceived not solely as an individual, but as an individual who is a product of his or her social and cultural context. As a result, systemic influences are seen as equally important as individual ones. Further, theories of counseling and psychotherapy are notorious for their one-dimensional nature. There are theories that can be described as primarily focusing on the feeling self (existential-humanistic), behaving self (behavioral), thinking self (cognitive), social self (interpersonal and family systems), or

historical self (psychodynamic). In many respects, these theories of counseling and psychotherapy fail to see the whole person. MCT conceptualizes people as more than thinking, feeling, or behaving beings; it also recognizes people as racial, cultural, spiritual, and political beings. Any theory that fails to acknowledge these other dimensions views only a limited portion of the human condition.

2. MCT expands the repertoire of helping responses. In translating the assumptions of counseling and mental health into practice, it becomes clear that certain specific guidelines for counselor behavior are considered "therapeutic." These are best explicated by what can be called therapeutic taboos derived from current and previous codes of ethics of the American Psychological Association (1995, 2002), American Counseling Association (1995), and American Association for Marriage and Family Therapy (1998): (1) Counselors do not give advice and suggestions (doing so may foster dependency); (2) counselors do not self-disclose personal thoughts and feelings (doing so is not professional); (3) counselors do not serve dual role relationships (doing so represents a conflict of interest); (4) counselors do not accept gifts from clients (doing so means a loss of objectivity); and (5) counselors do not barter (there is potential abuse of power). However, the American Psychological Association's (2002) code of ethics has revised some of their codes to allow multiple relationships that would not reasonably be expected to cause impairment or risk exploitation or harm to the client, and to allow bartering only if it is not clinically contraindicated and if the resulting arrangement relationship is not exploitative. In spite of these changes to the APA's ethics code, the role of the counselor is primarily to maintain objectivity, to place responsibility for change on the client, and to use relatively passive attending and listening. Yet, many multicultural psychologists have pointed out that "helping" as perceived by many people of Color involves the helper engaging in these taboo behaviors (Berman, 1979; Herring, 1999; L. C. Lee & Zane, 1998; Nwachuku & Ivey, 1991; Parham et al., 1999).

3. MCT advocates for alternative helping roles. As indicated earlier, the traditional counselor/therapist role is usually confined to a one-to-one, verbal-oriented process in the office that places the burden for change primarily on the client. The assumption is often that the problem resides within the client and, consequently, change must occur in the person. Even when problems are attributed to external conditions (an abusive spouse, an overbearing boss, or job discrimination), clients are encouraged to deal with the situation on their own. Seldom would it be considered appropriate for the counselor to actively intervene in the social system. MCT acknowledges the importance of the traditional counselor/therapist role, but believes that it is much too narrow and limiting, especially in working with racial/ethnic communities and clients. When, for example, the problems of clients of Color reside in prejudice, discrimination, and racism of employers, educators, neighbors, and/or organizational policies or practices in schools, mental health agencies, government, business, and our society, the traditional therapeutic role appears ineffective and inappropriate (Parham et al., 1999; Sue, 2001; Sue et al., 1996).

To provide adequate MCT, it is imperative that counselors become culturally competent. Briefly, becoming a culturally competent counselor involves a general transformation of one's own attitudes/beliefs, knowledge, and skills before MCT can be implemented on a professional level.

CULTURAL COMPETENCE

Consistent with the definition of MCT, culturally competent counselors and therapists exhibit expertise in their ability to aid racial/ethnic clients at both the individual/personal level and the organizational/societal level:

> Cultural competence is the ability to engage in actions or create conditions that maximize the optimal development of the client and client systems. Multicultural counseling competence is achieved by the counselor's acquisition of awareness, knowledge, and skills needed to function effectively in a pluralistic democratic society (ability to communicate, interact, negotiate, and intervene on behalf of clients from diverse backgrounds) and on an organizational/societal level, advocating effectively to develop new theories, practices, policies, and organizational structures that are more responsive to all groups.

Such a definition assumes that equal treatment in counseling and psychotherapy may represent biased or discriminatory treatment if the racial/cultural backgrounds of clients are ignored. Likewise, differential therapeutic treatment based on an understanding of different life experiences is not necessarily discriminatory. The goal of cultural competence is equal access and opportunity, which may dictate differential treatment (i.e., process, outcome, and roles).

One of the earliest attempts to define multicultural counseling competencies came from the work of the APA Division of Counseling Psychology (17) (now the Society of Counseling Psychology) committee in which multicultural competencies were conceptualized in a tripartite division: awareness, knowledge, and skills related to working effectively with racial/ethnic populations (Sue et al., 1982). Another group further refined these three divisions into 31 competencies (Sue et al., 1992) that formed the foundation for measures of multicultural counseling competencies (D'Andrea, Daniels, & Heck, 1991; LaFromboise, Coleman, & Hernandez, 1991; Ponterotto, Sanchez, & Magids, 1991; Sodowsky, Taffe, Gutkin, & Wise, 1994) and models for multicultural training (Carney & Kahn, 1984; Pedersen, 1994; Sabnani, Ponterotto, & Borodovsky, 1991).

Multicultural counseling competence is multidimensional and multifaceted, and its many properties have been described in greater detail elsewhere (Constantine & Ladany, 2001; Ridley, Baker, & Hill, 2000; Sue, 2001; Sue et al., 1992). Readers interested in a more detailed description should go to the original sources. Using the divisions of awareness, knowledge, and skills and concentrating primarily on racial-cultural competence in counseling, the following attributes must be present in mental health practitioners and systems of mental health delivery.

Racial-Cultural Awareness

According to the competency standards, becoming aware of one's own values, assumptions, and biases as they relate to issues of race and race relations is paramount to becoming racially-culturally competent. This awareness begins with the recognition that everyone possesses a racial and cultural heritage. Most people of Color are consciously aware of themselves as racial beings, yet most White Euro-Americans are not so aware (Carter, 1995; Helms, 1990, 1995, 2001; Sue et al., 1998). The invisibility of Whiteness makes it difficult for many White Americans to realize that many people of Color do not universally hold their assumptions and values. For example, that healthy development means becoming an individual or "one's own person" is taken as a given and implicitly used to judge normality and abnormality. In counseling practice, it may mean that counselors who value individualism may unintentionally impose it on a client of Color. A 21-year-old Latino student who desires to consult with his mother and father before making a change in his major in college may be perceived by the counselor as overly dependent and immature.

For White Euro-American counselors, understanding what their Whiteness means to them is crucial to becoming culturally competent. Studies on White identity development suggest that the greater the awareness of counselors as to their Whiteness, the greater their multicultural counseling competencies (Brown, Parham, & Yonker, 1996; Carter, 1995; Neville et al., 1996; Neville, Worthington, & Spanierman, 2001; Parker, Moore, & Neimeyer, 1998; Thompson & Carter, 1997; Vinson & Neimeyer, 2000). Related to this is the need for White people to understand the meaning of "White privilege," how they have benefited from the injustices of the past, and to redefine their Whiteness in a nonracist manner (Helms, 1995). Gaining an awareness and understanding of Whiteness and White privilege is perhaps the greatest challenge for White trainees and professionals.

Likewise, people of Color, while more aware of their racial heritage, need to understand and become aware of their own issues related to race relations. It is often difficult for persons of Color to divorce themselves from the pain and anger caused by years of invalidation and oppression by Whites (Sue, 2003). This resentment and suspiciousness may be justified, but can create a schism that may prove more harmful than helpful. Overcoming this barrier requires people of Color to understand their own racial identity development (Atkinson et al., 1998; Helms, 1996, 2001; Sue & Sue, 2003); to make distinctions between intentional and unintentional racism (Ridley, 1995); to realize that in many respects, Whites, too, are victims because they are socialized into oppressor roles without their informed consent (Sue, 1999, 2003); and to realize that the formation of mutual respect and understanding can come about only through building multicultural alliances. Last, persons of Color must begin to realize that much work also has to occur among themselves (African American-Asian American, Native American-Latino American, etc.); that race relations are more than a minority-majority issue, but involve interracial relations as well; and that we must avoid the "who's more oppressed trap," which serves to divide rather than unify.

Racial-Cultural Knowledge

Understanding the worldviews of visible racial/ethnic groups means acquiring accurate information related to the cultural heritage, life experiences, and historical background of the diverse groups in our society. Counselors who work with client populations different from their own must possess specific information about the group. To be effective in working with Asian American families, for example, counselors must understand how family values and structures may differ from their own: that the family is the psychosocial unit of operation for members (not individualism); that the norm for communication may be vertical rather than horizontal; that the family may be more patriarchical than egalitarian; and that interdependence, not independence, is the valued norm.

But having facts is not enough. Racial-cultural competence requires the ability to interpret and translate such knowledge into sociological and psychological consequences for clients. Counselors must be able to understand how race and culture affect personality formation, vocational choices, help-seeking behavior, the manifestation of psychological disorders, and the appropriateness or inappropriateness of counseling and therapy approaches. In other words, acquisition of knowledge requires an active and not a passive application. When one considers that such an understanding is required for all groups of Color (e.g., African Americans, Latino Americans, and Native Americans) in our society, the magnitude of our work becomes obvious. While it is impossible to fully understand all the different groups in our society, understanding one group different from our own is a giant first step toward becoming racially-culturally competent.

Further, racial-cultural knowledge is more than a simple understanding of the lifestyles, cultural values, and assumptions of the group. It is not just racial-cultural differences that are important, but how these differences are perceived by our society and the meaning attached to them. Often, White individuals perceive racial-cultural differences as deficits or equate them with deviance. Thus, while many African Americans may value passion and expressiveness in their verbal and nonverbal communications, Euro-Americans often interpret these as signs of inability to be rational, being impulsive, or being out of control. Likewise, Asian Americans who may value restraint of strong feelings may be labeled inhibited, out of touch with their feelings, or repressed. When decisions are based on such misinterpretations, mental health professionals may misdiagnose their clients of Color with detrimental consequences (e.g., being shunted into dead-end jobs, hospitalized, misdiagnosed as mentally ill or retarded, and given inappropriate forms of treatment).

Likewise, it is important for counselors to be cognizant of the sociopolitical forces that constantly impinge on the life circumstance of persons of Color. Their racial reality is often one of constant invalidation, stereotyping, prejudice, and discrimination. While individual bias is harmful to persons of Color, it is often institutional policies and practices that cause the greatest damage. Institutional racism may result in poverty, unemployment, lower quality of health care, low self-esteem, poor performance in school, and mental health problems. These negative consequences are not intrinsic to persons of Color nor their communities, but are wrought upon them by discriminatory forces in our social system. The racially-culturally competent counselor must have specific knowledge of how the social system operates and affects the lives of people of Color.

Racial-Cultural Skills

As previously outlined, many people of Color perceive helping differently from their White counterparts. Many traditional Asian Americans perceive the credible helper as an "expert" who has the answers and will dispense wisdom via advice, teaching, and helpful suggestions. The role of the client is to remain relatively passive, while the helper takes on a more active role (Sue & Sue, 1999). African Americans attribute higher credibility to helpers who are not averse to their own self-disclosures and are more likely to "be real" and "human" in interacting with clients. Maintaining distance and objectivity on the part of counselors may be perceived by Black clients as signs of detachment and insincerity, attributes likely to lower the trustworthiness of the helping professional (Parham, 1997). Racial-cultural counseling competence means that the therapeutic transactions that occur between counselors and racially different clients must be characterized by a wide repertoire of helping responses (Ivey, Ivey, & Simek-Morgan, 1997; Sue, 1990). Universal therapeutic taboos against giving advice and suggestions or against counselor self-disclosure must be reconceived as among the potentially helpful therapeutic responses available to counseling professionals.

The ability to engage in indigenous healing practices or to utilize indigenous healing systems is another racial-cultural skill that would increase the effectiveness of counselors. For example, Ho'oponopono, sweat lodge purification, meditation, the use of storytelling and fables, reading from passages of the Koran, spiritual and collective integration of the Black church, and rituals that center consciousness have their roots in ancient cultural traditions and are time-tested methods of healing (Parham et al., 1999; Sue & Sue, 2003). Counselors must begin to accept indigenous healing practices as legitimate means of helping. Those who are comfortable and skilled in their use might consider combining them with Euro-American techniques to maximize effectiveness. Techniques such as acupuncture, acupressure, meditation, and yoga are increasingly used by counselors and therapists to reduce anxiety, specific phobias, and substance abuse and to enhance self-confidence, personal control, and marital satisfaction (Alexander, Rainforth, & Gelderloos, 1991; Kwee, 1990; Walsh, 1995; West, 1987). Counselors who are unskilled in their use must avoid viewing these indigenous practices as "unscientific," akin to mysticism, or supernatural.

This last point brings us to a very important issue. Many racial/ethnic communities might view the use of these healing methods as sacrilegious when used by "outsiders." It is incumbent on the mental health professional to respect such beliefs: a characteristic of a culturally competent counselor. In such a situation, the counselor might act as a facilitator of indigenous healing practices (Atkinson, Thompson, & Grant, 1993) by referring culturally different clients to healers in the community while continuing to work with them. The ability to refer clients to community resources assumes that counselors are intimately connected to the communities they hope to serve. To become familiar with the client's community, helping professionals must leave their office and form liaisons with community leaders (Lewis, Lewis, Daniels, & D'Andrea, 1998). Doing so is more than a professional activity: It involves a very personal commitment to form relationships with the client's cultural community.

In addition to freeing oneself from the therapeutic taboos in traditional models of counseling and being able to honor, respect, and utilize indigenous healing methods, racial-cultural competence requires systemic intervention skills:

Culturally skilled counselors are able to engage in psychoeducational or systems intervention roles, in addition to their clinical ones. Although conventional counseling and clinical roles are valuable, other roles such as the consultant, advocate, adviser, teacher, facilitator of indigenous healing and so on may prove more culturally appropriate. (Sue et al., 1998, p. 42)

To become culturally competent, counselors and trainees must receive appropriate education and training. Counselors will not be able to adopt the awareness, knowledge, and skills necessary to be culturally competent without a proper restructuring of the education and training programs already in place.

IMPLICATIONS FOR EDUCATION AND TRAINING

The importance of developing racial-cultural competence in counseling and therapy is even more pressing in light of our changing demographics. The question before us is: What type of training programs and experiences are required to develop the awareness, knowledge, and skills necessary to work effectively with different racial-cultural groups? Fortunately, a growing professional literature provides us with many exciting and important models of multicultural training (Abreu, Chung, & Atkinson, 2000; Carney & Kahn, 1984; Kiselica, 1998; Munoz & Sanchez, 1996; Ponterotto, Alexander, & Grieger, 1995; Ridley et al., 2000; Ridley, Mendoza, Kanitz, Angermeier, & Zenk, 1994; Sue, 2001). Our discussion in this last section is mainly confined to outlining several important training requirements to aid trainees in developing racial-cultural competence:

1. First and foremost, directors of training programs must recognize that becoming racially-culturally competent is more than an intellectual exercise confined to book learning in the classroom. If dealing with issues of bigotry, bias, and unintentional racism were simply a matter of acquiring accurate information, we would have eliminated them years ago. Racism is deeply embedded in the psyche, held there by nested or embedded emotions, and cannot be unmasked without experiences that challenge the invalid assumptions and beliefs of trainees. Including course work on multiculturalism and the mental health of people of Color is important, but becoming truly competent requires "lived reality." The failure of traditional education and training programs is that they do not provide life experiences for trainees that force them to understand racial-cultural groups on an experiential level. Faculty must build into their academic requirements activities that include not only experiential activities and role-plays, but interactions with communities of Color: attending community forums and events, observing and participating in community celebrations, doing volunteer work, establishing relationships (personal rather than professional) with members of the community, serving on community committees and boards, and developing personal social friendships with people of Color. Such activities will help trainees to reduce their anxiety and fears, challenge stereotypes and biases, observe leadership in action, increase interactions with healthy members of the community, view racial/ethnic group members as "real people" rather than "objects of study," and increase awareness of community resources.

2. A strong antiracism component must be a part of the education and training program. Course work and experiential activities related to understanding oneself as a racial-cultural being are important facets of becoming racially-culturally competent. A useful starting point is the assumption that everyone possesses biases, prejudices, and racist attitudes and beliefs. Although these are not acquired by free choice, people are products of their cultural conditioning and must face the fact that no one is immune from inheriting the racial biases of their forebears. Addressing this issue means studying the manifestation of individual, institutional, and societal racism, how trainees are products of a biased system, how the mental health professions are culture-bound, and how traditional forms of assessment, diagnosis, and treatment may be biased against people of Color. Antiracism training is much enhanced through using White racial identity and people of Color identity development models to form the basis of course work and experiential exercises.

3. Becoming racially-culturally competent means breaking free from the narrow confines of counseling and therapy. The in-the-office, one-to-one remediation approach may be a helpful mode of treatment in some situations, but it is not the only helping mode available. For example, when the problems of clients of Color reside in systemic forces (unfair or biased policies and practices of our institutions and social policy), the racially-culturally competent helping professional must be able to intervene at an individual as well as a systemic level. Yet, our training programs do an inadequate job in helping trainees develop the skills necessary to effectively intervene in the social system. Training programs fail to teach psychoeducational skills, institutional intervention strategies, or advocacy techniques. Teaching clients how to interview and find jobs, advocating for change in a biased school system, forming liaisons with community leaders, meeting clients in their home, utilizing community resources, giving advice to clients on how to negotiate organizational structures, and offering consultation services are all activities that call for different professional roles played by helping professionals. Atkinson et al. (1998) have identified six helping roles in addition to the conventional counseling role: (1) advocate (representing the interests of a client or group; speaking on their behalf), (2) change agent (changing a social environment that may oppress), (3) consultant (collegial relationship toward prevention), (4) advisor (giving advice and suggestions), (5) facilitator of indigenous support systems (referring clients to or working with community support services: ethnic churches, service organizations, extended families), and (6) facilitator of indigenous healing methods (culture-specific methods and healers). These roles require almost revolutionary changes not only in the curriculum and practica/internships, but also in the professional definition of counseling psychology (Vera, Buhin, Montgomery, & Shin, this *Handbook,* this volume).

4. Graduate programs in psychology often overlook an important requirement for effective racial-cultural training: the invalid assumption that administrators, faculty, supervisors, and staff are culturally competent. How is it possible to teach students to be culturally competent when the faculty lack racial-cultural competence themselves? More often than not, educators are no different from their students in their awareness, knowledge, and skills concerning racial-cultural issues. Indeed, sometimes students are more sophisticated than their professors on matters of race, culture, and ethnicity. As a group, educators have been socialized into the

"academic protocol" that values objectivity, rational discourse, and the avoidance of emotionality. Often, discussions dealing with race, racism, and bigotry arouse intense feelings and reactions, which prevent one group from understanding another. Like their students, educators must work through their underlying biases, preconceived notions, prejudices, and stereotypes. The means by which this process occurs is most often through engaging and experiencing difficult dialogues. These occur when major differences in worldview, personality, and perspective are made public, are challenged, are found to be offensive to others, or trigger intense emotional responses. An individual or group engaged in a difficult dialogue feels at risk for potentially disclosing intimate thoughts, beliefs, or feelings generated by the topic at hand. These topics usually involve race, gender, sexual orientation, or disability. Professors need intensive and ongoing training so they can help their students recognize the importance of understanding, recognizing, and facilitating difficult dialogues in classrooms, therapy sessions, social gatherings, public forums, business and industry, municipalities, and other settings.

CONCLUSION

Developing racial-cultural competence requires a systematic effort on the part of training programs at every level of education. Understanding how the educational culture of the program enhances or negates the development of racial-cultural competencies is crucial to productive development (Sue, 1995, 2001). In other words, it does little good that individual instructors may present multicultural content to students when the very educational institution that employs them is filled with monocultural policies and practices. In many cases, organizational customs do not value or allow the use of racial-cultural knowledge or skills in the educational context. Educational institutions may even actively discourage, negate, or punish racial-cultural expressions among its faculty and students. Thus, it is imperative to examine the racial-cultural competence of institutions of higher learning as well. How we move educational and training institutions so that they become truly multicultural is a major challenge. The counseling profession stands at a major crossroad (Y. T. Lee, 1993): Will it continue the path of monoculturalism, or will it show the courage and conviction to move toward racial-cultural competence?

REFERENCES

Abreu, J. M., Chung, R. H. G., & Atkinson, D. R. (2000). Multicultural counseling training: Past, present, and future directions. *Counseling Psychologist, 28,* 641–656.

Alexander, C., Rainforth, M., & Gelderloos, P. (1991). Transcendental meditation, self-actualization and psychological health: A conceptual overview and statistical meta-analysis. *Journal of Social Behavior and Personality, 6,* 189–247.

American Association for Marriage and Family Therapy. (1998). *AAMFT code of ethics.* Washington, DC: Author.

American Counseling Association. (1995). *Code of ethics and standards of practice.* Alexandria, VA: Author.

American Psychological Association. (1995). *Ethical principles of psychologists and code of conduct.* Washington, DC: Author.

American Psychological Association. (2002). *Ethical principles of psychologists and code of conduct.* Washington, DC: Author.

American Psychological Association. (2003). Guidelines on Multicultural Education, Training, Research, Practice, and Organizational Change for Psychologists. *American Psychologist, 58*(5), 377–402.

Atkinson, D. R., Morten, G., & Sue, D. W. (1998). *Counseling American minorities* (5th ed.). Boston: McGraw-Hill.

Atkinson, D. R., Thompson, C. E., & Grant, S. K. (1993). A three-dimensional model for counseling racial/ethnic minorities. *Counseling Psychologist, 21,* 257–277.

Berman, J. (1979). Counseling skills used by black and white male and female counselors. *Journal of Counseling Psychology, 26,* 81–84.

Brown, S. P., Parham, T. A., & Yonker, R. (1996). Influence of cross-cultural training course on racial identity attitudes of white women and men: Preliminary perspectives. *Journal of Counseling and Development, 74,* 302–310.

Carney, C. G., & Kahn, K. B. (1984). Building competencies for effective cross-cultural counseling: A developmental view. *Counseling Psychologist, 12,* 111–119.

Carter, R. T. (1995). *The influence of race and racial identity in psychotherapy.* New York: Wiley.

Carter, R. T. (in press). Uprooting inequity and disparities in counseling and psychology: An introduction. In R. T. Carter (Ed.), *Handbook of racial-cultural psychology and counseling: Theory and research* (Vol. 1, pp. xv–xxviii). Hoboken, NJ: Wiley.

Carter, R. T., & Qureshi, A. (1995). A typology of philosophical assumptions in multicultural counseling and training. In J. G. Ponterotto, J. M. Casas, L. A. Suzuki, & C. M. Alexander (Eds.), *Handbook of multicultural counseling* (pp. 239–262). Thousand Oaks, CA: Sage.

Constantine, M. G., & Ladany, N. (2001). New visions for defining and assessing multicultural counseling competence. In J. G. Ponterotto, J. M. Casas, L. A. Suzuki, & C. M. Alexander (Eds.), *Handbook of multicultural counseling* (pp. 257–288). Thousand Oaks, CA: Sage.

D'Andrea, M., Daniels, J., & Heck, R. (1991). Evaluating the impact of multicultural counseling training. *Journal of Counseling and Development, 70,* 143–150.

Grencavage, L. M., & Norcross, J. C. (1990). Where are the commonalties among the therapeutic common factors. *Professional Psychology: Research and Practice, 21,* 372–378.

Harner, M. (1990). *The way of the shaman.* San Francisco: Harper & Row.

Helms, J. E. (1990). *Black and white racial identity: Theory, research, and practice.* New York: Greenwood Press.

Helms, J. E. (1995). An update of Helms's White and people of Color racial identity models. In J. G. Ponterotto, J. M. Casas, L. A. Suzuki, & C. M. Alexander (Eds.), *Handbook of multicultural counseling* (pp. 181–198). Thousand Oaks, CA: Sage.

Helms, J. E. (2001). An update of Helms's White and people of Color racial identity models. In J. G. Ponterotto, J. M. Casas, L. A. Suzuki, & C. M. Alexander (Eds.), *Handbook of multicultural counseling* (2nd ed., pp. 181–198). Thousand Oaks, CA: Sage.

Helms, J. E., & Richardson, T. Q. (1997). How "multiculturalism" obscures race and culture as differential aspects of counseling competency. In D. B. Pope-Davis & H. L. K. Coleman

(Eds.), *Multicultural counseling competencies: Assessment, education and training, and supervision* (pp. 60–79). Thousand Oaks, CA: Sage.

Herring, R. D. (1999). *Counseling with Native American Indians and Alaska Natives.* Thousand Oaks, CA: Sage.

Highlen, P. S. (1994). Racial/ethnic diversity in doctoral programs of psychology: Challenges for the twenty-first century. *Applied and Preventive Psychology, 3,* 91–108.

Highlen, P. S. (1996). MCT theory and implications for organizations/systems. In D. W. Sue, A. E. Ivey, & P. B. Pedersen (Eds.), *A theory of multicultural counseling and therapy* (pp. 65–85). Pacific Grove, CA: Brooks/Cole.

Ivey, A. E., Ivey, M., & Simek-Morgan, L. (1997). *Counseling and psychotherapy: A multicultural perspective.* Boston: Allyn & Bacon.

Katz, J. (1985). The sociopolitical nature of counseling. *Counseling Psychologist, 13,* 615–624.

Kiselica, M. S. (1998). Preparing Anglos for the challenges and joys of multiculturalism. *Counseling Psychologist, 26,* 5–21.

Kluckhohn, F. R., & Strodtbeck, F. L. (1961). *Variations in value orientations.* Evanston, IL: Row, Peterson.

Korchin, S. J. (1976). *Modern clinical psychology.* New York: Basic Books.

Kwee, M. (Ed.). (1990). *Psychotherapy, meditation and health.* London: East-West.

LaFromboise, T. D., Coleman, H. L. K., & Hernandez, A. (1991). Development and factor structure of the Cross-Cultural Counseling Inventory-Revised. *Professional Psychology: Research and Practice, 22,* 380–388.

Lee, L. C., & Zane, N. W. S. (1998). *Handbook of Asian American psychology.* Thousand Oaks, CA: Sage.

Lee, Y. T. (1993). Psychology needs no prejudice but the diversity of cultures. *American Psychologist, 48,* 1090–1091.

Lewis, J. A., Lewis, M. D., Daniels, J. A., & D'Andrea, M. J. (1998). *Community counseling.* Pacific Grove, CA: Brooks/Cole.

Munoz, R. H., & Sanchez, A. M. (1996). *Developing culturally competent systems of care for state mental health services.* Boulder, CO: WICHE.

Neville, H. A., Heppner, M. J., Louie, C. E., Thompson, E. C., Brooks, L., & Baker, R. (1996). The impact of multicultural training on white racial identity attitudes and therapy competencies. *Professional Psychology: Research and Practice, 27,* 83–89.

Neville, H. A., Worthington, R. L., & Spanierman, L. B. (2001). Race, power, and multicultural counseling psychology: Understanding White privilege and color-blind racial attitudes. In J. G. Ponterotto, J. M. Casas, L. A. Suzuki, & C. M. Alexander (Eds.), *Handbook of multicultural counseling* (pp. 257–288). Thousand Oaks, CA: Sage.

Nwachuku, U., & Ivey, A. (1991). Culture specific counseling: An alternative approach. *Journal of Counseling and Development, 70,* 106–111.

Paniagua, F. A. (1998). *Assessing and treating culturally diverse clients.* Thousand Oaks, CA: Sage.

Parham, T. A. (1997). An African-centered view of dual relationships. In B. Herlihy & G. Corey (Eds.), *Boundary issues in counseling* (pp. 109–112). Alexandria, VA: American Counseling Association.

Parham, T. A., White, J. L., & Ajamu, A. (1999). *The psychology of blacks: An African centered perspective* (3rd ed.). Englewood Cliffs, NJ: Prentice-Hall.

Parker, W. M., Moore, M. A., & Neimeyer, G. J. (1998). Altering white racial identity and interracial comfort through multicultural training. *Journal of Counseling and Development, 76,* 302–310.

Pedersen, P. B. (1994). *A handbook for developing multicultural awareness.* Alexandria, VA: American Counseling Association.

Ponterotto, J. G. (1997). Multicultural counseling training: A competency model and national survey. In D. B. Pope-Davis & H. L. K Coleman (Vol. Eds.), *Multicultural aspects of counseling series: Vol. 7. Multicultural Counseling competencies: Assessment, education, training, and supervision* (pp. 111–130). Thousand Oaks, CA: Sage.

Ponterotto, J. G., Alexander, C. M., & Grieger, I. A. (1995). Multicultural competency checklist for counseling training programs. *Journal of Multicultural Counseling and Development, 23*(1), 11–20.

Ponterotto, J. G., Sanchez, C. M., & Magids, D. M. (1991, August). *Initial development and validation of the Multicultural Counseling Awareness Scale (MCAS-B).* Paper presented at the annual convention of the American Psychological Association, San Francisco.

Reisman, J. (1971). *Toward the integration of psychotherapy.* New York: Wiley.

Ridley, C. R. (1995). *Overcoming unintentional racism in counseling and therapy: A practitioner's guide to intentional intervention.* Thousand Oaks, CA: Sage.

Ridley, C. R., Baker, D. M., & Hill, C. L. (2000, August). *Multicultural counseling competence: Reexamination, reconceptualization, and practical application.* Paper presented at the American Psychological Association Annual Convention, Washington, DC.

Ridley, C. R., Mendoza, D. W., Kanitz, B. E., Angermeier, L., & Zenk, R. (1994). Cultural sensitivity in multicultural counseling: A perceptual schema model. *Journal of Counseling Psychology, 41,* 125–136.

Sabnani, H. B., Ponterotto, J. G., & Borodovsky, L. G. (1991). White racial identity development and cross-cultural counselor training. *Counseling Psychologist, 19,* 76–102.

Schofield, W. (1964). *Psychotherapy: The purchase of friendship.* Englewood Cliffs, NJ: Prentice-Hall.

Sodowsky, G. R., Taffe, R. C., Gutkin, T. B., & Wise, S. L. (1994). Development of the Multicultural Counseling Inventory: A self-report measure of multicultural competencies. *Journal of Counseling Psychology, 41,* 137–148.

Stewart, E. C. (1971). *American cultural patterns: A cross-cultural perspective.* Pittsburgh, PA: Regional Council for International Understanding.

Sue, D. W. (1990). Culture specific techniques in counseling: A conceptual framework. *Professional Psychology: Research and Practice, 21,* 424–433.

Sue, D. W. (1995). Multicultural organizational development: Implications for the counseling profession. In J. G. Ponterotto, J. M. Casas, L. A. Suzuki, & C. M. Alexander (Eds.), *Handbook of multicultural counseling* (pp. 474–492). Thousand Oaks, CA: Sage.

Sue, D. W. (1999). Creating conditions for a constructive dialogue on "race": Taking individual and institutional responsibility. In J. Q. Adams & J. R. Welsch (Eds.), *Cultural diversity: Curriculum, classroom, and climate.* Chicago: Staff and Curriculum Developers Association.

Sue, D. W. (2001). Multidimensional facets of cultural competence. *Counseling Psychologist, 29,* 790–821.

Sue, D. W. (2003). *Overcoming our racism: The journey of liberation.* San Francisco: Jossey-Bass.

Sue, D. W., Arredondo, P., & McDavis, R. J. (1992). Multicultural competencies/standards: A pressing need. *Journal of Counseling and Development, 70,* 477–486.

Sue, D. W., Bernier, J. B., Durran, M., Feinberg, L., Pedersen, P., Smith, E., et al. (1982). Position paper: Cross-cultural counseling competencies. *Counseling Psychologist, 10,* 45–52.

Sue, D. W., Bingham, R., Porche-Burke, L., & Vasquez, M. (1999). The diversification of psychology: A multicultural revolution. *American Psychologist, 54,* 1061–1069.

Sue, D. W., Carter, R. T., Casas, J. M., Fouad, N. A., Ivey, A. E., Jensen, M., et al. (1998). *Multicultural counseling competencies: Individual and organizational development.* Thousand Oaks, CA: Sage.

Sue, D. W., Ivey, A. E., & Pedersen, P. B. (1996). *A theory of multicultural counseling and therapy.* Pacific Grove, CA: Brooks/Cole.

Sue, D. W., & Sue, D. (1999). *Counseling the culturally different: Theory and practice* (3rd ed.). New York: Wiley.

Sue, D. W., & Sue, D. (2003). *Counseling the culturally diverse: Theory and practice* (4th ed.). New York: Wiley.

Thompson, C. E., & Carter, R. T. (1997). An overview and elaboration of Helms's racial identity development theory. In C. E. Thompson & R. T. Carter (Eds.), *Racial identity theory: Applications to individual, group, and organizational interventions* (pp. 15–32). Mahwah, NJ: Erlbaum.

U.S. Census Bureau. (2000). *U.S. Census 2000, Summary Files.* Available from http://www.census.gov.

Vinson, T. S., & Neimeyer, G. J. (2000). The relationship between racial identity development and multicultural counseling competency. *Journal of Multicultural Counseling and Development, 28,* 177–192.

Walsh, R. (1995). Initial meditative experiences: Part I. *Journal of Transpersonal Psychology, 9,* 151–192.

Wehrly, B. (1995). *Pathways to multicultural counseling competence.* Pacific Grove, CA: Brooks/Cole.

West, M. (Ed.). (1987). *The psychology of meditation.* Oxford, England: Clarendon Press.

CHAPTER 2

Emerging Approaches to Training Psychologists to Be Culturally Competent

Joseph G. Ponterotto and Richard Austin

The critical importance of training psychologists and mental health professionals for work in an increasingly multicultural society is now unquestioned (see Atkinson, Brown, & Casas, 1996; Pope-Davis, Coleman, Liu, & Toporek, 2003; Sue et al., 1998). Continuing demographic transitions and evolving mandates of professional accrediting bodies demand that all mental health training programs address multicultural issues in a coordinated and thorough manner. First, with regard to census projections, it is now clear that the demographic face of the United States is changing rapidly. As of 1999, 28% of the U.S. population consisted of citizens of racial/ethnic minority backgrounds, namely, African Americans, Hispanic Americans, Asian Americans/Pacific Islanders, and American Indians. By the year 2050, the collective minority representation will reach 48%. The average growth rate per decade from the year 2000 to the year 2050 is projected to be as follows: White Americans 2.42%, African Americans, 10.82%, American Indians, 10.84%, Hispanic Americans, 27.62%, and Asian American/Pacific Islanders, 29.96% (U.S. Bureau of the Census, 2000). It is clear that psychologists working in all corridors of this country will be interacting increasingly with a culturally diverse clientele.

Second, multicultural training and competency evaluation is being increasingly emphasized in competency mandates issued by state education departments and licensing boards, by professional associations, and by managed care organizations. Professional organizations such as the American Psychological Association (1996), the American Counseling Association (1988), and the National Council on the Accreditation of Teacher Education Programs (2001) clearly specify multicultural training components in their accreditation criteria.

Recent surveys in professional specialties further document the increasing influence of cultural perspectives as a core component of training and practice. For example, in counseling psychology, a recent Delphi Poll of training directors on the future of the profession identified "commitment to issues of diversity" as the single greatest future core identification for the field over the next 10 years (Neimeyer & Diamond, 2001, p. 57).

Despite the overall momentum and increasing commitment to multicultural competence in the profession, there exists great variability in the procedures, mechanisms, and methods employed by psychology programs to integrate multiculturalism into their training mission. Understandably, some programs are more effective than others in adequately preparing students for the realities of multicultural practice and research.

The purpose of this chapter is to review select, creative, and emerging approaches to multicultural training. We believe that these models represent state-of-the-art training that facilitates more comprehensive integration of multicultural issues throughout the curriculum. The chapter is organized into three major sections. The first section reviews briefly the current status of multicultural training in professional psychology, summarizes a brief literature on training levels and designs, and introduces a popular integration model and evaluation tool. The second section describes two creative, experiential-focused multicultural course designs. The final major section reviews creative off-campus, community-centered, and international training initiatives. A goal of this chapter is to stimulate educators in professional psychology to think beyond traditional didactic multicultural learning and embrace more in vivo, highly interactive cross-cultural training.

STATUS OF MULTICULTURAL TRAINING IN PROFESSIONAL PSYCHOLOGY

Taken as a whole, survey evidence in the 1990s indicates that although programs in professional psychology have made great strides in addressing issues of diversity during training, there remains much progress to be made in terms of fully integrating multiculturalism as a central component of training. Reporting the results of a clinical psychology training survey, Bernal and Castro (1994) concluded that the specialty is equipping students with some cultural awareness, but not with adequate cultural proficiency and competence. Similar evaluations could be made from training survey data in school psychology (Rogers, Ponterotto, Conoley, & Wiese, 1992), counseling psychology and counselor education (Ponterotto, 1997), and community psychology (Suarez-Balcazar, Durlak, & Smith, 1994).

Two important studies have examined multicultural awareness levels in practicing psychologists, counselors, and educators. In a paper-and-pencil survey of practicing doctoral-level psychologists in counseling and clinical psychology, respondents indicated that though they worked with racial/ethnic minority clientele, only a small percentage felt professionally prepared and fully competent to do so (Allison, Crawford, Echemendia, Robinson, & Knepp, 1994).

Focusing specifically on White Caucasian Americans, D'Andrea and Daniels (2001) recently reported the results of a 16-year ongoing qualitative study (using interviews and observations) on White racism. Well represented among the sample were practicing psychologists, counselors, and educators. In examining White persons' reactions to issues of racism, the authors uncovered three emergent patterns. First, many respondents expressed "overt anger" at the current attention in the profession being devoted to multiculturalism and to acknowledging ongoing racism in the profession and in society. These respondents reported being tired of the pressure to be "politically correct." A second pattern emerging among the sample was a sense of "general apathy" toward racism. Finally, the third pattern identified was a sense of "intellectual detachment" among many White professionals who acknowledged the existence of ongoing racism but neglected to take action to combat various forms of oppression in their personal or professional lives.

D'Andrea and Daniels's descriptive qualitative study supports the notion that many White professionals, who dominate the profession numerically, are at lower to middle stages of racial identity development (Carter, 1995; Helms, 1995), which has been correlated to lower levels of multicultural counseling competence (Constantine, Juby, & Liang, 2001; Ottavi, Pope-Davis, & Dings, 1994; Vinson & Neimeyer, 2000).

With a brief review of the status of multicultural training in hand, we now turn to a discussion of varied training levels extant in the helping professions.

Multicultural Training Levels

On a general level, psychology training programs vary in the level of attention to and integration of multicultural issues in the curriculum. A helpful conceptualization is provided by D'Andrea and Daniels (1991), who characterize counseling training programs along two levels and four specific stages (see column 1 of Figure 2.1). The first level is called Cultural Encapsulation and is characterized by an almost nonexistent multicultural training approach spearheaded by a mostly White, middle-class male faculty. This level is divided into two specific stages, a Culturally Entrenched stage and a Cross-Cultural Awakening stage.

In the Culturally Entrenched stage, training programs provide minimal to no exploration of the issues related to the mental health needs of racial and ethnic minority persons. Training programs at this stage are based on the assumption that all counselors and client populations share the same basic beliefs about normality, appropriateness, and personal needs. In the second stage, Cross-Cultural Awakening, programs still do little to incorporate multiculturalism into training; however, a developing awareness of multicultural issues emerges. During this stage, multicultural

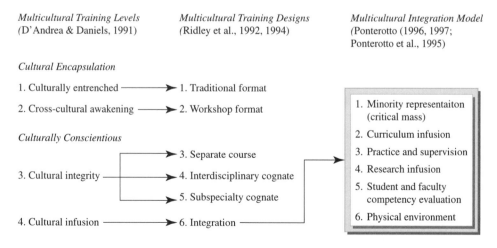

Figure 2.1   Classifications of multicultural counseling training levels and designs.

issues are introduced in some classes, and students are encouraged to attend multicultural training workshops.

In the second level of the D'Andrea and Daniels (1991) model, named Culturally Conscientious, faculty not only acknowledge the critical role that cultural, racial, gender, and class factors play in a person's overall development, but they also implement specific institutional changes to ensure that multicultural training is provided in a systematic fashion. The Conscientious level consists of two stages: Cultural Integrity and Cultural Infusion. The Cultural Integrity stage is characterized by increased attention to multicultural issues and the existence of a specific multicultural counseling course taught by a professor with multicultural expertise. Some programs may also offer multiple culture-centered courses organized as training cognates.

In the final stage, Cultural Infusion, programs fully and systematically integrate multicultural issues into the entire curriculum. Programs at this stage are committed to culturally diverse representation among students and faculty and integrate multicultural issues into all courses, externship supervision, comprehensive exams, research mentoring, and student/faculty competency evaluations. In a qualitative study (using extensive interviewing and program case studies) of the status of counseling programs vis-à-vis training levels, D'Andrea and Daniels (1991) determined that the majority of counseling training programs were operating at level 1, stage 2, the Cross-Cultural Awakening stage.

However, since the classic D'Andrea and Daniels (1991) article was published, significant multicultural progress has been made in a number of counseling programs nationwide. Examining the results of a national survey (Ponterotto, 1997) of counseling training, where 89% of programs require a multicultural course, 62% have multiple multicultural courses, and 58% attempt to integrate multicultural issues into all coursework, we would now place the majority of programs at level 2, stage 3, Cultural Integrity, with some reaching stage 4, Cultural Infusion.

Having examined various general levels of multicultural training, we now turn to a brief review of more specific training designs.

Multicultural Training Designs

Copeland (1982) was the first scholar to posit varied training designs, identifying the following four approaches: separate course, area of concentration (or subspecialty cognate), interdisciplinary approach, and integration. Also, Ridley and colleagues (Ridley, Espelage, & Rubinstein, 1997; Ridley, Mendoza, & Kanitz, 1992, 1994) expanded the list to include the traditional design and the workshop design, bringing the total to six approaches (see Column 2 of Figure 2.1). The traditional design does not acknowledge the salience of cultural factors in counseling, believing that psychological interventions developed by and for European Americans transcend cultures. The workshop design is regarded as an extension of the traditional design because it requires no changes in the existing curriculum. Rather, this design encourages students to attend workshops or in-service events concerning issues of diversity, which is a minor recognition of the importance of cultural dynamics in counseling.

In the separate course design, training programs usually offer one or two courses in their curriculum that aim to promote trainee competence in cross-cultural counseling. The separate course design was the most common approach to addressing multicultural issues (see Ridley et al., 1992, 1994, 1997), and for a number of model multicultural programs, the establishment of this separate course served as a stepping stone to fuller integration of multicultural issues. The interdisciplinary and subspecialty cognate designs go beyond the separate course model by conceptually linking a cluster of culture-based courses. Specifically, in the interdisciplinary approach, a trainee is encouraged to take multicultural courses in multiple disciplines, such as counseling, sociology, anthropology, and ethnic studies; in the subspecialty cognate, trainees complete sequence of courses in multicultural counseling in such areas as assessment, research, supervision, and family counseling.

The final program design is the integrated program, where multicultural issues are infused throughout the entire curriculum and training experience. In this design, multiculturalism is at the very core of all counseling and clinical training. An emphasis in most integrated programs is on the trainees' self-awareness of their own cultural socialization and the impact of their own worldview in understanding, relating to, and helping clients from diverse backgrounds. Additional emphases are placed on developing cultural knowledge of the groups one plans to work with and developing specific culturally relevant skills.

The consensus among multicultural specialists is that the integrated program design is not only the most fruitful, but perhaps the only feasible alternative to training culturally competent counselors and psychologists (e.g., Abreu, Chung, & Atkinson, 2000; Leach & Carlton, 1997; Ponterotto, 1998; Ridley et al., 1992, 1994). Studies of model multicultural programs in counseling and school psychology indicate that exemplar programs incorporate full multicultural integration in all aspects of program activity (Ponterotto, 1997; Rogers, Hoffman, & Wade, 1998). For a detailed case study of an exemplar integrated program, see Atkinson et al. (1996) and Ponterotto (1996), who describe and evaluate critically the University of California, Santa Barbara, Combined Ph.D. Program in Counseling/Clinical/School Psychology.

An Integration Model of Multicultural Training

Working from a counseling psychology base and examining nominated model multicultural training programs, Ponterotto, Alexander, and Grieger (1995) developed a competency model that outlined 22 specific areas of multicultural competency organized into six broad domains: minority representation, curriculum issues, practice and supervision, research considerations, student and faculty competency evaluation, and physical environment. The competency model is organized as a practical checklist to facilitate program development and multicultural goal setting. The Appendix to this chapter presents the latest 24-item (two items were added) version of the Multicultural Competency Program Checklist (see Appendix).

The multicultural program checklist has been used to examine the general status of counseling training programs nationwide (Constantine, Ladany, Inman, & Ponterotto, 1996; Ponterotto, 1997) and as part of specific case studies to evaluate select training programs (Ponterotto, 1996) and predoctoral internship centers (Manese, Wu, & Nepomuceno, 2001). Figure 2.1 presents a schema demonstrating the link between D'Andrea and Daniels's (1991) training levels, Ridley et al.'s (1992) training designs, and Ponterotto et al.'s (1995) integration model.

Having presented a brief review of multicultural training levels, multicultural program designs, and an integration model, the remainder of this chapter turns to a review of emerging training designs and strategies geared to more adequately preparing psychologists for multicultural practice and research. The following sections address innovative course-anchored training approaches and off-campus training initiatives.

COURSE-FOCUSED MULTICULTURAL TRAINING

Two innovative, experiential-focused, and course-anchored training approaches are found at Teachers College, Columbia University and the University of Maryland at College Park. Both courses are housed in Counseling Psychology programs.

Teachers College Racial Cultural Lab Course

For over a decade now, Teachers College, Columbia University has offered an innovative and required Racial Cultural Lab course. The course, designed by Professor Robert T. Carter, employs a variety of instructional strategies: didactic lectures, writing assignments, role-plays, and group process (see Carter, this *Handbook,* this volume).

Prior to the beginning of the course, each student is instructed to write an autobiography that includes how social class, religion, ethnicity, and race have played a role in his or her life development. The course is then divided into two sections. The first section employs a lecture format to disseminate information to students about a variety of multicultural issues. The second section, which is completed in smaller groups of six to eight students, involves an intense experiential process.

During this second portion of the class, each student is interviewed by the group members and the group leader. Based on his or her autobiography, the student responds to questions that include a discussion of how each identity (e.g., social class, religion, ethnicity, and race) influences his or her worldview. More specifically, the student explains how he or she affirms or disaffirms each identity and discusses any feelings of ambivalence related to these factors. During the course of the interview, which can last from one hour for each identity to several class periods, the students are constantly challenged by the instructor and the small group leaders to focus on the particular factor about which they have been questioned (see Carter, 1995, 2003).

The students keep journals that address their feelings about the process. They are required to write at least seven pages after each class day and hand in the journals to the instructor on a weekly basis. The instructor then responds to the students' comments by asking questions and sharing additional observations. The journal eventually becomes the transcript of the running dialogue between instructor and student.

During the second half of the semester, a training component is utilized in which students work in dyads and engage in role-plays designed to simulate different multicultural counseling experiences. The Multicultural Counseling Lab course can prove to be an extremely challenging experience, as students are forced to confront difficult issues in regard to their worldview, such as their own entrenched stereotypes, prejudices, privileges, and internalized racism.

Multicultural Immersion Experience Course

Pope-Davis, Breaux, and Liu (1997) proposed a Multicultural Immersion Experience class that combines affective and cognitive multicultural learning tools. The course is divided into three phases. The first phase requires students to identify a group that they perceive as being culturally different from their own (e.g., Asian Americans, Native Americans, gays and lesbians, bisexuals) within the university or the surrounding community. The student is then expected to immerse himself or herself in that group during the course of the academic semester, participating in the group's organizational events, social gatherings, presentations, and meetings.

Prior to immersing themselves in the identified group, students are assessed on their overall multicultural competence using self-report instruments (e.g., the Multicultural Counseling Inventory [MCI; Sodowsky, Taffe, Gutkin, & Wise, 1994]). The initial assessment serves as a baseline measure of the student's overall efficacy prior to the immersion experience. Upon completion of the course, students are again assessed in terms of multicultural competency to examine any growth or impasses in this area. Also, in preparation for the immersion experience, students write a brief autobiography that addresses their own issues of oppression, race, class, and gender in a manner that may link their experiences to that of the group in which they will be immersed.

The second phase of the course requires that the students maintain a journal describing and processing their immersion experiences. Journal entries are made daily or weekly and have no length restrictions. Journaling is an effective tool for processing feelings of discomfort or anxiety associated with the immersion experience. Students are also encouraged to use the journals to write down questions that may be discussed in class and as a source of further reflection (Pope-Davis et al., 1997).

The third and final phase of the Multicultural Immersion Experience course is the final presentation, in which the students and members of the immersed group lead a class discussion about their respective experiences. The remaining portion of the class includes the students' postexperience multicultural competency assessment and reflections on the journal. Other suggested activities can entail the students creating a syllabus for a potential course on the particular immersed group (Pope-Davis et al., 1997).

The Multicultural Immersion Experience is an intensive process that requires a great deal of coordination among various organizations within the university and the surrounding community. Notwithstanding the coordination challenges in running such a course, the immersion experience provides a significant contribution to the area of in vivo exposure, which many researchers suggest is lacking in multicultural competence training (Alderfer, this *Handbook,* this volume; McRae & Johnson, 1991; Ridley et al., 1994).

The Teachers College, Columbia University and University of Maryland multicultural courses are examples of creative course-anchored training currently taking place in some professional psychology programs. These courses extend the more traditional didactic and case study class designs to more directly deal with personal awareness and bias and in vivo cross-cultural interaction. In recent years, an important literature base has evolved that directly addresses challenges in and strategies for teaching multicultural psychology courses (e.g., Reynolds, 1995; Ridley et al., 1997; Vazquez, 1997).

Though quite innovative, the courses described previously are understandably limited in fully preparing students for the complexities of multicultural counseling and research because they are primarily campus-based. In the next section, we review training philosophies and model programs that literally immerse trainees in another culture.

OFF-CAMPUS MULTICULTURAL TRAINING

Immersion in a new cultural milieu forces trainees to examine their own cultural socialization as they experience firsthand variant and possibly conflicting worldviews. When immersed in another culture, without the possibility of retreat into one's home culture, the trainee is forced to negotiate the host culture and develop bicultural skills. Likewise, the immersion process may help advance racial (or ethnic, or religious) identity development. Bicultural skill development and higher stages of racial/ethnic identity development are important components of "multicultural personality" development, which is hypothesized to correlate with quality of life indicators and with enhanced effectiveness of psychologists and educators working in heterogeneous environments (Ponterotto, Costa, & Werner-Lin, 2002; Ponterotto, Mendelsohn, & Belizaire, 2003; Ramirez, 1999).

Among the most innovative immersion-focused multicultural training programs we identified in preparing this chapter were the ethnography-focused training at John F. Kennedy University and the international exchange programs at the State University of New York in Albany and the University of Georgia.

Ethnographic-Focused Model

One of the most creative and culturally integrated doctoral training programs in the United States is the Psy.D. Program in Psychology at John F. Kennedy (JFK) University in Orinda, California (Hocoy, 2000). The primary emphasis of the program is to train multiculturally proficient psychologists, and the chief route to this proficiency is the tool of ethnography rooted in cultural anthropology. More specifically, cultural anthropologists hold the position that genuine understanding of a culture comes only from living in the culture and, over time, assuming its worldview. The JFK program defines culture broadly to include but not be limited to race, ethnicity, class, gender, disability, age, sexual orientation, and religious/spiritual orientation.

The culturally intensive JFK University program includes three years of course work and practica, a diversity-related clinical dissertation project, and a one-year predoctoral internship. A foundation clinical training course, the Integrated

Professional Seminar (IPS), runs three successive years and integrates multicultural awareness/proficiency, legal and ethical issues, and group process. The first-year IPS is taught by a male and female professor team, where at least one professor is a scholar of Color. Roughly 10 students are assigned to each IPS class. Perhaps the most unique aspect of the program is the first-year practicum, which is a *non-clinical* ethnographic field placement where students are immersed in a cultural setting, novel to them, for at least 10 hours per week for a full academic year. The ethnographic immersion is intended to provide a paradigm shift in the way students view the world. The goal of this immersion is the development of genuine cultural empathy (see Ridley et al., 1994; Scott & Borodovsky, 1990) that can be acquired only through a lived immersion experience where the trainee becomes the minority in another cultural reality.

Importantly, no direct clinical service is provided during this practicum; in fact, clinical work is seen as an impediment to the ethnographic immersion. Trainees are expected to suspend or deconstruct their cultural and training worldview and learn the worldview of another culture. During the IPS, students learn basic ethnography research skills to help them process their lived experiences.

Students' placements are selected by the JFK training office to ensure that the setting is culturally novel to the trainee and where she or he will be a minority in the culture. Sample placements have included a Japanese retirement home, an inner-city drug rehabilitation center, a battered women's center, and a group home for persons managing cerebral palsy. Students serve as participant-observers in their setting, not as clinicians-in-training. Site supervisors are well aware of the participant-observer training goals, which are rooted in cultural anthropology, not psychology. For accountability in training mission and goals, each placement is visited each quarter by one of the IPS faculty.

Throughout the year-long immersion experience, students maintain a journal and submit process or reflective papers on alternate weeks. At semester's end, final integrative papers and a class presentation are required. Importantly, given the intense immersion and interaction characteristic of the placements, ethical issues around entering and withdrawing from the setting are emphasized throughout the year.

With regard to a more formal training evaluation, the faculty use the Multicultural Counseling Awareness Scale (MCAS; Ponterotto et al., 1996) to monitor self-reported multicultural competency development. Preliminary data document a statistically significant increase in multicultural competence after the first-year infusion experience (Dan Hocoy, personal communication, June 19, 1999).

International Exchange in Family Therapy Training

Though international exchange programs are common on the undergraduate level, such programs are rare in professional psychology training. However, perhaps no cultural immersion experience is as impactful as living abroad for an extended period of time where the American student is both the cultural and linguistic minority. Extended cultural immersion experiences abroad are likely to have a more profound impact on the trainee than a U.S.-based immersion experience because retreat back into the familiarity of one's own culture is more difficult.

Recently, the doctoral program in Counseling Psychology at the State University of New York at Albany (SUNY Albany) established an exchange program in family therapy practice and research with the Universidad de La Coruna in northwestern Spain (Friedlander, Carranza, & Guzman, 2002). The goal of the SUNY Albany-La Coruna international program is "to create a flexible, affordable exchange program, that would maximize the students' opportunity to experience one another's culture as well as grow professionally and personally" (Friedlander et al., 2002, p. 319). The exchange program is in its formative stages, with the alliance initially begun in 1988 as a result of cooperative research ventures between faculty at the respective institutions. At this writing, three Albany students have traveled to Spain, and one La Coruna student has trained at Albany. The exchange program is intended to be limited to one to two students per year to help maximize individualized programming.

The training at the Universidad de La Coruna is a nine-month, 35-credit program of study that includes 100 hours of supervised practicum in systemic family therapy, with a focus on structural, strategic, and solution-focused family therapy. Classes are held two evenings per week (total of eight class hours) and the exchange student participates in five to six hours of work-study per week assisting faculty with family-focused research projects. The training also includes regular colloquia, and students work under faculty in various local hospitals and community agencies. The first two students to participate in the La Coruna exchange stayed only two months each (as planned); the third student to visit enrolled in the full nine-month program and is also conducting his dissertation as part of the exchange experience (see details in Friedlander et al., 2002). Naturally, to participate in the full training program, fluency in Spanish is a requirement.

At present, one La Coruna student has stayed in Albany for a seven-week period and participated in courses, research, and clinic site visits. The facilitators of the exchange program hope to further develop the program in the future. The benefits of the exchange program to the students and the programs are well presented in Friedlander et al. (2002), as are descriptions of the logistic challenges involved in establishing such a program.

International Exchange Program in Social Work

In 1992, a social work exchange agreement was established between the University of Georgia and the Universidad Veracruzana (Xalapa, Mexico). After two years of planning and administrator visits between the two universities, the first team of three social work faculty and three social work students from the University of Georgia sojourned to Xalapa for a one-month stay. The students were chosen from an open application process and were granted 10 hours of course credit for their participation.

While in Xalapa, participants attended intense Spanish-language classes from 8 to 11 A.M. and 3 to 5 P.M. daily. The students were assigned to host families for living arrangements and to serve as a catalyst for language and culture knowledge acquisition. Regular field trips to social agencies, clinics, and hospitals were arranged, as was continuous contact with varied aspects of the Mexican culture as reflected in the geographic area (program specifics are outlined in Kilpartick, Nackerud, & Boyle, 1996).

Specific contact with Mexican schools of social work were arranged in Poza Rica, Veracruz, and in Minititlan, Veracruz. Formal professional presentations on varied social work topics were conducted regularly by professors from both participating universities. Throughout the month-long infusion experience, students and faculty kept reflective journals of their day-to-day experiences. The participants shared journals with one another and extracted common themes following grounded theory methodology. Exchange participants also completed the MCAS (Ponterotto et al., 1996; Ponterotto & Potere, 2003) before and after the sojourn, the results of which indicated score increases for all participants. The qualitative analysis of the reflective journals was particularly revealing; the results formed the core of an in-depth summary manuscript (cf. Kilpatrick et al., 1996).

CONCLUSION

The trend in emerging approaches to multicultural training in professional psychology appears to encompass movement away from a sole reliance on didactic, more abstract, and information-focused training designs toward embracing more experiential and interactive models of training. A paradigm shift is also reflected in the broadened role of culture, moving from an isolated focus on previously neglected racial/ethnic minority populations to a focus on culture as the core of all human interaction and clinical practice (cf. Sue, Ivey, & Pedersen, 1996).

The course- and community-focused training models summarized in this chapter possess a strong focus on the development of personal awareness of the trainee. Psychology students in these programs are led to examine their own socialization biases, to understand issues of power, privilege, and oppression, and to learn cultural empathy through in vivo cross-cultural interaction. In the context of heightened personal awareness as cultural beings, trainees are exposed to the worldviews and life experiences of culturally different citizens and clients. Culturally indigenous healing models and the intersection of Western and non-Western helping/healing models are also considered.

Particularly salient to the ethnographic training model of JFK University and the international exchange programs at SUNY Albany and the University of Georgia is a belief that infusion in another cultural milieu is critical to becoming multiculturally proficient. It is our belief that international exchange programs of at least one-year duration would be ideal in exposing American psychology graduate students to culturally diverse perspectives on daily living, family functioning, spirituality integration, symptom expression, and healing approaches. Naturally, faculty as well as students benefit from such exchange experiences.

In a society where systems of managed care are having increasing influence on the types and quality of mental health treatment available (see Atkinson, Bui, & Mori, 2001; Casas, Pavelski, Furlong, & Zanglis, 2001), it is essential that training programs in psychology work toward more culturally inclusive training models that are evaluated regularly using state-of-the art research methodologies. Recently, Quintana, Troyano, and Taylor (2001) provided a comprehensive review of quantitative issues and cultural validity considerations in research that can inform multicultural training evaluations. Likewise, Morrow, Rakhsha, and Castaneda (2001) reviewed a host of qualitative research methods that can be used effectively in multicultural research generally and training evaluation specifically.

We hope this chapter stimulates consideration of creative, in vivo training approaches for campus curriculum, externships, and predoctoral internships. Furthermore, we encourage training programs to evaluate carefully the impact of their training models on multicultural competence levels (cf. Pope-Davis et al., 2003).

APPENDIX

Multicultural Competency Program Checklist for Professional Psychology

	Competency	
	Met	Not Met
Minority Representation		
1. 30%+ faculty represent racial/ethnic minority populations.	_____	_____
2. 30%+ faculty are bilingual.	_____	_____
3. 30%+ students represent racial/ethnic minority populations.	_____	_____
4. 30%+ support staff (secretaries, graduate assistants) represent minority populations.	_____	_____
Curriculum Issues		
5. Program has a required multicultural course.	_____	_____
6. Program has one or more additional multicultural courses that are required or recommended.	_____	_____
7. Multicultural issues are integrated into all course work. Faculty can specify how this is done and syllabi clearly reflect this inclusion.	_____	_____
8. Diversity of teaching strategies and procedures employed in class (e.g., individual achievement and cooperative learning models are utilized).	_____	_____
9. Varied assessment methods used to evaluate student performance and learning (e.g., written and oral assignments).	_____	_____
Clinical Practice, Supervision, and Immersion		
10. Students are exposed to 30%+ multicultural clientele.	_____	_____
11. Multicultural issues are integral to on-site and on-campus clinical supervision.	_____	_____
12. Students have supervised access to a cultural immersion experience such as study abroad for at least one semester, or an ethnographic immersion in a community culturally different from that of the campus or the student's own upbringing.	_____	_____

	Competency	
	Met	Not Met

13. Program has an active Multicultural Affairs Committee composed of faculty and students. Committee provides leadership and support with regard to multicultural initiatives. _____ _____

Research Considerations

14. The program has a faculty member whose primary research interest is in multicultural issues. _____ _____
15. There is clear faculty research productivity in multicultural issues. This is evidenced by faculty publications and presentations on multicultural issues. _____ _____
16. Students are actively mentored in multicultural research. This is evidenced by student-faculty coauthored work on multicultural issues and completed dissertations on these issues. _____ _____
17. Diverse research methodologies are apparent in faculty and student research. Both quantitative and qualitative research methods are utilized. _____ _____

Student and Faculty Competency Evaluation

18. One component of students' yearly (and end-of-program) evaluations is sensitivity to and knowledge of multicultural issues. The program has a mechanism for assessing this competency. _____ _____
19. One component of faculty teaching evaluations is the ability to integrate multicultural issues into the course. Faculty are also assessed on their ability to make all students, regardless of cultural background, feel equally comfortable in class. The program has a mechanism to access this competency. _____ _____
20. Multicultural issues are reflected in comprehensive examinations completed by all students. _____ _____
21. The program incorporates a reliable and valid paper-and-pencil self-report assessment of student multicultural competency at some point in the program. _____ _____
22. The program incorporates a content-validated portfolio assessment of student multicultural competency at some point in the program. _____ _____

Physical Environment

23. The physical surroundings of the program area reflect an appreciation of cultural diversity (e.g., artwork, posters, paintings, languages heard). _____ _____
24. There is a Multicultural Resource Center of some form in the program area (or in the department or academic unit) where students can convene. Cultural diversity is reflected in the decor of the room and in the resources available (e.g., books, journals, films). _____ _____

REFERENCES

Abreu, J. M., Chung, R. H. G., & Atkinson, D. R. (2000). Multicultural counseling training: Past, present, and future directions. *Counseling Psychologist, 28,* 641–656.

Allison, K. W., Crawford, I., Echemendia, R., Robinson, L., & Knepp, D. (1994). Human diversity and professional competence: Training in clinical and counseling psychology revisited. *American Psychologist, 49,* 792–796.

American Counseling Association. (1988). *Accreditation procedures manual and application.* Alexandria, VA: Council for Accreditation of Counseling and Related Educational Programs.

American Psychological Association. (1996). *Guidelines and principles for accreditation of programs in professional psychology.* Washington, DC: Author.

Atkinson, D. R., Brown, M. T., & Casas, J. M. (1996). Achieving ethnic parity in counseling psychology. *Counseling Psychologist, 24,* 230–258.

Atkinson, D. R., Bui, U., & Mori, S. (2001). Multiculturally sensitive empirically supported treatments—An oxymoron. In J. G. Ponterotto, J. M. Casas, L. A. Suzuki, & C. M. Alexander (Eds.), *Handbook of multicultural counseling* (2nd ed., pp. 542–574). Thousand Oaks, CA: Sage.

Bernal, M. E., & Castro, F. G. (1994). Are clinical psychologists prepared for service and research with ethnic minorities? Report of a decade of progress. *American Psychologist, 49,* 797–805.

Carter, R. T. (1995). *The influence of race and racial identity in psychotherapy: Toward a racially inclusive model.* New York: Wiley.

Carter, R. T. (2003). Becoming racially and culturally competent: The racial-cultural counseling laboratory. *Journal of Multicultural Counseling, 31*(1), 20–30.

Casas, J. M., Pavelski, R., Furlong, M. J., & Zanglis, I. (2001). Advent of systems of care: Practice and research perspectives and policy implications. In J. G. Ponterotto, J. M. Casas, L. A. Suzuki, & C. M. Alexander (Eds.), *Handbook of multicultural counseling* (2nd ed., pp. 189–221). Thousand Oaks, CA: Sage.

Constantine, M. G., Juby, H. L., & Liang, J. J. C. (2001). Examining self-reported multicultural counseling competence and race-related attitudes among White marital and family therapists. *Journal of Marital and Family Therapy, 27,* 353–362.

Constantine, M. G., Ladany, N., Inman, A. G., & Ponterotto, J. G. (1996). Students' perceptions of multicultural training in counseling psychology programs. *Journal of Multicultural Counseling and Development, 24,* 241–253.

Copeland, E. J. (1982). Minority populations and traditional counseling programs: Some alternatives. *Counselor Education and Supervision, 21,* 187–193.

D'Andrea, M., & Daniels, J. (1991). Exploring the different levels of multicultural counseling training in counselor education. *Journal of Counseling and Development, 70,* 78–85.

D'Andrea, M., & Daniels, J. (2001). Expanding our thinking about white racism: Facing the challenge of multicultural counseling in the 21st century. In J. G. Ponterotto, J. M. Casas, L. A. Suzuki, & C. M. Alexander (Eds.), *Handbook of multicultural counseling* (2nd ed., pp. 289–310). Thousand Oaks, CA: Sage.

Friedlander, M. L., Carranza, V. E., & Guzman, M. (2002). International exchanges in family therapy: Training, research, and practice in Spain and the U.S. *Counseling Psychologist, 30,* 314–329.

Helms, J. E. (1995). An update of Helms's White and people of Color racial identity models. In J. G. Ponterotto, J. M. Casas, L. A. Suzuki, & C. M. Alexander (Eds.), *Handbook of multicultural counseling* (pp. 181–198). Thousand Oaks, CA: Sage.

Hocoy, D. (2000). *Ethnography as a tool of multicultural counseling training.* Unpublished manuscript, John F. Kennedy University, Orida, CA.

Kilpatrick, A., Nackerud, L., & Boyle, D. (February, 1996). *The road well-traveled: An international social work exchange program.* Paper presented at the annual meeting of the Council on Social Work Education, Atlanta, Georgia.

Leach, M. M., & Carlton, M. A. (1997). Toward defining a multicultural training philosophy. In D. B. Pope-Davis & H. L. K. Coleman (Eds.), *Multicultural counseling competencies: Assessment, education and training, and supervision* (pp. 184–208). Thousand Oaks, CA: Sage.

Manese, J. E., Wu, J. T., & Nepomuceno, C. A. (2001). The effect of training on multicultural counseling competencies: An exploratory study over a ten-year period. *Journal of Multicultural Counseling and Development, 29,* 31–40.

McRae, M. B., & Johnson, S. D. (1991). Toward training for competence in multicultural counselor education. *Journal of Counseling and Development, 70,* 131–135.

Morrow, S. L., Rakhsha, G., & Castaneda, C. L. (2001). Qualitative research methods for multicultural counseling. In J. G. Ponterotto, J. M. Casas, L. A. Suzuki, & C. M. Alexander (Eds.), *Handbook of multicultural counseling* (2nd ed., pp. 575–603). Thousand Oaks, CA: Sage.

National Council on the Accreditation of Teacher Education Programs (NCATE). (2001). *Professional standards for the accreditation of schools, colleges, and departments of education.* Washington, DC: Author.

Neimeyer, G. J., & Diamond, A. K. (2001). The anticipated future of counselling psychology in the United States: A Delphi poll. *Counselling Psychology Quarterly, 14,* 49–65.

Ottavi, T. M., Pope-Davis, D. B., & Dings, J. G. (1994). Relationship between white racial identity attitudes and self-reported multicultural counseling competencies. *Journal of Counseling Psychology, 41,* 149–154.

Ponterotto, J. G. (1996). Multicultural counseling in the twenty-first century. *Counseling Psychologist, 24,* 259–268.

Ponterotto, J. G. (1997). Multicultural counseling training: A competency model and national survey. In D. B. Pope-Davis & H. L. K. Coleman (Eds.), *Multicultural counseling competencies: Assessment, education and training, and supervision* (pp. 111–130). Thousand Oaks, CA: Sage.

Ponterotto, J. G. (1998). Charting a course for research in multicultural counseling training. *Counseling Psychologist, 26,* 43–68.

Ponterotto, J. G., Alexander, C. M., & Grieger, I. (1995). A multicultural competency checklist for counseling training programs. *Journal of Multicultural Counseling and Development, 23,* 11–20.

Ponterotto, J. G., Costa, C. I., & Werner-Lin, A. (2002). Research perspectives in cross-cultural counseling. In P. B. Pedersen, J. G. Draguns, W. J. Lonner, & J. E. Trimble (Eds.), *Counseling across cultures* (5th ed., pp. 395–420). Thousand Oaks, CA: Sage.

Ponterotto, J. G., Mendelsohn, J., & Belizaire, L. (2003). Assessing teacher multicultural competence: Self-report scales, observer-report evaluations, and a portfolio assessment. In D. B. Pope-Davis, H. L. K. Coleman, W. M. Liu, & R. L. Toporek (Eds.), *Handbook of multicultural competencies in counseling and psychology* (pp. 191–210). Thousand Oaks, CA: Sage.

Ponterotto, J. G., & Potere, J. C. (2003). The Multicultural Counseling Knowledge and Awareness Scale (MCKAS): Validity, reliability, and user guidelines. In D. B. Pope-Davis, H. L. K. Coleman, W. M. Liu, & R. L. Toporek (Eds.), *Handbook of multicultural competencies in counseling and psychology* (pp. 137–153). Thousand Oaks, CA: Sage.

Ponterotto, J. G., Rieger, B. P., Barrett, A., Harris, G., Sparks, R., Sanchez, C. M., et al. (1996). Development and initial validation of the Multicultural Counseling Awareness Scale (MCAS). In G. R. Sodowsky & J. C. Impara (Eds.), *Multicultural assessment in counseling and clinical psychology* (pp. 247–282). Lincoln, NE: Buros Institute of Mental Measurements.

Pope-Davis, D. B., Breaux, C., & Liu, W. M. (1997). A multicultural immersion experience: Filling a void in multicultural training. In D. B. Pope-Davis & H. L. K. Coleman (Eds.), *Multicultural counseling competencies: Assessment, education and training, and supervision* (pp. 227–241). Thousand Oaks, CA: Sage.

Pope-Davis, D. B., Coleman, H. L. K., Liu, W. M., & Toporek, R. L. (Eds.). (2003). *Handbook of multicultural competencies in counseling and psychology.* Thousand Oaks, CA: Sage.

Quintana, S. M., Troyano, N., & Taylor, G. (2001). Cultural validity and inherent challenges in quantitative methods for multicultural research. In J. G. Ponterotto, J. M. Casas, L. A. Suzuki, & C. M. Alexander (Eds.), *Handbook of multicultural counseling* (2nd ed., pp. 604–630). Thousands Oaks, CA: Sage.

Ramirez, M., III (1999). *Multicultural psychotherapy: An approach to individual and cultural differences* (2nd ed.). Boston: Allyn & Bacon.

Reynolds, A. L. (1995). Challenges and strategies for teaching multicultural counseling courses. In J. G. Ponterotto, J. M. Casas, L. A. Suzuki, & C. M. Alexander (Eds.), *Handbook of multicultural counseling* (pp. 312–330). Thousand Oaks, CA: Sage.

Ridley, C. R., Espelage, D. L., & Rubinstein, K. J. (1997). Course development in multicultural counseling. In D. B. Pope-Davis & H. L. K. Coleman (Eds.), *Multicultural counseling competencies: Assessment, education and training, and supervision* (pp. 131–158). Thousand Oaks, CA: Sage.

Ridley, C. R., Mendoza, D. W., & Kanitz, B. E. (1992). Program designs for multicultural training. *Journal of Psychology and Christianity, 11,* 326–336.

Ridley, C. R., Mendoza, D. W., & Kanitz, B. E. (1994). Multicultural training: Reexamination, operationalization, and integration. *Counseling Psychologist, 22,* 227–289.

Rogers, M. R., Hoffman, M. A., & Wade, J. (1998). Notable multicultural training in APA-approved counseling psychology and school psychology programs. *Cultural Diversity and Ethnic Minority Psychology, 4,* 212–226.

Rogers, M. R., Ponterotto, J. G., Conoley, J. C., & Wiese, M. J. (1992). Multicultural training in school psychology: A national survey. *School Psychology Review, 21,* 603–616.

Scott, N. E., & Borodovsky, L. G. (1990). Effective use of cultural role taking. *Professional Psychology: Research and Practice, 21,* 167–170.

Sodowsky, G. R., Taffe, R. C., Gutkin, T. B., & Wise, S. L. (1994). Development of the Multicultural Counseling Inventory: A self-report measure of multicultural competencies. *Journal of Counseling Psychology, 41,* 137–148.

Suarez-Balcazar, Y., Durlak, J. A., & Smith, C. (1994). Multicultural training practices in community psychology programs. *American Journal of Community Psychology, 22,* 785–798.

Sue, D. W., Carter, R. T., Casas, J. M., Fouad, N. A., Ivey, A. E., Jensen, M., et al. (1998). *Multicultural counseling competencies: Individual and organizational development.* Thousand Oaks, CA: Sage.

Sue, D. W., Ivey, A. E., & Pedersen, P. B. (1996). *A theory of multicultural counseling and therapy.* Pacific Grove, CA: Brooks/Cole.

U.S. Bureau of the Census. (2000). *Statistical abstract of the United States: 1999* (120th ed., Tables 16, 17, & 18). Washington, DC: U.S. Government Printing Office.

Vazquez, L. A. (1997). A systematic multicultural curriculum model: The pedagogical process. In D. B. Pope-Davis & H. L. K. Coleman (Eds.), *Multicultural counseling competencies: Assessment, education and training, and supervision* (pp. 159–183). Thousand Oaks, CA: Sage.

Vinson, T. S., & Neimeyer, G. J. (2000). The relationship between racial identity development and multicultural counseling competence. *Journal of Multicultural Counseling and Development, 28,* 177–192.

CHAPTER 3

Teaching Racial-Cultural Counseling Competence: A Racially Inclusive Model

Robert T. Carter

During the past few decades there has been an increase in the call for psychologists to become competent in working with people from a different racial and cultural perspective (see, Sue & Torino, this volume). Race and culture have been defined in various ways. Some definitions of culture refer to historically disenfranchised racial groups in the United States, while other definitions of culture have used what some people call a multicultural perspective that includes social groups who have experienced social oppression, such as women, gays and lesbians, and people with disabilities.

The push for developing racial-cultural competence began in the early 1970s. The most often cited instance of the call for cultural competence has been the work of education and training committees of Division 17 Society of Counseling Psychology of the American Psychological Association. The president of the Division at the time was Allen Ivey, who formed the committee to develop a definition and standards for what was then called cross-cultural counseling competencies (see Carter, this *Handbook,* Volume One). The position paper that resulted from the deliberations of the committee was published in *The Counseling Psychologist* in 1982 (Sue et al., 1982), then reissued, updated, and extended to organizations in 1998 (Sue et al., 1998).

In their position paper, Sue et al. (1982) defined cross-cultural counseling and outlined the knowledge, awareness, and skills needed to be culturally competent. Sue et al. also challenged the traditional and "culturally encapsulated" nature of psychology and counseling (Katz, 1985; Midgette & Meggert, 1991). One main issue regarding cultural competence, or what many call multicultural counseling competence, has been how to train counselors and psychologists. Training over the decades has moved from teaching about awareness to training for racial-cultural and multicultural competence (Carter, 2003; Sue et al., 1998; see also Constantine, Watt, Gainor, & Warren, this *Handbook,* Volume One). In Carter (2003), I describe development of the Racial-Cultural Counseling Lab and the racial-cultural competence training

I wish to thank Ma'at L. Lewis, Carla Hunter, Lisa Orbe, Erica King-Toler, Lillian Chiang, Heather Juby, Carol Wan, Karen Cort, Noah Collins, Alex Pieterse, and Leah DeSole for their comments and assistance on earlier drafts of this chapter.

model. In particular, I discuss how the course evolved from an awareness course to one based on students developing or showing minimal racial-cultural counseling competence. I also indicate when and how Johnson (1987) introduced the core of the training model into the curriculum at Teachers College, Columbia University. The laboratory course uses small-group structured interviews, lectures, skill building, and feedback to students about their learning (and other activities) to explore reference groups (i.e., gender, race, ethnicity, religion, and social class) as aspects of culture.

The current chapter therefore builds on the previous descriptions (Carter, 2003) of the Racial-Cultural Counseling Laboratory (Carter, 1995, 2000, 2001). The chapter adds more information about how counseling skills are integrated in the teaching about racial-cultural reference groups and the reactions and experiences of the teaching associates and further elaborates on other aspects of the course, such as the emphasis on understanding and dealing with resistance. Additionally, I describe the curriculum and the culturally based philosophy of the counseling master's and doctoral program at Teachers College, Columbia University. The program is aimed at the development of racially and culturally competent counselors and psychologists. I outline the courses in the curriculum that lead to competencies in racial-cultural counseling.

The teaching philosophy of the racial-cultural lab and the racism course are based on my (Carter, 1995) racially inclusive model of psychotherapy and training. My model argues that each person is socialized as a racial-cultural being, and his or her racial-cultural self becomes an important part of his or her personality structure. In other words, only by appreciating the significance of racial-cultural factors in one's own life can psychologists and counselors begin to appreciate the significance of racial-cultural factors in the lives of people in general and their clients specifically. I believe that racial-cultural competence is superordinate to counseling competence: It is not possible to be a competent counselor without being racially and culturally competent. However, as noted earlier, there are currently many ways to define and teach about racial-cultural or multicultural competence.

One of the core activities for counselors to become racially and culturally competent is for each student to become aware of his or her own racial-cultural worldview. Awareness of one's worldview helps one to be more effective as a counselor or therapist (Carter, 2001). Carter (2003) states:

> The self is the vehicle for cultural counseling knowledge and skill. Self-exploration is focused on the role and meaning of reference group memberships in the development and the integration of one's behavior, emotion, and beliefs as influenced by reference-group memberships. (p. 22)

Thus, the racially inclusive counseling competence model operates on the principle of personal exploration as the path to racial-cultural competence. The model uses the program's curriculum to build a foundation for the learning in the Racial-Cultural Counseling Laboratory course (called the Lab). I briefly describe a few of the courses that provide a foundation for the Lab (see also Sue & Torino, this volume).

Ponterotto and Austin (this volume) also describe the state of racial-cultural learning in programs around the country and note that graduate psychology training programs are increasingly offering training regarding racial-cultural or multicultural issues. Even though advocates of cultural competence emphasize the need to understand one's own worldview, most training approaches tend to focus on the cultural experiences of the "nondominant" groups, or people of Color.

The model of teaching and curriculum design presented here is based on race as the critical characteristic of cultural difference (see Carter, this *Handbook,* Volume One). The race-based approach assumes that sociorace defines cultural groups in North America; other reference group memberships, such as ethnicity, social class, gender, and religion, are understood within the context of racial group membership (Carter, 2000). Because the model does not hold the same assumptions as other approaches, not all reference group differences are considered in teaching the Lab course (e.g., sexual orientation, disability). Some classes in the curriculum approach racial-cultural differences from a diversity and/or multicultural perspective. Therefore, other reference groups are discussed in more detail in such courses. For instance, we have a Counseling Women course and recently offered a seminar on Counseling Lesbians, Gays, and Bisexuals. There are also elective courses on aging and the elderly.

Racial-cultural counseling competence is controversial: There is debate about how to define and understand what it entails for psychology and counselor training programs, and many argue that racial-cultural competence cannot be acquired through a single course (Carter, 1995; Helms & Cook, 1999; Sue, 2001). It is my belief that a training climate that holds racial-cultural competence as a prerequisite for competence as a counselor or therapist or psychologist is required. As I pointed out elsewhere (Carter, 2003), courses and expectations in training need to be both culturally focused (i.e., present information with a cultural perspective) and culture-specific (i.e., have specific content about race and culture). Thus, the training curriculum, 20 courses for master's level and 40 courses for the doctorate, should integrate knowledge, awareness, and skill about race and culture. Racial-cultural competencies in the context of an academic or internship postdoctoral training program should be acquired through didactic courses as well as experiential training and practica. In the next section, I describe the training program that uses the racial-cultural competence counseling experiential approach as a way to facilitate self-exploration.

THE TRAINING COMPONENTS

Both didactic and experiential courses can provide a racial-cultural context for learning. Two types of courses are available; one type is culturally focused (context-focused) and the other culture-specific (content-specific) (see Carter, 1995). Core psychology subject areas generally are not taught with a racial-cultural emphasis. However, it is possible to teach core courses, such as introductory theories, counseling skills, human development, organizational psychology, research methods, psychopathology, practica, and psychological testing and assessment, as culturally focused courses using a racial-cultural context. For instance, in courses that focus on counseling theories and human development, trainees should be taught about the cultural context in which the theories were developed. Also, almost all theories of human development and personality, as well as intervention techniques, taught in North America were developed within the cultural framework of dominant European American (i.e., White) racial-cultural patterns. The White American or European worldview assumes particular forms and mechanisms of perception, communication, language, relationship styles, and so forth. The theories and ways of understanding people are assumed to be universal and are often not examined for the ways in which the expectations of people and interactions are bound by the dominant culture's patterns (see Sue & Torino, this volume; Thompson, this volume). In learning about the cultural context in which these views were developed and about other worldviews (Asian, African, etc.), trainees and students will be able to recognize their own racially and culturally determined predispositions as natural aspects of themselves and others. Many courses in the curriculum at Teachers College are now taught with a cultural focus (theories of counseling, counseling skills, human development); as such, they include information and knowledge about racial-cultural issues and worldviews and the sociopolitical context of mainstream theories and ideas about human functioning.

Culture-specific courses expose students to cognitive, psychological, and emotional knowledge and experiences aimed at deepening trainees' and students' grasp of racial and cultural issues in society. Culture-specific courses should help students to understand that race and culture have many expressions and that all individuals have a race and culture that are affected by racism and other types of "isms." These courses also should be designed to help students to talk openly about culture, race, and "isms" and their impact on all people, not just people of Color. The following describes some of the culture-specific courses that serve as the core learning in our program. They are required of all students, both master's level and doctoral.

Multicultural Counseling and Psychotherapy

Multicultural Counseling and Psychotherapy is an overview lecture course that uses small discussion and work groups to explore different approaches to culture, race, mental health, and psychotherapy. In this course, human developmental and mental health theories are discussed in terms of cultural variation and how the core ideas contained in theories about human development and personality affect our understanding of wellness and illness. Students are also exposed to multicultural models, theories of human development, and counseling interventions. They explore traditional and cultural assumptions of and perspectives on normal and abnormal behavior, human functioning, and interpersonal relationships. In addition, using the cultural assumptions and perspectives that characterize each theory and intervention approach derived from it, students examine the various approaches offered by psychology for understanding and coping with cultural and racial variation in psychotherapy practice. Students are asked to work in small groups, select a topic about cultural issues, write papers, and engage in other learning activities.

Racism and Racial Identity in Psychology and Education

Students are also required to take either Racism and Racial Identity in Psychology and Education or Multicultural Counseling. A principal goal of the Racism course is to help students learn how racism affects both the oppressor and the oppressed and to increase students' ability to discuss racial issues with less emotion, which often characterizes such discussions. The exploration of cultural patterns of Americans is comparative and highlights specific American cultural practices, as reflected in worldview, thinking and language patterns, communication styles, and interpersonal activity. Next, the course provides a historical overview focusing on Asian, Latin, and African contributions to humankind. The historical overview demonstrates that historically disenfranchised groups lived in complex and elaborate civilizations long before the rise of European powers and that much that has occurred in history is not part of our mainstream educational material.

The historical overview is followed by an examination of racial inequality in the United States, specifically the relative influences of class, ethnicity, and race in the history and development of racism. The purpose of the material on social inequality is to teach students the critical role of race and culture in historical and current events. In particular, the material describes structural and institutionalized relationships in the colonies and today in the United States, wherein Blacks, Hispanics, Asians, and Native American Indians were and are relegated to low social status, while Whites, depending on ethnicity, were accorded greater access to positions of power and status (see Carter, this *Handbook,* Volume One). The course also examines the impact of racism on White Americans. Current events are followed by a focused discussion on racism with attention to its definition and meaning. The discussion about racism then incorporates racial identity theory and its corresponding research. Students learn that psychological variability, with respect to race and cultural identity, occur within each racial group. Video presentations and small group discussions supplement the didactic material.

It is important to note that the counseling theories, counseling skills, and group counseling courses are culturally focused, and the multicultural and racism courses are culture-specific.

THE RACIAL-CULTURAL COUNSELING LABORATORY

The Racial-Cultural Counseling Laboratory (Lab) is taken late in the program, in the second year for master's level and also for many doctoral students. Lab is primarily experiential, as noted previously. Prior to taking Lab, each student must fulfill several prerequisites: Students must take courses in counseling theories, basic counseling skills, group counseling, and racial identity and racism or the multicultural course. The Lab course is designed to build on the prior learning of students and to enhance self-exploration.

The Lab course is taught with the aim of building racial-cultural competence as endorsed by many professional associations (American Association for Counseling and Development, 1988, 1989; APA, 1990, 2003; Sue et al., 1982; Sue et al., 1998). Racial-cultural competence is imperative in the training of counselors and psychologists because each person develops and forms a sense of self and others in the context of race and culture. Each person's experience is racially and culturally bound.

The racial-cultural counseling competence (RCCC) approach (Carter, 2003) focuses on the concept of the counselor as person. The approach assumes that students in training bring to the profession a personal life in which they were taught about themselves as racial-cultural persons and socialized as members of gender, racial, social class, religious, and ethnic groups. Each person is taught through socialization to see himself or herself and others through the lens of his or her reference groups (Carter, 2001). The RCCC training conceptualizes the clinician as a racial-cultural person who brings to his or her counseling relationships a network of meaningful social identities and reference group affiliations. The reference groups and affiliations serve as both resources and barriers to the development of effective counseling and therapy relationships and interventions. Social group memberships as well as group affiliations influence the person as counselor on multiple levels: cognitively, behaviorally, and emotionally. The RCCC approach aims to facilitate students' awareness of the feelings, ideas, and behaviors about race and culture through reference groups as they assume the role of helper.

Overall, the Lab takes an integrative approach to training for racial-cultural competence (Sue, 2001). It emphasizes integrating the person as counselor through self-examination of affect, behavior, and cognition around racial-cultural concerns (Carter, 2001; Sue, 2001). The Lab consists of three major components: *didactic* (knowing that), *experiential* (knowing self), and *skill building* learning (knowing how). The class meets four hours each week of the semester: two hours in small groups (four to eight students per group), and two hours of lecture and readings (first half of the semester) and skill building (second half of the semester). The course is cotaught by the course professor and trained doctoral teaching associates (TAs).

The following descriptions of the course components include discussions of the specific content for each course element and TAs' perspectives on the rewards and challenges of the course. TAs who offered statements were five women (Asian, White, biracial, and African American) and two men (one White and one Black).

Lecture

The syllabus has an extensive required reading list for students. The readings include several books, book chapters, and journal articles (students are also asked to integrate readings into their journals). The focus of the reading is on providing information and varied points of view on the four reference groups. The professor primarily delivers the lecture and the TAs occasionally lecture on a particular topic. Thus, one goal of the *didactic* component of the course is to increase students' factual knowledge about nondominant and dominant reference groups. The readings show the stereotypes people hold and the role of between-group perceptions and provide information about sociopolitical relationships between various groups in our society. A strong emphasis in the lectures is on the clinical context and significance of reference group differences and similarities. Students sometimes think that their professional and personal lives do not intertwine; the lectures and readings deal with how the various personally based reference group memberships are often intertwined in one's life and therefore effect one's professional relationships. The lectures also serve as a large group setting enabling students to process their experiences of resistance and growth.

During the lecture, I have also of late given more time and attention to the connection between the reference group exploration and the use of effective counseling skills. The integration of effective counseling skills with racial-cultural knowledge is crucial, because sometimes students think it is possible to use generic techniques with all clients without regard to the importance of learning how to accept, understand, and be genuine in their interactions. Often, even those students with prior learning about racial-cultural contexts and racial-cultural-specific information do not fully grasp the ways that their reference groups influence their counseling effectiveness. As a way of emphasizing the skill-building aspect of the course I have also spent more time in the lecture component describing and giving illustrations of the importance of understanding an individual's experience from their perspective, a skill that is particularly important when dealing with racial-cultural information or differences. It has become apparent that students tend to hold on to the desire to interpret and explain personal dynamics and behavior as more valuable than struggling to understand the meaning of persons' experiences. Students tend to draw on their own life experiences to provide them with the source of understanding, an approach that becomes difficult when what they are being presented with is outside their frame of reference. I assist students to recognize that their own life experiences are a limited source of understanding because these experiences are influenced and informed by various racial-cultural orientations that may or may not facilitate understanding. Here I emphasize the need to use counseling skills (clarifying, perception checking, use of summary, reflection of feeling and content, focusing, etc.) for the purpose of understanding the interviewee/client from the client's point of view and thereby gaining an understanding of what is being said that comes from the experience of the interviewee/client and not the interviewer/counselor.

Another highly significant issue that is addressed in lecture is the distinction between group memberships and personal constructions of one's reference group. I have found it important to honor and respect each person's particular way of understanding his or her group identities. Many of us have developed unique and complex ways of understanding who we are, and as such, many personal constructions of group identities reflect efforts to reject or cope with group or social categories or with family dynamics. Some people seek comfort in unique and personally relevant group identities and find comfort in sometimes complex resolutions that are highly personal. I want to respect students' private, family, and personal lives and at the same time set a boundary for the small group self-exploration activity that is primarily about reference group memberships and less about one's personal group identity. Said another way, often we tell ourselves what it means to be in a group and that construction of a group membership is unique to each person. For instance, some students claim Catholicism as their religious group membership, yet acknowledge that they follow no rules or practices that are Catholic. In such cases, students may be preserving a family tradition although they themselves are nonreligious; in this context, the claim of being Catholic is a personal construction. We work hard to focus on social groups and the rules that determine membership, so that there is some external basis for membership and not just a person's uniquely constructed beliefs. We discuss the group and its rules for membership without altering a person's personal construction or beliefs. For instance, a woman may think of herself as poor because she is a student, but actually she belongs to the upper-middle-class reference group; a

Black student may contend that he has no race, that skin color is not relevant. We respect their beliefs yet ask students to discuss the meaning of their beliefs based on the social traditions and practices of their race as a reference group for other people and in society. We discuss the actual group membership, not the one constructed for personal reasons or temporary situations.

One TA made the observation that there is no single text that addresses the reference group or counseling issues associated with self-exploration of racial-cultural issues. Students in lecture often take a stance of wanting to get things right during the large group discussions, making it hard for them to participate. TAs often feel frustrated by the students' silence. One shared this perspective: "There is like a taboo to talk about the reference group issues. . . . It is like pulling teeth sometimes. . . . Students feel it is scary to share about these difficult topics. . . . The dynamic often reflects the larger society."

The Small Group

The small group is where students, led by a group facilitator and the course professor, focus on the use of their counseling skills to understand the interviewee and to gain a better understanding of his or her reference group memberships. The group leaders, usually advanced doctoral students who have taken the course, guide students' use of counseling skills, such as listening, attending, reflecting, confronting, and leading. The group leaders also provide input and feedback on each group member's learning throughout the course. Each group leader receives about two to three hours of training prior to the start of class and is supervised one and a half hours per week. One TA made this observation about supervision: "Seeing students struggle with the same things I do as a counselor . . . is an empowering position, but as a doctoral student in training, it is challenging to be a supervisor while also being a supervisee [under the professor]." The small groups are also co-led by the course professor. I rotate from group to group each week and in this way co-lead and model group and individual interventions for each TA.

Assignments: Foundations for Small Group Work

Five written assignments/activities are used to facilitate the self-exploration component of the Lab's small-group experience. The first of five precourse requirements is an autobiographical sketch that students are required to hand in on the first day of class. The autobiographical sketch covers the student's life span development with respect to five major reference group memberships: gender, religion, social class, ethnicity, and race. Students are asked to identify specific incidents that may have contributed to their development and knowledge in each reference group area. Often, the TA will read and react to the sketches. The task sometimes generates strong feelings, as one TA noted:

> I find it disturbing to hear a prevalence of internalized racism among the Asian students, and some Asian students with English as a second language see themselves as deficient because of that and it is hard to work with such negative self-perceptions.

For the second precourse requirement, students are asked to prepare a genogram of their family and friendship networks. The genogram and friend network focuses on and describes the specific reference group memberships (i.e., gender, religion, social class, ethnicity, and race) of each person in the network. Later in the course, each student presents the family and friend network information to his or her small group. The student uses the information to explore the racial-cultural composition of his or her intimate networks. Other small-group members are encouraged to use the information to better understand the student.

The third and new activity (introduced in 2004) is also completed before class begins. Students are asked to conduct a precourse interview with someone, not a relative, who is willing to discuss a personally relevant reference group issue. The student must tape and transcribe the interview and submit a written assessment of his or her use of counseling skills as well as how he or she dealt with the racial-cultural issues presented by the interviewee. The precourse interview and self-assessment is repeated at the course end as a postcourse task, so that students can experience directly their growth and development or lack of learning.

The fourth activity involves students' written responses to a set of structured questions that are used during the small group. The structured interview questionnaire asks students to consider and respond to questions about their four reference groups: religion, social class, ethnicity, and race (due to time limitations and the size of the classes—it takes about 4 hours or more for each student to be interviewed—the number of groups discussed have been limited). Some of the questions focus on how students feel about a group membership (e.g., ethnicity), how membership is affirmed, how the reference group has influenced their personal development, and what positive and negative generalizations people may have toward a member of the group. There are also three questions about how the reference group membership influences the student's role as a helper.

The fifth assignment is a weekly journal composed throughout the semester. The journal is divided into two sections: facts and affective experience. The factual section describes what occurred during the class meeting. In the affective/reactive section, students describe their emotional, behavioral, and intellectual responses to small group and class events in terms of their reference group memberships. To further students' knowledge, the course professor and TAs engage in a dialogue with the students through the journals by writing comments and questions to journal entries; students are required to respond to the comments and questions in the following week's journal. In this way, the professor and TAs have an opportunity to further develop students' learning about reference groups. Through journal dialogue, the trainer (the professor and/or the TA) can learn about the individual student's learning process and about the issues that are well understood and those that need further exploration. Regarding the journals and autobiographical sketches, one TA observed: "The six- to eight-page ongoing dialogue between the student and teaching assistant is fruitful and also a place where insights can be gained by both parties."

Another challenge is helping students learn the material and its emotional significance. Often, TAs must cope with challenges to their authority and role as teaching associate. As one TA put it: "One person challenged me in an indirect way . . . it was about his views against affirmative action and a challenge against me and the Asian professor." TAs report that it is often difficult to cope with the students' expression of anger and hostility that often emerges in reaction to the focus on racial-cultural issues in counseling. One experienced TA who had taught Lab several times observed:

> You get tired of seeing the same themes. You feel as though your previous group moved on, but when you get a new group of students you get the same themes all over again. For example, mostly White students will talk about wanting to learn about race from students of Color. It is tiring to teach on that level. It is challenging being patient enough for them to make shifts in world-view. It can be easy to just teach about race [and other reference groups] as opposed to letting them explore their own race [and other reference groups] in order to learn. It is draining to know that so many White people think that race is about people of Color. Seeing it four times in one night is overwhelming.

Another shared this experience:

> It [journal] usually starts out with subtle acting-out behaviors and denial that they know anything about [reference groups]. But as these more subtle behaviors get challenged (questioned and commented on), they up the ante and resort to more and more overtly hostile behaviors and attitudes. One student, for example, wrote his final journal all in huge (probably 28 point) font in order to meet the page limits when he clearly had nothing to say.

The Lab is extremely time consuming and demanding for the entire staff. One TA commented:

> The group members' struggles and acting-out force me to face my own group membership issues, including automatic assumptions and reactions. I must process my feelings and reactions in order to respond to them in an effective manner.

Another said: "It is very time-consuming [to read the journals] and requires a great deal of time and emotional energy outside the course." And at the same time, TAs report benefits from the process of working with students through the journal and the autobiographical sketch. One shares this viewpoint: "Reading the journals gives you a chance to see additional material that people are afraid to reveal. You get to nurture people and to discuss the things they might not otherwise bring up in the group." Another notes: "Journal dialogue also provides a place to [do] more in-depth processing that may not fit within the time limits of the group."

There is considerable emphasis in the class on the effective use and demonstration of counseling skills to gain an understanding of the interviewee and other group members. The students are expected to draw on knowledge from prior courses (group, counseling skills, practica, etc.), and we assume some basic skills.

There is one additional activity I should discuss. During the first meeting of the semester, once the small groups are formed (we form the groups so that there is diversity in terms of gender, race, age, etc., and we try to avoid having students who are intimate friends in the same group), students are asked to indicate from sight alone, without personal knowledge or discussion, each other's reference group memberships and to write these out on a rating form. We ask further that when indicating other group members' race, ethnicity, religion, and social class, the raters indicate the cues and clues used to make the rating. We conduct a general processing of the rating experience (both in small group and in lecture) without discussing the specific ratings. Rather, we explore students' experience doing the task. Typically, students reveal feeling uncomfortable and anxious. The processing often leads to a discussion of stereotypes and the source of our assumptions about people when it comes to reference group membership. Students enter the course with powerful and automatic generalizations (i.e., stereotypes), and the rating illustrates to students where their assumptions about people's group memberships come from. Evident from the ratings is the central role that race plays in our assumptions about people. Usually, students indicate that they use race to determine other group memberships, or, if race is not used, they draw on their personal relationships. They talk about how they could not tell a person's ethnicity, social class, or religion from sight, so they guess it from race. This activity also demonstrates how we use material or superficial information to make judgments about people. Prior to each student's interview, the other students in the small group share their ratings and the basis for the rating; that is, they have to say what they saw that led them to think someone was White, Asian, Buddhist, Christian, or middle class.

Small Group: Interviews and Interactions

Responses to structured questions are presented as a starting point for group interaction about reference group memberships. Students discuss their reference group memberships (e.g., religion, social class) and how they understand them, in terms of how each has affected their development, and what, if any, perceptions of others guided their behavior and so forth. Once the presentation (responses to the precourse questions) for one reference group is completed, the interviewee responds to questions from group members in their effort to gain a deeper and clearer understanding of the interviewee's reference group membership.

The integrative approach emphasizes students' affective, cognitive, and behavioral experience during the small group interactions. Understanding one's emotional and behavioral reactions is considered an important component of the small group learning. "Traditional mental health training programs focus on training students on how to interpret behavior instead of teaching them to understand behavior or the person's experience from that person's perspective." The therapist is held up as the expert or authority with the power to determine what is wrong and how it should be fixed. In the Lab, the emphasis is on attending to the person with the aim of understanding his or her experience and perspective, one TA notes, "is what makes Lab challenging. The focus for both the TA and the group is to understand and *not* interpret, which, surprisingly enough, takes significantly more energy and attention than expected." Yet the emphasis is consistent with racial-cultural learning in that it requires that one make the effort to grasp and accept the other person's experience, behavior, and meaning system.

There are three tasks for each student participating in the small group: (1) to practice and strengthen his or her counseling skills in a racial-cultural context, (2) to help the interviewee by working to understand the meaning and significance of his or her reference group memberships, and (3) through the interview process and the effort associated with helping someone understand themselves better, to gain insight into his or her own reference group memberships as the interviews proceed throughout the semester.

The focus on group memberships and redirecting discussion away from personal constructions plays a key role in this process. Students tend to be resistant to giving up their personal constructions; as illustrated earlier, the area of religious group membership seems to be especially challenging in this regard. To illustrate students will often identify as a "nonpracticing Catholic" or "a nonpracticing Baptist." Upon exploration, it quickly becomes evident that these students are in fact nonreligious, not participating in any aspect of formal religion. Often the students need to identify as "nonpracticing" is more related to a family or personal dynamic. As one TA notes:

> Students seem to experience the exploration of the various reference group memberships as the course professor and TA trying to take something away from them, when in reality, the goal of the self-exploration is to seek a more complete understanding of how students experience their reference group membership and to have their self-identification be more consistent with the reality of their day-to-day experience.

The distinction between personal construction and group membership helps students examine the reality of their lives and opens up more honest exploration of the social group and the meaning associated with it rather than the unique meaning each person may assign. The group membership focus also protects students from revealing details of family and private issues.

The TAs as group leaders must help the group members to work effectively with one another. Group leaders must also monitor their own biases and preferences. Instruct them to give equal time to each reference group, but each TA struggles in some way because of his or her own reference group issues. One shared this thought:

> It always feels like each [reference group] section could go on forever, it is hard to balance. Since I am partial to race, it is hard to know when is the best time to end that portion of the interview. Different people have a reference group that is more salient for them and you have to figure that out.

Another noted: "While you are aware of your own biases and theirs, you are trying to maintain or create a safe environment to explore."

In addition, how Whites react to the learning about race and culture is often a challenge. Race seems the most difficult group membership for students and staff, even though the course does not emphasize it over other reference group memberships. In fact, it is the last group to be discussed in the student's interview. One TA observed:

> I've seen Whites in group sometimes play things out . . . they have a notion that because they are White there is no way to talk about race. The person of Color or TA often has to take up the [lead] role, but [in reality] it is not necessary for the person of Color or TA to take the lead. The learning can get done in a group of White people, but they are slow to get that.

White students are often relieved when assigned a White TA, as one White TA noted:

> The most obvious thing is that White students expect me to protect them. When they arrive in group for the first day, they are visibly "relieved" and comment on this relief in their

journals that they got me as a TA. Boy are they surprised when I start to challenge them! Then their initial agreeable and participatory attitudes give way to various shades of anger and resentment that I won't "play the game."

A core aspect of the learning, addressed often in supervision, is the student's effective use of counseling skills in the small group, as well as maintaining balanced exploration of all four reference groups. Also, TAs must learn how to work both with individual group members and groups as a whole. In supervision, I emphasize the integration of thought and emotion, combined with sound counseling techniques that are racially and culturally appropriate, so the TAs have to work the balance between the skills instruction and supporting the students' emotional and cognitive learning. One TA describes the challenge this way:

> My biggest issue is balancing, going deeper, and being in touch with emotions and me being able to hold that. The balance between challenging and being supportive and ensuring that the members do that for each other is difficult. . . . It is hard when students drop important issues. . . . If everybody shuts down the TA has to step in. I would like to see the group members step up instead.

Another shares this: "Learning to genuinely engage in a process of trying to really understand another person's experience as they describe it is a huge part of the course. Students struggle with this." Yet another talks about the students' struggle to develop counseling skills:

> Making sure that students phrase questions appropriately, like not too many closed-ended questions . . . is a responsibility and a challenge that we have to address to help them be better counselors. The content and delivery are important.

TAs also report that the need to focus simultaneously on the three core aspects of the students' learning is both a challenge and a learning experience:

> In the small group it is difficult at times to focus on racial-cultural issues, the students' use of counseling skills, and on the students' attempts to understand the interviewee at the same time. A very helpful aspect of supervision is to explore ways in which TAs can be more effective in focusing on these three areas and to explore personal racial-cultural dynamics that might be impeding the TA in this area.

The most difficult aspect of the training is dealing with students' feelings and their projections of emotions associated with race and culture. Two TAs talk about their experience with projection and the feelings it engendered in them—notice that most of the discussion centers on race, yet I know that similar feelings occur regarding social class, ethnicity, and religion:

> A particular student expressed her thoughts and feelings about Black women being big and tough, which intimidates her. While I know intellectually she is potentially projecting on me, I'm trying not to project back on her. In such a situation, it is difficult not to get

angry . . . rather, I stay with the material because that is what the learning in the class, for me and the students, is all about . . . but it is still challenging.

For me it is hard . . . the students think I am supposed to be nice because I am an Asian woman . . . not being challenging. They are surprised by me, expecting me to be much nicer.

One aspect of the Lab that distinguishes it from other training approaches is that it is designed to stimulate self-exploration, part of which takes place in a very public setting. Self-exploration comes from having to move deeper in your representation and understanding of your thoughts, emotions, and actions. The small group is one of the primary places where that learning takes place. TAs are challenged by the task of pushing students to deeper levels of exploration and the task of getting the students in the group to also push each other. One TA points out: "Everybody wants to be nice to each other . . . the opposite of nice is confrontation in class . . . but nice is not to talk genuinely. That does a disservice to students." It is surprising to learn that we have to work against prior learning in Lab. Another TA noted: "Working through the unconditional positive regard students have learned in previous counseling training is tough to work with."

Race is used as a marker for other reference groups; this is most apparent in the ratings activity. Although the Lab uses a race-based perspective, race is not the primary focus of the course; however, it is the area that generates the most conflict and emotional struggle on the part of students and TAs. One TA describes the experience this way:

It is difficult to get people to own racist thoughts and ideologies. It is hard to get them to own and talk about how they adhere to racist ideas and behavior. Getting people to be honest and authentic is the hardest challenge.

A TA of Color points out: "I have encountered groups unwilling to work on race because I must be the expert . . . often there is an assumption that I am the only one with a race." Another notes: "It is difficult for people to be genuine and it is very obvious and hurtful when they are not."

It is clear that there are many challenges and struggles for the staff of the Lab. There are also rewards and benefits. One TA said:

Despite feeling anxious around what gets done, I don't feel personal responsibility for the students' growth. I know learning always comes out of the course and it is wonderful to be a part of something that touches so many people.

Another TA shared this about the course: "Through the supervision of other students I am challenged as in no other forum to address these [racial-cultural] issues personally as well as professionally." Another shares this:

The experience as a TA is an invaluable training opportunity because you are given the challenge to exercise your skills in a variety of domains (e.g., individual, group, race, and culture) while having live supervision to guide you. Never in my clinical training have I ever had a supervisor observe my clinical work in a naturalistic setting.

Skill Building

In the skill-building part of the course, students practice their knowledge of racial-cultural issues by working with each other. Skill building involves ensuring that students learn about their clinical strengths and weaknesses in the context of racial-cultural issues. Given the importance of emotional and psychological integration, being aware of and able to express one's affect as well as one's cognitive and behavioral experience is considered an objective of skills training. Simulated counseling sessions are utilized for skill building.

Pairs of students form counselor-client dyads and alternate as the client and the counselor. The presenting issues are students' actual experiences involving one or more reference group issues, and counselors draw on their skills and knowledge to assist the client. Simulations are 30- to 45-minute taped (audio or video) interactions that are observed by the TA and sometimes the professor. Each taped skill session is processed during a noninteractive (no discussion) review of the tape in which students are required to focus on uncovering aspects of the session that were not apparent during the interaction. The processing is facilitated by use of rating sheets that record the students' experiences as counselor and client. After the tape review of the session, the TA (and professor, rotating from group to group) leads a small group discussion about interventions where each member presents an analysis of his or her skills and comfort in the session, in particular how the reference group issue was handled.

Sometimes, TAs with less experience have more trouble with the skill session of the course, in part because there are multiple dyads in each group that must be monitored. TAs point out that "looking at four dyads at once is difficult."

The emphasis in the skill portion of the class, as noted earlier, is to have students practice dealing with racial-cultural issues in counseling and applying counseling skills effectively. Regarding the skill training and its complexity, one TA observes: "No matter what, the learning happens. While watching a dyad it is difficult to trust the process when you observe a student almost emotionally harming another student." Nevertheless, the process does have an important and powerful effect on the students' and TA's learning. Students sometimes want to focus on the counseling skills and overlook the racial-cultural learning. One TA shares this observation:

> It is challenging to integrate teaching students basic counseling skills and also focusing on racial-cultural counseling skill development. I've seen students easily talk about race, but not be able to effectively end the session. There is usually a pull by students to focus on generic counseling skills, but you must give them balanced feedback.

Watching students grow and learn is one of the rewards of teaching in the Lab. Yet, growth is not restricted to the students, but also takes place in the TAs and the professor. One TA talks about the experience this way:

> It is empowering to do this work for my own personal growth and development as well as my clinical training. I have become more comfortable talking about my various [reference group] identities and understanding what about my past and current experiences impact how I see myself and don't see myself in these [reference group] identities.

Another shares the reward of seeing learning take place: "Being able to see movement in the students and myself is rewarding. By the end, the White students at the very least aren't saying they are lucky to be born American." Another says, "As a TA you often see your own struggles and experiences through the eyes of your students serving as a constant reminder that you have grown but still have so much growth to experience. You are never above the learning."

Feedback

One of the unique and most controversial aspects of the course is that it is evaluative, providing students with constant feedback and interventions about their behavior and learning in the small group and journals, how and whether they adhere to the course guidelines, and how their learning is reflected in their skill building. Because the course is competence-based, feedback and evaluation are given to each student along a number of dimensions. Students are given feedback about their use of counseling skills (ability to listen, respond to, and reflect feelings, etc.), in small group, and skill training, and on how they use and communicate their racial-cultural knowledge. The teaching staff provide students with written feedback about their learning, emphasizing growth and obstacles to learning. Each student receives a written midsemester feedback report. If concern arises—when a student does not hand in a journal, comes to class late, does not interact in small group, or avoids racial-cultural issues—a written warning is given. Usually, students are advised that it is difficult to assess their learning given their behavior or lack of progress. At the end of the course, a final written feedback and assessment report about their learning in the course is provided.

In the final feedback and assessment, the professor and TA indicate whether and to what extent the student has demonstrated the minimal racial-cultural counseling competencies needed to pass the course. To pass, students must have shown that they were willing to engage in the process of learning. We do not require perfection or personality reconstruction to pass the course. We ask, and look throughout the semester, for students' effort to understand their reference group memberships. We ask if students were able to use effectively basic counseling skills and were able to help other students learn. Not all students pass the course. Many, but not all, students who do not pass are given an opportunity to continue learning in a future semester. The professor's and TAs' feedback and clinical judgment in regard to each student's racial-cultural competence makes the course an integral part of the program's curriculum (e.g., theories, counseling skills, practicum, internship). All final decisions about whether a student will continue his or her learning is made by the professor.

The model for training in mental health professions uses the supervision approach. Much of the teaching in mental health practice occurs through observation, feedback, and evaluation: The student's skills and abilities are observed in a range of settings and are evaluated by an established professional. Clinical judgment, exercised by experienced and established or advanced trainees, is at the core of our training methods and is highly valued. I think students benefit from intensive and highly structured experiences.

Some would argue that the evaluation in the Lab course does not make students feel safe. More important, some scholars contend that in teaching students about racial-cultural issues it is imperative to provide safe environments. I am not always sure what "safe" means, in this context. "Safe" is also used as a euphemism for racial characteristics of communities; that is, non-White and poor communities are "unsafe" areas. Sometimes it seems to mean free from evaluation and feedback. To others, safe may mean students are free to openly express themselves; the trade-off for the openness is a passing grade for the course or a grade based on some other activity, such as a paper. They might be right, and I may be mistaken about my belief that, due to their socialization, students will resist learning about race and culture unless it is required, and if required, the course should be delivered with the same seriousness, evaluation, and grading decisions about passing as other learning experiences, all of which have some evaluation and assessment.

CHALLENGES OF TEACHING FOR RACIAL-CULTURAL COMPETENCE

The challenges associated with teaching about race and culture have come from many places. My emphasis on learning or not passing the course has been a source of conflict with students, faculty, department chairpersons, deans, and other administrators. As long as students were being asked to be aware without assessment—they took the course as pass/fail and the pass was given without question—my colleagues were happy and so were students. Once students were held to a higher standard regarding the expectation that race and culture were important and racial-cultural competence was required, people from all directions objected. When students do not pass the class in the spring semester, they may claim that the course professor is preventing them from graduating. Yet, students typically take other courses in their final semester that they must pass in order to graduate. Conflicts and objections have swirled around the course and me for more than a decade: Efforts were made to discredit me and to remove the course from the required list of courses; students have appealed to higher levels to have their grade changed or their failure overturned. One TA notes:

> Most of the White students' resistance comes in very subversive ways—mostly via the journal—a virtual backstabbing, if you will. . . . This backstabbing extends beyond the course as White students who are asked to come back and "further their learning" often go to the dean or otherwise challenge their grades and try to trash the TA and professor in the process.

Despite these conflicts, for the most part, over the years, I have been supported and the efforts to discredit the course and me have failed. One reason is that the students are powerfully and positively affected by the experience. They develop competence to deal with and understand racial-cultural issues that other courses do not teach. The course is difficult and intense but in the end extremely valuable. The intensity is reflected in students' emotional reactions and defenses, which may manifest in two ways, as the work occurs on both an individual and a group level. On the individual level, resistance is exhibited through intellectualization, projection, and denial. It can be hard to reveal oneself to a group of people, and it may be threatening to a student's ego, so one way to react is through resistance. Part of the resistance seems to be that students are very attached to their personal constructions and find it hard to consider the meaning of their group membership beyond what they have told themselves. Thus, on a group level, students engage in silence and confusion about what they should do and how, as a way to avoid the work of the class.

I also think that students must have an opportunity to practice and understand racial-cultural issues and to develop competence and confidence before they are given responsibility for the lives of their clients, who, more often than not, will be different from them and will present with a range of distressful life experiences. I would rather students know through direct experience the feeling of vulnerability than to misunderstand another person's life situation, or worse, not be able to help a client because the student was blocked by unexamined racial-cultural issues. I believe it is my professional and ethical responsibility to ensure that students are prepared with an understanding of their socialization and racial-cultural roles and taught how to minimize the negative influences of those roles in counseling relationships. Students in training need to be observed and provided with corrective interventions and feedback to enhance their effectiveness as counselors and therapists.

As I noted elsewhere (Carter, 2003), many students report that the Lab evaluation seems different from other classes. Students often express the view that they should have equal input into their evaluation. I think this view exists because other courses tend not to focus as much on self-exploration, nor do courses focus on the individual student's reference groups. For some reason, counseling professionals and psychologists are ambivalent about providing feedback to students on their personal issues in experiential learning courses, practica, and field settings. So students have less experience receiving the type of feedback that takes place in Lab. As more students are becoming licensed professionals with fewer years of training, it may be necessary to set the reluctance aside and give the feedback to students and supervise their work more closely during training.

The feedback is given as corrective interventions focused on students' use of counseling skills and the integration of knowledge of self and others. The professor and the TAs work through students' defensive maneuvers that resist engaging in self-exploration and counseling skill development. We work to understand, and through that understanding soften the resistance so students can learn about their reference group memberships. We do so by attempting to augment the learning process by helping students understand the nature of their defenses in the small group and other sections of the course. One way we help students work through their defenses is by asking them to provide a self-assessment prior to our written feedback. Usually, we find that students' own evaluation mirrors our view of their learning, and the matching of perceptions helps students accept the feedback; thus, they work on the areas that we together have judged need improvement. The focus on understanding what the student is saying on his or her terms is a powerful tool in working through defenses. As stated earlier, we ask students, while learning about how they see the world through the lenses of reference groups, to sharpen their counseling skills. We require students to be better listeners, to be able to reflect and express emotions, to be able to understand another person from that person's perspective and experiences—all critical skills for any helping professional.

We recognize that the challenge to learn about oneself at the same time one is trying to strengthen and apply one's helping skills is quite daunting for many students. Nevertheless, we work with students to meet the challenge by giving feedback and by emphasizing professional and counseling skill development. To help students understand the feedback, we (the TA and professor) meet individually with each for the midterm and final feedback. Yet, for some, the fact of being given feedback is a struggle.

It is hard for many students, even those who sought out the training, to accept racial-cultural competence as an area in which they should be evaluated, in part because many aspects of the learning involve self-exploration and self-development. Some students contend that racial-cultural issues are personal beliefs and as such should not be the subject of their evaluations; they experience the feedback as personally threatening. We address these concerns in several ways. (1) We work hard to distinguish between personal beliefs and reference group memberships. That is, we ask students to explore what it means to be an American or to have been raised as middle class. In this way, we separate personal constructions of reference group experience from social group experience. (2) We discourage delving into family or personal stories in the course. (3) We focus students' attention on the group aspects of their experience.

Students' attitudes toward the course vary. Some students enter the course full of anticipation and interest in learning, and some are overly concerned about how they will do. Some are curious about what they will learn about themselves in terms of racial and cultural identity; others desire to augment their awareness due to a sense of professional responsibility; and still others attend class solely because the course is a program requirement.

Student experiences in the course can be characterized by a host of defenses and reactions intended to enhance or resist engaging in the course material. Most students are able to move from their initial, resistant stance to honestly engaging in the self-exploration process; however, there are students who ardently "stay stuck" and continue to vent their negative feelings toward the teaching staff. A typical response in these instances is expressing the feeling that the teaching staff is attempting to "sabotage" them by withholding critical information. Feedback and patient understanding usually prevail, and then most students focus on becoming racially and culturally competent.

Regarding the work and its benefits, one TA shared this viewpoint:

> The dual relationship with the professor binds you with the professor. You bond. It gives me profound respect for the professors. We see each other in a clinical sense. The professor gets to assist with your clinical development.

Others place being a TA in a professional context:

> Working as a teaching assistant in this course is often different from working in other courses. TAs for the course have a tremendous amount of responsibility when working with students, providing them with input/feedback, and ultimately evaluating their progress.

Given this responsibility we are professionals in training and are treated as such. The professor works with us and we do a lot of work. In a system which often attempts to remind us that we are students, this course demands a level of professionalism beyond the student status.

It's rewarding to see movement and it constantly gives me renewed energy to keep doing this work, even in spaces where it may not be accepted or appreciated (such as outside sites on externship). It also serves to remind me every time I teach that we still can not be complacent in our own program, even while we have a commitment to an integrative racial-cultural program.

One TA sees the benefits from a personal developmental perspective:

I often find myself thinking that while Lab is primarily about learning racial-cultural competence, it is also in essence learning to be a more effective human being, to be more genuine, understanding, and authentic in your personal interactions and relationships. In this sense being a TA is another opportunity for personal growth and a chance to facilitate this growth in others.

CONCLUSION

The Lab is a course with many layers and pieces, each element designed to facilitate the student's development along each of the three dimensions: knowing how (skill development), knowing that (racial-cultural knowledge), and knowing oneself (self-exploration). The course components are woven together to promote integration of students' thoughts, emotions, and actions regarding the role of racial-cultural factors in effective counseling relationships. The course focus on reference groups as aspects of culture provides an effective way to deconstruct the complex experiences of race and culture. I am clear and firm in my belief about the central role of self-exploration in learning about how to be a racially and culturally competent mental health professional. Finally, the feedback about the students' learning is imperative and an effective mechanism in the training. Without evaluation, students would not learn as effectively how each reference group contributes to their understanding of themselves as people and professionals. Maybe in the future more programs will hold students to a competence standard in classes that are designed to teach them about racial-cultural issues, especially as racial-cultural or multicultural competence standards have been in existence for over 30 years.

REFERENCES

American Association for Counseling and Development. (1988). *Ethical standards.* Alexandria, VA: Author.

American Association for Counseling and Development. (1989). *Bylaws.* Alexandria, VA: Author.

American Psychological Association. (1990). *Guidelines for providers of psychological services to ethnic, linguistic, and culturally diverse populations.* Washington, DC: Author.

American Psychological Association. (2003). Guidelines on Multicultural Education, Training, Research, Practice, and Organizational Change for Psychologist. *American Psychologist, 58*(5), 377–402.

Birnbaum, M. (1975). The clarification group. In K. Benne, L. Bradford, J. Gibb, & R. Lippet (Eds.), *The laboratory method of changing and learning.* Palo Alto, CA: Science and Behavior Books.

Carter, R. T. (1995). *The influence of race and racial identity in psychotherapy: Toward a racially inclusive model.* New York: Wiley.

Carter, R. T. (2000). Reimagining race in education: A new paradigm from psychology. *Teachers College Record, 102*(5), 864–896.

Carter, R. T. (2001). Back to the future in cultural competence training. *Counseling Psychologist, 29*(4), 787–789.

Carter, R. T. (2003). Becoming racially and culturally competent: The racial-cultural counseling laboratory. *Journal of Multicultural Counseling, 31*(1), 20–30.

Carter, R. T. (in press). Uprooting inequity and disparities in counseling and psychology: An introduction. In R. T. Carter (Ed.), *Handbook of racial-cultural psychology and counseling: Theory and research* (Vol. 1, pp. xv–xxviii). Hoboken, NJ: Wiley.

Constantine, M. G., Watt, S. K., Gainor, K. A., & Warren, A. K. (in press). The influence of Cross's initial Black racial identity theory in other cultural identity conceptualizations. In R. T. Carter (Ed.), *Handbook of racial-cultural psychology and counseling: Theory and research* (Vol. 1, pp. 94–115). Hoboken, NJ: Wiley.

Helms, J. E. (Ed.). (1990). *Black and white racial identity.* Westport, CT: Greenwood Press.

Helms, J. E., & Cook, D. A. (1999). *Using race and culture in counseling and psychotherapy.* Boston: Allyn & Bacon.

Johnson, S. D. (1987). Knowing that versus knowing how: Toward achievement expertise through multicultural training for counsel. *Counseling Psychologist, 15,* 320–331.

Katz, J. H. (1985). The sociopolitical nature of counseling. *Counseling Psychologist, 13*(4), 615–624.

Midgette, T. E., & Meggert, S. S. (1991). Multicultural counseling instruction: A challenge for faculties in the 21st century. *Journal of Counseling and Development, 70,* 136–141.

Sue, D. W. (2001). Multicultural facets of cultural competence. *Counseling Psychologist, 29*(6), 790–821.

Sue, D. W., Bernier, J. E., Duran, A., Feinberg, L., Pedersen, P., Smith, E. J., et al. (1982). Position paper: Cross-cultural counseling competencies. *Counseling Psychologist, 10,* 45–52.

Sue, D. W., Carter, R. T., Casas, J. M., Fouad, N. A., Ivey, A. E., Jensen, M., et al. (1998). *Multicultural counseling competencies: Individual and organizational development.* Thousand Oaks, CA: Sage.

CHAPTER 4

Multicultural Learning in Family Therapy Education

Charleen Alderfer

When the importance and the need for multicultural learning in family therapy training became evident, there was, for a few years, an ongoing debate about how the subject should be incorporated into the curriculum. One argument supported the infusion of the subject throughout the entire marriage and family therapy curriculum, including multicultural issues in every course. The other view, held by some family educators, supported the idea of one required course, which would provide an extensive and concentrated multicultural education to all students. While the single course model did not prohibit the inclusion of multicultural issues in other courses, it would ensure the uniform education of all students in marriage and family therapy programs. It should be noted that family therapy education uses the term "multicultural" to cover as many areas of difference as possible. My own experience has been that it is impossible to focus on each identified group and understand fully the experience of its members. Therefore, the course described in this chapter focuses on the self of the learner in relation to members of different identity groups.

In the beginning, race and gender were the major areas to be included in the educational programs. In the past 20 years, the definition of multicultural issues has expanded to more areas than just those two. Now we expect our students not only to have a thorough knowledge of race and the effects of racism in the United States, but we want them to understand the impact of gender on families for women as well as men and children; we want them to be prepared to work with a wide range of clients from ethnic backgrounds different from their own; understanding social class and its effects on families in relation to the larger society is a necessary element of their education; we expect them to work with gay and lesbian couples and families and to be aware of the special problems confronting those with an alternative lifestyle; we want them to be aware of the many aspects of spirituality and how it affects the treatment of a family. Underlying all of these expectations is the need to have our

I want to thank Clayton P. Alderfer for his comments, editorial advice, and general support in preparing this chapter.

students understand oppression and prejudice not only as they occur in our society, but, more important, as they occur within groups and within individuals.

How best can we, as teachers of potential family therapists, help students to meet all the challenges of a complex multicultural and diverse population? Our approach is not for students to learn the characteristics of every dimension of difference from self, but to learn the roots of their own identity and the effect of that identity on the understanding of difference. Our focus is to encourage students to learn about their own identity groups and their relationships to those identity groups that are different. The model for the class employs embedded intergroup theory (Alderfer, 1987), which is based on the premise that identity groups give messages to their members about what it means to be a member and, at the same time, provide perspectives on other groups. Both kinds of messages are carried with the group member as she or he encounters people who belong to other groups. From the theory's point of view, it is not only the individual who is generating a reaction from others, but also the individual as a representative of her or his multiple group memberships. Students begin by examining the development of their attitudes and values in their own family, a primary identity group. This model is designed not to ignore the characteristics of identity groups but to discuss those differences as they arise throughout the course and in the context of seeing clients.

This course focusing on multiculturalism is an important element in an educational program for training family therapists. The course has also been used with success in master's-level counseling programs. From the outset, students are expected to develop self-awareness as it pertains to the conduct of family therapy. Their first course in the family therapy program, Family of Origin, is based on the work of Murray Bowen (1978). In this course, students are asked to prepare a three-generation or more genogram of their own family. The Family of Origin course offers an initial opportunity to examine students' own racial and ethnic history. The instructor helps this process by discussing her or his own racial and ethnic experiences and by asking students to include these same dimensions in their own genogram presentations.

The aim of the family therapy program is to prepare students to work with families that are both similar to and different from their own. There are at least two ways in which knowledge of racial and ethnic dynamics influences the behavior of therapists. In the first instance, therapists need to take account of their own race and ethnicity when they meet and join with client families (e.g., Black therapist with White family). The second element involves therapists' readiness to work with unique elements of families from particular cultures or combinations of cultures (e.g., the roles of men and women in Italian families, the dynamics common to Catholic-Jewish families). As part of their training, students work with families under supervision in practicum and internship settings. Supervisors encourage students to observe and respond to racial and ethnic influences as they practice.

It is crucial to include a course that is concentrated and required as well as to infuse multicultural learning throughout an educational program for family therapists. This chapter presents a format for a course that meets students' need to understand the impact of systemic thinking as required in a family therapy program.

OVERVIEW OF THE COURSE

The course's duration is a standard academic semester of 14 weeks; each class meets for two and a half hours each week. Two major themes simultaneously permeate the class: learning about differences on an individual basis and learning about differences as a group member in relation to other groups. The learning of these themes is accomplished by working on individual issues through an exploration of one's family of origin in the context of identity groups.

After introductions, which include an example of each student's encounter with difference, students are asked to form identity groups based on race and ethnicity. We discuss the fact that Black-White relations have been central to problems in the United States even before the founding of the country as well as in the present. Race is rooted in people's interpretations of biological differences, such as skin color, hair texture, and body type. Ethnicity, which to some has a degree of correlation with race, is rooted in culture, learned patterns of behavior, and geographic regions. Students are encouraged to establish groups first on the basis of common race and then on the basis of common ethnicity. The number of groups on average is five and is dependent on size and the racial and ethnic composition of the class.

From time to time, students are reluctant or unwilling to form groups based on race or ethnicity. When this happens, they are encouraged to discuss their resistance. If the conversation does not end the resistance, students are then asked to find another basis of identity. Under these circumstances, people have formed groups on the basis of occupation or profession or generation (e.g., athletes, social workers, women over 40). We do not insist that students form groups based on race and ethnicity when they are clearly and explicitly reluctant to do so. In all but two classes offered over a period of 10 years, only two have elected not to form groups based on race and ethnicity. In spite of that choice, the topic of race and ethnicity stays with the class. Experience has taught me that when resistance to the initial formation based on race and ethnicity is too great, giving students a chance to move away from that resistance and find other bases for similarity increases their willingness to engage in the learning. Otherwise, an unproductive degree of energy is spent denying the effects of racial and ethnic group memberships. It is clear to me that more intergroup learning about race and ethnicity occurs when groups can be formed based on those identities.

Once the groups are formed and identified, we begin to work on the development of individual attitudes and values in relation to differences, which include race and ethnicity. As an introduction to the personal work, an overview of the historical roots of racism in the mental health professions is presented in the format of a "professional family of origin." This format is consistent with the manner in which students are asked to examine their own family's contributions to the development of the values and attitudes they hold toward differences.

One of the major theories of family therapy most frequently used in education and training is natural systems theory, developed and practiced by Murray Bowen (1978). Because most attitudes about differences are first learned from our family of origin, we begin the class by reading *Even the Rat Was White* (Guthrie, 1998).

This book describes the multiple abuses of people of Color as research subjects, often overlooked by psychologists. Guthrie also describes some questionable "research findings" about race based on inaccurate reporting of the results. Some of the more enlightening sections of the book, for White students, are the chapters on the struggles and the accomplishments of Black psychologists and the growth of Black colleges. Based on this book, there are lectures and discussions of our professional family of origin. The discussions of the lectures and readings are carried out within each of the identity groups. For instance, all groups tend to be appalled by the section on eugenics, but differences between African American groups and other racial and ethnic groups tend to appear around the topic of intelligence testing and the Bell curve; controversy about the reasons for different racial and ethnic group IQ evokes group and individual conflicts. One common denominator for almost all of the students, including those of Color, is the extent to which they are unaware of the prejudice and authority exercised over minority and oppressed groups by early psychology experimenters. Psychology is a professional ancestor of family therapy and, therefore, similar to our own ancestors, gives us a legacy to be both respected and challenged.

At the same time, we begin the work that is the foundation of self-learning. Students are given a series of questions about their own family of origin. These questions relate to the six areas of difference that are most relevant to the contemporary societal issues affecting the therapeutic relationship: race, gender, ethnicity, social class, sexual orientation, and spirituality. Each question deals with both the overt and covert messages given to the student by her or his family in relation to each of the six areas. (A more detailed explanation of the questions is provided in the section "Personal Family of Origin Questions.") Readings accompany each of the six areas of difference; foundational readings are taken from family therapy literature, others are current articles taken from magazines and newspapers. Lectures are based on the readings.

As the students in each of the identity groups become more cohesive, the discussion within each group becomes more intense. When groups report at the end of each session, the differences between them become evident. Students begin to get a sense of strong identification with their own group and also begin to see the areas where they are influenced by the group and where their individual family learning exerts a more powerful hold on their attitudes and behaviors. Many spirited discussions occur between groups.

Students in the class complete several written assignments. Each group also presents itself as a group to the class at the end of the semester. As a weekly assignment, each student keeps a journal highlighting the important learning in the class and any effects evident outside of class. Students are also asked to do an alternative assignment in which they attend a function or an event outside the identity group they have formed for the class. A written assignment asking them to assess their feelings prior to attending the event, during the event, and after the event is required; it is important for students to discover what behaviors contributed to any change of attitude. The final class is an ethnic dinner for which each student is asked to prepare food that is either a part of her or his ethnic heritage or family of origin heritage. This is fun, fattening, and provides serious reflection. Many students have never been in touch with their background through food, which tells them something about the degree of nurturing in their history.

In a presentation by each group, students are asked to present their group to the class by focusing on both differences and similarities within the group and, as best they can, between groups. They respond to the six areas of difference even if their group is based on something other than race and ethnicity; for example, a group of school counselors presented themselves and the effects of the six areas of difference on their work. A final question for each group relates to how the learning from this class will affect the work of each person as a family therapist.

This is not a particularly easy class to teach because the faculty person must be aware of the problems in all the areas of difference and must guard against defensiveness in response to the sometimes surprising issues that surface. It also requires a knowledge and understanding of groups and their functioning. One needs to be extensively prepared, though it is difficult to be prepared precisely for what is presented by the students in each class. The instructor's own values and beliefs are subject to challenge. It is not unusual for some students to look for vulnerabilities in the instructor and to challenge her or him. Teaching the class is both energizing and emotionally draining. The overall results are very rewarding.

KEY ELEMENTS OF THE COURSE

The following section includes the elements of the course listed in the syllabus. While it is important for the integrity of the course to include all elements, it is also possible to add others evolved by specific needs arising in a given class.

Six Areas of Difference

Of the several dimensions of difference, the topics of race and ethnicity are perhaps the most complex. At the core of these struggles is the history of slavery in the United States. Even after the civil rights movement and the activation of legislative changes, the relationship between Blacks and Whites continues to be strained by the effects of racism. The history of the United States also includes conflicts between ethnic groups, such as those between the English and the Germans, the Irish and the Italians, and, more recently, between Asians and Whites. The course begins with Guthrie's (1998) *Even the Rat Was White* to identify the role of race and racism in shaping biases still visible in psychology today.

The underlying assumption of the course is that most learning about individual differences occurs in one's family of origin through the transmission of both overt and covert messages. Covert messages about differences are often difficult to uncover, and they have a greater influence in the development of negative stereotypes. By examining the extent of the messages given to them in the following six areas of difference, students uncover the roots of present values and attitudes of which they were previously unaware:

1. *Race:* The most volatile and emotional difference due to the legacy of slavery and racism in the United States is African American. Hispanics and Asians are less difficult to discuss, and in the eastern part of the country, it is rare to

have any interaction with Native Americans. The discussions tend to be difficult and fraught with denial of racial problems.

2. *Gender:* This is one of the earliest differences experienced in the family. Most discussions are lively and, though they can be emotional, show progressive changes about the role of men and women in society across the generations.

3. *Ethnicity:* This difference brings out very strong identity with an ethnic group for some individuals; others express concern that they do not have an ethnicity or do not know what ethnicity means to them. Discussion focuses on the meaning of ethnicity and how it is carried on in the family.

4. *Social Class:* It is often difficult for students to discuss this difference as nearly everyone identifies as middle class. Further exploration allows them to designate areas within this difference, such as education, wealth, and geographic location.

5. *Sexual Orientation:* There is a lot of secrecy surrounding this difference. Traditional families seem reluctant to discuss sex and are loathe to discuss sexual orientation.

6. *Spirituality:* This difference is often the most readily discussed and, initially, the most superficial. As students become more involved with the subject, there are some very serious and touching conversations focusing both on the rigidity of some beliefs and the lack of spirituality in some lives.

The six areas of difference are the basis for class introductions, group formation, family of origin work, reading assignments, class discussions, written assignments, and group presentations. As students begin to understand how their attitudes toward these differences were shaped, they begin to understand their behavior in relation to groups and individuals who are unlike themselves (see also, Carter, this *Handbook,* this volume).

Initial Class Introductions

After an introduction to the class and the professor, students begin the first event of the course. They are given the six areas of difference with a brief explanation of each. They are then asked to present themselves to their classmates with the additional assignment of talking about an experience that is related to one of these areas. Introductions often begin slowly, with very tentative discussion in areas that seem relatively safe. Usually, religion or spirituality is one of the first areas of difference to be raised. Ethnicity is also frequently raised, but in a very gentle, benign way. A student might say, "I have no ethnicity, I am just American," and then go on to say that she has missed having a strong ethnic background, like "an Italian family." The more difficult areas of race and sexual orientation tend to appear later in the introductions. In one instance, a light-skin male African American spoke about racial profiling and of the importance to him of the words of W. E. B. DuBois reminding Black Americans that they live in two worlds. In another instance, a gay man said that he rarely spoke in public about being gay, but this forum allowed him to tell about the prejudice he had experienced. It is not unusual for a woman to talk about the abuse she has tolerated in a past relationship with a man. Immediately, the class becomes encompassed by difference and, for the most part, students begin to feel free to ask questions and promote discussion.

Assignments

The assignments give students the opportunity to apply their learning from class. The core assignments are important aspects of the course. Other assignments may be added depending on the composition and needs of the class.

Journals

Students are expected to keep a journal of reactions to each session of the class. They are encouraged to write about thoughts, feelings, and life events, both past and present, that are evoked by the class process. Journals are collected at the end of every third session and are read and returned to students with the comments of the instructor. Students are encouraged to respond either in class or in future journal entries. Contents of the journals frequently become ingredients of the class history and discussion.

While it is demanding for the instructor to read all the journals and to provide feedback, it is important to the students to know that their entries are being read and given serious consideration. They report feeling heard, understood, challenged, and able to confront the instructor. Some students write in their journals thoughts and feelings that they feel uncomfortable expressing in the class. Others find the journals a useful way to reflect on the complexities of the class.

Alternative Experience

A requirement of the course is for students to attend an event, a ceremony, or a place that is different from any in their identity group. They are also asked to write a paper describing the experience, paying particular attention to their personal reactions, the reactions of their family, and the reactions of members of the group they are entering.

Usually, there is some form of resistance focused on time or logistics, but not overtly to the assignment itself. The resistance, in whatever form, needs to be addressed as soon as it arises; it can be alleviated, but it also may carry over into the kind of experience selected. Some students choose relatively unthreatening ways to fulfill the requirement. For example, one woman attended the wedding of a family member who was marrying into a Christian faith different from her own. There is learning in this type of experience, but it tends to be more about families than about multiculturalism. Seeing this behavior as resistance, the instructor can speak to the student privately or respond through comments on the paper.

Other students meet the challenge head on. An Italian man who grew up in what he described as "an inner-city racist neighborhood" dressed in his best suit and attended an African American Baptist church service. He felt very out of place there and was welcomed by only a few of the members. Instead of reinforcing his prejudice, the experience caused him to examine how his own behavior might have affected the members of the church. A Jewish woman attended a Greek festival. She wandered about on her own for a while and then decided to sit at a table with some of the Greek women who were serving food at the festival. They struck up a lively conversation, and she returned home with a recipe for baklava and the phone number of one of the women. She became aware of inhibitions that had kept her from joining groups different from her own. In general, the alternative experience is enlightening for many of the students. It is also a measure for the instructor of how committed a student is to learning more about cultural differences.

Class Presentation

Each identity group is expected to make a presentation to the class. The first task is to define the characteristics of the group that give them an identity different from that of the other groups. They present ways they relate as a group and as individuals to the six areas of difference, thus allowing for a discussion of differences within as well as between groups. Their final task is to focus on how the learning in this class will inform their work as family therapists.

Creativity has become an exciting aspect of the presentations. In one group's presentation, each group member held a different colored ribbon. As each person spoke about a similarity to another group member, those people crossed ribbons. As they spoke about a difference, the ribbon was moved away. By the end of the presentation, there was a complicated interweaving of different colored ribbons. In another presentation, each group member brought childhood mementos that were meant to show the foundations of her or his beliefs and behaviors.

An active discussion about individual and group differences and similarities tends to follow each presentation. When students discuss how the learning affects their professional work, they begin the process of clinical application. They move toward an awareness of the areas they privilege in their work with clients and the areas they prejudice.

The Meal

The assignment for the final class is a meal of ethnic and family favorites. While the experience of eating is fun and tasty, it is also representative of the nurturing and caring that is a part of cultures and families. Students are asked to bring any sort of food that is identified with their cultural background or their family of origin. Many students spend time preparing a special dish; others get their moms to do it! Still others simply stop on the way to class and buy something (hopefully, something meaningful). The object of the assignment is to connect students with their own identity group in a nurturing way that they can share with other groups. All of these behaviors are part of the discussion during the meal.

One student made Irish soda bread. She said, "I can't believe how close I felt to my Irish heritage when I was making this bread. There were generations of women before me who did the exact same thing and I felt connected to them." Another woman brought an unusual combination of macaroni and broccoli. She said her family ate this when they were less well-off, and she associated the food with a great deal of warmth in her family.

There are group reactions to the food. In one class, the British Isles group waited behind the table to serve tea and biscuits to other students who came to them. At the same time, members of the Italian group were carrying large portions of pasta and antipasto to everyone in the room. These events provide an impetus for discussion and developing awareness.

The meal allows students to share another aspect of themselves. Eating together is an experience of intimacy and creates a communal atmosphere for the completion of unfinished business between groups and individuals.

Readings and Lectures

Readings include articles and chapters on diversity by family therapists as well as current events and interests of students. Lectures are based on the readings.

Readings

There are two ways of determining readings for the course. One is to use chapters from recognized family therapists who write about one or more of the six areas of difference. The traditional textbook is McGoldrick, Giordano, and Pearce (1996). Chapters are assigned as questions arise about specific ethnic groups, and students are encouraged to read chapters relevant to their present work and bring any issues occurring in their work to class for discussion. The readings are generally used on a regular basis and are included in the syllabus.

The other way of selecting readings is to determine the composition of the class, the interests of the students, and current social situations reported in the media. For example, a very popular article for a class composed of many athletes was taken from *Sports Illustrated* (Smith, 2001). It focused on the relationship between Allen Iverson, who is Black and an outstanding Philadelphia 76ers player, and Larry Brown, coach of the 76ers, who is White and Jewish. Because it was playoff time and this class was offered near Philadelphia, the article was well received. The athletes were happy, and no one missed the areas of difference being discussed. This class has been taught for the past few years in New Jersey, where racial profiling is a hot issue. When White students seek to deny its existence, there has been an African American student to present personal experiences to the contrary. Students are also encouraged to bring articles, poems, and other readings to class for discussion. Some of the most exciting interchanges have been sparked through the discussion of works contributed by both students and faculty. Both kinds of reading are important to the course, the first to understand where family therapists stand on the issues and the second to understand the divergent views of society.

Lectures

The lectures are drawn from both kinds of reading. Those taken from the family therapy literature must be updated as new writings appear. Those taken from the contemporary works are more demanding on the instructor; completely new lecture material must be created for every work added to the readings. Contemporary works also provide an opportunity for the instructor to keep up to date on the latest events and controversies in the six areas of difference.

Formation of Identity Groups

The substantive work on the six areas of difference is done in identity groups. When students are asked to form groups based on their racial and ethnic backgrounds, the instruction usually stimulates immediate discussion and reluctance. Some students have never been asked to think about their own ethnicity, some deny awareness of their ethnicity, and others readily find each other and move easily into a group. Students from families who have been in the United States for a long period of time seem less connected to their ethnic group than those who are first or second generation. Students of northern European heritage tend to be more reluctant to form groups than do those of southern European heritage. Often, there is only one representative of a group in the class, and this presents a problem as to where that person should go; for example, it is not unusual to have one Hispanic student or one African American student. One solution has been to put the singles together, as that is not unlike what occurs in society. A group constellation of single ethnic or racial group representatives allows for discussion of feelings about being in that situation.

If there is only one representative of a racial or ethnic group and there is no resolution to the problem of singleness, groups may be formed on the basis of other identities. Although this solution is workable, it makes the discussion more diffuse and diminishes the learning about ethnic and race difference based on group membership. When ethnicity and race are not the basis for the identity groups, other commonalities must be discovered. Students are then asked to form groups based on one of the other areas of difference. They can be very creative in the interpretation of this instruction; however, most often, the choices are based on such things as position in family, such as first and only children, youngest children, children of single parents, or being single parents themselves. Gender-based groups are rarely a choice because there are usually very few males in family therapy training programs. Women will frequently get into groups based on age, so there will be a 20-year-old group or a group of women over 40. We have had profession-based groups such as teachers and athletes; occasionally, religion is the basis of a group, but it tends to be prior religion, such as "recovering Catholic." Students give names to their groups; it is important to not discourage any chosen names, as naming is a telling aspect of identity.

The class convenes as a total group at each class session. The activities in that format are a report of any relevant personal events or current events during the week, a lecture, and a discussion of the assignments. Next, they work in identity groups on the area of difference for that class by responding to the family of origin questions. The final activity is a report and discussion by each group with special attention to differences and similarities both within and between identity groups.

Professional Family of Origin

The use of family of origin work is central to most of the programs designed for training family therapists (Bowen, 1978). In this course, the origin and development of the profession with regard to race and ethnicity is studied and discussed. As previously stated, Guthrie (1998) is the foundation reading for the lecture and discussion. Most students have a new awareness of the questionable generalization of the results of some of the early experiments: They question the early standardization of tests, and they are appalled by eugenics and those involved. In short, they learn that they cannot blindly accept the words of our professional family in the same way that they cannot blindly accept what they learned in their personal family of origin.

One White male student who was well-read and had a strong background in psychology stated in reference to what Guthrie (1998) had written, "I have never heard these things in all the psychology classes I have taken in both graduate and undergraduate programs." African American students are often more aware of these issues, particularly in light of the founding of the Black Psychologists Association in 1969, but they too tend to be unaware of the degree of early mistreatment of minorities by researchers.

Personal Family of Origin Questions

A set of questions forms a framework for the exploration of students' relationship to the six areas of difference based on learning from the family of origin (see Table 4.1). Working in the identity groups that have been formed, each student answers questions and discusses the responses with other group members. At the end of the specified period for discussion, each group reports to the entire class and intergroup discussion ensues. It is in this activity that group differences and similarities are observed and the effects of larger social systems and events on these dynamics are discussed. It is in this interaction that the effect of the group on individual behavior becomes evident. The task of the instructor is to highlight this area of discussion and to deal with the resistance that frequently arises when group phenomena are brought to the foreground.

One's Own Family and Others' Families

The first series of questions focuses on the examination of positive and negative messages about one's own family and about other families. Students often discuss their difficulty in doing this as they feel that they are betraying family secrets. It is important to help them through these feelings. The sense of betrayal becomes more intense when race and sexual orientation are the topics of consideration. Both the overt and covert aspects of the messages are specifically examined. Students tend to report that the more difficult and negative messages were covert in nature, while the more positive and easy messages were overt in nature. One exception tends to be in the area of race, where both kinds of messages were negative. Race messages frequently were stated when dating and marriage became focal in the family development. Another exception is in the area of sexual orientation, where there are few, if any, covert messages, and the topic was simply not discussed in families.

One's Own Groups and Others' Groups

The next set of questions is designed to help students begin to think about the group memberships of their family and how those memberships might influence the attitudes conveyed both inside and outside the family. After defining their various group memberships, students begin to develop an awareness of the different attitudes about other groups that are expressed in one way in their family and another

Table 4.1   Areas of Difference Questions

1. What messages, both positive and negative, did your family give you about your own family?
2. What messages, both positive and negative, did your family give you about other families?
3. Which of those messages were overt and direct?
4. Which of those messages were covert and indirect?
5. What attitudes, both positive and negative, about your own group memberships were expressed in your family?
6. Which of those attitudes could be expressed outside the family?
7. Which of those attitudes were expressed only within your family?
8. What messages, both overt and covert, did your family give you about your relationship to your own racial group?
9. What messages, both overt and covert, did your family give you about your relationship to other racial groups?
10. What messages, both overt and covert, did your family give you about your relationship to your own ethnic group?
11. What messages, both overt and covert, did your family give you about your relationship to other ethnic groups?
12. What messages, both overt and covert, did your family give you about your own gender group, and by whom were they given?
13. What messages, both overt and covert, did your family give you about the other gender group, and by whom were they given?
14. What messages, both overt and covert, did your family give you about your own social class?
15. What messages, both overt and covert, did your family give you about other social classes?
16. What messages, both overt and covert, did your family give you about your own sexual orientation?
17. What messages, both overt and covert, did your family give you about an alternative sexual orientation?
18. What messages, both overt and covert, did your family give you about your own religion and spirituality?
19. What messages, both overt and covert, did your family give you about other religions and spiritualities?
20. How do the messages given to you by your family create areas of prejudice in your work?
21. How do the messages given to you by your family create areas of preference in your work?

way in a more heterogeneous group. This realization of differences between family and nonfamily attitudes is another learning that causes some anguish. At this point, it is important to encourage students to continue exploring the effects of their family on their present interactions and to not blame themselves for acting according to what they have learned. It is an opportune time to help them consider alternative behaviors more in keeping with present views of themselves.

One Jewish male expressed his struggle with what he experienced as mixed messages and hypocrisy: "African Americans were a frequent presence in my grandparents' home, but at the same time, they [the family] made it clear to us in covert ways that we were to not to marry anyone of Color." It was not easy for him to talk about this family norm in a racially mixed class.

One's Own Race and Others' Race

Because of the history and legacy of violent race relations in this country, race is the most difficult of the six areas of difference to discuss openly. Therefore, we begin with race in order to deal directly with difficult issues up front. Generally, race is a part of the discussion in each of the other areas of difference. The questions about race focus on what each person has learned about race and race relations from their family of origin. If the class is in ethnic and racial groups, very clear differences about race arise between groups, and there tend to be greater similarities within groups. The family experiences of the African American group are very different from the other groups'. Often, White groups of all ethnicities express anxiety at the strong differences between themselves and African Americans in the class. Students begin to recognize that "We have grown up in different countries." The most obvious differences within all groups tend to be related to length of time in the United States, geographic locations of families of origin, social class, education, and generation.

Readings about race are assigned and discussed in the large group as well as in small groups. Group reports include responses to the questions and reactions to the readings. Hardy's (1993) discussion of the dilemmas and pain of an African American family therapist is a core reading. He not only writes eloquently about race in family therapy, but he is also one of the foremost contemporary educators and thinkers in the field. It is important for students to be aware that race is not the only contribution of people of Color in family therapy. In a class of largely young students, we used a provocative chapter from Bell (1992) focusing on a Black-White romantic relationship. The younger students were very caught up in this discussion of the relationship and were generally more accepting, whereas older students were less sure of how to deal with it. The conversation evoked age as a group membership and created a very lively interaction.

An African American male talked about watching "all-White TV as I was growing up and wondering why the Bradys had it so good, while my mom was in the kitchen making dinner after working all day and telling us not to watch that show." For many White students, this was the first time they heard directly how biased the media are and have been against African Americans. An Irish woman spoke apologetically in a racially mixed class: "We were told people of Color were lesser than White people. They were to be feared and not trusted. This was conveyed by the sheltered and protective ethnic community my parents grew up in." In this case, the message came not only from the family but from the community as well. For some, the depth of prejudice became more of a reality. A Polish woman discussed the covert racism in her family, who conveyed the message by simply having no African American friends and avoiding situations in which people of Color might be present. She added, "Now that I have my own children, I realize I am not as open-minded and free of prejudice as I once hoped."

The instructor must have a strong sense of her or his own racial identity to work with the emotions that arise in these kinds of discussions. It is impossible not to experience some of the anxiety, anger, fear, and shame expressed both overtly and covertly by students. Any evidence of defensiveness or negative response, verbal or nonverbal, will be immediately perceived by students and will hinder the discussion. On the other hand, it is important to confront the predominance of racial stereotypes and misconceptions with facts (i.e., lynchings, the violence of the KKK, driving while Black) and contrary evidence. A student who feels blamed or criticized for her or his opinion will withdraw from the group and affect not only individual learning, but group learning as well.

One's Own Gender and Others' Gender

This set of questions concerns not only how gender was discussed in families, but whether a male or female parent or relative passed most of the messages. Not surprisingly, both women and men get different messages from their mother than from their father. The content of the learning about gender is very much dependent on generation for women, but less so for men. Those few men in family therapy programs seem to have incorporated messages of altruism and nurturing from their family; this learning seems to come mainly from mothers. Women in the field seem to learn more about heterosexuality and "jobs to fall back on" from their father. Older women have received the same messages from their mother about professional work, but younger women have observed their mother in professional roles and are encouraged by both parents to find meaningful work.

All of the preceding generalizations are affected by race, ethnic group, socioeconomic class, and religion. Learning about one's gender identity is very much dependent on other areas of difference. For instance, White, lower socioeconomic classes often do not value education as much for women as do White, upper socioeconomic classes. Another example is fundamentalist religions, which view women as subservient to men.

Readings by Luepnitz (1988) and Hare-Mustin (1987) on gender in family therapy are discussed in the small groups. A most useful reading by Bograd (1990) discusses the unique issues of women therapists treating men, addressing power differentiation and how women in therapeutic relationships might react. Women often become aware of these concerns and are able to put words to some of the problems they have had working with men. In this context, men are able to discuss previously unidentified issues of working with women clients.

Students seem less inhibited and protective of their family when discussing gender. The identity groups have more in common in the area of gender than they do in any of the other areas. A White Italian English woman spoke about the covert messages in her family: "Women are intelligent, creative, and talented in their own spheres, but really are not as intelligent as men. The women in my family modeled lives of exterior propriety and inner psychological death." An African American woman talked about the covert injunctions to be strong: "My mother and father encouraged me and told me I could be whatever I wanted. They thought it was as important for me to have an education as it was for my brothers." A German Irish male related his family's use of jokes to belittle women: "Women in my family were demeaned and belittled in a sneaky way . . . always through sexual jokes."

Discussion of gender identity is often intense and seems to be more free of concerns about being "politically incorrect" than the discussions about race. As it is likely that there will be more women in the class than men, the instructor needs to find ways to keep the male point of view alive without directly aligning with those opinions; the same would be true for the female point of view if the class were largely male. The gender of the instructor has a marked impact on how these dynamics are handled. It is important to hear the voices of both sides and to be aware that the same dynamics being discussed are also being enacted in the classroom. A woman in charge has a very different effect on both genders than does a man in charge. It is important for the instructor to deal with this dynamic directly by acknowledging her gender in the context of the discussion.

One's Own Ethnic Group and Others' Ethnic Groups

Students often resist responding to the ethnicity questions. Their tendency is to want to deny the importance of ethnicity or to claim not to have an ethnicity. There is usually at least one group that has energy in relation to its ethnicity and that spurs other groups to look more deeply at themselves. The instructor must be prepared to deal with resistance by discussing with the group and eventually with the class the underlying reasons. Frequently, they arise from families giving messages to "blend in," "not be too Italian," and "go with the mainstream." Contrary to northern European ethnic groups, most groups of Color have little difficulty with their African American and Hispanic identities.

Readings for this area are taken from McGoldrick et al. (1996). Students first read about their own ethnic group and bring that to the discussion. This area of difference can lead to cohesiveness in the groups. When the ethnic groups are working, there is a sense of pride in who they are. For White students, there has also been a sense of shame and sadness for how African Americans and, to some degree, other ethnic groups have been treated by their White ancestors.

An example of an event that not only recreated history but also created significant learning occurred in a class with groups based on race and ethnicity. After a lengthy discussion about whether being Jewish was racial or religious, the Jewish students decided they wanted to form an identity group based on religion. Then, about a third of the way through the class, they changed their minds and wanted to be part of their own ethnic groups. The German Jews went to the German group, the Polish Jews went to the Slavic group, and the Russian Jews went to the Russian group. In each case, their own ethnic group rejected them, and at the end of that class, the Jews were once again a group. The lingering hurt of rejection, the microcosm of historical events, and the guilt of the rejecting were topics of discussion throughout the rest of the course. Journals were filled with feelings in relation to this event. It was a difficult time for the entire group, including the instructor, and the level of negativity meant that much processing was necessary. It is difficult to prepare for an experience that has the long historical impact, the societal prejudice, and the emotionality of this example. The instructor needs not only to know the biases and prejudices she or he brings to the class, but must have an understanding of the historical replication of the plight of the Jews. This is only one instance of the multilayered events that can occur in the class.

One's Own Social Class and Others' Social Class

Social class is a complex area of discussion. Most students tend to determine social class by socioeconomic standards and, therefore, claim middle-class membership. A few express pride at having been lower class and moved to their present position in the middle class. Few, if any, claim upper-class membership. When they begin to realize that not only money but education, type of employment, and other, less tangible factors affect social class, they have a more sophisticated conversation and begin to appreciate the nuances of social class.

Readings from Kliman and Madsen about the family life cycle in the context of social class in Carter and McGoldrick (1989) and Rank (2000) and about the effect of social class on families in Nichols et al. (2000) supplement the discussion. Often hidden in contemporary articles dealing with other areas of difference are references to social class that provide good lecture and discussion points. For example, Hardy (1993) focuses on the dilemma of being a Black professional in a largely White profession, thus subtly dealing with social class. In this case, students begin to connect their biases about race and social class. Often, the unexamined assumptions of some White students associate African Americans with lower social class. Hardy brings these assumptions into sharp focus, thus providing an arena for rich discussion.

An Italian woman whose master's degree was the highest of any woman in her family spoke of her brother being the star of the family but very distant from them: "He is a doctor and now in another class. I'm not sure he has more money than my husband and I, but he doesn't want to deal with people who he sees as having less education." Strong messages are given by one's family of origin that getting too far away from one's social class of origin on any dimension will make it hard to come home again. A Jewish male reported that the covert messages in his family were to use humor to demean those of a higher social class. Demeaning messages about social class linger and may provoke responses from the unconscious when the therapist is working with a family. If those messages, both overt and covert, remain unexamined within the psyche of the family therapist, they will manifest themselves in the treatment of the client.

One's Own Sexual Orientation and Others' Sexual Orientation

Aside from race, gay and lesbian issues are the most difficult areas of difference for students to discuss openly. Usually, students assume that everyone in the class is heterosexual. Unlike race, gay and lesbian sexual orientation is not easily identified. Therefore, students are initially very careful about what they say. Even when students identify themselves as gay or lesbian, there is often an awkward pause in the class process. Often, the group responses to the questions lead to more open conversation. Once opinions about sexual orientation are expressed, individuals will speak up about what they have learned from their family and how that learning influenced their feelings about the gay and lesbian community.

Bigner (2000) discusses the development of gay and lesbian families and provides a framework for working with these families. Articles by Markowitz (1991), Hersch (1991), and Dahlheimer and Fiegal (1991) present material useful both for students' personal learning and for their professional work with gay and lesbian clients and their families.

In many classes, gay and lesbian students have spoken about their sexual orientation from the beginning. One young Irish man who had recently come out spoke last in the introduction phase of the class. He talked about his work life and then, with only a brief hesitation, said, "I'm gay and I can't believe I just said that." He went on to become a major contributor to the class both by answering other students' questions and adding his own views of his experiences of being gay in his family. An Italian woman addressed the covert and secretive nature of sexuality in her family: "Sex and sexual orientation was never discussed from my grandmother's generation to my mother, and not much from my mother to me unless I broached the subject."

Sexual orientation carries messages, often unspoken in families, that are deep-seated and pervaded with negativity. Often, they come in the form of cruel jokes. Students who are able to relate these messages tend to do so with a mixture of sadness and shame.

One's Own Spirituality and Others' Spirituality

Spirituality and religion seem to be one of the easiest areas of difference for students to discuss. When given choices during the introductions, many students seem fairly at ease choosing spirituality to demonstrate the effect of a difference on their lives. Yet, in spite of the apparent comfort with religion, it becomes clear that many families give very strong messages about spirituality and religion, particularly in relation to marriage. In relation to gender, women in the family seem to carry the religious beliefs and behaviors. When the subject is a religion such as Islam, which is associated with people of Color, and now with political and terrorist activity, the discussion and feelings become more complex. Students then need to deal with their feelings and attitudes toward skin color and a religion that has become suspect by some groups in the United States. There are also ways of expressing spirituality that are not anchored in organized religion. Class discussions in relation to alternative expressions of spirituality broaden students' sensitivity to the spiritual lives of their clients (see Smith & Richards, this *Handbook,* Volume One).

There have been few consistent readings for the class in the area of spirituality. Prest and Keller (1993) wrote one of the earliest articles relating spirituality to family therapy, and it has been the most used reading. Recent articles relating spirituality to family therapy have been appearing in journals, and they are also used in the course. Among these are Frame (2000) and Fukuyama (2000), who provide conceptual frameworks for using the spirituality of the family in the therapeutic process. Myers (2000) provides an extensive analysis of spirituality in the United States and, though it is not specific to family therapy, offers useful concepts for application.

Students seem less restrained in speaking about spirituality. There is often a sense of pride in having a strong religious background and in overcoming certain dogmas so they could integrate a more personal spirituality into their lives. In particular, many of those raised Catholic express gratitude for their religious background and relief that they have become less bound by the rules of the religion. Those with weaker religious background express the need to find "an anchor." One young woman who had little organized religion in her family persuaded her father to go with her to a Quaker meeting for her alternative experience: "We felt so welcomed that we plan to go back next week." An Italian woman spoke to the issue of women as conveyors of religion in the family: "I was taught that it was important that I attend church every Sunday, but my father, like most men in the family, rarely went to mass. The men were exempt from this rule. I, therefore, received the covert message 'Do as I say, not as I do' in regard to spirituality." A Jewish male expressed an overt message: "My mother was the spiritual influence. She insisted that my family attend religious services."

Recently, some White fundamentalist students have reacted strongly against the idea of working with gay and lesbian clients. These students adhere to a strict interpretation of certain parts of the Bible and believe it would be against their religious values to even entertain the possibility of any kind of therapy with gays and lesbians except reparative work. As this is a relatively new experience in the class, we are working on ways to integrate their perspective into the course. However, there is the question of whether a person who is that determined not to be accepting of different lifestyles should even be a member of the mental health helping professions.

On the whole, religion and spirituality appear to carry fewer negative messages than do other areas of difference, and these messages are more easily processed in adulthood. If not examined, however, they remain powerful and affect the work of therapists with their clients.

STUDENTS' REACTIONS TO THE COURSE

Reactions are measured at the end of each course with a standardized form and open-ended questions designed to evaluate the content of the course and the performance of the instructor. Over the years, responses have been largely positive. Occasionally, students request more time for a specific area of difference, other readings, more lectures, and more discussion. There have not been concerns about the amount of self-exploration nor the time spent in groups. Students say they felt challenged to learn both by the content and the format.

Following is a sample of comments from both men and women, African American and Caucasian, and a variety of ethnic groups. Because evaluations do not include identification of the student, it is not possible to say if the students who responded are male or female, Black or White, or what membership they have to any of the other areas of difference.

> I learned a great deal from the class, both about multicultural perspectives and about myself.
>
> The course challenged me to think about myself and my biases.
>
> I feel better prepared to work with multiculturally different families.

This class aided in bringing circumstances in my life to my attention . . . aspects of my family and myself that I never thought about.

I felt the readings were written in a way that everyone could understand.

I really do have to say I gained a lot of new knowledge.

The instructor expressed her ideas and values and thus I felt comfortable doing the same.

EVALUATION

It is difficult to assign letter grades to a student's multicultural awareness. Class participation, the alternative assignment, and the group presentations are the basis for grading; evaluation, as a broader concept, is more easily accomplished in these activities. If there is anyone who is clearly demonstrating an inability to be open to differences, is unwilling to place herself or himself in a position to learn, or has disturbing journal entries, a conference with that student is scheduled. At that point, it is not only important to discuss what the difficulties are in this area, but whether family therapy is really the right choice of life work for this person.

The learning from this class is evident in other areas of the students' programs. Case presentations include references to differences clients show and how those differences might influence treatment. In supervision sessions, students bring up issues of difference and often refer to the multicultural class as their first encounter with the effects of difference on therapy. Many times they relate feeling more accepting of difference than are members of their family of origin. When observing students working with clients, the supervisor can see an inclusiveness of difference in sessions by students who have had the course as opposed to those who have not yet taken it.

CONCLUSION

This course is very rewarding and, simultaneously, very difficult to teach. Students become engaged in the process and are increasingly eager to learn about difference as the class progresses. They are also hesitant and often embarrassed about exposing the prejudices of their family. The instructor needs to walk a fine line between confronting the prejudice in an understanding way and shutting down further discussion in the process. Change does not occur by allowing negative attitudes toward other groups to persist.

The instructor has to be well prepared to deal with personal questions or affronts. It is important that the instructor allow her or his own feelings and values to be known to the class. If the instructor is not a participant in as well as a leader for the class, the students cannot respond freely. The race of the instructor and the composition of the class change the interaction. When anxiety is high, it is not unusual for a student to confront the instructor about the effects of the class. A White instructor with an all-White class will have a very different set of dynamics from a Black instructor with an all- or nearly all-White class. As this class has been run with White instructors and a largely White class, it would not be appropriate to speculate on the different dynamics in this chapter. That topic is deserving of its own chapter!

This course should not be the only exposure to multicultural learning in a marriage and family therapy program. Multicultural perspectives must be included in all classes, with attention given to each area of difference as it arises in the context of working with couples and families. Social injustice is an integral part of the problems faced by many families. The initial learning must focus on a student's family of origin, the seat of learning about all areas of difference.

SUPPLEMENTAL READINGS

Boyd-Franklin, N. (1989). *Black families in therapy: A multisystems approach.* New York: Guilford Press.

Boyd-Franklin, N. (2003). *Black families in therapy: Understanding the African-American experience* (2nd ed.). New York: Guilford Press.

Carter, R. (1995). *The influence of race and racial identity on psychotherapy.* New York: Wiley.

Freedman, E. H. (1985). *From generation to generation: Family process in churches and synagogues.* New York: Guilford Press.

Helms, J., & Cook, D. (1999). *Using race and culture in counseling and psychotherapy: Theory and process.* Boston: Allyn & Bacon.

Sowell, T. (1981). *Ethnic America: A history.* New York: Basic Books.

Sue, D. W., & Sue, D. (1990). *Counseling the culturally different: Theory and practice* (2nd ed.). New York: Wiley.

Sue, D. W., & Sue, D. (2003). *Counseling the culturally different: Theory and practice* (4th ed.). New York: Wiley.

Thompson, C., & Carter, R. (1997). *Racial identity theory: Application to individual, group, and organizational interventions.* Mahwah, NJ: Erlbaum.

REFERENCES

Alderfer, C. P. (1987). An intergroup perspective on group dynamics. In J. Lorsch (Ed.), *Handbook of organizational behavior* (pp. 190–222). Englewood Cliffs, NJ: Prentice-Hall.

Bell, D. (1992). *Faces at the bottom of the well: The permanence of racism.* New York: Basic Books.

Bigner, J. J. (2000). Gay and lesbian families. In W. C. Nichols, M. A. Pace-Nichols, D. S. Becvar, & A. Y. Napier (Eds.), *Handbook of family development and intervention.* New York: Wiley.

Bograd, M. (1990). Women treating men. *Family Therapy Networker, 14*(3), 54–58.

Bowen, M. (1978). *Family therapy in clinical practice.* New York: Aronson.

Carter, B., & McGoldrick, M. (1989). *The expanded family life cycle: Individual, family and social perspectives* (3rd ed.). Boston: Allyn & Bacon.

Dahlheimer, D., & Fiegal, J. (1991). Bridging the gap. *Family Therapy Networker, 15*(1), 44–53.

Frame, M. W. (2000). The spiritual genogram in family therapy. *Journal of Marital and Family Therapy, 26,* 211–216.

Fukuyama, M. A. (2000). Integrating spirituality into marriage and family counseling. *The Family Digest: International Association of Marriage and Family Counselors, 12*(4), 1, 7–9.

Guthrie, R. (1998). *Even the rat was white* (2nd ed.). Boston: Allyn & Bacon.

Hardy, K. (1993). War of the worlds. *Family Therapy Networker, 17*(4), 50–57.

Hare-Mustin, R. T. (1987). The problem of gender in family therapy theory. *Family Process, 26,* 15–27.

Hersch, P. (1991). Secret lives. *Family Therapy Networker, 15*(1), 36–42.

Luepnitz, D. A. (1988). *The family interpreted: Feminist theory in clinical practice.* New York: Basic Books.

Markowitz, L. M. (1991). Homosexuality: Are we still in the dark? *Family Therapy Networker, 15*(1), 27–35.

McGoldrick, M., Giordano, J., & Pearce, J. (1996). *Ethnicity and family therapy* (2nd ed.). New York: Guilford Press.

Myers, D. G. (2000). *The American paradox: Spiritual hunger in an age of plenty.* New Haven, CT: Yale University Press.

Prest, L. A., & Keller, J. F. (1993). Spirituality and family therapy: Spiritual beliefs, myths and metaphors. *Journal of Marital and Family Therapy, 19,* 137–148.

Rank, M. (2000). Socialization of socioecomonic status. In W. Nichols, M. Pace-Nichols, D. Becvar, & A. Napier (Eds.), *Handbook of family development and intervention* (pp. 129–142). New York: Wiley.

Smith, G. (2001). Mama's boys. *Sports Illustrated, 94*(17), 54–67.

Smith, T. B., & Richards, P. S. (2005). The integration of spiritual and religious issues in racial-cultural psychology and counseling. In R. T. Carter (Ed.), *Handbook of racial-cultural psychology and counseling: Theory and research* (Vol. 1, pp. 132–162). Hoboken, NJ: Wiley.

CHAPTER 5

The Ecology of Life Spaces: Racial Identity-Based Education and Training

Vivan Ota Wang

What does the twenty-first century hold in store for those challenged by racism and oppression? Unless changes occur in how all people recognize the impact of their racialized experiences and histories, misperceptions and misunderstandings about race and race relations will continue. Education and training can lead individuals to shift from *what* others imagine them to be to *who* they really are. They can *Learn to Be*.

According to the United Nations Educational, Scientific, and Cultural Organization's (UNESCO) International Commission on Education for the Twenty-First Century report (1996), *Learning to Be* is a fundamental principle in personal development for people striving to attain their ideals of freedom, liberty, and the pursuit of happiness. Learning to Be education in formal and vernacular forms must contribute to the all-around development of each individual: mind and body, intelligence, sensitivity, aesthetic sense, personal responsibility, and spiritual values. All human beings must be enabled to develop independent, critical thinking and form their own judgment, to determine for themselves what they believe they should do in different circumstances (p. 94).

In its simplest form, Learning to Be is more than an existential quest for knowledge and self-understanding. Learning to Be is personal and practical in its implications for creating realistic choices for attaining life goals. In the spirit of Learning to Be, racial identity development has particular significance. Based on understanding how oppression and power dynamics influence psychological and social development, racial identity theory provides a personally flexible and socially responsive paradigm for scholars and educators to understand and develop strategies for race-based dialogues.

By recognizing racial identity development as an essential life competence, people from all racial groups will be better equipped to navigate their personally and socially racialized experiences more effectively as fully integrated cognitive-affective individuals. Simply put, we cannot fully grasp what external realities mean for others until we know what Martin Buber has called the "I and Thou" for ourselves. Only when the existence of a racialized psychological and environmental reality is recognized as a reality can education serve as a catalyst allowing students and professionals alike to develop culturally responsive skill sets.

This chapter discusses the importance of Learning to Be through racial identity development and suggests racial identity theory as a requisite framework for developing racially-culturally competent education and professional training programs. A racial identity-based education and training model using didactic and experiential teaching methods is presented. Additionally, examples of how racial identity can be integrated into specific education programs and settings for a wide range of professionals (e.g., educators, attorneys, organizational consultants, and mental health professionals) are illustrated.

CRITICAL RACE THEORY

Critical race theory challenges the status quo by assuming that racism is normal and not an aberration in U.S. society (Delgado, 1995; Delgado & Stefanci, 2000). Because of race's embeddedness into what is considered ordinary and natural, critical race theory has suggested that the invisibility of racism (e.g., microaggressions, where subtle behaviors express passive aggressions, being ignored by a sales clerk) results in institutionalized degradation and exploitation of its victims and maintenance of an invisible status quo (unless compared with extreme injustices). Starting from the premise that social realities are self-interested cultural constructs, critical race theorists have suggested that mixed-race interests converge and are tolerated only when White self-interests are simultaneously promoted.

Thus, racial socialization is a powerful process that overtly and covertly communicates "difference" to White and visible racial-cultural people. Often translated into meanings of value and worth, these messages can create different environmental climates in the same physical location. As a result, given the same physical life spaces, people experience life differently depending on their own personal racialized, psychological realities interacting with the racialized attitudes imposed on them by people and/or institutions that surround them. For example, the DWB, FWB (Driving While Black or Followed While Black) phenomena (e.g., untrustworthiness) dramatically influence interpersonal interactions and potentials as well as broader matters such as housing and employment.

For Whites and visible racial-cultural people alike, notions of race influence how fairness, meritocracy, and justice are experienced. For example, when real-life inequities are witnessed or lived or when discussions of race and racism occur, some White people may feel guilty and hopeless. On the other hand, being race- or color-blind, dismissing race as irrelevant, asserting race as a personal preoccupation, or presuming (overtly or covertly) inferior characteristics of visible racial-cultural people and positive superior characteristics of White people maintains the social status quo. Thus, hoping that "the conspiracy of silence" about racism will make racism disappear, bell hooks rightfully states:

> This erasure, however mythic . . . allows for assimilation and forgetfulness. The eagerness with which contemporary society does away with racism, replacing this recognition with evocations of pluralism and diversity . . . further mask[s] reality. (1992, p. 176)

TRENDS IN EDUCATION AND TRAINING

In psychology and education, limited and insular theories and training models coupled with inexperienced professionals have perpetuated inequities and have continued disparities in educational achievement, mental health, and general well-being of White and visible racial-cultural people (Carter, 1995; Carter & Block, 1996; Carter & Gesmer, 1997; Cook, 1997; Fordham, 1996; Ota Wang & Briggs, 1997; Ponterotto & Casas, 1991; Ridley, Li, & Hill, 1998; Shem, 1978; D. Sue & Sue, 2003). Over the past 20 years, recognizing the power of education and professional training, researchers and educators have developed multicultural competence guidelines in hopes of meeting the needs of all students, clients, and helping professionals (D. Sue, Arredondo, & McDavis, 1992; D. Sue et al., 1982; D. Sue et al., 1998). Specifically, knowledge, awareness, and skills characterizing multicultural competence have provided a basis for many psychology and other professional education and training programs (Ota Wang, 1994; D. Sue et al., 1982; D. Sue et al., 1998).

One educational strategy to gain multicultural competence has been to learn about "members of the opposite race and different cultures" (Kiselica, 1998, p. 13) by studying visible racial-cultural people through structured cross-racial interactions, such as Beale's (1986) Cross Cultural Dynamic Encounter and Mio's (1989) Partners Program. These programs provide limited training because of their limiting presumption that only visibly racial-cultural people possess race and culture. This training focus on a "racial client" as the major distinguishing factor often results in tendencies to overgeneralize and homogenize members of various racial groups and ignore within-racial-group factors. At the same time, a training strategy focusing on these "othered" clients' cultural beliefs and values may misguide attention to the visible racial-cultural other rather than inward, toward self-understanding of the counselor's own cultural beliefs, values, and stereotypes that are largely ignored, remain unchallenged and are reinforced (Carter, this *Handbook,* this volume; Ridley, Espelage, & Rubinstein, 1997, p. 132; Sue & Torino, this *Handbook,* this volume).

Another teaching method has avoided race altogether by advocating for a unifying perspective of universal generalizabilty. This common factors approach views all humanity as being joined by unifying constructs (usually from the practitioner's worldview), as exemplified in Smith's (1985) stress-resistant delivery model, Atkinson, Thompson, and Grant's (1993) counseling racial/ethnic minority clients model, and Trevino's (1996) change process cross-cultural counseling model. By ignoring how racial socialization and racial identity attitudes shape worldviews, entire groups of people and communities are not acknowledged, thus making learning and the work about race even more impersonal.

These racial avoidances and displacements may be caused by the discomfort White people feel in race and racism discussions, especially when the focus and exploration become more personal in terms of what it means to be White. For instance, White people may view their Whiteness as (1) a bland, empty cultural space; (2) a nonidentity (e.g., non-Black, non-Asian); (3) the presence of an absence; (4) existing only as a contrast effect to visible racial-cultural people; and/or (5) intellectually nonexistent because race is a "social construction" (Cameron & Wycoff, 1998).

Additionally, critics have been frank about how terminology has been used or avoided by scholars to obscure race-based discussions (Bhopal & Donaldson, 1998; Carter, this *Handbook,* Volume One; Helms & Richardson, 1997). For example, when discussing race, researchers have used ethnicity, heritage, and geography (e.g., African/Black/African American; Asian/Pacific Islander/Eastern; White/Caucasian/European/Western; Hispanic/Latino) (Arredondo et al., 1996; Bhopal & Donaldson, 1998); vague terminology (e.g., multicultural, cross-cultural, people of Color) (Arredondo et al., 1996; D. Sue & Sue, 2003); or other constructs (e.g., social class) as race proxies. These inconsistencies have only added to the confusion of how to discuss race and race-related issues.

Until all people are able and willing to integrate race into personal understandings of who they are as people and professionals in a meaningful way, they will likely live and work in culturally encapsulated worlds that perpetuate systematic oppression (Wrenn, 1962, 1985). To this end, to teach effectively about race and racism, some educators have encouraged students to discuss their experiences of racism and feelings as racially socialized people, legitimating their experiences and using these experiences in the service of their learning (Carter, 1995; Kiselica, 1999; Ridley, 1995; Tatum, 1992; Tomlinson-Clarke & Ota Wang, 1999). As Tatum has described:

> If not addressed, these emotional responses can result in student resistance to oppression related content areas. Such resistance can ultimately interfere with the cognitive understanding and mastery of the material. Yet when students are given the opportunity to explore race-related material in a classroom where both their affective and intellectual responses are acknowledged and addressed, their level of understanding is greatly enhanced. (1992, pp. 1–2)

As a result, researchers have developed educational models that focus on understanding personal and societal racial socialization (Carter, 1995, this *Handbook,* this volume; Helms, 1984, 1995; Johnson, 1987; Ota Wang, 1998; Ridley, 1995; Tatum, 1992; Tomlinson-Clarke & Ota Wang, 1990), individual, cultural, and institutional racism and oppression (Pinderhughes, 1989), and White privilege (McIntosh, 1990). *It should be noted that scholars have identified the limited advantages and many disadvantages of single-course offerings in education and training programs and have suggested that developing programmatic experiences throughout a curriculum may provide more meaningful educational and training outcomes.* For further discussion of multicultural counseling training program development, refer to Ponterotto and Austin (this *Handbook,* this volume) and Ridley, Mendoza, and Kanitz (1994).

RACIAL IDENTITY TRAINING MODEL

Racial identity theory has provided frameworks for understanding personal experiences, perceptions, attitudes, behaviors, and responses about oneself and dominant and/or nondominant racial-cultural groups by allowing researchers to understand the existence and dynamics of intragroup variation (Helms, 1990, 2001). The critical roles and functions of racial-cultural identity developmental theory have rested on their utility for (1) understanding self-identification processes for members of all racial-cultural groups, (2) emphasizing person-social-cultural environmental interactions, and (3) influencing self-concept by interpreting interpersonal interactions. Significantly, a person's phenotype per se does not determine his or her psychological racial orientation. In fact, a person's overall psychological view of his or her racial group is the primary indicator of racial identity.

The minority (or people of Color [POC]) model is a five-status process of racial-cultural identity development (Helms, 1990, 2001; Helms & Cook, 1999) for visible racial group (VRG) people. In the POC model, POC refers to "Asian, African, Latino/Latina, and Native Americans living in the United States, regardless of the original continental origins of their ancestry" (Helms & Cook, p. 85). In the first status, *Pre-encounter,* VRG people have incorporated negative racial stereotypes of people from their own race-culture and overvalued and idealized Whites' cultural norms. Due to limited accurate information about their own cultural history, people at this status believe the negative racial-cultural stereotypes are true, reject people from their own racial-cultural group, and overvalue White European-oriented cultures. As these people develop an increased awareness of discrimination in the second status, *Encounter,* they may feel confused as they try to understand experiences that challenge their previously held beliefs of White superiority and VRG inferiority. Through this cognitive and emotional dissonance that challenges their notions about meritocracy, individuals develop greater positive views of their racial-cultural identity by becoming involved in learning about their own race and culture. In search of a new cultural identity, these people in *Immersion* affirm their culture, withdraw from White society, and denigrate "Whiteness" by becoming involved in an idealized racial-cultural heritage. In *Emersion,* these people become more accepting of the strengths and weaknesses of their own racial-cultural people and begin incorporating a more affirming and balanced racial-cultural identity. Next, intellectually assessing and responding to members of White groups characterizes *Integrative Awareness.* In the Integrative Awareness status, a positive VRG identity and maintenance of a balanced perspective of Whiteness is achieved and motivated by personal choices about one's identity preferences, rather than reacting to socially driven racialized information. Additionally, people at this status are able to reach beyond their own ascribed racial group affiliation and recognize personal and common group issues among other groups of oppressed people.

The White racial identity model is based on White people's acknowledging and accepting their Whiteness and those ways in which they collude with and benefit from racism. Through a two-step, five-status process (formerly identified as stages), Helms (1995) has theorized how a White person can abandon a racist identity and develop a nonracist White identity. The five White racial identity ego statuses are (1) Contact, (2) Disintegration, (3) Reintegration, (4) Pseudo-independence, and (5) Autonomy.

In *Contact* ego status, people are generally unaware of how they benefit from systemic racism. Because they deny the existence of race and racism, White people in Contact status are unaware of their own racial group membership and ignore the race of others. While they may avoid visible racial-cultural people or develop token friendships with VRG people to satisfy their curiosity, choosing to befriend a VRG person moves a White person into the *Disintegration* status, where the person's Whiteness becomes a more personally salient characteristic. Disintegration is characterized by internal conflict related to a growing awareness of unequal treatment VRG people experience compared to White people. At this status, White people become more aware of racism and feel conflicted and guilty over their own internal standards versus societal norms about race and race relations. Consequently, White people in the disintegration status may retreat into a White *Contact* society or move to the *Reintegration* status as a solution to this cognitive dissonance. Thus, the Reintegration status occurs as the White person seeks to regain psychological equilibrium by affirming his or her White racial superiority. At this status, distance is maintained from VRG people by negative stereotyped thinking about them. In the *Pseudo-independence* status, White people begin to accept the personal implications of being White and are likely to intellectualize racial issues before they develop an emotional understanding of race relations. In Pseudo-independence, the role White people have in perpetuating racism is intellectual. They seek to transform their own racist attitudes and/or behavior by helping VRG people become more similar to White people. While interpersonal interactions are initially limited to a few VRG people, as these interactions increase, White people are likely to move into the *Autonomy* status, where they can recognize their White racial identity as a valuable asset without a need to feel superior to others. At Autonomy, White people have internalized a positive White identity by integrating both an emotional and an intellectual appreciation for and respect of racial differences and commonalities (see also, Carter & Pieterse, this *Handbook,* Volume One; Thompson, this *Handbook,* this volume).

I now turn to the theoretical pedagogies of Lewin (1948) and Bronfenbrenner (1986) and describe how their life spaces and ecological models, respectively, serve as essential structural models for applying racial identity theory. A sequence of didactic and experiential learning experiences and implementation strategies for tailoring racial identity theory to profession-specific contexts (e.g., education, law, organizational consulting, and mental health) is illustrated.

ECOLOGY AND LIFE SPACES

Lewin's (1948) life space topology is the foundation of the racial identity training model (Ota Wang, 1994; Wang, 1993). Where psychological processes interact with environmental ecologies is a person's "life space," a place where values, feelings, and attitudes are formed (Lewin, 1948). Lewin suggests that power is a structural and psychological force that expands or limits a person's life space and mobility. For example, because people who experience discrimination and prejudice have more restricted movement and life spaces, the "same physical situations must . . . be described for different [groups of people] as a specifically different phenomenal and functional world" (p. 73).

Bronfenbrenner's (1986) ecological person-process-context system model organizes Lewin's life space model by providing multidimensional structures for examining how psychological, physical, and environmental influences such as racial identity development and race socialization affect individuals, communities, and society at large (Ota Wang, 1994). The ecological system includes (1) the *microsystem:* individual psychological understandings of self and interactions between other individuals (e.g., family members); (2) the *mesosystem:* institutions that directly influence individuals (e.g., home, schools, hospitals); (3) the *exosystem:* social, cultural, and political institutional structures that influence mesosystem policies (e.g., occupational settings, legislative bodies); and (4) the *chronosystem:* what accounts temporally for the time in which the system is influenced (e.g., history). For a more detailed discussion of ecological systems, see Bronfenbrenner (1986).

On one hand, for the racial identity training model, Bronfenbrenner's (1986) ecological model is a structural anchor for the training content area trilogy of power and oppression, personal relevance, and responsibility. Additionally, unlike traditional educational strategies that focus on individuals as analysis points, this approach structures a broad temporal context (*chrono-*) for understanding personal (*micro-*) feelings and experiences. Thus, lesson plans are purposefully ordered in a chrono-, exo-, meso-, and microsystem sequence to give students generous opportunities to learn how they fit (or don't) as racialized people in temporal-contextual systems. Importantly, by understanding how institutional and group norms are developed, maintained, dictate accessibility/inaccessibility, and shape policies regarding opportunities, services, and so on, students can learn about imposed, presumed, and chosen personal/professional roles and how "the system" interacts and systematically advantages or disadvantages individuals and groups depending on racial group affiliations.

On the other hand, racial identity theory is the affective anchor for the emotional scaffolding of racialized self-development and awareness. Overall, clarifying one's own racial identity statuses and developing a level of comfort and self-acceptance are necessary prerequisites when learning to relate to and function respectfully with people from all racial group affiliations (Banks, 1997; Carter, 1995; Helms, 1984, 2001). Additionally, racial identity theory becomes an effective means of teaching how the notion of meritocracy is driven by individualism and microsystem expectations that decontextualize the notions of race and racial identity from people.

Using didactic and experientially focused teaching methods, racial identity-based training provides a wide range of learning opportunities for students and practitioners across professions to explore and integrate their own cognitive and affective understandings of how racial socialization, racial group affiliation, and racial identity status(es) influence professional opportunities and personal development for themselves and those around them. In the following section, issues related to each of the three key themes are briefly discussed and illustrated for each ecological system.

THE POWER/OPPRESSION-PERSONAL RELEVANCE-RESPONSIBILITY TRILOGY

Oppression is a dynamic force by which one group in society achieves power, authority, and privilege through the control and exploitation of other groups. Specifically, structural and psychological oppression is the conscious *and* subconscious misuse and related experiences of power and authority.

Theme 1: Power and Oppression

Oppression is a psychic process in which a person attempts to cope with his [or her] fear and anxiety through the sacrifice of another's freedom. It is a process that struggles toward a homeostatic and controlled situation where all choices are predetermined and therefore completely expected. Oppression creates the cessation of feelings through the imposition of limits on thinking, feeling, self-expression, and behavior in hope that these limits will defend the individual against the anxiety he [or she] experiences in changing unpredictable and/or potentially or actually threatening situations. While the product of oppressive relationships is self oppression, the extreme consequence of oppression is a psychic death.

Consequently, teaching about power, oppression, and privilege can generate strong emotions (that people may want to avoid), ranging from guilt and shame to anger and despair. Additionally, if feelings (whatever they may be) are ignored or minimized, the consequences can be resistance to hearing, understanding, and learning race-related content, limiting a person's racial identity developmental potential. Thus, Pinderhughes writes:

> Those in power can also develop a tendency to deny their personal pain and ignore their experiences of powerlessness. This stance can be costly in terms of its potential for distorting reality and for denying and devaluing one's own feelings. (1989, p. 123)

Particular care must be taken to ensure that these avoidance mechanisms are not perpetuated. Samples of power and oppression teaching topics are in Table 5.1.

Theme 2: Personal Relevance

As outcomes of middle- and upper-class White male historical dominance in behaviors and thinking, acting, and perceptions, notions about meritocracy have guided what are considered socially and politically appropriate ways of thinking, feeling, and behaving (Scheurich, 1993). Fostered by individualism, the meritocratic myth is a veil of racial silence that often leaves race-based discussions intellectualized and superficially distanced and personally irrelevant. As a way of beginning more meaningful

Table 5.1   Sample of Power and Oppression Teaching Material

System	Example of Teaching Material
Chronosystem	Explore how racial group affiliations have been constructed and have changed in history up to the present time. Illustrate how "scientific, " social, and cultural systems have categorized and differentially pathologized and normalized racial groups.
Exosystem	Study issues of affirmative action legislation and how recent policy changes systematically disenfranchise and advantage various racial groups.
Mesosystem	Study how stereotyping and perceived attributions in schools influence teaching expectations and student academic performance.
Microsystem	Discuss people from the vantage point of various racial groups in the city where you live: quality of life issues ranging from characteristics and availability of housing, employment, education, and health care.

race-based dialogues, understanding racial identity theory can move all people (e.g., White, Black, Asian, American Indian) from cognitive understandings of what it means to be a racial person to more thoughtful and psychological understandings of how avoidance and minimization of race function in personal views of themselves and others. Exploring personally significant ways that race and racism have affected a person's own life can serve as validating experiences, not by preventing the collision of developmental processes and painful issues but by allowing the language and socialization to be less frightening when it does occur. As shown in Table 5.2, teaching self-generated knowledge can be a powerful tool for reducing the initial state of denial many people may experience.

Theme 3: Responsibility

Common individual emotional responses such as guilt, shame, embarrassment, or anger when talking and learning about racism (Carter, 1995; Helms, 1990, 2001) can nevertheless be experienced by people as atypical, pathological, and emotionally paralyzing. As people become aware and begin understanding how racism and oppression operate in their realities, they may feel more responsible about interrupting these cycles of oppression by identifying misinformation and adjusting their attitudes, beliefs, and behaviors. Thus, educators and trainers must be especially attentive to normalize these feelings as part of a developmental cognitive-affective learning process to prevent paralysis or intellectual entrenchment. As shown in Table 5.3, by communicating that decreasing prejudice and racism goes beyond intellectually grasping information about race and racial socialization, people will realize they must become their own race change agents.

EXPERIENTIAL TRAINING

By valuing how race-based assumptions can influence interpersonal interactions and understanding a person's personal racial reality, experiential education teaches

Table 5.2   Sample of Personal Relevance Teaching Materials

System	Example of Teaching Material
Chronosystem	Explore your own family U.S. immigration history and how zeitgeists and racial issues may have influenced familial occupational and financial choices and accomplishments.
Exosystem	Explore how societal stereotypes and expectations can influence employment and educational choices.
Mesosystem	Explore how organizations in your community may systematically reward and disenfranchise different racial groups (e.g., White privilege and presumed entitlements) in employment, housing, health care systems.
Microsystem	Discuss how microaggressions (e.g., being followed, not being helped when shopping) have personally influenced quality of life issues such as employment, renting or purchasing a home, applying to schools, receiving health care.
	Using a personal time line (e.g., critical events and incidents) from a racial vantage point, show how race has shaped personal attitudes and behaviors.

Table 5.3   Sample Issues of Responsibility Teaching Material

System	Example of Teaching Material
Chronosystem	Discuss the similarities and differences of current and late nineteenth- and early twentieth-century research and anthropometric efforts to scientifically distinguish racial groups. Explore what research methodology can be used to avoid race-biased research.
Exosystem	Discuss how local government officials and agencies influence allocation of resources for education, health, and safety and explore how racial identity attitudes can influence these decisions.
Mesosystem	Discuss how university communities and professional organizations that are informed and value intragroup racial identity statuses create supportive racial environments.
Microsystem	Write an autobiography at the beginning of training exploring how the role of race influenced your personal development. Given all of the information and awareness attained during training, revise the autobiography at the end of the training with extra attention to how race and racial identity issues have influenced previous unacknowledged life experiences and specific actions you have taken with this new information.

people how to become effective racial-cultural agents in their daily lives. Relying on previous didactic knowledge and beginning awareness, a focused experiential learning of personal racial self-exploration of how overt and covert displacements of power are experienced (e.g., microaggressions), power is exercised, and vulnerability is experienced can shift thinking and feelings from presumptions about *what people should be* to more personalized interactions based on *who people are.*

Applying an ecological systems approach, experiential training focuses on how people's feelings, attitudes, and behaviors about race occur at various levels of social and personal functioning. Specifically, concentrating on how racial identities are formed and maintained forces individuals to face and understand how they assign meanings that shape people and institutions around them. To this end, in a small group format, people are given the opportunity to identify and acknowledge their biases, blind spots, and strengths and the ways their perceptions, attitudes, and feelings have developed and are manifested in personal and workplace environments. By developing racial self-awareness and its associated physical and psychological benefits and consequences of maintaining or eliminating prejudices, individuals can begin to recognize the necessary personal commitment to living a more racially thoughtful, sensitive, and inclusive lifestyle.

In one approach, based on Johnson's (1987) "C" group model, the primary learning experience is an in-depth group interview. Here, individuals identify and examine personal feelings and understandings in which their reference group, society (chronosystem), institutions (exosystem), disciplines (mesosystem), and racial identity status (microsystem) have influenced the assumptions they make about themselves and others (Carter, this *Handbook,* this volume). Process journals serve as a record for people to document their observations, opinions, and feelings as their racial identity attitudes have evolved by the time the training has been completed. While some people are clearly more self-reflective and articulate about their own processes than others are, most experience the opportunity as a transforming process to examine and explore potentially provocative thoughts and feelings about race- and racial identity-based issues. This learning format also permits people to learn about the existence and value of intragroup variation, the lack of connection between expertise and racial group membership, and the recognition that exploring feelings and experiences about race, power, and oppression can be painful and isolating, yet immensely rewarding.

PROFESSIONAL APPLICATIONS OF THE RACIAL IDENTITY THEORY CORE MODE

Professionals from varied disciplines, including education, law, organizational consulting, and mental health, have become increasingly aware of the intentional and unintentional benefits and consequences of racism. While many have begun to voice their personal struggles over how to address race and racial identity issues in their own professions, accusations of racism, symbolic violence, and cultural imperialism have left many of them feeling helpless and paralyzed. Racial identity-based training offers a proactive way of implementing race-based training in professional training and education by modeling race-based dialogues as possible, productive, and

Table 5.4   New Racial Paradigm Matrix for Educators

System	Power and Oppression	Personal Relevance	Responsibility
Chronosystem	Discuss the history of the teaching profession and how various racial group affiliations have been represented in the profession.	Explore how your extended family experienced the educational system and how zeitgeists and racial issues have influenced academic achievements and/or failures.	Discuss how current test construction and uses influence education in admissions and academic placements. Explore how educators can better use and interpret these tests.
Exosystem	Study issues of affirmative action legislation and how it affects different racial groups' access to and quality of education.	Explore how race and racial identity attitudes influence professional expectations, attitudes, and behaviors.	Discuss how school districts allocate resources for schools. Explore how racial identity can influence these decisions.
Mesosystem	Study how stereotyping and perceived attributions influence teacher expectations of student academic performance.	Discuss what factors influenced your decision to accept a job (e.g., racial composition of colleagues, students, administrators).	Discuss how your knowledge of antidiscrimination laws influences your teaching style and classroom management.
Microsystem	Discuss how race and racial identity influence student ability grouping.	Explore how your educational experiences were influenced by a teacher's attitudes about race.	Explore first experiences with feeling different. How does this translate into the classroom?

useful. Specifically, the core didactic and experiential tripartite training model organizes content and context issues for a wide array of professionals to learn how race and racial identity affect them. Context-specific applications can then be used as ongoing learning tools. Tables 5.4 through 5.8 illustrate sample teaching matrixes for various disciplines.

CONCLUSION

To understand the comprehensive nature of how personal, group, and institutional racism and oppression influences all people and groups, a continuous dialogue must exist. If meaningful race relations are to occur, that dialogue must allow for open and thoughtful discussion. Specifically, racial-cultural training must go beyond didactic "other"-focused teaching methods and begin applying racial identity theory early in training so realistic understandings and conceptualizations can occur. For example, learning strategies have been shown to differ depending on when affectively based learning was taught. Students taught content knowledge early in their training often intellectually removed themselves from clinical interactions and focused on gathering "culture"-specific techniques based on their assumptions about

Table 5.5   New Racial Paradigm Matrix for Attorneys

System	Power and Oppression	Personal Relevance	Responsibility
Chronosystem	Explore how U.S. immigration patterns have influenced race and national origins definitions and immigration law.	Explore how laws affected your family's U.S. immigration.	Discuss how your racial group membership/ identity influences national policy. Explore ways you can advocate for more equitable immigration laws.
Exosystem	Explore how race and racial identity influence criminal law and death penalty cases.	For three or more generations, discuss how property and estate law influenced how your family owned property.	Discuss how race influences educational opportunities (e.g., clerkships). Explore ways you can influence equitable selection processes.
Mesosystem	Discuss how attitudes about race in your state and labor and employment law affect discrimination litigation.	Explore how race-based criteria (e.g., legacy, affirmative action) may have affected your law school admission.	Explore how race and racial identity may influence subspecialty choices; explore ways of achieving equitable representation.
Microsystem	Explore how race influences child custody cases.	Explore how race influences whom you choose as clients and who chooses you.	Explore how race and language ability influence legal access; explore ways you can create equitable access.

Table 5.6   New Racial Paradigm Matrix for Organizational Consultants

System	Power and Oppression	Personal Relevance	Responsibility
Chronosystem	Explore the history and historical significance of industrialization and how race and leadership influenced racial identity development.	Explore your own feelings and attitudes about the organization's purpose and history; explore how your feelings and attitudes affect consulting.	Explore how race has influenced the successes and failures of the organization; develop individual and group interventions that will not perpetuate institutional forms of racism.
Exosystem	Explore how race and racial identity influence the organization's capacity to collaborate and foster relationships with other community systems.	Within community and/or industry standards, understand how race and racial identity influence the organization's success/failure expectations. Explore how your feelings about success and failure influence the quality of services you provide.	Explore how race influences flexibility and adaptability of the organization. Create a written history. Explore how management can use racial identity development in policy decision making.
Mesosystem	Explore how race and racial identity influence role definition, responsibilities, and organizational decision making.	Observe and explore organizational parallel processes. Explore how your racial identity influences what is maximized, minimized, or ignored.	Explore how the organization understands the needs of the community it serves. Develop racially sensitive and responsive strategies for successful partnerships.
Microsystem	Discuss how race and racial identity influence individual and group work units and desired outcome.	Explore how race and racial identity influence embedded intergroup relations for you and other members in the organization. Examine how your own racial identity development influences organizational intervention strategies.	Explore how race and racial identity influence your commitment as a consultant to all clients.

what racial-cultural others should be. These individuals viewed racism and racial identity as interesting but not clinically relevant. Students who had an integrated didactic-affective experience course early in their training (where the course material served as a primary learning scaffold) reported increased racial awareness overall. When faced with cultural questions, their inquiries focused on how to better understand what race, cultural values, attitudes, and behaviors mean for themselves and their clients, rather than seeking culture-specific counseling interventions (Ota Wang,

Table 5.7   New Racial Paradigm Matrix for Health Care Professionals

System	Power and Oppression	Personal Relevance	Responsibility
Chronosystem	Study the history of medicine and how "scientific" research was used to understand population differences.	Explore how your understanding of the medical literature influences who receives care and under what conditions; explore health care disparities.	Explore how you have used racial categories in clinical practices and/or research projects and how your uses may have implied or reified biological/ genetic versus socially determined versus environmental interactions.
Exosystem	Explore how race composition and racial identity influence health practitioner training and research organizations' research objectives.	Explore how race and racial identity attitudes influence professional admittance, expectations, and advancement.	Develop mentoring programs for all racial groups to encourage and nurture the next generation of health care professionals.
Mesosystem	Explore how race categories are used when creating differential diagnoses.	Explore how race and racial identity influence clinical and research medical education; explore how race and racial identity issues influence bedside clinical practices.	Use accurate group/ population descriptions (e.g., ancestry, geography, self-identification) when doing clinical assessments and conducting research projects.
Microsystem	Identify how race and racial identity can influence peer review.	Explore how your race and racial identity influence your attitudes about disease causation and patient responsibility for treatment compliance and management.	Explore how race influences insurance coverage for medical services; explore ways you can ensure equitable access and coverage for all.

1998). These findings suggest the importance and necessity of including education in racial identity development and racial socialization as early as possible if all students are to be legitimated for who they are in the learning process and experience their optimal learning and developmental potential.

Multicultural training has incurred criticism. Many people who are developing and implementing multicultural training programs have not had any systematic training in multicultural issues (Pedersen, this *Handbook,* Volume One; Ridley et al., 1994). In contrast, one of the strengths of using a racial identity-based training model is that many of those who are developing and advocating this paradigm shift are scholars and educators who have been formally trained in multicultural issues and are effectively applying their own multicultural training to curriculum development and practice. Their training has enabled them more realistically to understand the complexity of race and racial identity in conducting research, teaching students,

Table 5.8   New Racial Paradigm Matrix for Mental Health Professionals

System	Power and Oppression	Personal Relevance	Responsibility
Chronosystem	Explore how psychology understood race using "scientific methodology." Discuss how race is understood in the context of mental health and psychopathology.	Draw a three- to four-generation family tree and explore your family's understanding of race in the context of the prevailing zeitgeist of that time; explore how racial identity influences family members' attitudes and behaviors.	Explore how race has influenced psychology research; through mentorship and course work, design relevant and nonbiased research studies.
Exosystem	Explore how race composition and racial identity influence professional mental health organizations with regard to membership and training objectives and goals.	Explore how race and racial identity attitudes influence professional expectations, personal attitudes, and behaviors.	Discuss how race influences insurance coverage for mental health services; explore ways you can ensure equitable coverage.
Mesosystem	Explore how stereotyping and perceived attributions of mental health professionals influence client preference and treatment expectations (e.g., YAVIS clients).	Explore how race and racial identity influence clinical supervision. Explore how race and racial identity issues can be incorporated into supervision.	Use systemic methods for accurate clinical assessments that take into account systemic qualities, personal qualities, and racial identity development. Explore how you can do more racially responsive assessments.
Microsystem	Identify microaggressions. Explore how individual microaggressions influence (1) issues of daily living and (2) the counseling process.	Explore how your race and racial identity influence your feelings and behaviors toward power and powerlessness; discuss how this influences your clinical judgment and skills.	Explore ways of maintaining personal and professional racial identity development (e.g., friendship networks). Improve multicultural competence in research and clinical work through continuing education/postdoctoral studies.

and implementing interventions. Their training has also provided an essential guide for how to teach about the complexity of what it means to be a racial-cultural person.

Thus, the success of racial identity-based training depends on the commitment of those who teach and train to work constantly on further developing themselves as racial-cultural people. Ideally, providing people an understanding of the environmental and psychological realities of everyday racism can be a catalyst for exploring the impact that racial socialization has on quality of life issues for the oppressor and the oppressed. For race work to occur, a supportive environment must be created: Institutional support must go beyond tolerance to engagement. Additionally, educators and trainers must work against the subtle and covert messages in educational and professional institutions that can create reluctant and unaccommodating environments for faculty, students, and professionals exploring racial-cultural issues.

Racial identity-based training provides a supportive structure for discussing issues of race, racism, and racial identity development in an open manner. Students and professionals alike must come to terms with their existence as racial people and the ways in which their racial identity development is relevant to their personal experiences, motivations, and behaviors. Thus, in the spirit of *Learning to Be,* learning goes beyond the struggle of helping others; what we must do is first learn to be ourselves.

As Carter has aptly stated:

> Struggle that comes from knowing oneself requires a personal commitment that often leads one through a painful journey and soul searching to become comfortable with [one's] racial socialization since race is treated as invisible in the social structure. (1995, p. 260)

If there is no struggle, there is no progress (Douglass, 1849):

> The whole history of progress of human liberty
> Shows that all concessions
> Yet made to her august claims
> Have been born of earnest struggle.
> If there is no struggle
> There is no progress.
> Those who profess to favor freedom,
> And yet deprecate agitation,
> Are men [and women] who want crops
> Without plowing up the ground,
> They want rain
> Without thunder and lightning.
> They want the ocean
> Without the awful roar of its waters.
> This struggle may be a moral one;
> Or it may be a physical one;
> Or it may be both moral and physical;
> But it must be a struggle.
> Power concedes nothing without a demand.
> It never did, and it never will.
> Find out just what any people
> Will quietly submit to
> And you have found the exact measure
> Of injustice and wrong
> Which will be imposed upon them,
> And these will continue till they are resisted . . .
> The limits . . . are prescribed
> By the endurance
> Of those [who] . . . [are] oppress[ed].
> Men [and Women] may not get all they pay for

in this world, but they pay for all they get.
If we ever get free
from the oppressions and wrong heaped on us,
we must pay for their removal.
We must do this
by labor,
by suffering,
by sacrifice,
and if needs be
by our lives and the lives of others.

—Frederick Douglass, 1849

REFERENCES

Arredondo, P., Toporek, R., Brown, S. P., Jones, J., Locke, D. C., Sanchez, J., et al. (1996). Operationalization of multicultural counseling competencies. *Journal of Multicultural Counseling and Development, 24,* 42–78.

Atkinson, D. R., Thompson, C. E., & Grant, S. K. (1993). A three-dimensional model for counseling racial/ethnic minorities. *Counseling Psychologist, 21,* 257–277.

Banks, J. A. (1997). *Teaching strategies for ethnic studies* (6th ed.). Needham Heights, MA: Allyn & Bacon.

Beale, A. V. (1986). A cross-cultural dyadic encounter. *Journal of Multicultural Counseling and Development, 14,* 73–76.

Bhopal, R., & Donaldson, L. (1998). White, European, Western, Caucasian, or What? Inappropriate labeling in research on race, ethnicity, and health. *American Journal of Public Health, 88,* 1303–1307.

Brofenbrenner, U. (1986). Recent advances in research on the ecology of human development. In R. K. Silbereisen, K. Eyferth, & G. Rudinger (Eds.), *Development as action in context: Problem behavior and normal youth development* (pp. 287–309). Heidelberg and New York: Springer-Verlag.

Cameron, S. C., & Wycoff, S. M. (1998). The destructive nature of the term Race: Growing beyond a false paradigm. *Journal of Counseling and Development, 70,* 277–285.

Carter, R. T. (1995). *The influence of race and racial identity in psychotherapy: Toward a racially inclusive model.* New York: Wiley.

Carter, R. T. (in press). Uprooting inequity and disparities in counseling and psychology: An introduction. In R. T. Carter (Ed.), *Handbook of racial-cultural psychology and counseling: Theory and research* (Vol. 1, pp. xv–xxviii). Hoboken, NJ: Wiley.

Carter, R. T., & Block, C. J. (1996). White racial identity attitude theories: A rose by any other name is still a rose. *Counseling Psychologist, 24*(2), 326–334.

Carter, R. T., & Gesmer, E. (1997). Applying racial identity theory to the legal system: The case of family law. In C. E. Thompson & R. T. Carter (Eds.), *Racial identity theory: Applications to individual, group, and organizational interventions* (pp. 219–235). Mahwah, NJ: Erlbaum.

Cook, D. (1997). The art of survival in white academia: Black women faculty finding where they belong. In M. Fine, L. Weis, L. C. Powell, & L. M. Wong (Eds.), *Off white—Readings on race, power, and society* (pp. 100–109). New York: Routledge.

Delgado, R. (Ed.). (1995). *Critical race theory: The cutting edge.* Philadelphia: Temple University Press.

Delgado, R., & Stefancie, J. (2000). *Critical race theory: The cutting edge* (2nd ed.). Philadelphia: Temple University Press.

Fordham, S. (1996). Racelessness as a factor in black students' school success: Pragmatic strategy or pyrrhic victory. In T. Beauboeuf-Lafontant & D. Smith Augustine (Eds.), *In Facing racism in education* (2nd ed., pp. 209–243). Cambridge, MA: Harvard Educational Review.

Helms, J. E. (1984). Toward a theoretical explanation of the effects of race on counseling: A Black and white model. *Counseling Psychologist, 12,* 153–165.

Helms, J. E. (Ed.). (1990). *Black and white racial identity: Theory, research, and practice.* New York: Greenwood Press.

Helms, J. E. (1995). An update of Helm's White and people of Color racial identity models. In J. G. Ponterotto, J. M. Casas, J. M. L. A. Suzuki, & C. M. Alexander (Eds.), *Handbook of multicultural counseling* (pp. 181–198). Thousand Oakes, CA: Sage.

Helms, J. E. (2001). An update of Helm's White and people of Color racial identity models. In J. G. Ponterotto, J. M. Casas, J. M. L. A. Suzuki, & C. M. Alexander (Eds.), *Handbook of multicultural counseling* (2nd ed., pp. 181–198). Thousand Oakes, CA: Sage.

Helms, J. E., & Cook, D. A. (1999). *Using race and culture in counseling psychotherapy.* Needham Heights, MA: Allyn & Bacon.

Helms, J. E., & Richardson, T. Q. (1997). How "multiculturalism" obscures race and culture as differential aspects of counseling competency. In D. B. Pope-Davis & H. L. K. Coleman (Eds.), *Multicultural counseling competencies—Assessment, education and training, and supervision* (pp. 60–79). Thousand Oakes, CA: Sage.

hooks, b. (1992). *Black looks: Race and representation.* Boston: South End.

Johnson, S. D. (1987). Knowing that versus knowing how: Toward achieving expertise through multicultural training for counseling. *Counseling Psychologist, 15,* 320–331.

Kiselica, M. S. (1998). Preparing Anglos for the challenges and joys of multiculturalism. *Counseling Psychologist, 26,* 5–21.

Kiselica, M. S. (Ed.). (1999). *Confronting prejudice and racism during multicultural training.* Alexandria, VA: American Counseling Association.

Lewin, K. (I 948). *Resolving social conflict.* New York: Harper.

McIntosh, P. (1992). White privilege and male privilege: A personal account of coming to see correspondences through work in women's studies. In M. L. Andersen & P. A. Collins (Eds.), *Race, class, and gender: An anthology.* Belmont, CA: Wadsworth.

Mio, J. S. (1989). Experiential involvement as an adjunct to teaching cultural sensitivity. *Journal of Multicultural Counseling and Development, 17,* 38–46.

Ota Wang, V. (1994). Cultural competency in genetic counseling. *Journal of Genetic Counseling, 3*(4), 267–277.

Ota Wang, V. (1998). Curriculum evaluation and assessment of multicultural genetic counselor education. *Journal of Genetic Counseling, 7*(1), 87–111.

Ota Wang, V., & Briggs, K. (1997, February). *The role of cognitive information processing and racial identity attitudes on causal attributions.* Paper presented at the 14th Annual Winter Roundtable on Cross-Cultural Psychology and Education, Teachers College, Columbia University, New York.

Pedersen, P. (2005). The importance of Cultural Psychology Theory for multicultural counselors. In R. T. Carter (Ed.), *Handbook of racial-cultural psychology and counseling: Theory and research* (Vol. 1, pp. 3–16). Hoboken, NJ: Wiley.

Pinderhughes, E. (1989). *Understanding race, ethnicity, and power in clinical practice.* Chicago: Free Press.

Ponterotto, J. G., & Casas, J. M. (1991). *Handbook of racial/ethnic minority counseling research.* Springfield, IL: Charles C Thomas.

Reynolds, A. L. (1995). Challenges and strategies for teaching multicultural counseling courses. In J. G. Ponterotto & J. M. Casas (Eds.), *Handbook of multicultural counseling* (pp. 312–330). Thousand Oaks, CA: Sage.

Ridley, C. R. (1995). *Overcoming unintentional racism in counseling and therapy.* Thousand Oaks, CA: Sage.

Ridley, C. R., Espelage, D. L., & Rubinstein, K. J. (1997). Course development in multicultural counseling. In D. B. Pope-Davis & H. L. Coleman (Eds.), *Multicultural counseling competencies: Assessment, education and training, and supervision* (Vol. 7, pp. 131–158). Thousand Oaks, CA: Sage.

Ridley, C. R., Li, L. C., & Hill, C. L. (1998). Multicultural assessment: Reexamination, reconceptualization, and practical application. *Counseling Psychologist, 26,* 827–910.

Ridley, C. R., Mendoza, D. W., & Kanitz, B. E. (1994). Multicultural training: Reexamination, operationalization, and integration. *Counseling Psychologist, 22,* 227–289.

Scheurich, J. J. (1993). Toward a white discourse on white racism. *Educational Researcher, 22,* 5–10.

Shem, S. (1978). *The house of God.* New York: Dell.

Smith, E. M. J. (1985). Ethnic minorities: Life stress, social support, and mental health issues. *Counseling Psychologist, 13,* 537–579.

Sue, D. W., Arredondo, P., & McDavis, R. J. (1992). Multicultural counseling competencies and standards: A call to the profession. *Journal of Counseling and Development, 70,* 477–486.

Sue, D. W., Bernier, J. E., Durran, A., Feinberg, L., Pedersen, P., Smith, E. J., et al. (1982). Position paper: Cross-cultural counseling competencies. *Counseling Psychology, 10,* 45–52.

Sue, D. W., Carter, R. T., Casas, J. M., Fouad, N. A., Ivey, A. E., Jensen, M., et al. (1998). *Multicultural counseling competencies.* Thousand Oaks, CA: Sage.

Sue, D. W., & Sue, D. (2003). *Counseling the culturally diverse: Theory and practice* (4th ed.). New York: Wiley.

Tatum, B. D. (1992). Talking about race, learning about racism: The application of racial identity development theory in the classroom. *Harvard Educational Review, 62,* 1–24.

Tomlinson-Clarke, S., & Ota Wang, V. (1999). A paradigm for racial-cultural training in the development of counselor cultural competencies. In M. Kiselica (Ed.), *Confronting prejudice and racism during multicultural training* (pp. 155–167). Alexandria, VA: American Counseling Association.

United Nations Educational, Scientific, and Cultural Organization. (1996). *Learning: The treasure within.* France: Author.

Wang, V. (1993). *Handbook of cross-cultural genetic counseling.* (Available from Vivian Ota Wang, Graduate School of Education, 10 Seminary Place, New Brunswick, NJ 08903).

Wrenn, C. G. (1962). The culturally encapsulated counselor. *Harvard Educational Review, 32,* 444–449.

Wrenn, C. G. (1985). Afterward: The culturally encapsulated counselor revisited. In P. B. Pedersen (Ed.), *Handbook of cross-cultural counseling and therapy* (pp. 323–329). Westport, CT: Greenwood Press.

CHAPTER 6

A Practical Coping Skills Approach for Racial-Cultural Skill Acquisition

Barbara C. Wallace

Sue (2003, p. xi) provides a frank and compelling guide for attaining liberation from engaging in racism and oppression that is largely directed toward Whites and others in the United States who "harbor racist beliefs and need to overcome them." Sue effectively explains "complicity in being either an active or passive participant in the oppression of others" and urges readers to "combat the injustices of racism" and "entertain the notion that you have oppressed others whether knowingly or unknowingly" (p. 45). On the other hand, when addressing people of Color, Sue acknowledges that racism "is a constant reality in our lives" and a "toxic force" (p. 257). Yet, "we have persevered and become stronger," despite having been "subjected to inhuman stressors," allowing for the identification of cultural strengths (p. 259).

Fully appreciating the rage that many African Americans, in particular, may feel in response to racism and oppression, hooks (1996) asserts:

> Collective failure to address adequately the psychic wounds inflicted by racist aggression is the breeding ground for a psychology of victimhood wherein learned helplessness, uncontrollable rage, and/or feelings of overwhelming powerlessness and despair abound in the psyches of black folks yet are not attended to in ways that empower and promote wholistic states of well-being . . . [T]he wounded African-American psyche must be attended to within the framework of programs for mental health care that link psychological recovery with progressive political awareness of the way in which institutionalized systems of domination assault, damage, and maim. (pp. 137–138)

By presenting a model for racial-cultural skill acquisition, this chapter further builds on those cultural strengths discussed by Sue (2003) and offers an approach consistent with hooks's (1996) recommendation to empower and promote holistic states of well-being that include an awareness of how institutionalized systems of racism and oppression function in the United States. Racial-cultural skill acquisition is the process by which individuals learn practical coping skills (specifically affective, behavioral, and cognitive coping responses) for deployment in response to the racism and oppression regularly encountered in institutions in the United States.

Clark, Anderson, Clark, and Williams (1999) assert that institutional racism "may reduce access to goods, services, and opportunities for African Americans in ways that have important health consequences" (p. 812). African Americans are exposed to disproportionate amounts of environmental stimuli that may be sources of chronic or acute stress, much of it interpersonally experienced (Clark et al., 1999). They explain that it is both the individual's evaluation or cognitive appraisal of the seriousness of an event and his or her coping responses that determine whether a psychological stress response will ensue. If "maladaptive coping responses are used, the perception of an environmental event as racist will trigger psychological and physiological stress responses" (p. 809). When maladaptive coping responses are not replaced with more adaptive ones, a state of heightened psychological and physiological activity persists. The negative effects of racism on health are reduced when adaptive coping responses are used, mitigating the potentially negative impact of an enduring psychological and physiological stress response (Clark et al., 1999).

The stress of racism and oppression includes the possibility that one may not perceive with certainty what are often covert, invisible dynamics. Wallace (1996, 2003) explains that violence has visible overt and invisible covert dimensions. The impact of violence includes assaults on the self-concept, identity, cognitions, affects, and consciousness of the victim of violence. This is consistent with hooks's (1996, p. 138) assertion that institutionalized systems of domination "assault, damage, and maim," leaving a "wounded African-American psyche." Thus, racial-cultural skill acquisition also needs to impact identity development, promoting positive progressive shifts as well as the acquisition of adaptive coping responses, given the range of harmful effects that follow from experiences of racism and oppression. The result of racial-cultural skill acquisition is attainment of vital strengths not only for surviving, but also for effective, adaptive, practical coping with the racism and oppression regularly encountered in U.S. institutions.

This chapter presents a model for racial-cultural skill acquisition with a focus on identity development stages for learning adaptive coping responses to racism and oppression. The chapter (1) discusses the rationale for a focus on adaptive affective, behavioral, and cognitive responses to racism and oppression; (2) briefly reviews current models of racial-cultural skill acquisition; (3) presents a recommended model for racial-cultural skill acquisition, a practical coping skills approach, that fosters adaptive affective, behavioral, and cognitive responses to racism and oppression; (4) provides a case example; and (5) concludes by offering suggestions for models of practice for racial-cultural skill acquisition.

AFFECTIVE, BEHAVIORAL, AND COGNITIVE COPING IN THE FACE OF STRESS: ILL HEALTH EFFECTS

Clark et al. (1999, p. 809) placed their hope on the possibility of being able to "identify coping responses that influence the relationship between perceived racism and stress responses." But they recognize a potential limitation of their model insofar as some individuals "may not report perceiving any stressor or may inhibit the expression of psychological responses (e.g., anger), yet show exaggerated physiological responses to stimuli" (p. 809). In addition, Clark et al. discussed psychological stress responses of anger, paranoia, anxiety, helplessness-hopelessness, frustration, resentment, and fear; any of these may lead to a variety of coping responses. For example, the psychological stress response of anger might lead to coping responses of anger suppression, hostility, aggression, verbal expression of anger, or use of alcohol or other drugs to blunt affect. There are also chronic affective states, with coping in response to these often manifesting as chronic behavioral patterns of passivity, overeating, avoidance, or efforts to gain control. Also, they report that passive and active coping responses to discrimination were found to be related to increased psychological distress, poorer well-being, and more chronic conditions among African Americans. A cognitive flexibility style for coping with perceived racism was associated with processing the racist content of the stimulus longer than for those who used a more active coping response. Passive coping responses to unfair treatment and discrimination were associated with hypertension and higher resting blood pressure levels (Clark et al., 1999).

Anger and anxiety may be maladaptive affective responses to the stress of racism and oppression, especially if states of psychological arousal persist. Suinn (2001) summarizes how stress, anger, and anxiety are hazardous to health, and the incontrovertible evidence that anger and anxiety are associated with increased vulnerability to numerous illnesses such as colds, sore throats, headaches, cancer, internal disease, and rheumatic arthritis and impairment of the immune system. Anxiety and anger also negatively impact cellular immunity and tolerance for pain that influences recovery from and adjustment to illness, in addition to being related to coronary artery blockage, cardiovascular disease, and cardiovascular death (Suinn, 2001).

There is a strong rationale for focusing on the development of adaptive affective, behavioral, and cognitive coping responses to the stress of racism and oppression as the core components of racial-cultural skill acquisition. One goal is to reduce ill health effects.

LEARNING ADAPTIVE AFFECTIVE, BEHAVIORAL, AND COGNITIVE RESPONSES TO STRESS

Suinn (2001) described a model for learning adaptive coping responses that uses a brief (six- to eight-session) highly structured cognitive-behavioral intervention that was initially used for anxiety arousal but extended to use with anger. The brief intervention exposes individuals to anxiety arousal through visualization and then seeks deactivation of the emotional arousal through relaxation skills, incorporating homework practice for generalization, self-monitoring, and gradual fading in of self-control skills (pp. 32–33). A body of research supports the efficacy of this approach with anxiety, and evidence of efficacy with anger is accumulating.

Gaston and Porter (2001) presented another model for teaching coping skills for use in stressful interpersonal interactions that trigger anger. They, too, placed emphasis on self-monitoring, the conscious execution of adaptive responses, and learning of self-control skills so that old, maladaptive responses are effectively replaced with new, adaptive coping responses. They cite four potential behavioral repertoires that are characterized by certain corresponding thoughts (cognitions) and feelings (affects) when an interpersonal environmental stimulus makes one angry: (1) a passive response, (2) a passive-aggressive response, (3) an aggressive response, and (4) an assertive and positive response. The goal is to facilitate the learning of an assertive and positive response that allows an individual to express "thoughts and feelings in an open, direct, and honest manner without being verbally or emotionally abusive to someone else" (p. 83). The assertive and positive verbal response is the opposite of a passive response, where an individual "repressed her thought and feelings and said nothing" (p. 93) as a defense. The passive-aggressive response involves a situation where a person has articulated "indirect hints" or behaviorally "done something sneaky to get revenge" (p. 93). This is also a defensive strategy, involving both avoidance and acting-out of aggressive behavior in an indirect manner. They describe the aggressive response through an example where one may "attack" and attempt to "hurt and humiliate," as an "out of control" reaction (p. 93). In sum, they recommend teaching individuals how to assess situations differently, self-monitor anger, respond with a positive assertive verbal response, talk to positive/optimistic supportive friends, and acquire a more positive attitude.

Folkman and Moskowitz (2000) discussed how coping processes that generate and sustain positive affect in the context of chronic stress constitute a special class of meaning-based coping responses. They review a body of research showing that positive affect promotes creativity and flexibility in thinking and problem solving and facilitates the processing of important, self-relevant information. Their longitudinal research findings with AIDS caregivers revealed three types of coping related to the occurrence and maintenance of positive affect: (1) positive reappraisal, (2) goal-directed problem-focused coping, and (3) the infusion of ordinary events with positive meaning. They explain positive reappraisal as "cognitive strategies for reframing a situation to see it in a positive light (seeing a glass half full as opposed to half empty)" (p. 650). Folkman and Moskowitz also argue that positive, meaning-based coping may permit a more resilient physiological response in the face of subsequent stress, providing protection from maladaptive neural, endocrine, and immune responses to chronic stress that could lead to disease (p. 649).

Thus, research evidence and practice models support the validity of focusing on the learning of adaptive affective, behavioral, and cognitive coping responses to the stress of racism and oppression. A focus on the learning of adaptive coping responses is consistent with tradition in the field of stress and coping (Lazarus, 2000).

CURRENT MODELS OF RACIAL-CULTURAL SKILL ACQUISITION

This review of current models of practice for racial-cultural skill acquisition is not exhaustive, but serves to describe contemporary trends in the psychological literature. For example, the race-based approach views racial identity as playing a decisive role in personality development, and a model of racial identity for all racial groups has evolved (Carter, 1995, 2000; Cross, 1971, 1991; Helms, 1995, 2001), including statuses for Blacks and people of Color (Africans, Latinos, Asians, Native Americans, and some immigrants) as well as Whites (Carter, 2000). In counseling or teaching to promote racial-cultural skill acquisition, there are four distinct pairs of relationships that are possible from a racial identity development perspective (Carter, 2000; Helms, 1984):

1. *Parallel,* where the person in power (counselor, teacher) and the person with less power (client, student) have the same level of racial identity development and, for example, the client/student "in this case, acquires no new information about how to deal with racial stimuli. Because the two persons in the example have similar perspectives, neither is given an opportunity to challenge his or her racial identity status beliefs" (p. 890).

2. *Regressive,* where the client/student has a more mature and advanced racial identity status than the counselor/teacher in a position of power, and the client/student may feel disregarded, devalued, and dismissed.

3. *Crossed,* where the counselor/teacher and the client/student have opposite racial identity ego statuses and conflict ensues, with the possibility that suppression may occur if the person in power has the less advanced status development.

4. *Progressive,* where the counselor/teacher, or power holder, has a more advanced racial identity status development than the client/student, allowing the aspirant to learn, grow, and understand his or her issues surrounding race and racial identity (Carter, 2000).

Sue and Sue (2003) support a training process for counselors that must include an assessment of trainees' stage of identity development and facilitates awareness of how the level of identity development impacts cross-cultural encounters. Sue and Sue provide a detailed explanation of the many characteristics of the culturally competent mental health professional; they articulate multicultural counseling competencies and what constitutes multicultural competence on the organizational level. Similarly, the objectives of multicultural competence, as well as the exact nature of the competencies deemed essential to counseling practice and being able to impact organizational life, have been presented (Sue et al., 1998). Counseling professionals have reached broad consensus regarding the concept of multiculturalism, describing in detail 10 specific characteristics (Sue et al., 1998). This body of work provides standards for a field seeking to meet the needs of developing trainees and current professionals.

There is an extensive guide bringing together expert views on how to conduct multicultural counseling (Ponterotto, Casas, Suzuki, & Alexander, 2001), and a theory of multicultural counseling and therapy (MCT) has been articulated (Sue, Ivey, & Pedersen, 1996) and thoughtfully critiqued (Parham, 1996; Pope-Davis & Constantine, 1996). Sue et al. (1996) explained that MCT theory is ultimately concerned with freeing individuals, families, groups, and organizations to generate new ways of thinking, feeling, and acting while developing a "cultural identity [that] represents a cognitive, emotional and behavioral progression through identifiable and measurable levels of consciousness, or stages" (p. 17).

Wallace (1996) provided a training curriculum for counselors, psychologists, and educators who may, in turn, adapt the curriculum for delivery to clients and community members, asserting that all need to learn a new set of "A, B, Cs" for coping in order to shift affects, behaviors, and cognitions and reverse social conditioning in the U.S. culture of violence. Wallace (2003) encouraged a paradigm shift away from our society's historical pattern of hierarchical domination and oppression (A/B) toward a nonhierarchical equality (A = B), describing these, respectively, as the old paradigm (A/B) or psychology of oppression, and the new paradigm (A = B) or psychology of liberation. Wallace asserted that movement from the old to the new paradigm (with corresponding shifts in affects, behavior, and cognitions) also involves a corresponding change in identity. Thus, the overall approach put forth is called a psychology of oppression, liberation, and identity development (Wallace, 2003).

Wallace, Carter, Nanin, Keller, and Alleyne (2003) integrated racial identity theory, identity development theory for sexual orientation, and identity development theory for people with disabilities with the concept of stages of change (DiClemente & Velasquez, 2002; Prochaska & DiClemente, 1982) and motivational interviewing (Miller & Rollnick, 1991, 2002). One result of this integration is the presentation of more generic identity development stages that apply to a variety of identities, whether racial or sexual (Wallace et al., 2003), as follows: a precontemplation stage/status (identity is the societal view of self, or not thinking about the issues), contemplation stage/status (the societal view of self is questioned, or thinking about the issues), preparation stage/status (a decision is made to start working on identity, or addressing the issues), action stage/status (actively working on identity or the issues for up to six months), maintenance stage/status (sustained work on identity or the issues for over six months), and a relapse stage/status (abandonment of active work on identity and related issues).

Given research findings from the fields of addiction, public health, and medicine (Burke, Arkowitz, & Dunn, 2002; Resnicow et al., 2002), Wallace et al. (2003) feel justified in asserting that the integration of identity development theory (for race, sexual orientation, and disability), stages of change, and motivational interviewing will accelerate the rate of movement across stages of change, for example, from a stage of precontemplation (not thinking about identity issues) to a stage of contemplation (thinking about identity issues). With regard to the contemplation stage, which is the equivalent of Sue and Sue's (2003) dissonance stage and Cross's (1991) pre-encounter stage, people "generally move into this stage slowly, but a traumatic event may propel some individuals to move into dissonance at a much more rapid pace" (Sue & Sue, 2003, p. 221). There is value in an approach like motivational interviewing that may accelerate the rate of movement across stages.

The rationale for Wallace et al.'s (2003) integration of identity development theory, stages of change, and motivational interviewing includes how the stages of change have "played an integral role in the development of motivational interviewing and brief interventions using a motivational approach. . . . Motivational interviewing can be used to assist individuals to accomplish the various tasks required to transition from the precontemplation stage through the maintenance stage" (DiClemente & Velasquez, 2002, p. 202). Also, a body evidence shows that adaptations of motivational interviewing "improved the rate of entry into [an action stage and] retention in intensive substance abuse treatment" (Burke et al., 2002, p. 219). There is evidence of efficacy when adaptations of motivational interviewing are extended to a variety of issues/problems, whether hypertension, diabetes, dual diagnoses, and eating disorders (Burke et al., 2002) or fostering diet and physical activity change, smoking cessation, medication adherence, and HIV prevention, cardiovascular management, screening for cancer, and engagement in infection-control procedures in international settings (Resnicow et al., 2002). Adaptations typically include key principles of motivational interviewing, such as inquiring about client concerns, creating cognitive dissonance between behaviors/cognitions and valued goals, exploring possible next steps, reviewing a menu of options, performing a decisional balance exercise (pros and cons of change), reinforcing "change talk" (expressed intention to change) so that change talk increases and resistance decreases, and allowing individuals to freely decide for themselves steps to pursue (Miller & Rollnick, 2002).

The stages of change also allow for the possibility of individuals cycling through the stages many times (Miller & Rollnick, 1991), consistent with how, in regard to racial identity development, "almost all models now entertain the possibility that development can vary (looping and recycling)" (Sue & Sue, 2003, p. 252). Sue and Sue described "an identifiable sequence that can occur in a linear or nonlinear fashion" (p. 254), even as they spoke about a stage process of identity development. Thus, the integration of identity development statuses, stages of change, and motivational interviewing (Wallace et al., 2003) represents a valuable contribution to the many existing and evolving identity development models described in the literature by others (e.g., Ponterotto et al., 2001; Sue & Sue, 2003).

The selected review of contemporary models of practice for racial-cultural skill acquisition contributes guiding principles in formulating this chapter's recommended practical coping skills approach. First, it is important to consider racial identity development in the United States, where racism/oppression abound. Second, racial-cultural skill acquisition, or being able to cope with the stress of racism and oppression (and foster practical coping skills in students, trainees, and clients), constitutes an important multicultural competency or standard for counselors and psychologists. Third, it is appropriate to focus on the learning and shaping of new ways of "feeling, acting, and thinking," or adaptive affective, behavioral, and cognitive coping responses, along with fostering corresponding progressive shifts in identity. Fourth, research supports integrating identity development theory, stages of change, and motivational interviewing to accelerate the rate of movement across identity stages/statuses, accelerate entrance into interventions, and enhance retention in interventions for racial-cultural skill acquisition.

A PRACTICAL COPING SKILLS APPROACH TO RACIAL-CULTURAL SKILL ACQUISITION: ADAPTIVE RESPONSES TO RACISM AND OPPRESSION

The recommended approach introduces stages of change for practical coping skills for racism and oppression with a special focus on affective, behavioral, and cognitive responses. The model represents a logical progression that builds on prior work

(Wallace et al., 2003) integrating identity development theory, stages of change, and motivational interviewing.

Stages of Change for Practical Coping Skills for Racism and Oppression: A Focus on Affective, Behavioral, and Cognitive Responses

The logic of introducing stages of change for practical coping skills for racism and oppression with a specific focus on affective, behavioral, and cognitive coping responses rests in a careful analysis of the work of Carter (2000). From my analysis, the work of Carter permits specification of the characteristic affects, behaviors, and cognitions for each identity stage/status, as shown in Table 6.1 (for Blacks and people of Color) and Table 6.2 (for Whites). Tables 6.1 and 6.2 also show how the identity statuses for Blacks and people of Color and for Whites, respectively, may be seen in relation to the more generic stages of change recommended for use by Wallace et al. (2003).

As Tables 6.1 and 6.2 indicate, the proposed integration of identity statuses and stages of change is not perfect. The integration of identity statuses and stages of change for Blacks and people of Color necessitates a mixed contemplation and determination stage that is commensurate with the encounter (Blacks) and dissonance (people of Color) statuses. Similarly, the integration of identity statuses and stages of change for Whites necessitates the development of three phases of contemplation: One involves Whites experiencing initial confusion; a second involves Whites experiencing confusion and making the "wrong" conclusion, with persistent behaviors suggesting active racism; and a third mixed contemplation and determination stage, where Whites experiencing confusion now go on to draw the "right" conclusion and decide to begin work developing a nonracist identity.

Given the many models of identity development for Blacks, Asian Americans, and Latinos/Hispanics, there is logic in moving toward models, such as one for racial-cultural development (Sue & Sue, 2003, p. 241), that can accommodate minority groups' "similar patterns of adjustment to cultural oppression" and be applied to White identity development as well. There is also logic in focusing on affects, behaviors, and cognitions, given how the "therapist is able to anticipate the sequence of feelings, beliefs, attitudes, and behaviors" that are "likely to arise" (p. 227) as individuals move across stages.

The work of Sue and Sue (2003) supports this chapter's taking the next logical evolutionary step in identity development theorizing: recognizing similar patterns of adjustment to racism and oppression for different racial and ethnic groups, acknowledging the possibilities of regression/relapse/looping/cycling, and focusing on the affects, behaviors, and cognitions characterizing each stage. However, Sue and Sue asserted that a "great deal of evidence is mounting that while identity may sequentially move through identifiable stages, affective, attitudinal, cognitive, and behavioral components of identity may not move in a uniform manner" (p. 233).

The mounting evidence of efficacy for the use of adaptations of motivational interviewing in promoting change for a wide range of problem behaviors (Burke et al., 2002) justifies the integration of stages of change, motivational interviewing, and

Table 6.1   Racial Identity Development Stages/Statuses for Blacks and People of Color: Affects, Behavior, and Cognitions

STAGE/Identity Status	AFFECTS	BEHAVIOR	COGNITIONS
PRECONTEMPLATION STAGE Pre-encounter (Blacks) Conformity (people of Color)	Negative feelings toward one's race or one's own group.	Behavior reflects preference for the dominant race.	Negative cognitions regarding one's race or one's own group.
CONTEMPLATION STAGE and PREPARATION STAGE Encounter (Blacks) Dissonance (people of Color)	Feelings of confusion, ambivalence, and anxiety. Feels open, determined to explore something new.	Behaviors that facilitate resolving inner conflict such as talking, reading. Behaviors of preparing to take action, seeking out new avenues for learning about identity issues.	Conflicting cognitions. Cognitive confusion. Decision made to explore identity issues by taking action.
ACTION STAGE Immersion-emersion (Blacks and people of Color)	Feelings of acceptance of one's own race and culture. Negative affect toward dominant culture and views.	New behavior of exploring one's own culture is attempted, rehearsed, and gains in strength.	New cognitions about one's race and culture reflect new knowledge.
MAINTENANCE STAGE Internalization (Blacks and people of Color) Internalization-commitment (Blacks) Integrative awareness (people of Color)	Feelings of security regarding self. Feelings of pride, fulfillment, self-confidence. Accepts and respects others. Feelings of peace, altruism, a desire to engage in social action for social justice. Humanistic feelings.	Stable behavior reflects balance in inter-acting with one's personal and dominant culture. Respectful behavior with others. Behaviors that constitute social action for social justice. Humanistic behaviors.	Cognitions are stable, flexible, and reflect respect for self/others. Cognitions reflect value for both one's personal and the dominant culture.

MOTIVATIONAL INTERVIEWING accelerates movement across stages.

105

Table 6.2   Racial Identity Development Stages/Statuses for Whites: Affects, Behavior, and Cognitions

STAGE/Identity Status	AFFECTS	BEHAVIOR	COGNITIONS
PRECONTEMPLATION STAGE Contact	Feelings of superiority over others. Feelings of enjoying white privilege.	Behaviors consistent with white privilege.	Cognitions consistent with white privilege. Endorses concept that personal effort leads to rewards.
CONTEMPLATION STAGE Disintegraton	Feelings of confusion, ambivalence, anxiety. Feelings of alliance with Whites.	Behaviors consistent with white privilege. New behavior of dialogue or reading to resolve confusion.	Holds conflicting cognitions, such as racial inequality exists, yet one is in alliance with other Whites.
CONTEMPLATION STAGE (wrong conclusion) Reintegraton	Feels confusion, ambivalence, anxiety. Settles into feelings of superiority.	Behaviors consistent with white privilege. Continues reading, dialogue behaviors.	Cognitions reflect defenses of intellectualization, rationalization, denial. Concludes whites deserve benefits.
CONTEMPLATION STAGE (right conclusion) and PREPARATION STAGE Pseudo-independence	Continuing feelings of confusion, ambivalence, anxiety. Starts to feel open to explore something new. Then, begins to feel determined to explore something new.	Some behaviors still consistent with white privilege. Dialogue and reading on issues as new behavior. Prepared to try new behavior.	Finally concludes that racism should be abandoned, as a new cognition. Holds the cognition that it is time to pursue development of a nonracist identity, and corresponding behaviors.
ACTION STAGE Immersion-Emersion	Feels a new self-pride without racism. Developing new acceptance and respect of others as new feelings.	New non-oppressive behavior is attempted, rehearsed, gains strength.	New cognitions on whiteness, matters of race, equity are developing as new knowledge is gained.
MAINTENANCE STAGE Autonomy	More mature feelings of self-pride, genuine acceptance and respect for diverse others. Develops feelings of altruism, commitment to social action for social justice.	Stable behaviors that are non-oppressive. Behaviors of social action for social justice for all.	Stable cognitions on whiteness, race, equity and increasingly more mature cognitions on social action and social justice.

MOTIVATIONAL INTERVIEWING accelerates movement across stages.

identity development models. For, yet another advantage from the integration may be enhancement of an individual's internal motivation to change his or her behavior while using techniques that also foster change in affects and cognitions via resolution of ambivalence—a key component of motivational interviewing (Miller & Rollnick, 2002).

Thus, specifically for the task of racial-cultural skill acquisition, it is valid to present both stages of change for practical coping skills for racism and oppression, and the affective, behavioral, and cognitive coping responses common to each identity stage. This is illustrated in Table 6.3. Table 6.3 also suggests how motivational interviewing may accelerate the rate of movement across stages of change (see arrow in table) for coping with racism and oppression. The table also indicates how maladaptive coping tends to prevail in the stages of precontemplation (not thinking about adaptive coping responses to racism and oppression), contemplation (thinking about acquiring adaptive coping responses to racism and oppression), and preparation (preparing to learn adaptive coping responses to racism and oppression). However, adaptive coping tends to prevail in the stages of action (engaged in actively learning and practicing adaptive coping responses to racism and oppression) and maintenance (generalizing and refining adaptive coping responses to racism and oppression for greater than six months). There is also the possibility of entering a relapse stage, with maladaptive coping responses prevailing once again.

Recommended Assessment Questions

There are a number of recommended assessment questions. The questions help to determine an individual's stage of change, as well as the type, quality, and specific nature of his or her responses to racism and oppression.

Assess Stage of Change for Coping with Racism and Oppression

- Is the individual in a stage of precontemplation? Or, is the individual not even thinking about adaptive coping responses to racism and oppression?

- Is the individual in a contemplation stage? Or, is the individual thinking about acquiring adaptive coping responses to racism and oppression?

- Is the individual in a preparation stage? Or, is the individual preparing to learn adaptive coping responses to racism and oppression, having made a decision to do so?

- Is the individual in an action stage? Or, is the individual engaged in actively learning adaptive coping responses to racism and oppression?

- Is the individual in a maintenance stage? Or, is the individual actively engaged in generalizing and refining adaptive coping responses to racism and oppression, having been engaged in an active learning process for a period greater than six months?

- Is the individual in a relapse stage? Or, has the individual returned to the use of maladaptive coping responses after a period of active engagement in adaptive coping responses to racism and oppression?

Table 6.3 Stages of Change for Practical Coping Skills for Racism and Oppression

IDENTITY STAGE	AFFECTIVE RESPONSES	BEHAVIORAL RESPONSES	COGNITIVE RESPONSES
I. PRECONTEMPLATION (not thinking about adaptive coping responses to racism and oppression; maladaptive responses prevail) II. CONTEMPLATION (thinking about acquiring adaptive coping responses to racism and oppression; maladaptive responses prevail) III. PREPARATION (preparing to learn adaptive coping responses to racism and oppression; maladaptive responses prevail)	In stages I, II, and III, anger, anxiety, fear, and frustration, etc..., as psychological arousal, may persist and lead to increased vulnerability to illness. A calm response, and/or generating and sustaining positive affect are ideal/adaptive coping. Positive and adaptive affective responses include humor/glee, amusement, joy, and love; affects of acceptance, respect and empathy may occur in response to viewing social conditioning as responsible for creating racism and oppression. Positive affect promotes creativity and flexibility in thinking and problem solving, and facilitates the processing of information.	In stages I, II, and III, passive (self-destructive overeating, drug/alcohol use), passive-aggressive (hostile), or aggressive (violent) behavioral responses prevail. Assertive verbal behavior is ideal/adaptive response to stress of racism/oppression. Avoidant behavior may be adaptive or maladaptive, depending on situation. Bodily behavior includes physiological responses of arousal such as higher resting blood pressure, hypertension, etc...; it may persist and lead to increased vulnerability to illness. A calming behavioral response is ideal/adaptive, including any behavior (deep breathing, exercise, yoga, etc...) or relaxation technique that effectively diffuses physiological arousal. Seeking out social support is also adaptive, especially with positive and optimistic peers. And, engaging in social action/advocacy for social justice is ideal.	In stages I, II, and III, conscious perception and processing may or may not occur as a cognitive response to racism/oppression. Any cognitive appraisals that trigger psychological and physiological stress responses or an arousal that persists are maladaptive. Ideal/adaptive cognitive responses include: positive reappraisal (eq. "glass is _ full"); goal-directed problem solving (eq. "What I have to do is...."); infusion of racist/oppressive events with positive meaning (eq. "I will grow from surviving this."); calming self-talk (eq. "I am calm, centered, and balanced."); and, spiritual self-talk ("Let Go, Let God").
IV. ACTION (engaged in actively learning and practicing adaptive coping responses to racism and oppression; adaptive responses prevail)	In stage IV, psychological arousal is diffused via calm and/or adaptive responses of positive affect listed above (humor/glee, acceptance, respect, empathy, etc...).	In stage IV, positive assertive behavior, or avoidant behavior (as appropriate), calming behavioral responses, or others listed above (exercise, social support, social action, etc...) are adaptive.	In stage IV, conscious perception of racism/oppression with responses that do not trigger persisting arousal are adaptive. Examples are listed above.
V. MAINTENANCE (generalizing, refining adaptive coping responses to racism and oppression for > 6 months; adaptive responses prevail)	In stage V, given practice effects, affective responses are consistently adaptive and reflect generalization, refinement, and sophistication.	In stage V, given practice effects, behavioral responses are consistently adaptive and reflect generalization to more situations, refinement, and sophistication.	In stage V, given practice, cognitive responses are consistently adaptive and reflect generalization, refinement, etc...
VI. RELAPSE (maladaptive responses prevail)	Maladaptive affective responses return in stage VI.	Maladaptive behavioral responses return in stage VI.	Maladaptive cognitive responses return in stage VI.

MOTIVATIONAL INTERVIEWING accelerates movement across stages.

Assess Prevalence, Quality, Type, and Nature of Maladaptive Coping Responses

- Which are more prevalent: maladaptive or adaptive coping responses to racism and oppression?

- What are the individual's specific patterns of maladaptive affective, behavioral, and cognitive coping in response to racism and oppression?

- Do prevalent maladaptive affective responses include anger, anxiety, fear, or frustration—as commonly experienced states of psychological arousal that persist, following exposure to racism and oppression, potentially leading to an increased vulnerability to illness?

- Do prevalent behavioral responses include passive, self-destructive, or defensive strategies, such as overeating or drug/alcohol use, in response to exposure to racism and oppression? Or, do maladaptive passive-aggressive behaviors occur, such as hostile acts in response to racism and oppression? Or, do maladaptive aggressive behaviors occur, such as violence in response to racism and oppression? Is there avoidant behavior in response to racism and oppression, and does it seem appropriate or maladaptive? Does bodily behavior in response to racism and oppression include physiological responses of arousal, such as a higher resting blood pressure, that may persist and lead to an increased vulnerability to illness (e.g., hypertension)?

- Do prevalent cognitive responses include the conscious perception of what seems to constitute racism and oppression, as well as any cognitive processing of the events? Do any cognitive appraisals occur in response to the perception of racism and oppression? Do the individual's cognitive appraisals trigger psychological and/or physiological states of arousal that persist, suggesting maladaptive cognitive coping?

Assess Adaptive Coping Responses in Precontemplation, Contemplation, and Preparation Stages

- Do adaptive affective responses ever occur in reaction to racism and oppression, such as a calm feeling state or a strategy for generating and sustaining positive affective states, including humor, amusement, joy, and love? Or, do adaptive affective responses of acceptance, respect, and empathy ever occur, perhaps in response to viewing the social conditioning of others as responsible for creating racism and oppression? Do affective responses prevent persisting states of psychological arousal or provide effective diffusion of psychological arousal, suggesting that they are adaptive?

- Do adaptive behavioral responses ever occur in response to racism and oppression, such as those that create a state of calm (deep breathing, exercise, yoga, etc.), providing effective diffusion of physiological arousal?

- Do adaptive cognitive responses ever occur in response to racism and oppression, such as cognitive appraisals that effectively prevent or diffuse states of psychological and physiological arousal? Do cognitive responses include positive reappraisal (e.g., "The glass is half full"), goal-directed problem solving (e.g., "What I have to do is X, so that I get outcome Y and eliminate possibility Z"), or the infusion of racist/oppressive events with positive meaning (e.g., "I will grow from surviving this experience of racism and oppression, gaining new knowledge and refined coping skills")? Does the individual use self-talk that serves to create a state of calm, whether via affirmations ("I am calm, centered, and balanced") or spiritual self-talk ("Let Go and Let God!" or "God has a better plan than I can imagine"), as forms of adaptive cognitive coping?

Assess Prior and Newly Acquired Adaptive Coping Responses in the Action Stage

- Is the individual showing evidence of taking action in deploying both prior and newly acquired adaptive affective, behavioral, and cognitive responses when racism and oppression are encountered? Are those adaptive affective, behavioral, and cognitive responses that are taught (to clients in sessions, to students in classrooms, to trainees in practica) being practiced in and generalized to real-world situations involving racism and oppression? Are adaptive affective, behavioral, and cognitive responses gradually increasing in prevalence, while maladaptive responses are decreasing?

Assess Adaptive Responses in the Maintenance Stage

- Are the individual's adaptive affective, behavioral, and cognitive responses successfully generalizing to a variety of new situations where racism and oppression are encountered? Are the individual's adaptive affective, behavioral, and cognitive responses evidencing increasing refinement and sophistication in response to both ongoing and newly encountered situations involving racism and oppression, reflecting practice effects over time? Is the individual showing increasing creativity and flexibility in deploying adaptive responses and tailoring them to both ongoing and newly encountered situations involving racism and oppression?

Assess for Maladaptive Coping Responses/Relapse in the Action and Maintenance Stages

- Do maladaptive affective, behavioral, or cognitive responses ever return? Is the return of maladaptive coping responses a temporary occurrence that is followed by a return to adaptive affective, behavioral, and cognitive responses, as may occur in any learning process, and is the prevalence of maladaptive coping responses decreasing in frequency of occurrence over time? Or, does the relapse involve a persistent pattern of maladaptive affective, behavioral, and cognitive coping responses that are reemerging after a substantial period of successful deployment of adaptive coping responses to racism and oppression?

Assess Maintenance Stage for Quality of Identity Development

- Does identity development for the individual reflect awareness as one who consistently adaptively copes with racism and oppression? Is the individual presenting over time a progressively more mature, stable, and internalized identity as one who adaptively copes with racism and oppression? Does the individual perceive self as someone who engages in social action for social justice or advocacy work, consistent with attaining the highest ideals associated with identity development? Does the individual seek out and/or respond to opportunities to foster organizational multicultural competence and combat racism and oppression in institutions in the United States as a social activist for social justice?

Implications of Assessment Findings

Assessment findings allow interventions to be tailored to individual clients/students/trainees in order to meet them "where they are" in the change process. Individuals may also be matched to interventions in light of their stage of change and characteristics as either a precontemplator, contemplator, or person in an action, maintenance, or relapse stage. Persons in all stages benefit from working with professionals who can feel genuine empathy, acceptance, and respect for where individuals are in the change process—whether in a painful relapse or a naïve state of precontemplation.

When an individual is in a precontemplation stage he will benefit from a tailored intervention involving the delivery of information or psychoeducation to increase their awareness or raise their level of concern. Recommended motivational interviewing techniques include reflective listening, summarizing, and affirming an individual as he describes his situation, or giving the person freedom to make their own decisions; these are typically effective in helping the individual move to a state of contemplation (DiClemente & Velasquez, 2002). The person in a contemplation stage will benefit from motivational interviewing techniques that help the individual to explore her concerns, consider the pros and cons of change (decisional balance), resolve her ambivalence/confusion, and thereby accelerate her rate of movement to a preparation and/or action stage. In addition, careful listening, summarizing, feedback, double-sided reflection ("on the one hand . . . yet on the other hand"), affirmation, and increasing self-efficacy to change are vital in this stage. An individual in a preparation stage who has decided to learn adaptive affective, behavioral, and cognitive responses may need assistance in making a plan of action and accessing interventions to facilitate the learning process, whether being matched to counseling sessions, classroom course work, practicum training opportunities, workshops, seminars, or a book club following a pertinent reading list. Offering a menu of options is also helpful, allowing the individual in preparation to select what he or she prefers, while a professional can gently warn against a change plan that seems inappropriate or ineffective (DiClemente & Velasquez, 2002).

Integrating the work of Miller and Rollnick (2002) and Marlatt and Gordon (1985), specific recommendations may be made for those in the action, maintenance, and relapse stages. An individual in an action stage is now actively engaged in counseling sessions, or taking courses/practica, attending workshops/seminars, and/or reading and learning about how to adaptively cope. Interventions tailored for such an individual should include cognitive-behavioral skill-building interventions, opportunities to role-play and rehearse adaptive responses, and the delivery of reinforcement and feedback that allows for refining coping responses and increasing the individual's self-efficacy to cope in a specific situation. A person in action also benefits from motivational interviewing techniques to strengthen his or her commitment to continue to pursue change. Also helpful is learning how to anticipate and cope with specific high-risk situations for a return to maladaptive coping, for managing high-risk situations for relapse, and for preventing relapse. Individuals must learn how to prevent a lapse (or some return to maladaptive coping) from turning into a full-blown relapse. Persons in a maintenance stage may benefit from the use of motivational interviewing techniques to further strengthen their commitment to the performance of adaptive affective, behavioral, and cognitive coping responses to racism and oppression. They also benefit from ongoing cognitive-behavioral interventions to help them refine their coping strategies, as well as interventions to further increase their feelings of self-efficacy in being able to cope successfully in specific situations involving racism/oppression. An individual in relapse may benefit from motivational interviewing techniques to resolve any ambivalence about beginning the task (once again) of deploying adaptive coping responses (positive assertive verbal responses, etc.) and/or relinquishing maladaptive responses (avoidance, overeating, drug/alcohol use, violence). Persons in a relapse stage may also need assistance in restoring their sense of hope that they can change, once again.

Additional Guidance for Professionals Regarding Fostering Adaptive Responses

Table 6.3 serves as an important guide in how to foster racial-cultural skill acquisition. However, more guidance to professionals may be given. First, regardless of race, ethnicity, or culture, what is presented in Table 6.3 applies to all who need to learn adaptive responses to racism and oppression. A professional of any race or ethnicity may seek to both acquire for themselves and foster in others (clients, students, trainees) practical skills for coping with racism and oppression. A few examples are given to support this assertion. Second, professionals may benefit from more detailed guidance regarding how to foster adaptive affective, behavioral, and cognitive coping, going beyond what appears in Table 6.3.

As Table 6.3 suggests, there are a variety of potential adaptive affective responses to racism and oppression, ranging from amusement to acceptance and empathy. A White, Latino/Hispanic, Asian, and African American may each, for example, struggle with powerful feelings of anger over witnessing racism and oppression. Or, they might all learn to deploy the adaptive affective response of feeling acceptance, respect, and empathy for a racist oppressor as a result of viewing him or her as a product of social conditioning in the United States. Generally, such adaptive affective responses reflect learning to cope with the experience of powerful affects or feelings arising in the inner self when facing the stress of racism and oppression. Adaptive affective responses include learning how to regulate and modulate affective reactions and feelings when faced with other people's words, gestures, or actions as a racist and oppressor. Prolonged states of psychological arousal suggest the need to learn how to better regulate and modulate affective reactions.

Adaptive behavioral responses may include those listed in Table 6.3, as well as walking away from certain situations, as opposed to assertively speaking up. Often, avoiding a situation is adaptive to prevent a negative outcome, such as being fired from a job that one depends on for income. In the United States, it may be easier or safer for a White or Asian to speak up in some situations, whereas there might be a greater risk of police brutality or termination from work if an African American or Latino/Hispanic spoke up against racism/oppression. An African American, for example, might have to resort more often to other adaptive behavioral responses, such as deep breathing, exercise, or seeking out social support from positive and optimistic peers. All racial and ethnic group members must rely on such adaptive responses at times. There may be times when an adaptive behavioral response also includes avoiding a situation, stimulus, or trigger that may enrage one to the point where one's health is placed at risk. At other times, avoidance may be only a temporary adaptive behavioral strategy until newly acquired adaptive behavioral responses have been sufficiently role-played, refined, and strengthened, such as making a positive assertive verbal remark. Adaptive behavioral responses generally involve conscious execution of active, assertive reactions to what is happening in racist oppressive environments versus remaining passive and perhaps having a physiological arousal that persists, potentially damaging health. Ideally, adaptive behavioral responses permit avoidance of persistent states of physiological arousal, such as when a relaxation response is produced from deep breathing, progressive muscle relaxation, exercise, or social support.

Following and going beyond what is presented in Table 6.3, adaptive cognitive responses may include the process of perceiving and processing an event that seems worthy of classification as racism and oppression. For a White who is just beginning the task of overcoming his or her racism, to begin to perceive and process events in society as racist and oppressive may be a monumental step. Similarly, it is an important step for a new immigrant of Color who is naïve to being targeted for racism and oppression in the United States, to begin to perceive and process events that deserve classification as racism and oppression. African Americans, on the other hand, may more readily perceive events as racist and oppressive because of the long legacy of U.S. racism targeted against them. However, an African American opponent of affirmative action, or someone claiming to be color-blind, for example, might be as naïve as a new immigrant and fail to perceive and process events as racist and oppressive until some traumatic event occurs.

Regardless of race, ethnicity, or cultural background, in coping with racism and oppression that is perceived (perhaps finally!), adaptive cognitive responses include the making of positive reappraisals, goal-directed problem solving, and the infusion of events with positive meaning. However, individuals from different racial, ethnic, or cultural groups might have characteristic patterns of engagement in positive reappraisal, problem solving, and infusing positive meaning into events that reflect cultural, religious/spiritual, educational, or acculturation influences. For example, there is spiritual self-talk ("Let Go and Let God!" and "I am too blessed to be stressed") that is characteristic of many African Americans. African Americans may have learned, by necessity, to deploy such self-talk in response to racism and oppression, especially when to speak up may have meant violent beating, lynching, or, in more contemporary times, police brutality or dismissal from work. Historically, prayer and religious/spiritual beliefs have also guided African Americans in formulating characteristic forms of positive reappraisal and the infusion of events with positive meaning, for example, "God is trying to tell me something" and "God is working here." Goal-directed problem solving for African Americans, Latinos/Hispanics, and Asians might involve the following: "If I complain or say anything, then I may lose my job and end up not being able to take care of my family."

Wallace (1996) referred to self-talk as *internal cognitive coping,* given what individuals say to themselves, typically silently. Calming self-talk can serve as vital anger management and be used to diffuse psychological and physiological arousal; it can also be combined with cognitive imagery, such as the visualization of sitting by a lake, mountain, or beautiful garden. Calming self-talk may involve the delivery of affirmations ("I am calm, centered, and balanced") or a reminder to count to 10 or walk away.

Wallace (1996) identifies *external cognitive coping* as another adaptive cognitive response. Technically, this also constitutes the adaptive behavioral response of delivering a positive assertive verbal response; what starts as a carefully formulated cognition may then be delivered aloud as overt verbal behavior. External cognitive coping involves statements to be delivered aloud to others, such as the following: "I am concerned about what is happening here in this institution." A White individual or African American or other person of Color may respond with such external cognitive coping in response to institutional racism and oppression. For an African American being confronted or harassed at work, external cognitive coping might include the following statements being carefully formulated, rehearsed/role-played in the action stage and then delivered aloud to the offender: "Is this something you'd like to discuss? I am not available for discussion right now. Perhaps at a later time?" Such a positive assertive verbal response may bring closure to an incident of harassment, allow the individual being harassed to seek out social support from positive optimistic peers, or seek advice from a counselor, lawyer, or ombudsman.

The Importance of Good Self-Observation and Self-Monitoring

Self-observation and self-monitoring, specifically, the skill inherent in observing and reporting accurately one's experiences in the real world, has been called cultivation of a self-observing ego (Wallace, 1996). Information from self-observation may be brought to counseling, allowing for receipt of instruction, rehearsal, and tailored role-plays covering those coping strategies recommended for future deployment in the racist and oppressive situation. Or, an individual may confer with positive and optimistic allies (peers, counselor, lawyer, ombudsman) and receive feedback about what needs to be done next or the type of adaptive coping recommended for deployment in the next encounter. Moreover, the ability to self-observe or self-monitor means being able to stop oneself from performing a maladaptive affective, behavioral, or cognitive response in certain situations; this is how extinction of maladaptive coping responses may occur in the action stage, even as newly acquired coping responses are being practiced in counseling sessions and generalized to the real world. The ability to engage in self-observation or self-monitoring also translates into the ability to consciously direct oneself to perform an adaptive practical coping skill—replacing the prior maladaptive response. Homework for clients, students, and trainees that includes self-monitoring (journaling, logs) fosters self-observation and is vital for racial-cultural skill acquisition.

CASE EXAMPLE ILLUSTRATING PRODUCTIVE TECHNIQUES FOR RACIAL-CULTURAL SKILL ACQUISITION

A case example illustrates the utility of the recommended model for racial-cultural skill acquisition. The case demonstrates the importance of focusing on client acquisition of practical coping skills (adaptive affective, behavioral, and cognitive responses) for racism and oppression.

The Case of Mr. K.C.: Racism and Oppression in Seeking Access to Job Training

Mr. K.C. is a 43-year-old, 6′2″, 220-pound African American man with a high school diploma who recently lost lucrative employment. Mr. K.C. arrived at one of our sessions angry, sharing his story of outrage.

"That man! That man! I did everything you said. That's it!" In this manner, Mr. K.C. described his experiences coping with the stress of a racist and oppressive Caucasian male serving in the role of gatekeeper for access to highly valued job training opportunities.

Mr. K.C. was eloquent in explaining: "I was polite. I listened to him putting up all sorts of obstacles. And I responded to each one. He did not have anything else to put on the table to block me. He stalled and said we had to meet two more times. I smiled, said thank you, and extended my hand to shake his. He acted like he did not want to shake my hand." Mr. K.C. imitated the gatekeeper's behavioral movements, suggesting great hesitancy. Smiling, Mr. K.C. then described how the gatekeeper finally responded: "He shook my hand and I wished him a good day." Mr. K.C. continued, "I did everything you said." Indeed, he had gone beyond my recommendations by improvising the handshake—which seemed like a well-executed *adaptive behavioral response*—effectively diffusing some of the hostility and hate he felt coming from the racist gatekeeper.

I provided immediate reinforcement and praise, striving to further increase his sense of self-efficacy. The client had successfully generalized to the real world the adaptive responses we had role-played and rehearsed in therapy. Consistent with this training in adaptive cognitive responses to racism and oppression in prior sessions, he successfully engaged in *internal cognitive coping,* wherein he was thinking internally one thing ("You racist jerk"), while he also deployed *external cognitive coping* and said something else aloud ("Thank you"). At the same time, he engaged in the *adaptive affective response* of remaining calm, smiling, and appearing pleasant (and even joyful). All of these adaptive responses served to prevent this racist gatekeeper from receiving confirmation of negative stereotypes he held about Mr. K.C. The gatekeeper could not dismiss Mr. K.C. as an angry and rude Black man who could be justifiably barred from job training opportunities because he could be easily provoked to violence. Instead, Mr. K.C. demonstrated that he was a pleasant and polite man who was adaptively coping with racism and oppression.

Mr. K.C. had also engaged in excellent self-observation and self-monitoring and was able to provide detailed descriptions of his coping responses deployed in the gatekeeper's office. I told him how proud I was of him.

We went on to discuss future strategy (thereby engaging in the *adaptive cognitive response of goal-directed problem solving*) for the next encounter in the gatekeeper's office. More examples of what he might have to do (*adaptive behavioral responses*) and say (*adaptive cognitive responses*) were role-modeled by me for him and then practiced by Mr. K.C. in role-play. Through praise, I reinforced his role-play performance, increasing his self-efficacy to cope in future office interactions with the gatekeeper. At the end of the role-play, the client smiled broadly and thanked me. He spontaneously elaborated on how he could use certain things this gatekeeper had already said and done to his advantage in their next office meeting; this showed his *ability to have cognitive flexibility and problem-solve, as adaptive cognitive responses.*

The client then talked about his desire to have a meeting with this gatekeeper's boss to discuss the gatekeeper's unfair, racist pattern of dealing with African Americans. However, the timing for that meeting seemed inappropriate. I brainstormed aloud the likely outcomes, role modeling *goal-directed problem-solving as an adaptive cognitive response.* The client decided against a meeting with the gatekeeper's boss, stating, "I'm okay now. I'll meet with him two more times. But he was an hour late for one meeting. I was on time. And he didn't come in one day and had to reschedule. But I was there each time. As long as I know that you know what is going on I'm okay. I'm not going to let him stop me. It may take two months, whereas before he was in that position it was a fast, streamlined process. I know. I've been around a long time. I watched a lot of people go through the process of getting job training before he was hired. I just didn't follow through with job training before he got here, because I got a great job. Then I lost it. He has no right to put up all these obstacles to block me. But he's doing the same thing to other people, too. He acts like I'm not ready to work. Yet, I was working!"

The client elaborated: "I talk to people. A lot of people are being held back because he is in that position. He sits on their paperwork for weeks. I should get together a petition and get all these people I know to sign it. Then I'll send it to the agency head. He's holding people back. It's not fair. It wasn't this way before he got here." In this manner, he reflected a willingness to engage in the *adaptive behavioral responses of social action for social justice and advocacy* on behalf of the oppressed—also indicating positive, progressive identity development.

A week later, the client returned for his next therapy session and freely shared, "I asked around a little bit. Only two people are even at the stage I'm at, but having the same experience. The rest aren't there yet. They're not ready for referral for job training. So, I'm not going to do the petition. *I'm going to leave it in God's hands.* If you're going to throw up a brick wall, I may have to go another way. I may have to get another agency to help me. *I'm asking God, 'What decision should I make?'* Should I stay with the agency or move on? My stubbornness to stay may be to fight him. If I leave, will he have won? Will I be running away? I've run away before. I'm tired of running away. I've put a lot of time into that paperwork. But, I may have to go somewhere else." In this manner, the client used *spiritual self-talk as an adaptive cognitive response.*

Three months later, Mr. K.C. was in a job training class, having successfully deployed adaptive affective, behavioral, and cognitive coping responses to racism and oppression. But why did he have to wait so long?

CONCLUSION: SUGGESTIONS FOR MODELS OF PRACTICE FOR EFFECTIVE RACIAL-CULTURAL SKILL ACQUISITION

Given the recent call by Sue (2003) for Whites socialized in the United States to overcome their racism and oppression, two logical questions follow: How long will it take? How intrinsically motivated are beneficiaries of White privilege to change, even if they are given a practical guide?

As the case of Mr. K.C. illustrated, African Americans are tired of waiting, as racist gatekeepers for access to everything from job training to employment, educational opportunities, bank loans, and mortgages "sit" on their paperwork. Sue (2003, p. 255) eloquently articulates how people of Color in general are "tired," being left to wonder "if things will get better." Until Whites change and successfully overcome their racism, or given the belief that racism "will always be with us" (Sue, 2003, p. 270), African Americans, in particular, as well as all others in the United States must learn adaptive affective, behavioral, and cognitive responses to racism and oppression, or racial-cultural skill acquisition. This chapter's recommended model for racial-cultural skill acquisition—a practical coping skills approach—should prove of value to professionals in their work with clients, students, and trainees.

It is recommended that other racial identity development theorists consider potential benefits from integrating stages of change and motivational interviewing in their models. The stages of change provide a common framework that facilitates comparisons across models, also contributing a common language that is clear and concise when referring to identity stages/statuses across models. Motivational interviewing introduces the concept of accelerating the rate of movement across stages/identity statuses. Motivational interviewing provides new hope that, with regard to Whites, movement toward change in surrendering personal complicity in racism and oppression and in challenging racist and oppressive institutional practices can be accelerated and that intrinsic motivation can be enhanced through the use of motivational interviewing techniques. For African Americans, Latinos/Hispanics, Asians, and new immigrants (e.g., Africans), motivational interviewing may accelerate the rate of racial-cultural acquisition or the learning of practical coping skills for racism and oppression. Otherwise, movement across stages of change for practical coping skills for racism and oppression may be "a gradual process" where people generally move "slowly," unless "a traumatic event may propel some individuals to move" at a "much more rapid pace" (Sue & Sue, 2003, p. 221). Moreover, motivational interviewing may also enhance entrance into and retention in interventions promoting racial-cultural skill acquisition (Burke et al., 2002; Resnicow et al., 2002).

If the integration of motivational interviewing has been successful in the fields of addiction, public health, and medicine in fostering everything from alcohol and drug abstinence, diet and physical activity change, smoking cessation, medication adherence, HIV prevention, cardiovascular management, screening for cancer, and engagement in infection-control procedures in international settings (Miller & Rollnick, 2002; Resnicow et al., 2002), why not apply it to the field of multiculturalism, specifically to the task of racial-cultural skill acquisition? Future research needs to determine the efficacy of motivational interviewing techniques when applied to the task of moving individuals across stages of change for acquiring practical coping skills for racism and oppression. Research should also determine whether or not the recommended approach to racial-cultural skill acquisition promotes progressive movement across stages of change for practical coping skills for racism and oppression and the learning of adaptive affective, behavioral, and cognitive responses.

REFERENCES

Burke, B. L., Arkowitz, H., & Dunn, C. (2002). The Efficacy of Motivational Interviewing and Its Adaptations: What We Know So Far. In W. R. Miller & S. Rollnick (Eds.), *Motivational interviewing: Preparing people for change* (2nd ed., pp. 217–250). New York: Guilford Press.

Carter, R. T. (1995). *The influence of race and racial identity in psychotherapy: Toward a racially inclusive model.* New York: Wiley.

Carter, R. T. (2000). Reimagining race in education: A new paradigm from psychology. *Teachers College Record, 102*(5), 864–897.

Clark, R., Anderson, N. B., Clark, V. R., & Williams, D. R. (1999). Racism as a stressor for African Americans: A biopsychosocial model. *American Psychologist, 54*(10), 805–816.

Cross, W. E. (1971). The Negro-to-Black conversion experience: Toward a psychology of Black liberation. *Black World, 20,* 13–27.

Cross, W. E. (1991). *Shades of Black: Diversity in African American identity.* Philadelphia: Temple University Press.

DiClemente, C., & Velasquez, M. M. (2002). Motivational interviewing and the stages of change. In W. R. Miller & S. Rollnick (Eds.), *Motivational interviewing: Preparing people for change* (2nd ed., pp. 201–216). New York: Guilford Press.

Folkman, S., & Moskowitz, J. T. (2000). Positive affect and the other side of coping. *American Psychologist, 55*(6), 647–654.

Gaston, M. H., & Porter, G. K. (2001). *Prime time: The African American woman's complete guide to midlife health and wellness.* New York: Ballantine.

Helms, J. E. (1984). Toward a theoretical model of the effects of race on counseling: A Black and white model. *Counseling Psychologist, 12,* 153–165.

Helms, J. E. (1995). An update on Helms's White and people of Color racial identity models. In J. Ponterotto, J. M. Casas, L. A. Suzuki, & C. M. Alexander (Eds.), *Handbook of multicultural counseling* (pp. 181–198). Thousand Oaks, CA: Sage.

Helms, J. E. (2001). An update on Helms's White and people of Color racial identity models. In J. Ponterotto, J. M. Casas, L. A. Suzuki, & C. M. Alexander (Eds.), *Handbook of multicultural counseling* (2nd ed., pp. 181–198). Thousand Oaks, CA: Sage.

hooks, b. (1996). *Killing rage: Ending racism.* New York: Henry Holt.

Lazarus, R. S. (2000). Toward better research on stress and coping. *American Psychologist, 55*(6), 665–673.

Marlatt, G. A., & Gordon, J. R. (Eds.). (1985). *Relapse prevention: Maintenance strategies in the treatment of addictive behaviors.* New York: Guilford Press.

Miller, W. R., & Rollnick, S. (1991). *Motivational interviewing: Preparing people to change addictive behavior.* New York: Guilford Press.

Miller, W. R., & Rollnick, S. (Eds.). (2002). *Motivational interviewing: Preparing people for change.* New York: Guilford Press.

Parham, T. (1996). MCT theory and African-American populations. In D. W. Sue, A. Ivey, & P. B. Pedersen (Eds.), *A theory of multicultural counseling and therapy* (pp. 177–199). Pacific Grove, CA: Brooks/Cole.

Ponterotto, J. G., Casas, J. M., Suzuki, L. A., & Alexander, C. M. (Eds.). (2001). *Handbook of multicultural counseling* (2nd ed.). Thousand Oaks, CA: Sage.

Pope-Davis, D., & Constantine, M. G. (1996). MCT theory and implications for practice. In D. W. Sue, A. Ivey, & P. B. Pedersen (Eds.), *A theory of multicultural counseling and therapy.* Pacific Grove, CA: Brooks/Cole.

Prochaska, J. O., & DiClemente, C. C. (1982). Transtheoretical therapy: Toward a more integrative model of change. *Psychotherapy: Theory, Research, and Practice, 18,* 276–288.

Resnicow, K., DiLorio, C., Soet, J. E., Borreli, B., Ernst, D., Hecht, J., et al. (2002). Motivational interviewing in medical and public health settings. In W. R. Miller & S. Rollnick (Eds.), *Motivational interviewing: Preparing people for change* (2nd ed., pp. 251–269). New York: Guilford Press.

Sue, D. W. (2003). *Overcoming our racism: The journey to liberation.* New York: Wiley.

Sue, D. W., Carter, R. T., Casas, J. M., Fouad, N. A., Ivey, A. E., Jensen, M., et al. (1998). *Multicultural counseling competencies: Individual and organizational development.* Thousand Oaks, CA: Sage.

Sue, D. W., Ivey, A., & Pedersen, P. B. (Eds.). (1996). *A theory of multicultural counseling and therapy.* Pacific Grove, CA: Brooks/Cole.

Sue, D. W., & Sue, D. (2003). *Counseling the culturally diverse: Theory and practice* (4th ed.). New York: Wiley.

Suinn, R. M. (2001). The terrible twos—anger and anxiety: Hazardous to your health. *American Psychologist, 56*(1), 27–36.

Wallace, B. C. (1996). *Adult children of dysfunctional families: Prevention, intervention, and treatment for community mental health promotion.* Westport, CT: Praeger.

Wallace, B. C. (2003). A multicultural approach to violence: Toward a psychology of oppression, liberation, and identity development. In B. C. Wallace & R. T. Carter (Eds.), *Understanding and dealing with violence: A multicultural approach* (pp. 3–39). Thousand Oaks, CA: Sage.

Wallace, B. C., Carter, R. T., Nanin, J. E., Keller, R., & Alleyne, V. (2003). Identity development for "diverse and different others": Integrating stages of change, motivational interviewing, and identity theories for race, people of Color, sexual orientation, and disability. In B. C. Wallace & R. T. Carter (Eds.), *Understanding and dealing with violence: A multicultural approach* (pp. 41–91). Thousand Oaks, CA: Sage.

CHAPTER 7

Issues of Language Diversity: Training Culturally Competent and Confident Therapists

Marie Faubert and Don C. Locke

The history of language in the United States is a very painful one. As waves of immigrants came from non-English-speaking parts of Europe, they were made to feel inferior, excluded, and unqualified. People were judged ignorant or uneducated if they spoke in halting, nonstandard English (Walsh, 1991). Even those who came from English-speaking countries but spoke other than standard English or spoke with devalued accents were discriminated against by the dominant society.

Some families maintained their mental health by speaking the mother tongue in the home and in their place of worship and by speaking standard English in the marketplace for economic survival. Devalued, European immigrant families often taught their children their native language. In the extensive experience of the first author, French, Italian, Polish, Lithuanian, German, and Jewish immigrants established their own schools for families who wanted to maintain the native language. There were few, if any, public schools available for immigrant families who wanted to teach the "language of the hearth" respectfully and successfully to their children. Worse, students were ridiculed for speaking a "foreign" language or having an accent, which sounded "funny."

Other families rejected their first language. Their children did not learn the mother tongue. There are residual feelings of resentment among significant numbers of their descendants when newer immigrants demand the right to maintain their first language. "My grandparents had to give up their language and learn English. Why can't *they*?" is heard in classrooms and at family gatherings.

African Americans suffered trauma as they interfaced with the dominant cultures in the countries to which they were brought as persons held in slavery. In chains in the Western Hemisphere, they were stripped of their names and their languages. They were forced to give up any public recognition of their African past. They were forbidden to learn to read and write. Creatively, African immigrants and their descendants developed unique language forms throughout the Americas and the Caribbean (Sidnell, 2001; Yaron, 2000).

Immigrants from Asia had experiences similar to those of non-English-speaking Europeans and Africans. Their language usage styles and sounds were ridiculed publicly in newspapers, comedy routines, and schools. Research provides evidence that Asian Americans have suffered great pain in their struggle to learn English and thereby become accepted (Tsai, Ying, & Lee, 2001).

Native Americans have endured similar losses of traditional languages. The U.S. federal schools had as a goal to strip indigenous children of their native language and cultural beliefs and practices. Much psychological pain resulted. Native people are presently struggling to relearn their languages and teach them to their children (Reyhner & Tennant, 1995).

This chapter reflects on the salience of language diversity issues in therapy, provides ways of helping psychology and counselor education students learn how to use language diversity in therapy, and makes some recommendations toward enhancing language competence.

SALIENCE OF LANGUAGE DIVERSITY ISSUES IN THERAPY

"In addition to speech, each language carries with it an unspoken network of cultural values" (Reyhner & Tennant, 1995, p. 279). In other words, language is more than words, and translation must be more than literal (Bonomi et al., 1996; Matsumoto, 1994; Stewart & Bennett, 1991; Trimble, this *Handbook,* Volume One). Yet, in spite of the salience of language as an essential aspect of culture, language has not been a major part of the cultural competency dialogue. One of the few places where it is addressed is in Locke (1998), who includes its consideration as part of his paradigm. Furthermore, there has been a dearth of research addressing the salience of language directly in therapy.

Indirectly Related Studies

The significant studies regarding language do not report research related directly to the salience of language in therapy. Publications, for the most part, are in areas of language deficit; typical examples are the reports of Berndt and Mitchum (1997) on cerebral autosomal dominant arteriopathy with subcortical infarcts and leukoencephalopathy disease, Harris and Filley (2001) on brain disease affecting language, and Mimura et al. (2001) on nonfluent aphasia.

Pena (2001) found that language and cultural diversity impact on the validity of evaluating children's vocabulary, and that effective clinical interviews and sensitive feedback are necessary before diagnoses of language impairment can be made. This study can provide a background for developing understanding of how important first-language meanings are to children in therapeutic encounters. Berry (1999) provided evidence for the salience of the language of therapy when he found that using Spanish with Mexican American women resulted in greater compliance with treatment during pregnancy.

Directly Related Studies

Research more directly related to the use of language in therapy is focused on Spanish-first-language clients. Altarriba and Santiago-Rivera (1994) documented the stressors in the lives of Spanish-speaking people in the United States, such as the "language barrier, poverty, and discrimination in education and employment" (p. 388), and demonstrated success in using indigenous communication styles. They also investigated the impact of using more than one language in the same sentence or paragraph and acculturation issues in planning effective counseling strategies. Their article pointed out significant challenges in assessment and planning and executing interventions for therapists who are not fluent in the language of their clients.

Both Altarriba and Santiago-Rivera (1994) and Bradford and Muños (1993) addressed the use of translators in therapy. Three of the many problems inherent in using a translator are:

> Both client and counselor might become frustrated with the extra time it takes to translate information . . . concerns about confidentiality can surface, creating client discomfort . . . the counselor might hesitate in forming conclusions because of the difficulty involved in accurately matching client speech and body language. (Altarriba & Santiago-Rivera, 1994, p. 55)

Another dilemma is the loss of meaning in translation. Translators interpret the meaning of what speakers say to listeners, and interpretation can lead to misunderstanding when translators interpret for therapists and for clients. Translation "may interfere with the therapeutic alliance" (Altarriba & Santiago-Rivera, 1994, p. 391), and information may be distorted, resulting in errors in communication. The same words in the same language may have different meanings in different places. Spanish in Puerto Rico is not the same as Spanish in México. The use of interpreters is expensive, and this interferes with the use of language as a "therapeutic modality" (Altarriba & Santiago-Rivera, 1994, p. 392).

In spite of the problems, however, Bradford and Muños (1993) have demonstrated that carefully trained interpreters can be used effectively in therapy as long as the limitations are taken into consideration. They developed a thoroughly planned strategy and demonstrated its use with a case study in which translation was "direct and concurrent" (p. 53). *Direct* translation meant "offering a literal rendering of the patient's words" (p. 53); that is, no interpretation was allowed. The direct approach requires that therapists are able to read the body language and nonverbals of clients—no easy task. *Concurrent* translation meant that the translation was "occurring simultaneously with the patient's speaking" (p. 53). In a related study, Lin and Cheung (1999) pointed out that research with Asian American groups in the United States suggested that, although Asian Americans underutilize mental health facilities (Sue, 1990, 2001), they use them more frequently when the therapists are culturally competent and can speak the native language of the client.

Dearth of Research

Toppelberg and Shapiro (2000) reviewed 10 years of research on children with communication disorders and found that most of the studies considered only monolingual, English-speaking children. Presently, many children are erroneously evaluated, misdiagnosed as having learning disabilities, and misplaced in special education classes when they are simply struggling to learn English (Geisinger, 1992; Pena,

2001; Valenzuela, 1999). Including studies such as that of Toppelberg and Shapiro in curriculum can provide opportunities to sensitize psychology and counselor education students concerning the limitations of studies done with monolingual, English-speaking children.

Pope-Davis, Ligiero, Liang, and Codrington (2001) summarized the content of the *Journal of Multicultural Counseling and Development* for 15 years prior to the issue in which their article appeared. They found 14 categories, and language was not one of them. The neglect of a serious consideration of how language diversity affects and influences psychotherapy is blatant. Given that psychotherapy is talk-laden, this dearth of consideration in a journal committed to cultural and diversity issues is one indication of the absence of consideration of language issues in psychotherapy in general. Given the salient place that language plays in psychotherapy, it is imperative that language take center stage in research and, concurrently, in the pedagogy preparing counseling psychologists and professional counselors.

Language diversity is becoming an essential component of the present conversation in the United States in education and other fields (Lyon, 1996; Ovando & McLaren, 2000; Richard-Amato, 1996; Valenzuela, 1999). Psychotherapy has some catching up to do. It is necessary that psychology and counselor education programs make the study of language diversity fundamental to their programs.

Those who prepare future therapists in psychology or counselor education programs often are themselves muted by the lack of value the dominant culture places on being multilingual, and consequently, they do not know the importance or have the expertise to engage in pedagogy with students preparing to work with clients whose first language is not English (Freire, 1973, 1985, 1993a, 1993b, 1994a, 1994b, 1998; Gadotti, 1994).

LEARNING HOW TO USE LANGUAGE DIVERSITY EFFECTIVELY

Professors of psychology or counseling who successfully facilitate in their students respect for the principal language of clients not only communicate that they value multilingualism, but provide opportunities in class for students to demonstrate their multilingualism. This can be accomplished if the professor is multilingual or if some of the students in the class are multilingual. For example, a simple activity is for students to read poetry in their first language and explain it to the other members of the class.

In one class, the first author had three students who had three different primary languages read the Prologue to Saint John's Gospel in their primary language. After the reading, the Egyptian American student described the experience this way: "I felt supported. You listened to me with respect. I don't get an opportunity to speak in the language that I use in my home outside of my home very often. I am with other Arabic speakers when I speak Arabic outside my home. This has been an affirming experience. Thank you." The members of the class expressed their appreciation for this experience and mentioned that they now realized on an affective level the importance of language in therapy. If students hear colleagues speaking different languages, then the feelings of being left out because they do not know what is being said are minimized, and students are better able to use the first language of clients effectively.

If both professor and students are monolingual English, then videotapes, DVDs, CDs, the Internet, guests, or other vicarious experiences must be introduced into the classroom to develop knowledge, abilities, and skills in working with clients whose first language is not English. Students can be sent into communities where a language other than English is spoken. Sitting with a group of people who are having a lively conversation in a language that one does not understand can enhance the sensitivity of students to the challenges of clients who are struggling to understand and be understood.

Relationship between Therapist and Client

Research supports the significance of the quality of the relationship between therapist and client (Fiedler, 1950). Clients, as well as students, state that they feel *valued, affirmed, and respected* when they have been able to speak their own language in therapy. Clients can be encouraged to express their feelings in their first language whether or not the therapist is fluent in their language.

For example, in a role-play, a student "counselor" listened to a student "client" share her joys, fears, and anxieties concerning the maturing of her son. The client was having a difficult time articulating her feelings in English. When she was invited by the counselor to speak in her first language, the client's demeanor changed, her tone of voice became softer, and her speech became slower. The counselor asked the client if it would be all right if he paraphrased what he thought he heard her say in her first language. Subsequently, client and counselor engaged in a dialogue about the experience. This was a teachable moment in which the other students in the class learned that one does not have to understand a language to use it effectively in therapy.

Accurate Understanding of Cognitions and Feelings

The problem of understanding is compounded exponentially when the first language of the therapist is different from the first language of the client. It has been said that individuals feel like different people when they move from one language to another (Guttfreund, 1990). Others have explained that it was impossible to get into an activity because they could not feel adequately in English (S. Hanna, personal communication, September 6, 1999; M. Salazar, personal communication, October 10, 1998). Others who are bilingual have said that they speak in the language that "comes into their head," that the language chosen is automatic and related to the context of place and people (M. Faubert Lopez-Velasco & J. Faubert Lopez-Velasco, personal communication, March 10, 2000).

Encouraging bilingual students in class to *cross-code* (to speak interchangeably in more than one language in one sentence or paragraph) acknowledges their need to speak in the language in which they are thinking and feeling. In addition, support provides an environment in which bilingual students are affirmed and monolingual students are given the opportunity to appreciate the skills of their classmates.

Finally, it is imperative that students appreciate the struggles of second-language English speakers and that they become more acutely aware of the limitations of being monolingual.

Even when therapists are well acquainted with the first language of clients, there can be misunderstanding. Students can be taught to check the accuracy in interpretation of cognitions and feelings. Enhancing understanding of cognitions and feelings of clients on the part of therapists is one purpose of the development of basic microskills. When more than one language is involved, the complexity is much greater.

RECOMMENDATIONS TO ENHANCE LANGUAGE COMPETENCE

The Locke paradigm (Locke, 1998) introduces the salience of language in therapy, and the application of Freire's model to therapy and training of language-effective therapists is explained in Locke and Faubert (1999). When students reflect on their own language experiences, they become sensitive to the language issues of their classmates and future clients: Spanish speakers can share that they had their hands slapped with a ruler when they spoke Spanish on the playground; Arabic speakers can share that they had to fight to keep their children out of special education classes when teachers thought their children had language disorders because they were struggling with English; African American students can share the pain they felt when they realized how devalued their language was outside their communities and how hard some worked to unlearn their cultural language.

Sometimes students are surprised when they begin to make meaning of their personal language experiences. One student shared that her father never got over the experience of going to school in the first grade knowing only French. He had shared with his children what it was like to be ridiculed, to have to go home to his grandmother, who could neither read nor write English, and explain what a report card was and the meaning of what was on it. For this 7-year-old, this experience was traumatic and remembered throughout his life and shared with his children.

In one class, an Anglo-American student said that she felt deprived because she could speak only English and had no experience of learning another language (see Appendix). She said that she felt envious of those in the class who could call on thoughts and emotions from more than one perspective. Other students comforted her in her personal feelings of inadequacy and told her that they valued her honesty.

Opportunities to use classroom experiences to enhance an appreciation of client issues are almost limitless. Through dialoguing, role-playing, and perusing research literature, students can strengthen their skills in using language diversity effectively in therapy. Master's theses and dissertations can be written to add to the growing body of research on the subject of using language diversity to enhance the success of therapy.

Academic Classes

If a counselor education program is to be most effective, it must be included in all counseling courses, even theory-based courses, and there should be opportunities for practice. This practice can include demonstrations of counseling by professors, role-playing, and videotapes on which students illustrate effective use of micro-skills and cultural competence directly related to language use. Both academically rigorous discussions and practice provide grist for improved understanding of the significance of language in psychology and professional counseling.

It is recommended that students' practice activities not be evaluated in any way that affects their grades so that students can feel comfortable in their experiences of open dialogue for the purpose of enhancing therapy skills and developing cultural competence and confidence. Most effective is a balance between academic content and consciousness raising:

> Effective teaching for the purpose of preparing culturally competent counselors involves both *conscientization* and praxis phases and includes raising awareness, encouragement to action, and vigorous reflection. (Locke & Faubert, 1999, p. 44)

A requirement in preparing therapists is to recognize the "complex issues, dilemmas, and challenges provided by the situation and circumstances" (Anderson, 1997, p. 245) offered by language differences as an opportunity to enhance therapists' abilities to be instruments of consciousness raising and not of oppression (Freire, 1973, 1993a, 1994b, 1998). Language difference among students can provide penetrating, profound, and personal opportunities in the program to enhance cultural competence and confidence. Consequently, those who are preparing therapists to be effective with clients whose first language is other than English must be able to use the teachable moments that arise in the classroom to enhance appreciation for the unique issues relevant to language diversity in therapy.

Those coming to the United States from nations whose languages are devalued not only are expected to learn English, but are expected to forget the language with which they came. For clients, this expectation is "subtractive" (Valenzuela, 1999, p. 26). What Valenzuela writes about language-different children in schools is often true of language-different clients in counseling sessions:

> They [schools] neither reinforce their native language skills nor their cultural identities . . . the organization of schooling has been historically implicated in the devaluation of the Spanish language, Mexico, Mexican culture, and things Mexican. . . . American institutions have responded *additively* to immigrant groups who come to the United States either as members of an educated class or as speakers of high-status languages. For newcomers who speak a nonstandard linguistic variety, emanate from rural backgrounds, or are nonliterate, U.S. society had been much less welcoming. . . . While possessing an accent in a high-status language is perceived positively and may even constitute an advantage, the same does not hold true for members of historically subordinate groups. (p. 26)

The loss of language can also mean the loss of a sense of identity (E. Gonzalez, personal communication, September 16, 2000). Therefore, the lack of acceptance of a first language on the part of therapists can communicate disrespect for the identity of language-different clients. Like color, the lack of respect for language difference can be used as a "marker for ethnicity" (Valenzuela, 1999, p. 26), resulting in being devalued by insensitive therapists. This is especially true for many Mexican Americans, whether they are recent immigrants or have been in the United States for many generations.

African men, women, and children landed in the Western Hemisphere not only with a land base, culture, and tradition (Carter, 1989) but with many different languages. In the United States, Africans with similar linguistic backgrounds were separated because people who could communicate were a threat of resistance in the oppressive system of slavery. This linguistic separation resulted in the creolization of language. African tones and grammatical patterns were applied to the new language; consequently, many Africanisms survive in African American English (Baugh, 1990).

In addition, social judgments influence the choice of language. Because linguistic patterns are designed to gain respect from those from whom one wants respect (Baugh, 1990), counseling psychology and counselor education students must develop an appreciation for African American sound and content and value them when colleagues or clients use them. An effective way the professor can help students appreciate African American linguistic content and patterns is by reading aloud from works in dialect, such as the poem "Little Brown Baby" by Paul Lawrence Dunbar (Hughes & Bontemps, 1970). This poem is written in African American English. An African American female student shared the inner conflict she felt when she heard the poem because she worked so hard to lose her "Black speech." This same student shared that she often has felt embarrassed when she finds herself using "Black speech" with her friends and that with this exercise and others, she has been able to integrate and resolve her feelings. She remarked that she now feels more comfortable being "bi-dialectic and bi-accentual" (Baugh, 1990).

Counseling psychology and counselor education students who are developing awareness of African American language need to know its African origins and its relationship to linguistic diversity. They need to become sensitive to possible internal conflicts among African Americans when they are choosing registers of language. Choice of register, style, dialect, and accent often depends on the situation in which African Americans find themselves (Baugh, 1990). The classroom is a place to foster appreciation for the complexity of clients' language choices in therapy.

In addition, students need to become aware of national and regional language differences. The United States is a very large nation, and bidialect and biaccent variations either heighten or limit understanding between therapists and clients. As there are social stratification implications in the choice of dialect or accent used in conversation, for example, working-class, middle-class, and upper-class registers, choices can either enhance or inhibit conversation between therapists and clients (Baugh, 1990).

These and other experiences and conversations in classes enhance the cultural competence and confidence of counseling psychology and counselor education students. African American students benefit by reflecting on issues about which they may not have thought for some time; Latin American, Asian American, and Native American students integrate their experiences of language with African American experiences of language and much sharing and mutual support can take place.

European American students have the opportunity to reflect on what they have heard their parents, grandparents, or great-grandparents say about having had a first language devalued and used as a marker for ethnicity (Valenzuela, 1999). Students who have recently come to the United States from various parts of the world can begin to develop an appreciation for racial issues in the United States. U.S. students who represent the dominant culture become aware of their valuing system for African American phonemes, use of words, and grammatical constructions and how their attitudes will translate to clients in therapy sessions.

Psychology and counseling programs need to consider the place that language diversity plays in developing skills for effective counseling. Presently in the United States, whether or not language diversity issues in counseling are examined in programs will affect the retention of language-diverse students and the effectiveness of all students with future clients. All levels of the university must be committed to openly supporting language diversity. Academic knowledge and awareness of issues of language diversity in counseling must be requirements for professors and students. Professors need to apply the consideration of language diversity issues to enhance the quality of programs (Villarreal, 1999) if professional therapists will be culturally competent and confident in the future. The optimal environment to operationalize such programs includes faculty and students from various language groups and racial and ethnic backgrounds. When professors can teach in languages other than English, when students hear professors speaking in languages other than English, and when students witness mutual respect among diverse faculty members, students see models of respect for diversity, including language diversity (Locke & Faubert, 1999).

The Practicum Class

David was a counselor education student enrolled in practicum class. He was conducting a small group session with seven Latino adolescents. The purpose of the session was to help the young men sharpen their negotiating, decision-making, and task-completing skills as a group. David cannot speak Spanish. The young men are bilingual Spanish-English.

David gave the directions in English. The students asked for clarification in English. David gave the students 45-centimeter-long wooden planks, one fewer than the number of young men in the group. Written on the planks were the words *support apoyo, opportunity oportunidad, encouragement dar ánimo, cooperation cooperación, conviction convencido,* and *influence influencia.* These words were chosen because David had been working with these ideas with the young men during their previous sessions. He had asked one of the Spanish-speaking students in his practicum class to help him prepare the planks. The task that the young men had to accomplish was to get from one point to another, about two meters in distance, while stepping only on the planks. After having addressed themselves to the task with gusto, the young men successfully achieved their goal on the second try.

As soon as the group members began to work together to perform the task as David had instructed them, they moved to Spanish. This was the language that they spoke to one another outside of the group and to their parents. Spanish was the language that would make them feel most comfortable as they negotiated the assignment. David demonstrated nonverbally his comfort with the students speaking Spanish in the group. He exhibited respect for the students and for the language the students spoke.

After the activity was completed, the language comfortably returned to English to accommodate David. He and the members of his group talked about the significance of the activity, the reasons for the words being on the planks, and the skills that the young men used to complete the task. David and his group members closed by talking about transferring the skills they had used to succeed in the activity to their families, places of worship, high school, community, and future professions.

David demonstrated a skill that is pivotal to effective therapy: He provided an environment where clients can find their voice:

> I became keenly aware that the voice is not something to be given by those in power. Voice requires struggle and the understanding of both its possibilities and limitations. The most educators [professional psychologists and counselors] can do is to create structures that would enable submerged voices to emerge. It is not a gift. Voice is a human right. It is a democratic right. (Macedo, 1994, p. 4)

The dominant discourse (Anderson, 1997; Gergen, 1999; Holzman & Morss, 2000) overpowers the word spoken from the point of view of clients who come from populations who speak languages that are traditionally devalued. Psychology and counseling training programs are human systems, which "are language- and meaning-generating systems" (Anderson, 1997, p. 3). Students in practicum classes have unique ways of knowing and conversing, and this diversity of knowing and conversing is manifested in the languages that they use. Training programs must develop the skills in their students to enhance their sensitivities to language difference.

The diversity of knowing and conversing demonstrated by multilingualism provides grist for conversation in practicum classes. By sharing their experiences with their first clients, students engage in reciprocal and complementary learning and have the opportunity to practice the humility necessary for genuine dialogue (Freire, 1993a). Psychology and counselor education programs, therefore, become conversations in humility facilitated by professors who respect, value, and integrate the points of view, interpretations, and life experiences of students. The languages in which dialogue takes place demonstrate the salient place that language diversity plays in therapy and counseling. To paraphrase:

> Any group of students, even if homogeneously organized, has diverse [language], learning styles, agendas, and kinds of expertise. All members contribute [in the language characteristic of them]; no [language] is better or more important than another. All [languages] are valued, considered equally important, and viewed as the seeds of [a new way of making meaning of the world]. (Anderson, 1997, p. 245)

When the cultures and languages of professors and students interface, there can be clashes of understanding. There will be struggle because language can be subtle. When professors and students enter into reciprocal pedagogy (Freire, 1993a,

1994a; Locke & Faubert, 1999), there can be misunderstanding exacerbated by language difference among members, resulting in need for clarification. However, the reverberation of reciprocal valuing of language, the tenor and tone of culture, is like the beat of the drum in a wonderful jazz ensemble. It can all come together in the rhythm and symbols of authentic dialogue, and confident, culturally competent professionals can be the result.

Finally, effective pedagogy that maximizes using language difference is a "process of reflective, integrative, and participative thought, feeling, and practice" (Locke & Faubert, 1999, p. 57). Reflection requires conversation with self, and more often than professors might think, this conversation takes place in a language other than standard English. To be participative is to use conversation to make meaning of the world with others. The conversation between professors and students and among students engages students in a journey of reciprocal understanding that will be applied in therapy. This understanding is enhanced when language difference is valued and made part of the public discourse in the classroom.

SUMMARY

This chapter introduced some theories, research, and strategies for enhancing appreciation for language diversity in preparing culturally competent and confident therapists. It has drawn on disciplines outside of psychology and counseling. Both academic and practicum classes have been considered. There is much research and practice left to be done. It is recommended that the conversation on cultural competence and confidence include an in-depth study of language diversity and its role in effective counseling.

APPENDIX

How Does It Feel?

Psychology and counseling students who are monolingual English need the experience of what it feels like to be in a situation where they are struggling to understand and be understood. In addition, students for whom English is not their first language benefit from the practice of sharing their experiences about what it is like to struggle to understand and be understood in English.

One exercise that has been effectively used in a counselor education class to enhance understanding of language diversity was designed and presented by María Salazar, a bilingual professional school counselor, while she was a graduate student. It is used here with her permission (M. Salazar, personal communication, January 15, 2002).

The purpose of this activity is to enhance the appreciation for language-different clients and their families in a school or agency setting. María is introduced in English by another person because she does not want the participants to hear her speak English. The person who introduces her explains that this will be a unique experience. María introduces the activity in Spanish: "I will read a short story about a

Mexican American family. As I read the story, I want each of you to listen very carefully to the content of the story and to ask as many questions as is necessary because at the end of the story I will be giving a short quiz."

María writes on the chalkboard *Clase de Literatura México-Americana.* Each member is given the following short story, which María reads aloud to them:

A los tres niños los dejaban en casa cuando se iban a trabajar porque al viejo no le gustaba que anduvieran los niños en la labor haciendo travesuras o quitándoles el tiempo a los padres. Habían tratado de llevarlos con ellos y mantenerlos en el carro pero se había puesto muy caliente el día y muy bochornoso y hasta se habían puesto enfermos. Desde entonces decidieron dejarlos en casa major, aunque eso sí, todo el día andaban bien preocupados por ellos. En lugar de echar lonche iban a casa a comer a medio día y así se daban cuanta de que si estaban bien o no. Ese siguiente lunes se levantaron como siempre de madrugadita y se fueron a trabajar. Los niños se quedaron bient dormiditos. (Rivera, 1987, pp. 44–45)

After reading the story, María summarizes it in Spanish. She then distributes the following quiz, reads the questions, and gives the students five minutes to complete the quiz. She deliberately does not extend much empathy to the students for taking a test in a language that most of the participants either cannot read at all or can read only with differing degrees of struggle. These directions are designed not to be particularly sensitive to the limitations of language of many of the participants:

Exámen

Nombre completo: _____

Fecha: _____

Escribe una sola oración para contestar las siguientes preguntas y escribe las respuestas con lápiz por favor. Si tienes alguna pregunta sobre las prejunta levanta la mano por favor y te ayudaré lo más pronto possible.

1. ¿Cuál es el título de esta pequeña historia México-Americana?
2. ¿Quien es el autor de las historia que acabamos de leer?
3. ¿Cúales son los nombres de los personajes de la historia y cúales son sus edades?
4. ¿De que se trata la historia?
5. ¿Que tragedia occurrió en esta historia?
6. ¿Quien fue el único de los niños que sobrevivió esta tragedia?

María continues by asking the participants to write the feelings and thoughts that they experienced during the activity. After giving the students about 10 minutes to reflect and write, she invites them to share their feelings and thoughts. She asks the students what they think it means to be sensitive to someone else's feelings or needs regarding language. She invites the students to imagine themselves in the place of children and adults who have similar experiences every day in schools and agencies.

María suggests to her classmates that they learned how difficult it is to know how someone else is feeling, especially when trying to communicate in a second language.

She reminds her colleagues that they can become sensitive to the feelings of others in spite of first-language differences. The counselor education students express their appreciation to María for this experience.

REFERENCES

Altarriba, J., & Santiago-Rivera, A. L. (1994). Current perspectives on using linguistic and cultural factors in counseling the Hispanic client. *Professional Psychology: Research and Practice, 25,* 388–397.

Anderson, H. (1997). *Conversation, language, and possibilities: A postmodern approach to therapy.* New York: Basic Books.

Baugh, J. (1990, September). *Linguistic diversity and conflict among African Americans.* Symposium conducted at North Carolina State University, Raleigh.

Berndt, R. S., & Mitchum, C. C. (1997). Lexical-semantic organization: Evidence from aphasia. *Clinical Neuroscience, 4,* 57–63.

Berry, A. B. (1999). Mexican American women's expressions of the meaning of culturally congruent prenatal care. *Journal of Transcultural Nursing, 10,* 203–212.

Bonomi, A. E., Cella, D. F., Hahn, E. A., Bjordak, K., Sperner-Uterweger, B., Gangeri, L., et al. (1996). Multilingual translation of the Functional Assessment of Cancer Therapy (FACT) quality of life measurement system. *Quality of Life Research, 5,* 309–320.

Bradford, D. T., & Muños, A. (1993). Translation in bilingual psychotherapy. *Professional Psychology: Research and Practice, 24,* 52–61.

Carter, M. J. (1989). *Why African American.* Garrison, NY: Graymoor.

Fiedler, F. (1950). The concept of an ideal therapeutic relationship. *Journal of Counseling Psychology, 14,* 239–245.

Freire, P. (1973). *Education for critical consciousness* (M. B. Ramos, Trans.). New York: Continuum. (Original work published 1969)

Freire, P. (1985). *The politics of education: Culture, power, and liberation* (D. Macedo, Trans.). South Hadley, MA: Bergin & Hadley.

Freire, P. (1993a). *Pedagogy of the oppressed: New revised 20th-anniversary edition* (M. B. Ramos, Trans.). New York: Continuum.

Freire, P. (1993b). *Pedagogy of the city* (D. Macedo, Trans.). New York: Continuum.

Freire, P. (1994a). *Pedaogy of hope: Reliving pedagogy of the oppressed* (R. R. Barr, Trans.). New York: Continuum. (Original work published 1992)

Freire, P. (1994b). *Paulo Freire on higher education: A dialogue at the National University of New Mexico.* Albany: State University of New York Press.

Freire, P. (1998). *Teachers as cultural workers: Letters to those who dare to teach* (D. Macedo, D. Koike, & A. Oliveira, Trans.). Boulder, CO: Westview.

Gadotti, M. (1994). *Reading Paulo Freire: His life and work* (J. Milton, Trans.). Albany: State University of New York Press.

Geisinger, K. F. (1992). Fairness and selected psychometric issues in the psychological testing of Hispanics. In K. F. Geisinger (Ed.), *Psychological testing of Hispanics* (pp. 17–42). Washington, DC: American Psychological Association.

Gergen, K. J. (1999). *An invitation to social construction.* Thousand Oaks, CA: Sage.

Guttfreund, D. G. (1990). Effects of language usage on the emotional experience of Spanish-English and English-Spanish bilinguals. *Journal of Consulting and Clinical Psychology, 58,* 604–607.

Harris, J. G., & Filley, C. M. (2001). CADASIL: Neurophychological findings in three generations of an affected family. *Journal of the International Neuropsychological Society, 7,* 768–774.

Holzman, L., & Morss, J. (Eds.). (2000). *Postmodern psychologies, societal practice, and political life.* New York: Routledge.

Hughes, L., & Bontemps, A. (Eds.). (1970). *The poetry of the Negro. (1746–1970).* Garden City, NY: Doubleday.

Lin, K. M., & Cheung, F. (1999). Mental health issues for Asian Americans. *Psychiatric Services, 50,* 774–780.

Locke, D. C. (1998). *Increasing multicultural understanding: A comprehensive model* (2nd ed.). Thousand Oaks, CA: Sage.

Locke, D. C., & Faubert, M. (1999). Innovative pedagogy for critical consciousness in counselor education. In M. S. Kiselica (Ed.), *Confronting prejudice and racism during multicultural training* (pp. 43–58). Alexandria, VA: American Counseling Association.

Lyon, J. (1996). *Becoming bilingual: Language acquisition in a bilingual community.* Philadelphia: Multilingual Matters.

Macedo, D. (1994). *Literacies of power: What Americans are not allowed to know.* Boulder, CO: Westview Press.

Matsumoto, D. (1994). *People: Psychology from a cultural perspective.* Pacific Grove, CA: Brooks/Cole.

Mimura, M., Oda, T., Tsuchiya, K., Kato, M., Ikeda, K., Hori, K., et al. (2001). Corticobasal degeneration presenting with nonfluent primary progressive aphasia: A clinicopathological study. *Journal of the Neurological Sciences, 183,* 19–26.

Ovando, C. J., & McLaren, P. (Eds.). (2000). *The politics of multiculturalism and bilingual education: Students and teachers in the cross fire.* Boston: McGraw-Hill.

Pena, E. D. (2001). Assessment of semantic knowledge: Use of feedback and clinical interviewing. *Seminars in Speech and Language, 22,* 51–62.

Pope-Davis, D. B., Ligiero, D. P., Liang, C., & Codrington, J. (2001). Fifteen years of the *Journal of Multicultural Counseling and Development:* A content analysis. *Journal of Multicultural Counseling and Development, 29,* 226–238.

Reyhner, J., & Tennant, E. (1995). Maintaining and renewing native languages. *Bilingual Research Journal, 19,* 279–304.

Richard-Amato, P. A. (1996). *Making it happen: Interaction in the second language classroom: From theory to practice* (2nd ed.). White Plains, NY: Longman.

Rivera, T. (1987). . . . . *y no se lo tragó la tierra.* Houston, TX: Arte Publico.

Sidnell, J. (2001). Conversation turn-taking in Caribbean English Creole. *Journal of Pragmatics, 33,* 1263–1290.

Stewart, E. C., & Bennett, M. J. (1991). *American cultural patterns: A cross-cultural perspective* (Rev. ed.). Yarmouth, ME: Intercultural.

Sue, D. W. (1990). Culture-specific strategies in counseling: A conceptual framework. *Professional Psychology: Research and Practice, 21,* 424–433.

Sue, D. W. (2001). Surviving multiculturalism and racism: A personal and professional journey. In J. G. Ponterotto, J. M. Casas, L. A. Suzuki, & C. M. Alexander (Eds.), *Handbook of multicultural counseling* (2nd ed., pp. 45–54). Thousand Oaks, CA: Sage.

Toppelberg, C. O., & Shapiro, T. (2000). Language disorders: A 10-year research update review. *Journal of the American Academy of Child and Adolescent Psychiatry, 39,* 143–152.

Trimble, J. E. (in press). An inquiry into the measurement of ethnic and racial identity. In R. T. Carter (Ed.), *Handbook of racial-cultural psychology and counseling: Theory and research* (Vol. 1, pp. 320–359). Hoboken, NJ: Wiley.

Tsai, J. L., Ying, Y.-W., & Lee, P. A. (2001). Cultural predictors of self-esteem: A study of Chinese American females and male young adults. *Cultural Diversity and Ethnic Minority Psychology, 7,* 284–297.

Valenzuela, A. (1999). *Subtractive schooling: U.S.-Mexican youth and the politics of caring.* Albany: State University of New York Press.

Villarreal, A. (1999). Rethinking the education of English language learners: Transitional bilingual education programs. *Bilingual Research Journal, 23,* 11–45.

Walsh, C. E. (1991). *Literacy as praxis: Culture, language, and pedagogy.* Norwood, NJ: Ablex.

Yaron, M. (2000). Mixed languages: A functional-communicative approach. *Bilingualism: Language and Cognition, 3,* 79–99.

CHAPTER 8

Racial-Cultural Training for Group Counseling and Psychotherapy

Mary B. McRae and Ellen L. Short

Although there is a growing literature on multicultural counselor training that focuses on individual counseling and psychotherapy (Atkinson, 2003; Atkinson, Morten, & Sue, 1989, 1997; Casas, 1984; McRae & Johnson, 1991; Pedersen, 1991, this *Handbook,* Volume One; Sue & Sue, 1999, 2003), we know little about racial-cultural training in group counseling and psychotherapy. The purpose of professional training is to prepare counselors and psychologists to help people who may come from a variety of racial and cultural groups to function better interpersonally and in groups and organizations. If groups are indeed a microcosm of the larger society (Yalom, 1985), then a focus on issues such as race and culture in the training literature for group counseling and psychotherapy seems to be crucial in the preparation of mental health professionals. The demographic transitions of the twenty-first century as well as the need for group treatment with large clinical populations suggest that racial-cultural factors will become increasingly important.

Racial and cultural factors are an integral part of daily life in many places in the United States. Race

> refers to a group of people who share biological features that come to signify group membership and the social meaning such membership has in the society at large. Race becomes the basis for expectation regarding social roles, performance levels, values, and norms and mores for group, nongroup and in-group members. (Jones, 1993, p. 9)

Goldberger and Veroff (1995) identify traditional definitions of culture as groups of people who share a common history, geographic region, language, rituals, beliefs, values, rules, and laws (Johnson, this *Handbook,* Volume One). Additionally, contemporary definitions of culture in a pluralistic society mark individuals with shared characteristics as members of a group. Thus, groups identified by race, gender, class, ethnicity, sexual identity, disability, and age may call themselves "cultures," and be regarded as such by others, despite their membership in the larger culture and dissimilarities of history, language, rules, beliefs, and cultural practices. Our use of the term "racial-cultural" in this chapter embodies these definitions as they apply to group training for counseling and psychotherapy.

The purpose of racial-cultural group training is to teach trainees to work competently with people from diverse racial-cultural backgrounds and to provide an emotional and corrective or transforming experience in their lives. The paucity of existing literature concerning racial-cultural aspects of training in group counseling and psychotherapy reflects the profession's ambivalence about fully incorporating components of race and culture into research, training, and curricula. The ambivalence may be related to the difficulties inherent in systemic and institutionalized structures in academic environments, which are often resistant to exploring certain topics, in much the same way that groups may tend to suppress and exhibit reluctance to explore sensitive and uncomfortable topics.

In a larger social-historical context, this ambivalence about exploring race and culture also has its roots in the American cultural experience (Carter, this *Handbook,* this volume). Toni Morrison (1992) in *Playing in the Dark: Whiteness and the Literary Imagination,* states, "In matters of race, silence and evasion have historically ruled literary discourse" (pp. 10–11). She further states that silence and evasion have historically been viewed as effective methods of enforcing the invisibility of the African American presence in the dominant culture. This condition of invisibility perpetuates the emergence of an "other" to which one group can compare itself via the use of racist stereotypes and projections. While Morrison's focus is on African Americans, the "other" can easily be any disenfranchised group. We may hypothesize, therefore, that the inability to fully explore and embrace issues of race and culture in curricula and group psychotherapy training programs may be an example of reinforcing long-held patterns of denial of the pervasiveness of racial-cultural dynamics in institutionalized environments.

In many academic and training environments, for example, issues of member inclusion/exclusion exist primarily along racial-cultural lines, along with stereotyped assumptions about differences. Moreover, the composition of these environments is often representative of power differentials that exist in society. Despite the existence of these conditions, however, academic and training institutions are often reluctant to assess their internal racial and cultural climates. This reluctance has very often led to the development of curricula and training models that are etic and ethnocentric in content (Highlen, 1994; Sue & Torino, this *Handbook,* this volume). In light of rapidly changing demographics in client/patient care, the lack of curricula and training on racial-cultural factors is not only harmful to emerging professionals, it is also unethical. Highlen cites the importance of doctoral programs developing methods with which to assess internal levels of institutional commitment to multiculturalism and diversity. Implicit in this perspective is the belief that systemic functioning greatly impacts the quality of training that students receive. Thus, academic environments, organizationally, are very much like groups, which are, as Yalom (1985) suggests, a microcosm of the larger society. A focus, therefore, on issues of race and culture at the institutional level *and* in the training literature for group counseling and psychotherapy is crucial to the education and training of mental health professionals.

In this chapter, we provide a brief overview of some of the major issues considered in the traditional group counseling and psychotherapy training literature. This is a literature that has addressed racial-cultural factors minimally, not taking advantage of the fact that groups are a microcosm of society in which race and culture are an integral part of the daily experience of many individuals who live in urban or racially heterogeneous environments. We then examine the scant training literature on group counseling and psychotherapy that has addressed racial-cultural factors, and present group relations theory as a framework for group counseling and psychotherapy training. Last, we make some recommendations for future training and research.

TRADITIONAL MODELS OF GROUP TRAINING

Group counseling and psychotherapy are considered by some to be a multidimensional laboratory for living (Yalom, 1985, 1995). This means that those being trained in this area must be prepared to address the multitude of issues that confront us in our daily lives. The traditional literature's approach to training has been more etic (racially and culturally generalized) than emic (racially and culturally specific), assuming that the methods and concepts can be generalized to all trainee and client populations (Johnson, 1990). The etic view can be problematic because of its reliance on a Eurocentric point of view that espouses the application of generalized definitions of social reality; whether there is a method of training that is appropriate for groups consisting of individuals from different racial-cultural groups needs to be explored. A method that encourages collaborative dialogue that is meaningful and engaging and allows differentiation of culture, style, and personality is needed. Traditional models for training in psychology and multicultural counselor education have been focused primarily on teaching trainees to *know that* cultural differences exist and secondarily on teaching them to *know how* to apply racial/cultural awareness and knowledge (Carter, this *Handbook,* this volume; McRae & Johnson, 1991). The question of how to engage across differences needs to be a primary consideration in group training of counselors and psychologists.

Traditional models for group counseling and psychotherapy training have focused on methods and process. The methods that have been identified as most useful are didactic and include observation of experienced clinicians, a personal group experience, practice, and supervision (Conyne, Wilson, Kline, Morran, & Ward, 1993; Kibel, 1987; Klein, Bernard, & Singer, 1992; Shaffer & Galinsky, 1989; Yalom, 1985, 1995). While most agree that training should include the study and discussion of group theory and engage the trainee in some type of group experience, few go as far as Yalom (1985), who suggests personal psychotherapeutic work for trainees.

Some of the etic models that have been developed for experiential learning provide a framework for studying racial-cultural factors in group training. However, they tend not to address racial-cultural factors in a direct manner as an integral part of the training process, but merely as an assumption that needs testing and further exploration. Glass and Benshoff (1999) developed a processing model that can be used in training to help group members identify and examine their experiences in groups. They propose a structure for thinking about and intervening with groups for more effective facilitation of the learning process. The model focuses on three stages: reflecting, understanding, and applying. In each of these stages the trainee is taught to focus on the activity, the relationship to and in the group, and the self. Smaby, Maddux, Torres-Rivera, and Zimmick (1999) developed a similar model. They identify the stages of counseling as exploring, understanding, and acting. They claim that their model also teaches intuitive and responsive skills, such as appropriate self-disclosure, immediacy, and confrontation skills. Each of these models call for reflection, exploring, understanding, and applying what one learns about others interpersonally.

The traditional models reviewed provide methods and processes for "knowing that" and "knowing how" to work with groups. However, they provide no mention of "knowing that" racial-cultural issues exist in all groups, some more salient than others, and "knowing how" to manage racial-cultural issues in groups (Carter, this *Handbook,* this volume).

Working across differences such as race and culture requires awareness of self and others, understanding of racial and cultural differences, and a willingness to develop skills that enhance interpersonal communication (Sue, Bingham, Porche-Burke, & Vasquez, 1999). The establishment of professional standards for the training of group workers has been helpful in developing basic competencies for evaluation, understanding theories, leadership styles, principles of group dynamics, ethical concerns, and therapeutic factors, and methods for recruiting and selecting members. The Association for Specialists in Group Work, a division of the American Counseling Association, endorsed principles for diversity-competent group workers in 1999. The notion that issues of race and culture were important concepts to be addressed in group counseling and psychotherapy was a crucial step forward.

APPROACHES TO RACIAL-CULTURAL GROUP TRAINING

There is a scarcity of literature on racial and cultural factors in training for group counseling and psychotherapy. Race and culture are considered elements of the social structure and dimensions of human representation (Omi & Howard, 1994). Racial-cultural group training can help trainees to explore both positive and negative attributions made to individuals and to racial-cultural groups in the form of stereotypes, attitudes, feelings, and behaviors.

The early literature on racial-cultural factors focused more on learning about how differences influenced groups rather than on training; the later literature began to address training issues as well. Much of the literature on interracial group psychotherapy published in the 1970s and early 1980s described the relationships among members as dichotomous and polarized along racial lines, with the African American members being angry and hostile and those of European descent being defensive and guilty (Brayboy, 1971; Burke, 1984; Kibel, 1972; Patterson & Smits, 1974). The literature also must be considered in a social-historical context. For example, the Black civil rights movement in the United States in the late 1960s and early 1970s highlighted differences between racial groups. It was an era when the nigrescence linear stage models of racial identity were developed and introduced, thus further emphasizing the impact of society on the development of psychological theories and research focusing on race (Constantine & Wilton, this *Handbook,* this volume).

The methods for training in group work have rarely considered their relevance to trainees from different racial and cultural backgrounds. While the positives and the negatives of each of the training methods have been identified (Berger, 1996), no studies were found that indicate whether the didactic or experiential method is preferred or most useful for trainees from different racial and cultural groups. We know little about the preferred racial or cultural composition or racial and cultural climate of training groups (Davis, 1981). Choice of training methods is most often based on the phase of professional education of trainees, class size, and availability of resources. Berger notes that class composition should also be considered, but viewed confrontations between trainees from different backgrounds as problematic and a reason to move to more structured or didactic methods that would contain anxiety. However, attempts to contain anxiety in mixed racial-cultural groups may be related to concerns about allowing some of the emotions associated with prejudice and oppression to surface in a training setting. In our view, confrontation and conflict can create opportunities to learn about differences. Excessive containment of these emotions in the training room may impede the trainees' emerging awareness and understanding of these processes as well as the development of management skills for future use with client populations.

One concern in interracial groups that has received little attention is that of racial composition and balance (Davis, 1979). Davis did a study using undergraduate students to explore the racial preferences of Blacks and Whites for the composition of group members. His work suggested that Blacks and Whites have different conceptions of what constitutes the proper racial balance in a group. Black people seem to prefer groups with equal numbers of Whites and Blacks, whereas White people seem to prefer groups that are proportionate to societal representation. For example, if Whites see themselves as being in the majority or 70% of the population, then they are more comfortable in a group in which they are the majority.

Racial composition is related to status in groups. Those in the majority group often have more status than those in the minority. Status incongruence in groups relates to power, authority, leadership, and member roles. Tsui and Schulz (1988) suggested that in racially mixed groups, the power relationship between the "minority" and the "majority" must be understood before dealing with cultural differences. Tsui and Schulz purport that those who set the norms of the group are the majority and that attempts to engage the minority through "premature requests for disclosure" or feedback may be an invasion of personal boundaries (p. 137). Those who belong to racial-cultural groups in the minority may perceive the requests as demands by the powerful collective to educate them about "the minority experience." The responsibility for working across differences becomes that of the "minority group" and not the group as a whole.

Racial issues in groups are often associated with power, privilege, and prejudice in this society. Racial issues in groups may also be associated with cultural dynamics concerning language and verbal participation. For example, group norms may be enforced by the majority members who place value on verbal fluency and demonstrations of intellectual acuity that may feel uncomfortable to some group members. The majority voice in the group has long been demonstrated as a call for conformity in social psychology and may influence those in the minority to question their own judgment when confronted by those in the majority (Asch, 1952, 1956). The pressure in groups is to conform to the norms of the group. Thus, the question in diverse racial-cultural groups is: Who sets the norm and how?

The literature that focuses directly on group training using racial and cultural factors is minuscule. Larry Davis (1981), a professor of social work, wrote one of the earliest articles that focused specifically on racial issues in training of group workers (Hurdle, this *Handbook,* this volume). He suggested that group practitioners learn about racial dynamics in groups, such as leader-member status and the impact of racial composition in the group. The methods of training recommended were racial consciousness raising in classrooms, role-play, and closely supervised practica that provide an opportunity to practice with clients from different racial and cultural backgrounds.

Davis and colleagues developed a framework for leadership of multiracial groups (Davis, Galinsky, & Schopler, 1995). This framework, called RAP (recognize, anticipate, and problem-solve), is intended to alert practitioners to potential problem areas, identify underlying racial dynamics, validate concerns, and guide the selection of appropriate interventions. Their model actively engages the practitioner in addressing a wide number of concerns that have been identified as important in multiracial groups. It calls for the practitioner to be self-aware as well as aware of the group's racial dynamics. The need for self-assessment of one's own racial and cultural attitudes and values has been a continuing premise for multicultural training (Carter, 2001; McRae & Johnson, 1991). The RAP model also notes the need to acknowledge racial and ethnic differences that exist in the group and discuss their salience and the awkwardness people feel as it surfaces in the group. The problem-solving component of the model calls for the leader to use interventions and goals that are culturally appropriate and acceptable to the group and to convey respect and genuineness through behavior. Stopping the action of the group and confronting racial problems between members directly in accordance with predetermined rules is deemed by the authors to be helpful in developing skills for use outside of the group (Hurdle, this *Handbook,* this volume).

Another approach to training that seems to have potential is one that engages the trainee in a search for basic parameters, such as spatial, time, and emotional boundaries, that can be considered in terms of cultural similarities and differences and their meanings to groups (Falicov, 1995). The practitioners explore their own values and life experiences in four parameters—ecological context, migration/acculturation, organization, and life cycle—to develop self-awareness before working with others from different racial-cultural backgrounds. This approach is important in training group leaders to examine systemic issues and to heighten awareness about the location of knowledge and their own professional and personal culture. Other authors have called for more effective multicultural training of group workers and provide an overview of the major issues to be considered, such as racial identity development and racial consciousness (Greeley, Garcia, Kessler, & Gilchrist, 1992).

GROUP RELATIONS MODEL: AN OPTION FOR RACIAL-CULTURAL GROUP TRAINING

Most of the work reviewed on group counseling and psychotherapy training suggests that didactic observation and experiential learning that provides an opportunity for reflection on here-and-now experiences, understanding of the relationship between theory and experience, and application has proved most beneficial. Yalom (1985, 1995) suggests that here-and-now feelings are the major discourse that drives the life of the group and "facilitates the development and emergence of each member's social microcosm" (p. 135), making the group more vital and engaging each member more intensely. Group process involves close attention to what occurs in the here-and-now experience of the group. Identifying these processes as they occur in the here and now has been identified as crucial to trainee learning (Wiggins & Carroll, 1993).

In keeping with the emphasis on the here and now, we offer the group relations model for racial-cultural group training. The model was developed at the Tavistock Institute for Human Relations in the United Kingdom and later brought to the United States. The theoretical roots of the model can be traced to Wilfred Bion, Melanie Klein, and Kurt Lewin. The group relations approach encompasses all that the literature reviewed in this chapter suggests is important for training of future professionals in racial-cultural group work. Conceptually, this model uses systems and psychodynamic theory to explore its premise that the individual acts on behalf of the group, given the group norms and the cultural context in which the group occurs. Within each group or system, there are boundaries, authority issues, roles, and tasks to be considered that will vary according to the culture of the group. The group functions on a number of levels: intrapsychic, interpersonal, group, and intergroup (Wells, 1990). Thus, we need to consider the individual personality characteristics, interpersonal relations, the group as a whole, and relationships between subgroups.

The psychodynamics of the group can be understood from the perspective of object relations and interpersonal theory. Object relations theory addresses psychological defenses that are used in interactions with others. Interpersonal theory addresses the relational aspects of these interactions. The most commonly used defenses in groups are splitting and projective identification. At a basic level, splitting refers to the process of dividing the world (and others) into all good and all bad (Reed & Noumair, 2000). Reed and Noumair describe splitting as the

> polarization of specific characteristics as contained within individuals or subgroups, whereby all of a particular quality is perceived as being contained within one, and all of its opposite contained within another. (p. 58)

Projective identification is the process by which undesirable or ambivalent aspects of the self or group are projected onto other individuals or groups. The individual or group receiving the projection is subtly encouraged to unconsciously identify with the projections and behave as if they are a reality. Their identification with the projections is on behalf of the group as a whole.

When individuals in groups express the feelings of others, they are considered to have a "valence," or an unconscious disposition for such expression, or they are exhibiting prescribed societal roles related to their demographic characteristics. Fenster (1996) suggested that polarization between racial groups may occur as a possible mechanism of defenses such as resistance, intellectualization, and projective identification. Fenster indicated that intellectualization may be used as a defense by group members in the majority to focus on superficial cultural or racial attributes of those members in the minority. Cheng, Chase, and Gunn (1998) suggested that splitting and projective identification are major defenses used in mixed racial-cultural groups to protect against feelings of inadequacy and vulnerability.

Racial and cultural issues in mixed groups may be related to power differentials and authority and class hierarchies that exist in society. Demographic variables such as race, culture, class, sexual orientation, gender, and disability often represent differences between group members that may carry negative, uncomfortable evaluations and stimulate feelings about inclusion and exclusion. Given that inclusion/exclusion is one of the issues that all groups struggle with, any kind of difference, visible or invisible, will serve as a catalyst for feelings about membership to emerge. Stereotyped assumptions about differences also influence a group member's perception of self and others. Members who belong to the dominant racial-cultural group may perceive themselves or be perceived as powerful and privileged; members who belong to the nondominant group may perceive themselves as powerless or powerful, given the particular context of the group. The ways members from different groups interact is considered by some to be directly related to issues of power and authority relations (Bennis & Shepard, 1974; Bion, 1959; Ota Wang, this *Handbook,* this volume). The intersection of racial-cultural factors and power, authority, and interpersonal relations seem central to any discussion of group processes (Ramsey, 1997) and are an integral part of study in the group relations model.

It has been suggested that one of the best ways to teach group psychotherapy is through group dynamics (Kibel, 1987). Group dynamics involve the study of the structure and function of groups and a focus on group behavior, specifically the interactions that occur among persons in groups (Microsoft Encarta Encyclopedia, 1999). A number of studies have been conducted on group dynamics, covering factors such as projection (Kivlighan, Marsh-Angelone, & Angelone, 1994), stages of group development (Kivlighan & Mullison, 1988), group process variables (e.g., therapeutic relationship, therapeutic interventions, and therapeutic factors; Fuhriman & Burlingame, 1990; Yalom, 1985), and power and authority relations (Bennis & Shepard, 1974; Bion, 1959). However, few have studied how racial and cultural issues impact these dynamic factors. Widely held assumptions concerning the scarcity of power in our society lead to questions about who has power, access, and control of material resources and the ability to shape and influence decisions and agendas; these are all crucial points to study (Reed & Noumair, 2000). Given the fact that racial and cultural factors often represent power, authority, and class or status hierarchies in society, the lack of attention to them may be reflective of existing societal structures that perpetuate the invisibility and institutionalization of a dominant culture in which privileges are readily available to some subgroups and not to others. Understanding the confluence of stereotypes, projection, and interpersonal style that exists within the group process would increase our ability to negotiate and collaborate among and between racial and cultural groups in society (Carter, this *Handbook,* this volume). The group relations model addresses power hierarchies that exist and provides a foundation to examine systemic structures and their relationships to racial-cultural factors.

Slavson (1956) provided the premise for further consideration of the group relations model for racial-cultural group training many years ago. In one of the earliest articles dealing with racial and cultural factors in group psychotherapy, the author provides a description of his work with Jewish, "Negro," and Irish groups (Slavson, 1956). According to Slavson, historical experiences and cultural patterns accounted for most of the differences in group therapy between those from different racial-cultural groups. He suggested that a social-historical context of the group experience was the most important distinction. He states: "From our observations of the racial groups of patients it would seem that they are fundamentally the same as to psychologic needs, anxieties, and motivations" (p. 161). Slavson suggested that the social and historical context made a difference in peoples lives: He attributed what he called "weak family cohesiveness" among Negroes to slavery; he attributed "the neurotic fatalistic reactions" of the Irish to "centuries of famine, poverty, and often inhumane treatment . . . at the hands of their conquerors, the English" (p. 158). Historically and culturally, we develop different ways of being and managing our everyday lives (Carter & Pieterse, this *Handbook,* this volume).

While Slavson (1956) used the most negative aspects to account for differences in the lives of people he worked with, we are now aware of the wealth of positive aspects of each racial-cultural group. The point that he did make that we believe holds true is that psychologically, the needs, anxieties, and motivations of individuals are more similar than different. Thus, the historical and cultural patterns may cause individuals to respond differently in their behaviors, but emotionally from similar places. Slavson suggested and Yalom (1985) verified in his work that certain curative factors in groups, such as instillation of hope, universality, or knowing that one is not alone in what one is feeling, catharsis (expression of emotions), altruism, reenactment of family dynamics for corrective experiences, and interpersonal learning, are constant across differences. We believe that the group relations model provides a mechanism for learning about and experiencing emotions and understanding them in the context of the group and broader society.

The group relations model provides opportunities to focus on the role of the individual in the context of the group as a whole: boundaries, authority, and tasks of the group or institution. The model also provides a unique template for understanding the psychodynamic processes that occur within and between various social identity groups. The framework is clearly identified and open for study by all those who participate. The group relations model has potential for training students to become more aware and alert to racial and cultural factors as they relate to systemic and psychodynamic processes. Because this model provides opportunities to learn through experience and reflection, using both intellect and emotions without neglecting one for the other, it allows students to try out new behaviors and discuss them as they learn. This experiential focus provides the opportunity to explore interactions in the here and now as they occur. Thus, cognitions, behaviors, and emotions are allowed to surface together for identification and possible exploration. The power of such experiences for racial-cultural group training has the potential to significantly enhance trainee learning.

Continued use of the group relations model for training counselors and psychologists reflects the importance of utilizing and expanding existing models to include racial and cultural group dynamics. The systems and psychodynamic approach of the model seems particularly appropriate for training in racial and cultural factors in groups, mainly because it encompasses opportunities to observe behaviors, identify feelings, and apply them to other settings. What is needed in future explorations of the model is a focus on understanding the various behaviors of individuals from different racial-cultural backgrounds. For example, how is behavior from members of various racial-cultural groups understood, and what is the mechanism for training those who use the model to become more aware of different behavioral responses? How is behavior linked to emotions for various racial-cultural groups, and what training tools are needed to better understand the connections? Are Slavson's (1956) and Yalom's (1985) assumptions and findings about curative factors across groups valid? Are modifications of the group relations model needed to better understand behaviors of different racial and cultural groups? Is there a universal model for training that works for diverse groups? At this point, what exists is mostly anecdotal data. Thus, research on the appropriateness of various models of training needs to be a priority on our agenda.

CONCLUSION: NEW DIRECTIONS FOR TRAINING AND RESEARCH

The lack of an abundant body of literature and research concerning race and culture in group counseling and psychotherapeutic training is unfortunate. The situation can, however, be viewed as an opportunity to expand on existing theories and create new models for the future. Training models for the future should continue to incorporate practitioner self-assessment of racial and cultural attitudes, and these models should facilitate the training of practitioners of European descent *and* practitioners of Color working with diverse groups. Training methods should also expand on traditional psychodynamic theory and continue to explore the defense mechanisms of splitting, projection, and projective identification and group process in relation to race, ethnicity, and culture. Issues of power, authority, leadership, dependency, and interdependency in groups should be included in relation to these variables. Additionally, training models that espouse worldviews that are non-Eurocentric should be introduced. Finally, group counseling and psychotherapy training models should incorporate time-limited and brief forms of group therapy with diverse populations in applied settings (see Hurdle, this *Handbook,* this volume).

It would be advantageous for researchers and practitioners involved in developing racial-cultural group counseling and psychotherapy training programs to explore existing links between societal events that illuminate the complexities of race, ethnicity, and culture (e.g., in areas of politics, race/gender-power dynamics) in a group relations context. Creating links between the external environment of the world to the internal academic environment in training facilitates an ability to apply learned theory in relevant contexts, as well as a knowledge of group functioning that is not bound solely by ivory tower, elitist perspectives.

This chapter has addressed some of the major issues that currently exist in the profession and the literature regarding the racial-cultural factors of group counseling and psychotherapy training. It has also provided the reader with key suggestions for continued development of training programs that incorporate race and culture as important, integral components of group life, instead of merely peripheral, superficial aspects to be focused on haphazardly, or not at all. If the profession of counseling psychology is going to continue to impact and serve society in a meaningful way, it is imperative that academic programs develop and implement curricula and group counseling and psychotherapy training programs that foster a perspective embodying a breadth of knowledge of, and sensitivity to, the complexities of race, ethnicity, and culture in group life.

REFERENCES

Atkinson, D. R., Morten, G., & Sue, D. W. (1989). *Counseling American minorities: A cross-cultural perspective* (4th ed.). Dubuque, IA: Brown.

Atkinson, D. R., Morten, G., & Sue, D. W. (1997). *Counseling American minorities: A cross-cultural perspective* (5th ed.). Dubuque, IA: Brown.

Atkinson, D. R., Morten, G., & Sue, D. W. (2003). *Counseling American minorities: A cross-cultural perspective* (6th ed.). Dubuque, IA: Brown.

Asch, S. E. (1952). *Social psychology.* Engelwood Cliffs, NJ: Prentice-Hall.

Asch, S. E. (1956). Studies of independence and conformity: A minority of one against a unanimous majority. *Psychological Monographs, 70*(Whole No. 416).

Bennis, W. G., & Shepard, H. A. (1974). A theory of group development. In G. S. Gibbard, J. J. Hartmann, & R. D. Mann (Eds.), *Analysis of groups* (pp. 127–153). San Francisco: Jossey-Bass.

Berger, R. (1996). A comparative analysis of different methods of teaching group work. *Social Work with Groups, 19,* 79–89.

Bion, W. R. (1959). *Experiences in groups.* New York: Basic Books.

Brayboy, T. (1971). The Black patient in group therapy. *International Journal of Group Psychotherapy, 2,* 288–293.

Burke, A. W. (1984). The multi-racial small group: Theoretical issues and practical considerations. *International Journal of Social Psychiatry, 30,* 89–95.

Carter, R. T. (2001). Back to the future in cultural competence training. *Counseling Psychologist, 29*(6), 787–789.

Carter, R. T., & Pieterse, A. L. (in press). Race: A social and psychological analysis of the term and its meaning. In R. T. Carter (Ed.), *Handbook of racial-cultural psychology and counseling: Theory and research* (Vol. 1, pp. 41–63). Hoboken, NJ: Wiley.

Casas, J. M. (1984). Policy, training, and research in counseling psychology: The racial/ethnic minority perspective. In S. D. Brown & N. Lent (Eds.), *Handbook of counseling psychology* (pp. 785–831). New York: Wiley.

Cheng, W. D., Chase, M., & Gunn, R. W. (1998). Splitting and projective identification in multicultural group counseling [Abstract]. *Journal for Specialists in Group Work, 23*(4), 372–387.

Constantine, M. G., & Wilton, L. (in press). The role of racial and cultural constructs in the history of the multicultural counseling movement. In R. T. Carter (Ed.), *Handbook of racial-cultural psychology and counseling: Theory and research* (Vol. 1, pp. 64–77). Hoboken, NJ: Wiley.

Conyne, R. K., Wilson, F. R., Kline, W. B., Morran, D. K., & Ward, D. E. (1993). Training group workers: Implications of the new ASGW training standards for training and practice. *Journal for Specialists in Group Work, 18,* 11–24.

Davis, L. (1979). Racial composition of groups. *Social Work, 24,* 208–213.

Davis, L. (1981). Racial issues in the training of group workers. *Journal of Specialists in Group Work, 6,* 155–159.

Davis, L. E., Galinsky, M. J., & Schopler, J. H. (1995). RAP: A framework for leadership of multiracial groups. *Social Work, 40,* 155–165.

Falicov, C. J. (1995). Training to think culturally: A multidimensional comparative framework. *Family Process, 34,* 373–388.

Fenster, A. (1996). Group therapy as an effective treatment modality for people of Color. *International Journal of Group Psychotherapy, 46,* 399–416.

Fuhriman, A., & Burlingame, G. (1990). The consistency of matter: A comparative analysis of individual and group process variables. *Counseling Psychologist, 18,* 6–63.

Glass, J. S., & Benshoff, J. M. (1999). PARS: A process model for beginning group leaders. *Journal for Specialists in Group Work, 24,* 15–27.

Goldberger, N. R., & Veroff, J. B. (1995). *The culture and psychology reader.* New York: New York University Press.

Greeley, A. T., Garcia, V. L., Kessler, B. L., & Gilchrist, G. (1992). Training effective multicultural group counselors: Issues for a group training course. *Journal for Specialists in Group Work, 17,* 196–210.

Highlen, P. S. (1994). Racial/ethnic diversity in doctoral programs in psychology: Challenges for the twenty-first century. *Applied and Preventive Psychology, 3,* 91–108.

Johnson, S. D. (1990). Toward clarifying culture, race, and ethnicity in the context of multicultural counseling. *Journal of Multicultural Counseling and Development, 18,* 41–50.

Johnson. S. D., Jr. (in press). Culture, context, and counseling. In R. T. Carter (Ed.), *Handbook of racial-cultural psychology and counseling: Theory and research* (Vol. 1, pp. 17–25). Hoboken, NJ: Wiley.

Jones, J. (1993). Psychological models of race. In J. D. Goodchilds (Ed.), *Psychological perspectives on human diversity in America* (pp. 3–46). Washington, DC: American Psychological Association.

Kibel, H. D. (1972). Interracial conflicts as resistance in group psychotherapy. *American Journal of Psychotherapy, 26,* 555–562.

Kibel, H. D. (1987). Contributions of the group psychotherapist to education on the psychiatric unit: Teaching through group dynamics. *International Journal of Psychotherapy, 37,* 3–29.

Kivlighan, D. M., Marsh-Angelone, M., & Angelone, E. O. (1994). Projection in group counseling: The relationship between members' interpersonal problems and their perceptions of the group leader. *Journal of Counseling Psychology, 41,* 99–104.

Kivlighan, D. M., & Mullison, S. (1988). Participants' perception of therapeutic factors in group counseling: The role of interpersonal style and stage of group development. *Small Group Behavior, 19,* 452–468.

Klein, R. H., Bernard, H. S., & Singer, D. L. (Eds.). (1992). *Handbook of contemporary group psychotherapy: Contributions from object relations, self psychology, and social systems theories.* Madison, CT: International Universities Press.

McRae, M. B., & Johnson, S. D. (1991). Toward training for competence in multicultural coun-selor education. *Journal of Counseling Development, 70,* 131–135.

Microsoft Encarta Encyclopedia. (1999). *Kurt Lewin: Group dynamics* [CD-ROM]. Abstract from: 1298 Part No. X04-711982-1020032.

Morrison, T. (1992). *Playing in the dark: Whiteness and the literary imagination.* New York: Vintage Books.

Omi, M., & Howard, W. (1994). *Racial formation in the United States from 1960's to the 1990's* (2nd ed.). New York: Routledge.

Patterson, D. L., & Smits, S. J. (1974). Communication bias in Black-white groups. *Journal of Psychology, 88,* 9–25.

Pedersen, P. (in press). The importance of Cultural Psychology Theory for multicultural coun-selors. In R. T. Carter (Ed.), *Handbook of racial-cultural psychology and counseling: Theory and research* (Vol. 1, pp. 3–16). Hoboken, NJ: Wiley.

Pedersen, P. B. (1991). Multiculturalism as a generic approach to counseling. *Journal of Coun-seling and Development, 70,* 6–12.

Ramsey, M. (1997). Exploring power in multicultural counseling encounters. *International Journal for the Advancement of Counseling, 19,* 277–291.

Reed, G. M., & Noumair, D. A. (2000). The tiller of authority in a sea of diversity: Empower-ment, disempowerment, and the politics of identity. In E. B. Klein, F. Gabelnick, & P. Herr (Eds.), *Dynamic consultation in a changing workplace* (pp. 51–79). Madison, CT: Psychoso-cial Press.

Shaffer, J., & Galinsky, M. D. (1989). *Models of group therapy* (2nd ed.). Englewood Cliffs, NJ: Prentice-Hall.

Slavson, S. R. (1956). Racial and cultural factors in group psychotherapy. *International Jour-nal of Group Psychotherapy, 2,* 152–165.

Smaby, M. H., Maddux, C. D., Torres-Rivera, D., & Zimmick, R. (1999). A study of the effects of a skills-based versus a conventional group counseling training program. *Journal for Spe-cialists in Group Work, 24,* 145–152.

Sue, D. W., Bingham, R. P., Porche-Burke, L., & Vasquez, M. (1999). The diversification of psychology. A multicultural revolution. *American Psychologist, 54*(12), 1061–1069.

Sue, D. W., & Sue, D. (1999). *Counseling the culturally different: Theory and practice* (3rd ed.). New York: Wiley.

Sue, D. W., & Sue, D. (2003). *Counseling the culturally diverse: Theory and practice* (4th ed.). New York: Wiley.

Tsui, P., & Schulz, G. L. (1988). Ethnic factors in group process: Cultural dynamics in multi-ethnic therapy groups. *American Journal of Orthopsychiatry, 58,* 136–142.

Wells, L. (1990). The group as a whole: A systematic socioanalytic perspective on interper-sonal and group relations. In J. Gillette & M. McCollom (Eds.), *Groups in context: A new perspective on group dynamics* (pp. 49–85). New York: Addison-Wesley.

Wiggins, J. D., & Carroll, M. R. (1993). Back to the basics: Perceived and actual needs of group leaders. *Journal for Specialists in Group Work, 18,* 24–29.

Yalom, I. D. (1985). *The theory and practice of group psychotherapy* (3rd ed.). New York: Basic Books.

Yalom, I. D. (1995). *The theory and practice of group psychotherapy* (4th ed.). New York: Basic Books.

CHAPTER 9

The Working Alliance, Therapy Ruptures and Impasses, and Counseling Competence: Implications for Counselor Training and Education

William Ming Liu and Donald B. Pope-Davis

Why do some clients stay in counseling and others do not? What are the most important aspects of therapy that keep clients in counseling? What do culturally diverse clients want in a counselor? How are issues of counseling effectiveness and attrition related in a cultural context? Questions of how to best work with clients place the focus of counseling on the potential impact of cultural variables such as race and ethnicity, on the therapeutic dyad, and on how all these variables potentially contribute to client retention and attrition. But how can psychologists best conceptualize and use relationship variables in understanding the way culture and therapy work, and what are some potential problems that may arise in the therapy relationship? Although the racial and cultural counseling literature has provided a glimpse, the extant research literature has yet to fully understand the client's experience in therapy and the relationship variables related to positive therapy outcomes. Hence, our chapter focuses on exploring some of the potential factors associated with therapy hurdles and moving past barriers that may impede an effective counseling relationship. We discuss the importance of recognizing and resolving culturally based impasses and ruptures as a part of developing rapport with and understanding of the client and creating the space for new dialogues between client and counselor to appear.

Before beginning, it is important to define some terms. For us, culturally based therapy impasses are defined as stalls and problems in the therapy relationship between client and counselor resulting from the inappropriate or ineffective use of culture in therapy by the counselor. That is to say, the counselor, in an attempt to demonstrate his or her cultural competency (i.e., cultural knowledge, awareness, and skills of a particular cultural group) or develop a rapport with the client, may use culture, such as the racial similarities or dissimilarities between client and counselor, to discuss the racial dynamics of the counseling relationship. Because the client may not be interested in discussing the racial dynamics of the relationship, a stall or incongruency in the relationship arises, which we define as a culturally based therapy impasse or rupture.

Our intention is not to say that culturally based impasses occur only in racially or culturally dissimilar dyads; they can occur between two people who come from similar racial and cultural backgrounds. Our intent is to highlight how culture may be used ineffectively in the counseling relationship, and how the ineffective use of culture in therapy may lead to a rupture or stall in the therapy relationship that needs to be addressed by the counselor. To accomplish the goal of understanding cultural counseling ruptures and impasses, the first step is to define the therapeutic relationship. Second, we define impasses and, more specifically, racial and cultural therapy impasses. Finally, we address the need to focus on the therapeutic relationship in counselor training and supervision.

RACIAL AND CULTURAL COUNSELING COMPETENCIES AND THE THERAPY RELATIONSHIP

Culturally diverse individuals are defined as people who may regard themselves as different from another person based on, for instance, race, gender, or sexual orientation. Being racially and culturally competent, an aspect of multicultural counseling competencies, is the ability to work with culturally diverse clients in counseling (Pedersen, 1996; Ponterotto, Casas, Suzuki, & Alexander, 1995, 2001; Pope-Davis & Coleman, 1997; Sue, Arredondo, & McDavis, 1992; Sue, Ivey, & Pedersen, 1996). The need to be culturally competent is due to the current and future growth of racial and ethnic communities in the United States (Hall, 1997; Pedersen, 1991; Sue et al., 1992; Sue, Bingham, Porche-Burke, & Vasquez, 1999). Because of the growing racial and ethnic diversity, racial and cultural competency research has permeated much of counselor training and research (e.g., Pope-Davis, Reynolds, Dings, & Nielson, 1995; Sodowsky, Kuo-Jackson, Richardson, & Corey, 1998; Speight, Thomas, Kennel, & Anderson, 1995) and spawned various models of multicultural counseling (Ponterotto, Fuertes, & Chen, 2000).

Racial and cultural counseling research has also matured and evolved (Ponterotto et al., 2000). At first, it seemed that much of the research underpinning cultural competencies was built on client preferences and perceptions of racially similar and different counselors. The premise was to understand the racial and cultural variables tied to client retention and attrition. The research suggested that client preferences could vary according to cultural trust and mistrust (Poston, Craine, & Atkinson, 1991), sex role (Blier, Atkinson, & Geer, 1987), acculturation (Gim, Atkinson, & Kim, 1991), race and ethnicity (Atkinson & Lowe, 1995; Coleman, Wampold, & Casali, 1995; Hess & Street, 1991; Lin, 1994), intent to use services (Akutsu, Lin, & Zane, 1990), counseling style (i.e., directive versus nondirective; Atkinson & Matsushita, 1991), language (Faubert & Locke, this *Handbook,* this volume; Flaskerud & Liu, 1991; Lin, 1994), and presenting issue (Abbott, Tollefson, & McDermott, 1982). Hence, multiple variables were implicated in client retention. Although any variable could be a key factor, the research was not definitive about which variables were the most important, but the research did suggest the importance of culture in the therapy relationship.

Racial and cultural competency research also focused on counselor competencies (Coleman, 1997; Constantine, 2000; Constantine & Ladany, 2000; Ladany, Inman, Constantine, & Hofheinz, 1997; Worthington, Mobley, Franks, & Tan, 2000). The intent was to understand how a counselor's cultural competency might translate to clinical practice activities, such as case conceptualization. The assumption underlying much of this research was that, if counselors were culturally competent, they would be able to develop effective therapy relationships. Accordingly, clients would respond positively to counselors who were able to understand the client's worldview (Kim & Atkinson, 2002; Pope-Davis, Liu, Toporek, & Brittan-Powell, 2001). The problem was that there was no extant research to support the assumptions, no research on the efficacy of counseling with culturally competent counselors, and no process-related research on racial and cultural counseling competencies (Abreu, Chung, & Atkinson, 2000; Pope-Davis et al., 2001; Yutrzenka, 1995). Hence, a gap existed between theory, research, and counseling practice.

To address the missing connection between theory and research, the new question arising from racial and cultural competency research has focused on the client's experiences (Pope-Davis et al., 2001). For example, in one research project examining the client's experiences with culturally competent counselors, Sodowsky et al. (1999) examined multicultural competencies among counselors, supervisors, and clients. Thirty master's- and doctoral level-counseling students working with students in an English as a Second Language (ESL) afterschool program were surveyed. The results showed that the working alliance between client and counselor increased by the end of the counseling relationship and supported the notion that cultural competency on the part of the counselor may facilitate an effective counseling relationship with the client.

Focusing on real clients in therapy, Pope-Davis et al. (2002) used grounded theory, a qualitative methodology, to investigate the counseling experiences among 10 former clients who self-disclosed being in a cross-cultural counseling dyad. These cross-cultural dyads consisted of mixed gender, sexual orientation, racial, and ethnic relationships. The results showed that clients did appreciate the counselor's use of culture in therapy, but it depended on the salience and meaningfulness of culture in the client's life, whether or not the client believed culture was related to the presenting issue, how culture was discussed in the session, and the perceived strength of the counseling relationship. The clients in the study appreciated the interest expressed by counselors about the client's culture and felt that the counselor's cultural interest reflected the counselor's cultural competency. Counselors were not perceived as having an overall cultural competency, but were seen as having cultural competency in some areas (e.g., gender) and not competent in other areas (e.g., race). Yet, the important issue for the client was getting his or her needs met, and if the needs were met, then the counselor was given leniency in other areas of the therapy relationship. In other words, if the cultural competency of the counselor was useful in meeting the needs of the client, then the client would likely be forgiving of the counselor if mistakes were made in therapy. Thus, a potential link between cultural competency, therapy impasses, and the therapy relationship was implied by the findings.

THERAPY RUPTURES AND IMPASSES

From the Pope-Davis et al. (2002) study of client experiences, results suggested that the manner in which counselors introduced culture into counseling and the perceived intentions of the counselor contributed to either positive therapy outcomes or therapy ruptures and impasses. But what are ruptures and impasses? Theoretically, impasses are defined as a "deadlock or stalemate that causes therapy to become so difficult that progress is no longer possible and termination occurs" (Hill & Nutt-Williams, 2000, p. 693). Ruptures are less severe, but are still temporary disruptions in the therapeutic alliance (Hill & Nutt-Williams, 2000). In the Pope-Davis et al. (2002) study, cultural issues (e.g., sexual orientation, age, race), when discussed, sometimes led to therapy stalls or impasses. The ability of the therapists to recognize and resolve ruptures and impasses appeared to be related to either positive or negative outcomes (i.e., attrition) in therapy as reported by the clients. Liu (2001) found a similar result among clinicians who experienced ruptures around racial and cultural issues in therapy that lead to a constant strain on the working alliance until termination.

Thus, the variability to which culture was attended to and discussed by the counselor in session highlights two issues not currently addressed in cultural competency research and training. The first is the need to focus on the process of therapy and how the cultural competency of the clinician operates in each session and throughout the course of therapy (Fuertes, Costa, Mueller, & Hersh, this *Handbook,* Volume One). The second issue that has not been focused on is how counselors use "culture" in therapy, culture's association to the therapy relationship, and what to do when therapy stalls as a result of culture. Therefore, a need exists to help clinicians recognize and resolve impasses and ruptures in the therapeutic relationship that may be created by cultural issues in therapy (either use or nonrecognition).

The reason for targeting therapy ruptures and impasses is simple. Therapists, at any experience level, tend to make mistakes in therapy that result in stalls or interruptions in the therapy goals and tasks. Some relationship problems may occur because a therapist, experimenting with his or her own cultural competencies around cultural issues, attempts to use culture in therapy when it may disrupt the therapeutic process. For instance, the counselor may feel that the client should discuss racial and cultural similarities and differences in the therapy relationship, or the counselor may attempt to demonstrate his or her cultural sensitivity by talking about racially and culturally based experiences such as racism, homophobia, or sexism. In such cases, the introduction of culture into the therapy process may take attention away from another client process (i.e., silence) or presenting issue, or the use of culture may be focused on a cultural issue that is not salient for the client. The overuse of culture or the forcing of culture into therapy may reflect a number of counselor struggles, such as anxiety, unresolved issues around a particular cultural issue, or unfamiliarity with talking about culture. All of these counselor reactions may in part be construed broadly as countertransference (Chin, 1993).

It is important that therapy impasses be recognized, addressed, and resolved for therapy to proceed positively and effectively. But in addressing impasses, additional issues may arise that are not directly linked to the therapy relationship.

For instance, the therapist may attempt to discuss the racial dynamics or cultural differences between client and counselor in the therapy relationship. By starting a dialogue with the client about racial dynamics or cultural differences, issues of racism, power, and oppression may be elicited that need to be discussed. But along with the cultural concerns that need to be discussed, it may also be important for the counselor to address the potential therapy impasse created by the mention of race and culture. In other words, a culture-related impasse raises the additional need to discuss issues such as race and racism as a part of, and along with, the therapy relationship. However, for this discussion to take place between client and counselor, a strong working relationship needs to exist.

So far, we have alluded to the components of the therapeutic relationship, such as the alliance and countertransference. The following section elaborates further the theoretical components of the therapeutic relationship and their applicability to multicultural counseling competencies.

THE THERAPEUTIC RELATIONSHIP

The therapeutic relationship is considered by some to be one of the principal healing tools in counseling (Bordin, 1979; Gelso & Carter, 1985; Sexton & Whiston, 1994). It consists of three interdependent parts: the working alliance, a transference configuration (transference and countertransference), and the real relationship (Gelso & Carter, 1994). The components of the relationship are rooted in psychodynamic theories (Patton & Kivlighan, 1997) and may be limited in their application to some people regardless of cultural background. For example, clients who are not interested in developing insight may not appreciate counselor nondirectiveness or other psychodynamic therapy interventions such as free association and dream interpretation. Although there are limitations to psychodynamic therapy (Carter, 1995) and therapy impasse research has not addressed the meaningfulness of culture in the relationship (Safran, Muran, Samstag, & Stevens, 2002), the concept of the therapeutic relationship and impasses do have general applications to counseling that extend beyond the psychodynamic framework (Bordin, 1979; Grencavage & Norcross, 1990; Kelly, 2000). Authors have also proffered various ways that psychodynamically based counseling can be used effectively with cultural minority clients (Ivey, D'Andrea, Ivey, & Simek-Morgan, 2002).

The therapeutic relationship can be conceptualized as the

> interpersonal process by which the therapist and client attempt to help the client achieve a post-therapy state that is better in some way than the one in which he or she entered therapy. (Helms & Cook, 1999, p. 159)

In other words, the therapeutic relationship represents the negotiated tasks and goals between counselor and client; the strength of the relationship will necessarily impact the outcome of therapy. Even though the therapeutic relationship seems to have general applications regardless of cultural background of the client, the empirical literature is limited because the research on therapy ruptures and impasses are either only theoretical or based predominantly on White clients and samples (e.g., Hill,

Nutt-Williams, Heaton, Thompson, & Rhodes, 1996; Kivlighan & Shaughnessy, 2000; Rhodes, Hill, Thompson, & Elliot, 1994). Because the empirical data are limited, discussions about the therapeutic relationship and its applications to non-White clients should be considered speculative and applied with some sensitivity to this missing aspect in the research.

Transference Configuration

The therapeutic relationship revolves around three interdependent components. The first is the transference configuration, consisting of the client's transference and the counselor's countertransference. Client transference is defined as

> the repetition of past conflicts with significant others, such that feelings, attitudes, and behaviors belonging rightfully in those relationships are displaced onto the therapist; and countertransference is the therapist's transference to the client's material, both to the transference and the nontransference communications presented by the client. (Gelso & Carter, 1994, p. 297)

In a counseling relationship where culture may be an important factor for client, counselor, or both, the transference configuration can easily represent the extent to which the client repeats behaviors and attitudes that were learned from other interactions, either familial or extrafamilial. Some previously learned behaviors and attitudes might be culturally based. Countertransference, though, represents the feelings and behaviors that clinicians need to be aware of in session, as some of these reactions to clients may not be based on the actual therapy material but on issues the therapist needs to struggle with outside of the therapy relationship. For instance, countertransference typically can appear for counselors when working with clients who create discomfort or anxiety (Gelso, Fassinger, Gomez, & Latts, 1995).

Carter (1995) has noted that the construct of transference and countertransference has potential limitations with racially and culturally diverse clients. Specifically, counselors focused on understanding transference and managing countertransference could "miss the centrality of race in an individual's intrapsychic and identity structure" (p. 72), and too much focus on the intrapsychic aspects of the client could obscure the contextual issues of the client's problems. Chin (1993) and Ivey et al. (2002) posit that countertransference has cultural applications, as a counselor's prejudicial attitudes will certainly manifest as some reaction to the client. Moreover, several researchers have attempted to incorporate culture into the constructs of transference and countertransference (Ivey et al., 2002; Leong, Wagner, & Tata, 1995). Authors have offered suggestions to practitioners about addressing the different cultural values between psychoanalysis and patient values (Cabaniss, Oquendo, & Singer, 1994), incorporating indigenous parental constructs into psychodynamic theories (Chin, 1993; Comas-Diaz & Minrath, 1985; Scheidlinger, 1999), encouraging counselors to understand their racially and culturally based countertransference (Comas-Diaz & Jacobsen, 1995; Holmes, 1992), understanding the client's experience in psychodynamic therapy (Aslami, 1997), recognizing the counselor's homophobia (Frost, 1998), and understanding the transference onto minority therapists (Tang & Gardner, 1999). This sample of research and theory suggests that there may be some applicability of the transference configuration to culturally diverse peoples.

The Real Relationship

The second component of the therapy relationship is the real relationship. Essentially, the real relationship is the connection between client and therapist that is genuine and honest and is relatively free from distortions caused by transference and countertransference. Gelso and Carter (1994) suggest that the real relationship is "that dimension of the total relationship that is essentially nontransferential, and is thus relatively independent of transference" (p. 297). The real relationship is composed of two dimensions. The first dimension is genuineness or the "ability and willingness to be what one truly is in the relationship—authentic, open, and honest" (p. 297). The second dimension is realistic perceptions or "perceptions uncontaminated by transference distortions and other defenses" (p. 297). The real relationship is the empathic bond between client and counselor that exists independent of distortions in the relationship. In other words, the real relationship is the "interactive nature of the personal relationship between the client and counselor that is based on direct, genuine, and undistorted interactions" (Sexton & Whiston, 1994, p. 11).

The Working Alliance

Finally, the working alliance is perceived to be the most important aspect of the relationship if therapy is to proceed and to be effective (Bordin, 1979; Gelso & Carter, 1994; Grencavage & Norcross, 1990; Horvath, 2000; Safran, Muran, & Samstag, 1994). Research suggests that positive ratings of the working alliance typically result in favorable therapy outcomes (Safran et al., 1994; Safran & Segal, 1990) and symptom reduction (Mallinckrodt, 1996). It is important to remember that research supporting the working alliance has typically been conducted on mostly White participants and thus may have limited generalizability to non-White and non-middle-class clients.

In the therapeutic relationship, the working alliance, as it is defined in the psychodynamic literature, is "the alignment or joining of the reasonable self or ego of the client and the therapist's analyzing or 'therapizing' self or ego for the purpose of the work" (Gelso & Carter, 1994, p. 297). Simply, the working alliance refers to the counselor's capacity with the client to negotiate collaborative goals and tasks in the therapy relationship for the expressed purpose of achieving a posttherapy state that is better than the pretherapy state (Helms & Cook, 1999). As a construct, the working alliance has strong connections to counseling with culturally diverse individuals because of its reliance on the collaborative relationship and negotiating goals and tasks. The stronger the working alliance, the better able client and counselor are to develop therapy goals, tasks, and an emotional bond.

RACIAL-CULTURAL APPLICATIONS OF THE THERAPEUTIC RELATIONSHIP

While all three components of the therapeutic relationship are intimately related to culture and counseling, of interest to this chapter is the working alliance and its relationship to therapy impasses that result from a misapplication of a counselor's self-perceived cultural competencies. The working alliance, with its emphasis on joining together for therapy work and negotiating tasks and goals, is relevant to cultural competencies because therapists sometimes have an agenda that is not congruent with the client's agenda or purpose for being in counseling (Pope-Davis et al., 2001). Comprehending the misalignment in therapy goals and tasks may help us to understand one variable in premature termination among minority clients. This is not to infer that counselors should not confront the client or engage in difficult dialogues with clients. In fact, engaging in difficult dialogues with clients may be a reflection of a robust working alliance. Rather, this is to suggest that counselors need to be sensitive to ruptures and impasses resulting from cultural issues that lead to therapy attrition.

If the working alliance is strong, the therapy relationship may be able to withstand incongruent agendas, tasks, and goals, to some extent, as a process of therapy. This issue of incongruent agendas may be meaningful for counselors in training. As they start to learn about counseling processes and cultural issues and concerns (e.g., racial dynamics, gender conflict, ableism), there may be some interest on their part to overinclude these issues in therapy as a way to master this discourse with clients. Clients, however, may not realize that counselors in training are using culture and race for the client's benefit, and consequently, incongruencies arise. The key in the working alliance will be the resiliency of the client and the ability of the counselor to recognize and process these incongruencies and impasses in therapy.

IMPASSES

Impasses in therapy are sometimes referred to as breaches, ruptures, or interruptions (Safran & Segal, 1990). In the past, therapy impasses have been conceptualized as a problem from the client that arises because of some deficiency or incapacity of the client to be "real" or "actualized" (Newirth, 2000). While this definition has a strong psychodynamic valence, the notion of impasses can be readily translatable to other therapeutic schools (e.g., cognitive-behavioral; Deffenbacher, 1999; Safran & Segal, 1990; Safran et al., 1994) as conflicts and stalls that arise in therapy. Ruptures and impasses are considered a cocreated product of therapist and client that needs to be addressed. In this case, impasses are not about the incapacity of the client; rather, the impasse represents a product, and sometimes an unintended consequence of an intervention, within the counseling relationship.

Therapists often perceive impasses as negative (Hill et al., 1996). Impasses may result from a variety of issues: client history of interpersonal problems, lack of agreement between therapist and client, interference in the therapy process by others, transference, therapist mistakes, and therapist personal issues (Hill et al., 1996). Counselor's negativity toward impasses may arise from a sense that impasses reflect on the competency of the clinician, especially when the impasse is a result of cultural material introduced by the clinician.

Confusing for many clinicians is that impasses may manifest in several different ways in session. Traditionally, clinicians must work to decide if the therapy impasse is actually an impasse or is reflective of some other therapy process. Impasses may manifest under several themes in counseling. For instance, Safran and Segal's (1990) seven impasse themes are: (1) overt expression of negative sentiments (e.g., client attacks the therapist's competence); (2) indirect communication of negative sentiment (e.g., client becomes withdrawn); (3) disagreement about the goals or tasks of therapy (e.g., client wants more strategies and advice); (4) compliance (e.g., client acquiesces rather than confronts); (5) avoidance maneuvers (e.g., client skips from topic to topic); (6) self-esteem-enhancing operations (e.g., client defends himself or herself to regain sense of worth); and (7) nonresponses to interventions (e.g., client does not make use of therapy intervention). Impasses that arise due to a counselor's misapplication of or inattention to culture in counseling may manifest in several ways that the counselor must seek to recognize and resolve. Consequently, not only is the client coping with the therapy rupture or impasse, but exacerbating the impasse may be culture-related issues that were not previously known. For instance, the counselor forces the topic of gender into a cross-gender dyad (female counselor and male client). The client may not be ready to discuss gender issues or gender issues are not salient to the current concerns for the client. By forcing some gender topic in the counseling relationship, the male client may experience a rupture of the working alliance. Exacerbating the rupture may be feelings of resentment, anger, and frustration toward a perceived feminist counselor (either man or woman). Now, the counselor must not only work to reconcile the therapy relationship, but must also address the political issues that are tied into being perceived as a feminist. Addressing one without the other may not repair the relationship fully, and consequently, attrition may occur.

Additional work is also demanded of the clinician to discern, based on his or her clinical intuition and training, if an impasse theme is really related to some therapy rupture and breach (e.g., Ridley, 1984; Thompson, Worthington, & Atkinson, 1994), or if it is a culturally based style of communication (e.g., acquiescence to authority is typical in Asian American styles of communication; Helms & Cook, 1999; Sue & Sue, 1999, 2003). For instance, clients who limit their self-disclosure may be manifesting a particular cultural communication style when working in a mixed-race or mixed-gender dyad (Nickerson, Helms, & Terrell, 1994). That is, the client's reticence may be discomfort resulting from unfamiliarity in working with a man or woman or racially dissimilar other. The consequence of misreading, misinterpreting, or not recognizing therapy issues could lead to attrition from therapy.

Culturally Based Therapy Impasses

Sue and Sue (1999, 2003) list a number of counselor assumptions that may lead to conflict and misinterpretation in therapy. Culturally bound values such as focusing on the individual, expecting verbal and emotional expression, insight, and self-disclosure are some specific counselor values that may lead to therapy conflicts (see also Sue & Torino, this *Handbook,* this volume). Class-bound assumptions and language barriers are also potential sources of therapy conflict. These therapy conflicts are largely situated in the potential cultural differences between client and counselor. However, conflicts in therapy may also result when counselors who are developing sensitivity and competency with cultural differences misapply culture in therapy. Consequently, conflicts and ruptures may be construed as cultural impasses.

To repeat our earlier statement, our intention is not to say that culturally based therapy impasses occur only in culturally different dyads. In fact, a White male counselor working with a White male client could face a culturally based impasse if the counselor attempts to use antisexist and antihomophobic language to challenge the client's adherence to traditional masculine norms. The impasse here is created because the counselor attempts to demonstrate his nontraditional masculinity without fully recognizing or respecting, for example, the masculine socialization experiences of the client that have shaped his masculine role subscription. Similarly, the White male counselor could face an impasse with the same client if he attempts to overidentify with the client's masculine experiences (e.g., using sexist language to denigrate women). In either case, an impasse or rupture in the therapeutic alliance may occur as a result of cultural incongruities even though client and counselor are of the same race and gender.

Again, a culturally based therapy impasse may be regarded as a stall or difficulty in the therapy relationship resulting from incompatible goals and tasks between client and counselor. The incompatibility may arise due to the inappropriate use of culture in counseling. Contributing to the impasse may be the client's positive or negative appraisal of the counselor's cultural competency. Working together, the two factors may contribute to a cultural therapy impasse. The clinician needs to be aware of how the two factors function together in the relationship.

When clinicians attempt to use a culturally based intervention in therapy, the impasse may arise because the intervention "activates an important interpersonal schema" (Safran & Segal, 1990, p. 158). For instance, in some cases, mentioning or overemphasizing issues of race or discussing the racial dynamics of the therapy relationship may cause the client to feel uncomfortable because he or she is not ready to talk about race. Incongruent goals and objectives between counselor and client, especially as they relate to the readiness of the client to discuss issues of race, may create too much anxiety, dissonance, and confusion such that the client is unable to articulate feelings of discomfort. Consequently, the client may manifest a number of different coping responses as a reaction to this intervention (e.g., withdrawal, verbal reticence, agitation). In this example, the impasse resulted from the counselor's intentional use of race in session as a means to explore how the client feels about working with a racially dissimilar counselor because the counselor believes the research literature demands such a discussion. Or the issue of race is too discomforting for the clinician, who avoids the discussion altogether (e.g., Burkard, Ponterotto, Reynolds, & Alfonso, 1999; Ridley, 1984; Thompson et al., 1994). The specific intervention is important because cultural competency–based interventions introduce into the session not only a therapy-related task but also culture. As a result, the client may be asked to respond to multiple levels of intervention: the therapy intervention itself, the cultural context and meta-communication by the therapist, or both simultaneously.

But culturally competent counselors should feel empowered and comfortable introducing or using some aspect of culture (e.g., race, sexual orientation, social class) in therapy. When the counselor is comfortable using culture in therapy, the intentions are to understand the client better. The use of culture is one of many intentional techniques a counselor can use to understand the clients. Other techniques are getting and giving information; using focus, cognitions, feelings, and insight; suggesting and reinforcing change; offering hope, support, and clarification; challenging and setting limits; working toward catharsis and behavior and self-control; countering resistance; and examining therapist needs and the relationship (Hill & O'Grady, 1985). In some cases, though, the counselor attempts to master two skills at once. With such dual intention, the anxiety of attempting to master two skills simultaneously in therapy may create impasses that could not be foreseen by the therapist. When impasses occur, the ability of the therapist to recognize and resolve issues is one indicator of therapist overall competency.

An impasse may also arise when the therapist's intention and intervention, combined with a culture-related comment, are received by an unexpecting or unprepared client. Culturally based impasses may occur when, for example, the therapist forces a cultural issue into a session when it is unwarranted, does not recognize cultural issues presented by the client, or does not recognize broad cultural issues underlying the context of the problem. In the Pope-Davis et al. (2000) qualitative study, clients remarked that they would repeatedly mention some aspect of their culture for the counselor to integrate and address in the session; when these attempts failed, the client then experienced an overall lack of empathy from the therapist that may have been initiated from this incapacity to address culture. An impasse may also occur when a therapist's intervention is not culturally sensitive: if, for instance, the therapist suggests an intervention that challenges not only the client's presenting issues but also the worldview of the client such that anxiety around the suggestion increases. Then the client has difficulty discerning between his or her presenting issue and the conflicts that arise from worldview differences. Finally, an impasse may result from a culture-related comment in an unsuccessful attempt to build rapport. In this case, the therapist makes a comment about how he or she has friends like the client, has traveled to the client's country of origin, or admires the client's culture (e.g., the therapist says he or she likes jazz to a Black client). The client becomes unsure how to use this information in therapy and it becomes a point of disengagement from therapy and the counselor.

Because many of the ideas presented thus far are theoretical, an example is provided to illustrate a multicultural rupture and impasse in counseling.

---------------------------------- **Case Example** ----------------------------------

An Asian American male counselor in a doctoral-level practicum experience is seeing a Vietnamese gay male client. The client is 24 years old and is currently enrolled as an undergraduate. The presenting issue for the client is his increasing difficulty with studying and feelings of apathy toward his schoolwork; he would like counseling to cure him of his apathy.

The client has a strong accent, and so the counselor assumes that the client is relatively low in acculturation. In probing the client's family and relationships, the counselor discovers that the client is currently living with a White male whom he met through an Internet chat room. Immediately, the counselor begins to think that the client is also in the conformity status of racial identity. Finally, when probed on his openness to his family about his sexual orientation, the client relates that his family knows nothing about his orientation.

With these three dimensions of culture operating—the client's acculturation level, his racial identity, and his gay identity—the counselor begins to focus on the culture-related issues rather than on the presenting issue of the client. In the third session, the counselor starts to focus on the acculturation level of the client's family and openness to his sexual orientation. The counselor also probes into the client's social support and campus activities (e.g., participation in the Asian American Council and the Lesbian, Gay, Bisexual Alliance). As the counselor starts on this thread of discovery, the client becomes increasingly reticent in therapy. The client begins to stare at the counselor whenever questions about his culture, history, family, or identity are brought up. Eventually, the client calls to cancel a meeting and never returns to therapy.

In this case, the foci for the counselor are the various cultures and possible reference groups the client brings into session rather than the presenting issue of the client. In an effort to tie in the various cultural elements of the client to make sense of his presenting issue, the counselor introduces additional variables that were not initiated by the client. The client is asked to struggle with these additional issues (e.g., racial identity, sexual orientation, acculturation) as a part of therapy even though it is unclear if the client is interested or ready to discuss these concerns.

Although certainly a working alliance rupture did take place, the client may have been unsure about how to approach the therapy relationship. Because the issues of culture were forced into the session, the therapy relationship became secondary to the cultural issues. Furthermore, because the counselor was unaware of the rupture that had occurred, the slow withdrawal of the client in session was not recognized. Eventually, the combination of factors led to the client's termination from counseling.

COUNSELOR TRAINING

One pertinent issue that arises from the current discussion is counselor training. Counselor training becomes an excellent opportunity for trainees to develop the resiliency and ability to cope with culturally based therapy impasses. Linked with the development of counseling skills, the resolution of impasses should become an integral aspect of self and other awareness. Counselor training can also be a good environment in which trainees can practice culture-related dialogues, recognize and resolve ruptures and impasses, and become more accustomed to and familiar with cultural-related discourses in therapy (Carter, this *Handbook,* this volume).

Recognizing the Impasse

Ruptures, conflicts, breaches, and impasses in the therapy process are important and significant parts of therapy (Safran, 1993) and should be emphasized in training. Impasses represent significant issues in therapy that not only may lead to client attrition but may also signal counselor impairment. As part of recognizing therapy impasses, the counselor needs to become aware of the affective consequences of therapy ruptures and impasses, such as feelings of anger and disappointment, boredom, and defensiveness (Hill et al., 1996). Trainees also need to be aware of the other ways they cope with these impasses. For instance, when trainees struggle in session, they are likely to produce incongruent behaviors, such as displaying annoyance or anger, advancing their own agenda, becoming directive, talking too much, or shutting down (Williams, Judge, Hill, & Hoffman, 1997). In coping with their anxiety in session, counselors may avoid or become overinvolved in the session, focus on the client, become self-aware, or become self-involved (e.g., suppress their feelings; Williams et al., 1997).

Another way of understanding therapy impasses is for counselors to be aware of their own behaviors that may initiate counseling ruptures and impasses. For instance, therapists need to be aware of interventions made, their intentions for choosing certain interventions, and client reactions to the intentional use of culture as an intervention (Hill, 1992). The key is to have some rationale for using a particular intervention in session that helps the counselor understand the client better.

Awareness of client responses is important because the likelihood of clients hiding their negative reactions may be high (Hill, 1992; Watson & Greenberg, 2000). Clients may obscure their negative reactions by increasing certain cultural styles of behavior. For instance, some clients may become more reticent, avoid eye contact, arrive late to session and request to leave early, or start to dispute therapy goals and tasks. The therapist needs to discern whether the client is exhibiting behaviors and attitudes that are related to an impasse or to the therapy goals. Recognizing the impasse early is important: Typically, by the time therapists recognize an impasse, some damage to the relationship has already been done (Hill, 1992).

Resolving the Impasse

Counselors should be aware that there is no one established formula for detecting and resolving therapy impasses (Omer, 2000). Rather, the resolution of therapy impasses should be construed as a multisession event that can be revisited in an attempt to strengthen the working alliance (Omer, 2000). In other words, like any other relationship impasse, resolution of the impasse by client and counselor is not simple or always immediate. In dynamic therapy, the process of resolving the impasse can also serve as a model and exemplar for how the client can resolve other conflicts in his or her life (Brossart, Willson, Patton, Kivlighan, & Multon, 1998; Elliott et al., 1990; Safran, 1993). The therapy session essentially serves as the vehicle for new schemas to be modeled, developed, and practiced (Elliott et al., 1990). Similarly, engaging clients in and helping them become comfortable with culture-related dialogues in a significant relationship may help clients to engage in other difficult dialogues throughout their life. This does not mean that client and counselor must engage in culturally based dialogues; instead, the dialogues are one way the client can begin to understand himself or herself as a racial being living in a racially and culturally diverse society (Thompson, this *Handbook,* this volume).

Research has shown that when clients perceive a strong working alliance and are willing to assert their negative feelings in the misunderstanding and therapists are able to remain flexible and accepting, they are likely to resolve the impasse (Rhodes et al., 1994). In contrast, those therapists who had a poor relationship, were unwilling to discuss or allow client negative feelings, and had a general lack of awareness of the client were likely to encounter attrition in therapy.

Safran and Segal (1990) posit several strategies for resolving impasses. First, the counselor should attend to the rupture in the working alliance. Attending to the working alliance is especially important because clients may be reluctant to communicate their experience with conflict. For instance, clients may experience the impasse but still want to retain a positive image of themselves and the counselor (Hill, Gelso, & Mohr, 2000; Kelly, 2000). Second, therapists should be aware of their own reactions and feelings. Being aware of one's feelings is an important barometer of the therapy relationship and the ability to take responsibility in the relationship. Third, the counselor should look for ways to accept responsibility. In other words, the counselor should investigate and explore, with and without the client, various ways that he or she may have initiated the rupture and impasse. Modeling taking responsibility for creating a culturally based therapy problem may help the client explore different ways to initiate difficult dialogues in his or her life. Moreover, the counselor's approach and attitude may communicate to the client how to cope with various feelings of anger, frustration, and vulnerability when struggling with potentially provocative issues. Fourth, the therapist should try to empathize with the client's experience and attempt to imagine himself or herself as the client in the same situation. Fifth, the counselor could attempt to maintain the stance of the participant-observer. This may be a problem for some counselors, as this stance assumes that the problem lies with the client. In a culturally based rupture or impasse, the counselor may be the initiator and so may have difficulty trying to extricate himself or herself from a discourse with the client that he or she initiated. The suggestion of maintaining the stance of a participant-observer could be reframed as a suggestion for counselors to look for ways to create new dialogues with the client that will de-escalate tension between them, but always acknowledging and recognizing that the rupture or impasse was created by the counselor and now needs to be resolved by the counselor and the client together.

It is important to keep in mind that in a counseling context where culture is salient, the resolution of the impasse, as mentioned earlier, takes on other meanings. It is not just about resolving the rupture in the relationship. It is also about the culture-related dialogues that must take place between client and counselor and building a new therapy framework in which these issues can be integrated into therapy and the relationship. In a sense, the topic has been breached, and refusal to address these issues not only complicates the relationship but may fit into a larger nontherapy society in which issues of culture (e.g., race, gender, sexual orientation) are minimized, avoided, or dismissed in significant relationships. Thus, resolving the impasse means that the therapist must be an active participant in framing issues of culture in therapy and the therapeutic relationship.

Supervision

Supervision plays an important role in understanding therapy and developing strategies to resolve impasses. For one, supervision can help the trainee to understand that misunderstandings that occur in therapy can be positive events (Bordin, 1979). That is, trainees should expect some decline in the working alliance during phases of counseling when the client is being challenged the most and is struggling significantly

(Kivlighan & Shaughnessy, 2000). The decline in the working alliance can also be modeled in the supervision relationship and working alliance (Ladany, Ellis, & Friedlander, 1999). Trainees should understand that the decline in the working alliance eventuates in greater improvement in the client's perceived benefit from counseling when compared to a linear or stable (i.e., no peaks or valleys) working alliance (Kivlighan & Shaughnessy, 2000).

Because the supervision working alliance can translate into the therapy working alliance (Patton & Kivlighan, 1997), the capacity of the supervision relationship to embrace culture-related discourses becomes an important practice environment for trainees. The supervision working alliance is an important relationship where trainees should feel comfortable, willing to be challenged, and ready to discuss therapy impasses that were created by their overzealous interventions (e.g., Chen & Bernstein, 2000). However, the supervisee also may look toward the supervisor's cultural competency and willingness to address culture-related material in the supervision relationship (Bashshur et al., 2000; Ladany et al., 1997). Thus, a trainee will look to the supervisor as a model of how to talk about and resolve culturally based therapy impasses.

Just as a therapeutic impasse can give counselors a glimpse into core issues and conflicts of the client (Safran, 1993), the observed and reported ruptures and impasses in supervision can also provide a glimpse into issues with which the trainee is struggling. The recognition of culturally based therapy impasses is important in training because there may be a tendency for trainees to present themselves as culturally proficient. The need to present a competent façade may be a result of competing pressures of professionalism and the sense that "incompetent" trainees are also likely to carry a stigma akin to being ignorant or racist. The combination of the different pressures may lead some counselors in training to demonstrate their cultural competency to the detriment of their clients. Supervisors need to be sensitive to and aware of the performance anxiety that trainees struggle with and how these demands may manifest in therapy (see also Chen, this *Handbook*, this volume).

CONCLUSION

This chapter focused on the notion of therapeutic impasses that are created by the misapplication or misuse of culture-related material in a therapy session. The result of the misapplication may present multiple problems in the therapy relationship that need to be resolved. The first issue faced by client and counselor is the rupture that occurred in the working alliance that needs to be recognized and repaired. The second is the culture-related material that sometimes worked to obscure and exacerbated the rupture in the working alliance. The role of the clinician is to engage the client in essentially three dialogues: the working alliance relationship, how culture is related to their relationship, and finding some way for culture to become a part of the therapeutic relationship. These are the difficult dialogues that the clinician needs to become comfortable with in session. Nonrecognition of these ruptures can certainly lead to ineffective therapy or client attrition.

REFERENCES

Abbott, K., Tollefson, N., & McDermott, D. (1982). Counselor race as a factor in counselor preference. *Journal of College Student Personnel, 23,* 36–40.

Abreu, J. M., Chung, R. H. G., & Atkinson, D. R. (2000). Multicultural counseling training: Past, present, and future directions. *Counseling Psychologist, 28,* 641–656.

Akutsu, P. D., Lin, C. H., & Zane, N. W. S. (1990). Predictors of utilization intent of counseling among Chinese and white students: A test of the proximal-distal model. *Journal of Counseling Psychology, 37,* 445–452.

Aslami, B. A. (1997). Interracial psychotherapy: A report of the treatment of inner-city adolescents. *Journal of the American Academy of Psychoanalysis, 25,* 347–356.

Atkinson, D. R., & Lowe, S. M. (1995). The role of ethnicity, cultural knowledge, and conventional techniques in counseling and psychotherapy. In J. G. Ponterotto, J. M. Casas, L. A. Suzuki, & C. M. Alexander (Eds.), *Handbook of multicultural counseling* (pp. 387–414). Thousand Oaks, CA: Sage.

Atkinson, D. R., & Matsushita, Y. J. (1991). Japanese-American acculturation, counseling style, counselor ethnicity, and perceived counselor credibility. *Journal of Counseling Psychology, 38,* 473–478.

Bashshur, M., Brittan-Powell, C., Codrington, J., Kelley, W., Liang, C., Ligiero, D., et al. (2000, August). *Critical incidents multicultural supervision: Exploring supervisee and supervisor experiences.* Paper presented at the annual meeting of the American Psychological Association, Washington, DC.

Blier, M. J., Atkinson, D. R., & Geer, C. A. (1987). Effect of client gender and counselor gender and sex roles on willingness to see the counselor. *Journal of Counseling Psychology, 34,* 27–30.

Bordin, E. S. (1979). The generalizability of the psychoanalytic concept of the working alliance. *Psychotherapy: Theory, Research, and Practice, 16,* 252–260.

Brossart, D. F., Willson, V. L., Patton, M. J., Kivlighan, D. M., Jr., & Multon, K. D. (1998). A time series model of the working alliance: A key process in short-term psychoanalytic counseling. *Psychotherapy, 35,* 197–205.

Burkard, A. W., Ponterotto, J. G., Reynolds, A. L., & Alfonso, V. C. (1999). White counselor trainees' racial identity and working alliance perceptions. *Journal of Counseling and Development, 77,* 324–329.

Cabaniss, D. L., Oquendo, M. A., & Singer, M. B. (1994). The impact of psychoanalytic values on transference and countertransference: A study in transcultural psychotherapy. *Journal of the American Academy of Psychoanalysis, 22,* 609–621.

Carter, R. T. (1995). *The influence of race and racial identity in psychotherapy: Toward a racially inclusive model.* New York: Wiley.

Chen, E. C., & Bernstein, B. L. (2000). Relations of complementary and supervisory issues to supervisory working alliance: A comparative analysis of two cases. *Journal of Counseling Psychology, 47,* 485–497.

Chin, J. L. (1993). Transference. In J. L. Chin, J. H. Liem, M. A. Domokos-Cheng Ham, & G. K. Hong (Eds.), *Transference and empathy in Asian American psychotherapy: Cultural values and treatment needs* (pp. 15–33). Westport, CT: Praeger.

Coleman, H. L. K. (1997). Conflict in multicultural counseling relationships: Source and resolution. *Journal of Multicultural Counseling and Development, 25,* 195–200.

Coleman, H. L. K., Wampold, B. E., & Casali, S. L. (1995). Ethnic minorities' ratings of ethnically similar and European American counselors: A meta-analysis. *Journal of Counseling Psychology, 42,* 55–64.

Comas-Diaz, L., & Jacobsen, F. M. (1995). The therapist of Color and the white patient dyad: Contradictions and recognitions. *Cultural Diversity and Mental Health, 1,* 93–106.

Comas-Diaz, L., & Minrath, M. (1985). Psychotherapy with ethnic minority borderline clients. *Psychotherapy, 22*(2), 418–426.

Constantine, M. G. (2000). Social desirability attitudes, sex, and affective and cognitive empathy as predictors of self-reported multicultural counseling competence. *Counseling Psychologist, 28,* 857–872.

Constantine, M. G., & Ladany, N. (2000). Self-report multicultural counseling competence scales: Their relation to social desirability attitudes and multicultural case conceptualization ability. *Journal of Counseling Psychology, 47,* 155–164.

Deffenbacher, J. L. (1999). Cognitive-behavioral conceptualization and treatment of anger. *Journal of Clinical Psychology, 55,* 295–309.

Elliott, R., Llewelyn, S. P., Firth-Cozens, J. A., Margison, F. R., Shapiro, D. A., & Hardy, G. (1990). Assimilation of problematic experiences by clients in psychotherapy. *Psychotherapy, 27,* 411–420.

Flaskerud, J. H., & Liu, P. Y. (1991). Effects of an Asian client-therapist language, ethnicity and gender match on utilization and outcome of therapy. *Community Mental Health Journal, 27,* 31–42.

Frost, J. C. (1998). Countertransference considerations for the gay male when leading psychotherapy groups for gay men. *International Journal of Group Psychotherapy, 48*(1), 3–24.

Fuertes, J. N., Costa, C. I., Mueller, L. N., & Hersh, M. (in press). Psychotherapy process and outcome from a racial-ethnic perspective. In R. T. Carter (Ed.), *Handbook of racial-cultural psychology and counseling: Theory and research* (Vol. 1, pp. 256–276). Hoboken, NJ: Wiley.

Gelso, C. J., & Carter, J. A. (1985). The relationship in counseling and psychotherapy: Components, consequences, and theoretical antecedents. *Counseling Psychologist, 13,* 155–243.

Gelso, C. J., & Carter, J. A. (1994). Components of the psychotherapy relationship: Their interaction and unfolding during treatment. *Journal of Counseling Psychology, 41,* 296–306.

Gelso, C. J., Fassinger, R. E., Gomez, M. J., & Latts, M. G. (1995). Countertransference reactions to lesbian clients: The role of homophobia, counselor gender, and countertransference management. *Journal of Counseling Psychology, 42,* 356–364.

Gim, R. H., Atkinson, D. R., & Kim, S. J. (1991). Asian-American acculturation, counselor ethnicity and cultural sensitivity, and ratings of counselors. *Journal of Counseling Psychology, 38,* 57–62.

Grencavage, L. M., & Norcross, J. C. (1990). Where are the commonalities among the therapeutic common factors? *Professional Psychology: Research and Practice, 21,* 372–378.

Hall, C. C. I. (1997). Cultural malpractice: The growing obsolescence of psychology with the changing U.S. population. *American Psychologist, 52,* 642–651.

Helms, J. E., & Cook, D. A. (1999). *Using race and culture in counseling and psychotherapy: Theory and process.* Boston: Allyn & Bacon.

Hess, R. S., & Street, E. M. (1991). The effect of acculturation on the relationship of counselor ethnicity and client ratings. *Journal of Counseling Psychology, 38,* 71–75.

Hill, C. E. (1992). Research on therapist techniques in brief individual therapy: Implications for practitioners. *Counseling Psychologist, 20,* 689–711.

Hill, C. E., Gelso, C. J., & Mohr, J. J. (2000). Client concealment and self-presentation in therapy: Comment on Kelly (2000). *Psychological Bulletin, 126,* 495–500.

Hill, C. E., & Nutt-Williams, E. (2000). The process of individual therapy. In S. D. Brown & R. W. Lent (Eds.), *Handbook of counseling psychology* (3rd ed., pp. 670–710). New York: Wiley.

Hill, C. E., Nutt-Williams, E., Heaton, K. J., Thompson, B. J., & Rhodes, R. H. (1996). Therapist retrospective recall of impasses in long-term psychotherapy: A qualitative analysis. *Journal of Counseling Psychology, 43,* 207–217.

Hill, C. E., & O'Grady, K. (1985). List of therapist intentions illustrated in a case study and with therapists of varying theoretical orientations. *Journal of Counseling Psychology, 32,* 3–22.

Holmes, D. E. (1992). Race and transference in psychoanalysis and psychotherapy. *International Journal of Psychoanalysis, 73*(1), 1–11.

Horvath, A. O. (2000). The therapeutic relationship: From transference to alliance. *Journal of Clinical Psychology, 56,* 163–173.

Ivey, A. E., D'Andrea, M., Ivey, M. B., & Simek-Morgan, L. (2002). *Theories of counseling and psychotherapy: A multicultural perspective* (5th ed.). Boston: Allyn & Bacon.

Kelly, A. E. (2000). Helping construct desirable identities: A self-presentational view of psychotherapy. *Psychological Bulletin, 126,* 475–494.

Kim, B. S. K., & Atkinson, D. R. (2002). Asian American client adherence to Asian cultural values, counselor expression of cultural values, counselor ethnicity, and career counseling process. *Journal of Counseling Psychology, 49,* 3–13.

Kivlighan, D. M., & Shaughnessy, P. (2000). Patterns of working alliance development: A typology of clients' working alliance ratings. *Journal of Counseling Psychology, 47,* 362–371.

Ladany, N., Ellis, M. V., & Friedlander, M. L. (1999). The supervisory working alliance, trainee self-efficacy, and satisfaction. *Journal of Counseling and Development, 77,* 447–455.

Ladany, N., Inman, A. G., Constantine, M. G., & Hofheinz, E. W. (1997). Supervisee multicultural case conceptualization ability and self-reported multicultural competence as functions of supervisee racial identity and supervisor focus. *Journal of Counseling Psychology, 44,* 284–293.

Leong, F. T. L., Wagner, N. S., & Tata, S. P. (1995). Racial and ethnic variations in help-seeking attitudes. In J. G. Ponterotto, J. M. Casas, L. A. Suzuki, & C. M. Alexander (Eds.), *Handbook of multicultural counseling* (pp. 415–438). Thousand Oaks: Sage.

Lin, J. C. H. (1994). How long do Chinese Americans stay in psychotherapy? *Journal of Counseling Psychology, 41,* 288–291.

Liu, W. M. (Chair.). (2001, August). *Multicultural competency based treatments: Mental health, treatments, and therapy failures.* Presented at the 109th Annual Convention of the American Psychological Association, San Francisco.

Mallinckrodt, B. (1996). Change in working alliance, social support, and psychological symptoms in brief therapy. *Journal of Counseling Psychology, 43,* 448–455.

Newirth, J. (2000). Impasses in the psychoanalytic relationship. *Journal of Clinical Psychology, 56,* 225–231.

Nickerson, K. J., Helms, J. E., & Terrell, F. (1994). Cultural mistrust, opinions about mental illness, and Black students' attitudes toward seeking psychological help from white counselors. *Journal of Counseling Psychology, 41,* 378–385.

Omer, H. (2000). Troubles in the therapeutic relationship: A pluralistic perspective. *Journal of Clinical Psychology, 56,* 201–210.

Patton, M. J., & Kivlighan, D. M., Jr. (1997). Relevance of the supervisory alliance to the counseling alliance and to treatment adherence in counseling training. *Journal of Counseling Psychology, 44,* 108–115.

Pedersen, P. B. (1991). Multiculturalism as a generic approach to counseling. *Journal of Counseling and Development, 70,* 6–12.

Pedersen, P. B. (1996). The importance of both similarities and differences in multicultural counseling: Reaction to C. H. Patterson. *Journal of Counseling and Development, 74,* 236–237.

Ponterotto, J. G., Casas, J. M., Suzuki, L. A., & Alexander, C. M. (Eds.). (1995). *Handbook of multicultural counseling.* Thousand Oaks, CA: Sage.

Ponterotto, J. G., Casas, J. M., Suzuki, L. A., & Alexander, C. M. (Eds.). (2001). *Handbook of multicultural counseling* (2nd ed.). Thousand Oaks, CA: Sage.

Ponterotto, J. G., Fuertes, J. N., & Chen, E. C. (2000). Models of multicultural counseling. In S. D. Brown & R. W. Lent (Eds.), *Handbook of counseling psychology* (3rd ed., pp. 639–669). New York: Wiley.

Pope-Davis, D. B., & Coleman, H. L. K. (Eds.). (1997). *Multicultural counseling competencies: Assessment, education and training, and supervision.* Thousand Oaks, CA: Sage.

Pope-Davis, D. B., Liu, W. M., Toporek, R., & Brittan-Powell, C. (2001). How do we identify cultural competence in counseling: Review, introspection, and recommendations for future research. *Cultural Diversity and Ethnic Minority Psychology, 7,* 121–138.

Pope-Davis, D. B., Reynolds, A. L., Dings, J. G., & Nielson, D. (1995). Examining multicultural counseling competencies of graduate students in psychology. *Professional Psychology—Research and Practice, 26,* 322–329.

Pope-Davis, D. B., Toporek, R. L., Ortega-Villalobos, L., Ligiero, D. P., Brittan-Powell, C. S., Liu, W. M., et al. (2002). A qualitative study of clients' perspectives of multicultural counseling competence. *Counseling Psychologist, 30,* 355–393.

Poston, W. S. C., Craine, M., & Atkinson, D. R. (1991). Counselor dissimilarity: Confrontation, client cultural mistrust, and willingness to self-disclose. *Journal of Multicultural Counseling and Development, 19,* 65–73.

Rhodes, R. H., Hill, C. E., Thompson, B. J., & Elliott, R. (1994). Client retrospective recall of resolved and unresolved misunderstanding events. *Journal of Counseling Psychology, 41,* 473–483.

Ridley, C. R. (1984). Clinical treatment of the nondisclosing client: A therapeutic paradox. *American Psychologist, 39,* 1234–1244.

Safran, J. D. (1993). Breaches in the therapeutic alliance: An arena for negotiating authentic relatedness. *Psychotherapy, 30,* 11–24.

Safran, J. D., Muran, J. C., & Samstag, L. W. (1994). Resolving therapeutic alliance ruptures: A task analytic investigation. In A. O. Horvath & L. S. Greenberg (Eds.), *The working alliance: Theory, research, and practice* (pp. 225–258). New York: Wiley.

Safran, J. D., Muran, J. C., Samstag, L. W., & Stevens, C. (2002). Repairing alliance ruptures. In J. C. Norcross (Ed.), *Psychotherapy relationships that work: Therapist contributions and responsiveness to patients* (pp. 235–254). New York: Oxford University Press.

Safran, J. D., & Segal, Z. V. (1990). *Interpersonal process in cognitive therapy.* New York: Basic Books.

Scheidlinger, S. (1999). On concepts of amae and the mother-group. *Journal of the American Academy of Psychoanalysis, 27,* 91–100.

Sexton, T. L., & Whiston, S. C. (1994). The status of the counseling relationship: An empirical review, theoretical implications, and research directions. *Counseling Psychologist, 22,* 6–78.

Sodowsky, G. R., Kuo-Jackson, P. Y., Richardson, M. F., & Corey, A. T. (1998). Correlates of self-reported multicultural competencies: Counselor multicultural social desirability, race, social inadequacy, locus of control racial ideology, and multicultural training. *Journal of Counseling Psychology, 45,* 256–264.

Sodowsky, G. R., Webster, D., Yang, Y., Liu, J., Germer, J., Lynne, E. M., et al. (1999, August). *Empirical validity of multicultural competencies: Counselor, client, and supervisor self-reports.* Paper presented at the annual meeting of the American Psychological Association, Boston.

Speight, S. L., Thomas, A. J., Kennel, R. G., & Anderson, M. E. (1995). Operationalizing multicultural training in doctoral programs and internships. *Professional Psychology: Research and Practice, 26,* 401–406.

Sue, D. W., Arredondo, P., & McDavis, R. J. (1992). Multicultural counseling competencies and standards: A call to the profession. *Journal of Counseling and Development, 70,* 477–486.

Sue, D. W., Bingham, R. P., Porche-Burke, L., & Vasquez, M. (1999). The diversification of psychology: A multicultural revolution. *American Psychologist, 54,* 1061–1069.

Sue, D. W., Ivey, A. E., & Pedersen, P. B. (1996). Basic assumptions of a theory of multicultural counseling and therapy. In D. W. Sue, A. E. Ivey, & P. B. Pedersen (Eds.), *A theory of multicultural counseling and therapy* (pp. 13–29). Pacific Grove, CA: Brooks/Cole.

Sue, D. W., & Sue, D. (1999). *Counseling the culturally different: Theory and practice* (3rd ed.). New York: Wiley.

Sue, D. W., & Sue, D. (2003). *Counseling the culturally diverse: Theory and practice* (4th ed.). New York: Wiley.

Tang, N. M., & Gardner, J. (1999). Race, culture, and psychotherapy: Transference to minority therapists. *Psychoanalytic Quarterly, 68,* 1–20.

Thompson, C. E., Worthington, R., & Atkinson, D. R. (1994). Counselor content orientation, counselor race, and Black women's cultural mistrust and self-disclosures. *Journal of Counseling Psychology, 41,* 155–161.

Watson, J. C., & Greenberg, L. S. (2000). Alliance ruptures and repairs in experiential therapy. *Journal of Clinical Psychology, 56,* 175–186.

Williams, E. N., Judge, A. B., Hill, C. E., & Hoffman, M. A. (1997). Experiences of novice therapists in prepracticum: Trainees', clients', and supervisors' perceptions of therapists' personal reactions and management strategies. *Journal of Counseling Psychology, 44,* 390–399.

Worthington, R. L., Mobley, M., Franks, R. P., & Tan, J. A. (2000). Multicultural counseling competencies: Verbal content, counselor attributions, and social desirability. *Journal of Counseling Psychology, 47,* 460–468.

Yutrzenka, B. A. (1995). Making a case for training in ethnic and cultural diversity in increasing treatment efficacy. *Journal of Consulting and Clinical Psychology, 63,* 197–206.

CHAPTER 10

Racial-Cultural Training for Supervisors: Goals, Foci, and Strategies

Eric C. Chen

The pressing need for mental health professionals to develop competence in an increasingly diverse society has been widely acknowledged in the counseling and psychology fields and embraced in many training programs in recent years (e.g., Ponterotto, 1997; Quintana & Bernal, 1995; Ridley & Kleiner, 2003; Speight, Thomas, Kennel, & Anderson, 1995). Not surprisingly, the past decade has witnessed considerable advances in the curricula, courses, and training experiences proposed to prepare mental health professionals for the development of multicultural or racial-cultural competence (e.g., Abreu, Chung, & Atkinson, 2000; Pope-Davis, Coleman, Liu, & Toporek, 2003; Tyler & Guth, 1999).

More recently, the American Psychological Association's (APA; 2003) "Guidelines on Multicultural Education, Training, Research, Practice, and Organizational Change for Psychologists," attending to ethnic and racial minority groups as well as those from biracial, multiethnic, and multiracial backgrounds, calls for psychologists to identify strategies that will allow them to enhance their effectiveness in multi-cultural or racial-cultural contexts, that is, in "interactions between individuals from minority ethnic and racial groups in the United States and the dominant European-American culture" (p. 378). Although multiculturalism has been generally interchanged with diversity to include cultural dimensions such as race, ethnicity, language, sexual orientation, gender, age, disability, socioeconomic status, education, and religious and spiritual orientation, all critical aspects of an individual's personal identity, this chapter, in accordance with the APA guidelines, uses the term "multicultural" narrowly to connote racial-cultural interactions among all racial-ethnic groups in the United States. Despite widespread endorsement of the multicultural counseling competencies model, the implicit assumption that multicultural or racial-cultural awareness, knowledge, and skills translate into effective practice remains unsubstantiated (Constantine & Ladany, 2000; Ponterotto, Fuertes, & Chen, 2000).

Clinical supervision provides an effective mechanism for facilitating the development of supervisees' racial-cultural competencies through timely and specific feedback on efforts to transfer awareness, knowledge, and skills to clinical practice (Chen, 2001; Liu & Pope-Davis, this *Handbook,* this volume; Martinez & Holloway,

1997; Vasquez, 1992). Moreover, Ladany, Inman, Constantine, and Hofheinz's (1997) research suggests that supervisees are more likely to consider racial-cultural factors in case conceptualization when the supervision environment supports an open examination of individual differences. Supervisors who fail to attend to racial-cultural factors in the supervisory relationship are ill-prepared to facilitate supervisees' development of multicultural competencies or to monitor the welfare of clients in multicultural counseling (Bernard & Goodyear, 2004). Consequently, supervisees' efforts to work effectively with a diverse clientele may be hindered.

This chapter constitutes an attempt to improve racial-cultural training for clinical supervisors by synthesizing three areas of the relevant literature: clinical supervision, multicultural counseling and training, and counselor education. Throughout the chapter, the term "multicultural" will be used interchangeably with "racial-cultural," in line with the APA's (2003) guidelines and in accordance with the focus of this volume. Following the convention suggested by Bernard and Goodyear (2004), distinctions are made between the supervisor training (educator-trainee) and supervision (supervisor-supervisee) contexts because the former is much more limited in scope and more specific in purpose. The terms "supervisor educator" or "educator" refer to any mental health professional who provides training to enhance the supervision competencies of another professional, referred to as a "supervisor trainee" or "trainee." The educator, among other possibilities, could be a faculty member teaching a course on supervision for doctoral students or a senior psychologist providing supervision for other staff members who are training to become competent supervisors. Occasionally, when a more delimited term seems necessary to designate the supervision context, I use "supervisor" and "supervisee" as appropriate. Although the chapter incorporates the perspectives of both supervisor educators and trainees, the focus is on racial-cultural training for supervisors, as well as on pedagogical considerations in the design and implementation of the training program.

Several assumptions guiding the chapter need to be clarified. First, a number of general supervisor training approaches and frameworks are available in the supervision literature, and interested readers may refer to Bernard and Goodyear (2004) and Goodyear and Guzzardo (2000) for a review of these models and for existing empirical support, respectively. Because race and ethnicity are among myriad critical cultural variables (e.g., religion, sexual orientation) that can influence the supervision process and outcome, the chapter, which focuses on only two of these critical variables, is intended to complement rather than replace these models.

Second, the chapter is predicated on the conceptualization of race and ethnicity as dynamic variables that exert powerful influences on interpersonal encounters across diverse contexts. Helms (1994) identifies three different ways of conceptualizing race or racial factors:

> (a) nominal classification, meaning demographic categories; (b) cultural referent, which pertains to the customs, traditions, and values hypothetically related to group affiliations; and (c) socio-racial delineations, implying shared sociopolitical experiences. (p. 164)

Similarly, Ho (1995) suggests that internalized culture should not be confused with membership in a racial or ethnic group, implying that practitioners should attempt to integrate each client's identity at the individual, group, and universal levels and their interactions, rather than solely focusing on group membership (Leong, 1996).

The third assumption is that racial-cultural training occurs in an interpersonal context, commanding attention to both the relationship and the contextual aspects of the training. As in any interpersonal relationship, educators and trainees must establish a solid foundation on which to explore the potential minefields of misunderstanding, disagreement, and conflict. Moreover, documentation of parallel process phenomena in the supervision literature (cf. Bernard & Goodyear, 2004) highlights the importance of recognizing reciprocal contextual influences in racial-cultural training among three contexts of interpersonal transactions: counseling (counselor-client), supervision (supervisor-supervisee), and supervisor training (educator-trainee). As such, effective racial-cultural training for supervisors cannot be developed without adequate attention to the ways in which the goals, foci, and strategies of racial-cultural training for supervisors are influenced by these three interlocking relationship contexts.

The remainder of the chapter is composed of three sections. The first section presents an overview of the primary goals, focus areas, and main strategies of racial-cultural training. The discussion is organized according to the major roles and functions of the educator, including teacher, counselor, supervisor, and advocate. Next, a case example is presented as an illustration for the use of the interactional approach to supervision of supervisor trainees in practice. The final section concludes the chapter with closing comments regarding the demanding and complex nature of supervisor training.

SUPERVISOR TRAINING: GOALS, FOCI, AND STRATEGIES

When designing training experiences for trainees, the educator needs to keep in mind two distinct but related questions. The first question: *What* do I need to know? is directed toward trainees and is content-oriented, with a particular focus on the requisite knowledge and skills in developing racial-cultural competencies. The second question: *How* do I help trainees know what they need to know and, further, transfer that knowledge into practice? is aimed at the educator and is primarily pedagogical in nature. Although these two questions differ with respect to their emphasis on *declarative knowledge* versus *procedural knowledge* (Anderson, 1993), or *knowing that* versus *knowing how* (Carter, this *Handbook,* this volume; Johnson, 1987), the educator ultimately faces the daunting task of helping trainees proceduralize the declarative knowledge about racial-cultural issues in supervision.

A criticism of existing multicultural competencies and training models is that they tend to be described in abstract and often philosophical terms that defy specification and offer little guidance for the practitioner (Alvarez & Piper, this *Handbook,* this volume; Leong, 1996; Mollen, Ridley, & Hill, 2003; Ponterotto et al., 2000). In an attempt to address this shortcoming, an elucidation of the typical roles taken by the educator and the goals, functions, foci, and strategies fundamental to each role is presented in Table 10.1. However, in actuality, the roles of the educator as teacher, counselor, supervisor, and advocate are interrelated and overlap in varying degrees

Table 10.1 Goals, Functions, Foci, and Strategies for Racial-Cultural Training for Supervisors

	ROLES OF SUPERVISOR EDUCATOR			
	Teacher	Counselor	Supervisor	Advocate
Goal	• To raise supervisors' awareness about racial-cultural issues in supervision and counseling • To expand supervisors' knowledge and skill base about racial-cultural factors that affect the supervision relationship and process	• To create a receptive atmosphere of trust and safety • To identify and overcome obstacles that may interfere with the acquisition and application of declarative knowledge	• To support the integration of cognitive learning with supervision practice • To safeguard the welfare of supervisees and clients	• To identify and remediate an existing problem with an external source for supervisor trainees • To promote and embrace multiculturalism within the system
Function	• Instructing • Demonstrating • Coaching • Guiding • Inspiring	• Exploring • Facilitating • Empathizing • Encouraging • Supporting	• Inquiring • Evaluating • Modeling • Focusing • Consulting	• Informing • Challenging • Defending • Problem solving • Promoting
Focus	• The learning of supervisor trainees individually and as a group	• Intra- and interpersonal dynamics	• Individual supervisor's supervision practice	• Characteristics, assumptions, policies, resources, and practices of systemic contexts
Strategy	*Didactic Instruction* • Lecture and readings • Case analysis • Small group discussions *Experiential Activities* • Journal writing • Portfolio • Interviews • Skill training (e.g., role plays) • Laboratory exercises (e.g., triad model) • Guided imagery	• Individual and group counseling skills • Communicating concerns to trainees, supportive in tone, yet specific in purpose • Anticipating problems • Setting ground rules • Discussing confidentiality • Building group norms	• Tape review • Reviewing session notes • Reflective inquiry • Case conference • Group consultation	• Ongoing internal and external evaluation • Dialogue with supervisor trainees, colleagues, and administrators

throughout the training process. The relative importance of each depends on several factors, including the training format and the characteristics of trainees. The capacity of trainees to address the complexity of race and ethnicity in the context of supervision, for example, is directly related to their level of professional development (Bernard, 1994) and needs to be considered by the educator when determining the appropriate roles in the training process.

Although broad and somewhat arbitrary in nature, the typology presented in Table 10.1 delineates variables, concepts, and issues that are likely to impact the supervisor training. This framework may be used in conjunction with a model such as Ridley, Mendoza, and Kanitz's (1994) Multicultural Program Development Pyramid (MPDP) as a starting point for designing graded learning activities and experiences that meet the needs of trainees. A key aspect of the MPDP is a 10 by 10 grid in which *learning objectives* (e.g., displaying culturally responsive behaviors, cultural empathy) intersect with *instructional strategies* (e.g., participatory learning, introspection). The delineation of the roles of the educator provides a framework for the implementation of specific objectives and strategies, such as those described in Ridley et al.'s model. Individual characteristics of trainees and the educator further determine the specific interrelation of the various roles of the educator. The following sections independently discuss the various roles of the educator.

The Role of Teacher

As teacher, the educator instructs and advises trainees, particularly those with limited prior exposure to racial-cultural issues. The focus is placed on the learning needs of trainees, and a thorough assessment of the general counseling and racial-cultural competencies of trainees guides the design of didactic and experiential training exercises. The two principal goals are to heighten trainees' awareness of racial-cultural issues in counseling and supervision and to enhance their knowledge and skills about racial-cultural factors salient to the supervision relationship and process. In essence, the educator helps trainees assemble the necessary conceptual foundation of awareness and knowledge, from which their supervisory skills are sharpened in their actual supervision practice. Training strategies (see Table 10.1) include both didactic instruction and experiential activities (Bernard & Goodyear, 2004; Reynolds, 1995, this *Handbook*, this volume).

Didactic Instruction

The didactic component of training addresses two major content areas: (1) general racial-cultural issues and (2) issues and challenges specific to supervision. First, the APA's (1993, 2003) guidelines and the literature on the multicultural counseling competencies model (Arredondo, 1999; Arredondo et al., 1996; Pope-Davis et al., 2003; Sue, Arredondo, & McDavis, 1992) expose trainees to general racial-cultural issues, including professional and ethical expectations of mental health professionals in working with a diverse clientele. Didactic training should continue beyond these relatively static conceptualizations to include dynamic, heuristic constructs, such as worldviews (e.g., Ibrahim, 1991; Ibrahim, Roysircar-Sodowsky, & Ohnishi, 2001), racism and oppression (e.g., D'Andrea & Daniels, 2001; Van Dijk, 1993), racial-cultural identities (e.g., Atkinson, Morten, & Sue, 1998; Cross, 1995; Helms, 1995, 2001), and acculturation (e.g., Berry & Kim, 1988). Specific attention should be given to their manifestations in the counseling or supervision process.

The second content area, which involves common problems or issues in supervision, includes over- and underinterpretations of the influence of race and culture, avoidance of racial-cultural issues, and interactions dictated by a fear of being perceived as culturally insensitive, or worse, as racist (Helms & Cook, 1999; Leong & Wagner, 1994). Furthermore, concerns salient to dyads of White supervisors and supervisees of Color, described in detail by Fong and Lease (1997), include issues of unintentional racism, power dynamics, miscommunication, distrust, and vulnerability in supervision. According to Fong and Lease, White supervisors' unintentional racism (e.g., "color blindness") may be associated with their ignorance of, or discomfort with, racial-cultural issues and is manifested in their minimizing or avoiding the discussion of such issues in supervision. The evaluative power inherent in the role of supervisor, coupled with the privilege afforded as a member of the majority in society, underscores the complexity of power dynamics in this supervision relationship. Miscommunication in the interracial supervision dyad occurs when differences in communication styles, verbal and nonverbal, are not monitored appropriately. If not addressed successfully, each of these issues, individually and collectively, is likely to contribute to a sense of distrust and vulnerability between the supervisory participants.

Conversely, supervisors of Color with White supervisees may face challenges such as supervisor patronization and supervisee resistance. Supervisor patronization may occur either when White supervisees increasingly depend on their supervisors' racial-cultural competencies for guidance and assurance or when they overemphasize racial-cultural issues in circumstances where other variables are more critical (Remington & DaCosta, 1989). On the other hand, supervisors of Color may experience supervisee resistance when the supervisors' level of competence is called into question, both overtly and covertly, by their White supervisees (Priest, 1994).

Disparities between supervisors and supervisees on levels of racial identity status or racial-cultural competencies, independent of race or ethnicity, present potential challenges in supervisory relationships. Helms's (1990, 1995; Helms & Cook, 1999) interactional model contends that race is an integral part of the identity of racial minorities who experience racial oppression on a constant basis; in comparison, those who reap social privileges may be less aware of their racial selves. Extending Helms's model to clinical supervision, Cook (1994) maintains that the racial identity ego status of supervisory participants is likely to influence their supervisory interactions, and by providing a comprehensive account of different configurations of racial identity interaction in supervision (e.g., *parallel, progressive,* and *regressive*), she offers insight into the ways in which racial-cultural issues are approached or avoided in the supervision process. In addition, the supervisory relationship may be difficult to negotiate if the supervisor has more knowledge and technical skills of a specific theoretical orientation than the supervisee, but the supervisee has more knowledge, experience, or skills than the supervisor in working with people of Color (Aponte & Johnson, 2000; Fukuyama, 1994). According to Cook, these relationships may be characterized as regressive. Supervisors, for example, may be effective in the use of interpretation and become aware of the different aspects of interpretation that influence its effect. In contrast, the supervisee, despite cultural awareness and sensitivity, may not be cognizant of the limitations or the debilitating effects that the unexamined aspects of this interpretation technique may have.

Experiential Activities

An overemphasis on the didactic component of the learning process may lead to an intellectual exercise, often obscuring the complexity of racial-cultural issues in supervision and allowing trainees to minimize the need to examine their own racial-cultural beliefs and assumptions (Reynolds, 1995, this *Handbook,* this volume). Hence, didactic instruction should be accompanied by learning activities that are primarily experiential in nature and aim to expand the "comfort zone" of trainees in interacting with individuals across racial-cultural divides (Carter, 2003). Experiential activities encourage trainees to shift their perceptions of race and culture from static background variables to subtle but powerful influencers in the interpersonal encounter.

To be effective, the educator should design a series of experiential exercises from low to high levels of anxiety, with consideration of the level of safety and trust displayed in the training environment. When there is a moderate to high level of safety and trust, specific racial-cultural counseling experiential exercises or approaches (e.g., Carter, 2003; Pedersen, 2000) may be adapted and utilized to increase trainees' *cognitive empathy* (Scott & Borodovsky, 1990) in interracial interactions. As discussed by Bernard and Goodyear (2004), a worst-case scenario may be created and discussed to allay trainees' anxiety by encouraging trainees to work in small groups to develop and describe several "absolutely awful" supervision skits in relation to both race and culture. When used with an appropriate balance of anxiety and trust, experiential exercises encourage trainees to take personal risks and to be open to their own experiences and mistakes so that valuable lessons may be learned. Following a didactic discussion of general and unique racial-cultural issues in supervision, the educator may use experiential and cooperative learning activities, such as role playing, case studies, or guided imagery, to facilitate trainees' exploration of potential plans and strategies when confronted with challenging issues in supervision.

The Role of Counselor

Unlike the teacher role, which places emphasis on facilitating trainees' acquisition of declarative knowledge (Anderson, 1993), the educator engages in the counselor role when trainees' learning seems to be inhibited by their own personal beliefs, experiences, or needs. An example is supervisor trainees' *cultural countertransference* (Vargas, 1989), which arises from their limited experience with clients of Color or supervisees of Color or from their past experiences with a specific racial-cultural group. Because the discussion of race and culture in supervision requires a high degree of involvement that is grounded in personal experience, values, and beliefs, the educator is called on to employ counseling skills to manage these challenges with sensitivity and appropriate concern for the needs of trainees. Interventions aimed at identifying obstacles that may interfere with racial-cultural learning should consider both intra- and interpersonal dynamics in the training group. Intervention strategies may be utilized at the individual or group level, depending on the source of obstacles. When there is evidence, for instance, that the learning process is stalled by a group phenomenon, a group-level intervention strategy would be more appropriate and effective.

Individual-Level Intervention Strategies

When trainees' personal characteristics interfere with the acquisition and application of knowledge and skills or negatively affect the learning experience of others in the group, the educator has the responsibility to be active in exploring these issues with them privately. Prior to exploration with individual trainees, however, the educator should identify specific issues or concerns that affect their professional functioning, along with specific examples and target goals. Without clarification from the educator, trainees may feel undue pressure by the educator to address personal issues, which may be intrusive, if not unethical (Bernard & Goodyear, 2004). Using a variety of counseling skills, notably active listening, paraphrasing, empathy, and clarification, the educator is more likely to be successful in facilitating open discussions that are supportive in tone but specific in purpose.

Group-Level Intervention Strategies

When exploring racial-cultural factors and issues, the educator should take a proactive approach by anticipating problems, establishing ground rules (e.g., confidentiality), and building norms. At the onset of racial-cultural training, sufficient time must be allotted so that trainees can establish their ground rules through a discussion of personal safety and boundaries in the learning environment. Acting as a *norm shaper* (Yalom, 1995), the educator helps group members explore their reactions in various challenging scenarios, thus building constructive communicative and procedural norms. As a *participant-observer,* the educator remains cognizant of the developmental stage of the group and the therapeutic factors at work at each stage.

One task involves monitoring both subtle and obvious interpersonal dynamics that emerge in the process. Subtle dynamics are harder to detect and therefore more difficult to address than overt challenging group dynamics (e.g., conflicts, subgrouping). Trainees of Color, for example, may be pressured or expected by other members in the group to assume responsibility for exploring racial-cultural issues (Cook, 1994). To minimize the anxiety surrounding the topic of race, group members may neutralize the topic by using "culture" and other euphemisms instead of "race" (Helms & Cook, 1999). Although intervention strategies relative to each of these subtle challenges are much more complicated, group counseling skills, especially process illumination and linking, are particularly useful in facilitating the development of trainees, both individually and as a group (Chen, Thombs, & Costa, 2003).

The Role of Supervisor

The supervision format is a highly valuable training component because without supervision, trainees' gains in racial-cultural awareness and knowledge do not translate readily into improved practice (Ancis & Ladany, 2001; Chen, 2001; Constantine, 2003). In supervision with the educator, trainees experience the complex interacting forces that influence the definition and negotiation of interpersonal relationships. They observe how the educator, as supervisor, navigates through this complex process. Furthermore, trainees learn how to apply didactic information by way of the supervision experience. The primary aim of the educator in the supervisor role, therefore, is to solidify trainees' racial-cultural competencies through the integration of cognitive learning into supervision practice. The secondary aim is to monitor the performance of trainees to maximize benefits and to prevent or minimize any adverse impact on their supervisees, and by extension, the clients.

Unlike the roles of teacher or counselor, where the focus is placed on either the content being learned or the characteristics of supervisor trainees and general interpersonal dynamics, the supervisor role commands attention to supervisor trainees' behavior in action and, more specifically, to the degree to which racial-cultural knowledge and skills are applied in the supervision session. In the supervisor role, the educator may face the double temptation of functioning as a "remote counselor" (to the client) or as a "remote supervisor" (to the trainee's supervisee). To avoid these traps, the educator should engage with trainees in responding to the following question derived from Paul's (1967) query about individual therapy: *What* supervision strategies are most effective for *this* supervisee, given her or his levels of professional development and racial-cultural training and competencies, in order to best serve *that* specific client under *that* unique set of circumstances?

As shown in Table 10.1, common supervision strategies include tape review, review of session notes, sharing written observations, journals, reflective inquiry (discussed later), case conference, and group consultation (Bernard & Goodyear, 2004). A great number of potentially helpful perspectives or models related to racial-cultural supervision have been developed (e.g., Ancis & Ladany, 2001; Brown & Landrum-Brown, 1995; Lopez, 1997); two others (Helms & Cook, 1999; Martinez & Holloway, 1997) seem particularly relevant to supervisor training and are described later. A third approach (Chen, 2001) is elaborated and applied to group supervision as a case example.

The Helms and Cook Approach

In Helms and Cook's (1999) view, racial-cultural factors affect the intrapersonal and interpersonal dynamics in the supervision relationship, as well as the supervisee's concurrent functioning in the counseling process. Racial-cultural issues exert an ongoing influence on supervision encounters, although more saliently in some interactions than in others. Helms and Cook encourage supervisors to utilize a here-and-now focus to uncover and clarify the nature of racial identity interactions (Cook, 1994) in the supervision relationship. Applying Yalom's (1995) concept of process illumination to supervision, they suggest that supervisors move sequentially from *experiencing* to *illumination* in the interactive process.

The experiencing phase requires supervisors and supervisees to reflect on the supervision and counseling relationships, respectively, and to ask What is going on here, right now? Helms and Cook (1999) list other specific questions for supervisees to explore:

> At what point did you notice the client's race (or culture)? How does it feel when a person of my race makes such observations about your client? What do you think about what I just said? What do you usually do when you feel like this? How similar to your client's feelings about you is what you're feeling about me right now? (p. 286)

Similarly, the supervisor poses questions that promote reflection on her or his own race-based assumptions about clients and supervisees and the infiltration of her or his worldview on supervisees' conceptualizations and diagnoses of clients.

A mere exploration of the experience, however, is not complete without illumination, which characterizes the second phase. When an event is experienced and its racial-cultural components are clarified and examined fully, the supervisory participants gain a cognitive understanding of the influence of race-culture on the interpersonal transaction. This approach allows them to generalize the interpersonal learning from the current interaction to other situations.

The Martinez and Holloway Approach

Martinez and Holloway (1997) extend the systems approach to supervision (Holloway, 1995) to examine racial-cultural issues in supervision. At the core of the systems approach to supervision is the supervisory relationship, which operates in a teaching-learning context. Several factors influence how specific learning tasks and teaching strategies are linked to the supervisor trainee's professional development: (1) tasks: *what* is the teaching topic of supervision; (2) functions: *how* is the supervisor trainee teaching; and (3) contextual factors encompassing the characteristics of client, supervisee, supervisor, and institution. Thus, the supervisory relationship reins in the supervision process with tasks and functions that assist the supervisee in the acquisition of skills necessary to perform important counseling functions.

Martinez and Holloway's (1997) approach connects the principles of racial-cultural training with the practice of supervision by asserting that the supervision relationship, which is shaped by participants' expectations, racial-cultural identities, and attitudes, empowers supervisor trainees to systematically explore and examine racial-cultural issues. Trainees are encouraged to learn how to use the systems approach to supervision as a language for describing salient events in supervision across multiple relational contexts. The sources of racial-cultural challenges and issues that emerge in the relational contexts of the systems approach to supervision may then be identified and addressed appropriately.

An Interactional Approach to Clinical Supervision

Although initially proposed to guide clinical supervisors as they facilitate the development of multicultural competencies of counselor trainees, the interactional approach to clinical supervision described by Chen (2001) may also be used as a link between the principles of racial-cultural training and the practice of supervisor educators. The interactional approach places a premium on interpersonal communication as a window into the nature of interpersonal relationships and into the characters of the interacting participants (Chen & Bernstein, 2000). Through critical incidents in interpersonal encounters in supervision, clinical supervisors reveal much about themselves, both personally and professionally, and the way they approach supervision. Integral to the interactional perspective are the concepts of *intentionality* and *reflection.*

Intentionality refers to the supervisor's purposeful selection of behavior responses from a range of alternatives in order to achieve specific goals. Two distinct aspects of intentionality warrant clarification. The reason aspect, or why the supervisor acts in certain ways, deals with both the understanding of the antecedent conditions of the supervisor's behaviors and the rationale for choosing particular behaviors, response modes, skills, or interventions in lieu of other alternatives. The plan aspect, or what the supervisor has in mind for the supervisee, brings into focus the anticipated effect of the behavioral response on the supervisee's cognition, affect, or behavior.

The second concept, reflection, centers on the supervisor's diligent behavior in undergoing active, persistent, and deliberate consideration of any covert beliefs or tacit assumptions in light of the evidence that supports them and the immediate consequences they evoke. Reflection on these helpful and hindering moments in clinical supervision is important for advancing the supervisor's understanding of how racial-cultural issues are manifested during the supervision session. Through reflective inquiry, the supervisor can identify and address different problems in the supervisory working alliance, such as ruptures, misunderstandings, or impasses (Liu & Pope-Davis, this *Handbook,* this volume).

In the context of supervisor training, the educator in the interactional approach functions mainly as a participant-observer in the training process. Similar to the role of inquirer in Kagan's (1976, 1980) interpersonal process recall method, the educator guides the exploration of salient interpersonal transactions from supervisor trainees' sessions. Specifically, the educator raises questions relative to each of the four phases in the reflective inquiry process: (1) *describing,* or recalling and articulating the critical incidents in vivid detail; (2) *informing,* or uncovering meanings that are derived from and embedded in these interpersonal transactions, from the perspectives of both interactants; (3) *confronting,* or identifying, challenging, and evaluating assumptions and choices made relative to the given consequences; and (4) *planning,* or developing specific goals and action strategies for future sessions. An illustration of this sequence is provided in the case example.

Grounded in the empirical and conceptual bases, the interactional approach is well suited for the educator who endeavors to provide racial-cultural training on several fronts. First, it establishes a learning environment that is characterized by support and challenge. Trainees may examine and question their unwarranted assumptions, stereotypes, and beliefs in a manner that allows them to adjust the reason and plan aspects of their intentionality in future supervision sessions. Second, the approach focuses on the examination of critical incidents in interpersonal encounters, particularly incidents, interactions, and processes in clinical supervision that may be related to or influenced by the race-ethnicity of the supervisor, supervisee, or clients, or any stereotypes and assumptions about race-ethnicity. As such, this approach is similar to Helms and Cook's (1999) model in placing emphasis on "racial events" (Helms, 1995) and on trainees' here-and-now experiences of racial-cultural issues. The approach is trainee-centered in the sense that the racial-cultural events to be examined are provided by the trainees, and recommendations generated from the reflective inquiry process correspond to the specific needs and developmental levels of the trainees. Third, as in Martinez and Holloway (1997), the approach seeks to motivate trainees to become self-directing and self-monitoring in their supervision practice. Trainees are encouraged to become their own critics and to develop curiosity about the meaning of their interactants' behaviors and responses, thus increasing their effectiveness in supervision.

The Role of Advocate

Racial-cultural training needs to be implemented at the institutional, program, curriculum, instructional, and individual levels in order for change to occur and endure (Aponte & Aponte, 2000). The institutional system itself is made up of individuals; consequently, it is not immune from biased practice. Although oppression may be manifested at the interpersonal, institutional, and societal levels, its corrosive power at the systemic level is much greater and often goes unchallenged (Atkinson, Thompson, & Grant, 1993). Thus, the system context of the supervision or learning environment plays a vital role in trainees' learning experience and educators' effectiveness in supervision (Chambers, Lewis, & Kerezsi, 1995). The development of racial-cultural competencies calls for a collaborative effort at multiple levels, including the institutional, program, curriculum, and instructional levels. Rooney, Flores, and Mercier (1998) and Ponterotto (1998), for instance, have identified contextual influences as key aspects that greatly impacted their own experiences in racial-cultural counseling as students and as a counselor educator, respectively.

Therefore, aside from the aforementioned roles, supervisor educators need to serve as advocates when contextual conditions may hamper or sabotage racial-cultural training. As advocates, educators focus on the contexts surrounding the supervisor training, with two goals in mind: first, to identify and remediate an existing problem with an external source for trainees, and second, to promote and embrace racial-cultural awareness within the system. In pursuing these goals, educators strive to model for the trainees an ongoing concern for issues and factors outside the supervisory and counseling relationships that may affect, positively or negatively, the development of racial-cultural competencies of trainees.

Strategically, it may prove fruitful for systemic biases or problems relative to race and culture to be located and explored first within the specific training group. These organizational concerns may involve inconsistency or incompatibility in different areas (e.g., mission statement, organizational policies and practices, resources, space and facility) or at various levels (e.g., administration, training, service delivery) and may be ideological or structural in nature. Because these concerns or conditions may not be obvious to educators, an ongoing process of self-examination is crucial, followed by a dialogue with trainees and colleagues in the system. If individuals in power do not seem to be aware of the conditions or characteristics in question, advising them of the impact that these conditions are having on the learning of trainees would be an appropriate step. If the overall organizational setting is not responsive to the learning needs of supervisor trainees or their supervisees, however, educators should pursue alternative courses of action with or for trainees while consulting with colleagues to bring about change. Initiatives may include the following: challenging or confronting the source of the problem on be-half of trainees; defending trainees' roles, functions, and responsibilities; and pro-moting changes or solutions that may better address the needs of trainees.

— Case Example: An Interactional Approach to Supervision of Trainees —

The case example is intended to illustrate the utility and steps of the interactional approach in racial-cultural training for supervisors in a context of group supervision. The discussion focuses on group supervision for several reasons. First, group supervision is probably the most frequently used modality for supervision of trainees (Bernard & Goodyear, 2004). Second, the complexity inherent in the group format is often challenging for educators. Third, there are certain advantages to group supervision as opposed to individual supervision, such as monitoring trainees' performances in a relatively ego-protected environment, the availability of multiple sources of feedback, and the relative ease with which vicarious learning may take place (Fong & Lease, 1997; Martinez & Holloway, 1997).

Vignette

A faculty member conducts regular group supervision sessions for doctoral students who are being trained as supervisors, and each of the doctoral students supervises a group of master's-level counseling students. After a brief silence at the beginning of a group supervision session, Kathy, a female member in a group of mostly White supervisor trainees and a Jewish counseling psychology doctoral student in her late twenties with extensive counseling experience, requests to use some time to discuss her own supervision group. As required in the supervision course, Kathy has pro-vided three group supervision sessions for three counselor trainees, all in their mid-twenties: Mary, Jennifer, and Tom.

She describes her supervisees as follows. Mary is a Black woman completing her practicum at a high school in a suburban area with large Black and Hispanic popu-lations. She expressed comfort with being in the counselor role and attributed it to her three years of prior experience working with adolescents. Her career goal is to work at a high school as a school counselor addressing the career choices and devel-opmental issues of high school juniors and seniors.

Jennifer is a Black woman with no prior counseling experience. She is currently working as a practicum student at a Catholic high school. At the outset, she experi-enced high anxiety about adjusting to the counselor role. She felt like an "imposter" and worried about not knowing what to say or do during a counseling session. She expressed relief that the supervision group was relatively small, as she tends to be shy and more hesitant to speak in large group settings.

Tom, who is White, is doing his first practicum in a high school with a diverse student population. He indicated that his selection of this practicum site was based on his motivation to broaden his cultural exposure and competencies. During the first supervision session, he described his own Catholic schooling as regimented and nondiverse, recalling, "There were three Blacks in the school and they were as active and as White as any other White person." His experience has been enlightening, and he has valiantly struggled to empathize with his clients and to balance the multiple issues of cultural values, religious beliefs, and client concerns.

Reflective Inquiry Process

In accordance with the first phase of the interactional approach, *describing,* the supervisor educator invites Kathy to describe in detail a specific critical incident in her supervision session while raising specific questions: "What actually happened? What were you hearing your supervisees say and observing them do?" Upon reflection, Kathy expresses her discomfort about the "racial undertones" that went undetected in her third session. Specifically, whenever Jennifer requested suggestions regarding her work with clients, Mary often quickly offered responses that seemed to be quick fixes and not grounded theoretically or empirically. Furthermore, Kathy recalls feeling that her efforts to explore with Jennifer were sabotaged by Mary, who often plays the role of "expert" or "supervisor." Some of Kathy's suggestions for Jennifer were met with Mary's skepticism, as evidenced by her response, "That's not practical." Kathy observed that during the session there seemed to be an increased level of interaction between Mary and Jennifer, while both Kathy and Tom remained unusually quiet, particularly during the latter part of the session.

In the next phase, *informing,* the educator asks Kathy to direct her attention to the meanings she derives from these transactions. Specifically, the educator and the trainees in the group pose: "What was your own reaction, overt and covert, when you experienced the 'racial undertones' during these moments? In what way did this event stand out for you? What might it mean from each of your supervisees' perspectives?" Kathy indicates that she feels discouraged, impatient, and frustrated that her group is not making much progress. Specifically, she recalls feeling slighted, challenged, and "dethroned" by Mary, who seems to exude a confidence that exceeds her level of professional development. While feeling more connected with both Jennifer and Tom because they seem open and cooperative, she feels "excluded" by Mary and Jennifer because she perceives that they have formed a special bond because of their race. As if walking on eggshells, Kathy admits that she experiences fear and discomfort that her supervisees, particularly Mary and Jennifer, may accuse her of racial-cultural insensitivity or, even worse, of racist attitudes if she addresses this "racial undertone." She also expresses concern about Tom's behavior in supervision, as he seems to be increasingly withdrawn and less involved. She wonders to what extent Mary and Jennifer might be repelled by the racist remarks that Tom made during the first session.

The third phase, *confronting,* involves uncovering Kathy's intentionality preceding her behaviors in the session. Questions to consider are the following: "What was the possible range of alternatives for you to respond to this 'racial undertone'? How did you choose to act the way you did from among the alternatives? How did you explain this event from your perspective, and from your supervisees' perspectives, individually and jointly?"

Kathy describes her desire for each of her supervisees to benefit from her supervision. She wants each of them to feel included in the group and experience a sense of belonging, "despite individual differences," but she is held back by her own doubts. She indicates that she is hesitant to challenge Mary's perceived counseling competencies due to her own lack of experience in working with youth of Color. She also fears that addressing Tom's racist comments from the first session would only make him more withdrawn and would therefore threaten group cohesion. In addition, her perception of the "subgroup" of Mary and Jennifer is further complicating the development of group cohesion. Without addressing these issues promptly and effectively, however, she is concerned that the subsequent supervision may "derail" from the ideal course.

After enough response has been generated from Kathy, members in the supervisor group are encouraged to participate more fully in the confronting phase by sharing their own reactions, thoughts, or comments from the perspectives of supervisor or supervisee. In doing so, possible intervention strategies may be expanded and accompanied by the increased range of supervisor intentionality. Feedback from the group involves several areas:

- The supervisory relationship may feel awkward for every member in the group, particularly for Kathy and Mary. This is because Mary, as a trainee, has more knowledge, experience, or skills in working with youth of Color than does Kathy, a fact that is rarely acknowledged directly by all members in the supervision group.

- The bond between Mary and Jennifer seems to be interpreted by Kathy as an intentional act to exclude Tom and Kathy. What are alternative hypotheses? How likely is it that the bond between Mary and Jennifer formed as a result of their similarity in race, sex, and status as counselor trainees working in high school settings?

- Kathy seems to perceive individual differences as obstacles to be overcome, as opposed to opportunities that would deepen interpersonal understandings.

- Both Kathy and Mary seem to share similar needs to feel competent or helpful. To what extent do Kathy's needs, coupled with her task-oriented supervisory style, interfere with her goal of building a cohesive group?

Finally, accompanying the *planning* phase are the following questions: "How might what happened suggest to you what you should attend to during the next session? What would you like to see happen next? To what end? What are the implications for your supervision practice?" In light of her own reflections, as well as the feedback from the group, Kathy reports a new understanding of this critical event and the nature of the interpersonal relationships built in her supervision group. Recognizing the limitations of her supervisory style and the impact of her own needs on her group, she identifies building group cohesion as her primary goal for the next session. Specifically, she plans to state matter-of-factly to her group that due to racial and sex differences, there will be times when she will need them to help her understand their perspectives, and that she welcomes the opportunity to discuss these issues further in their supervision sessions. Moreover, Kathy believes that she could strengthen her connections with each supervisee in the following ways:

- She could connect with Jennifer by emphasizing their similarity in terms of the "novice" status and their feelings of insecurity in the professional development process, as both are supervisor and counselor in training. She would encourage her not to devalue her own experience, learning, and instinct as a budding counselor.

- With Mary, Kathy could build their working alliance by acknowledging Mary's contributions to the group, particularly for Jennifer, due to her extensive knowledge, experience, and skills in working with youth of Color. She could communicate to Mary that she values her contribution to the group's learning and hopes that Mary will benefit from the group as well.

- With Tom, she could encourage him to share his experience as the only man in the group, reinforce his efforts to increase his racial-cultural competencies, and support him in using this group as a laboratory to examine racial-cultural issues, as well as other individual differences, that may occur in the future.

Following the planning phase, the educator shifts the focus from Kathy to the entire supervisor-training group and asks members to reflect on their learning, in terms of both content and process. The reflection is intended as a mechanism to identify emergent themes, convergent and divergent, among members' reactions so that learning can be consolidated, feedback given, and a parallel process may occur from the supervisor-training group to Kathy's supervision group.

Comments

This case example depicts the process through which the educator draws out a trainee's tacit assumptions and beliefs that influence the direction of her interventions. This example is not intended to direct educators on how to function as supervisors but to illustrate the potential that the interactional approach has to offer. The supervision group as a "social microcosm" (Yalom, 1995) provides a context in which sociocultural roles and expectations may be explored and negotiated. Educators in their role as supervisors of training groups thus function to foster such an examination and to offer the opportunity for increased sensitivity and appreciation for racial-cultural issues. Ideally, trainees' stereotypical views and behaviors may be relinquished for new, more adaptive ones. Therapeutic factors and concepts of group dynamics, such as cohesion and competition, take on a new spin when viewed through the lens of race and culture. Indeed, reflective inquiry as a "multilayered analysis penetrates each relationship and enhances the opportunity to both recognize the context in which each issue emerges and how this influences other contexts" (Holloway, 1995, p. 163).

CONCLUSIONS

Incorporating race and culture into clinical supervision training is neither an easy nor a short-term task for educators. Each of the interrelated interpersonal contexts, namely, counseling, supervision, and supervisor training, is composed of individuals who bring unique social and cultural values, beliefs, and expectations to each interpersonal encounter. Educators thus face the daunting task of keeping these complex, interacting sociocultural forces in mind while striving to create and set in motion the machinery of supervisor training and to keep it operating with maximum effectiveness.

Although educators are required to play several roles simultaneously, the demands, expectations, and anxiety of trainees are no less intimidating. In discussing supervisee anxiety in clinical supervision, Olk and Friedlander (1992) argue that supervisees often have to navigate several roles, which may be contradictory at times. On one hand, as learners, they are expected to remain motivated, eager to learn, and open to feedback from their supervisors. On the other hand, they must ensure that their supervisors will continue to evaluate their performance favorably. Furthermore, they may be expected to act as clients in supervision by disclosing any personal issues that may get in the way of their effective professional functioning, with the looming concern in their mind that in doing so, they may be perceived as incompetent. Supervisor trainees may find themselves in a similarly vulnerable position in racial-cultural training, and educators should be particularly cautious, patient, and supportive in order to alleviate feelings of anxiety and vulnerability.

In collaboration with educators, trainees can create, share, apply, and master knowledge and skills in this learning process. Through a mixture of teaching and learning strategies and activities, trainees and educators can engage in a broad spectrum of cognitive, affective, and social interactions that permit collaborative, inquiry-based learning. The idiosyncrasies of particular supervisors, individually and as a group, however, are not amenable to the simple application of a cookbook approach. The suggested goals, focus areas, and strategies presented in this chapter are by no means prescriptive or exhaustive. Rather, they represent an effort to stimulate the creative thinking of educators in developing effective training activities and experiences for supervisors as they endeavor to become more proficient and culturally responsive in clinical practice.

REFERENCES

Abreu, J. M., Chung, R. H. G., & Atkinson, D. R. (2000). Multicultural counseling training: Past, present, and future directions. *Counseling Psychologist, 28,* 641–656.

American Psychological Association. (1993). Guidelines for providers of psychological services to ethnic, linguistic, and culturally diverse populations. *American Psychologist, 48,* 45–48.

American Psychological Association. (2003). Guidelines on multicultural education, training, research, practice, and organizational change for psychologists. *American Psychologist, 58,* 377–402.

Ancis, J. R., & Ladany, N. (2001). A multicultural framework for counselor supervision. In L. J. Bradley & N. Ladany (Eds.), *Counselor supervision: Principles, process, and practice* (3rd ed., pp. 63–90). Philadelphia: Brunner-Routledge.

Anderson, J. R. (1993). *Rules of the mind.* Hillsdale, NJ: Erlbaum.

Aponte, J. F., & Aponte, C. E. (2000). Educating and training professionals to work with ethnic populations in the twenty-first century. In J. F. Aponte & J. Wohl (Eds.), *Psychological intervention and cultural diversity* (2nd ed., pp. 250–267). Needham Heights, MA: Allyn & Bacon.

Aponte, J. F., & Johnson, L. R. (2000). Ethnicity and supervision: Models, methods, processes, and issues. In J. F. Aponte & J. Wohl (Eds.), *Psychological intervention and cultural diversity* (2nd ed., pp. 268–285). Needham Heights, MA: Allyn & Bacon.

Arredondo, P. (1999). Multicultural counseling competencies as tools to address racism and oppression. *Journal of Counseling and Development, 77,* 102–108.

Arredondo, P., Toporek, R., Brown, S. P., Jones, J., Locke, D. C., Sanchez, J., et al. (1996). Operationalization of the multicultural counseling competencies. *Journal of Multicultural Counseling and Development, 24,* 42–78.

Atkinson, D. R., Morten, G., & Sue, D. W. (1998). Within-group differences among racial/ethnic minorities. In D. R. Atkinson, G. Morten, & D. W. Sue (Eds.), *Counseling American minorities: A cross-cultural perspective* (5th ed., pp. 21–50). Boston: McGraw-Hill.

Atkinson, D. R., Thompson, C. E., & Grant, S. K. (1993). A three-dimensional model for counseling racial/ethnic minorities. *Counseling Psychologist, 21,* 257–277.

Bernard, J. M. (1994). Multicultural supervision: A reaction to Leong and Wagner, Cook, Priest, and Fukuyama. *Counselor Education and Supervision, 34,* 159–171.

Bernard, J. M., & Goodyear, R. K. (2004). *Fundamentals of clinical supervision* (3rd ed.). Boston: Allyn & Bacon.

Berry, J. W., & Kim, U. (1988). Acculturation and mental health. In P. Dasen, J. W. Berry, & N. Sartorius (Eds.), *Health and cross-cultural psychology* (pp. 207–236). Newbury Park, CA: Sage.

Brown, M. T., & Landrum-Brown, J. (1995). Counselor supervision: Cross-cultural perspectives. In J. G. Ponterotto, J. M. Casas, L. A. Suzuki, & C. M. Alexander (Eds.), *Handbook of multicultural counseling* (pp. 263–286). Thousand Oaks, CA: Sage.

Carter, R. T. (2003). Becoming racially and culturally competent: The racial-cultural counseling laboratory. *Journal of Multicultural Counseling and Development, 31,* 20–30.

Chambers, T., Lewis, J., & Kerezsi, P. (1995). African American and white American students: Cross-cultural preparation programs. *Counseling Psychologist, 23,* 43–62.

Chen, E. C. (2001). Multicultural counseling supervision: An interactional approach. In J. G. Ponterotto, J. M. Casas, L. A. Suzuki, & C. M. Alexander (Eds.), *Handbook of multicultural counseling* (2nd ed., pp. 801–824). Thousand Oaks, CA: Sage.

Chen, E. C., & Bernstein, B. L. (2000). Relations of complementarity and supervisory issues to supervisory working alliance: A comparative analysis of two cases. *Journal of Counseling Psychology, 47,* 485–497.

Chen, E. C., Thombs, B., & Costa, C. I. (2003). Multicultural competencies in group therapy: Process and tasks. In D. B. Pope-Davis, H. L. K. Coleman, W. M., Liu, & R. L. Toporek (Eds.), *Handbook of multicultural competencies in counseling and psychology* (pp. 456–477). Thousand Oaks, CA: Sage.

Constantine, M. G. (2003). Multicultural competence in supervision: Issues, process, and outcomes. In D. B. Pope-Davis, H. L. K. Coleman, W. M. Liu, & R. L. Toporek (Eds.), *Handbook of multicultural competencies in counseling and psychology* (pp. 383–391). Thousand Oaks, CA: Sage.

Constantine, M. G., & Ladany, N. (2000). Self-report multicultural counseling competence scales: Their relation to social desirability attitudes and multicultural case conceptualization ability. *Journal of Counseling Psychology, 47,* 102–115.

Cook, D. A. (1994). Racial identity in supervision. *Counselor Education and Supervision, 34,* 132–141.

Cross, W. E. (1995). The psychology of Nigrescence: Revising the Cross model. In J. G. Ponterotto, J. M. Casas, L. A. Suzuki, & C. M. Alexander (Eds.), *Handbook of multicultural counseling* (pp. 93–122). Thousand Oaks, CA: Sage.

D'Andrea, M., & Daniels, J. (2001). Expanding our thinking about white racism: Facing the challenge of multicultural counseling in the 21st century. In J. G. Ponterotto, J. M. Casas, L. A. Suzuki, & C. M. Alexander (Eds.), *Handbook of multicultural counseling* (2nd ed., pp. 289–310). Thousand Oaks, CA: Sage.

Fong, M. L., & Lease, S. H. (1997). Cross-cultural supervision: Issues for the White supervisor. In D. B. Pope-Davis & H. L. K. Coleman (Eds.), *Multicultural counseling competencies: Assessment, education and training, and supervision* (pp. 380–407). Thousand Oaks, CA: Sage.

Fukuyama, M. A. (1994). Critical incidents in multicultural counseling supervision. *Counselor Education and Supervision, 34,* 142–151.

Goodyear, R. K., & Guzzardo, C. R. (2000). Psychotherapy supervision and training. In S. D. Brown & R. W. Lent (Eds.), *Handbook of counseling psychology* (3rd ed., pp. 83–108). New York: Wiley.

Helms, J. E. (Ed.). (1990). *Black and white racial identity: Theory, research, and practice.* Westport, CT: Greenwood.

Helms, J. E. (1994). How multiculturalism obscures racial factors in the therapy process: Comment on Ridley et al. (1994), Sodowsky et al. (1994), Ottavi et al. (1994), and Thompson et al. (1994). *Journal of Counseling Psychology, 41,* 162–165.

Helms, J. E. (1995). An update of Helms's White and people of Color racial identity models. In J. G. Ponterotto, J. M. Casas, L. A. Suzuki, & C. M. Alexander (Eds.), *Handbook of multicultural counseling* (pp. 181–198). Thousand Oaks, CA: Sage.

Helms, J. E. (2001). An update of Helms's White and people of Color racial identity models. In J. G. Ponterotto, J. M. Casas, L. A. Suzuki, & C. M. Alexander (Eds.), *Handbook of multicultural counseling* (2nd ed., pp. 181–198). Thousand Oaks, CA: Sage.

Helms, J. E., & Cook, D. A. (1999). *Using race and culture in counseling and psychotherapy: Theory and process.* Boston: Allyn & Bacon.

Ho, D. Y. F. (1995). Internalized culture, culturocentrism, and transcendence. *Counseling Psychologist, 23,* 4–24.

Holloway, E. L. (1995). *Clinical supervision: A systems approach.* Thousand Oaks, CA: Sage.

Ibrahim, F. A. (1991). Contribution of cultural worldview to generic counseling and development. *Journal of Counseling and Development, 70,* 13–19.

Ibrahim, F. A., Roysircar-Sodowsky, G., & Ohnishi, H. (2001). Worldview: Recent developments and needed directions. In J. G. Ponterotto, J. M. Casas, L. A. Suzuki, & C. M. Alexander (Eds.), *Handbook of multicultural counseling* (2nd ed., pp. 801–824). Thousand Oaks, CA: Sage.

Johnson, S. D. (1987). Knowing that versus knowing how: Toward achieving expertise through multicultural training for counseling. *Counseling Psychologist, 15,* 320–331.

Kagan, N. (1976). *Influencing human interaction.* Mason, MI: Mason Media.

Kagan, N. (1980). Influencing human interaction—eighteen years with IPR. In A. K. Hess (Ed.), *Psychotherapy supervision: Theory, research and practice* (pp. 262–286). New York: Wiley.

Ladany, N., Inman, A. G., Constantine, M. G., & Hofheinz, E. W. (1997). Supervisee multicultural case conceptualization ability and self-reported multicultural competence as functions of supervisee racial identity and supervisor focus. *Journal of Counseling Psychology, 44*, 284–293.

Leong, F. T. L. (1996). Toward an integrative model for cross-cultural counseling and psychotherapy. *Applied and Preventive Psychology: Current Scientific Perspectives, 5*, 189–209.

Leong, F. T. L., & Wagner, N. S. (1994). Cross-cultural counseling supervision: What do we know? What do we need to know? *Counselor Education and Supervision, 34*, 117–131.

Lopez, S. R. (1997). Cultural competence in psychotherapy: A guide for clinicians and their supervisors. In C. E. Watkins, Jr. (Ed.), *Handbook of psychotherapy supervision* (pp. 570–588). New York: Wiley.

Martinez, R. P., & Holloway, E. L. (1997). The supervision relationship in multicultural training. In D. B. Pope-Davis & H. L. K. Coleman (Eds.), *Multicultural counseling competencies: Assessment, education and training, and supervision* (pp. 325–349). Thousand Oaks, CA: Sage.

Mollen, D., Ridley, C. R., & Hill, C. L. (2003). Models of multicultural counseling competence: A critical evaluation. In D. B. Pope-Davis, H. L. K. Coleman, W. M. Liu, & R. L. Toporek (Eds.), *Handbook of multicultural competencies in counseling and psychology* (pp. 21–37). Thousand Oaks, CA: Sage.

Olk, M., & Friedlander, M. L. (1992). Trainees' experiences of role conflict and role ambiguity in supervisory relationships. *Journal of Counseling Psychology, 39*, 389–397.

Paul, G. (1967). Strategy in outcome research in psychotherapy. *Journal of Consulting Psychology, 31*, 109–118.

Pedersen, P. B. (2000). *A handbook for developing multicultural awareness* (3rd ed.). Alexandria, VA: American Counseling Association.

Ponterotto, J. G. (1997). Multicultural counseling training: A competency model and national survey. In D. B. Pope-Davis & H. L. K. Coleman (Eds.), *Multicultural counseling competencies: Assessment, education and training, and supervision* (pp. 111–130). Thousand Oaks, CA: Sage.

Ponterotto, J. G. (1998). Charting a course for research in multicultural counseling training. *Counseling Psychologist, 26*, 43–68.

Ponterotto, J. G., Fuertes, J. N., & Chen, E. C. (2000). Models of multicultural counseling. In S. D. Brown & R. W. Lent (Eds.), *Handbook of counseling psychology* (3rd ed., pp. 639–669). New York: Wiley.

Pope-Davis, D. B., Coleman, H. L. K., Liu, W. M., & Toporek, R. L. (Eds.). (2003). *Handbook of multicultural competencies in counseling and psychology.* Thousand Oaks, CA: Sage.

Priest, R. (1994). Minority supervisor and majority supervisee: Another perspective of reality. *Counselor Education and Supervision, 34*, 152–158.

Quintana, S. M., & Bernal, M. E. (1995). Ethnic minority training in counseling psychology: Comparisons with clinical psychology and proposed standards. *Counseling Psychologist, 23*, 102–121.

Remington, G., & DaCosta, G. (1989). Ethnocultural factors in resident supervision: Black supervisor and white supervisees. *American Journal of Psychotherapy, 43*, 398–404.

Reynolds, A. L. (1995). Challenges and strategies for teaching multicultural counseling courses. In J. G. Ponterotto J. M. Casas, L. A. Suzuki, & C. M. Alexander (Eds.), *Handbook of multicultural counseling* (pp. 312–330). Thousand Oaks, CA: Sage.

Ridley, C. R., & Kleiner, A. J. (2003). Multicultural counseling competence: History, themes, and issues. In D. B. Pope-Davis, H. L. K. Coleman, W. M. Liu, & R. L. Toporek (Eds.), *Handbook of multicultural competencies in counseling and psychology* (pp. 3–20). Thousand Oaks, CA: Sage.

Ridley, C. R., Mendoza, D. W., & Kanitz, B. E. (1994). Multicultural training: Reexamination, operationalization, and integration. *Counseling Psychologist, 22,* 227–289.

Rooney, S. C., Flores, L. Y., & Mercier, C. A. (1998). Making multicultural education effective for everyone. *Counseling Psychologist, 26,* 22–32.

Scott, N. E., & Borodovsky, L. G. (1990). Effective use of cultural role taking. *Professional Psychology: Research and Practice, 21,* 167–170.

Speight, S. L., Thomas, A. J., Kennel, R. G., & Anderson, M. E. (1995). Operationalizing multicultural training in doctoral programs and internships. *Professional Psychology: Research and Practice, 26,* 401–406.

Sue, D. W., Arredondo, P., & McDavis, R. J. (1992). Multicultural competencies and standards: A call to the profession. *Journal of Multicultural Counseling and Development, 20,* 64–88.

Tyler, J. M., & Guth, L. J. (1999). Using media to create experiential learning in multicultural and diversity issues. *Journal of Multicultural Counseling and Development, 27,* 153–165.

Van Dijk, T. A. (1993). *Elite discourse and racism.* Newbury Park, CA: Sage.

Vargas, L. A. (1989). *Training psychologists to be culturally responsible: Issues in supervision.* Paper presented at a symposium at the 97th Annual Convention of the American Psychological Association. New Orleans, LA.

Vasquez, M. J. T. (1992). Psychologists as clinical supervisor: Promoting ethical practice. *Professional Psychology: Research and Practice, 23,* 196–202.

Yalom, I. D. (1995). *The theory and practice of group psychotherapy* (4th ed.). New York: Basic Books.

CHAPTER 11

Applications of Racial-Cultural Supervision

Amy L. Reynolds

I am completing my predoctoral internship that I decided to do in a large city so I could work with more racially diverse clients. My caseload is very diverse and I am learning so much. However, my supervisor never seems to discuss race or other cultural issues and I feel uncomfortable bringing them up myself. This has been a big disappointment because I didn't expect to have this problem when I discovered that my supervisor was a person of Color. Now I find myself relying on the other interns for support around multicultural issues and concerns. Somehow I thought this time it would be different.

—Latino doctoral student completing his
internship at a VA hospital

I am a faculty member in a clinical psychology program and have been supervising doctoral students for over 15 years. My goal is to be "color-blind" and help my supervisees work effectively with all clients. I don't ignore race, but I think it is more important for students to have grounding in theory and treatment planning. There are multicultural counseling courses that help them learn how to be multiculturally competent. I care about all of our students and can't figure out why the students of Color rarely seek me out as a mentor. I really just don't understand what they expect of me.

—White male faculty member teaching at a
predominately White university

I am completing my first practicum at a nearby college counseling center and have been really enjoying the experience. I like working with my supervisor but I am having difficulty because I have no idea how he views me. He is Japanese American and is very indirect in his feedback. I want him to tell me more of what I am doing wrong and how to make it better but he never does. I want to talk with him about it but I am not sure what to say. Usually I am very assertive and have no problem asking for what I need. Why am I feeling and acting so differently now?

—White female graduate student in counseling psychology

These statements and numerous others like them are all too familiar in academic and training programs in psychology today. Many practitioners and faculty members are struggling with creating supervision experiences that assist graduate students, interns, and new professionals in their development of racial-cultural competence. Several studies have found that trainees and graduate students report dissatisfaction with supervision or have difficulty utilizing supervision as a tool for enhancing their racial-cultural awareness and skills (Duan & Roehlke, 2001; Fukuyama, 1994; Ladany, Lehrman-Waterman, Molinaro, & Wolgast, 1999; Reynolds, Schaefer, Saud, & Blackburn Lue, 2002). Their concerns include a lack of racial-cultural sensitivity by supervisors, having to get racial-cultural supervision needs met outside of supervision by other students or professionals, supervisors ignoring or overinterpreting race or culture, and cross-cultural communication problems (Liu & Pope-Davis, this *Handbook,* this volume).

The training gap in racial-cultural issues appears to be one of the major contributors to the difficulties experienced in supervision. Constantine (1997) reported that many supervisors have not been adequately trained to address racial-cultural issues in supervision and may not be equipped to effectively conceptualize the concerns of diverse clients and provide meaningful support to supervisees struggling to incorporate racial-cultural awareness and skills into their therapy. Helms and Cook (1999) further stated that many supervisors do not know how to address race and culture in the here and now with their supervisees, even though they are able to use those same here-and-now skills in teaching supervisees how to be effective therapists generally (Chen, this *Handbook,* this volume).

Supervision is generally regarded as a vital component in helping students integrate their theoretical knowledge of psychological and counseling issues (Holloway, 1995; Martinez & Holloway, 1997); however, the literature has only begun to explore how to use supervision to integrate racial-cultural issues into the counseling process and to increase racial-cultural competencies (Brown & Landrum-Brown, 1995; Constantine, 1997; Helms & Cook, 1999; Reynolds & Baluch, 2001). Although much of this literature focuses more broadly on multicultural supervision, exploring issues of race and culture are almost always central to the exploration of these issues. Given the essential role supervision plays in the personal and professional development of counselors (Bernard, Goodyear, & Bernard, 2004; Holloway, 1995), more models that have been empirically tested and research about how supervision has helped or hindered the integration of racial-cultural issues are needed (Reynolds et al., 2002).

The purpose of this chapter is to briefly review the status of the multicultural and racial-cultural supervision literature, provide illustrations of how racial and cultural issues influence the supervision process, and make concrete suggestions regarding effective racial-cultural supervision techniques and approaches. Case studies are used to illustrate how supervisors and supervisees can enhance the racial-cultural competence of their work with supervisees and clients, respectively.

RACIAL-CULTURAL ISSUES IN SUPERVISION

The investigation of cultural and racial issues in counseling and the counseling relationship has generated considerable research in recent years, and yet the information on racial-cultural supervision is still somewhat limited (Brown & Landrum-Brown, 1995; Leong & Wagner, 1994; McNeill, Hom, & Perez, 1995). When Leong and Wagner reviewed the broader multicultural supervision literature, they found the information was predominantly theoretical, and not empirically based. Since their groundbreaking literature review in the mid-1990s, there has been a significant increase in the amount of supervision literature addressing racial-cultural issues. Constantine (2001b) reported that there has been a "relative explosion of recent empirical writings in the area of multicultural supervision" (p. 98).

Recent publications have described various supervision models, techniques, and approaches for incorporating racial-cultural concerns into the supervision process (Chen, this *Handbook,* this volume; Constantine, 1997; D'Andrea & Daniels, 1997; Duan & Roehlke, 2001; Garrett et al., 2001; Helms & Cook, 1999; Hird, Cavalieri, Dulko, Felice, & Ho, 2001; Reynolds & Baluch, 2001). Such integration of racial-cultural issues is extremely important because traditional supervision theories and models are monocultural and ethnocentric (Daniels, D'Andrea, & Kim, 1999). Although more publications have been exploring the effect of race and racial identity on the supervision and counseling processes (cf. Cook, 1994; Cook & Paler Hargrove, 1997; Duan & Roehlke, 2001; Fong & Lease, 1997; Helms & Cook, 1999), these writings have often focused on how to assist White supervisees or supervisors increase their racial-cultural competence through supervision. However, more multicultural scholars have begun to broaden the exploration to focus on how to address the diverse array of racial-cultural dyads possible in supervision, including supervisors of Color working with White supervisees and supervisors and supervisees of Color working together (Banks-Johnson, 2002; Cook, 1994; Helms & Cook, 1999; Ladany, Brittan-Powell, & Pannu, 1997; Ladany, Inman, Constantine, & Hofheinz, 1997). Priest (1994) addressed race as a variable in supervision by exploring concerns that may arise when the supervisor is a person of Color and the supervisee is White. Other writers have discussed the unique training and supervisory needs of students of Color (McNeil et al., 1995) and how the intercultural dynamics of the supervisory triad (i.e., supervisor, supervisee/counselor, client) are affected by each participant's worldview (Brown & Landrum-Brown, 1995).

The limited empirical and theoretical literature addressing racial-cultural supervision attests to the need for more research and exploration in the area. Supervision is an extremely important and powerful relationship that offers students and new professionals the chance to learn how to integrate issues of race and culture into counseling theory and techniques (Martinez & Holloway, 1997). Supervision can provide counselors in training with concrete opportunities to more fully explore and experience racial-cultural issues, such as worldview, racial/cultural identities, cultural values, power, and oppression, which may arise in both therapeutic and supervisory relationships. An important study by Constantine (2001a) found that addressing racial-cultural issues in supervision was a significant predictor of multicultural counseling self-efficacy. In addition, supervision can potentially play an essential role in the integration of racial-cultural issues into a trainee's personal and professional identities.

Exploration of actual case studies is an ideal medium in which to illustrate how racial and cultural issues and challenges affect supervision (cf. Chen, 2001, this

Handbook, this volume; Cook & Paler Hargrove, 1997; Daniels et al., 1999). Significant issues such as cross-racial supervisory dyads, transference and countertransference in supervision, and how to discuss racial-cultural issues in supervision are addressed.

---------------------------------- **Case Studies** ----------------------------------

Megan, a 24-year-old White woman, is a second-year graduate student in counseling psychology. After two practicum experiences in her department's training clinic, she recently began an assistantship in the counseling center at her university. Megan's counseling skills are well developed for her level of experience, and she is typically able to build effective relationships with her clients. The counseling center is located in an institution with fewer than 10% students of Color, so trainees have limited opportunities to work with students of Color. Megan attended a predominantly White university for her undergraduate degree and has had few significant working or personal relationships with people of Color. She is aware of her limited experience and is eager to work with clients who are racially different from her. Her supervisor, Marcia, is an African American woman who has been a therapist and supervisor for 12 years. Marcia, although trained at a predominantly White institution, has spent much of her life living and working in the African American community. Marcia has pursued professional development in multicultural counseling because she felt her training was inadequate in helping her to work effectively with clients who were different from her.

Megan is pleased to have two African American clients and wants to develop good working relationships with them. She is frustrated that she is having difficulty building a connection with one of her African American clients. She worries that the client does not trust her and wonders if it is because she is White. She looks to Marcia for answers and specific feedback about how to work effectively with this client, but Marcia is more interested in helping Megan find her own answers. Although they often discuss the racial dynamics in the therapy relationship, they never explore the racial differences in their supervisory relationship. On several occasions, there has been some miscommunication in supervision, and Marcia is unaware that Megan is becoming somewhat hesitant about expressing her thoughts and feelings in supervision.

This case exemplifies some of the key issues being explored in the racial-cultural supervision literature. In this situation, the supervisor is comfortable examining the dynamics of culture and race in the therapy relationship in supervision. The supervisee is actively exploring how to work effectively with an African American client and is invested in developing those skills. Having an open and questioning attitude sets the stage for a productive supervisory relationship that has the potential to enhance the racial-cultural competence of the supervisee. Megan's desire to get concrete feedback from Marcia is likely influenced by both her developmental level as a therapist and her assumption or expectation that Marcia, as an African American, knows best how to work with African American clients. Beginning therapists often focus on the expertness of their supervisors and want more structured and didactic supervisory relationships (Bernard & Goodyear, 1992, 2004; Holloway, 1995).

Communication difficulties can occur when there is a cross-racial dyad, especially when there are power differences in the relationship. There are many differences in communication styles, relationship expectations, and racial attitudes that may influence how each individual communicates and perceives the communication of the other. Although supervisors of Color are likely to have many White supervisees, most White supervisees have limited opportunities to be supervised by people of Color. Megan's assumptions about her African American supervisor likely shape her expectations and perceptions, especially when working with African American clients. As the supervisor, Marcia's comfort level with self-disclosure, especially on racial issues, may be influenced by her sense of competence and any concerns she might have about how she is perceived as a professional of Color. Priest (1994) highlighted how concerns about how others perceive them and the challenges of self-examination may be a unique consideration or dilemma for supervisors of Color.

The most prominent barrier to effective racial-cultural supervision in this case study appears to be the lack of attention to racial and cultural issues in the supervisory relationship. While the supervisor is comfortable addressing racial issues when examining the relationship between the counselor and the client, she hesitates to initiate similar conversations regarding the supervisory relationship. Ignoring the impact of racial or cultural issues on the supervisory relationship can create or heighten conflict and miscommunication (Brown & Landrum-Brown, 1995; Cook, 1994; Daniels et al., 1999; Helms & Cook, 1999). According to Gatmon et al. (2001), addressing cultural issues in the supervisory relationship

> may serve to enhance the supervisory relationship, strengthen the supervisory working alliance, foster a better learning environment in cross-cultural supervisory dyads, and support the acquisition of multicultural competence. (p. 103)

Helms and Cook (1999) emphasized the importance of directly considering and addressing racial and cultural dynamics in supervision and therapy. They believed that race and culture "influence the intrapersonal and interpersonal dynamics of the supervision as well as the supervisees' quality of functioning in the therapy process in response to supervision" (p. 283). Helms and Cook advocated approaching race using a here-and-now focus, which emphasizes the interactive process between the beliefs and racial identity of the supervisees and supervisors and their effect on supervision. Given the power differential in the supervision relationship and the potential anxiety the here-and-now approach can generate, it is vital that the supervisor initiate such conversations. The use of self-disclosure and openness to exploring racial and cultural issues on a personal level can be a very positive and affirming approach to introducing such discussions in supervision (Cook & Paler Hargrove, 1997; Porter, 1995).

The significance of such open communication is further evident in the parallel process occurring across therapy and supervision in this particular case study. In relationships with both her client and her supervisor, Megan is struggling to feel a connection and may feel misunderstood. While it is unclear how much of these feelings are the result of developmental issues versus cross-cultural communication issues, further dialogue that directly addresses issues of race and culture is warranted. By using more process communication in supervision that explores cultural issues, Marcia may help Megan express herself and build more open and meaningful relationships with both her client and her supervisor.

Robert, a 41-year-old White male student in counseling, is in his first practicum experience in the departmental counseling clinic. Robert is returning to graduate school for his doctorate after over 15 successful years of working in the corporate world. While Robert's communication and influencing skills are well developed due to his outgoing personality and extensive work experiences, he is less skilled in important microcounseling skills and characteristics, such as active listening, empathy, and paraphrasing. Robert believes his work experience has prepared him to work with a diverse client caseload; however, he has had few experiences working with people who are racially different from him. His supervisor is Pam, a 33-year-old White female assistant professor who graduated four years ago with her doctorate degree.

Robert is the second person in his family to receive a doctorate and he comes from a professional family. He has always been successful in his endeavors and it has been a challenge for him at times to be in the learner role. He has always operated in a White world and has limited understanding of how people of other races and cultures live. He had hoped to have a more experienced supervisor and possibly one who was of a different racial background so that he could learn from that person. Pam, whose parents did not attend college, has often lived and worked in racially integrated settings. Pam's friendships and professional interests reflect an interest in embracing other cultures and people who have different life experiences than her own. Pam has sought out additional training to help her be more sensitive and skilled with clients who are racially different from her. She is comfortable openly discussing racial and cultural issues with both clients and supervisees.

Pam views Robert as someone who struggles to be authentic with clients who are racially different from him. She sees him as being open to others but lacking the self-awareness necessary for being culturally sensitive as a counselor. She initiates several conversations about racial-cultural issues, and although it takes them a while, they ultimately create a positive relationship in which Robert is able to explore how he interacts and works with clients who are racially different from him. Robert eventually admits that he was reluctant to discuss cultural issues with Pam because he was unsure if she could help him with those issues. Later conversations also addressed how being White affected their relationships with people of Color and how they viewed their own cultural differences within supervision.

This case is an excellent example of how cultural issues exist even in supervisory relationships where both the supervisor and the supervisee are White. Racial-cultural issues influence how individuals view themselves and others even when they are racially similar. Despite their racial similarities, both Pam and Robert have had very different life experiences that affected their racial identity, attitudes, and ability to form genuine relationships with people who are racially or culturally different from them. Often, in racially similar relationships (either in counseling or supervision), issues of race and culture are not addressed. Individuals, especially in White/White dyads, often assume that unless there are visible racial or cultural differences, there is nothing to discuss. However, such attitudes negate the diverse and complex nature of race and culture and how influential it is for all individuals. Pam and Robert had other differences that likely affected their experiences as White individuals. There were social class differences that likely influenced opportunities in their lives, such as where they lived and what type of relationships they formed. There also were differences in how they each experienced their racial identity given these diverse life experiences. In fact, there were probably as many cultural differences in this relationship as there were in the previous case study that involved a cross-racial supervisory relationship.

To provide culturally sensitive and appropriate supervision, supervisors need to address racial-cultural issues in all supervisory relationships, not just in cross-racial relationships. It is important for supervisors to explore how supervisees view themselves as racial-cultural beings and their related attitudes and life experiences. By expressing an interest in these issues, supervisors develop a deeper understanding of their supervisees and express respect for the importance of racial-cultural issues and dynamics. According to Daniels et al. (1999), "Culture needs to be one of the lenses that supervisors and supervisees use to frame their supervisory experiences" (p. 202).

In this case example, Pam as the supervisor takes the initiative to explore racial-cultural issues. Without her commitment, it is unlikely that racial-cultural issues would have been addressed in supervision unless Robert had a client of Color (and even then the focus probably would have been on the client). There are few role models or discussions in the literature to assist White individuals in learning how to discuss racial-cultural issues among themselves, so it makes sense that Pam and Robert had to struggle somewhat until they could develop the level of trust and openness necessary to discuss such complex and emotionally powerful issues as race, class, and culture. Ochs (1997) provided an excellent example of how to address issues of race and culture in a White counselor/White client dyad.

Dinah, a 32-year-old Native American female student in clinical psychology, is completing her predoctoral internship at an urban VA hospital. She did her coursework at a predominantly White midwestern university, where most of her clients were White. She was raised in a Native American community and has had limited experience with non-Native racial minorities. All of her supervisors were White until her internship, when she was assigned to work with Luis, who is a Puerto Rican male.

Luis completed his own doctorate about 25 years ago and has been working at the VA ever since. Luis is an excellent supervisor and typically has positive and well-developed relationships with his supervisees. He has had little training in multicultural counseling but has a fair amount of experience working with clients who are racially different from him. Luis has had limited contact with and knowledge of Native American culture.

Dinah has a racially diverse caseload and feels challenged by the diversity of her clients' life experiences, values, and cultures. She is very interested in understanding her clients' worldviews and cultural experiences. Her counseling and interpersonal style are very consistent. She focuses on listening and making observations and is often quiet. Dinah wants her supervisory relationship with Luis to be successful, but she is struggling. Although Dinah has great respect for Luis's clinical skills, she finds his supervisory style to be confrontational at times. Luis is helping her work more effectively with her clients, and Dinah believes she is growing as a therapist. Luis is sometimes frustrated because he thinks Dinah is too passive with her clients and that she spends too much time focusing on cultural issues. Because of several uncomfortable interactions, Dinah no longer brings up cultural issues in supervision and works hard to address issues that she thinks Luis values. Recently, she has begun to speak with some of the other interns and staff members about racial-cultural issues in therapy in order to get those supervision needs met.

This case illustrates how such important dynamics as racial identity, cross-cultural communication, and cultural knowledge can have a powerful impact on the supervisory relationship. As a supervisor, Luis is excellent at helping his supervisees assess their skill levels and work more effectively with their clients. However, his supervisee, Dinah, is interested in understanding the cultural aspects of her clients and wants to use supervision to further her multicultural awareness, knowledge, and skills. While their supervisory relationship has a lot of potential, there are several significant barriers to a positive working alliance. As an advanced trainee, Dinah appears interested in a more collegial relationship with her supervisor that allows her to speak openly about her questions and concerns. Her desire is fairly typical for advanced supervisees, and if they are unable to get those needs met in supervision, they may turn elsewhere (Reynolds et al., 2002). Efforts to get supervision needs met outside of supervision introduces troubling ethical issues about ensuring the well-being of the client, which is one of the central responsibilities of supervision.

Important theoretical work by racial identity scholars (cf. Carter, 1995; Cook & Paler Hargrove, 1997; Helms, 1990; Helms & Cook, 1999) has provided models and strategies for exploring how racial identity can affect relationship dynamics in either therapeutic or supervisory relationships. Racial identity "operates as a filter for one's thoughts, feelings, and behaviors and shapes [one's] worldview" (Carter, 1995, p. 114) and influences one's relationships and interactions. Many of the racial identity models are developmental in nature and suggest various statuses or stages that some individuals may experience as they become more conscious of their racial identity. Helms (1990) offered a racial identity interaction model that suggests that relationships are strongly affected by the expression of individuals' racial identity. It is essential that supervisors have some awareness of the racial identity literature in order to provide more effective and relevant racial-cultural supervision.

Much has been written about how race and racial identity can affect communication style, expression of feelings, cultural value orientations, and interpersonal relationships (Carter, 1995; Carter & Pieterse, this *Handbook,* this volume; Helms & Cook, 1999; Thompson & Carter, 1997). Racial identity has been shown to influence supervisees' level of racial-cultural competence and their perceptions of their supervisor's level of competence as well as the supervisory relationship (Ladany, Brittan-Powell, et al., 1997). Helms and Cook (1999) further suggested that whether individuals are of similar or divergent levels of racial identity (meaning they view their race and its meaning in their lives in similar or disparate ways) might have a profound impact on the supervisory relationship and process. Racial identity has been found to influence the supervisee's views and insights about the supervisory relationship (Ladany, Brittan-Powell, et al., 1997). In the case study explored here, it appears that the centrality of race and culture differs for the supervisor and the supervisee. It has been suggested that such crossed racial dyads are more problematic when those with less power (the supervisee) have more heightened awareness of their race and culture (Helms & Cook, 1999). Many multicultural experts have emphasized the importance of supervisors being comfortable addressing issues of race and culture in the supervision process, especially on a personal level (Chen, this *Handbook,* this volume; D'Andrea & Daniels, 1997; Helms & Cook, 1999). Such role modeling can have a profound effect not only on the supervisory relationship but also on the personal and professional development of the supervisee (Cook & Paler Hargrove, 1997).

Difficulty in directly addressing issues of race and culture in the supervision process is affected by several factors. A lack of experience and comfort in examining racial-cultural issues on a personal level may make it difficult for supervisors to open up and share their own thoughts and feelings about such potentially powerful issues. Depending on when and how one was trained as a supervisor, such intimate self-disclosures may feel uncomfortable and even be viewed as inappropriate. In addition, because research shows that many supervisors have received little training in multicultural counseling or how to incorporate racial-cultural issues into supervision (Constantine, 1997), they may feel insecure about taking the risk to disclose such personal insights with their supervisees.

Limited contact with specific racial groups, such as occurred in the previous case example, also may make it difficult to anticipate or understand potential racial and cultural issues and their influence on the interpersonal process in both therapy and supervision dyads. Without an appreciation of Native culture and its impact on communication, Luis is lacking important insight into Dinah and how her culture may affect her therapy and communication style. Likewise, because Dinah lacks experience with other people of Color, she may not understand how her supervisor's communication style is influenced by his culture.

Finally, transference and countertransference issues and reactions to race and culture can create significant barriers to healthy working supervisory relationships unless they are faced and confronted directly (Carter, 1995). Miscommunication in a cross-cultural dyad, such as appeared to be occurring between Luis and Dinah, could be influenced by multiple factors such as lack of cultural knowledge, transference/countertransference issues, racial bias, family upbringing, positive/negative racial interactions and experiences, and racial identity differences. Supervisors need the insight and ability to sense such conflicts in supervision and intervene effectively.

STRATEGIES FOR EFFECTIVE RACIAL-CULTURAL SUPERVISION

Although there is no unified model of racial-cultural supervision, there are reoccurring themes and issues addressed in the literature. Effective racial-cultural supervision is one of many tools that may be used to assist in the development of racial-cultural competence in counselors and psychologists. For supervision to be effective in the development of therapists, addressing racial-cultural issues must be viewed as fundamental to the process of supervision. Just as the field of multicultural counseling has redefined what it means to be a competent counselor, the racial-cultural supervision literature must have a similar effect on the research and practice of supervision.

Four prominent themes are explored in the broader multicultural supervision literature and in this chapter's case studies that have immediate implications for effective supervision strategies. First, it is vital that issues of culture, race, and difference be actively explored in supervision. These discussions of difference must not just focus on the therapeutic relationship but must also be included when analyzing and exploring the supervisory relationship (Cook, 1994; Helms & Cook, 1999). Helms and Cook argued that acknowledgment of racial-cultural issues is necessary for promoting positive and progressive supervisory relationships. It is not enough to help supervisees be more effective by addressing racial and cultural issues only in the context of therapy. The impact of racial-cultural dynamics on the supervisory relationship must also be addressed (Gatmon et al., 2001; Helms & Cook, 1999). Although this chapter has focused primarily on issues of race and culture, it is just as important that gender, sexual orientation, and other key social identity variables be viewed as the responsibility of supervision (Constantine, 1997; Gatmon et al., 2001; Porter, 1995).

Second, the power dynamics in the supervision process and their impact on the ability of both supervisor and supervisee to freely address racial and cultural issues must be acknowledged and explored (D'Andrea & Daniels, 1997; Porter, 1995). Supervisors must take the initiative in identifying and discussing racial and cultural issues because fears about evaluation may make it too difficult for supervisees to introduce the conversation (Brown & Landrum-Brown, 1995; Reynolds et al., 2002). Unless supervisors increase their own racial-cultural competence in supervision, supervisees are likely to turn to other students and professionals to get their racial-cultural supervision needs met (Reynolds et al., 2002). Therefore, it is vital that supervisors prioritize their professional development in the areas of racial-cultural counseling and supervision so they are able to provide the most effective and culturally relevant supervision.

A third theme, racial identity, has become a major research topic in racial-cultural supervision. Understanding the effect of diverse racial identities across supervisory dyads warrants ongoing research and exploration (Helms & Cross, 1999; Priest, 1994). It is more significant to understand how supervisors and supervisees (as well as clients) make meaning of their race and culture than it is to know their cultural background. According to Garrett et al. (2001), it is important for

> supervisors to become more fully aware of their own cultural identity, more knowledgeable about various racial or cultural groups and cultural nuances that differ from their own, as well as seeking out formal training in multicultural counseling. (p. 155)

Finally, a fourth theme is the importance of considering developmental influences and realities on the incorporation of racial and cultural issues in supervision. Supervisors must take into account the supervisees' level of experience and training with racial and cultural issues as they attempt to address the racial-cultural dynamics in the therapeutic and supervisory relationship (Carney & Kahn, 1984; Chen, this *Handbook,* this volume; Lopez et al., 1989; Sabnani, Ponterotto, & Borodovsky, 1991). Understanding supervisees' developmental level of counseling skill as well as their level of racial-cultural awareness and comfort will allow supervisors to make more relevant, meaningful, and effective interventions.

Considering significant themes in the literature that can assist supervisors in increasing the racial-cultural competence of their supervisees is essential to the development of effective supervision and competent counselors. Unfortunately, many supervisors have not been trained to consider culture or race as a significant factor in either counseling or supervision and may be struggling to develop the necessary attitudes, knowledge, and skill to do so. Supervisors can take important steps to increase their competence and confidence in directly working with racial-cultural issues and concerns.

The first and most important step involves additional training. Through relevant professional conferences, videotapes, and literature, supervisors can increase their awareness, knowledge, and skills in addressing racial-cultural issues. Nothing can replace the value of professional development that is specifically created for expanding and enhancing racial-cultural supervision skills. To take that first step, supervisors must be willing to acknowledge what they don't know and take the time and energy to learn more. Networking with professionals in their agency, institution, or school or region or state is an additional approach to gathering information and provides important support for supervisors. Any time new skills are being developed and applied, more opportunities are needed to practice those skills and get feedback and supervision. Using peers for support and supervision is an ideal but often overlooked way to enhance skills and abilities.

Exploring developmental models of multicultural competence in counselors (cf. Carney & Kahn, 1984; Chen, this *Handbook,* this volume; Lopez et al., 1989; Sabnani et al., 1991) and applying them to the supervision process is another useful approach to understanding how to develop competence in racial-cultural supervision. Viewing the acquisition of supervision skills in a racial-cultural context from a developmental perspective has significant heuristic value. Examining these parallels will not only increase a supervisor's empathy for the counselor's process but will heighten the supervisor's understanding of the attitudes, knowledge, and skills necessary to assist graduate students and new professionals in their development of racial-cultural competence.

Finally, if supervisors engage with their supervisees openly and focus on the process of supervision and the relationship they develop, they will undoubtedly receive on-the-job training that can help them develop the specific skills they need to assist their supervisees. By initiating the exploration of racial-cultural issues and encouraging dialogue, supervisors give permission for supervisees to struggle openly with their fears and concerns. By acknowledging that they too are learning in this area, supervisors can create honest relationships where they don't feel the need to suggest that they know more than they know or have more skills than they do. In this manner, the process of incorporating racial-cultural competence in supervision can enhance the skills and enrich the overall experience for the supervisor and the supervisee.

CONCLUSION

The racial-cultural supervision literature has steadily expanded over the past 20 years. There are developmental models that can be applied to cultural aspects of supervision (cf. Carney & Kahn, 1984; Chen, this *Handbook,* this volume; Lopez et al., 1989; Sabnani et al., 1991) and theoretical models that centralize and crystallize cultural and racial concerns in their conceptualization of effective supervision (cf. Brown & Landrum-Brown, 1995; Chen, 2001; Garrett et al., 2001). If the counseling profession is committed to increasing the level of racial-cultural competence of counselors, then it is vital that supervision and, more specifically, the supervisory relationship be more fully studied and understood as a means for counselors to more effectively infuse racial and cultural issues and dynamics into their practice. Supervision is an ideal environment for racial and cultural issues to be addressed and for theoretical notions of multicultural competence to be applied and taught to the next generation of counselors and psychologists.

To use supervision to assist in the development of racial-cultural competence, it is vital that the counseling and psychology profession make a strong commitment, in terms of expectations and resources, to retrain and reeducate professionals who have had no or limited training in racial-cultural issues. If supervisees are going to use supervision to integrate and apply racial-cultural competence, supervisors need a basic level of racial-cultural and multicultural awareness, knowledge, and skills to assist in that process (Constantine, 1997; D'Andrea & Daniels, 2001). Finally, what we define as effective and meaningful supervision will need to change to incorporate racial-cultural realities and issues into the training and supervision process. Unless our core definitions and assumptions about supervision and therapy begin to change, transforming the counseling and psychology profession to more fully and freely incorporate the dynamic and complex realities of multiculturalism may not be possible.

REFERENCES

Banks-Johnson, A. (2002). Perceptions of the supervisory relationship: Minority supervisors working with minority supervisees. *Dissertation Abstracts International, 63*(1-A), 94.

Bernard, J. M., Goodyear, R. K., & Bernard, J. M. (2004). *Fundamentals of clinical supervision.* (3rd ed.). Boston: Allyn & Bacon.

Brown, M. T., & Landrum-Brown, J. (1995). Counselor supervision: Cross-cultural perspectives. In J. G. Ponterotto, J. M. Casas, L. A. Suzuki, & C. Alexander (Eds.), *Handbook of multicultural counseling* (pp. 263–286). Thousand Oaks, CA: Sage.

Carney, C. G., & Kahn, K. B. (1984). Building competencies for effective cross-cultural counseling: A developmental view. *Counseling Psychologist, 12,* 111–119.

Carter, R. T. (1995). *The influence of race and racial identity in psychotherapy: Toward a racially inclusive model.* New York: Wiley.

Chen, E. C. (2001). Multicultural counseling supervision: An interactional approach. In J. G. Ponterotto, J. M. Casas, L. A. Suzuki, & C. Alexander (Eds.), *Handbook of multicultural counseling* (2nd ed., pp. 801–824). Thousand Oaks, CA: Sage.

Constantine, M. G. (1997). Facilitating multicultural competency in counselor supervision: Operationalizing a practical framework. In D. B. Pope-Davis & H. L. K. Coleman (Eds.), *Multicultural counseling competencies: Assessment, education and training, and supervision* (pp. 310–324). Thousand Oaks, CA: Sage.

Constantine, M. G. (2001a). Multiculturally-focused counseling supervision: Its relationship to trainees' multicultural counseling self-efficacy. *Clinical Supervisor, 20,* 87–98.

Constantine, M. G. (2001b). Perspectives on multicultural supervision. *Journal of Multicultural Counseling and Development, 29,* 98–101.

Cook, D. A. (1994). Racial identity in supervision. *Counselor Education and Supervision, 34,* 132–141.

Cook, D. A., & Paler Hargrove, L. (1997). The supervisory experience. In C. E. Thompson & R. T. Carter (Eds.), *Racial identity theory: Applications to individual, group and organizational interventions* (pp. 83–95). Mahwah, NJ: Erlbaum.

D'Andrea, M., & Daniels, J. (1997). Multicultural counseling supervision: Central issues, theoretical considerations, and practical strategies. In D. B. Pope-Davis & H. L. K. Coleman (Eds.), *Multicultural counseling competencies: Assessment, education and training, and supervision* (pp. 290–309). Thousand Oaks, CA: Sage.

Daniels, J., D'Andrea, M., & Kim, B. S. K. (1999). Assessing the barriers and changes of cross-cultural supervision: A case study. *Counselor Education and Supervision, 38,* 191–204.

Duan, C., & Roehlke, H. (2001). A descriptive "snapshot" of cross-racial supervision in university counseling center internships. *Journal of Multicultural Counseling and Development, 29,* 131–146.

Fong, M. L., & Lease, S. H. (1997). Cross-cultural supervision: Issues for the white supervisor. In D. B. Pope-Davis & H. L. K. Coleman (Eds.), *Multicultural counseling competencies: Assessment, education and training, and supervision* (pp. 387–405). Thousand Oaks, CA: Sage.

Fukuyama, M. A. (1994). Critical incidents in multicultural counseling supervision: A phenomenological approach to supervision research. *Counselor Education and Supervision, 34,* 142–151.

Garrett, M. T., Borders, L. D., Crutchfield, L. B., Torres-Rivera, E., Brotherton, D., & Curtis, R. (2001). Multicultural superVISION: A paradigm of cultural responsiveness for supervisors. *Journal of Multicultural Counseling and Development, 29,* 147–158.

Gatmon, D., Jackson, D., Koshkarian, L., Martos-Perry, N., Molina, A., Patel, N., et al. (2001). Exploring ethnic, gender, and sexual orientation variables in supervision: Do they really matter. *Journal of Multicultural Counseling and Development, 29,* 102–113.

Helms, J. E. (1990). *Black and white racial identity: Theory, research, and practice.* Westport, CT: Praeger.

Helms, J. E., & Cook, D. A. (1999). Using race and culture in therapy and supervision. In J. E. Helms & D. A. Cook (Eds.), *Using race and culture in counseling and psychotherapy: Theory and process* (pp. 277–298). Boston: Allyn & Bacon.

Hird, J. S., Cavalieri, C. E., Dulko, J. P., Felice, A. A. D., & Ho, T. A. (2001). Visions and realities: Supervisee perspectives of multicultural supervision. *Journal of Multicultural Counseling and Development, 29,* 114–130.

Holloway, E. L. (1995). *Clinical supervision: A systems approach.* Thousand Oaks, CA: Sage.

Ladany, N., Brittan-Powell, C., & Pannu, R. (1997). The influence of supervisory racial identity interaction and racial matching on the supervisory working alliance and supervisee multicultural competence. *Counselor Education and Supervision, 36,* 285–305.

Ladany, N., Inman, A. G., Constantine, M. G., & Hofheinz, E. W. (1997). Supervisee multicultural case conceptualization ability and self-reported multicultural competence as functions of supervisee racial identity and supervisor focus. *Journal of Counseling Psychology, 44,* 284–293.

Ladany, N., Lehrman-Waterman, D., Molinaro, M., & Wolgast, B. (1999). Psychotherapy supervisor ethical practices: Adherence to guidelines, the supervisory working alliance, and supervisee satisfaction. *Counseling Psychologist, 27,* 443–475.

Leong, F. T., & Wagner, N. (1994). Cross-cultural counseling supervision: What do we know? What do we need to know? *Counselor Education and Supervision, 34,* 117–131.

Lopez, S. R., Grover, K. P., Holland, D., Johnson, M. J., Kain, C. D., Kanel, K., et al. (1989). Development of culturally sensitive psychotherapists. *Professional Psychology: Research and Practice, 20,* 369–376.

Martinez, R. P., & Holloway, E. L. (1997). The supervision relationship in multicultural training. In D. B. Pope-Davis & H. L. K. Coleman (Eds.), *Multicultural counseling competencies: Assessment, education and training, and supervision* (pp. 325–349). Thousand Oaks, CA: Sage.

McNeill, B. W., Hom, K. L., & Perez, J. A. (1995). The training and supervisory needs of racial and ethnic minority students. *Journal of Multicultural Counseling and Development, 23,* 246–258.

Ochs, N. (1997). White counselor and white client: The case of Mrs. Ames. In C. E. Thompson & R. T. Carter (Eds.), *Racial identity theory: Applications to individual, group, and organizational interventions* (pp. 69–82). Mahwah, NJ: Erlbaum.

Porter, N. (1995). Supervision of psychotherapists: Integrating anti-racist, feminist, and multicultural perspectives. In H. Landrine (Ed.), *Bring cultural diversity to feminist psychology: Theory, research, and practice* (pp. 163–176). Washington, DC: American Psychological Association.

Priest, R. (1994). Minority supervisor and majority supervisee: Another perspective of clinical reality. *Counselor Education and Supervision, 34,* 152–158.

Reynolds, A. L., & Baluch, S. (2001). Racial identity theories in counseling: A literature review and evaluation. In C. L. Wijeyesinghe & B. W. Jackson (Eds.), *New perspectives on racial identity development: A theoretical and practical anthology* (pp. 153–181). New York: New York University Press.

Reynolds, A. L., Schaefer, K., Saud, K., & Blackburn Lue, K. (2002). *Multicultural issues in supervision: Incorporating student voices.* Unpublished manuscript.

Sabnani, H. B., Ponterotto, J. G., & Borodovsky, L. G. (1991). White racial identity development and cross-cultural training: A stage model. *Counseling Psychologist, 19,* 76–102.

Thompson, C. E., & Carter, R. T. (Eds.). (1997). *Racial identity theory: Applications to individual, group, and organizational interventions.* Mahwah, NJ: Erlbaum.

CHAPTER 12

Postdoctoral Training in Racial-Cultural Counseling Competence

Charles R. Ridley and Debra Mollen

The importance of postdoctoral training in professional psychology has been widely discussed in recent years by researchers, burgeoning psychologists, and seasoned practitioners. Adequate preparation of new psychologists has implications both for the profession itself and the public at large. The nascent discussions have focused on the considerable value of postdoctoral training (Belar et al., 1993; R. Brown, 1996; Graham & Fox, 1991; Wiens, 1993), the needs and opinions of trainees and new professionals (France & Wolf, 2000; Stewart & Stewart, 1998; Stewart, Stewart, & Vogel, 2000), and the developing identity and related concerns of trainees (Kaslow, McCarthy, Rogers, & Summerville, 1992).

Although there has been general agreement on the importance of postdoctoral training, specific models to guide postdoctoral training are scarce. To its credit, the National Conference on Postdoctoral Training in Professional Psychology, held in Ann Arbor, Michigan, in 1992, identified valuable components that such training ideally provides: a commitment to the scientist-practitioner model, opportunities for psychologists to achieve greater professional competence, the provision of role models, and ongoing evaluation of new psychologists that ensures self-correction and continuing development (Belar et al., 1993). The proceedings from the conference also stressed the importance of "the development of innovative models that improve service delivery to under-served populations and address emerging societal needs" (Larsen et al., 1993, p. 9). We agree with the proceedings. Each of the components is important, but, in our opinion, innovative models are especially invaluable for guiding the training that impacts the next generation of practicing psychologists.

Four years after the Ann Arbor conference, however, there still appeared to be a dearth of innovative models. R. Brown (1996) lamented that

> the need to discuss new models and curricula is so critical that *Professional Psychology: Research and Practice* published last summer a "call" for information on training programs that are innovative with respect to setting, content, or funding. (p. 506)

Farberman (2000) stressed the need to have consistent policies to guide preparation for independent practitioners and called attention to current training mandates that focus more on the accrual of clinical hours to the detriment of the quality of the training experience. Similarly, Wiens (1993) noted earlier that "most people are just doing postdoctoral training, but not developing curriculum, requirements, exit exams, or anything of that sort" (p. 417).

Concurrent with the discourse on postdoctoral training has been considerable attention paid to the importance of multicultural counseling training (Abreu, Chung, & Atkinson, 2000; Ridley, Mendoza, & Kanitz, 1994). The word "multicultural" has long been used, and it is referenced in this chapter where appropriate. However, we focus our discussion of the term primarily on racial-cultural psychology. We acknowledge that a wide range of sociopsychological variables are relevant to understanding people. We further believe that race and culture are particularly salient in that individuals of visible racial/cultural groups are often subjected to racism, oppression, and disenfranchisement. For a more comprehensive examination of terminology and meanings, refer to Ridley (1995), Helms and Cook (1999), and Ridley, Baker, and Hill (2002a).

Ample discussion regarding the need for doctoral training to comprehensively address changing demographics, client diversity, and trainee resistance to issues of race and culture has occurred (Ridley & Thompson, 1999). Despite the agreed upon importance of racial-cultural training, a number of shortcomings have been found in doctoral training programs and at predoctoral internship sites. These shortcomings include a reliance on the separate course model as opposed to more comprehensive training regimes, difficulty addressing trainee resistance, failure to link course work and practical experience, inadequate measurement of training outcomes, negligible time devoted to racial-cultural training, insufficient opportunities to practice with diverse clients, and insufficient supervision pertaining to racial-cultural issues (Abreu et al., 2000; Chen, this *Handbook,* this volume; Constantine & Ladany, 1996; Lee et al., 1999; Murphy & Wright, 1995; Quintana & Bernal, 1995; Reynolds, this *Handbook,* this volume).

It seems clear that two areas deemed critical for the development of competent practicing psychologists—postdoctoral training and racial-cultural counseling training—are problematic. In spite of a general consensus that both domains are of crucial importance to the field, there remains a dearth of comprehensive training models, an absence of sufficient measures to evaluate trainees, and a gap between the areas rated important and those to which reasonable time and effort have been devoted.

The purpose of this chapter is to describe the key issues and set forth the advanced competencies pertinent to postdoctoral training in racial-cultural counseling. We organize the chapter into three major sections. First, we discuss core training themes pertinent to postdoctoral issues in general as well as those themes particularly relevant to racial-cultural counseling training. Next, we discuss key advanced racial-cultural counseling competencies that can be incorporated into postdoctoral training. Finally, we make recommendations for future research and training.

CORE TRAINING THEMES

A theme is a subject of discourse common to all or most of the forms of a paradigm. In this section, we examine core training themes, dividing them into two subsections: postdoctoral and racial-cultural training themes.

Postdoctoral Training Themes

A review of the extant literature on postdoctoral training yielded five general themes that need to be addressed when planning training models.

Balancing Didactic and Experiential Activities

Blending training experiences for new psychologists maximizes their potential impact. Discussions from the 1992 Ann Arbor meeting led to an agreement that both didactic and experiential training activities are essential for developing competent practitioners. Didactic and experiential activities ideally include skill acquisition, theoretically driven conceptualization, knowledge of legal and ethical principles, managing service delivery with research endeavors, and studying models of consultation, supervision, program development, and evaluation (Larsen et al., 1993).

A balanced approach to multicultural training has been emphasized as well. Considering the potential for trainee resistance, Abreu et al. (2000) suggested that multicultural training begin with didactic, cognitive instruction before giving experiential, affective-based instruction. Beginning with didactic instruction may reduce initial anxiety that trainees often experience and facilitate later experiential activities. Considering the importance of multicultural training, the ubiquity of multicultural issues in the field, and the likelihood of resistance, postdoctoral training sites should include myriad learning opportunities. Key instructional strategies are lectures, hands-on exercises, supervision, reading and writing assignments, role-playing, modeling, technology-assisted training, introspection, and involving trainees in research (Ridley et al., 1994).

Creating a Systematic, Organized Training Experience

Designing and executing a well-thought-out, systematic postdoctoral training program increases the likelihood that emerging psychologists will have greater competence to practice. A reliance on prescribed training programs embarks on "the need for a formal system of postdoctoral education that relates to the realities of current psychological practice and is sensitive to the important social problems that have not yet been systemically addressed" (Graham & Fox, 1991, p. 1033). Approaching the creation of training programs purposefully and thoroughly lends itself to overcoming the more arbitrary means by which postdoctoral training tended to occur previously (e.g., Wiens, 1993).

Evaluating to Yield Self-Correction

Evaluating the process and outcome of training is critical to helping trainees attain competence. Unfortunately, the common evaluation method of using checklists is laden with potential pitfalls. For example, Kruger and Dunning (1999) found that individuals who performed in the lowest quartiles in tests of grammar and logical reasoning most significantly overestimated their ability compared to individuals who scored in higher quartiles, and that incompetent individuals failed to detect competent performance in their peers. The researchers demonstrated that meta-cognitive skills mitigate incompetence and improve individuals' ability to predict accurately performance in others and in themselves. They defined metacognitive skills as "the ability to know how well one is performing, when one is likely to be accurate in judgment, and when one is likely to be in error" (p. 1121).

Practitioners are no less prone to making such errors, and due to the often unregimented nature of psychological practice, they may be more inclined than others to inaccurately gauge their efficacy. In a study that examined counselor effectiveness based on several client- and counselor-generated measures, Lafferty, Beutler, and Crago (1989) found:

> Patients of less effective therapists felt less understood by their therapists than did the patients of more effective therapists, but less effective therapists perceived their patients as somewhat more involved in the therapy process and reported being more directive and supportive than did more effective therapists. (p. 78)

Because professional self-evaluation is difficult for many psychologists, achieving an accurate understanding of one's ability as a psychologist based on postdoctoral training programs requires ongoing evaluation that serves to facilitate self-awareness and self-correction in trainees (Larsen et al., 1993).

Specifying Learning Objectives

Participants at the Ann Arbor conference in 1992 agreed that both broad-based components and specific training objectives are crucial factors in the creation and execution of effective postdoctoral training programs (Larsen et al., 1993). Specification of such objectives provides clarity, delineates expectations, and functions as a baseline for ongoing programmatic and individual evaluation. VandeCreek, Knapp, and Brace (1990) reported that mandatory continuing education for licensed psychologists is more effective when learning objectives are specified. Ridley and Thompson (1999) asserted that clear learning objectives can be useful in minimizing trainee resistance.

Linking Training and Practice

Proceedings from the Ann Arbor conference firmly connect training and practice. While endorsing the scientist-practitioner model, the proceedings state that the purpose of postdoctoral training is to facilitate competence in the professional practice of psychology and not solely to advance research competence (Larsen et al., 1993). Making the linkage between training and practice adds to the quality of training programs by providing a sound approach that increases clinical utility and gives trainees a substantive knowledge and practice base (VandeCreek et al., 1990). The linkage is strongest when the concept of competence is clearly defined. Unfortunately, competence in professional psychology has been inadequately defined (Ridley et al., 2002a). Corey and Herlihy (1996) noted:

> Without an agreed-upon definition of competence, it is difficult for ethically conscientious counselors to determine exactly where their boundaries of competence lie and to recognize when they are in danger of exceeding them. (p. 219)

Racial-Cultural Training Themes

Five themes specific to multicultural counseling training are identified in the literature and described in this section.

Providing Organizational and Leadership Support

Ridley and Thompson (1999) argued the need for a top-down commitment to racial-cultural training. The commitment serves to model the desirable behavioral and attitudinal expectations anticipated of support personnel, staff psychologists, and trainees. Individual stakeholders will be more likely to embrace racial-cultural psychology as relevant and meaningful if it is apparent in the behavior and attitudes of an organization's leadership (Evans, Delphin, Simmons, Omar, & Tebes, this *Handbook*, this volume; Ridley & Thomson, 1999; Sue et al., 1998). D'Andrea and Daniels (1999) asserted that administrators and policymakers should be included in creating antiracist climates in training milieus. Finally, Reynolds (1997) pointed out the great discrepancy between changing racial-cultural curricula in organizations and actually changing those organizations:

> Many of the training programs seem to focus on content information about the various underrepresented groups and have not fully included the oppression or social justice agenda in their teaching efforts. For counseling programs to integrate multicultural issues effectively, they must utilize systemic and systematic approaches that examine the underlying organizational structure of the program and social justice issues. (p. 215)

Creating a Safe and Supportive Training Environment

Because racial-cultural psychology is a sensitive topic—one laden with passion, emotion, and controversy—training directors need to create safe, supportive environments so that the relevant issues can be discussed openly and without threat. Kiselica (1998) illustrated this point well when he delineated some of the critical components of an effective training environment for multicultural training. Among such critical components are balancing gentle confrontation with ongoing support, sharing the joy that can readily characterize learning about multiculturalism, and being willing to engage in trainer self-disclosure. Tomlinson-Clarke and Wang (1999) concurred, emphasizing that without a clear intention to create such an environment, subtle and covert messages can be communicated, inciting defensiveness and resistance among trainees.

Preevaluating Trainees' Racial-Cultural Counseling Competence

Although valid measures of racial-cultural counseling competence are still emerging, postdoctoral training sites should preevaluate emerging psychologists' comfort and competence in racial-cultural psychology before training begins. Trainers can gain valuable information about individual variation in background, experience, and areas for development pursuant to racial-cultural counseling competence. Without this information, trainers may jump to erroneous conclusions about trainees' needs, interests, and competence. Rooney and Flores (1998) reported that being cognizant of individual differences allows conceptualization along a continuum rather than forced into either/or thinking; focuses trainers effectively on a lifelong pursuit rather than the limited content scope perspective; and takes into account how various teaching modalities affect trainees differently, depending on where they fall on the developmental continuum.

Tailoring Training to the Developmental and Competency Levels of Trainees

Once there is a sound preevaluation, training programs can be tailored to meet the needs of postdoctoral psychology trainees. Mobley and Cheatham (1999) offered some timely suggestions. They suggested that the primary objective of their racial-cultural training model is for educators to "gain increased awareness, sensitivity, and knowledge about their own racial-cultural heritage as well as the racial-cultural heritage of the counselors in training" (p. 91). In doing so, educators would stay attuned to developmental differences. The tripartite model includes learning about self, which encompasses conducting a cultural self-assessment, engaging in self-reflection, and gauging one's responses to sociopolitical and cultural events in society; learning about others, which consists of using available resources to conduct an anthropological-type study to examine various cultural groups; and learning about the self in relation to others, which involves seeking feedback from others about how one is perceived as a racial-cultural being (see also Carter, this *Handbook,* this volume; Sue & Torino, this *Handbook,* this volume). Although the model was developed for counselor educators and not trainees per se, it is relevant to all professionals interested in pursuing racial-cultural counseling training.

Confronting, Addressing, and Surmounting Trainee Resistance

Ridley and Thompson (1999) view resistance as purposeful behavior intended to thwart the change process. Accordingly, they proposed seven strategies to help trainers manage resistance associated with racial-cultural training: creating an optimal training environment; utilizing a systems perspective for understanding resistance; recognizing resistant behavior; confronting trainee resistance; elucidating learning objectives; taking a nondefensive posture regarding resistance; and helping trainees identify the sources of their resistance. Although it is a relatively new area of research, confronting trainee resistance is a central component of effective racial-cultural training. Apathy and other negative reactions may be addressed by tailoring specific parts of training curricula to these very areas using both didactic and experiential techniques (Abreu et al., 2000).

STATE LICENSURE AND CONTINUING EDUCATION

The graduate degree is the hallmark credential for establishing professional competence. At the same time, licensure and certifications offer additional assurance to the public who access the services of practicing psychologists (Welfel, 1998). The regulation and enforcement of the practice of psychology is based on statutes at the state level, and each state has its own statutes.

We assert that counseling competence is competence in racial-cultural counseling (Carter, this *Handbook,* this volume). In taking this position, we argue that one of the criteria of professional competence is the ability and committed intention to incorporate racial and cultural data beneficially in counseling. Therefore, we hold that racial-cultural counseling competence should be a requirement of state licensure. For professionals to stay abreast of developments in the field and meet licensure requirements, they need continuing education. We recommend that states adopt our proposed advanced competencies as one means of licensing psychologists.

ADVANCED RACIAL-CULTURAL COUNSELING COMPETENCIES

Racial-cultural counseling training is burgeoning with new information and competencies (e.g., Abreu et al., 2000; Sue, 2001). Most doctoral programs probably cannot devote the necessary time and space in their curricula to adequately train students in this area. Nevertheless, we argue that racial-cultural training is essential in light of our view that clinical competence always entails racial-cultural competence. We propose four advanced competencies that should be integrated into postdoctoral training curricula. Before we present the advanced competencies, we briefly describe the basic dimensions of racial-cultural competence (see Figure 12.1). We believe the dimensions are foundational for attaining the advanced competencies.

There are seven counseling competencies we deem important: conceptualizing therapeutic change, utilizing cultural self-awareness, communicating cross-culturally, individualizing therapeutic change, incorporating cultural data, using therapeutic interventions, and evaluating process and outcome. Conceptualizing

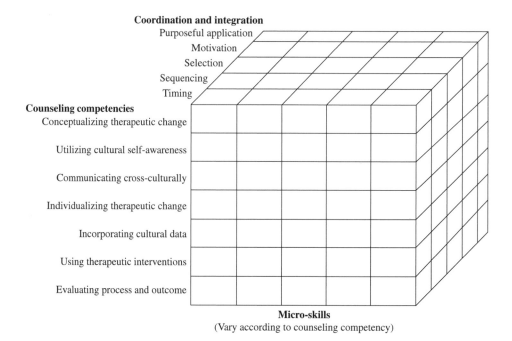

Figure 12.1 Dimensions of racial-cultural counseling competence.

therapeutic change refers to having a coherent model for understanding therapeutic change. Utilizing cultural self-awareness is possessing a keen understanding about one's culture and using self-awareness to facilitate the therapeutic change process. Communicating cross-culturally means purposefully considering culture in the "exchange of messages and the creation of meaning" (Gudykunst, 1998, p. 9). Individualizing therapeutic change is defined as tailoring case conceptualization, treatment planning, and therapeutic interventions to reflect individual differences. Incorporating cultural data refers to integrating cultural data across all phases of treatment. Using therapeutic interventions is implementing a diverse array of treatment modalities intended to strengthen the therapeutic relationship and facilitate meaningful change. Finally, evaluating process and outcome means examining the counseling process and determining its effectiveness.

In addition, each of the competencies has its own set of microskills, which are the building blocks that contribute to successful attainment of each competency. We do not describe the many possible microskills because of space limitations. However, here is an example in the competency of incorporating cultural data: using a client's cultural values in making a psychological assessment. Finally, the competencies and microskills require coordination and integration. This coordination is necessary because racial-cultural counseling competence is more than the rote execution of the competencies. Coordination and integration refer to the fluid execution of the various competencies and microskills. Coordination and integration consist of purposeful application, motivation, selection, sequencing, and timing.

Organizational Consultation

As counseling has historically focused on individual change, training that includes organizational consultation may be met initially with considerable surprise and resistance. The value in training new psychologists to think and act from systemic frameworks, as opposed to merely individualistic conceptualizations, cannot be overstated. Such broad-based thinking has implications for social justice and for creating enduring, meaningful, and powerful change (Reynolds, 1997; Sue et al., 1998). Rather than merely offering didactic training on organizational consultation, every effort should be made for postdoctoral training to incorporate the guidelines delineated in the literature so that new psychologists have a compelling example from which to draw.

Sue et al. (1998) delineated several characteristics of effective multicultural organizations that should be incorporated into postdoctoral training sites. These characteristics should be incorporated both into the inherent structure of the site and into the training curriculum itself. A top-down approach is necessary to create an environment conducive to organizational change. When influential stakeholders adapt and express a strong commitment to multiculturalism, the other players in the organization are more likely to follow suit. Rewriting organizations' mission statements reinforces the commitment to multiculturalism. Devising action plans that address systemic change is also of critical importance. An organization should formulate independently operating teams that assess and monitor its progress on an ongoing basis, and feedback from key stakeholders needs to be sought and incorporated.

Postdoctoral trainees also need to be taught about accountability in organizations. Key stakeholders should know precisely what their responsibilities are regarding racial-cultural change. Organizations should consider racial-cultural competence in their hiring and promotion of employees and ought to have delineated goals, expectations, and guidelines to reflect this. Mentoring across all levels of an organization— not just those in the highest strata—is important. Understanding and encouraging the constructive coalition of various racial-cultural groups is also important in the consultation process. Finally, real change must be systemwide and must go beyond the boundaries of the organization if the larger societal issues of racism, oppression, and injustice are to be addressed and, ultimately, conquered (Sue et al., 1998).

Supervision

In recent years, the topic of multicultural supervision has begun to permeate the literature. Although there is a range of concerns, prominent issues stand at the forefront. The first issue pertains to the need to incorporate culture into supervisory relationships (Chen, this *Handbook,* this volume; Reynolds, this *Handbook,* this volume). A number of pragmatic suggestions have been offered.

Stone (1997) proposed a four-stage process to facilitate productive supervisory relationships. The first stage entails building an appropriate learning set that begins in doctoral-level training and continues through advanced practica, predoctoral internship, and postdoctoral training. This first-stage learning set includes the valuing and respecting of cultural differences and the integration of experiential and instructional activities. Racial identity development models, acculturation theory, and idiographic perspectives can be employed to help complement the learning set and assess the trainee's own level of ethnic-racial identity development (D'Andrea & Daniels, 1997; Stone, 1997). Second, concrete experiences enhance and build on the learning set. Sufficient time and effort should be focused on racial-cultural counseling issues in supervision. Such focus can occur through tape review, transcript analysis, and supervisor-supervisee dialogue that explores cultural themes in depth. Third, reflection and analysis of cultural themes should occur in both individual and group supervision models. The inclusion of group supervision is highlighted as a particularly salient feature of training, as it encompasses a more collectivistic approach than the traditional dyad allows. Finally, Stone (1997) argued that some sort of action, such as organizing relevant projects that contribute to social justice or contributing to ongoing research and publication, should be taken to concretize the process.

M. Brown and Landrum-Brown (1995) emphasized the inclusion of cultural information as it pertains to all three parties involved in the therapeutic relationship: the counselor/supervisee, the supervisor, and the client. In addition to attending to issues of ethnicity and race, the authors examined eight dimensions of worldview incongruence that need to be incorporated into effective multicultural supervision. Among these eight dimensions are differences in ethos (guiding beliefs), epistemology (how one knows), and axiology (values).

The second issue pertains to the need for supervisors who were trained before the multicultural movement to get additional education and update their skills. Along these lines, an interesting point has been raised and addressed in the literature (Constantine, 1997; D'Andrea & Daniels, 1997): Many trainees may enter postdoctoral work with a greater understanding of multiculturalism than their supervisors (Reynolds, this *Handbook,* this volume). This presents a scenario that may arouse anxiety in the supervisors, as the traditional model of supervision emphasizes the power differential, with the supervisor instructing and acting as an expert consultant to the trainee. Several practical strategies have been suggested for addressing this scenario, including trainers' assessment of their multicultural competence; developing more collegial, egalitarian supervisory relationships with trainees to foster collaborative learning; and developing relationships with "cultural ambassadors" outside the training site who can serve as valuable resources regarding the various groups that form the cultural community (D'Andrea & Daniels, 1997). Constantine (1997) concurred with D'Andrea and Daniels's suggestions but supplemented them with her own suggestions. She emphasized the importance of supervisors taking responsibility for educating themselves, for setting the tone for discussing multicultural themes, and for actively seeking feedback from trainees and clients regarding the quality of multicultural competence offered in the placement. Constantine's suggestions depart from traditional supervision models, but they offer the possibility of increased awareness and education to both trainees and trainers at postdoctoral sites.

Program Development/Evaluation

As the field of counseling psychology continues to evolve and change in response to an increasingly multicultural population, professional demands vary and become more diverse (Ponterotto & Austin, this *Handbook,* this volume). Apart from traditional responsibilities such as offering direct services to individuals and conducting assessments, psychologists now engage in a host of other tasks, such as program development and evaluation. This diversification of tasks has distinct implications for racial-cultural training; programs need to be racially and culturally sensitive to their target populations.

One useful model for program development created for use in educational settings has applicability to counseling psychology (Aiello & Bullock, 1999). The model consists of three phases and eight stages, each of which clearly specifies the desirable outcomes. The first phase is the Paradigm Shift Phase, also called Preparation, in which the targeted group first becomes amenable to the program development and then works with the psychologist to develop a mission statement. The Preparation phase has particular salience for members of underrepresented groups who may not be used to the inclusion model in which their opinions are sought and incorporated. The second phase is the Reorganization Phase, also called Implementation, in which restructuring begins, problem-solving efforts are generated, and staff development and training occurs. The third phase is the Realization Phase, also called Institutionalization, in which careful monitoring and evaluation of the previous phases begins; ongoing resources are provided; support services are expanded as needed; and data, generated from the program development, can be used to inform other interested professionals.

There are several critical factors that have particular relevance to program development and evaluation with diverse populations (Nastasi, Varjas, Sarkar, & Jayasena, 1998). The process begins with assessing an organization's stage of commitment to change. Using a six-point scale, psychologists can survey key stakeholders to see how enthusiastic, resistant, or indifferent they may be to development of new programs.

The process continues with an emphasis on collaboration with the stakeholders. Then there is intentional collection and incorporation of cultural data into the process of design; this enables psychologists to develop models and programs that are responsive to culture. Finally, there is emphasis on the specific context in which the program is to be implemented; this consideration of context increases "the likelihood of program acceptability, proper implementation, and sustainability" (Nastasi et al., 1998, p. 260).

Primary Prevention

Prevention involves proactive activities targeted predominantly at high-risk groups who have yet to be affected by the condition to be prevented (Albee & Ryan-Finn, 1993). Prevention is advantageous to both the profession and to the public at large. It can stop destructive behaviors from ever occurring, delay a problem, reduce the impact of a given problem, promote factors known to increase physical and emotional well-being, and support larger institutions that work for similar purposes (Romano & Hage, 2000). Further, it has practical significance, as prevention is cost-effective to both the public and organizations such as managed care companies and other health insurance providers.

Regarding racial-cultural issues, prevention has particular applicability and implications for postdoctoral training. As Romano and Hage (2000) asserted:

> Preventionists must be aware of the historical, social, and political factors that contribute to institutional racism, poverty, and oppression, which in turn place particular groups as well as entire communities at risk for physical and emotional distress. (p. 746)

The authors also emphasized the importance of developing and maintaining multicultural competence in order to create effective prevention strategies. Of particular salience in devising prevention programs is establishing constructive dialogue between psychologists and the groups they intend to help, so that communication can facilitate the development of strategies in which the targeted population will be seriously invested.

Hage (2000) gave an example of how she considered social and cultural factors in primary prevention. She explored ways to prevent male violence against female intimates. She sought to establish the relationship between the cycle of violence and how a patriarchic society legitimizes men's dominance over women and how economic conditions may support the patriarchy. She also considered racial-ethnic factors that are important in the prevention strategies she elucidates. She cited evidence that White women and Black women respond differently to domestic violence and do not make use of community resources with similar frequency. She concluded that prevention programs ought to be differentially targeted.

IMPLICATIONS AND INTEGRATION

The dimensions of racial-cultural counseling competence and the advanced competencies are relevant facets for postdoctoral training programs in light of the core training themes delineated earlier in the chapter. The first such theme, balancing didactic and experiential activities, necessitates myriad training experiences. Both theoretical conceptualization and skills acquisition were identified as important components for training at the 1992 Ann Arbor meeting (Larsen et al., 1993). The dimensions of racial-cultural counseling competence are theoretically based yet consist of microskills that practitioners must acquire to achieve competence.

The second theme identified was creating a systematic, organized training experience. The model and the advanced competencies lend themselves to the development of a curriculum that includes racial-cultural training. The model consists of an integration of critical components identified as those most salient in the multicultural counseling literature. The coordination and integration of the various facets of the model are among its most important features. The precise structure of the model lends itself to the type of organized training experience identified as critical in the literature generated from the national conference.

The third core theme was regular evaluation to yield self-correction. The concept of self-evaluation is explicit in the model. The seventh competency, evaluating process and outcome, requires practitioners to seek comprehensive feedback from a variety of sources to gauge their effectiveness in treatment. Because we acknowledge that competence is not equated with perfection, it is anticipated that counselors sometimes will err. Of critical importance is learning how to monitor one's progress so that correction can occur.

The fourth theme was specification of learning objectives. The dimensions of racial-cultural counseling competence and advanced competencies delineate several critical components. The components of the dimensions of racial-cultural counseling competence can easily be expressed in terms of specific learning objectives trainees need to master. Practitioners can be asked to describe the model, explain the theoretical structure, and apply it to counseling cases. In addition, the microskills of the model provide clear objectives that lend themselves to the development of new curricula.

The fifth theme identified was linkage of training and practice. The model and advanced competencies have the structure needed to accomplish this task. They have relevance for both didactic teaching and practical application. The model and the competencies provide the theoretical structure deemed important by the stakeholders at the National Conference on Postdoctoral Training in Professional Psychology. They also are inherently linked to actual case examples so that training and practice can continue to inform and enrich each other.

CONCLUSION

The need for comprehensive multicultural training has been established. Although doctoral programs provide initial exposure to multicultural counseling competence, the breadth of material needed to be covered by the curriculum, coupled with the extensive multicultural literature, does not permit graduate training to adequately address this domain. A foundational model of the dimensions of racial-cultural counseling competence has been proposed. In addition to the model, four advanced competencies were described for postdoctoral training.

Postdoctoral training is in need of standardization that addresses the central components common to all practitioners. Future research should continue to focus on developing effective theoretical-based models that address the most relevant aspects of practice. Including new psychologists in the development and evaluation of such models provides an additional perspective and increases the likelihood that trainees will be more invested in such curricula. The advanced competencies should continue to be refined and supplemented as the responsibilities of new psychologists continue to develop and become crystallized.

REFERENCES

Abreu, J. M., Chung, R. H. G., & Atkinson, D. R. (2000). Multicultural counseling training: Past, present, and future directions. *Counseling Psychologist, 28,* 641–656.

Aiello, J., & Bullock, L. M. (1999). Building commitment to responsible inclusion. *Preventing School Failure, 43,* 99–103.

Albee, G. W., & Ryan-Finn, K. D. (1993). An overview of primary prevention. *Journal of Counseling and Development, 72,* 115–123.

Belar, C. D., Bieliauskas, L. A., Klepac, R. K., Larsen, K. G., Stigall, T. T., & Zimet, C. N. (1993). National conference on postdoctoral training in professional psychology. *American Psychologist, 48,* 1284–1289.

Brown, M. T., & Landrum-Brown, J. (1995). Counselor supervision: Cross-cultural perspectives. In J. C. Ponterotto, J. M. Casas, L. A. Suzuki, & C. M. Alexander (Eds.), *Handbook of multicultural counseling* (pp. 263–286). Thousand Oaks, CA: Sage.

Brown, R. A. (1996). Training in professional psychology: Are we addressing the issues? *Professional Psychology: Research and Practice, 27,* 506–507.

Constantine, M. G. (1997). Facilitating multicultural competency in counseling supervision: Operationalizing a practical framework. In D. B. Pope-Davis & H. L. K. Coleman (Eds.), *Multicultural counseling competencies: Assessment, education and training, and supervision* (pp. 310–324). Thousand Oaks, CA: Sage.

Constantine, M. G., & Ladany, N. (1996). Students' perceptions of multicultural training in counseling psychology programs. *Journal of Multicultural Counseling and Development, 24,* 241–254.

Corey, G., & Herlihy, B. (1996). Competence. In B. Herlihy & G. Corey (Eds.), *Ethical standards casebook* (5th ed., pp. 217–228). Alexandria, VA: American Counseling Association.

D'Andrea, M., & Daniels, J. (1997). Multicultural counseling supervision: Central issues, theoretical considerations, and practical strategies. In D. B. Pope-Davis & H. L. K. Coleman (Eds.), *Multicultural counseling competencies: Assessment, education and training, and supervision* (pp. 290–309). Thousand Oaks, CA: Sage.

D'Andrea, M., & Daniels, J. (1999). Understanding the different psychological dispositions of white racism: A comprehensive model for counselor educators and practitioners. In M. Kiselica (Ed.), *Confronting prejudice and racism during multicultural training* (pp. 59–88). Alexandria, VA: American Counseling Association.

Farberman, R. K. (2000). When is a new psychologist ready for independent practice? *Monitor on Psychology, 31*(8), 44–47.

France, C. M., & Wolf, E. M. (2000). Issues related to postdoctoral education and training in professional psychology: Results of an opinion survey. *Professional Psychology: Research and Practice, 31*(4), 429–434.

Graham, S. R., & Fox, R. E. (1991). Postdoctoral education for professional practice. *American Psychologist, 46,* 1033–1035.

Gudykunst, W. B. (1998). *Bridging differences: Effective intergroup communication* (3rd ed.). Newbury Park, CA: Sage.

Hage, S. M. (2000). The role of counseling psychology in preventing male violence against female intimates. *Counseling Psychologist, 28,* 797–828.

Helms, J. E., & Cook, D. A. (1999). *Using race and culture in counseling and psychotherapy: Theory and process.* Boston: Allyn & Bacon.

Kaslow, N. J., McCarthy, S. M., Rogers, J. H., & Summerville, M. B. (1992). Psychology postdoctoral training: A developmental perspective. *Professional Psychology: Research and Practice, 23,* 369–375.

Kiselica, M. S. (1998). Preparing Anglos for the challenges and joys of multiculturalism. *Counseling Psychologist, 21,* 5–21.

Kruger, J., & Dunning, D. (1999). Unskilled and unaware of it: How difficulties in recognizing one's own incompetence lead to inflated self-assessment. *Journal of Personality and Social Psychology, 77,* 1121–1134.

Lafferty, P., Beutler, L. E., & Crago, M. (1989). Differences between more and less effective psychotherapists: A study of select therapist variables. *Journal of Consulting and Clinical Psychology, 57,* 76–80.

Larsen, K. G., Belar, C. D., Bieliauskas, L. A., Klepac, R. K., Stigall, T. T., & Zimet, C. N. (Eds.). (1993). *Proceedings of the National Conference on Postdoctoral Training in Professional Psychology.* Washington, DC: Association of Psychology Postdoctoral and Internship Centers.

Lee, R. M., Chalk, L., Conner, S. E., Kawasaki, N., Jannetti, A., LaRue, T., et al. (1999). The status of multicultural counseling training at counseling center internship sites. *Journal of Multicultural Counseling and Development, 27,* 58–75.

Mobley, M., & Cheatham, H. (1999). R.A.C.E.—racial affirmation and counselor educators. In M. S. Kiselica (Ed.), *Confronting prejudice and racism during multicultural training* (pp. 89–106). Alexandria, VA: American Counseling Association.

Murphy, M. C., & Wright, B. V. (1995). Multicultural training in university counseling center predoctoral psychology internship programs: A survey. *Journal of Multicultural Counseling and Development, 23,* 170–181.

Nastasi, B. K., Varjas, K., Sarkar, S., & Jayasena, A. (1998). Participatory model of mental health programming: Lessons learned from work in a developing country. *School Psychology Review, 27,* 260–277.

Quintana, S. M., & Bernal, M. E. (1995). Ethnic minority training in counseling psychology: Comparisons with clinical psychology and proposed standards. *Counseling Psychologist, 23,* 102–122.

Reynolds, A. L. (1997). Using the multicultural change intervention matrix (MCIM) as a multicultural counseling training model. In D. B. Pope-Davis & H. K. Coleman (Eds.), *Multicultural counseling competencies: Assessment, education and training, and supervision* (pp. 209–226). Thousand Oaks, CA: Sage.

Ridley, C. R. (1995). *Overcoming unintentional racism in counseling and therapy: A practitioner's guide to intentional intervention.* Thousand Oaks, CA: Sage.

Ridley, C. R., Mendoza, D. W., & Kanitz, B. E. (1994). Multicultural training: Reexamination, operationalization, and integration. *Counseling Psychologist, 22,* 227–289.

Ridley, C. R., & Thompson, C. E. (1999). Managing resistance to diversity training: A social systems perspective. In M. S. Kiselica (Ed.), *Confronting prejudice and racism during multicultural training* (pp. 3–24). Alexandria, VA: American Counseling Association.

Romano, J. L., & Hage, S. M. (2000). Prevention and counseling psychology: Revitalizing commitments for the 21st century. *Counseling Psychologist, 28,* 733–763.

Rooney, S. C., & Flores, L. Y. (1998). Making multicultural education effective for everyone. *Counseling Psychologist, 26,* 22–33.

Stewart, A. E., & Stewart, E. A. (1998). Trends in postdoctoral education: Requirements for licensure and training opportunities. *Professional Psychology: Research and Practice, 29,* 273–283.

Stewart, A. E., Stewart, E. A., & Vogel, D. L. (2000). A survey of interns' preferences and plans for postdoctoral training. *Professional Psychology: Research and Practice, 31*(4), 435–441.

Stone, G. (1997). Multiculturalism as a context for supervision: Perspectives, limitations, and implications. In D. B. Pope-Davis & H. L. K. Coleman (Eds.), *Multicultural counseling competencies: Assessment, education and training, and supervision* (pp. 263–289). Thousand Oaks, CA: Sage.

Sue, D. W. (2001). Multidimensional facets of cultural competence. *Counseling Psychologist, 29,* 790–821.

Sue, D. W., Carter, R. T., Casas, J. M., Fouad, N. A., Ivey, A. E., Jensen, M., et al. (1998). *Multicultural counseling competencies: Individual and organizational development.* Thousand Oaks, CA: Sage.

Tomlinson-Clarke, S., & Wang, V. O. (1999). A paradigm for racial-cultural training in the development of counselor cultural competencies. In M. S. Kiselica (Ed.), *Confronting prejudice and racism during multicultural training* (pp. 155–168). Alexandria, VA: American Counseling Association.

VandeCreek, L., Knapp, S., & Brace, K. (1990). Mandatory continuing education for licensed psychologists: Its rationale and current implementation. *Professional Psychology: Research and Practice, 21,* 135–140.

Welfel, E. R. (1998). *Ethics in counseling and psychotherapy: Standards, research, and emerging issues.* Cincinnati, OH: Brooks/Cole.

Wiens, A. N. (1993). Postdoctoral education—-training for specialty practice: Long anticipated, finally realized. *American Psychologist, 48,* 415–422.

PART II

Critical Issues in Racial-Cultural Practice

CHAPTER 13

Psychological Theory and Culture: Practice Implications

Chalmer E. Thompson

Well-conceived theories of personality and identity development, cognitive, affective, and moral development, and adaptation and coping are intended to inform sound mental health practice. Psychotherapists and counselors rely on theories of behavior and human development to guide them in facilitating psychological health in their clients, with "psychological health" variously defined as the elimination of unwanted or destructive symptoms, the promotion of self-actualization, the enhancement of spirituality, and so forth. *How* psychological health is defined and experienced is linked inextricably to culture, that is, the norms, rules, roles, and worldviews that people adopt to make sense of and function in the world (e.g., Brislin, 1993; Carter, this *Handbook,* this volume; Draguns, 1996; Landrine & Klonoff, 1996; Pedersen, Conner, Dragun, & Trimble, 2002; Sue & Torino, this *Handbook,* this volume). Given that culture informs human experience, it follows that theorists who enfold cultural factors as integral to human experiences provide crucial knowledge to psychotherapists. Theories that account for culture and research that supports attendant premises of theories form the basis for competent and ethical practices.

Amply documented are criticisms leveled against both psychological theorists and researchers for treating culture as an ancillary or overlooked aspect of human development and functioning (e.g., Carter, this volume; Comas-Diàz, 2000; Fanon, 1968; Miller, 1999; Moghaddam & Studer, 1997; Rogler, 1999; Sue & Sue, 1999, 2003). Miller captures the essence of much of the criticism by stating that basic psychological theory is generally perceived as "formulations of universal psychological processes and mechanisms, which are merely filled in by cultural parameters" (p. 87). Key to this perception of psychological theory is the assumption that dominant groups can legitimately be seen as possessing universal processes and therefore as prototypical relative to nondominant group members. Furthermore, theory development and research on the cultural systems that shape the psychological processes of dominant group members *as* dominant group members appear generally to be deemed irrelevant to theory development and research (with notable exceptions in recent years; e.g., Ancis & Szymanski, 2001; D'Andrea & Daniels, 1999; Gushue & Carter, 2000; Neville, Worthington, & Spanierman, 2001). On the other hand, when theorists and researchers "fill in" cultural parameters, they do so primarily by directing their attention to people from non-dominant cultural groups.

For example, when Teyber (2000) cautions therapists to be familiar with the experiences of "particular groups" when applying interpersonal processes in psychotherapy, he cites as an illustration that therapists need to "know that African Americans' history includes slavery and racial discrimination" (p. 21). The author therefore suggests that certain information about African Americans can be important to practitioners in their work with these clients. The author also stresses that therapists need to be flexible in their work regarding client response specificity or, rather, the individual qualities of each person shaped by different socializing influences, including culture.

But because African Americans as a racial-cultural group (and later, other non-White groups) are mentioned to the exclusion of Whites, it can be concluded by the reader that it is only these former populations that have cultural or racial concerns worth pointing out. Might the therapist gain something by having certain knowledge about Whites? Consistent with the practice of inserting material to enhance practitioners' work with African Americans, might practitioners also be well-advised to know that White Americans' history includes slavery and pressures to condone systems of racial persecution and exploitation? Might cultural and sociopolitical knowledge influence the therapeutic interaction involving different racial-cultural dyadic combinations? In the examples here of African American and White American history, the focus is on negative information. However, it should be noted that the inclusion of positive and contemporary aspects of race and culture would be essential. *Also essential is information on how any of this information is systematically linked to psychological processes and therefore to assessment and treatment.*

In Teyber's (2000) defense, it can be argued that he merely omitted examples related to Whites as a racial-cultural group. To be sure, my intention is not to demonize the author or his work (which I generally admire), but rather to illustrate a tendency that occurs with many theorists and is likely the result of an implicit process of conditioning. Stated plainly, I propose that many received psychological theories tend to omit or selectively attend to culture and race as psychological processes because theorists are conditioned to assume that *dominant culture* is (1) standard and therefore culturally and racially neutral and (2) relatively separate from *nondominant culture*. These assumptions very likely are accompanied by the conclusion that "others," non-dominant group members, have a culture that is relevant for study because they are not culturally and racially neutral. How this tendency of fragmenting cultural realities influences theory development and, ultimately, therapy with *all* clients is discussed in this chapter.

Miller (1999) urged psychologists to contemplate culture not only as integral to psychological functioning, but also as a *patterning of psychological processes* that needs to be incorporated into all types of psychological inquiry. Therefore, I also explore the complexities of culture and then devote specific attention to a theory of patterned processes that is relevant to the therapist's ability to best work with cultural information. I propose that racial identity theory is valuable in the therapist's understanding of the interdependence of people within and across different cultural contexts. At the conclusion of the chapter, I reconstruct Teyber's (2000) conceptualization by systematically including factors related to race and culture.

CULTURE AND SOCIALIZATION:
MACROSYSTEMS PROCESSES

Moghaddam and Studer (1997) stated that culture prescribes correct behavior, "the way people *should* do things" (p. 193). The correctness of behavior depends on several factors, including the characteristics of the person and the situation. For example, the authors refer to variations in how people differ relative to *positions in social space* and their *social roles*. Examples of positions in space are the employer and employee in occupational space and the child and father in kin space. Social roles refer to the behaviors prescribed for a person in a given position. An example of social roles includes how a child, father, employer, or employee are expected to behave. *Norms* refer to prescriptions for behavior in particular settings, such as correct behavior at a funeral as opposed to a wedding. *Rules* are prescriptions for behavior for people in specific social roles, for example, how priests are to behave at a christening as opposed to a funeral or wedding. Finally, Moghaddam and Studer described how positions, roles, norms, and rules are all part of a *normative system* that clarifies correct behavior for persons in situations. The authors stated that normative systems are internalized through processes of socialization (Bowser, this *Handbook,* Volume One; Yeh & Hunter, this *Handbook,* Volume One).

From the massive collection of writings in anthropology, we know that history is an important aspect of culture. Culture consists of traditions passed down through generations and modified ostensibly by the presence of and/or eventual integration between people from different cultures. Language, art, artifacts, and music are considered aspects of cultural traditions. Moreover, transformations in cultural tradition are the result of migrations, invasions, and other events that are notable to members of cultural groups and their way of life. The invasion of one or more cultures in one society will likely mean that intercultural immersion will differ in quality in comparison to societies in which people come together in relative harmony. Still, it is likely that there exists stability in original cultures and in the normative systems that have been created even as changes occur in different societies (see Brislin, 1993; Carter & Pieterse, this *Handbook,* Volume One; Martín-Baró, 1994). Indeed, culture can be recreated and refashioned in order for certain groups to endure oppression. Therefore, culture needs to be understood not merely as conformance to certain norms and rules, but also as a means to capitalize on prior normative systems to navigate new and changing structures. Culture can thus be said to connect the present and the past.

Structures of domination and oppression, such as racism, sexism, and class exploitation, are cultivated over time and across regions of society. Conversely, individuals and groups have resisted and continue to resist domination. Forces of domination and resistance commingle, working simultaneously. At a macrosystems level, forces of domination promote practices that privilege members of the dominant group and marginalize members of the subordinate group. Both privileging and marginalizing practices reflect efforts to normalize a way of being for people and their relationships between and within ascribed groups. Further, privileging certain groups and marginalizing others is an intertwined practice that is supported by institutional structures, such as mainstream media and schooling, child rearing, and "acceptable" language and discourse, that selectively attend to, deny, and generally distort aspects of reality for the purpose of maintaining an unfairly stratified status quo (for discussions on racism as a structure of domination, see Neville et al., 2001; Thompson, in press; Thompson & Carter, 1997; Thompson & Neville, 1999). For example, although history is important to the sustaining of culture, structures of domination can influence cultural socializing practices by downplaying or erasing certain aspects of history.

I focus attention next on how macrosystem-level processes play a role in individual adaptation.

INDIVIDUAL PSYCHOLOGICAL PROCESSES RELATED TO RACE AND CULTURE

Recursively influencing the process of cultural socialization at the microsystems level are individuals whose lives are entangled in the weave of domination and resistance. Macrosystem processes help to define normative systems and feed into the construction of identity in all members in a society. The identities of dominant group members can be nurtured, as in the United States, by a conditioning that encourages a sense of superiority or entitlement in matters of oppression. In the absence of conditions or external forces to counter this conditioning, as in the case of social movements (e.g., Sarason, 1996; Williams, 1988), dominant group members may thrive on the knowledge, however distorted, of their superiority or relative entitlement compared to subordinate group members. This distorted knowledge can be fiercely protected when the individual is unable or unwilling to confront the moral dilemma of acknowledging the evidence of unfair stratification on the one hand, and believing in equality, justice, and meritocracy on the other.

Racial identity theorist Janet Helms (e.g., 1995, 2001) proposed that when people are confronted with this dissonance, they can enter into a process of moral development during which they work through their belief in referent group superiority and their belief in the inferiority of others. Alternatively, they may justify the superiority of themselves and their referent group and, conversely, justify the inferiority of others. Helms proposed that for many dominant group members, both paths of coping with the dissonance occur simultaneously and with different thrusts, depending on individual and contextual factors. However, successfully working through the dissonance will be difficult when the person is emotionally, cognitively, and conatively tied to a reality in which his or her deservedness, superiority, and referent group loyalty is reinforced and when the ability for resolving moral decisions is diminished. Working through the dissonance is complicated further when the individual possesses a low tolerance for experiencing uncomfortable emotions that will likely emerge when the fictitiousness of his or her stature is realized more fully (see Thompson & Carter, 1997). The person may also strike out against or dismiss the perspectives of others whom he or she perceives as causing these emotions. If dominant group members pursue a path of moral strivings, then they will find a need to ultimately disengage themselves from a "them versus us" perspective and construct a way of being that reflects the moral inclusion of people within broader humanity (Thompson, 2004).

Members of subordinate groups are not passive in the process of domination. Indeed, it is the lack of passivity that can provoke stronger efforts to dominate. Subordinate group members can variously act to resist, even under threat of harm or death. Historical accounts of the battles between Whites and Native Americans during the first 200 years of the European invasion and of the uprisings of African-descended people against Whites during the formative years of slavery provide glimpses of these outward attacks against extermination and subjugation. But over the course of history, and with less violent and more institutionalized domination, members of subordinate groups still practice resistance, as well as conformity to and acceptance of the sociopolitical status quo (Sue & Sue, 1999, 2003).

Operating within structures of domination *and* resistance, members of subordinate groups, too, carve out identities in which they attempt to make sense of and work through the reality of oppression. They discover emotions like anger and rage and, concomitantly, a need to manage these emotions. If the expression of these emotions casts them further into the margins, say, by being labeled, avoided, chastised, or killed, then they can experience hopelessness toward the prospects of change. They may find alternative ways to express themselves, perhaps by relating only to racially similar others in constructive or nonconstructive ways, or by suppressing their emotions and, subsequently, becoming explosive and misdirected in their expressions. When subordinate group members can no longer tolerate being treated as devalued members in society and are unable to tap into meaningful ways of opposing the domination, they may turn their emotions inward and toward their referent group members whom they deem deserving of their collective fate. Some subordinate group members may relent or contribute to the perpetuation of oppressive systems of stratification. They may glorify and associate only with dominant group members either physically, if possible, or psychologically. They may think of themselves as superior because of how White their skin appears, how fluent their English is, or how materially successful they are relative to others in their referent group. They experience a moral struggle similar to that of dominant group members—the primary difference is that subordinate group members are doing so in reaction to a system of dehumanization. In other words, they can dissociate themselves racially-culturally—not necessarily separating themselves entirely from their referent group, but segmenting themselves to inflate their status within that group (see Thompson, in press).

In contrast, with hope and a legacy of endurance, members of the subordinate group can avail themselves of constructive ways of resisting. They can instead construct or restore a positive sense of self and referent group identity. Similar to dominant group members, there are moral overtones to the reconstruction of self. Reconstruction of positive identities has to occur with regard for all humans, including dominant group members (Thompson, in press).

Structures of domination and oppression influence culture by differentially and unfairly defining the norms and rules that people follow and the roles they assume. Consequently, people who are socialized in the broader culture learn, often implicitly, what is expected of them within sociopolitical hierarchies. The individual may choose not to conform to these expectations, but in making the choice to disengage from societal norms, he or she can experience unpleasant or even dire consequences, such as being subjected to violence. Conversely, consequences can be positive, such as overturning sinister codes of conduct in a particular setting and instigating more sweeping change at community or regional levels. A confluence of forces, including extent of violence, situational and sociological timing, and amount and manner of social support, conspires to dictate certain outcomes.

Complex perspectives of the rules, norms, and roles that shape cultural systems reveal important information about the processes in which people learn and relate to others. Socializing processes informed by culture and sociopolitical forces occur in child-rearing practices and are detectable in occupational settings, within family groups, and in public spheres. And relevant to this discussion on socialization is the *interdependence* in the construction of societal and individual identities: Members of the dominant group depend on subordinate group members to help them construct images of themselves (dominant group members) as neutral, superior, and deserving; consequently, members of subordinate social groups have to be viewed as subjective, inferior, and undeserving, a view that subordinate group members may then internalize (Helms, this *Handbook,* Volume One). These interdependent influences are established as a result of the yoked existence between dominant and subordinate groups (Thompson, in press).

The foregoing discussion is embedded in racial identity theory (see Helms, 1995, 2001; Helms & Cook, 1999; Thompson & Carter, 1997). I refer to the theory for the purpose of focusing specifically on one of its basic premises: the dynamic interdependence of people both within and across different cultural groups.

Structures of domination, such as racism, create pathologies in everyday life. One manifestation of this pathology is the normative practice of fragmenting and distorting the notion of culture. This fragmentation is present when there is an assumption that culture can be filled in to explain basic psychological theory. It also is present when there is an assumption of cultural homogeneity in research on the mental health of subordinate cultural groups, whereby relatively little attention is paid to the diversity that exists within these groups (see Rogler, 1999).

Hence, people in racialized societies may learn over time to fragment certain aspects of culture that they find appealing (e.g., admiring "different" language, art, communication styles) and distancing themselves from reminders of ongoing marginalization. Irrespective of race and culture, people may also perceive "others" and themselves in a disjointed fashion. For example, although negative experiences of oppressed groups may be acknowledged, as in Teyber's (2000) example of African Americans, some people may find it difficult to recognize the connection between the experience of African Americans and those of White Americans (Helms, this *Handbook,* Volume One). Meanwhile, a more holistic perspective of people and of reality can reveal the real humanity of people and present opportunities for eradicating continued injustices. Fragmented views of reality can spawn behaviors that are patronizing and distancing, perpetuating conflicts between groups, fermenting divisions within groups, and prompting fragmented views about the self.

This practice of fragmentation brings us as humans no closer to understanding the totality of a people and their experiences. In the context of psychological practice, it also brings the therapist no closer to an understanding of the self in connection with culture. It is in this context that interdependence would seem essential to successful practice.

IMPLICATIONS OF FRAGMENTATION TO THEORY DEVELOPMENT AND PRACTICE

Approaching culture as an aspect of the self is to embrace an important aspect of reality. However, in societies where there is or has been domination, forcible expulsion, or colonization, there may also exist tendencies to define culture in a reduced or dismissive manner. What occurs when race and culture are dismissed or distorted from psychological theories is the proclivity to focus away from these societal forces and instead emphasize intrapsychic factors that influence psychological phenomena. Martín-Baró (1994), the creator of liberation theology who was later assassinated in war-torn El Salvador, argued:

> Psychology has created a fictionalized and ideologized image of what it means to be human, based on its own ahistoricism and bias toward individualism. This false image presents the individual as bereft of history, community, political commitment, and social loyalties. A still shot, it captures a moment and calls that Us, making it seem that what we are during some frozen, circumscribed moment is all that we can or will ever be. In this distorted picture . . . we cannot hope to comprehend ourselves and our realities, but what is perhaps worse, we are likely to accept what it says about us as right and immutable. (p. 5)

I propose that the failure of theorists to see the whole, the present as connected to the past, and people as linked together with an array of human strengths and weaknesses can inhibit the potential of practitioners to help create meaningful change in their clients' lives.

Theorists need to understand that culture constitutes an essential perspective to basic psychological processes, as do biological, sociological, and historical perspectives (see Miller, 1999). They can contribute substantively to the practices of therapists when they treat aspects of culture as patterned processes that can be enfolded into concepts of personality, performance, and coping. Lines of development in theory and inquiry can help improve constructs and theories presumed universal, tailor them according to the particular cultural systems of the group being investigated, or define emerging constructs.

Importantly, with little or limited awareness about sociopolitical reality, it can become easy for therapists to perceive the goals of psychotherapy as centered primarily on the person *as extracted from* his or her cultural context (for dominant group members) or *as embedded within* a cultural context that is mysteriously detached from a highly interdependent context (for subordinate group members). The problem in both cases is that there is an absence of knowledge and understanding about the interdependent relationship between dominant and subordinate group processes and, therefore, a fragmented perception of reality and of the person as a racial-cultural being.

Several problems arise when therapists collude in fragmented realities. First, they may assume that the environment is relatively nonpolitical or neutral, making the perspectives of those who point out these realities suspect or even exaggerated.

So, although therapists may be sympathetic to the horrors of discrimination, forcible removal, or exploitation, they can lack an understanding of the impact of dehumanizing experiences on clients, particularly when the therapist views these experiences as aberrational or nonsystemic. Therapists who collude in a fragmented view of reality, self, and others are inclined to distort presenting information and can feel hopeless about ways to effect needed change. Absent an understanding of the broader context and historical events that have an impact on dehumanizing experiences, it becomes fairly easy to minimize feelings of client hopelessness or rage. It would seem that the ability of therapists to relate authentically to clients would mean having the wherewithal to take into account the varied aspects of their own and their clients' existence. Clients profit when therapists are cognitively and affectively capable of viewing the world and its contents without distortion.

Another implication of this fragmented reality is that the therapist can implicitly encourage clients *not* to see the urgency of societal problems as relating to their psychological problems. Clients therefore assume the role of someone who is blinded to or distorts this reality—yet another manifestation of macrosystem processes (see Thompson & Neville, 1999). When the therapist is a dominant group member, turning a blind eye to reality serves to covertly perpetuate his or her benefactor status. When the client also is a dominant group member and has issues related to his or her status or with members from subordinate groups, the inability of the therapist to attend to the role of these sociopolitical and cultural issues as knottily tied to client psychological health is yet another means of perpetuating injustice.

Helms (1995, 2001) and Thompson and Carter (1997) proposed that therapists who have integrated a complex understanding of race and culture into their conceptualizations of mental health assume roles that serve the client beyond the immediate individual needs. They invite the possibility that race and culture are associated with client concerns. They recognize that stature is imposed and are mindful of how sociopolitical hierarchies based on race, gender, sexual orientation, and social class have an impact on the client and the therapist-client dynamics. Therapists utilize advanced racial identity schemata to allow for a thorough and complex rendering of client complaints. Advanced racial identity schemata are characterized by an approach versus avoidance of reality, and confidence in self and with one's interactions with others. Therapists who operate using advanced status schemata have an appreciation of how structures of disadvantage separate and divide humankind. As such, advanced status therapists are committed to addressing manifestations of dehumanizing structures of oppression.

Parallel to an awareness of the patterned ways in which people can and cannot relate to one another, advanced status therapists are aware of the experiences that help inform them of their clients' experiences. These therapists know that language, norms, and roles are the products of tradition and relating in one's world. They also come to respect that culture is shaped by context. Culture also helps to shape their clients' worldview about relationships, including the therapist-client relationship, and is to be regarded and understood. Advanced status therapists know that client response specificity is essential.

Drawing from the literature on Posttraumatic Stress Disorder and refugee "careers," advanced status therapists are also aware that people encounter a range of traumatic, displacing experiences that can produce stress (Carter, Forsyth, Mazulla, & Williams, this *Handbook,* this volume; Prendes-Lintel, 2001). Research on traumatic and posttraumatic stress has directed much of its attention to the moderating variables that help explain adaptation and coping of people who have been forcibly removed and the subject of brutal violence. Similarly, advanced status therapists also are aware of the relatively large body of research on acculturation for different racial groups (see Cortes, Rogler, & Malgady, 1994; Kim & Abreu, 2001; Kohatsu, this *Handbook,* Volume One; Rogler, Cortes, & Malgady, 1991; Szapocznik, Santisteban, Kurtines, Perez-Vidal, & Herves, 1984). A person's readiness and temperament for change and the circumstances surrounding immigration and emigration, such as war, prior exposures to different cultures, and the quality of living conditions in new environments, are critical in formulating models of adjustment and adaptation. Future complementary models to inform their work would ultimately include the experiences not only of those who transfer to and from different cultural environments, but also of those from the host culture. It would be intriguing, for example, to examine the adaptation issues of German residents who lived through the Holocaust and who now are experiencing the influx of Turks in Germany. Attention to dominant group processes could help them form a more complete picture of reality and of their positioning within it.

Finally, advanced status therapists are able to acknowledge the interdependent nature of cultural construction. By perceiving therapy as a transformational experience that extends beyond individual needs frozen in time, these therapists perceive therapy as a process of empowerment that extends to community and societal fortitude. The discovery of therapy as a means to empower clients as cultural and sociopolitical beings involves having the therapist become aware of his or her stature within human-created hierarchies and, using this awareness, to overcome the barriers to successful therapy process and outcome.

A RECONSTRUCTED THEORY OF INTERPERSONAL PROCESSES IN THERAPY

I believe that Teyber's (2000) conceptualization of interpersonal processes in therapy can generally be valuable to practitioners. From a cultural standpoint, it operates under an assumption that insight is valuable to the client and that there is generally some ease in discussing issues between the therapist and client—assumptions not necessarily shared by clients across cultures (e.g., Atkinson, Morten, & Sue, 1998; Sue & Sue, 1999, 2003). However, I attempt here to discuss aspects of the theory I perceive as valuable and ways to modify it to be more racially and culturally appropriate. In brief, I recommend that therapists adopt an interpersonal theoretical stance or sensibility that is inclusive of cultural and sociopolitical factors.

The primary assumption of interpersonal processes theory is that people come to understand themselves and their world based on their interactions with others (Teyber, 2000). Patterns of relating form over the course of their development when there is relative consistency in rewards for behaviors that are considered appropriate. For inappropriate behaviors there are consequences that are effective in dampening the frequency of the behavior or extinguishing it altogether. In some families, the system of rewards and consequences is based on the pathologies of one or more family members, such as a parent with narcissistic tendencies who doles out rewards and punishments that objectify other family members. Such parents are unable to relate authentically because of their need for wholeness and completion; they are unable to give or reciprocate in healthy ways. Children develop patterns of behaving that are both healthy and unhealthy. However, with an erratic system of rewards and a concomitant reward structure that contributes to a denial of the problem within the family, the child develops patterns that become rigidly fixed. These fixed patterns are developed to maintain a system of pathology and, therefore, constrain the individual in his or her development throughout the life span from approaching people and situations.

The context in which these fixed patterns occur is not only familial, but also racial and cultural. This latter factor is one to which Teyber (2000) occasionally alludes but does not address sufficiently. People reside in contexts in which there is a denial of problems and a diminution of extant pathology. Therapists who strive to bring wholeness to the lives of children from traumatized or dysfunctional households actually hold key ingredients to their work when they are able to perceive the interrelatedness of race and culture with psychological processes.

I propose that there are exceptional advantages when therapists adopt interpersonal process sensibilities to psychotherapy that integrate aspects of liberation psychology. I define liberation psychology as that study of the human condition that summons a reality of social injustice and inequality rather than dismisses it. Liberation psychology also extends to practice whereby those who are aware of structural oppression also equip themselves to disrupt patterns of injustice (see Thompson & Carter, 1997). Psychologists can do so by examining the patterns of injustice as they are played out in the interactions of clients with themselves or with others in their environment.

As an interpersonal therapist, I have to make very careful, ethical decisions about the care of clients. For example, clients who have experienced a personal crisis, are grieving over the loss of a loved one, or who need assistance adjusting to a mental illness as they transition from an institution to everyday life probably think little about oppression and their participation in it. It can be argued that clients who experience patterns of dysfunctional relationships, are addicted to alcohol and/or drugs, are incarcerated, or are interested in undergoing a transformation of their personality also think little about the impact of oppression on their lives. But decisions about *how* and *when* issues of oppression are integrated into counseling and psychotherapy are as varied as the clients themselves. For example, a personal crisis may surface past problems, or one's admission of a debilitating mental disorder can bring on emotions that also stem from acculturative stress. My efforts reflect a way of being and, therefore, may be realized in therapy or supervision by a set of questions that allows the client to reveal information that he or she may not have readily revealed at the outset.

It is notable that I approach my practice of psychotherapy by attuning to all aspects of the clients' lives and problems *inclusive of* those aspects that affect their sense of morality and overall being in the world (e.g., Martín-Baró, 1994; Thompson, in press). In my view, liberation psychology aims to empower people to eliminate the structures that frustrate a sense of communal well-being and, thus, a sense of individual and familial well-being. I use this integration of interpersonal processes theory and liberation psychology in my role not only in psychotherapy, teaching, supervision, but also in my work as a community activist.

I focus attention on the relational dynamics between therapist and client as data to discern some of the person's past and ongoing patterns of interactions with others in his or her environment (Teyber, 2000). I believe that psychotherapy not only is a dialectical exchange in which the therapist helps clients by reinforcing mechanisms that improve psychological functioning, but it also is a relationship that can be instructive to both the therapist's and client's lives. That the client's reality is different from mine is important to our work, as is the fact that our realities occur interdependently outside and inside of therapy. For me to perceive my client as human, I also need to appreciate his or her wholeness and work through any prejudices or stereotypes I harbor that could obstruct an authentic relationship. Importantly, I also look for signs throughout the course of the relationship that the client has imposed certain judgments of me based on my presumed affiliations or loyalties within our larger cultural context. I also know that I can make unfair assumptions about clients on the basis of physical cues. These assumptions can obstruct therapy; consequently, I try to be mindful of them and, where appropriate, check the veracity of these assumptions. I also believe that by expressing my appreciation of different cultural approaches to communicating, I learn how best to convey any assumptions that I have about factors that I presume to be integral to treatment when these factors may not be important or salient to the client. For example, I am persuaded that insight is important to facilitating therapeutic change, but my use of it is quite broad and accommodates the needs, readiness, and worldview of the client. I also attend to survival needs as a priority in my work and, therefore, consider my knowledge of and collaboration with community resources to be essential to my work.

Given the silence and codification that surrounds society regarding issues of race and its impact on institutions, it is not surprising that people are accustomed to use silence or code words. I have learned and continue to learn ways to respond to the deflection, again being sensitive to my clients' cultural and sociopolitical lenses and to timing in the therapy. I believe that approaches to therapy need to anticipate the possibility that clients will refer to matters pertaining solely to culture and largely downplay issues related to racism. Clients may conceal issues related to race, believing that their racial experiences are irrelevant to the therapy or that mention of race will create discomfort in the relationship. For some clients, the concealment of race is driven by the desire to have the therapist erase any stereotypes that their physicality evokes. Client suspicions about therapist assumptions are very important, and therapists need to develop a skill base for introducing matters that can compromise the quality of the counseling relationship. Compromising need not mean that the relationship is doomed to failure because of the stops and starts that can occur in developing rapport. I believe that the therapist's objective is to create a dialectical relationship wherein the anxiety that arises when people form any relationship is embraced rather than avoided. Indeed, the clients can learn a great deal when they take risks, experience being misunderstood, and become informed about their own misunderstanding when the therapist approaches clients as people whom they see as fully human.

CONCLUSION

Once culture is perceived as a force that is integral to the self and thus is connected to history and context, theorists and therapists can make better use of the growing research on patterned processes related to adaptation, coping, identity development, and psychological functioning. An important first step is to recognize the patterns of interdependent relating that are circumscribed by societal dysfunction and inequality. Ignoring the patterns, however nondeliberate, can propel therapists to perpetuate the dysfunction in treatment. Perpetuating the dysfunction occurs when therapists fail to attend to clients holistically—inclusive of cultural and sociopolitical factors—and likewise when the therapist has little direction in knowing how to resolve manifestations of the client's participation in oppression and internalized oppression. A perpetuation of dysfunction can also occur in the process of therapy. For example, subordinate group clients might unwittingly place a high premium on the fictive superiority of the dominant group therapist, and the therapist proffers little or no intervention to pierce the fiction of sociopolitical hierarchies dramatized in the therapy relationship.

I propose that a reconstructed theory of interpersonal processes can assure client response specificity when the therapist is keenly aware of his or her role in an unfair society. In my estimation, well-informed therapists can better help their clients when they themselves work through identity issues and position themselves as change agents who serve the needs of their clients and not their own needs for approval, worth, and affiliation based on a pathological status quo.

REFERENCES

Ancis, J., & Szymanski, D. M. (2001). Awareness of white privilege among white counseling trainees. *Counseling Psychologist, 29,* 548–569.

Atkinson, D. R., Morten, G., & Sue, D. W. (1998). *Counseling American minorities* (5th ed.). Boston: McGraw-Hill.

Bowser, B. P. (in press). The role of socialization in cultural learning: What does the research say? In R. T. Carter (Ed.), *Handbook of racial-cultural psychology and counseling: Theory and research* (Vol. 1, pp. 184–206). Hoboken, NJ: Wiley.

Brislin, R. (1993). *Understanding culture's influence on behavior.* Fort Worth, TX: Harcourt Brace Jovanovich.

Carter, R. T., & Pieterse, A. L. (in press). Race: A social and psychological analysis of the term and its meaning. In R. T. Carter (Ed.), *Handbook of racial-cultural psychology and counseling: Theory and research* (Vol. 1, pp. 41–63). Hoboken, NJ: Wiley.

Comas-Diàz, L. (2000). An ethnopolitical approach to working with people of Color. *American Psychologist, 55,* 1319–1325.

Cortes, D. E., Rogler, L. H., & Malgady, R. G. (1994). Biculturality among Puerto Rican adults in the United States. *American Journal of Community Psychology, 22,* 707–721.

D'Andrea, M., & Daniels, J. (1999). Building on our knowledge of racism, mental health, and mental health practice: A reaction to Thompson and Neville. *Counseling Psychologist, 27,* 224–238.

Draguns, J. G. (1996). Humanly universal and culturally distinctive: Charting the course of cultural counseling. In P. B. Pedersen, J. G. Draguns, W. J. Lonner, & J. E. Trimble (Eds.), *Counseling across cultures* (4th ed., pp. 1–20). Thousand Oaks, CA: Sage.

Fanon, F. (1968). *Black skin, white masks.* New York: Grove Press.

Gushue, G. W., & Carter, R. T. (2000). Remembering race: White racial identity attitudes and two aspects of social memory. *Journal of Counseling Psychology, 47,* 199–210.

Helms, J. E. (1995). An update of Helms's White and people of Color racial identity models. In J. Ponterotto, J. M. Casas, L. A. Suzuki, & C. M. Alexander (Eds.), *Handbook of multicultural counseling* (pp. 181–198). Thousand Oaks, CA: Sage.

Helms, J. E. (2001). An update of Helms's White and people of Color racial identity models. In J. G. Ponterotto, J. M. Casas, L. A. Suzuki, & C. M. Alexander (Eds.), *Handbook of multicultural counseling* (2nd ed., pp. 181–198). Thousand Oaks, CA: Sage.

Helms, J. E. (in press). Challenging some misuses of reliability as reflected in evaluations of the White racial identity attitude scale. In R. T. Carter (Ed.), *Handbook of racial-cultural psychology and counseling: Theory and research* (Vol. 1, pp. 360–390). Hoboken, NJ: Wiley.

Helms, J. E., & Cook, D. A. (1999). *The use of race and culture in counseling and psychotherapy.* Boston: Allyn & Bacon.

Kim, B. K., & Abreu, J. M. (2001). Acculturation measurement: Theory, current instruments, and future directions. In J. G. Ponterotto, J. M. Casas, L. A. Suzuki, & C. M. Alexander (Eds.), *Handbook of multicultural counseling* (pp. 394–424). Thousand Oaks, CA: Sage.

Kohatsu, E. L. (in press). Accultration: Current and future directions. In R. T. Carter (Ed.), *Handbook of racial-cultural psychology and counseling: Theory and research* (Vol. 1, pp. 207–231). Hoboken, NJ: Wiley.

Landrine, H., & Klonoff, E. A. (1996). *African American acculturation: Deconstructing race and reviving culture.* Thousand Oaks, CA: Sage.

Martín-Baró, I. (1994). *Writings for a liberation psychology.* Cambridge, MA: Harvard University Press.

Miller, J. G. (1999). Cultural psychology: Implications for basic psychological theory. *Psychological Science, 10,* 85–91.

Moghaddam, F. M., & Studer, C. (1997). Cross-cultural psychology: The frustrated gadfly's promises, potentialities, and failures. In D. Fox & I. Prilleltensky (Eds.), *Critical psychology: An introduction* (pp. 185–201). Thousand Oaks, CA: Sage.

Neville, H. A., Worthington, R. L., & Spanierman, L. (2001). Race, power, and multicultural counseling psychology: Understanding white privilege and color-blind racial attitudes. In J. G. Ponterotto, J. M. Casas, L. A. Suzuki, & C. M. Alexander (Eds.), *Handbook of multicultural counseling* (pp. 257–288). Thousand Oaks, CA: Sage.

Pedersen, P. B., Draguns, J. G., Conner, W. S., & Trimble, J. E. (2002). *Counseling across cultures* (5th ed.). Thousand Oaks, CA: Sage.

Prendes-Lintel, M. (2001). A working model in counseling recent refuges. In J. G. Ponterotto, J. M. Casas, L. A. Suzuki, & C. M. Alexander (Eds.), *Handbook of multicultural counseling* (pp. 729–752). Thousand Oaks, CA: Sage.

Rogler, L. H. (1999). Methodological sources of cultural sensitivity in mental health research. *American Psychologist, 54,* 424–433.

Rogler, L. H., Cortes, D. E., & Malgady, R. G. (1991). Acculturation and mental health status among Hispanics: Convergence and new directions for research. *American Psychologist, 46,* 585–597.

Sarason, S. B. (1996). *Barometers of change: Individual, educational, and social transformation.* San Francisco: Jossey-Bass.

Sue, D. W., & Sue, D. (1999). *Counseling the culturally different* (3rd ed.). New York: Wiley.

Sue, D. W., & Sue, D. (2003). *Counseling the culturally diverse* (4th ed.). New York: Wiley.

Szapocznik, J., Santisteban, D., Kurtines, W., Perez-Vidal, A., & Hervis, O. (1984). Bicultural effectiveness training: A treatment intervention for enhancing intercultural adjustment in Cuban American families. *Hispanic Journal of Behavioral Sciences, 6,* 317–344.

Teyber, E. (2000). *Interpersonal process in psychotherapy: A relational approach* (4th ed.). Belmont, CA: Wadsworth/Thomson Learning.

Thompson, C. E. (2004). Awareness and identity: Foundational principles in multicultural counseling. In T. B. Smith (Ed.), *Practicing multiculturalism: Internalizing and affirming diversity in counseling psychology* (pp. 35–56). Boston: Allyn & Bacon.

Thompson, C. E. (in press). Racial identity and peace education: Tools for the teacher in all of us. *Interchange.*

Thompson, C. E., & Carter, R. T. (1997). *Racial identity theory: Applications to individual, group, and organizational interventions.* Hillsdale, NJ: Erlbaum.

Thompson, C. E., & Neville, H. A. (1999). Racism, mental health, and mental health practice. *Counseling Psychologist, 27,* 155–223.

Williams, J. (1988). *Eyes on the prize: America's civil rights years, 1954–1965.* Hamondsworth, Middlesex, England: Penguin Books.

Yeh, C. J., & Hunter, C. D. (in press). The socialization of self: Understanding shifting and multiple selves acress cultures. In R. T. Carter (Ed.), *Handbook of racial-cultural psychology and counseling: Theory and research* (Vol. 1, pp. 78–93). Hoboken, NJ: Wiley.

CHAPTER 14

Integrating Theory and Practice:
A Racial-Cultural Counseling Model

Alvin N. Alvarez and Ralph E. Piper

A graduate student learns in her cross-cultural counseling course that racial identity theory involves an individual's intrapsychic reactions to racism (Helms & Cook, 1999). Prior to beginning his work at a local school district, a consultant reads that collectivism, spirituality, and interdependence are salient values of the majority culture in this particular district. A practitioner attends a conference seminar that highlights the role of acculturation theory (Kohatsu, this *Handbook,* Volume One; Padilla, 1980) in working with immigrant communities. Although each scenario is seemingly different, a common question binds each of these individuals. That is, how does one bridge the gap between racial-cultural counseling theory (RCT) and racial-cultural practice? At an abstract level, racial-cultural information and theories of racial-cultural counseling per se may be relatively straightforward to comprehend conceptually. Nevertheless, both practitioners and practitioners in training continue to struggle with questions of how theories of racial-cultural counseling (e.g., racial identity, acculturation), as well as their understanding of the values, beliefs, and history of a given community, can facilitate their ability to deliver culturally competent services.

While the need to link RCT to practice is intuitively understandable, the framework for doing so remains surprisingly absent in the literature. Indeed, given the attention that has been devoted to developing standards of cross-cultural competence (American Psychological Association, 2003; Ponterotto & Austin, this *Handbook,* this volume; D. Sue, Arredondo, & McDavis, 1992; D. Sue & Torino, this *Handbook,* this volume), as well as developing training models (Pedersen, 1977b; A. Reynolds, 1997), training exercises (Katz, 1978; Singelis, 1998), curriculum designs (Adams, Bell, & Griffin, 1997; Carter, this *Handbook,* this volume; A. Reynolds, 1995), and so forth, the absence of a framework for linking RCT to practice is particularly striking. The absence of a framework seems to be due in large part to the fact that, in general, race and culture have not been included as factors in theories of counseling. Instead, they are often presented as an addendum to the psychological canon, rather than as an integral part of it. Nevertheless, in a profession that has actively strived to promote cross-cultural competence as a requisite professional foundation (D. Sue et al., 1992), logic suggests that a framework is needed to assist practitioners in utilizing the racial-cultural counseling literature to inform and enhance the cultural responsiveness of their services. To this end, the central goal of the current chapter is to examine the role of RCT in facilitating the delivery of culturally sensitive services.

Specifically, the current chapter focuses on the practical interrelationships between RCT and clinical practice. Although we recognize that helping relationships may include various forms of service, for example, advocacy and consultation, we have chosen to focus the current chapter on exploring the counseling relationship for the sake of depth rather than breadth (see Vera, Buhin, Montgomery, & Shin, this *Handbook,* this volume). Moreover, to provide practical examples of translating theory into practice, Helms's theory of racial identity (1990, 2001) is used for illustrative purposes throughout this chapter. Consequently, we begin with a brief overview of Helms's (2001) theory of racial identity. Next, we address the philosophical assumptions underlying RCT and the relationship between philosophy and practice. Last, we present a model that delineates the role of RCT in informing various aspects of counseling.

RACIAL IDENTITY THEORY

Whereas there are several racial and cultural theories that might be useful for illustrative purposes, we refer mainly to Helms's (2001) racial identity model due to its prominence in the literature and presumably its familiarity to most readers. Moreover, Helms's (1994) contention regarding the need to clarify the conceptual imprecisions in terms such as multiculturalism, race, and ethnicity is particularly consistent with this *Handbook*'s attempt to focus specifically on racial and cultural counseling (Carter, this *Handbook,* this volume).

Racial identity development involves a process by which individuals in socioracial groups move from racial identity statuses characterized by self-denial to identity statuses characterized by self-affirming attitudes concerning their respective socioracial group, members of other socioracial groups, and ultimately themselves as racial beings (Carter, 1995; Carter & Pieterse, this *Handbook,* Volume One; Helms, 2001). Helms has argued that each racial identity status is associated with qualitatively distinct affects, behaviors, and cognitions around issues of race and racism. In effect, racial identity is an intrapsychic construct that is an integral part of one's personality (as opposed to a demographic characteristic) and as such has psychological relevance. Hence, racial identity statuses have an impact on how individuals interpret and internalize racial and environmental information, thus contributing to their racial worldview (Ota Wang, this *Handbook,* this volume).

Of particular relevance to counseling, Helms (1990, 2001) suggests that the counseling process and racial dynamics in a therapeutic dyad are reflective of the dominant racial identity statuses of both the counselor and the client (Wallace, this *Handbook,* this volume). Helms theorized that the interaction between the racial identity statuses of the counselor and the client expresses itself in four distinct therapeutic relationships: parallel, progressive, regressive, and crossed, which is considered a subtype of progressive or regressive relationships. In a parallel dyad, counselor and client operate from similar racial identity statuses, socializations, and attitudes, thereby creating a relationship characterized by harmony and the absence of conflict. In a progressive dyad, the counselor's racial attitudes are more mature than those of the client. Hence, in progressive dyads, it is possible that the counselor can assist the client in movement toward a more mature racial identity ego status. In contrast, regressive dyads occur when the client's racial identity development is more mature than that of the counselor. Conflict can arise between the counselor and the client as the client reacts to the perceived racial immaturity of the counselor. In a crossed dyad, the counselor and the client are at opposite ends of the racial identity spectrum, resulting in conflict and confusion in the relationship rather than a clear and coherent engagement of racial issues and attitudes. Given the scope of Helms's (2001) racial identity theory, we believe it is a particularly appropriate model for examining how RCT can inform various points in the counseling process (Wallace, this *Handbook,* this volume).

RACIAL-CULTURAL COUNSELING PHILOSOPHY

Part of the inherent difficulty in applying RCT to practice lies in the fact that RCT is not a single unified theory, nor is it associated with any single individual (Cheatham et al., 2001). Rather, numerous scholars and practitioners have contributed to a body of literature bound more by common philosophical assumptions than by strict adherence to any one theory of personality or psychopathology. Indeed, such a strict adherence to any one explanation for human behavior runs counter to the pluralistic philosophy that infuses RCT. Nevertheless, as a first step in integrating RCT with practice, a review of Sue, Ivey, and Pedersen's (1996) metatheory, that is, a theory about theories, of multicultural counseling and therapy may be useful in highlighting core philosophical assumptions that infuse theories of racial-cultural counseling (D. Sue & Torino, this *Handbook,* this volume). Indeed, the current chapter is based on the premise that the practice of racial-cultural counseling is influenced by, if not rooted in, one's philosophical assumptions about oneself as a counselor, as well as assumptions about one's client, the therapeutic relationship, and the sociopolitical and sociocultural context in which that relationship is embedded. Although Sue et al.'s metatheory deals specifically with the broader rubric of multicultural counseling, it is our belief that their propositions are still relevant for racial and cultural counseling.

D. Sue et al. (1996) presented the following propositions: (1) Western and non-Western models of helping are developed in specific cultural contexts, representing distinct and equally valid worldviews; (2) treatment needs to consider the totality of and interrelationships between the counselor's and the client's identities at multiple levels of experience (individual, group, universal) and contexts (individual, familial, and cultural); (3) the racial and cultural identities of both the counselor and the client influence how problems are defined as well as the process and goals of counseling; (4) the ultimate goal of cross-cultural counseling training is to expand the counselor's repertoire of interventions such that they are culturally consistent with the life experiences, values, and beliefs of the client; (5) multiple helping roles, other than conventional, individual counseling, may be salient in different cultural contexts; and (6) a central goal of cross-cultural counseling is to expand one's consciousness of oneself in relation to the social systems in which one is embedded (e.g., family, group, organizations).

In essence, the implications of D. Sue et al.'s (1996) proposals call on practitioners to recognize that multiple approaches to counseling may be equally effective, and that cultural sensitivity may require counselors to approach their work from a stance of flexibility rather than rigidity. That is, racial-cultural counseling challenges counselors to question their own assumptions of, explanations about, and solutions for a client's concerns. Thus, as a first step in applying RCT to practice, it may be helpful for counselors to recognize that, philosophically, one of the central foundations of racial and cultural counseling, is one's willingness to question, to explore, and to accept as valid those cultural worldviews and experiences that are different from one's own (Thompson, this *Handbook,* this volume).

INTEGRATING RACIAL-CULTURAL COUNSELING THEORY AND PRACTICE

A central challenge in the process of translating RCT into practice lies in the manner in which both practitioners and students interpret the task. One of the central barriers in applying RCT to practice may reflect practitioners' assumptions about the limited role of theories. All too frequently, practitioners interpret the task to mean What interventions are suggested by this theory? rather than How does this theory influence counseling? The former question implicitly limits the role and utility of a theory to the level of specific interventions, whereas the latter suggests that theory may be useful at various points along the counseling process, including the implementation of actual interventions. Hence, the former question assumes that theories may be of little use to practitioners if they fail to prescribe explicit interventions.

Given that racial-cultural counseling clearly involves more than just the implementation of a series of interventions and that it requires counselors to utilize assessment, diagnostic, and evaluation skills, the challenge for many counselors has been to understand how RCT can influence various phases of racial-cultural counseling. To assist counseling practitioners in applying RCT to practice, the following section outlines a model that describes how theory may influence practice at various points in the process.

Although various authors have addressed the application of theory to practice (Hansen & Freimuth, 1997; McEwen, 1996), these models fail to address specifically how racial and cultural theories of counseling can inform one's practice and the counseling relationship. Indeed, McEwen's model was primarily intended for student affairs practitioners, whereas Hansen and Freimuth's model focused primarily on integrating one's theoretical orientation into practice. To bridge this seemingly critical gap in the literature, we present the current model with the intent of stimulating both practitioners and scholars to further clarify the relationship between RCT and practice. The model outlines six points at which RCT may be integrated into practice: (1) self assessment, (2) diagnostic assessment, (3) inquiry and reflection, (4) diagnosis, (5) interventions, and (6) outcomes. Although every RCT may not have implications at each phase of counseling, the entire model is presented with the intent of challenging practitioners to broaden their understanding of the utility of RCT.

Although readers may be tempted to apply the current model in a linear and sequential fashion, we believe that the fluid and dynamic nature of counseling precludes such a simplistic application of the model. Indeed, it is our hope that practitioners will cycle through and revisit the various points of the model, on an as-needed basis, as they engage in a circular and continuous process of examining and reexamining themselves and their counseling relationships with specific clients. Relatedly, in using racial identity theory to illustrate our model, we have posed sample questions for practitioners to ask themselves as they attempt to apply racial identity theory to actual counseling. We would caution practitioners against using the sample questions as an exhaustive or prescriptive guide to applying racial identity theory or RCT to all clients. Instead, given the complexities of racial-cultural counseling and the uniqueness of each client, it is our hope that practitioners regard these sample questions merely as starting points for learning how to apply racial identity theory and RCT in relatively broad terms. The cultural competence of practitioners will ultimately be measured by their ability to adapt the broad principles and questions we have posed in this chapter to the nuances of working with a specific client.

Self-Assessment

Because each practitioner is culturally encapsulated (Wrenn, 1962), theories can be of use in assisting practitioners to examine their own personal assumptions, biases, and worldviews. Such a self-examination process can and should occur even before practitioners work with a specific client. As a central assumption of racial-cultural counseling, various authors (e.g., Helms & Cook, 1999; D. Sue et al., 1996) have long argued that both practitioners and their clients have implicit and explicit assumptions about their roles and the process of counseling that are shaped by their cultural and racial worldviews (Kwan, this *Handbook,* Volume One). The counselors' assumptions or worldviews are the default filters that practitioners use to understand the world and the information that they may receive from it. Thus, it would be natural to expect that practitioners have personal and informal theories about human behavior that reflect their own cultural socialization and personal experiences and biases (Carter, this *Handbook,* this volume; Thompson, this *Handbook,* this volume).

Insofar as practitioners do have such biases, RCT may provide them with a structured framework for posing questions that challenge their own awareness and assumptions of themselves and their clients. Indeed, even before beginning a session, RCT and the questions it poses may help practitioners to assess the strengths and limitations in their own knowledge about a given client or community. Therapists who take an active role in exploring their own racial attitudes and racial identity tend to be more able to identify and attend to overt and covert racial issues and dynamics as they occur in therapeutic dyads and groups. Many of our colleagues who have participated in only rudimentary explorations of race or culture, seem to have difficulty finding a starting place from which they can begin to engage racial and cultural issues. They may have attended diversity workshops or seminars or taken a course in cultural or racial awareness that have provided them with some heightened sense that race and culture are important variables to consider (Wallace, this *Handbook,* this volume). Nevertheless, they continue to struggle with how to incorporate racial and cultural sensitivity into their daily work. They often ask, "How do we begin to incorporate this material? Where do we start?"

We believe, as Carter (1995, this *Handbook,* this volume) and others have noted, that to truly understand the dynamics of race and culture in therapy, one must first engage in a self-examination of one's own racial identity and attitudes. One way of beginning to engage in racial-cultural self-examination is to begin reading material about race, racial identity, and culture and attempting to apply it to oneself. For instance, reading about racial identity theory (Helms 1990, 2001; Helms & Cook, 1999) should serve as an impetus for practitioners to ask questions about their own racial socialization, their own attitudes regarding race and racism, and their assumptions about how such attitudes might influence the counseling process. For instance, do they regard race as an uncomfortable topic to discuss? What were they taught about their own race, either implicitly or explicitly? Do they believe that the counselor's or client's race should be raised in session regardless of whether the client raises the topic? Similarly, learning about the cultural values, beliefs, and history of a particular community should also serve as a catalyst for a counselor's self-examination. What was I taught about this community? What values are similar to and different from my own? What experiences have I had with individuals from this community? These questions may serve as starting points for practitioners to assess their understanding of themselves and their clients (Liu & Pope-Davis, this *Handbook,* this volume).

Although learning and reading about racial and cultural theories can prove to be an enlightening process for counselors, reading alone and asking oneself such questions is insufficient because readers may or may not begin to engage in their own exploration process. Borrowing from Buddhist traditions, the concept of mindfulness (D. Reynolds, 1984) is particularly salient for counselors as they engage in a process of self-examination. To engage in mindfulness essentially requires one to pay close attention to one's own processes. That is, one's thinking, feeling, behavior—everything that makes up the self—becomes subject to the ongoing scrutiny of the observer (read: counselor). Thus, as counselors read about racial identity theory and pose some of the questions we noted earlier, we would also encourage counselors to be mindful of the reactions, thoughts, images, memories, and so forth that are elicited by racial identity theory. It is this level of mindfulness and the openness that is explicit in such a process that may provide counselors with a beginning understanding of their baseline attitudes toward race and culture. Although racial and cultural counseling theories per se will not transform an individual into a culturally competent counselor, being mindful of one's internal experience as one is exposed to RCT is a first, yet critical, step toward such competence.

Diagnostic Assessment

A central tenet of RCT argues that counselors need to recognize and understand their clients in context(s) (Carter, 1997; Helms & Cook, 1999; D. Sue et al., 1996). These contexts can include, but are not limited to, family, community, culture, and race. Accordingly, each context must be taken into account when one is attempting to assess a client's understanding of the external world, thereby providing crucial data regarding the context in which the client's psychological makeup may have developed (Ota Wang, this *Handbook,* this volume). Failure to assess the contexts of a person's life may lead the counselor to misinterpret information from the client, which in turn can lead to misdiagnosis and quite possibly inappropriate treatment modalities. Thus, to avoid misdiagnosis, a culturally responsive diagnostic assessment is a critical initial step in the counseling relationship.

To assist practitioners in conducting an effective assessment, RCT may expand counselors' understanding of a client by helping them to recognize their clients and themselves as cultural and racial beings with potentially distinct worldviews. In practice, a culturally effective assessment may be reflected in a counselor's ability to ask questions of a client that include factors or experiences (e.g., oppression, the salience of family or religion, normative help-seeking styles) that may be different from the practitioner's own experiences. Hence, RCT may influence the assessment process by raising questions that counselors may not have considered previously.

For example, the counselor who reads that spirituality (Smith & Richards, this *Handbook,* Volume One) may be salient to a particular community may want to ask about the role of clergy in a client's help-seeking process or perhaps ask a question about the role of divine intervention or fate in a client's healing process. Likewise, the client's revelation that she comes from a refugee family (Arredondo, this *Handbook,* this volume; Prendes-Lintel, 2001) may prompt the counselor to assess the potential losses the family may have endured (e.g., status, security, home, relatives) and their relationship to the client's attitudes about her academic and career success. Similarly, to incorporate racial identity theory into a diagnostic assessment, we routinely ask clients for information about their background, including what area of the country (or world) they come from, where their parents were born, what their neighborhood is like, and how they identify themselves both culturally and racially. In some cases (e.g., an African American client who identifies with a White referent group, or a White client who identifies with an Asian referent group), we may ask questions that address the difference between the client's "apparent" racial phenotype and his or her racial group affiliation (e.g., "It's interesting that you appear to be African American yet you don't seem to have many connections to that group. How does that work for you?" or "I wonder how it feels for you to look different from most of your friends"). The answers to such questions may provide information that is useful in understanding a client's racial worldview, racial group affiliations, and racial attitudes. Thus, by expanding therapists' understanding of the range of different racial and cultural worldviews, RCT may enhance the process of assessment by expanding the range of assessment questions and topics that practitioners are aware of or willing to ask in an effort to better understand the subjective experiences of their clients.

Inquiry and Reflection

Beyond guiding counselors with questions to pose in their assessment, various theorists (Carter, 1995; Helms & Cook, 1999; Pedersen, 1997a) have long recognized that racial-cultural counseling is not a simple matter of asking the "right" questions, but rather a dynamic and continually evolving process. In effect, both people in the room are recognized as bringing racial and cultural identities into the session that move, shift, collide, and contribute to the therapeutic relationship (Helms & Cook, 1999; D. Sue et al., 1996). Hence, a counseling session should serve as a catalyst for bringing to the counselor's awareness his or her own issues, attitudes, and feelings regarding culture and race, as well as be a catalyst for consideration of the client's attitudes, feelings, and behaviors regarding the very same issues. It may also be an opportunity for counselors to begin to reflect and ask questions about what happened in the session for both their client and themselves: what was helpful, what was not helpful, and how to approach the next session in a way that will facilitate the process. RCT can be helpful at this juncture by providing the counselor with a framework for reflecting on the impact of intercultural or interracial variables on the actual counseling process as well as each individual's perceptions of and contributions to that process.

Hence, rather than using RCT as static pieces of information about a particular client or community, RCT can contribute to an understanding of racial-cultural counseling as a fluid and dynamic process. That is, RCT may help counselors to recognize racial-cultural counseling as a fluid process by guiding them in (1) developing initial questions, (2) formulating working hypotheses about the client, (3) testing these hypotheses against the information provided by the client in a cyclical process of revising and modifying their working hypotheses, and (4) including themselves in the equation. Thus, RCT can become an integrated part of understanding the dynamics of the counseling process, rather than perceived as a taboo or unworkable addendum.

For instance, racial identity theory (Helms, 2001) suggests that individuals have one or more ego identity statuses that they use to interpret race-related events, and that the statuses shift in dominance. Applying racial identity theory during inquiry and reflection thus requires practitioners to combine their clinical skills, their knowledge of racial identity theory, and their observations of their client's racial attitudes to construct initial questions and working hypotheses about the genesis, content, and context of the client's dominant racial identity status, the session dynamics, and the race-related transference and countertransference issues that stem from these dynamics. Drawing on racial identity theory, it is reasonable to believe that some ego status is dominant in a client at each session. Determining which ego status may be dominant is part of the discovery process—a process that starts with initial questions such as: Who is this person racially? What are the factors in his life that have contributed to his current worldview? What constitutes a race-related event for him? Does his racial identity appear to be ego-syntonic or ego-dystonic with his other identities or with his behaviors? The answers to such initial questions may then lead to a working hypothesis about the client's racial worldview and his dominant racial identity status.

Moreover, in applying racial identity theory to inquiry and reflection, counselors must simultaneously ask these questions of themselves: Who am I as a racial being at this moment? How does my sense of myself as a racial being influence my work with this person? What are my feelings about who I perceive this client to be racially? What are my reactions to this person's racial worldview? To the extent that the counselor has a better understanding of his or her own racial worldview, the client's racial worldview, and the interaction between the two, such an understanding may also provide the counselor with greater clarity about the session dynamics and the client-counselor relationship. However, given the ever-changing dynamics of counseling, RCT and the manner in which theory can inform inquiry and reflection is, by necessity, a dynamic and ongoing process requiring a continual evaluation and reevaluation of the counseling relationship.

Diagnosis

Formulating a diagnosis for a client is a process that involves the intersection of client data and *DSM* criteria. Yet, even with all of this information, diagnosis can still be a complex issue—the outcome of which, one hopes, is an accurate picture of the client's strengths, distresses, and history and the relationship of these factors to the concerns that originally brought the client into therapy. The more accurately one can construct a diagnostic picture, the more likely it is that one will choose appropriate treatment modalities and options that will be helpful to the client.

During a diagnostic formulation, the counselor evaluates the client's reported behaviors, feelings, attitudes, and thoughts. Some symptoms may seem reasonable and appropriate, whereas others may seem to be manifestations of some form of psychological distress or illness. The counselor's decision regarding which factors are appropriate and which are not is based in part on the aforementioned data and criteria as well as clinical intuition. In turn, clinical intuition is based in part on the counselor's racial and cultural worldview, which provides the filters that guide the counselor's assumptions about which client factors are more or less healthy.

RCT can be useful in the process of diagnostic formulation by helping the counselor expand his or her worldview to include some behaviors, thoughts, attitudes, and feelings that may at first seem unreasonable, but are in fact culturally appropriate for the client. For instance, in some Latin cultures, having an *ataque de nervios* (a physical expression of distress) is a culturally appropriate expression of distress and simultaneously a cathartic release of that distress (American Psychiatric Association, 2000; Oquendo, 1995). However, counselors who are unfamiliar with such subtleties of Latin cultures may mistake the client's behavior for the onset of psychosis. Such misdiagnoses may lead to unnecessary hospitalization and psychopharmacological treatment for the client. Similarly, counselors unfamiliar with some of the subtleties of African American culture (Cook & Wiley, 2000) may mistakenly interpret an African American client's report of hearing God talk to her as the onset of a schizophrenic episode, and similar unwarranted treatment may result.

Given that racial and cultural issues often are not presented as the client's primary presenting problem, RCT may be a useful diagnostic tool in detecting how the client's underlying racial and cultural attitudes may contribute to his or her presenting issues. We have treated many students who report having concerns about perfectionism. Often, these students develop low self-esteem, depression, and sometimes obsessive-compulsive disorder rituals as reactions to feeling "less than perfect" or "not good enough." Although the core presenting issues may revolve around self-esteem and depression, we have found that for White students as well as for students of Color, underlying racial attitudes and identities influence their belief that to be "perfect" is synonymous with being White (or, "White enough"). In such cases, the accurate assessment of clients' racial identity is crucial because of its integration in the presenting symptoms. Thus, symptom relief is contingent on the therapist's ability to diagnose and to address simultaneously the client's racial identity, cognitive distortions, and behavioral manifestations.

These examples are not presented to suggest that whenever such behaviors are exhibited one should immediately understand them as culture-bound syndromes.

Indeed, there may be situations when they may represent the onset of a mental illness. However, the examples and the discussion of the relevance of RCT to the diagnostic process are meant to inform counselors that there is more than one way to interpret such behaviors, and that each should be considered to the fullest before a conclusion and subsequent course of treatment is decided on.

Interventions

Insofar as RCT is not a single, unified theory of personality or psychopathology, the challenge of linking RCT to specific interventions lies in the fact that RCT, as a body, does not necessarily prescribe a cohesive set of interventions or treatments in working with clients. Indeed, one philosophical foundation of RCT challenges the etic perspective that interventions are universally applicable to clients from all racial and ethnic groups (D. Sue et al., 1996). Nevertheless, the need remains for practitioners to understand the role of interventions with RCT. Consequently, it may be helpful to examine how RCT may influence the manner in which practitioners regard and choose the interventions they implement with their clients.

Fundamentally, RCT challenges practitioners to examine the cultural assumptions of their services and the degree to which their assumptions are consistent with the worldviews of the communities being served. With regard to specific interventions, RCT may be a catalyst for practitioners to critique the underlying assumptions in the interventions they implement. For instance, does this intervention integrate culturally consistent sources of help, such as indigenous healers or community elders? Is this intervention mindful of interpersonal (e.g., family, friends, clergy) resources who might have a stake in or reaction to the intervention? Is this intervention consistent with clients' normative beliefs about themselves, their interpersonal connections, their environment, and their status in that environment? Is this intervention consistent with how the client identifies herself or himself racially and culturally? Does the intervention take into consideration the historical and sociopolitical realities of the community in which this client lives? By including such questions in the treatment equation, counselors begin to consider not only the proximal factors of the case, but the distal factors as well, so that they may be better able to choose culturally appropriate interventions (Helms & Cook, 1999). Practitioners may obtain a better understanding of the need to go beyond the intrapsychic world of the client (proximal factors) by recognizing the role of extrapsychic factors, such as institutions and groups (distal factors), that may affect the client's optimal functioning and well-being.

For instance, racial identity theory (Helms, 2001) may be useful in identifying appropriate interventions for some clients of Color who exhibit what appear to be paranoid behaviors. Drawing on racial identity theory, it may be that the client is operating from a racial identity status that is characterized by hypervigilance around race and racial issues. Moreover, an examination of her environment (e.g., a predominantly White college campus) may reveal that the client is simply reacting to racial or cultural environmental stressors that may be more salient for her than for members of other racial-cultural groups (Carter, Forsyth, Mazzula, & Williams, this *Handbook,* this volume; Smedley, Myers, & Harrell, 1993). In such a case, both RCT in general and racial identity in particular suggest that counselors should develop interventions that support and advocate for rather than automatically pathologize the client. Hence, a reasonable intervention might be at the distal (as opposed to proximal) level. That is, the counselor may need to address one or more environmental factors by calling them to the attention of administrators who may have the authority to change them (Vera et al., this *Handbook,* this volume). Similarly, assuming that the client does operate from a status of racial hypervigilance, it may be important for counselors to recognize and respect the emotional intensity and possible anger associated with the client's period of racial identity development. At the proximal level, it may be helpful for counselors to validate the client's emotions and the difficulty of living under a racially oppressive environment (Alvarez, 2002). As a result, the counselor's intervention and advocacy may be critical to strengthening the counseling relationship by helping the client to feel supported in what may be a less than hospitable environment.

In other cases, clients of Color may have very close ties to their family or friends that, from a Western perspective, appear to be unhealthy enmeshments. However, in some cultures, such close ties provide strength and support to clients (McGoldrick, Giordano, & Pearce, 1996) who may not find support in environments that value individualism and independence rather than collectivism and interdependence. Attempting to intervene in a way designed to lessen the perceived enmeshment may prove damaging not only to the client's main source of support, but to the counseling relationship as well. The counselor who examines both proximal and distal factors of the client's worldview is more likely to be effective at discerning the appropriate level and manner of treatment. In effect, RCT challenges practitioners to recognize that interventions need not be limited to the individual client and that effective service delivery may require intervening with systems external to the client, such as families, community agencies, and health care systems. Consequently, although RCT may not necessarily prescribe specific interventions with a given client, the integration of RCT into one's professional repertoire may increase the likelihood that one's interventions are consistent with and respectful of clients and their worldviews.

Outcomes

RCT may also be of predictive utility to practitioners insofar as the theory outlines specific counseling outcomes. While counselors may rely on their relationship-building and assessment skills to refine and enhance the effectiveness of their interventions, inherent uncertainties in the counseling relationship still pose a challenge to any practitioner. In particular, counselors are often unclear about the impact of counseling on their clients. Regardless of the centrality of race and culture in relation to the client's presenting concerns, counselors are ultimately concerned with whether or not clients experience a shift in their ability to cope with their presenting problems. Nevertheless, insofar as race and culture are central to or intertwined with the presenting problems, RCT may be helpful to practitioners in describing potential race- and culture-related counseling outcomes.

For instance, in her racial identity interaction process model, Helms (2001) predicted that the dynamics in a counseling relationship would be reflective of the interaction between the dominant racial identity statuses of both the counselor and client. As one result of this interaction, her theory suggests, racial identity maturation in the client will be a more probable counseling outcome insofar as the counselor operates from a status of racial identity that is more sophisticated than the client's

(Helms & Cook, 1999). According to racial identity theory, clients should leave counseling with a more sophisticated understanding of themselves as racial beings, as well as a more sophisticated understanding of racial issues and dynamics.

Although race and culture will clearly not be central to every client's presenting concern, race and culture may be contributing factors for the counselor to consider. In cases where race and culture are salient, RCT in general and racial identity theory in particular may be useful in generating questions for counselors that examine the progress and outcome of the racial and cultural aspects of the case. For example, in working with a client who is initially in denial of race and culture, questions such as: Does the client react to racial issues in a manner that is different from when he began counseling? Is the client willing to explore the racial and cultural aspects of herself? Can the client recognize racism? may all be derived from racial identity theory as a means of monitoring the outcomes of counseling. To evaluate the strengths or limitations in their overall work with a particular client, practitioners may want to ask themselves how their work compares with the outcomes predicted by a particular racial-cultural theory. Despite the imprecise nature of counseling and the fact that the complexities of such a relationship will never be wholly predictable, RCT may be helpful to practitioners insofar as it can clarify potential counseling outcomes as well as provide a systematic framework for critiquing and reviewing the overall efficacy of their services.

CONCLUSION

The current model was presented to serve as a catalyst for practitioners and scholars to further discuss and explicate how RCT can inform various points along the process of racial-cultural counseling. Hansen and Freimuth (1997) observed that although students complete a course on counseling theories and a practicum course on techniques and interventions, the linkage between the two courses is rarely addressed in the formal curriculum. Hence, the linkage between theory and practice often remains implicit and left to the imagination of students to integrate. However, particularly in a climate of fiscal and professional accountability (Waehler, Kalodner, Wampold, & Lichtenberg, 2000), the need for an explicit linkage between theory and practice is clear. Consequently, whether in practicum courses, internship seminars, or continuing education courses, both scholars and educators may need to reexamine the extent to which the link between RCT and practice has been made explicit. Indeed, if RCT is truly a "fourth force" (Pedersen, 1999, this *Handbook,* Volume One) to be infused and integrated into how practitioners regard themselves, their clients, and the counseling relationship, then the linkage between racial-cultural counseling theory and practice should be explicit in all phases of the counseling process.

REFERENCES

Adams, M., Bell, L. A., & Griffin, P. (1997). *Teaching for diversity and social justice: A sourcebook.* New York: Routledge.

Alvarez, A. N. (2002). Racial identity and Asian Americans: Supports and challenges. In C. M. Kodama, M. K. McEwen, A. N. Alvarez, C. Liang, & S. Lee (Eds.), *Working with*

Asian American college students: New directions for student services (pp. 33–43). San Francisco: Jossey-Bass.

American Psychiatric Association. (2000). *Diagnostic and statistical manual of mental disorders* (4th ed., text rev.). Washington, DC: Author.

American Psychological Association. (2003). Guidelines on multicultural education, training, research, practice, and organizational change for psychologists. *American Psychologist, 58*(5), 377–402.

Carter, R. T. (1995). *The influence of race and racial identity in psychotherapy: Toward a racially inclusive model.* New York: Wiley.

Carter, R. T. (1997). Race and psychotherapy: The racially inclusive model. In C. E. Thompson & R. T. Carter (Eds.), *Racial identity theory: Applications to individual, group, and organizational interventions* (pp. 97–108). Mahwah, NJ: Erlbaum.

Carter, R. T. (in press). Uprooting inequity and disparities in counseling and psychology: An introduction. In R. T. Carter (Ed.), *Handbook of racial-cultural psychology and counseling: Theory and research* (Vol. 1, pp. xv–xxviii). Hoboken, NJ: Wiley.

Carter, R. T., & Pieterse, A. L. (in press). Race: A social and psychological analysis of the term and its meaning. In R. T. Carter (Ed.), *Handbook of racial-cultural psychology and counseling: Theory and research* (Vol. 1, pp. 41–63). Hoboken, NJ: Wiley.

Cheatham, H., D'Andrea, M., Ivey, A. E., Ivey, M. B., Pedersen, P., Rigazio-DiGilio, S., et al. (2001). Multicultural counseling and therapy: I. Metatheory—Taking theory into practice. In A. E. Ivey, M. D'Andrea, M. B. Ivey, & L. Simek-Morgan (Eds.), *Theories of multicultural counseling and psychotherapy: A multicultural perspective* (5th ed., pp. 291–328). Boston: Allyn & Bacon.

Cook, D. A., & Wiley, C. Y. (2000). African American spiritual traditions. In P. S. Richards & A. Bergen (Eds.), *Handbook of psychotherapy and religious diversity* (pp. 369–396). Washington, DC: American Psychological Association.

Hansen, N. E., & Freimuth, M. (1997). Piecing the puzzle together: A model for understanding the theory-practice relationship. *Counseling Psychologist, 25*(4), 654–673.

Helms, J. E. (1990). *Black and white racial identity: Theory, research, and practice.* Westport, CT: Greenwood Press.

Helms, J. E. (1994). How multiculturalism obscures factors in the therapy process: Comment on Ridley et al. (1994), Sodowsky et al. (1994), Ottavi et al. (1994), and Thompson et al. (1994). *Journal of Counseling Psychology, 41*(2), 162–165.

Helms, J. E. (2001). An update of Helms's White and people of Color racial identity models. In J. G. Ponterotto, J. M. Casas, L. A. Suzuki, & C. M. Alexander (Eds.), *Handbook of multicultural counseling* (2nd ed., pp. 181–198). Thousand Oaks, CA: Sage.

Helms, J. E., & Cook, D. A. (1999). *Using race and culture in counseling and psychotherapy: Theory and process.* Needham Heights, MA: Allyn & Bacon.

Katz, J. H. (1978). *White awareness: Handbook for anti-racism training.* Norman: University of Oklahoma Press.

Kohatsu, E. L. (in press). Accultration: Current and future directions. In R. T. Carter (Ed.), *Handbook of racial-cultural psychology and counseling: Theory and research* (Vol. 1, pp. 207–231). Hoboken, NJ: Wiley.

Kwan, K. (in press). Racial salience: Conceptual dimensions and implications for racial and ethnic identity development. In R. T. Carter (Ed.), *Handbook of racial-cultural psychology and counseling: Theory and research* (Vol. 1, pp. 115–131). Hoboken, NJ: Wiley.

McEwen, M. K. (1996). The nature and uses of theory. In S. R. Komives & D. B. Woodard, Jr. (Eds.), *Student services: A handbook for the profession* (3rd ed., pp. 147–163). San Francisco: Jossey-Bass.

McGoldrick, M., Giordano, J., & Pearce, J. K. (1996). *Ethnicity and family therapy* (2nd ed.). New York: Guilford Press.

Oquendo, M. A. (1995). Differential diagnosis of ataque de nervios. *American Journal of Orthopsychiatry, 65*(1), 60–65.

Padilla, A. M. (1980). *Acculturation: Theory, models, and some new findings.* Boulder, CO: Westview Press.

Pedersen, P. B. (1997a). *Culture-centered counseling interventions: Striving for accuracy.* Thousand Oaks, CA: Sage.

Pedersen, P. B. (1997b). The triad model of cross cultural training. *Personnel and Guidance Journal, 56,* 94–100.

Pedersen, P. B. (1999). *Multiculturalism as a fourth force.* Philadelphia: Brunner/Mazel.

Pedersen, P. B. (in press). The importance of Cultural Psychology Theory for multicultural counselors. In R. T. Carter (Ed.), *Handbook of racial-cultural psychology and counseling: Theory and research* (Vol. 1, pp. 3–16). Hoboken, NJ: Wiley.

Prendes-Lintel, M. (2001). A working model in counseling recent refugees. In J. G. Ponterotto, J. M. Casas, L. A. Suzuki, & C. M. Alexander (Eds.), *Handbook of multicultural counseling* (2nd ed., pp. 729–752). Thousand Oaks, CA: Sage.

Reynolds, A. L. (1995). Challenges and strategies for teaching multicultural counseling courses. In J. G. Ponterroto, J. M. Casas, L. A. Suzuki, & C. M. Alexander (Eds.), *Handbook of multicultural counseling* (pp. 312–330). Thousand Oaks, CA: Sage.

Reynolds, A. L. (1997). Using the Multicultural Change Intervention Matrix (MCIM) as a multicultural counseling training model. In D. B. Pope-Davis & H. L. K. Coleman (Eds.), *Multicultural counseling competencies: Assessment, education and training, and supervision* (pp. 209–226). Thousand Oaks, CA: Sage.

Reynolds, D. K. (1984). *Playing ball on running water.* New York: Quill.

Singelis, T. M. (1998). *Teaching about culture, ethnicity, and diversity: Exercises and planned activities.* Thousand Oaks, CA: Sage.

Smedley, B. D., Myers, H. F., & Harrell, S. P. (1993). Minority status stresses and the college adjustment of ethnic minority freshmen. *Journal of Higher Education, 64*(4), 434–452.

Smith, T. B., & Richards, P. S. (in press). The integration of spiritual and religious issues in racial-cultural psychology and counseling. In R. T. Carter (Ed.), *Handbook of racial-cultural psychology and counseling: Theory and research* (Vol. 1, pp. 132–160). Hoboken, NJ: Wiley.

Sue, D. W., Arredondo, P., & McDavis, R. J. (1992). Multicultural counseling competencies and standards: A call to the profession. *Journal of Multicultural Counseling and Development, 20,* 644–88.

Sue, D. W., Ivey, A. E., & Pedersen, P. B. (Eds.). (1996). *A theory of multicultural counseling and psychotherapy.* Pacific Grove, CA: Brooks/Cole.

Waehler, C. A., Kalodner, C. R., Wampold, B. E., & Lichtenberg, J. W. (2000). Empirically supported treatments (ESTs) in perspective: Implications for counseling psychology training. *Counseling Psychologist, 28*(5), 657–671.

Wrenn, G. (1962). The culturally encapsulated counselor. *Harvard Educational Review, 32,* 444–449.

CHAPTER 15

The Use of Race and Ethnicity in Psychological Practice: A Review

Kevin Cokley

A review of the psychotherapy literature reveals a paucity of articles dealing with race and ethnicity as psychological constructs in psychological practice. Whereas topics such as empirically supported treatments, prescription privileges, psychological assessment, ethics, the health care system, and children and families receive frequent mention in the psychological practice literature, there are very few substantive psychotherapy articles that incorporate race and ethnicity as important topics. While these topics are certainly important in the ever-changing landscape of psychotherapy, the changing demographics of the United States will have a significant impact on the practice of psychotherapy. Too often in psychotherapy research race and ethnicity are treated as simply demographic variables to be merely acknowledged and controlled rather than treated as complex social constructs involving deeply ingrained beliefs, attitudes, and psychological processes that impact every aspect of psychological practice.

Of the textbooks related to the major theories of psychotherapy, only one substantively addresses issues of race, ethnicity, and culture (Ivey, D'Andrea, Ivey, & Simek-Morgan, 2002). A cursory review of the psychotherapy literature through the psychology database PsycINFO using the keywords race, ethnicity, and psychotherapy confirms that race and ethnicity are examined primarily as demographic variables, whereas more psychologically oriented concepts such as racial identity, ethnic identity, acculturation, and cultural mistrust are practically nonexistent. The strict demographic usage of race and ethnicity as variables is consistent with what Helms (1994) has called nominal classification and what Phinney (1996) has called ethnic group categorization, where client and/or therapist racial self-designation (e.g., Black or White) or ethnic self-designation (e.g., African American, Mexican American) is assumed to have sufficient explanatory power of specific attitudes and behaviors. This approach was taken by DeWeaver (1992), who surveyed social workers in private practice to determine if race and gender affected their choice of part-time or full-time private practice. DeWeaver found that although there was not a significant relationship between race and type of practice or gender and type of practice, there was a significant interaction of race and gender, such that White women preferred part-time private practice and Black women preferred full-time private practice. DeWeaver noted that White women tended to use private practice to supplement their income, whereas Black women tended to use private practice as their primary income. Other published psychotherapy research, such as process research, has focused on the race of clients and therapists (Fuertes, Costa, Mueller, & Hersh, this *Handbook,* Volume One; Hill, Nutt, & Jackson, 1994). Still other demographic approaches have examined issues in psychotherapy supervision. For example, S. Williams and Halgin (1995) examined the differences in the training and supervision of minority students compared to White students. To their credit, they discussed the inappropriateness of assigning clients solely on the basis of race.

Typically, literature that addresses race and ethnicity in psychotherapy research examines such issues as who seeks psychotherapy, who drops out from psychotherapy, racial barriers to psychotherapy, client preferences for client-therapist ethnic similarity, and therapist attitudes about client-therapist ethnic similarity (Gray-Little & Kaplan, 2000). In this vein, the most common treatment of race and ethnicity issues in psychotherapy deals with issues of transference and countertransference. An example of this treatment can be found in Holmes (1992), where race (e.g., three cases involved a Black therapist and Black patient, and two cases involved a Black therapist and White patient) was examined for the degree to which it could serve as a useful vehicle for the expression of transference reactions. The impact of race and ethnicity on transference and countertransference has been examined in interracial group psychotherapy (McRae & Short, this *Handbook,* this volume; White, 1994) for its relevance in psychoanalytic treatment (Downing, 2000) and as "cultural factors" of the therapeutic relationship (Gelso & Mohr, 2001).

The majority of the psychotherapy literature on race and ethnicity examines Black/White patient dyads. One of the handful of articles that goes outside of the Black/White paradigm was published by Tang and Gardner (1999), where clinical experiences of Chinese American and African American therapists were examined. The authors reported that for African American therapists, projections are most often based on racial stereotypes, whereas for Chinese American therapists, projections are most often based on cultural stereotypes.

In spite of the relatively monolithic treatment of race and ethnicity in the psychotherapy literature, there is growing recognition that more sophisticated treatments of these constructs are overdue. Comas-Diaz (1992) discussed stages in the development of psychotherapy with ethnic group members and suggested that mainstream assumptions of normal behavior, psychological healthiness, and relationships would eventually be infused by the norms of people of Color.

Other sophisticated treatments of race and ethnicity use culture-specific approaches in therapy. For example, in working with African American clients, psychologists and other mental health professionals are beginning to incorporate more Africentric perspectives in their clinical practices to provide more culturally sensitive services. Morris (2001) suggests that an Africentric approach can be used to conceptualize, evaluate, and diagnose African Americans. Elligan and Utsey (1999) describe a case study of an African American male support group that utilizes an Africentric approach. Gregory and Harper (2001) describe a specific approach, NTU therapy, which employs a multifaceted approach toward delivering therapeutic services grounded in an Africentric worldview. Jwigonski (1996) asserts that

Africentric theory can be used to more effectively build on the strengths of African Americans. In a recently published book, Parham (2002) and other contributors give the most detailed and sophisticated treatment to date of African-centered approaches in counseling people of African descent. The limitations of Africentric approaches have been pointed out in work with African American women (C. Williams, 1999), yet these and other racial- and ethnic-specific therapeutic approaches are going to become increasingly more important as the demographics continue to shift to an ethnic minority majority (Ponterotto & Austin, this *Handbook,* this volume; D. Sue & Torino, this *Handbook,* this volume).

To move beyond simple demographic treatments of race and ethnicity requires recognizing them as complex social constructs. Constructs are most often thought of as concepts or ideas that are believed to exist in some measurable form. All proposed psychological states of being, such as self-esteem and happiness, are constructs because, although they cannot be seen and do not exist in physical form, people experience them as feelings or emotions that are then labeled. It is widely believed by most social scientists that race and, to a lesser extent, ethnicity are primarily social constructions of beliefs involving an interplay of fact, fiction, and hyperbole. No one is immune to holding a set of beliefs about race and ethnicity, and psychologists in practice are certainly no exceptions (Carter & Pieterse, this *Handbook,* Volume One; Johnson, this *Handbook,* Volume One; Juby & Concepción, this *Handbook,* Volume One). However, although we know that psychologists possess beliefs about race and ethnicity, we do not know a lot about how the constructs of race and ethnicity should be used in clinical work. To that end, this chapter provides a review of suggested methods of incorporating constructs of race and ethnicity in clinical work.

The first section provides a brief overview of race as a construct. The definition of race is reviewed, and implications for clinical work are discussed. The second section provides a brief overview of ethnicity as a construct. The definition of ethnicity is examined, and methods for incorporating it into counseling are explored.

DEFINING RACE

Although psychologists have argued that the use of race as a construct is fraught with problems (Yee, Fairchild, Weizmann, & Wyatt, 1993), many, if not most, psychologists continue to use it. Race is constructed as a group of people distinguishable from another group of people based on physical traits, such as skin color, body type, hair texture, and various sizes and shapes of the nose and lips. Historically, three different races have been described—Mongloid, Negroid, and Caucasoid—each of which can be distinguished from each other based on the aforementioned features (Carter & Pieterse, this *Handbook,* Volume One; Kwan, this *Handbook,* Volume One). Additionally, each race is believed to be characterized by certain psychological traits and physical capabilities. It is beyond the scope of this chapter to review the literature regarding the numerous problems with scientifically defining race. The reader is referred to Smedley (1993) for a thorough discussion of the history, evolution, and problems of the race construct. Suffice it to say that a strict phenotypical definition of race is extremely problematic because there is not one physical trait possessed by a racial group that cannot be shared by another racial group. Furthermore, there is a tremendous amount of within-group variability of physical traits (Shreeve, 1994) and physical abilities. Yet, in spite of these problems, most people know what is meant by the word race (Helms & Cook, 1999). The reality is that the construct of race persists as fact in the face of dubious and disproven scientific claims of validity. This is evidence that race is socially constructed and functions as a pragmatic heuristic in the lives of most people.

Implications of Race for Counseling

Helms and Cook (1999) have stated that "a goal of the therapist should be to make explicit implicit socioracial and sociocultural messages" (p. 17). This statement suggests that for a therapist to be considered racially and culturally competent, he or she must be able to (1) decode external messages internalized by the client as subtle expressions of racialized or racist thinking and (2) help the client to identify and ultimately eradicate unconscious, internalized racial messages. Of course, the therapist's ability to acquire these skills is predicated on a willingness to engage in the necessary introspective work of critically examining and challenging her or his own racial attitudes and biases in a never-ending process of personal growth. Simply put, a therapist cannot help a client decode, identify, and eradicate racial messages if the therapist cannot do so for herself or himself.

The therapist's race and level of racial self-awareness can influence the conceptualization of a client's problem and thus dramatically change the course of therapy (Thompson, Alvarez, & Piper, this *Handbook,* this volume). Take, for example, the following fictionalized transcript of a client I have seen for the past year. The client, whom I call Keshia, is an African American woman trying to get into medical school. She presented with issues of test anxiety surrounding the MCAT and low confidence. It is important to note that there was nothing explicitly racial about her problems mentioned by her in the intake interview.

Keshia: I don't feel comfortable talking with my instructor about the problems I'm having with this class.

Therapist: What do you think is causing your discomfort?

Keshia: I'm not sure. Well, I think it is because she has a condescending attitude toward me.

Therapist: How is she condescending toward you?

Keshia: Well, whenever I ask her to explain a concept to me, she always comes across like, "You poor child. Let me help you because you really don't understand this difficult material." And I don't like that at all.

Therapist: Does she actually say something like this to you?

Keshia: No.

Therapist: Well, why do you think that she is being condescending to you?

Keshia: I don't know. I just feel it. I can read people, and she just comes across as condescending.

Therapist: What is your professor's race?

Keshia: She is White.

Therapist: Could race have anything to do with how you're feeling?

Keshia: Hmmm, well, now that you've mentioned it, I think so. I grew up in a predominantly Black environment and I attended predominantly Black schools where there were mostly Black teachers. I've always done well in school. This teacher looks at me like I'm some poor Black student who isn't intelligent enough to learn the material. I think that's what really bothers me.

In this dialogue, I decoded the external "helping" message given by the professor and received by Keshia as an interaction that was perceived at an unconscious level as racialized. As a result, I asked a question about race to follow my clinical instincts. Obviously, we don't know the intent of the professor. However, in this instance, intent is less important than addressing and validating how Keshia experienced the offer of help. A racially and culturally competent therapist needs to be able to decode external messages for potential racial themes even when the client is unaware of them (Liu & Pope-Davis, this *Handbook,* this volume).

Although race or race-related problems had never explicitly been mentioned by Keshia in our prior sessions, I had systematically been decoding the messages that she had been sharing with me. She mentioned on more than one occasion the difficulties she had adjusting to this environment. Plus, she was in a program that was geared toward increasing the number of ethnic minority students in medical school. I did not explicitly ask her about race immediately. It was only after careful consideration of these and other signs that I followed my clinical intuition and asked the race question.

At this point, I should note the actual circumstances of how she came to be my client. She initially requested a female therapist, but because none was available, I was assigned to her. After acknowledging her request, I asked her if it would be a problem if I worked with her. She then disclosed that what she really meant was that she did not want a White male therapist. In essence, she associated a male therapist with a White therapist. She explained that she felt that a White male therapist could not really relate to her and that he might be patronizing toward her. It was in this context that I began speculating about other potential racial themes.

Cultural Mistrust

Keshia appears to be exhibiting classical signs of what Watkins, Terrell, Miller, and Terrell (1989) have called cultural mistrust. Cultural mistrust consists of feelings of mistrust toward White people and institutions that are controlled by White people. As has been pointed out by Helms (1994), the term cultural mistrust is really a misnomer, because what Watkins et al. really seem to be describing is racial mistrust. Regardless of the terminology, cultural mistrust is a race-related construct that all therapists should be knowledgeable about when working with people of Color. White therapists in particular need a thorough understanding of the history of oppression of people of Color and how this history, combined with current discriminatory practices, facilitates high levels of cultural mistrust among people of Color. It is my belief that White therapists generally have no idea how pervasive cultural mistrust is among people of Color, and if confronted with evidence of its pervasiveness, could become discouraged about their ability to effectively counsel ethnic minorities. That is why racial-cultural training is essential for becoming a racially and culturally competent therapist (Wallace, this *Handbook,* this volume).

Incorporating Research on Race in Therapy

As mentioned earlier, I was now more open to exploring other racial themes with Keshia. In particular, I wanted to explore with Keshia her thoughts regarding the MCAT. Keshia's presenting problems were very consistent with research dealing with African Americans, standardized tests, and a phenomenon called stereotype threat. Take, for example, this fictionalized transcript of my work with Keshia:

Therapist: How do you feel when you take the MCAT?

Keshia: Um, I get very nervous. My stomach starts to hurt, and my heart starts beating faster. It gets worse because of all the people taking the test with me. I wish that I could be in a room by myself where I would not be distracted.

Therapist: Have you always had these reactions to standardized tests?

Keshia: Yes, for as long as I can remember. When I took the SAT I felt the same way.

Therapist: Why do you think you react that way?

Keshia: I don't know. I guess maybe it's the pressure of having to do well.

Therapist: So, do you believe that your performance on the test is an accurate indicator of your true abilities?

Keshia: No, I mean, I know the material. I do well in classes. I just can't demonstrate my knowledge of what I really know on the test.

Therapist: Is that why you react that way and get so upset just thinking about the test?

Keshia: Yes, I believe so.

Therapist: It seems like your feelings about yourself are tied to your performance on the MCAT. In other words, when you perform poorly, you tend to be down on yourself.

Keshia: Yes, you're absolutely right.

Therapist: Could it also be possible that maybe you get so nervous and upset because you believe that your performance on the test says something about you as a Black person and about Black people in general?

Keshia: [hesitation] That's a really good question. I've never really thought about it like that. I think you have a point. Maybe that's why I feel so uncomfortable sometimes with my professors. I don't want them to think that Black people can't do well on this test.

In this dialogue, it can be seen that my line of questioning was driven by my racial awareness and knowledge of research about a phenomenon called stereotype threat (Steele, 1992; Steele & Aronson, 1995). Steele has argued that the standardized test performance of African American students (and other groups of students for whom a stereotype is made salient) is depressed by an unconscious fear that their performance will confirm stereotypes about Black intelligence. Historically, we know that of all the stereotypes about Blacks, perhaps the most trenchant is the belief that Blacks are less intelligent than Whites. Given the emotionally charged nature of this topic, one can easily imagine that it may never be brought up in a therapeutic context. Yet, it should be apparent that my knowledge of research on race greatly influenced my conceptualization of Keshia's problem and thus ultimately influenced the course of therapy. I helped Keshia identify the unconscious racial message of Black intellectual inferiority which she had internalized and which was partially responsible for her anxiety.

A therapist that was not racially and culturally competent might have chosen to take a strict cognitive-behavioral approach in working with Keshia. A cognitive-behavioral approach would simply conceptualize Keshia's test anxiety as stemming from faulty cognitions about the MCAT and its overall importance in the grand scheme of things. The therapeutic goal would be to change her thoughts about the MCAT such that she would no longer place so much importance on its scores and would not see the scores as making some statement about her individual ability. While that approach is certainly adequate, it would fail to help Keshia develop insight into the racialized nature of her anxiety, which, if left unconscious, would manifest itself again. In essence, it would be akin to only taking medication to treat a major depressive episode: The symptoms may go away, but they will return if the underlying thoughts and self-evaluation responsible for the depression aren't changed.

DEFINING ETHNICITY

A long-standing problem in the psychological literature is the inconsistent definition and usage of the term ethnicity (Juby & Concepción, this *Handbook,* Volume One). Narrowly defined, ethnicity is determined by one's country of origin, language spoken, and religion practiced. Carter (1995) defines ethnicity as belonging to an ethnic group, which "can refer to one's national origin, religious affiliation, or other type of socially or geographically defined group" (p. 13). Helms and Cook (1999) state that ethnicity "refers to the national, regional, or tribal origins of one's oldest remembered ancestors and the customs, traditions, and rituals handed down by these ancestors" (p. 19). Phinney (1996) states that ethnicity can be conceptualized in three ways: (1) ethnic group classification, (2) ethnic identity, and (3) minority status. Phinney also correctly notes that some people use ethnicity and race interchangeably. This broadly defined and liberal usage of ethnicity assumes that members of ethnic groups share the same physical features.

An examination of these definitions reveals problems inherent in their practical application. For example, the designation of American refers to a national origin, thus presumably an ethnicity. However, the reality is that saying that one is American is much less meaningful and useful as an ethnic designation than saying that one is Chinese, which is also a national origin. This is because the United States is the most diverse nation in the world; its heterogeneity renders an American ethnic label subject to much interpretation and therefore of dubious utility. China is a much more homogeneous nation; thus, a Chinese ethnic label becomes more meaningful. Using language as a definitive marker of ethnicity is also problematic. For example, English is the official language of the United States, but there are several groups that share English as their primary language who would clearly not be categorized as being of the same ethnic background (i.e., African Americans and European Americans). Similarly, the use of religion as a marker of ethnicity is problematic. The practice of Judaism is typically associated with being Jewish, which is considered to be an ethnicity. But what about those persons of Jewish ancestry who are not practicing Jews? The use of religion as a marker of ethnic identity is also problematic with Latinos/as: Although many Latinos/as are Catholic, others practice different variants of Christianity. In spite of these problems, the markers of nationality, religion, and language give us a starting point to begin to identify the contours of what constitutes an ethnic group (see Carter & Pieterse, this *Handbook,* Volume One; Trimble, this *Handbook,* Volume One).

Unlike race, most people are less sophisticated about ethnic groups and typically don't know what is meant by ethnicity. People tend to see ethnicity and race as the same, so that Mexicans, Mexican Americans, and Puerto Ricans are seen as being racially and ethnically the same (i.e., Hispanics). Similarly, Chinese, Chinese Americans, Japanese, and Japanese Americans are seen as being racially and ethnically the same (i.e., Asians).

Implications of Ethnicity for Counseling

Given the challenges of defining and therefore understanding ethnicity, what characteristics mark an ethnically and culturally competent therapist? I believe that for a therapist to be considered ethnically and culturally competent, she or he must be able to (1) identify those constituent elements of ethnicity (i.e., language, religion, cultural values) that may serve as proximal variables contributing to the client's difficulties and (2) help the client understand and negotiate ethnic or cultural processes (e.g., acculturation, enculturation) that may have a bearing on the client's problems.

The therapist's level of cultural competence can also influence the conceptualization of a client's problem and thus dramatically change the course of therapy. Take, for example, the following fictionalized transcript of a client I saw recently. The client, whom I call James, is an international student from Somalia. He presented with issues of interpersonal difficulties, depression, and low confidence. It is important to note that there was nothing explicitly cultural about his problems mentioned by him in the intake interview.

Therapist: I read on your intake sheet that you are having some interpersonal difficulties. Could you tell me a little more about the nature of your difficulties?

James: [stuttering] I, well, I don't know. I am having trouble making friends here.

Therapist: How so?

James: [stuttering] I don't know. I'm finding that people are different here.

Therapist: Did you have trouble making friends in Somalia?

James: [hesitation] No, not really. I mean, I've never been a very outgoing person, but in Somalia I never had trouble making friends.

Therapist: Do you think that it has something to do with cultural differences between Somalians and Americans?

James: Yes, I think so.

Therapist: From your observation and experience, what differences do you see between Americans and Somalians?

James: [stuttering and hesitation] Well, I, I, it's hard to say.

Therapist: Take your time. There is no rush or pressure here.

James: [stuttering] I, I think that Americans and Somalians think of friendship differently.

Therapist: How so?

James: Well, I think that for Somalians, when we call someone a friend, we take it more seriously than Americans. Here, it seems that Americans call each other friends, but don't treat each other the way Somalians treat friends. It, it seems rather superficial.

Here it can be seen that there are some obvious cultural issues to be addressed. James was coming from a collectivist culture where friendships were probably fewer but more valued. He was now experiencing an individualist American culture where, arguably, quantity of friendships are more important than quality of friendships. However, before I could start patting myself on the back for being a culturally competent therapist, I was still missing a piece of the puzzle.

Therapist: Are there any Americans that you have met that you hang out with?

James: Yes, I have met some.

Therapist: How do they treat you?

James: They are nice to me. They invite me to go out with them.

Therapist: Do you feel as though you have connected with them?

James: [stuttering] Uh, sometimes yes. But a lot of times no.

Therapist: Can you give me an example of when you had a difficult time connecting with them?

James: [Hesitation, stuttering] Uh, I, I can't think of an example.

At this point I was confused. I could not figure out why, if he really was having a difficult time connecting with his American friends, he could not think of one example to share with me. I began to think more about how we were relating. I noticed that James had trouble at times communicating his thoughts to me, which sometimes made it difficult to understand him. What if this was occurring with his American friends? I decided to pursue this possibility.

Therapist: James, do you think that your American friends always understand what you're saying?

James: No, I don't think so.

Therapist: Why do you think that?

James: Because a lot of times I'll say something and they will have a sort of blank expression on their faces. When they respond to me, it often does not have to do with what I just said.

Therapist: How do you respond when it is apparent that they don't understand you?

James: It, it makes me feel very self-conscious. The harder I try to make them understand, the worse it gets. Then I end up withdrawing and talking less.

Therapist: Do you think this may be why you feel as though you're not connecting with them?

James: [hesitation] Yes, I believe that's the reason.

Identifying language as a contributing factor to James's difficulties should have been obvious (Faubert & Locke, this *Handbook,* this volume). However, I was suffering from what Wrenn (1962) has called cultural encapsulation. I took for granted that he was comfortable with English, which was not his first language. It was only when I began using myself as a clinical instrument that I began to gain insight into the origin of James's difficulties. Once I was able to identify language as an issue significantly contributing to James's difficulties, I felt as if I made a breakthrough in our work together.

Acculturation

Recall that the second condition that I identified for culturally competent therapy is helping the client understand and negotiate ethnic cultural processes, such as acculturation. Acculturation is the process of adopting the majority culture and is an ethnicity-related construct (Kohatsu, this *Handbook,* Volume One). Culturally competent therapists should be familiar with how acculturation operates as an important factor in the mental health of ethnic minorities. Consider the following fictionalized transcript of a client I saw for a year. The client, whom I call Yamzi, is a 20-year-old Japanese international student presenting with issues of depression, interpersonal difficulties, and sexual frustration. Yamzi has been in the country for three years.

Therapist: What is the nature of your interpersonal difficulties?

Yamzi: I can't find a girlfriend. Everywhere I look I see guys and girls together.

Therapist: Why is it so important for you to have a girlfriend?

Yamzi: Because I get lonely. I just want to be able to spend time with someone who cares about me.

Therapist: That certainly is understandable. Have you ever had a girlfriend?

Yamzi: No, not really. There was a girl I really liked who I thought liked me, but it turns out she didn't like me.

Therapist: Could you tell me more about her?

At this point, Yamzi proceeded to tell me about the girl that he liked. Later in the session, he began disclosing more intimate information.

Therapist: You mentioned on your intake form that you were experiencing sexual frustration. Could you say some more about that?

Yamzi: [looking somewhat uncomfortable] It is sort of embarrassing to talk about.

Therapist: I don't want you to feel embarrassed. I am not judging you. You can say anything you want to here.

Yamzi: Well, I am always horny. I want to have sex really badly.

Therapist: That's understandable. It is a natural urge. So, you're not sexually active?

Yamzi: I am a virgin. But I very badly want to have sex.

Therapist: Is that why you want to have a girlfriend?

Yamzi: Yes, I think so. Besides, everyone is having sex. I am the only person not having sex.

Therapist: Why do you say that?

Yamzi: Because that's all my friends talk about. Who they got with . . .

Therapist: Are you talking about other Japanese international students?

Yamzi: No, I'm talking about my American friends. All of them are having sex. I'm probably the only 20-year-old college student who has not had sex.

This is a beautiful illustration of how acculturation can be one source of psychological problems. Yamzi has left a traditional Japanese culture where sex and sexuality are not displayed as openly as they are in the more sexually permissive American culture. He has been bombarded with cultural messages that everyone is having sex. So the saying "When in Rome, do as the Romans do" has particular salience in his case. His frustration is most likely the result of a clash in cultural values. He was raised in a culture of understated sexual expression, and now he was trying to be more American (i.e., have sex). This was a central theme through much of my work with him.

CONCLUSION

This chapter provides a brief review of how the constructs of race and ethnicity have typically been used in the psychotherapy literature. Most of the psychotherapy literature treats race and ethnicity as demographic variables. The most common application of this approach examines the psychoanalytic concepts of transference and countertransference in mixed (and same) racial counseling dyads. Next, I reviewed how Africentric approaches are increasingly being used as culturally sensitive therapeutic modalities. Following this brief review, I provided an outline of methods to incorporate race, ethnicity, and related constructs in clinical work. I provided definitions of race and ethnicity and discussed the problems inherent in them and their usage. I then considered how knowledge of the race and ethnicity research literature can guide clinical work in conceptualizing clients' problems. Fictionalized transcripts of real clients were used to demonstrate how knowledge of race, ethnicity, and related constructs and the extant literature were incorporated and applied in my clinical work with ethnic minority clients.

This chapter has been offered to help raise the awareness of therapists about the limitations of treating race and ethnicity as simply demographic categories, To paraphrase Helms and Cook (1999), this chapter has been offered to help therapists better understand the complex ways that race and ethnicity impact the lives of everyday people, as well as the psychotherapy process. It is my belief that racial-cultural psychology is *the* driving force behind the multiculturalism movement. Furthermore, I agree with Carter (1995) that race continues to be the most "elusive, perplexing, troubling, and enduring aspect of life in the United States" (p. 1). If clinical work in psychology is to remain relevant in the lives of all people, it must recognize that the constructs of race and ethnicity should not be viewed as merely demographic characteristics that are primarily areas of sociological inquiry. Race and ethnicity are, and have always been, legitimate topics of psychological inquiry.

REFERENCES

Carter, R. T. (1995). *The influence of race and racial identity in psychotherapy: Toward a racially inclusive model.* New York: Wiley.

Carter, R. T., & Pieterse, A. L. (in press). Race: A social and psychological analysis of the term and its meaning. In R. T. Carter (Ed.), *Handbook of racial-cultural psychology and counseling: Theory and research* (Vol. 1, pp. 41–63). Hoboken, NJ: Wiley.

Comas-Diaz, L. (1992). The future of psychotherapy with ethnic minorities. *Psychotherapy, 29,* 88–94.

DeWeaver, K. (1992). Race, private practice, and psychotherapy: An empirical examination and discussion. *Psychotherapy in Private Practice, 11,* 49–67.

Downing, D. (2000). Controversies in psychoanalytic education: The issue of race and its relevance in psychoanalytic treatment. *Psychoanalytic Review, 87,* 355–375.

Elligan, D., & Utsey, S. (1999). Utility of an African-centered support group for African American men confronting societal racism and oppression. *Cultural Diversity and Ethnic Minority Psychology, 5,* 156–165.

Fuertes, J. N., Costa, C. I., Mueller, L. N., & Hersh, M. (in press). Psychotherapy process and outcome from a racial-ethnic perspective. In R. T. Carter (Ed.), *Handbook of racial-cultural psychology and counseling: Theory and research* (Vol. 1, pp. 256–276). Hoboken, NJ: Wiley.

Gelso, C., & Mohr, J. (2001). The working alliance and the transference/countertransference relationship: Their manifestation with racial/ethnic and sexual orientation minority clients and therapists. *Applied and Preventive Psychology, 10,* 51–68.

Gray-Little, B., & Kaplan, D. (2000). Race and ethnicity in psychotherapy research. In C. Snyder & R. Ingram (Eds.), *Handbook of psychological change: Psychotherapy processes and practices for the 21st century* (pp. 591–613). New York: Wiley.

Gregory, W., & Harper, K. (2001). The NTU approach to health and healing. *Journal of Black Psychology, 27,* 304–320.

Helms, J. E. (1994). How multiculturalism obscures racial factors in the therapy process: Comment on Ridley et al. (1994), Sodowsky et al. (1994), Ottavi et al. (1994), and Thompson et al. (1994). *Journal of Counseling Psychology, 41,* 162–165.

Helms, J. E., & Cook, D. A. (1999). *Using race and counseling in counseling and psychotherapy: Theory and process.* Boston: Allyn & Bacon.

Hill, C. E., Nutt, E. A., & Jackson, S. (1994). Trends in psychotherapy process research: Samples, measures, researchers, and classic publications. *Journal of Counseling Psychology, 41,* 364–377.

Holmes, D. (1992). Race and transference in psychoanalysis and psychotherapy. *International Journal of Psycho-Analysis, 73,* 1–11.

Ivey, A. E., D'Andrea, M., Ivey, M. B., & Simek-Morgan, L. (2002). *Theories of counseling and psychotherapy: A multicultural perspective.* Boston: Allyn & Bacon.

Johnson, S. D. (in press). Culture, context, and counseling. In R. T. Carter (Ed.), *Handbook of racial-cultural psychology and counseling: Theory and research* (Vol. 1, pp. 17–25). Hoboken, NJ: Wiley.

Juby, H. L., & Concepción, W. R. (in press). Ethnicity: The term and its meaning. In R. T. Carter (Ed.), *Handbook of racial-cultural psychology and counseling: Theory and research* (Vol. 1, pp. 26–40). Hoboken, NJ: Wiley.

Jwigonski, M. (1996). Challenging privilege through Africentric social work practice. *Social Work, 41*, 153–161.

Kohatsu, E. L. (in press). Acculturation: Current and future directions. In R. T. Carter (Ed.), *Handbook of racial-cultural psychology and counseling: Theory and research* (Vol. 1, pp. 207–231). Hoboken, NJ: Wiley.

Kwan, K. (in press). Racial salience: Conceptual dimensions and implications for racial and ethnic identity development. In R. T. Carter (Ed.), *Handbook of racial-cultural psychology and counseling: Theory and research* (Vol. 1, pp. 115–131). Hoboken, NJ: Wiley.

Morris, E. (2001). Clinical practices with African Americans: Juxtaposition of standard clinical practices and Africentricism. *Professional Psychology—Research and Practice, 32*, 563–572.

Parham, T. (2002). *Counseling persons of African descent: Raising the bar of practitioner competence.* Thousand Oaks, CA: Sage.

Phinney, J. (1996). When we talk about American ethnic groups, what do we mean? *American Psychologist, 51*(9), 918–927.

Shreeve, J. (1994). Terms of estrangement. *Discover,* 57–63.

Smedley, A. (1993). *Race in North America: Origin and evolution of a worldview.* San Francisco: Westview Press.

Steele, C. (1992). Race and the schooling of African-Americans. *Atlantic Monthly, 269*(4), 68–78.

Steele, C. M., & Aronson, J. (1995). Stereotype threat and the intellectual test performance of African-Americans. *Journal of Personality and Social Psychology, 69*, 797–811.

Tang, N., & Gardner, J. (1999). Race, culture, and psychotherapy: Transference to minority therapists. *Psychoanalytic Quarterly, 68*, 1–20.

Trimble, J. E. (in press). An inquiry into the measurement of ethnic and racial identity. In R. T. Carter (Ed.), *Handbook of racial-cultural psychology and counseling: Theory and research* (Vol. 1, pp. 320–359). Hoboken, NJ: Wiley.

Watkins, C. E., Terrell, F., Miller, F., & Terrell, S. L. (1989). Cultural mistrust and its effects on expectational variables in Black client-White counselor relationships. *Journal of Counseling Psychology, 36*, 447–450.

White, J. (1994). The impact of race and ethnicity on transference and countertransference in combined individual/group therapy. *Group, 18*, 89–99.

Williams, C. (1999). African American women, afrocentrism and feminism: Implications for therapy. *Women and Therapy, 22*, 1–16.

Williams, S., & Halgin, R. (1995). Issues in psychotherapy supervision between the White supervisor and the Black supervisee. *Clinical Supervisor, 13*, 39–61.

Wrenn, C. G. (1962). The culturally-encapsulated counselor. *Harvard Educational Review, 32*, 444–449.

Yee, A. H., Fairchild, H. H., Weizmann, F., & Wyatt, G. E. (1993). Addressing psychology's problems with race. *American Psychologist, 48*, 1132–1140.

CHAPTER 16

The Impact of Cultural Variables on Vocational Psychology: Examination of the Fouad and Bingham Culturally Appropriate Career Counseling Model

Kris Ihle-Helledy, Nadya A. Fouad, Paula W. Gibson, Caroline G. Henry, Elizabeth Harris-Hodge, Matthew D. Jandrisevits, Edgar X. Jordan III, and A. J. Metz

Cultural variables play a role in our increasingly diverse society and need to be examined with regard to social, economic, and political systems and organizations, including the realm of psychology. According to Sue, Bingham, Porché-Burke, and Vasquez (1999), the need for psychology to address issues of race, culture, and ethnicity has never been more urgent. In January 2001, the National Multicultural Conference and Summit II (NMCS-II) hosted by the American Psychological Association Divisions 17 (Counseling Psychology), 35 (Society for the Psychology of Women), 44 (Society for Psychological Study of Lesbian and Gay Issues), and 45 (Society for the Psychological Study of Ethnic Minority Issues) was held to examine current issues in ethnic minority psychology. One recommendation that resulted from NMCS-II was for the field of psychology to tackle issues such as racism, oppression, and privilege by expanding our current theories and comprehension of diversity issues (Bingham, Porché-Burke, James, Sue, & Vasquez, 2002). One way to address changes that need to be made in both training and education is through research. In keeping with the NMCS-II, it is crucial that research focus on cultural competence (Bingham et al., 2002).

Vocational psychologists are increasingly paying attention to cultural variables (Swanson & Gore, 2000). Over the years, vocational psychologists have recognized the limitations of career theories for large segments of the population and the lack of attention to the role of structural and cultural factors that might influence an individual's career choices and behaviors (Fitzgerald & Betz, 1994). However, it appears as though vocational theorists have all but ignored the career development processes of racial and cultural group members (D. Brown, 2002). As suggested by Fouad and Byars (2002), clients from differing cultural contexts may require different counseling variables and processes, or may require different emphases on the same variables and processes. As practitioners, researchers, and scholars, it behooves us to operate within empirically grounded frameworks. For example, some authors have discussed the impact of cultural variables in the career counseling process (e.g., Bingham & Ward, 1994; Fouad & Bingham, 1995; Leong, 1985, 1993; Leong & Hartung, 1997; Ward & Bingham, 1993). Others have posited the role of being a person of Color interacting with mainstream U.S. society and its implications for career development (Carter & Swanson, 1990; Evans & Herr, 1994; Hackett & Byars, 1996; Helms & Piper, 1994).

While the field of vocational psychology has a better understanding of the role of culture in influencing occupational choice, the field has less understanding of how cultural variables impact the career counseling process. It has been identified that racial and cultural group members encounter barriers such as discrimination and racism, which White group members are not as likely to encounter (e.g., Arbona, 1996; Evans & Herr, 1994; Fitzgerald & Betz, 1994; Fouad & Byars, this *Handbook,* Volume One; Leung, 1995). Moreover, theorists in the field are aware that independent decision making has been the focus of more traditional career counseling, which tends to be linear and emphasizes individualistic approaches and values as opposed to incorporating collectivistic approaches and values. Neville, Gysbers, Heppner, and Johnston (2003) identified five tenets associated with traditional career counseling that are areas of caution when working within a multicultural career counseling frame. In brief, the five tenets are (1) Individualism and autonomy are universally desirable; (2) each client has a certain level of affluence; (3) opportunities are available to all individuals who work hard; (4) work is central in people's lives; and (5) the career counseling process is linear. It remains unclear whether this traditional emphasis is suitable for racial and cultural group members (Swanson & Fouad, 1999).

Scholars in multicultural vocational psychology (i.e., vocational psychology that incorporates cultural contextual variables) have asserted that traditional career counseling tends to operate on Western-based values and processes (e.g., individuation, linear processes) rather than on collectivistic, less rational decision-making models (Fouad & Bingham, 1995; Jackson & Neville, 1998; Leong & Brown, 1995). More specifically, scholars have called for career counseling to be multiculturally competent: to explicitly incorporate culture into career counseling, transforming career counseling into a more cultural-centered process (e.g., Bingham & Ward, 1994; Fouad, 1993, 1995; Fouad & Arbona, 1994; Leong & Serafica, 1995; Neville et al., 1998; Sue & Sue, 2003; Swanson, 1993; Swanson & Fouad, 1999; Ward & Bingham, 1993).

This chapter examines the role of race and ethnicity in various areas of the career counseling process to give practitioners greater knowledge about the role of culture in career counseling and provides recommendations for culture-centered career counseling. It is noteworthy that the approach in this chapter related to cultural differences in career counseling does not stem from a cultural deficit orientation but rather from the orientation of pluralism or cultural diversity (Sue & Sue, 2003). Cultural values and sociopolitical contexts influence worldviews and identity development and vary across groups (Carter, this *Handbook,* this volume; Fiske, Kitayama, Markus, & Nisbett, 1998; Fouad & Bingham, 1995; Fouad & Brown, 2000; Helms, 1990). It is assumed in this chapter that all clients operate within a cultural context; thus, culture becomes a critical variable to consider in the career counseling process. All persons are believed to be influenced by such factors as gender social-ization, racial identity and background, socioeconomic status, sexual orientation, and ability/disability (Swanson & Fouad, 1999). All of these factors shape one's en-vironment as well as one's responses to it (Swanson & Fouad, 1999). Therefore, it is especially crucial for a career-counseling model to consider such varying contextual influences; three models have done exactly that.

The first model is a five-stage model proffered by Leong and Hartung (1997). This model includes cultural differences in the recognition of career and vocational problems (i.e., stage 1), the role of culture in seeking help and services (i.e., stage 2), the evaluation of career and vocational problems (i.e., stage 3), culturally appro-priate career interventions (i.e., stage 4), and the outcome of the career intervention (i.e., stage 5).

Another model, by Leung (1995), centers on career interventions and has three levels: systemic (e.g., career-related programs in schools), group (e.g., group career counseling that centers on one racial and ethnic group), and one-to-one (e.g., indi-vidual client-counselor dyads framed by the cultural beliefs of the client). Leung's model includes both career and educational outcomes. Educational outcomes are critical in this model, as they impact the career development of people of Color and can counteract the cyclic relationship of poverty and discrimination (Leung, 1995).

Fouad and Bingham (1995) provide a third model, the Culturally Appropriate Career Counseling Model (CACCM), which uses structural (i.e., racism, discrim-ination, and oppression) and cultural factors as a frame to define a culturally ap-propriate career counseling process. A culture-centered career counseling process recognizes that all clients incorporate similar variables in making career decisions (e.g., interests, abilities, values, and family considerations). However, culture in-fluences the weight that individuals place on values such as family, the role of work in one's life (ranging from central to peripheral), and social status and whether the values are generally more collectivistic or individualistic (Swanson & Fouad, 1999). For example, culture may influence a focus on the centrality of work in an individual's life, with some individuals "working to live" and others "living to work" (D. Brown, 2002).

In the CACCM (Fouad & Bingham, 1995), the career counseling process occurs in a cultural context. Specifically, culture is identified as a critical variable that en-ters into each of the seven steps of the model and addresses process, goals, and interventions at a more micro level than the Leong and Hartung (1997) model. However, while the Fouad and Bingham model assumes that career counseling must incorporate culture into each step, it is unclear whether this process results in more effective outcomes for all clients. In accordance with the resolution that resulted from the NMCS-II, the purpose of this chapter is to examine the relationship of cul-tural variables, specifically race and ethnicity, on various aspects of the career counseling process. Thus, this chapter aims to guide counselors on how to work with clients; in contrast, career development theories focus on explaining voca-tional behavior (e.g., career choice, work adjustment, career progress) and are more fully discussed by Fouad and Byars in Volume One of this *Handbook*.

In this chapter, the role of cultural variables in each step of the Fouad and Bing-ham (1995) CACCM is explored. Empirical studies in vocational psychology that examine the relationship between culture and various aspects of the career counsel-ing process are examined in relation to the stages in the CACCM. This review is not intended to explicitly test Fouad and Bingham's model but to test their assumption that culture does influence career counseling at various stages in the process. Given the calls for multiculturally competent career counseling (e.g., Bingham & Ward, 1994; Fouad, 1993, 1995; Fouad & Arbona, 1994; Leong & Serafica, 1995; Neville et al., 2003; Sue & Sue, 2003; Swanson, 1993; Swanson & Fouad, 1999; Ward & Bingham, 1993), reviewing the empirical literature in relationship to the CACCM also provides one way to clarify what is empirically known about culturally appro-priate career counseling.

The criteria for inclusion in this review were (1) research articles that used an empirical research design, (2) publication within the past 20 years, and (3) research that identified race or ethnicity as an independent variable. Empirical studies were used to enable a comparison of quantitative findings using an effect size calcula-tion (B. Thompson, 2002). Recent studies (past 20 years) were reviewed to incor-porate current findings in the field. Finally, as previously described, the intent was to examine the role of race and ethnicity in the stages of career counseling, and thus, race and ethnicity were the two cultural variables being examined in the CACCM (Fouad & Bingham, 1995). Focusing on articles that used race or ethnic-ity as an independent variable allowed comparison across articles. However, it should be noted that this emphasis had the limitation of precluding other relevant articles, such as those that focused on the relationship between racial identity atti-tudes and counselor preference (e.g., Carter & Akinsulure-Smith, 1996; Helms & Carter, 1991).

Two procedures were employed to identify studies that fit the criteria. First, the PsychInfo and Educational Resource Information Center (ERIC) databases and the Social Science Abstracts were explored using broad search terms such as "career counseling," "counseling," and "culture" and narrower search terms such as "career barriers," "race," and "ethnicity." As empirical research articles were identified, each reference list was examined for possible additional articles that fit the three criteria for inclusion.

For articles that met the criteria for inclusion, all of the individual results were converted into effect sizes; this facilitated the comparison of results across studies (Cohen, 1998; Mullen, 1989; B. Thompson, 2002). Calculation of effect sizes pro-vides a common metric across studies to determine the clinical or practical signifi-cance of studies, rather than merely relying on statistical significance, which is heavily influenced by sample size (B. Thompson, 2002). Effect sizes can generally be measured in two ways: as the standard difference between two means or as a cor-relation between an independent variable and individual scores on a dependent vari-able; the correlation is called the effect size correlation (Rosnow & Rosenthal, 1996). Effect sizes are rarely reported in empirical investigations. When the means and standard deviations were reported in the reviewed studies, the effect sizes were calculated and are reported in this review. The coefficient calculated for the effect size is reported as *ES* throughout this review. Readers are referred to B. Thompson (2002) for a discussion of significance and Mullen (1989) for a discussion regarding meta-analysis. This review also followed Cohen's (1988) suggestion that small, medium, and large effect sizes are reflected in effect sizes of $r = .1, .3$, and $.5$, respectively.

This chapter includes an overview of the Fouad and Bingham (1995) model, followed by a separate section on each step. Each section consists of the description of that step of the CACCM and a review of the empirically grounded knowledge base regarding the role of culture related to that step. We then provide a general discussion related to the results and the limitations of the reviewed research. Included at the close of this chapter is a summary and recommendations section for culturally centered vocational practice based on the empirical review.

OVERVIEW OF THE CULTURALLY APPROPRIATE CAREER COUNSELING MODEL

Prior to entering the first step of the CACCM, both the counselor and the client prepare for counseling. Preparation for the counselor includes the development of cultural competence (Bingham & Ward, 1994; Cheatham, 1990; Sue, Arredondo, & McDavis, 1992). A counselor preparing for cross-cultural counseling must have awareness, knowledge, and skills related to her or his respective culture and others' culture, a range of counseling techniques (Sue et al., 1992), and a client who presents with career-related concerns (Fouad & Bingham, 1995). Once this stage is set, the first step of CACCM involves establishing rapport and a culturally appropriate relationship. Similar to the personal counseling process, flexibility, suspension of stereotypes and assumptions, and attention to the counselor role the client wants are imperative in the establishment of a therapeutic alliance.

In Step 2 of the model, counselors help clients identify career issues of concern (i.e., "What is troubling the client?") that may fall into the following five categories: cognitive (D. Brown & Brooks, 1991), social/emotional (e.g., D. Brown & Brooks, 1991; Gysbers & Moore, 1987; Spokane, 1991), behavioral (e.g., D. Brown & Brooks, 1991; Gysbers & Moore, 1987; Spokane, 1991), environmental, and external barriers, or some combination thereof. In the CACCM, it is essential to examine career issues in the client's cultural context. Cognitive beliefs may include faulty processing or irrational beliefs regarding career decision making. An example of a social/emotional concern may be a client dealing with anger or anxiety at work in relationship to racism that impedes her or him from fulfilling work-related opportunities (e.g., advancement). The anxiety may manifest itself in behavior when a client is persistently late to work. Environmental elements, such as working conditions and coworkers, are directly linked to the working environment. External barriers are divergent from environmental issues; they may include racism, sexism, oppression, or discrimination (i.e., any restriction that the client experiences that is outside of her or his control). External barriers are explicitly delineated in this model because career choice for many racial and cultural individuals incorporates a balance between factors outside of and within one's control.

Step 3 of the model addresses the impact of cultural variables on career issues (e.g., values, influence of dominant culture on aspirations). The primary question here is "How do cultural variables influence career decisions?" Fouad and Bingham (1995) present a sphere of concentric circles to help identify the way that culture may influence vocational behavior. A description of the sphere moving from the innermost circle to the outermost circle includes the core or unique aspects of the individual (i.e., biological factors), gender (i.e., role expectations), family (i.e., definitions, expectations, and values), racial or ethnic group (i.e., cultural factors such as racial identity development and worldview), and dominant group (i.e., structural factors such as barriers, definitions, and expectations). The sphere is dynamic and interrelated through the concentric circles; therefore, the influential strength of each or the interactive strength of each concentric circle may vary over time. For example, as one gains a greater sense of racial identity, the fourth sphere may increase in influential strength and the outermost concentric circle (i.e., dominant culture) will have less influence on one's vocational choice. In this way, the spheres of influence will vary for each individual and may expand or shrink throughout one's lifetime. (See Figure 9.2; Fouad & Bingham, 1995, for the spheres of influence.)

Step 4 includes culturally appropriate career counseling processes and goals that are grounded in the client's worldview. An example of an inappropriate process for a client whose culture values family and emphasizes collective values is solely addressing the implications of a career goal for the individual, rather than including her or his family in the process. An example of an inappropriate goal for this female client is the selection of a nontraditional career for women, a career choice grounded in dominant U.S. society values.

Step 5 includes establishing culturally appropriate counseling interventions, which requires the incorporation of cultural variables and linking interventions to client-defined and culturally contextualized career issues. For example, group interventions may be effective with racial and culturally diverse people (Bowman, 1993). Culturally appropriate interventions may also involve family in the career counseling process and encourage clients to access same-cultural group and same-sex group role models (Bowman). Assessment of interests and values, a traditional aspect of career counseling, may also constitute one aspect of intervention. It is critical that counselors are aware of how culture may influence vocational assessment and provide alternative means to assist in identifying and clarifying variables important to the client's decision-making process (Fouad, 1993). For example, vocational interest assessment results may be the basis of a decision for some clients, while for those from more collectivistically oriented cultures, interest information may hold less weight in a decision than family preferences for a career choice.

Only Steps 1 through 5 are included in this review, as these steps appear to be most critical to the career counseling process. The last two steps (decision making and implementation and follow-up) typically mark the closing of the career counseling process; because we are most interested in the actual career counseling process, these last two steps are not part of the focus of our review. (See Figure 9.1; Fouad & Bingham, 1995, for a snapshot view of the CACCM.)

Step 1: Establishing a Culturally Appropriate Relationship

Step 1 of Fouad and Bingham's (1995) CACCM is the establishment of a culturally appropriate relationship. This first step is similar to the concept of building a sound working alliance in that the core conditions of warmth, genuineness, and positive regard are satisfied. The addition of multicultural empathy (Ivey, D'Andra, Simek-Morgan, 2002; Ivey, Ivey, & Simek-Morgan, 1993) and understanding is what differentiates establishing a culturally appropriate relationship from the basic rapport building in the therapeutic relationship. The three-stage model of multicultural empathy includes (1) listening to and observing the client's comments and understanding how the client prefers to be related to; (2) responding to the client's words and constructs while using basic attending skills; and (3) clarifying statements with the client (i.e., check out counselor's understanding with the intention of the client; Ivey, Ivey, & Simek-Morgan).

A considerable amount of research underscores the salience of the therapeutic relationship on counseling outcomes; the relationship has been identified as one of the most critical aspects of the counseling process (Gelso & Carter, 1994). Horvath and Symonds (1991) found a small to medium effect size between alliance and therapeutic outcome ($ES = .26$). What remains unknown is the impact that cultural variables have on establishing a culturally appropriate relationship. Our intent was to quantitatively review the role that cultural variables have on the establishment of a culturally appropriate relationship; however, no research studies that fit our criteria for inclusion were found in the vocational psychology literature. The criteria were loosened and the domain of vocational psychology was broadened to general counseling psychology. Still, only 15 studies provided the necessary statistical information to calculate effect sizes. Of the 15 studies, 14 were analogue in nature and used college or high school students in their sample, while the remaining study was conducted with a clinical population at a mental health center.

The independent variables explored in the 15 studies included (1) counselor race (either racially similar or dissimilar to the sample population); (2) participants' cultural mistrust level using the Cultural Mistrust Inventory (Terrell & Terrell, 1981); (3) participants' level of acculturation (dichotomized into high or low levels) using either the Acculturation Rating Scale for Mexican Americans (ARSMA; Cuellar, Harris, & Jasso, 1980) or an adaptation of it; and (4) counselor content orientation (culturally responsive statements used or not used). The dependent variables included (1) ratings of counselor credibility using the Counselor Expertness Rating Scale (Atkinson & Carskaddon, 1975); (2) ratings of counselor attractiveness, expertness, and trustworthiness using the Counselor Rating Form-Short Version (Corrigan & Schmidt, 1983); and (3) ratings of counselor cultural competence using the Cross-Cultural Counseling Inventory-Revised (LaFromboise, Coleman, & Hernandez, 1991). Many of the studies utilized multiple independent and dependent variables and yielded an average sample size of 115.

Results

Eleven studies examined the effect of counselor race on racial and ethnic minority participants' perceptions of counselor credibility and competence (Abreu &

Gabarain, 2000; Atkinson, Casas, & Abreu, 1992; Atkinson & Matsushita, 1991; Gim, Atkinson, & Kim, 1991; Hess & Street, 1991; Ponce & Atkinson, 1989; Ramos-Sanchez, Atkinson, & Fraga, 1999; Ruelas, Atkinson, & Ramos-Sanchez, 1998; C. Thompson, Worthington, & Atkinson, 1994; Wade & Bernstein, 1991; and Watkins & Terrell, 1988). Overall, effect sizes across these studies ranged from small to medium (i.e., .17 to .38). Most of these studies found that people of Color provided higher credibility and cultural competency ratings to racially similar counselors than to racially dissimilar counselors. Our findings were consistent with meta-analytic findings of Coleman, Wampold, and Casali (1995).

Seven of the studies examined the effect of participant level of acculturation on perceptions of counseling (Abreu & Gabarain, 2000; Atkinson et al., 1992; Atkinson & Matsushita, 1991; Gim et al., 1991; Hess & Street, 1991; Pomales & Williams, 1989; Ponce & Atkinson, 1989; Ponterotto, Alexander, & Hinkston, 1988; Price & McNeil, 1992; Ruelas et al., 1998; and Ramos-Sanchez et al., 1999). Typically, level of acculturation, cultural commitment, and generation of immigration in the studies were dichotomized into high/low acculturation, strong/weak cultural commitment, and first/third generation of immigration. Most of these studies found that low-acculturated, strongly committed, first-generation participants gave higher credibility and competency ratings to racially similar counselors who used culturally responsive content; high-acculturated, weakly committed, third-generation participants gave higher credibility and competency ratings to White counselors who did not use culturally responsive content. Effect sizes in these seven studies ranged from .20 to .56. The largest effect size (.56) was found in a college setting (community colleges and university) where first- and second-generation Mexican American college students gave higher ratings of counselor credibility, as measured by the Counselor Effectiveness Rating Scale (CERS), than did their respective third-generation peers (Ramos-Sanchez et al., 1999). Counselors in the study were all identified as Hispanic American (most of whom indicated Spanish as their primary language), though country of origin was not delineated (Ramos-Sanchez et al., 1999). Ramos-Sanchez et al. did not find any significant gender differences for counselor preference by generation.

Three studies examined the use of culturally responsive content by counselors and its effect on clients' ratings of counselor credibility and competence (Atkinson et al., 1992; Gim et al., 1991; C. Thompson et al., 1994). These studies found that counselors who acknowledged the importance of culture in participant problems were perceived as more credible and culturally competent than counselors who ignored cultural variables. Atkinson et al. explored the level of acculturation (i.e., low, medium, or high) for Mexican American community college students on their ratings of counselor credibility and perceptions of cultural competence (i.e., cultural responsiveness). Overall Atkinson, Casas, and Abreu indicated that when the counselor—regardless of counselor ethnicity or participant acculturation—was portrayed as culturally responsive, the highest cultural competence ratings were revealed. In contrast, low cultural competence ratings for the counselor were revealed when the counselor was culturally unresponsive, again, regardless of counselor ethnicity or participant acculturation. Effect sizes across these three studies ranged from .05 to .40. Gim, Atkinson, and Kim reported the largest effect size (.40) for Asian American college students who gave more positive ratings to a culturally sensitive versus a culturally blind counselor.

Two studies examined participant level of cultural mistrust and its effect on Black-White counseling relationships (C. Thompson et al., 1994; Watkins & Terrell, 1988). Results reported by Thompson, Worthington, and Atkinson and Watkins and Terrel revealed that highly mistrustful Black participants rated the White counselor as less credible, less accepting, less trustworthy, and less expert than the Black counselor, with small to medium effect sizes (i.e., .15 to .28). In addition, the Black participants, when paired with a White counselor, gave fewer self-disclosures and stated that they expected less in terms of counseling outcomes. Watkins and Terrell found the largest effect size (i.e., .28) when highly mistrustful Black college students regarded the White counselor as less credible and less able to help them with the following four problem areas: (1) anxiety, (2) shyness, (3) inferiority feelings, and (4) dating difficulties.

Overall, there is a small effect size between culture and establishing a working alliance. Culture appears to make the most difference in the working therapeutic alliance when the therapist is perceived as culturally competent (as rated by the client) and when clients are relatively recent immigrants.

Step 2: Identification of Career Issues

In the second step of Fouad and Bingham's (1995) CACCM, counselors help clients identify career issues of concern. The literature reviewed for Step 2 of the model demonstrated two clear lines of research: One line explored both perceived career opportunities and perceived career barriers; the other focused on the examination of vocational and educational aspirations and expectations. As a result, Step 2 of the model is divided into two parts: Perceived Career Opportunities and Barriers, and Aspirations and Expectations: Career and Education.

Part I Perceived Career Opportunities and Barriers

Issues that impede the likelihood of clients reaching their career goals are often referred to as career barriers. Studies included here focused on the perception of career barriers, perceived occupational opportunities, and perceived occupational discrimination for one's own cultural group and, at times, for cultural group members outside of one's cultural group. Self-reported race was the independent variable used in all of the studies. All seven studies sampled students; three sampled college students (Luzzo, 1993; Slaney, 1980; Slaney & Brown, 1983) and the remaining four studies sampled high school students (Chung & Harmon, 1999; Lauver & Jones, 1991; McWhirter, 1997; McWhirter, Hackett, & Bandalos, 1998).

Results

Effect sizes ranged from small to the upper end of the medium range (i.e., $ES = .0$ to .68). Chung and Harmon (1999) reported the largest effect size; they assessed perceived occupational opportunity and discrimination for Black and White high school students. Results revealed that White students perceived greater occupational opportunity for Blacks ($ES = .68$) than did the Black students for themselves.

Furthermore, the Black students perceived more occupational discrimination for Blacks in general ($ES = .35$) than did the White students for Whites. Luzzo (1993) investigated the perceptions of past and future career development barriers for Black, Hispanic, White, Filipino, and Asian undergraduate students. Using an open-ended questionnaire, Luzzo found a significant relationship between race and past racial identity barriers ($ES = .33$), as well as between race and future racial identity barriers ($ES = .29$). Black participants were most likely to report past and future racial identity barriers, and White participants were least likely to do so.

McWhirter (1997) measured the perceived barriers of Hispanic and White high school students to educational and career goals and found that Hispanic girls anticipated significantly more racial discrimination in their future jobs ($ES = .35$) than did White girls. Using a similar scale, McWhirter et al. (1998) found that White high school girls perceived a greater likelihood of encountering many barriers to their career and educational goals ($ES = .26$) than did Hispanic high school girls. This finding ran counter to the expectation that White students would perceive fewer barriers than students from racially and culturally diverse groups. The perception of barriers (e.g., vocational and educational) may influence the career goals identified by the individual holding the perception. Slaney and Brown (1983) examined the number and distribution of factors that might impede career goals for Black and White college men. Significant differences were not found in the number of factors perceived; however, significant differences were revealed in the distribution of factors. Specifically, White college men considered school-related issues (e.g., low grades, program entry difficulties, boredom, dissatisfaction with college) to be career goal impediments more often than did Black college men ($ES = .18$). One possible explanation for this finding may be that White college students in this sample connected their school-related issues with future career-related pursuits and did not expect external barriers to be critical to this process. Another possible explanation is that the Black students in the study may view external barriers (e.g., racism or discrimination) as being more salient factors related to career goal obstacles.

Part II Aspirations and Expectations: Career and Education

Five investigations fit the three criteria for inclusion here. The five studies explored aspirations and expectations (i.e., career and education). While the overarching independent variable was culture (i.e., variables that create a context and worldview for individuals), special attention was given to race and gender. None of the studies identified how race was measured beyond self-report indices. Thus, it is unclear if race was measured through an open-ended request such as "Please fill in the blank with the racial group or groups with which you identify yourself," or a "check all boxes that apply" request. Career aspirations, career expectations, educational aspirations, educational expectations, occupational prestige, and occupational sex typing were identified as dependent variables. All of the investigations sampled college students except one, which explored gifted high school juniors (Leung, Conoley, & Scheel, 1994). All studies included both men and women, except one all-female study (Murrell, Frieze, & Frost, 1991).

Results

Effect sizes ranged from .0 to .67. Two of the studies that examined the role of race on career aspirations did so by assessing career aspirations in an open-ended format, coding the responses (e.g., prestige level) for analyses of racial and gender group differences (Arbona & Novy, 1991; Murrell, Frieze, & Frost, 1991). Arbona and Novy found no racial differences by gender in Holland-type analysis of career aspiration. Gender differences by group were revealed in career aspirations for Hispanic women (*ES* = .11) and White women (*ES* = 0.14); that is, women reported lower career aspirations than men within the same racial group. Gender effects were also reported for career expectations by Hispanic and White women (*ES* = .17 and .26, respectively; Arbona & Novy, 1991). Murrell, Frieze, and Frost explored career and educational aspirations of Black and White women by classifying occupations into categories of male-dominated (MDO) and female-dominated (FDO) occupations so that educational and career aspirations could be explored by occupational gender. The largest effect size (.67) in their study corresponded to a strong positive correlation between the number of children desired by and the career plans of Black women intending to enter FDOs. A medium effect size for the same relationship between desired number of children and plans to enter an FDO was reported for White women (*ES* = .32). Overall, women aspiring to MDOs demonstrated higher educational and career aspirations than did women planning on FDOs (*ES* = .17 and .36, respectively).

Chung, Loeb, and Gonzo (1996) explored different factors predicting career and educational aspirations for Black college students. The strongest effect size in the study (.30) was the socioeconomic status (SES) of the father's occupation relating to the career aspiration reported by the students. There were no significant differences between the Black men and women for career aspirations. Yet, the same Black women aspired to higher educational degrees than did the Black men (*ES* = .12).

Leung, Ivey, and Suzuki (1994) examined career choice through an occupational checklist, which had a corresponding single letter Holland code and was then rated for prestige level and gender traditionality. Racial group differences (i.e., Asian versus White) were negligible. However, Asians reported higher interest in the Investigative domain (*ES* = .24) and for MDOs (*ES* = .21) than their White counterparts. Leung, Ivey, and Suzuki also found significant differences for occupational prestige by gender (i.e., men higher than women; *ES* = .23) and race (i.e., Asian group members higher than White group members; *ES* = .15). A large effect size (.63) corresponded to the sex typing of occupations by gender, as evidenced by male students scoring significantly higher on the male dominance index (MDI) than did women, regardless of race.

Overall, race and ethnicity seemed to have a small effect size on career barriers and aspirations in general, with one exception: Persons of Color clearly perceived that occupational opportunities might be circumscribed due to race, whereas White students were less likely to perceive that restriction in opportunity for themselves or students of Color.

Step 3: Assessment of Effects of Cultural Variables

The impact of cultural variables on career issues was explored in Step 3 of the CACCM (Fouad & Bingham, 1995). Nine studies were found that empirically examined cultural influences on career-related variables and were usable for this study. One of the studies was excluded (Bae & Chung, 1997), as our research review focuses on culture in the United States. Career variables under study included career values, interests, maturity, satisfaction, self-efficacy, and identity. Cultural influences were defined in terms of ethnic and cultural affiliation, racial identity, and acculturation. The studies incorporated into the present review examined a range of career issues as dependent variables: career values (Weathers, Thompson, Robert, & Rodriguez, 1994), career satisfaction (Holder & Vaux, 1998), career maturity (Lundberg, Osborne, & Miner, 1997; Powell & Luzzo, 1998), career exploration (C. Brown, Darden, Shelton, & DiPoto, 1999), career-related self-efficacy (C. Brown et al., 1999), vocational identity and vocational hope (Jackson & Neville, 1998), and career interests (Park & Harrison, 1995). Again, culture was the overarching dependent variable, with special attention to race, level of acculturation, within-group (i.e., racial) differences (Park & Harrison, 1995), racial identity, national culture, and perceived race-related work stressors.

Miranda and Umhoefer (1998) explored acculturation as a measure of cultural influence on career variables. Jackson and Neville (1998) explored racial identity on vocational identity and vocational hope. Weathers et al. (1994) used the Career Values Survey to assess the relationship between Black racial identity development and the career values of a sample of Black women college students at a predominantly White university. Lundberg et al. (1997) compared the career maturity of Hispanic and White high school students through the use of the Decision-Making and the World of Work Information subscales of the Career Development Inventory (CDI). Holder and Vaux (1998) used the Minnesota Satisfaction Questionnaire to identify the extent to which race-related occupational stress affected job satisfaction for Black professionals working in predominantly White work environments. Park and Harrison (1995) explored the influence of racial affiliation on career interests. Powell and Luzzo (1998) used the Career Maturity Inventory (CMI) to examine whether differences exist in career maturity between Black and White urban high school students. C. Brown et al. (1999) used the school form of the Career Decision-Making Self-Efficacy Scale to explore differences between White and racially and culturally diverse students from urban and suburban high schools.

Results

Results of the studies reviewed for Step 3 yielded effect sizes that ranged from .01 to .61. Miranda and Umhoefer (1998) recorded the largest effect size among a sample of Hispanic career counseling clients born outside the United States. Acculturation and use of the English language predicted scores on the Career Self-Efficacy Scale ($ES = .61$).

Medium effect sizes were found with respect to the influence of scores on the Racial Identity Attitudes Scale (RIAS: Helms, 1990) on the vocational identity and vocational hope of a sample of Black college students (Jackson & Neville, 1998). Interestingly, although Jackson and Neville presented results indicating that racial identity attitudes significantly impacted both vocational identity and hope for women in the study, the effect size calculated for men in the study demonstrated a medium effect size for the influence of racial identity attitude on vocational identity and hope for men as well ($ES = .35$). Weathers et al. (1994) reported a similar medium effect (.38) for the impact of Black racial identity on the career values of Black female college students. The findings provide evidence that racial identity does influence the career values of Black women. Lundberg et al. (1997) indicated that Hispanic and White high school students differed on both the Decision-Making ($ES = .34$) and World of Work ($ES = .41$) subscales of the Career Decision Inventory. Holder and Vaux (1998) found a medium effect size for the impact of race-related work stressors on the career satisfaction of a sample of Black professionals in predominately White work environments ($ES = .41$).

Park and Harrison (1995) revealed mostly small effect sizes for the influence of racial affiliation on career interests. Differences between Asian and White college students on Self-Directed Search subscale scores yielded effect sizes ranging from small to medium (.11 to .32). Powell and Luzzo (1998) revealed small effect sizes, ranging from .13 to .26, for racial comparisons on career maturity. Negligible to small effects were noted for racial comparisons of career exploration beliefs and attitudes, as well as career decision-making self-efficacy, among urban and suburban samples of high school students (i.e., ES ranged from .06 to .24; C. Brown et al., 1999).

Overall, effect sizes were small for interests- and values-related career factors (e.g., Park & Harrison, 1995; Powell & Luzzo, 1998), while racial identity and generational status had a larger effect on career identity (e.g., Jackson & Neville, 1998; Weathers et al., 1994).

Step 4: Setting Culturally Appropriate Counseling Process and Counseling Goals

Research reviewed in Step 4 of the Fouad and Bingham (1995) model examined culturally appropriate counseling processes and goals. The processes and goals were examined separately due to a clear delineation of these domains as separate lines of research.

Culturally Appropriate Process

While a number of studies have discussed culturally appropriate processes in career counseling, only three fit the empirical criteria used for inclusion in this review (Abreu, 2000; Coleman, 1998; Fuertes, 1999). The identified independent variables examined in the investigations included (1) gender, (2) education level, (3) participant race, (4) counselor race, (5) accent, (6) counseling competence, and (7) acculturation. The dependent variables included (1) cross-cultural counseling competencies, (2) counselor effectiveness, (3) emotional bond to the counselor, and

(4) willingness to work with the counselor. Each of the studies sampled college student populations.

Results

The effect sizes for this part of Step 4 ranged from .14 to .44. Abreu (2000) revealed significant main effects for counselor ethnicity, participant sex, and level of acculturation on the 17 Expectations about Counseling-Brief Form (EAC-B) scales. The main effect for ethnicity yielded an effect size of .26; for sex, an effect size of .26; and for the interaction between counselor ethnicity and sex, an effect size of .24. Abreu reported, "Students will have higher expectations for counseling as a process that addresses their problems within the immediacy of the counseling relationship when their counselor is ethnically similar rather than ethnically dissimilar" (p. 137). Coleman (1998) found significant differences in participants' evaluation of counselor's competence ($ES = .44$), as well as a significant between-group difference (i.e., undergraduate students versus graduate students) as indicated by the effect size of .23. Finally, there was a small effect size reflecting an interaction between the participants' training and their evaluation ($ES = .16$). Fuertes (1999) demonstrated that the counselor's accent is another factor to be considered in the career counseling process. Counselor accent (i.e., Hispanic counselors) influenced the participation level of individuals in the investigation (i.e., Asians and Blacks; $ES = .22$).

Participants rated counselors who were competent in their basic counseling skills (e.g., core conditions such as warmth and basic listening skills such as paraphrasing, reflection) and also able to demonstrate multicultural counseling competence (e.g., awareness, knowledge, and skills related to self and culture of client), as assessed by the Cross-Cultural Counseling Inventory (LaFromboise et al., 1991), more highly than counselors who were not competent in basic counseling skills and multicultural counseling skills (Coleman, 1998). In general, the findings underscore the role of cultural variables in the career counseling process. Specifically, the counselor's race, perceived counseling competence (as rated by participants/clients), and counselor accent influenced expectations of and participation level in the counseling process.

Goals

What about the role of culture in goal setting in career counseling? A total of 15 studies were reviewed for inclusion in the review; however, only three fit the criteria. The three studies that were included examined the relationship between race and expectations for counseling and race and perception of effectiveness of counseling (Kenney, 1994; Kunkel, 1990; Lee & Mixon, 1995).

Results

Lee and Mixon (1995) examined how Asian and White students differed in their perceptions of (1) helpfulness of counseling, (2) counselor characteristics, and (3) general reactions to the counseling experience. Results demonstrated that Asian students have different expectations from the counseling process when compared to White students, as evidenced by a large effect size (.46). Kenney (1994) and Kunkel (1990) examined expectations for counseling using the EAC-B. Kunkel compared Hispanic and White college students' expectations for counseling, revealing that acculturation level significantly affected expectations about the counseling process, as evidenced by a medium effect size (.31). Post hoc F comparisons revealed that only two EAC-B variables contributed to this effect: expectations for counselor Directiveness and Empathy. For each of these variables, White-oriented respondents expressed the lowest expectations, and Hispanic-oriented respondents reported the highest expectations. Kenney compared counseling expectations of Black, Asian, and White college students. With an effect size for race and EAC-B scales of .17, Kenney concluded that Black students had lower expectations of personal commitment to the counseling process than did White students and that Black students also had lower expectations for facilitative conditions than did Asian students. According to Kenney, Asian students expected more counselor expertise than did Black or White students. The results of the three studies (Kenney; Kunkel; Lee & Mixon) demonstrated how race affects students' expectations for counseling.

Step 5: Culturally Appropriate Intervention

There is a dearth of quantitative literature on culturally appropriate career interventions. Bowman (1993) has documented a lack of material on career intervention strategies for racially and culturally diverse people. The paucity of empirical research does not appear to be unique to career counseling; it appears to be an issue systemic to counseling. Of the 53 studies reviewed for possible inclusion in the review for Step 5 of the Fouad and Bingham (1995) model, none fit the three criteria required for inclusion (Fuertes, Costa, Mueller, & Hersh, this *Handbook,* Volume One).

Through the review of the literature related to Step 5, it was determined that interventions could be categorized as either programs (e.g., D'Andrea & Daniels, 1992; Rea-Poteat & Martin, 1991; Rodriguez & Blocher, 1988) or strategies/training (e.g., Hardy & Laszloffy, 1992; McCollum & Carroll, 1998; Murry & Mosidi, 1993; Pedersen, 1997; Swanson, 1993; Watts-Jones, 1997). Most of the studies that examined the role of culture (e.g., race) in career interventions were qualitative in nature; thus, they are not included in this review. Participant feedback forms often were used to evaluate the effectiveness of these interventions. In general, the qualitative studies concluded with recommendations for culturally sensitive programs or interventions. The recommendations advocated for group interventions, family involvement, role models, mentors, career education at earlier ages, and the evaluation of counselor's own biases and stereotypes.

CONCLUSIONS

The purpose of this research review was to explore the relationship that cultural variables have in each of the first five steps of the Fouad and Bingham (1995) CACCM. Overall, there appears to be some preliminary validation for the influence of cultural variables in the career counseling process. In Step 1 of the CACCM, culture was found to play a role in the establishment of a therapeutic relationship. Levels of acculturation and cultural mistrust influenced preference for racially similar counselors. There was some support (i.e., Atkinson & Lowe, 1995) for the use of culturally responsive content resulting in greater client willingness to return for counseling, satisfaction with counseling, and depth of self-disclosure. Limitations of the studies included in Step 1 were (1) a lack of investigation of within-group differences, (2) utilization of predominantly analogue studies, (3) restricted sample populations (e.g., students only), and (4) the absence of choices for other counselor characteristics (e.g., gender, social class, sexual orientation, education level) that might also be salient (or even more salient than race) in counselor preference.

The identification of career issues, Step 2, was divided into perceived career opportunities and barriers, and aspirations and expectations: career and education. Overall, limited differences were revealed between racial groups for perceived career barriers. Of the significant findings in the perceived opportunities and barriers section (total of 20), 14 translated into small effect sizes. Most of the studies in this review examined the number of career barriers perceived without consideration for the severity or intensity of those barriers. The studies reviewed in this chapter have begun to help us gain a better understanding of the relationship between race and ethnicity and career barriers, but further research needs to be conducted to fully capture and comprehend the relationship between race and career barriers. For aspirations and expectations: career and education, very little of the variance in aspirations was accounted for by a racial or ethnic category. In fact, the findings generally reflected gender as being more salient to aspirations and expectations. Some of the gender differences in the studies reviewed might reflect an inherent expectation of barriers in workplace and educational settings. The findings also supported the notion that women perceive a challenge to the balance of home life and pursuit of a career, especially for those considering male-dominated occupations (Murrell, Frieze, & Frost, 1991).

The results of the nine studies reviewed in the assessment of effects of cultural variables, Step 3, generally provided some evidence that for the most part, culture has a small to medium effect on many career issues, and in some cases has a large impact. In particular, cultural variables were found to impact career self-efficacy and career values. The small to medium effect sizes reported provide initial support for the importance of cultural assessment in vocational counseling. Attending to the cultural influences of career issues of clients will facilitate more culturally competent conceptualization of clients and their respective needs.

Step 4 of CACCM, setting culturally appropriate counseling process and counseling goals, was divided into two sections: culturally appropriate process and culturally appropriate counseling goals. The first section had only three studies that fit the criteria. In general, it appears that people from racial and ethnic groups perceive counselors as having a higher degree of overall competence as a counselor. Culture (i.e., race and ethnicity) influenced the expectations held about the counselor and the counseling process. Individuals from racial and ethnic backgrounds who demonstrated a high degree of openness, tolerance, and acceptance of differences and similarities in self and others had a stronger anticipated alliance with the counselor. Overall, these findings demonstrate the importance of a culture-centered perspective for fostering effective counseling. In culture-centered practices, psychologists recognize that all individuals, including themselves, are influenced by different contexts, including the historical, ecological, sociopolitical, and disciplinary. "If culture is part of the environment, and all behavior is shaped by culture, then culture-centered counseling is responsive to all culturally learned patterns" (Pedersen, 1997, p. 256). A culture-centered focus suggests to the psychologist the consideration that behavior may be shaped by culture, the groups to which one belongs, and cultural stereotypes, including those about stigmatized group members (Gaertner & Dovidio, 2000; Major, Quinton, & McCoy, 2002; Markus & Kitayama, 1991; Steele, 1997).

In the second section of Step 4, only three studies fit the inclusion criteria. Overall, it appeared as though race influenced the expectations held about counseling, and those expectations varied according to ethnic group membership. Although the studies explored constructs relating to the process of counseling, none appeared to examine the specific goals of counseling and whether they differed by cultural groups.

In Step 5, culturally appropriate intervention, most of the studies were qualitative in nature and so were not included in this synthesis. Clearly, this is an area of much needed future research.

SUMMARY AND FUTURE DIRECTIONS

The findings revealed in this research review provide some preliminary evidence of the role that culture has on the career counseling process. However, the paucity of empirically grounded research precludes any firm conclusions. In some of the research reviewed, gender was more salient to career constructs than was race or ethnicity. Methodological concerns spanned the independent review: (1) within-group differences were often unexplored; (2) many of the studies were analogue; (3) sample populations were restricted (e.g., college or high school participant); (4) how information regarding race and/or ethnicity was gathered was not always reported; (5) level of acculturation or identity development indices were not always included; and (6) culture was operationalized in different ways and was not uniformly measured. These limitations affect the generalizability of the results to other populations (e.g., older adult populations).

Although the research clearly has a number of limitations, there are nonetheless a number of implications for the practice of career counseling:

1. The racial/ethnic similarity of client and counselor appears to be important for people of Color; the role of cultural competence has been revealed to be critical to people of Color as well. Counselors are strongly encouraged to be aware of themselves as cultural beings (i.e., actually having a culture to which one belongs and by which one is influenced), to be culturally centered, and to gain cultural knowledge of other cultural groups.

2. Counselors are strongly encouraged to understand clients' worldviews and the values and beliefs to which they ascribe before moving through the rest of the career counseling process. A client's values may affect the goals and processes of counseling.

3. Racial/ethnic clients do not have different career dreams and aspirations than White clients, but do have real barriers in accomplishing those dream and ones that tend to differ from White clients. Counselors are strongly encouraged to be aware of the effects of discrimination on their clients, the effects of being a member of a stigmatized group, and their respective implications on the career goals and aspirations of their clients.

4. Career counselors use a variety of assessment tools, and the research appears to suggest that they may use assessments to assess interests and values with racial/ethnic clients as they would White clients. Counselors are encouraged to note that relying on information from an interest inventory to make a career decision is typical of clients with an individualistic orientation. In other words, clients from a more collectivistically oriented culture may use the information from an interest inventory in conjunction with other factors in career choice, such as family obligations.

5. Counselors are encouraged to clarify expectations of counseling and be flexible to varying needs of clients. The client's worldview, cultural values, and culture-of-origin attitudes toward counseling all influence this process; therefore, it is critical that counselors operate in a culture-centered framework.

Future research needs to continue to focus on the effectiveness of career counseling for various populations and to answer the question Does the inclusion of a culture-centered focus make a difference in the effectiveness of career counseling? One of the most critical areas for further investigation is appropriate and effective career interventions. Future research needs to address some of the limitations mentioned earlier, as well as continue with replication to provide stronger evidence of these preliminary findings. The implications of researching the relationship that cultural variables have to career counseling are profound given the changing demographics of the United State. Thus, research related to cultural variables and the career counseling process will shape the training and practices of those in helping professions, as well as inform community-based education and outreach programming.

REFERENCES

Abreu, J. M. (2000). Counseling expectations among Mexican American college students: The role of counselor ethnicity. *Journal of Multicultural Counseling and Development, 28,* 130–142.

Abreu, J. M., & Gabarain, G. (2000). Social desirability and Mexican American counselor preferences: Statistical control for a potential confound. *Journal of Counseling Psychology, 47,* 165–176.

Arbona, C. (1996). Career theory and practice in a multicultural context. In M. L. Savickas & W. B. Walsh (Eds.), *Handbook of career counseling theory and practice* (pp. 45–54). Palo Alto, CA: Davies-Black.

Arbona, C., & Novy, D. M. (1991). Career aspirations and expectations of Black, Mexican American, and White students. *Career Development Quarterly, 39,* 231–239.

Atkinson, D., & Carskaddon, G. (1975). A prestigious introduction, psychological jargon, and perceived counselor credibility. *Journal of Counseling Psychology, 22,* 180–186.

Atkinson, D., Casas, A., & Abreu, J. (1992). Mexican American acculturation, counselor ethnicity and cultural sensitivity, and perceived counselor competence. *Journal of Counseling Psychology, 39,* 515–520.

Atkinson, D., & Lowe, S. (1995). The role of ethnicity, cultural knowledge, and conventional techniques in counseling and psychotherapy. In J. G. Ponterotto, J. M. Casas, L. A. Suzuki, & C. M. Alexander (Eds.), *Handbook of multicultural counseling* (pp. 387–414). Thousand Oaks, CA: Sage.

Atkinson, D., & Matsushita, Y. (1991). Japanese American acculturation, counseling style, counselor ethnicity and perceived counselor credibility. *Journal of Counseling Psychology, 38,* 473–478.

Bae, K., & Chung, C. (1997). Cultural values and work attitudes of Korean workers in comparison with those of the United States and Japan. *Work and Occupations, 24,* 80–96.

Bingham, R. P., Porché-Burke, L., James, S., Sue, D. W., & Vasquez, M. J. T. (2002). Introduction: A report on the National Multicultural Conference and Summit II. *Cultural Diversity and Ethnic Minority Psychology, 8,* 75–87.

Bingham, R. P., & Ward, C. M. (1994). Career counseling with ethnic minority women. In W. B. Walsh & S. Osipow (Eds.), *Career counseling with women* (pp. 165–195). Hillsdale, NJ: Erlbaum.

Bowman, S. L. (1993). Career intervention strategies for ethnic minorities. *Career Development Quarterly, 42,* 14–24.

Brown, C., Darden, E. E., Shelton, M. C., & DiPoto, M. C. (1999). Career exploration and self-efficacy of high school students: Are there urban/suburban differences? *Journal of Career Assessment, 7,* 227–237.

Brown, D. (2002). The role of work and cultural values in occupational choice, satisfaction, and success: A theoretical statement. *Journal of Counseling and Development, 80,* 48–56.

Brown, D., & Brooks, L. (1991). *Career counseling techniques.* Boston: Allyn & Bacon.

Carter, R. T., & Akinsulure-Smith, A. M. (1996). White racial identity and expectations about counseling. *Journal of Multicultural Counseling and Development, 24,* 218–228.

Carter, R. T., & Swanson, J. L. (1990). The validity of the Strong Interest Inventory with Black Americans: A review of the literature. *Journal of Vocational Behavior, 36,* 195–209.

Cheatham, H. (1990). Africentricity and career development of African Americans. *Career Development Quarterly, 38,* 334–346.

Chung, Y. B., & Harmon, L. W. (1999). Assessment of perceived occupational opportunity for Black Americans. *Journal of Career Assessment, 7*(1), 45–62.

Chung, Y. B., Loeb, J. W., & Gonzo, S. T. (1996). Factors predicting the educational and career aspirations of Black college students. *Journal of Career Development, 23,* 127–135.

Cohen, J. (1988). Set correlation and contingency tables. *Applied Psychological Measurement, 12,* 425–434.

Coleman, H. (1998). General and multicultural counseling competency: Apples and oranges? *Journal of Multicultural Counseling and Development, 26,* 147–155.

Coleman, H., Wampold, B., & Casali, S. (1995). Ethnic minorities' ratings of ethnically similar and European American counselors: A meta-analysis. *Journal of Counseling Psychology, 42,* 55–64.

Corrigan, J. D., & Schmidt, L. D. (1983). Development and validation of revisions in the counselor rating form. *Journal of Counseling Psychology, 30,* 64–75.

Cuellar, I., Harris, L. C., & Jasso, R. (1980). An acculturation scale for Mexican American normal and clinical populations. *Hispanic Journal of Behavioral Sciences, 2,* 199–217.

D'Andrea, M., & Daniels, J. (1992). A career development program for inner-city youth. *Career Development Quarterly, 40,* 272–280.

Evans, K. M., & Herr, E. L. (1994). The influence of racial identity and the perception of discrimination on the career aspirations of African American men and women. *Journal of Vocational Behavior, 44,* 173–184.

Fiske, A. P., Kitayama, S., Markus, H. R., & Nisbett, R. E. (1998). The cultural matrix of social psychology. In D. T. Gilbert & S. T. Fiske (Eds.), *The handbook of social psychology* (Vol. 2, 4th ed., pp. 915–981). New York: McGraw-Hill.

Fitzgerald, L. F., & Betz, N. E. (1994). Career development in cultural context: The role of gender, race, class, and sexual orientation. In M. L. Savickas & R. W. Lent (Eds.), *Convergence in career development theories* (pp. 103–118). Palo Alto, CA: Consulting Psychologists Press.

Fouad, N. A. (1993). Cross-cultural vocational assessment. *Career Development Quarterly, 10,* 4–14.

Fouad, N. A. (1995). Career behavior of Hispanics: Assessment and intervention. In F. T. L. Leong (Ed.), *Career development and vocational behavior of racial and ethnic minorities* (pp. 165–192). Mahwah, NJ: Erlbaum.

Fouad, N. A., & Arbona, C. (1994). Careers in a cultural context. *Career Development Quarterly, 43,* 96–104.

Fouad, N. A., & Bingham, R. (1995). Career counseling with racial/ethnic minorities. In W. B. Walsh & S. H. Osipow (Eds.), *Handbook of vocational psychology* (2nd ed., pp. 331–366). New York: Erlbaum.

Fouad, N. A., & Brown, M. T. (2000). Role of race and social class in development: Implications for counseling psychology. In S. D. Brown & R. W. Lent (Eds.), *Handbook of counseling psychology* (3rd ed., pp. 279–408). New York: Wiley.

Fouad, N. A., & Byars, A. M. (2002). *Work: Cultural perspectives on career choices and decision-making.* Manuscript submitted for publication.

Fouad, N. A., & Byars, A. M. (in press). Work: Cultural perspectives on career choices and decision-making. In R. T. Carter (Ed.), *Handbook of racial-cultural psychology and counseling: Theory and research* (Vol. 1, pp. 232–255). Hoboken, NJ: Wiley.

Fuertes, J. N. (1999). Asian Americans and African Americans initial perceptions of Hispanic counselors. *Journal of Multicultural Counseling and Development, 27*(3), 122–132.

Fuertes, J. N., Costa, C. I., Mueller, L. N., & Hersh, M. (in press). Psychotherapy process and outcome from a racial-ethnic perspective. In R. T. Carter (Ed.), *Handbook of racial-cultural psychology and counseling: Theory and research* (Vol. 1, pp. 256–276). Hoboken, NJ: Wiley.

Gaertner, S. L., & Dovidio, J. F. (2000). *Reducing intergroup bias: The common ingroup identity model.* Philadelphia: Psychology Press.

Gelso, C. J., & Carter, J. A. (1994). Components of the psychotherapy relationship: Their interaction and unfolding during treatment. *Journal of Counseling Psychology, 41,* 296–306.

Gim, R., Atkinson, D., & Kim, S. (1991). Asian American acculturation, counselor ethnicity and cultural sensitivity, and ratings of counselors. *Journal of Counseling Psychology, 38,* 57–62.

Gysbers, N. C., & Moore, E. J. (1987). *Career counseling: Skills and techniques for practitioners.* Englewood Cliffs, NJ: Prentice-Hall.

Hackett, G., & Byars, A. M. (1996). Social cognitive theory and the career development of African American women. *Career Development Quarterly, 44,* 332–340.

Hardy, K. V., & Laszloffy, T. A. (1992). Training racially sensitive family therapists: Context, content, and contact. *Families in Society, 73,* 364–370.

Helms, J. E. (Ed.). (1990). *Black and White racial identity: Theory, research, and practice.* Westport, CT: Greenwood Press.

Helms, J. E., & Carter, R. T. (1991). Relationships of White and Black racial identity attitudes and demographic similarity to counselor preferences. *Journal of Counseling Psychology, 38,* 446–457.

Helms, J. E., & Piper, R. E. (1994). Implications of racial identity theory for vocational psychology. *Journal of Vocational Behavior, 44,* 124–138.

Hess, R., & Street, E. (1991). The effect of acculturation on the relationship of counselor ethnicity and client ratings. *Journal of Counseling Psychology, 38,* 71–75.

Holder, J. C., & Vaux, A. (1998). African American professionals: Coping with occupational stress in predominantly White work environments. *Journal of Vocational Behavior, 53,* 315–333.

Horvath, A. O., & Symonds, B. D. (1991). Relation between working alliance and outcome in psychotherapy: A meta-analysis. *Journal of Counseling Psychology, 38,* 139–149.

Ivey, A. E., Ivey, M. B., & Simek-Morgan, L. (1993). *Counseling and psychotherapy: A multicultural perspective.* Boston: Allyn & Bacon.

Ivey, A. E., D'Andra, M., Ivey, M. B., & Simek-Morgan, L. (2002). *Theories of counseling and psychotherapy: A multicultural perspective* (5th ed.). Boston: Allyn & Bacon.

Jackson, C. C., & Neville, H. A. (1998). Influence of racial identity attitudes on African American college students' vocational identity and hope. *Journal of Vocational Behavior, 53,* 97–113.

Kenney, G. E. (1994). Multicultural investigation of counseling expectations and preferences. *Journal of College Student Psychotherapy, 9,* 21–39.

Kunkel, M. A. (1990). Expectations about counseling in relation to acculturation in Mexican-American and Anglo-American student samples. *Journal of Counseling Psychology, 37,* 286–292.

LaFromboise, T., Coleman, H., & Hernandez, A. (1991). Development and factor structure of the cross-cultural counseling inventory revised. *Professional Psychology: Research and Practice, 22,* 380–388.

Lauver, P. J., & Jones, R. M. (1991). Factors associated with perceived career options in American Indian, White, and Hispanic rural high school students. *Journal of Counseling Psychology, 38*(2), 159–166.

Lee, W. M. L., & Mixon, R. J. (1995). Asian and Caucasian client perceptions of the effectiveness of counseling. *Journal of Multicultural Counseling and Development, 23,* 48–56.

Leong, F. T. L. (1985). Career development of Asian Americans. *Journal of College Student Personnel, 26,* 539–546.

Leong, F. T. L. (1993). The career counseling process with racial-ethnic minorities: The case of Asian Americans. *Career Development Quarterly, 42,* 26–40.

Leong, F. T. L., & Brown, M. T. (1995). Theoretical issues in cross-cultural career development: Cultural validity and cultural specificity. In W. B. Walsh & S. H. Osipow (Eds.), *Handbook of vocational psychology* (2nd ed., pp. 143–180). Hillsdale, NJ: Erlbaum.

Leong, F. T. L., & Hartung, P. J. (1997). Career assessment with culturally-different clients: Proposing an integrative-sequential conceptual framework for cross-cultural career counseling research and practice. *Journal of Career Assessment, 5,* 183–202.

Leong, F. T. L., & Serafica, F. C. (1995). Career development of Asian Americans: A research area in need of a good theory. In F. T. L. Leong (Ed.), *Career development and vocational behavior of racial and ethnic minorities* (pp. 67–102). Hillsdale, NJ: Erlbaum.

Leung, S. A. (1995). Career development and counseling: A multicultural perspective. In J. G. Ponterotto, J. M. Casas, L. A. Suzuki, & C. M. Alexander (Eds.), *Handbook of multicultural counseling* (pp. 549–566). Thousand Oaks, CA: Sage.

Leung, S. A., Conoley, C. W., & Scheel, M. J. (1994). The career and educational aspirations of gifted high school students: A retrospective study. *Journal of Counseling and Development, 72,* 298–303.

Leung, S. A., Ivey, D., & Suzuki, L. (1994). Factors affecting the career aspirations of Asian Americans. *Journal of Counseling and Development, 72,* 404–410.

Lundberg, D. J., Osborne, W. L., & Miner, C. (1997). Career maturity and personality preferences of Mexican-American and Anglo-American adolescents. *Journal of Career Development, 23,* 203–213.

Luzzo, D. A. (1993). Ethnic differences in college students' perceptions of barriers to career development. *Journal of Multicultural Counseling and Development, 21,* 227–236.

Major, B., Quinton, W. J., & McCoy, S. K. (2002). Antecedents and consequences of attributions to discrimination: Theoretical and empirical advances. In M. P. Zanna (Ed.), *Advances in experimental social psychology* (Vol. 34, pp. 252–330). New York: Academic Press.

Markus, H. R., & Kitayama, S. (1991). Culture and the self: Implications for cognition, emotion, and motivation. *Psychological Review, 98,* 224–253.

McCollum, V., & Carroll, J. (1998). Career development issues and strategies for counseling African Americans. *Journal of Career Development, 2,* 41–52.

McWhirter, E. H. (1997). Perceived barriers to education and career: Ethnic and gender differences. *Journal of Vocational Behavior, 50,* 124–140.

McWhirter, E. H., Hackett, G., & Bandalos, D. L. (1998). A causal model of the educational plans and career expectations of Mexican American high school girls. *Journal of Counseling Psychology, 45*(2), 166–181.

Miranda, A. O., & Umhoefer, D. L. (1998). Acculturation, language use, and demographic variables as predictors of the career self-efficacy of Latino career counseling clients. *Journal of Multicultural Counseling and Development, 26,* 39–51.

Mullen, B. (1989). *Advanced basic meta-analysis.* Hillsdale, NJ: Erlbaum.

Murrell, A. J., Frieze, I. H., & Frost, J. L. (1991). Aspiring to careers in male- and female-dominated professions: A study of Black and White college women. *Psychology of Women Quarterly, 15,* 103–126.

Murry, E., & Mosidi, R. (1993). Career development counseling for African Americans: An appraisal of the obstacles and intervention strategies. *Journal of Negro Education, 62,* 441–447.

Neville, H. A., Gysbers, N. C., Heppner, M. J., & Johnston, J. (2003). Empowering life choices: Career counseling in cultural contexts. In N. C. Gysbers, M. J. Heppner, & J. Johnston (Eds.), *Career counseling: Process, issues, and techniques* (2nd ed., pp. 50–76). Boston: Allyn & Bacon.

Park, S. E., & Harrison, A. A. (1995). Career-related interests and values, perceived control, and acculturation of Asian-American and Caucasian-American college students. *Journal of Applied Social Psychology, 25,* 1184–1203.

Pedersen, P. B. (1997). *Culture-centered counseling interventions: Striving for accuracy.* Thousand Oaks, CA: Sage.

Pomales, J., & Williams, V. (1989). Effects of level of acculturation and counseling style on Hispanic students' perceptions of counselor. *Journal of Counseling Psychology, 36,* 79–83.

Ponce, F., & Atkinson, D. (1989). Mexican American acculturation, counselor ethnicity, counseling style, and perceived counselor credibility. *Journal of Counseling Psychology, 36,* 203–208.

Ponterotto, J., Alexander, C., & Hinkston, J. (1988). Afro American preferences for counselor characteristics: A replication and extension. *Journal of Counseling Psychology, 35,* 175–182.

Powell, D. F., & Luzzo, D. A. (1998). Evaluating factors associated with the career maturity of high school students. *Career Development Quarterly, 47,* 145–158.

Price, B., & McNeill, B. (1992). Cultural commitment and attitudes toward seeking counseling services in American Indian college students. *Professional Psychology: Research and Practice, 23,* 376–381.

Ramos-Sanchez, L., Atkinson, D., & Fraga, E. (1999). Mexican Americans' bilingual ability, counselor bilingualism cues, counselor ethnicity, and perceived counselor credibility. *Journal of Counseling Psychology, 46,* 125–131.

Rea-Poteat, M. B., & Martin, P. F. (1991). Taking your place: A summer program to encourage nontraditional career choices for adolescent girls. *Career Development Quarterly, 40,* 182–188.

Rodriguez, M., & Blocher, D. (1988). A comparison of two approaches to enhancing career maturity in Puerto Rican college women. *Journal of Counseling Psychology, 35,* 275–280.

Rosnow, R. L., & Rosenthal, R. (1996). Computing contrasts, effect sizes, and counternulls on other people's published data: General procedures for research consumers. *Psychological Methods, 1,* 331–340.

Ruelas, S., Atkinson, D., & Ramos-Sanchez, L. (1998). Counselor helping model, participant ethnicity and acculturation level and perceived counselor credibility. *Journal of Counseling Psychology, 45,* 98–103.

Slaney, R. B. (1980). An investigation of racial differences on vocational variables among college women. *Journal of Vocational Behavior, 16,* 197–207.

Slaney, R. B., & Brown, M. T. (1983). Effects of race and socioeconomic status on career choice variables among college men. *Journal of Vocational Behavior, 23,* 257–269.

Spokane, A. R. (1991). *Career interventions.* Englewood Cliffs, NJ: Prentice-Hall.

Steele, C. M. (1997). A threat in the air: How stereotypes shape intellectual identity and performance. *American Psychologist, 52,* 613–620.

Sue, D. W., Arredondo, P., & McDavis, R. J. (1992). Multicultural competencies and standards: A call to the profession. *Journal of Multicultural Counseling and Development, 2,* 64–88.

Sue, D. W., Bingham, R. P., Porché-Burke, L., & Vasquez, M. (1999). The diversification of psychology: A multicultural revolution. *American Psychologist, 54,* 1061–1069.

Sue, D. W., & Sue, D. (2003). *Counseling the culturally diverse: Theory and practice* (4th ed.). Hoboken, NJ: Wiley.

Swanson, J. L. (1993). Integrating a multicultural perspective into training for career counseling: Programmatic and individual interventions. *Career Development Quarterly, 42,* 41–49.

Swanson, J. L., & Fouad, N. A. (1999). *Career theory and practice: Learning through cases.* Thousand Oaks, CA: Sage.

Swanson, J. L., & Gore, P. A. (2000). Advances in vocational psychology theory and research. In S. D. Brown & R. W. Lent (Eds.), *Handbook of counseling psychology* (3rd ed., pp. 233–269). New York: Wiley.

Terrell, F., & Terrell, S. (1981). An inventory to measure cultural mistrust among Blacks. *Western Journal of Black Studies, 5,* 180–185.

Thompson, B. (2002). "Statistical," "practical," and "clinical": How many kinds of significance do counselors need to consider? *Journal of Counseling and Development, 80,* 64–71.

Thompson, C., Worthington, R., & Atkinson, D. (1994). Counselor content orientation, counselor race, and Black women's cultural mistrust and self-disclosures. *Journal of Counseling Psychology, 41,* 155–161.

Wade, P., & Bernstein, B. (1991). Culture sensitivity training and counselor's race effects on Black female clients' perceptions and attrition. *Journal of Counseling Psychology, 38,* 9–15.

Ward, C. M., & Bingham, R. P. (1993). Career assessment of ethnic minority women. *Journal of Career Assessment, 1,* 246–257.

Watkins, C., & Terrell, F. (1988). Mistrust level and its effects on counseling expectations in Black client-White counselor relationships. *Journal of Counseling Psychology, 35,* 194–197.

Watts-Jones, D. (1997). Toward an African American genogram. *Family Process, 36,* 375–383.

Weathers, P. L., Thompson, C. E., Robert, S., & Rodriguez, J. (1994). Black college women's career issues: A preliminary investigation. *Journal of Multicultural Counseling and Development, 22,* 96–105.

CHAPTER 17

Diagnosis in Racial-Cultural Practice

Tamara R. Buckley and Deidre Cheryl Franklin-Jackson

Within the past two decades, the United States has experienced a growing number of visible racial and ethnic group members (Ponterotto & Austin, this *Handbook,* this volume). With the increasing presence of immigrants, African Americans, Asian Americans, Latino, and Native Americans, psychological assessment and clinical diagnosis must address complexities that arise with diversity and reject the American assumption that the "melting pot" of assimilation will level out major cultural differences or make them peripheral to individuals' everyday lives (Weinfeld, 1994). Culture and race have a powerful impact on the diagnosis, formulation, treatment, and prognosis of medical and psychiatric illness (Alarcon, Westermeyer, Foulks, & Ruiz, 1999), yet the clinical interactions of race, culture, and psychopathology have not been examined systematically for almost two decades (Beiser, 1985; Favazza & Oman, 1978). To increase accurate assessment and diagnosis, diagnostic systems need to be continuously revised, and racial and cultural factors need to be considered in the clinical diagnostic process. In this chapter, we explore how the sociocultural, political, and historical environment impact psychiatric diagnosis; we also offer suggestions for addressing these factors in assessment and diagnostic practices.

RACIAL DISPARITIES IN PSYCHIATRIC PREVALENCE RATES

The prevalence rates for any type of mental illness indicate that 32% of all American adults have experienced a psychiatric disorder at some time in their lives, with Whites having the lowest rates (32%), followed by Hispanics (33%), and Blacks (38%) (Epidemiological Catchment Area Study [ECA]; Robins & Regier, 1991). The prevalence rates for schizophrenia reveal a similar picture. Historical prevalence rates for schizophrenia frequently indicate higher rates for Blacks in comparison to Whites (Jaco, 1960; Malzberg, 1959; Simon, Fleiss, Gurland, Stiller, & Sharpe, 1973; Vitols, Walters, & Keeler, 1963). Other studies indicate the same pattern (e.g., Strakowski et al., 1995). However, in a large epidemiological study, lifetime prevalence rates of schizophrenia (e.g., proportion of the sample who ever experienced this disorder) among Black, Hispanic, and White people were not statistically different after controlling for socioeconomic status, age, gender, and marital status (Kessler et al., 1994; Robins & Regier, 1991).

Prevalence rules for affective disorders are more variable than for schizophrenia. Estimates of affective disorders indicate that Blacks have a significantly lower lifetime prevalence rate of depression in comparison with Whites (Kessler et al., 1994). Lifetime prevalence rates of depression among Chinese Americans, however, were higher than for Whites (Takeuchi et al., 1998). Among Hispanics, prevalence rates of affective disorder were mixed, with some studies indicating higher rates for Hispanics in comparison to Whites (Robins & Regier, 1991) and other studies indicating lower rates of affective disorders in Hispanics compared to Whites (Kessler et al., 1994). Finally, the ECA study reported almost no differences in Major Depressive Disorder among Blacks, Hispanics, and Whites after controlling for demographic characteristics (Robins & Regier, 1991).

Taken together, these studies indicate some inconsistent findings; yet among most studies, people of Color are found to have higher rates of psychiatric diagnoses and more severe psychiatric conditions than Whites. Although epidemiological and comparative studies are important for generating data about the number of cases of a given disease for racial and ethnic groups (Draguns, 2000), these studies rarely provide explanations for racial disparities in psychiatric prevalence rates.

FOUNDATIONS OF PSYCHIATRY AND PSYCHOLOGY

Since its inception, psychology has attempted to distinguish itself from philosophy, religion, and other disciplines that explore the human psyche by focusing on measurement and experimentation (Carter & Pieterse, this *Handbook,* Volume One; Schultz & Schultz, 1996). By holding to the ideals of scientific experimentation and adopting parameters used in medicine, psychology has maintained its connection to medicine and the medical model, which is concerned with causes and effects. When using a medical model, people are often regarded objectively as patients or subjects, and clinical practice aims to distill physical malfunction involved in the illness into a disease classification or diagnosis. Psychology and psychiatry have adopted similar practices. Most practitioners aim to classify patients objectively, according to disease type. Yet psychiatric illnesses and assessments are far from objective. In psychology and psychiatry, the malfunction involved in illness is generally unknown at initial assessment. Rather, the etiology of dysfunction often becomes clear following multiple contacts between clinician and patient (Alarcon, 1995; Jones & Gray, 1986; Wallace, this *Handbook,* this volume). Psychological diagnosis requires a complex frame of reference, knowledge about the etiology of mental illness and disease in a variety of racial and cultural groups, mastery of assessment techniques and strategies, and objectivity in the definition of pathology, symptoms, and treatments (Alarcon, 1995):

> Deductions made from an examination of the mental state cannot be viewed as being equivalent to a medical description of the state of a bodily organ since these are described in terms that have objective validity. What a doctor finds in a mental status examination is as much a reflection of the observer as the patient, which is the result of an interaction rather than a one-sided observation. (p. 117)

Yet, in an attempt to fit clinical symptoms into rigidly specified diagnostic criteria (Branch, this *Handbook,* this volume; Kleinman, 1988), the subjectivity and complexity of human suffering is often minimized.

Moreover, diagnostic practices in psychology and psychiatry were developed using a Western framework and are based on a medical model of illness that was developed in Europe over the past 300 years (Fernando, 2001). Although Western medical science is considered by some to be objective, it has its own assumptions and cultural biases deeply rooted in cultural traditions; consequently, Western science is, at best, limited and restrictive in terms of recognizing psychopathology beyond Western borders (Mezzich, Kleinman, Fabrega, & Parron, 1996). The ideologies represented in many personality theories and in conceptualizations of illness also represent a Western worldview (Fernando, 2001).

Cross-Cultural Considerations in Psychiatry and Psychology

More recently, scholars have described psychiatric assessment as the most challenging issue in the cross-cultural study of psychopathology (e.g., Tsai, Ying, & Lee, 2000) and delineated how race and culture influence mental health assessment, diagnosis, and treatment (Fernando, 2001; Guarnaccia, Guevara-Ramos, Gonzales, Canino, & Bird, 1992; Rogler, 1993). For example, Rogler suggests that culture suffuses multiple levels of the assessment and diagnostic process, not just a single phase. The assessment of psychiatrically relevant symptoms is the first level where culture influences what is considered to be psychopathology and the subsequent diagnosis (Branch, this *Handbook,* this volume; Rogler, 1993). Judgment about whether a symptom qualifies as psychotic involves implicit cultural assumptions (Guarnaccia et al., 1992) because culture shapes the phenomenology of symptoms themselves and their content, meaning, and expression (Mezzich, Otero, & Lee, in press). The psychiatric classification systems in the United Sates and in the world are "local cultural phenomena which express borrowed and created elements" (Alarcon et al., 1999, p. 459). Culture is relevant to how an individual experiences distress (Kleinman, 1977; Ota Wang, this *Handbook,* this volume) and his or her willingness to disclose symptoms (Dohrenwend, 1966; D. Sue & Torino, this *Handbook,* this volume) and to the evaluation of symptom severity in diagnostic assessment (Rogler, 1993; Suzuki, Kugler, & Aguiar, this *Handbook,* this volume). For example, if an Asian patient is aware that his culture's marital customs are devalued in Western society, he may disclose very little to a White clinician about himself and his personal life. The client's limited disclosure may be interpreted by the clinician as secretive, devious, or paranoid. In reality, the client's behavior may be a healthy response to a situation in which he feels a need to protect himself. His limited disclosure may also reflect a cultural tradition of keeping personal matters within the family. Multicultural psychologists suggest that thoughts and behaviors considered inappropriate and pathological in one cultural context may be viewed positively by individuals from other cultural groups and backgrounds (Sue & Sue, 1999, 2003).

The second level of cultural influence concerns how symptoms are configured into disorders (Rogler, 1993). Culture is manifested through diagnostic rationales and decisions to group symptoms into patterns. For example, Anorexia Nervosa includes a group of culture-bound symptoms that can be grouped into a syndrome primarily seen in Western cultures (Mezzich et al., in press). Culture also configures symptoms by framing how behavior is expressed (Egeland, Hostettler, & Eshleman, 1983; Wallace, this *Handbook*, this volume), and it coalesces symptoms into culture-bound syndromes, such as the *amok*, originally reported in Malaysia; the *kora*, reported in southeast Asia; and *ataques de nervios* principally reported among Latinos from the Caribbean. Each of these syndromes includes characteristics unique to a specific culture, ethnic group, or region (Huges, Simons, & Wintrob, 1992). For example, ataque de nervios (translated as "an attack of nerves") is an anxiety disorder characterized by psychophysiological reactions, such as trembling, shouting, and aggression, that is prevalent among Hispanics and Mexican Americans (Canino & Canino, 1993). Because this configuration and expression of symptoms is rarely seen among other ethnic groups, the syndrome is not classified as an anxiety disorder in the standard multiaxial system of the *Diagnostic and Statistical Manual of Mental Disorders IV-TR* (*DSM-IV-TR;* American Psychiatric Association, 2000). Instead, culture-bound syndromes such as ataque de nervios are located in the Appendix of the *DSM-IV-TR*. The methods used to combine symptoms into disorders are culturally variable and must therefore be modified according to the cultural setting (Canino, Bird, & Shrout, 1987).

The third level of cultural influence in psychiatric assessment involves the interpersonal situation or the diagnostic interview (Branch, this *Handbook*, this volume; Rogler, 1993). Race and culture infuse the diagnostic interview because the clinical encounter is often intercultural and requires an understanding of interracial/cultural dynamics (Mezzich et al., in press). Racial and cultural factors can have a profound impact on diagnostic outcome, particularly when the client and the diagnostician are not culturally similar and when the client is not familiar with the language used by the clinician (Kirmayer, Groleau, Guzder, Blake, & Jarvis, 2003). Therapeutic situations that increase racial and cultural distance between clinician and client increase diagnostic error in assessing the type and severity of the illness (Rogler, 1989). Language difficulties are a concrete example of a cultural factor that can lead to cultural misunderstanding, incomplete assessment, inaccurate diagnosis, inadequate or inappropriate treatment, or a failed therapeutic alliance. Kirmayer and colleagues (2003) found frequent misdiagnoses and poor treatment by clinicians when cultural symptoms and language difficulties were not considered in the assessment process (Faubic & Locke, this *Handbook*, this volume).

Conducting a psychiatric assessment with a client who has a different racial or cultural background from the clinician is complicated because mental health is not isolated from other aspects of personality (Carter, 1995, this *Handbook*, this volume). Mental health is not only about biology and psychology but also encompasses race, culture, ethnicity, and social organization. To accurately assess and treat the client, a clinician should understand how race and culture can impact an individual on multiple levels. Without this recognition that race and culture impact behaviors, symptoms, and wellness, inaccurate assessment and diagnosis is frequent because of racial and cultural bias. Although clinicians may be expert in their own culture and language, most clinicians do not consider how their own racial and cultural background can influence interactions or reactions between themselves and their clients (Thompson, this *Handbook*, this volume).

In addition, assessment systems are embedded within a particular cultural-historical and political context that shapes and conditions the thought process and values of both clinician and client. With the history of racial and ethnic prejudice, racism, and stereotypes in the United States, clinicians may classify behavior that is different from their own as inappropriate and distorted. These prejudices and stereotypes can impact the recognition and evaluation of symptoms and psychopathology when making diagnostic decisions. For example, a Black person's anger and distrust might be perceived as paranoid thinking (Fernando, 2001). In addition, because television images often portray Blacks as dangerous, inferior, and violent, a clinician might erroneously project these attributes onto his Black client.

DIAGNOSTIC AND STATISTICAL MANUAL OF MENTAL DISORDERS

There are also concerns about the universality of the *Diagnostic and Statistical Manual of Mental Disorders* (*DSM*), which is the primary mental health classification system used for psychiatric diagnosis in the United States. Tsai and colleagues (2000) state that the *DSM-IV-TR* is fraught with shortcomings, even when applied in Western settings. Additional challenges arise when using the *DSM* with non-Western cultural and ethnic groups because of its reliance on clinical diagnosis, which may obscure cultural differences or similarities in specific symptoms. Multicultural psychologists and psychiatrists have debated the cultural validity of the *DSM* (Rogler, 1996), arguing that culture should be systematically addressed in the manual because culture is rooted in the meaning of mental disorder (Wakefield, 1992) and in the diagnostic process (Rogler, 1993). The cultural validity of the *DSM* is particularly important because practitioners often refer to it to construct meaning about psychological concerns and personality styles presented by their clients, without considering the relative nature of the diagnostic system and the cultural biases in the classification system (D'Andrea, 1999). Culture informs the overall conceptualization of a diagnostic system, which is a product of its times and circumstances (Mezzich et al., 1999). Therefore, psychiatric classification systems require continuous revisions because they are embedded in society and culture (Brody, 1990) and need to change with advances in scientific knowledge (Brody, 1990; Frances, Pincus, & Widiger, 1990). As a discipline, psychiatry has failed to acknowledge the social milieu or the biases in the assessment process that are endemic in the culture in which psychiatry has grown (Fernando, 2001). Indeed, psychiatry has only recently acknowledged cultural influences in diagnosis by developing cultural formulations to certain diagnoses.

Mezzich and colleagues (1999) argue that the entire multiaxial system should be examined from the perspective of racial and cultural influences. For example, in the classification of mood disorders on Axis I, the clinical expression of symptoms is a function of culture. In the classification of personality disorders on Axis II, disclaimers can be applied to practically every personality disorder when described in different cultural segments of the population. On Axis III, the classification of medical disease may even have cultural variations in the presentation of physical symptoms. The psychosocial stressors captured in Axis IV reflect culturally determined circumstances of individuals and groups. Finally, the overall functioning of the individual reported on Axis V reflects the individual's reporting style and assessment of symptoms, which is influenced, to a great extent, by the cultural context of events occurring in that person's life (Mezzich et al., 1999).

Resistance to examining cultural influences in diagnoses may be, in part, because of the conflict between the perceived objectivity of a disease model and the perceived subjectivity of a racially and culturally inclusive model (Alarcon, 1995; Branch, this *Handbook,* this volume; D. Sue & Torino, this *Handbook,* this volume; Thompson, this *Handbook,* this volume). Racial and cultural considerations in psychiatric assessment are often seen as competing with objectivity and the existing biomedical system, rather than adding to scientific rigor and accuracy (Rogler, 1996). Instead, practitioners rely on the strict use of psychodynamic theories and the *DSM-IV-TR* to construct meaning from what they consider to be appropriate, inappropriate, and pathological thoughts and behavior. Following these practices, clinicians often magnify clients' problems and minimize their personal strengths (Ivey & Ivey, 1998). To ameliorate the tendency toward psychopathology, Ivey and Ivey created a developmental framework for thinking about personality disorders that links psychodynamic concepts with a positive and culturally respectful assessment of client strengths. Their framework is unique because it recognizes the possible strengths as well as weaknesses that might be expected when working with clients who have a personality disorder such as Avoidant. Ivey and Ivey also recommend a variety of treatment approaches that draw on varying theoretical approaches, including multicultural, cognitive-behavioral, psychodynamic, developmental, and existential-humanistic.

THEORETICAL AND CONCEPTUAL CONSIDERATIONS FOR CROSS-CULTURAL ASSESSMENT AND DIAGNOSIS

The transcultural psychiatry literature has begun to delineate how cultural factors influence the assessment process, however, this literature does not include theoretical considerations to systematize approaches for addressing racial and cultural factors in assessment, diagnosis, and treatment. Several concepts and theories in counseling psychology may provide a framework for better understanding the complexity of the clinical interaction, particularly when the client and the mental health practitioner have different worldviews arising from differences in race and culture, education, socioeconomic status, or religious background (Alvarez & Piper, this *Handbook,* this volume).

Racial identity theory is one such theory that addresses the complexity of interactions. In the early 1970s, scholars in counseling psychology began developing theories of Black racial identity to capture the varied psychological experiences of Black people in the United States. Black racial identity theory highlighted the notion that there is within-racial-group variability regarding Black people's attitudes and beliefs about their own and other racial groups (Cross, 1971; Parham & Helms, 1981). Several years later, scholars developed a theory of White racial identity (Helms, 1990) and of minority identity development (Atkinson, Morten, & Sue, 1979; Constantine, Watt, Gainor, & Warren, this *Handbook,* Volume One); Constantine & Wilton, this *Handbook,* Volume One. For illustrative purposes, we briefly review

Black racial identity theory, rather than review racial identity theories for other racial groups. Briefly, Helms's (1990) developmental model of Black racial identity includes four racial identity statuses that are linked to ego development. Helms's model describes how Blacks can move from having self-degrading racial identity attitudes to self-enhancing racial identity attitudes in which they are secure about their racial identity and appreciate people from other racial and cultural backgrounds.

Racial identity theory has important implications for interpersonal interactions, such as the clinical interaction between clinician and patient. Carter's (1995) racially inclusive model examines how racial identity impacts interactions, which subsequently influences the process and outcome of therapeutic encounters, whether they are one-time clinical evaluations or longer-term counseling relationships. For example, in a clinical interview between patient and client, each person's racial identity will impact the interaction. It is important, therefore, for clinicians to be aware that individuals from all racial groups may identify with their group in a variety of ways, from positive to negative. The client's racial attitudes, beliefs, thoughts, and feelings will also impact his or her description of and willingness to disclose symptoms, as well as his or her comfort with the clinician. Simultaneously, the clinician's racial attitudes, beliefs, thoughts, and feelings will also influence the clinical interaction, irrespective of the racial group to which he or she belongs. For example, a Black clinician that has a less evolved Black racial identity may be very dissimilar from his Black client who has an evolved Black racial identity (Reynolds, this *Handbook,* this volume).

In addition to racial influences, culture, particularly level of acculturation, is an important variable in clinical interactions and assessment (Kohatsu, this *Handbook,* Volume One). Individuals in cultural groups vary in the extent to which they endorse the values, norms, and beliefs of their cultural group, although there may be some cultural similarities that shape the experience and expression of distress (Tsai et al., 2000). Understanding an individual's cultural orientation or level of acculturation can help a clinician assess how that individual's expressions of distress are influenced by culture, which may limit misdiagnosis (Dana, 1998). For instance, studies highlight differences in psychiatric prevalence rates among U.S.-born and non-U.S.-born ethnic minorities. In a study of Mexican American immigrants and Mexican-born Americans, there was a negative relationship between length of time in the United States and level of Unipolar Depression. Rates of Unipolar Depression were lowest for recent immigrants, higher for those who had been in the United States for 13 years or more, and highest for those born in the United States (Vega, Kolody, Aguilar-Gaxiola, & Alderete, 1998). Level of acculturation or length of stay in the United States can also affect language proficiency, which is a frequent barrier in psychiatric assessment and diagnosis (Tsai et al., 2000). According to Tsai and colleagues, language equivalence—the extent to which a word, concept, or norm can be considered relevant and applicable to the group that is being assessed—is the primary challenge when conducting psychiatric assessments with people who have a language different from that of the interviewer (Tsai et al., 2000). Conceptual equivalence—the extent to which the construct assumes the same meaning across cultures—is another important consideration in cross-cultural assessment. For example, in the

United States, "dependency" is considered a negative attribute, whereas in Japan it is considered the cultural ideal for interpersonal relationships (Doi, 1973; Yeh & Hunter, this *Handbook,* Volume One).

SUGGESTIONS FOR INCREASING THE ACCURACY OF ASSESSMENT AND DIAGNOSIS

Having an awareness and understanding of distinctions within and between racial and ethnic groups and of language barriers is critical for increasing the accuracy of assessment and diagnosis. With this understanding, scholars will be better equipped to address racial and ethnic disparities in psychiatric diagnostic prevalence rates. There is also a need to systematically integrate existing theories, concepts, and research from psychology into training programs. This integration would help trainees better understand how individual differences impact assessment and diagnosis and lead to misdiagnosis. Training is essential for developing cross-cultural competence (Carter, this *Handbook,* this volume; Pontoretto & Austin, this *Handbook,* this volume; D. Sue & Torino, this *Handbook,* this volume). It is unreasonable to expect clinicians to have an understanding of racial and cultural issues in diagnosis without adequate training. To this end, graduate programs in psychology and medical schools should include cross-cultural courses throughout the core curriculum so that students develop an awareness of racial and cultural issues in psychiatric assessment and evaluation and have an awareness of their own biases and assumptions.

There is also a need for more comprehensive psychiatric evaluations that emphasize the clinical interview as a tool for gaining an understanding of the patient in conjunction with information gleaned from collateral sources. Highlighting the clinical interview might also help the clinician gain a better understanding of the patient's sociocultural background, which could help to distinguish culturally bound behavior from behavior that reflects actual psychopathology (Branch, this *Handbook,* this volume; Westermeyer, 1987). In addition, there is a need to use alternative methods for gathering information to understand the individual, such as behavioral reports from family members, friends, and school personnel.

Finally, in the clinical arena and in research it is important that the field continue to refine its use of language. Within the past 20 years, psychology and psychiatry have recognized that consideration of culture is important for accurate diagnosis and treatment. In this same time period, the field has seemingly moved away from exploring race as a factor in diagnosis. Race is rarely examined as an explanatory construct in the literature with respect to research, theory, and the diagnostic process, although it is an important aspect of an individual that is unalterable. Whereas race was examined in early studies of mental health, more recently, possibly due to an increase of immigrants in the United States, the field seems to have moved away from an explicit focus on race and has instead begun to discuss culture. There may also be some confusion about the distinction between race and culture, so that the terms are being used interchangeably. In any case, we are not arguing that one construct is more important than the other, but it is our hope that clinicians and researchers will examine both race and culture and continue to delineate the differences between the two constructs. Because race is often the first identifiable feature of an individual, it is important that race continue to be included in research examining health disparities.

REFERENCES

Alarcon, R. D. (1995). Overview: White norms and psychiatric diagnosis of Black patients. *American Journal of Psychiatry, 138*(3), 279–285.

Alarcon, R. D., Westermeyer, J., Foulks, E. F., & Ruiz, P. (1999). Clinical relevance of contemporary cultural psychiatry. *Journal of Nervous and Mental Diseases, 187*(8), 465–471.

American Psychiatric Association. (2000). *Diagnostic and statistical manual of mental disorders* (4th ed., text rev.). Washington, DC: Author.

Atkinson, D. R., Morten, G., & Sue, D. W. (1979). *Counseling American minorities: A cross-cultural perspective.* Dubuque, IA: W. C. Brown.

Beiser, M. (1985). The grieving witch: A framework for applying principles of cultural psychiatry to clinical practice. *Canadian Journal of Psychiatry, 30*(2), 130–141.

Brody, E. B. (1990). Biomedical science and the changing culture of clinical practice. *Journal of Nervous & Mental Disorders, 178,* 279–281.

Canino, I. A., & Canino, G. J. (1993). Psychiatric care of Puerto Ricans. In A. C. Gaw (Ed.), *Culture, ethnicity and mental health* (pp. 467–500). Washington, DC: American Psychiatric Press.

Canino, G. J., Bird, H. R., & Shrout, P. E. (1987). The prevalence of specific psychiatric disorders in Puerto Rico. *Archives of General Psychiatry, 44,* 727–735.

Carter, R. T. (1995). *The influence of race and racial identity in psychotherapy: Toward a racially inclusive model.* New York: Wiley.

Carter, R. T. & Pieterse, A. L. (in press). Race: A social and psychological analysis of the term and its meaning. In R. T. Carter (Ed.), *Handbook of racial-cultural psychology and counseling: Theory and research* (Vol. 1, pp. 41–63). Hoboken, NJ: Wiley.

Constantine, M. G., Watt, S. K., Gainor, K. A., & Warren, A. K. (in press). The influence of Cross's initial black racial identity theory on other cultural identity conceptualizations. In R. T. Carter (Ed.), *Handbook of racial-cultural psychology and counseling: Theory and research* (Vol. 1, pp. 94–114). Hoboken, NJ: Wiley.

Constantine, M. G., & Wilton, L. (in press). The role of racial and cultural constructs in the history of the multicultural counseling movement. In R. T. Carter (Ed.), *Handbook of racial-cultural psychology and counseling: Theory and research* (Vol. 1, pp. 64–77). Hoboken, NJ: Wiley.

Cross, W. E. (1971). The negro-to-conversion experience: Toward a psychology of Black liberation. *Black World, 20,* 13–27.

Dana, R. H. (Ed.). (1998). *Understanding cultural identity in intervention and assessment.* Thousand Oaks, CA: Sage.

D'Andrea, M. (1999). Alternative needed for the *DMS-IV* in a multicultural-postmodern society. *Counseling Today, 41,* 44, 66.

Dohrenwend, B. P. (1966). Social status and psychological disorders: An issue of substance and an issue of method. *American Sociological Review, 31,* 14.

Doi, T. (1973). *The anatomy of dependence* (John Bester, Trans., 1st ed.). New York: Harper & Row.

Draguns, J. G. (2000). Psychopathology and ethnicity. In J. Aponte (Ed.), *Psychological intervention and cultural diversity* (pp. 41–58).

Egeland, J. A., Hostetter, A. M., & Eshleman, S. K. (1983). Amish study III: The impact of culture on the diagnosis of bipolar illness. *American Journal of Psychiatry, 140,* 67–71.

Favazza, A. R., & Oman, M. (1978). Overview: Foundations of cultural psychiatry. *American Journal of Psychiatry, 135,* 293–303.

Fernando, S. (2001). *Mental health, race and culture* (2nd ed.). New York: Palgrave.

Frances, A., Pincus, H. A., & Widiger, T. A. (1990). *DSM-IV:* Work in progress. *American Journal of Psychiatry, 147,* 1439–1448.

Guarnaccia, P. J., Guevara-Ramos, L. M., Gonzales, G., Canino, G. J., & Bird, H. (1992). Cross-cultural aspects of psychotic symptoms in Puerto Rico. *Research Community Mental Health, 7,* 99–110.

Helms, J. E. (1990). *Black and white racial identity: Theory, research, and practice.* Westport, CT: Greenwood Press.

Huges, C. C., Simons, R. C., & Wintrob, R. M. (1992). Selected glossary of culture bound symptoms. In J. E. Mezzich, A. Klien, H. Fabrega, B. Good, G. Johnson-Powell, K. M. Lin, et al. (Eds.), Revised cultural proposal for *DSM-IV.* Pittsburgh, Technical Report, *DSM* NIMH group on culture and diagnosis (pp. 161–168).

Ivey, A. E., & Ivey, M. B. (1998). Reframing *DSM-IV:* Positive strategies from developmental counseling and therapy. *Journal of Counseling and Development, 76,* 334–350.

Jaco, E. G. (1960). *The social epidemiology of mental disorders.* New York: Russell Sage Foundation.

Jones, B. E., & Gray, B. A. (1986). Problems in diagnosing schizophrenia and affective disorders among blacks. *Hospital and Community Psychiatry, 37*(1), 61–65.

Kessler, R. C., McGonagle, K. A., Zhao, S., Nelson, C. B., Hughes, M., Eshleman, S., et al. (1994). Lifetime and 12-month prevalence of *DSM III-R* psychiatric disorders in the United States. *Archives General Psychiatry, 51,* 8–19.

Kirmayer, L. J., Groleau, D., Guzder, J., Blake, C., & Jarvis, E. (2003). Cultural consultation: A model of mental health service for multicultural societies. *Canadian Journal of Psychiatry, 48,* 3.

Kleinman, A. (1977). Depression somatization and the "new cross-cultural psychiatry." *Social Science Medicine, 11,* 3–10.

Kleinman, A. (1988). *Rethinking psychiatry.* New York: Free Press.

Kohatsu, E. L. (in press). Acculturation: Current and future directions. In R. T. Carter (Ed.), *Handbook of racial-cultural psychology and counseling: Theory and research* (Vol. 1, pp. 207–231). Hoboken, NJ: Wiley.

Malzberg, B. (1959). Mental disease among Negroes. *Mental Hygiene, 43,* 457–459.

Mezzich, J. E., Kirmayer, L. J., Kleinman, A., Fabrega, H., Jr., Parron, D. L., Good, B. J., et al. (1999). The place of culture in *DSM-IV. Journal of Nervous and Mental Diseases, 187*(8), 457–464.

Mezzich, J. E., Kleinman, A., Fabrega, H., & Parron, D. L. (1996). *Culture and psychiatric diagnosis.* Washington, DC: American Psychiatric Press.

Mezzich, J. E., Otero, A. A., & Lee, S. (in press). International psychiatric diagnosis. In H. I. Kaplan & B. J. Sadock (Eds.), *Comprehensive textbook of psychiatry* (7th ed). Baltimore: Williams & Wilkens.

Parham, T. A., & Helms, J. E. (1981). The influence of Black students' racial attitudes on preferences for counselor's race. *Journal of Counseling Psychology, 28,* 250–257.

Robins, L. N., & Regier, D. A. (1991). *Psychiatric disorders in America: The epidemiological catchment area study.* New York: Free Press.

Rogler, L. H. (1989). The meaning of culturally sensitive research in mental health. *American Journal of Psychiatry, 146,* 296–303.

Rogler, L. H. (1993). Culture in psychiatric diagnosis: An issue of scientific accuracy. *Psychiatry, 56,* 324–327.

Rogler, L. H. (1996). Framing research on culture in psychiatric diagnosis: The case of the *DSM-IV. Psychiatry, 59,* 145–155.

Schultz, D. P., & Schultz, S. E. (1996). *A history of modern psychology.* (6th ed.). Orlando, FL: Harcourt Brace & Company.

Simon, R. J., Fleiss, J. L., Gurland, B. J., Stiller, P. R., & Sharpe, L. (1973). Depression and schizophrenia in hospitalized Black and White mental patients. *Archives of General Psychiatry, 28,* 509–512.

Strakowski, S. M., Lonczak, H. S., Sax, K. W., West, S. A., Crist, A., Metha, R., et al. (1995). The effects of race on diagnosis and disposition from a psychiatric emergency service. *Journal of Clinical Psychiatry, 56*(3), 101–107.

Sue, D. W., & Sue, D. (1999). *Counseling the culturally different: Theory and practice* (3rd ed.). New York: Wiley.

Sue, D. W., & Sue, D. (2003). *Counseling the culturally diverse: Theory and practice* (4th ed.). New York: Wiley.

Takeuchi, D. T., Chung, R., Lin, K. M., Shen, H., Kurasaki, K., Chun, C. A., et al. (1998). Lifetime and twelve-month prevalence rates of major depressive episodes and dysthymia among Chinese Americans in Los Angles. *American Journal of Psychiatry, 155,* 1407–1414.

Tsai, J. L., Ying, Y. W., & Lee, P. A. (2000). The meaning of "being Chinese" and "being American": Variation among Chinese American young adults. *Journal of Cross-Cultural Psychology, 31,* 302–322.

Vega, W. A., Kolody, B., Aguilar-Gaxiola, S., & Alderete, E. (1998). Lifetime prevalence of *DSM III-R* psychiatric disorders among urban and rural Mexican-Americans in California. *Archives of General Psychiatry, 55,* 771–778.

Vitols, M. M., Walters, H. G., & Keeler, M. H. (1963). Hallucinations and delusions in White and Negro schizophrenics. *American Journal of Psychiatry, 120,* 472–476.

Wakefield, J. D. (1992). The concept of mental disorder: On the boundary between biological facts and social values. *American Psychologist, 47,* 373–388.

Weinfeld, M. (1994). Ethnic assimilation and the retention of ethnic cultures. In J. W. Berry & J. A. Laponce (Eds.), *Ethnicity and culture in Canada* (pp. 228–266). Toronto, Ontario, Canada: University of Toronto Press.

Westermeyer, J. (1987). Cultural factors in clinical assessment. *Journal of Consulting and Clinical Psychology, 55,* 471–478.

Yeh, C. J., & Hunter, C. D. (in press). The solialization of self: Understanding shifting and multiple selves across cultures. In R. T. Carter (Ed.), *Handbook of racial-cultural psychology and counseling: Theory and research* (Vol. 1, pp. 78–93). Hoboken, NJ: Wiley.

CHAPTER 18

Assessment Practices in Racial-Cultural Psychology

Lisa A. Suzuki, John F. Kugler, and Lyndon J. Aguiar

Practicing psychologists today are faced with client populations of increased racial/ethnic diversity. Assessment practices and psychological tests that have been used for decades on White middle-class clients are being challenged as they are applied to other populations (e.g., immigrants). While critical statements have been made about the application of standardized measures with racially and culturally marginalized* populations, there has been little empirical data in the literature to examine this issue adequately (e.g., Sattler, 1992). Nevertheless, criticisms of tests and assessments have led to court cases and legislative rulings that have also impacted the field, dictating to some extent the ways different psychological assessment procedures and standardized instruments may be used and with what populations (GoPaul-McNicol & Armour-Thomas, 2002; Valencia & Suzuki, 2001). Many respected researchers and practitioners continue to face heated debate when assessing diverse racially/ethnically marginalized populations because of past transgressions and continuing misconceptions surrounding testing (e.g., Valencia & Suzuki, 2001).

The purposes of this chapter are (1) to examine the impact of cultural context in testing; (2) to review past and present approaches to testing; (3) to provide a brief discussion regarding the process of assessment; (4) to highlight issues of cultural bias, cultural loading, and equivalence; (5) to explore current practice with regard to test development procedures and methods used to establish the psychometric integrity of various instruments; and (6) to discuss implications surrounding the use of select personality assessment and cognitive ability measures in relation to culturally diverse populations.

CULTURAL CONTEXT AND TESTING

Much of the research in the area of multicultural assessment has focused on the use of particular instruments and the examination of different psychological constructs as they apply to diverse racial/ethnic populations. Research needs to go beyond the

---

*The term *marginalized* refers to those outside of the *mainstream* not only with respect to racial/ethnic identification but also socioeconomic status, educational level, and so on.

rudimentary examination of group differences in testing, and instead focus on the cultural context of testing practices. This can be accomplished by differentiating the value that various cultures place on tests and testing methods. In the mainstream American culture, there are a number of assumptions that underlie the use of tests and other assessment procedures in diagnosis and intervention. First, many test practices imply that valuable information can be obtained through examination of samples of behavior in standardized settings. The efficiency with which this test information is gathered is often an important promotional feature of a test. Prolonged engagement with any test taker may be seen as inefficient and unnecessary. However, gathering extensive background information may be critical to accurate interpretation of the test data obtained for members of marginalized racial and ethnic groups. Individuals from racially and culturally marginalized groups may not value the practice of time-limited test situations.

The second assumption in the mainstream culture that is widely held by practitioners is that psychological constructs (e.g., intelligence, personality factors) are etic (universal) in nature. Therefore, instruments are often translated, renormed, and restandardized into different languages for use with diverse populations in different cultural contexts. However, research in the area of ability testing indicates that although there may be a common core of cognitive skills, these may manifest differently depending on cultural context (Sternberg & Kaufman, 1998). For example, some groups may value and reward social intelligence over academic aspects of intelligence. Thus, scoring well on an intelligence test may have less value in that cultural context.

Third, most testing instruments measure products in terms of a static score. For example, cognitive tests are often based on the notion that there is one correct answer. In addition, the actual process that the individual test taker uses to arrive at a particular answer is often not addressed. Little attention is paid to the fact that the same task may tap different aspects of cognitive processing. For example, some cultures may emphasize meticulousness and thoughtfulness over speed; this difference could potentially impact an individual's score given that many tests are time-limited and bonus points may be given for quick performance (Branch, this *Handbook,* this volume; Helms, this *Handbook,* this volume; Trimble, this *Handbook,* this volume).

PAST AND PRESENT APPROACHES TO TESTING

It was during the 1900s that mental testing and personality assessment became widely accepted in the United States. This period has sometimes been referred to as the *Psychometric Movement.* It was during this time that the administration of group intelligence tests grew in the United States as screening of ability for different military duties occurred during World War I and World War II. In 1939, David Wechsler developed the Wechsler Bellevue Intelligence Scale, the precurser to the popular series of Wechsler intelligence scales now in existence. The success of ability tests also coincided with the growing popularity of personality measures during the 1900s (Cohen & Swerdlik, 1999). By the late 1930s it is estimated that 4,000 published tests were in existence (Cohen & Swerdlik, 1999). Currently, that number has increased to approximately 20,000 new tests published and developed each year, according to the American Psychological Association (Cohen & Swerdlik, 1999). Cognitive and personality tests are commonly used in educational, employment, and health settings.

Embedded in the wide acceptance of mental and personality measures are a number of assumptions that guide traditional test practices today. Researchers and clinicians who use tests adhere to the notion that psychological characteristics (i.e., states and traits) exist and can be measured and quantified in terms of scores. Furthermore, it is understood that scores have meaning and can be useful in making diagnoses as well as planning educational and psychological interventions. For decades tests were administered to members of diverse racial/ethnic groups without consideration of cultural context or environmental factors (e.g., limited opportunities or exposure). It is important to note that contextual understanding by the evaluator is crucial for all individuals in the assessment process. Failure to obtain information (e.g., historical, educational, political, social) may lead to inappropriate interpretations of test scores. This is most evident in challenges to the testing enterprise that were eventually raised in courts of law. In particular, issues related to the use of various cognitive ability tests in the placement and tracking of racially/ethnically marginalized students led to a number of court cases and legal decisions. A review of court cases involving pupils, from the *Yearbook of School Law* (American Council on Education, 1997) was conducted by Valencia and Suzuki (2001) and indicated that legal concerns regarding students from racially/culturally marginalized groups (e.g., African Americans and Hispanics) focused on five areas: (1) the use of tests as part of admissions, (2) educational tracking of students, (3) testing of nonnative English-speaking students, (4) the use of tests as promotion and graduation requirements (high-stakes testing), and (5) the classification of mentally retarded students. In these court cases, testing procedures in the educational system were noted to negatively affect students from marginalized racial and ethnic groups from the early 1960s to the mid-1980s. Current test development practices have addressed issues of diversity and led to greater attention to potential sources of bias in mental testing (see "Contemporary Test Development Procedures" in this chapter).

As noted in the following sections of this chapter, the recognized limitations of applying cognitive ability testing and personality assessments with members of diverse populations have led to an increased emphasis on integrating background information in understanding test results and behavior. In addition, many test manuals report the importance of interpreting test results with caution when they are administered to members of any racial/ethnic group for whom the test was not specifically normed. Most of the popular tests in the areas of cognition (e.g., Wechsler Scales) and personality (e.g., Minnesota Multiphasic Personality Inventory [MMPI]; see section in this chapter) are normed on nationally representative standardization samples with respect to race/ethnicity, socioeconomic status, educational attainment, and so on (Branch, this *Handbook,* this volume). Finally, there have been greater efforts to develop alternative testing procedures (e.g., nonverbal tests, translated and renormed versions of tests, measures with modified scoring procedures).

Most of the instruments and procedures described in this chapter are based on an etic perspective. That is, we discuss measures that were designed to identify universal psychological constructs. Etic measures are not sensitive to unique cultural interpretations of the construct(s) being assessed (nor do they claim to be). On the other hand, emic measures (e.g., Tell-Me-A-Story [TEMAS]; Costantino, 1987) were developed in specific sociocultural contexts and are designed to be particularly sensitive to the unique dimensions of abilities in particular cultural groups. However, only a few emic measures are currently available, and each is designed for specific racial/ethnic cultural groups.

UNDERSTANDING THE PROCESS OF ASSESSMENT

It is important for readers to understand the major distinction between assessment and testing. Cohen and Swerdlik (1999) put forth the following definitions:

> For our purposes, we will define *psychological assessment* as the gathering and integration of psychology-related data for the purpose of making a psychological evaluation, accomplished through the use of tools such as tests, interviews, case studies, behavioral observation, and specially designed apparatuses and measurement procedures. We will define *psychological testing* as the process of measuring psychology related variables by means of devices or procedures designed to obtain a sample of behavior. (p. 5)

Therefore, assessment is a process of evaluation that includes both qualitative (e.g., background information, observation) and quantitative (e.g., standardized test scores) data as part of the evaluation process. Assessment, according to this view, is a more inclusive term and incorporates the testing process.

The clinical interview forms the foundation of the assessment process. Though there are numerous standard interview formats (e.g., intake interview, mental status examination), it is important to note that many do not draw significant attention to cultural issues vital to the understanding of racial/ethnic group members. Salient information regarding historical, familial, economic, social, and community issues are often absent from the background information sections of evaluation reports (Suzuki & Kugler, 2001; Takushi & Uomoto, 2001). The collection of background information is critical to the interpretation of test results (both scores and test behavior) given reported scoring differences between various racial/ethnic groups and immigrant and refugee populations (Suzuki, Ponterotto, & Meller, 2001).

Cultural Bias, Cultural Loading, and Issues of Equivalence

Concerns regarding cultural bias, cultural loading, and psychological equivalence are often noted in the testing literature as issues that can severely limit the applicability of various measures with diverse populations. Cultural bias refers to a "systematic error in the estimation of some 'true' value for a group of individuals" (Reynolds, 1982, p. 186). This definition implies a psychometric determination of test or item bias. Van de Vijver and Poortinga (1997) note that all tests are prone to bias when used with marginalized members of a population.

Types of test bias include method bias, item bias, and construct bias. Method bias relates to systematic differences in the administration of a test to different groups (e.g., allowing a particular group more time to complete a time-limited test). Item bias refers to systematic group differences in responses to particular items of a test (e.g., a greater portion of individuals from a particular group incorrectly respond to a particular item compared to other groups). Construct bias pertains to the inadequacy of a test to measure constructs across different groups (e.g., the construct may not have the same meaning across different groups; therefore, a test developed in one cultural context is not directly applicable to another). All of these forms of bias are often taken into consideration during the test development process, but no test can be completely free of these biases (Trimble, this *Handbook,* Volume One).

Cultural loading refers to the fact that all tests reflect information that is valued in the particular cultural context in which the test was developed. For example, when tests are translated into different languages, item content may need to be modified to maintain cultural relevance. When the Wechsler scales were translated for use in Japan, items on the Information subtest were changed to reflect more relevant facts (e.g., a question on distance between two U.S. cities was changed to two cities in Japan).

In addition to content, the ways test items are presented and the format in which responses are recognized are also subject to cultural loading (e.g., Dahlstrom, 1986; Trimble, this *Handbook,* Volume One). For example, response formats such as scales assume that an individual test taker will be able to represent his or her feelings regarding a particular item in terms of a numerical or spatial scaling. Similarly, the true/false format presumes that the test taker will be able to represent his or her answer in an absolute dichotomous format indicating one correct response. People in different cultures may not view their emotions as either dichotomous or measurable on a numerical scale, as evident in response tendencies. For example, on a Likert scale, individuals from particular groups may place their ratings most often at the extremes, while responses of another group may fall most often in the middle. This should not be viewed as a limitation on the part of the individual being assessed but as a lack of sensitivity to the preferences of particular groups.

Related to cultural loading are concerns regarding issues of equivalence. Poortinga (1983) characterized the main issue of equivalence as "the problem of whether, on the basis of measurements and observation, inferences in terms of some common psychological dimensions can be made in different groups of subjects" (p. 238). Issues of equivalence have major implications for multicultural assessment practices. Helms (1992) summarized a number of forms of equivalence that may potentially impact test performance. Her work specifically focuses on cognitive ability testing. Two forms of equivalence she has discussed are conceptual and functional. Conceptual equivalence is present when the information contained in the test items is equally familiar to members of different racial/ethnic groups (e.g., a question regarding the number of days in a week would be equally familiar to all groups). Functional equivalence implies that test scores have a consistent meaning for different racial/ethnic groups (e.g., a score of 100 on an intelligence measure means the person is average regardless of group membership). Conceptual and functional are just a two of the forms of equivalence noted in the literature (see also, Trimble, this *Handbook,* Volume One).

Due to the complexity of factors that can impact the process of assessment, it is critical that professionals take into consideration the implications of cultural bias, cultural loading, and issues of equivalence at all phases of the assessment process, from test development to the actual interpretation of test scores.

CURRENT TEST DEVELOPMENT PROCEDURES AND METHODS USED TO ESTABLISH PSYCHOMETRIC INTEGRITY

The psychometric integrity of various tests is established through test procedures that take into consideration issues of reliability and validity. Given issues of cultural bias, cultural loading, and equivalence, a number of methods have been developed to address concerns regarding the use of tests with diverse racial/ethnic populations. These methods include procedures implemented during the development phase and those used during the establishment of the statistical reliability and validity of a test.

Contemporary Test Development Procedures

Test development procedures for most current psychological instruments in the areas of cognitive and personality assessment include attention to concerns related to race/ethnicity. It should be noted that many of the following practices are conducted after the initial version of the test is developed but prior to standardization. These practices do not necessarily eliminate but may reduce bias and increase awareness of potential issues that may impact test performance by members of different racially and ethnically marginalized groups. In addition, test items may be changed or removed based on findings that indicate bias. However, the underlying theoretical assumptions of that test remain unchanged. Test developers that do not employ these practices run the risk of creating instruments with unknown levels of bias. Professionals who assess individuals from diverse backgrounds should be extremely wary of such measures.

Fairness Review

Test developers often employ the efforts of experts to review test content and administration procedures for potential sources of bias, cultural loading, and equivalence. In this process, items viewed as being problematic are reworded or removed from the measure. Concerns have arisen, however, regarding the use of community experts without providing guidance as to what constitutes bias (Helms, 1997). That is, experts are often left to their own devices in reviewing test content.

Census-Based Standardization Sampling

Members of different racially/ethnically marginalized groups are represented in the sample in numbers that are proportional to their overall existence in the general population. This sample forms the foundation of the norming of the test and is used to establish the initial validity and reliability of the measure (Helms, this *Handbook*, Volume One). Other validity and reliability studies often follow, usually conducted by other researchers rather than the test author(s). Despite these efforts, concerns have been raised regarding the small numbers of racially and ethnically marginalized group members in particular standardization samples (Valencia & Suzuki, 2001). For example, the Leiter-R (Roid & Miller, 1997) standardization sample includes 1,138 Caucasians, 286 African Americans, 217 Hispanics, 55 Asians, and 23 Native Americans. The Kaufman Brief Intelligence Test (Kaufman & Kaufman, 1990) uses the "other" category to refer to members of the standardization sample that are not

White, Black, or Hispanic. It should be noted that this census-based sampling procedure may result in very small numbers of particular racial/ethnic group members,
given their relatively small percentage in the overall U.S. population. Test developers
use national norms to suggest that the instrument is appropriate for all members of
the U.S. population. This claim is potentially misleading given the small numbers
from racial/ethnic and marginalized groups whose contribution to the overall norming will have been minimal. An example is the inclusion of 23 Native Americans in
the norming sample of the Leiter-R (Branch, this *Handbook,* this volume).

Some test developers have conducted racial/ethnic oversampling to enable the
specific examination of scores obtained by different groups on the test. Thus, they
include larger numbers of individuals from particular racial and ethnic groups
above and beyond their proportional representation in the overall population. When
this oversampling is done, an evaluator can compare a client's scores to the overall
standardization sample or the supplemental norms for a particular racial/ethnic
group. Tests such as the Wechsler Intelligence Scale for Children III (Wechsler,
1991) incorporate an oversampling procedure.

Attention to Related Stratification Variables

Other stratification variables related to race/ethnicity are controlled for in the
standardization sample of many measures. For example, most cognitive measures
include attention to region of the country, socioeconomic status, urban/rural location, community size, parental occupation, and so on. This ensures to some extent
that the standardization sample will be reflective of the overall population to which
the measure will be applied. These variables have been found to vary between different racial/ethnic groups.

Development of Sociocultural Norms

Tests like the Kaufman Assessment Battery for Children (K-ABC; Kaufman &
Kaufman, 1983) include norms by race/ethnicity and parental education. Separate
norms were developed in addition to those provided based on the entire standardization sample. Thus, examiners may make use of these sociocultural norms when
they determine that it is more appropriate to compare a client to norms based on his
or her specific racial or ethnic group.

Reported Reliability and Validity Studies with Specific
Racial/Ethnic Groups

Test manuals may include attention to reliability and validity information for different racial/ethnic groups. Specific studies may be conducted to address the validity
of a particular measure with different racially and ethnically marginalized groups.

Sophisticated Statistical Examination of Item Responses and
Racial/Ethnic Group Performance

In the case of cognitive ability tests, item response theory and Rasch modeling are
methods of examining item difficulty levels by racial/ethnic grouping. These procedures are often incorporated in test development procedures.

Despite the availability of these procedures to reduce bias in testing, a significant number of published test manuals do not sufficiently address racial/ethnic group differences. Often, information regarding the profile of scores obtained for different racial groups is not provided. This information can be vital in formulating appropriate interpretations of the test scores obtained.

Reliability

Reliability refers to the consistency of measurement for a particular test. "More technically it is a proportion that indicates the ratio between the true score variance on a test and the total variance" (Cohen & Swerdlik, 1999, p. 146). There are different forms of reliability, such as test-retest, alternate forms, and split half reliabilities. Reliability estimates take into consideration sources of error variance, that is, test construction (e.g., content sampling), administration, scoring, and interpretation. Sources of error may vary depending on the cultural context of the individual being tested.

One source of error may be introduced during test administration. An individual's motivation and attention may vary depending on environmental conditions or the way test material is presented. For example, it was reported to one of the authors that school personnel in a low-income community administered statewide achievement tests in a standardized format in the new school library. Unfortunately, due to budget constraints, the library was not air-conditioned and the temperature during the testing reached above 90 degrees, likely impacting student performance.

Other sources of error in administration include the examiner's general demeanor and behavior. Different cultures have different norms of behavior that can impact the testing situation. For example, when testing Native American children, where the examiner sits, his or her tone of voice, and the amount of eye contact can potentially influence the examinee's response to the testing situation (Suzuki, Vraniak, & Kugler, 1996).

Research has also indicated that students who view tests as detrimental to their overall achievement may not perform well. For example, Steele and Aronson (1998) have written extensively regarding the "stereotype threat" that impacts the test performance of African Americans. They note that when a stereotype

> alleges an importantly negative quality—like the low intelligence stereotypes alleged for blacks and Latinos—the expectations that come with it can be quite unnerving, and stereotype threat can have critically disruptive effects. (Aronson, 2002, p. 282)

The research on stereotype threat indicates that test performance can be modified depending on the context in which the measures are administered. For example, when test instructions removed the relevance of the stereotype (e.g., nonevaluative judgments about ability), the performance for African American students increased (Steele & Aronson, 1998).

Traditional measures of reliability (i.e., test-retest, split half, and alternate form) do not take into consideration the cultural factors that can impact score consistency. Instead, these reliabilities, based on statistical correlations, assume a linear relationship between obtained scores. As noted in the preceding discussion, there are a multitude of factors that can impact test scores, increasing error variance and thereby impacting the reliability of a test. By introducing error, these factors lower the estimate of the "true score." For example, individuals who take a test on two separate occasions but under significantly different test conditions will most likely obtain discrepant scores, resulting in a lower estimate of test-retest reliability.

One of the primary reasons for examining the reliability of a test is related to the concept of validity. Reliability is a necessary but insufficient condition for validity. A test cannot be valid if it is not reliable. Two prerequisites of validity are that a test must consistently measure a construct and scores cannot fluctuate merely by chance (i.e., error). The following section addresses forms of validity in relation to cultural differences.

Validity

Validity refers to the *meaningfulness* of a test score or interpretation of an assessment procedure (i.e., those that do not yield a quantitative score). There are different forms of validity, often presented in test manuals, including content validity, construct validity, and criterion-related validity (see also, Helms, this *Handbook,* Volume One).

Content Validity

Content validity is assessed based on the judgment of those who are experts in the domains measured by the test (Geisinger, 1998). Content experts are asked to address how well the test items reflect the characteristics of the construct being measured.

Experts or members of particular racially and ethnically marginalized groups often assess content validity through fairness evaluations. As noted earlier in the test development section, these reviews are often subject to criticism given the lack of guidelines provided in reviewing test content.

Geisinger (1998) notes that related to content validity is the issue of "instructional validity," which focuses primarily on the legal implications (e.g., unequal educational access to resources and its effects on use of high-stakes testing) of test use:

> Instructional validity is concerned with the determination of whether specific subgroups in the population whose education differs in some substantive ways from that of the majority of the population have been exposed to the instruction that is assumed and is covered on the examination. (pp. 26–27)

Based on knowledge regarding the limited educational resources in a number of racially and ethnically marginalized communities, it appears feasible that in many situations, instructional validity may not be maintained. Instructional validity might be established by measuring a number of factors in a school or district, such as standardized reading and math scores, the amount of funding per student, class size, average number of years of experience per teacher, and turnover rate of teachers. Schools in low socioeconomic status communities that are composed of primarily marginalized groups compare poorly with other schools on these factors. Therefore, caution should be taken in the interpretation of test scores obtained in suboptimal learning conditions, particularly on those measures that are related to acquired knowledge and/or academic skills. Individuals from racially and ethnically marginalized groups may not have been exposed to the content required to obtain a correct response.

Construct Validity

Construct validity refers to a "judgment about the appropriateness of inferences drawn from test scores regarding individual standings on a variable called a 'construct'" (Cohen & Swerdlik, 1999, p. 197). The definitions of particular constructs may vary depending on cultural context. For example, Sternberg and Kaufman (1998) provide a review of studies conducted on culturally based definitions of "intelligence." Given these differences, one may hypothesize that the definition of intelligence that is adhered to by test developers may impact the establishment of construct validity. This may be seen in the controversies that have arisen regarding the use of intelligence tests with racially and ethnically marginalized group members. One attempt to address this issue has been increased attention to the importance of understanding multiple intelligences in examining the abilities of diverse racial/ethnic populations (Armour-Thomas & GoPaul-McNicol, 1998).

Criterion-Related Validity

Criterion-related validity is used to describe the relationship between a test score and some current or future variable to be assessed. The "criterion may be broadly defined as the standard against which a test or a test score is evaluated" (Cohen & Swerdlik, 1999, p. 182). Predictive validity is a critical form of criterion validity. as the usefulness of many instruments is dependent on how well they can predict future behavior. One important purpose of criterion validity studies is to determine whether differential prediction by racial/ethnic grouping is present for a particular measure:

> Differential prediction occurs when the relationship between the predictor test and the criterion is significantly different across groups . . . for example, a test might be valid in one sample and invalid in another . . . [with regard to ability tests]. To date, however, little evidence of differential prediction has been found in the psychometric literature when one compares with majority populations either ethnic groups or groups based on disability. (Geisinger, 1998, p. 27)

Although Geisinger concludes that there is no clear differential prediction with respect to racial/ethnic grouping, it is important to note that challenges may be raised in reference to the criterion used. For example, grade point average has been used as the criterion for many intelligence tests. Grades however, may not be assigned equitably given teachers' preconceptions regarding students from different racial/ethnic groups. Therefore, in these situations, the criterion of grade point average would not be a valid indicator of the predictive quality of an intelligence test.

A related form of criterion validity has been termed "consequential validity" (Geisinger, 1998). This has been defined as "the study of both the intended and unintended consequences that occur when testing is implemented" (p. 28). Concerns with respect to consequential validity may be seen in the increased use of high-stakes testing (i.e., testing that results in long-term consequences that impact education, employment, and health services). Differential passing rates (i.e., groups differ in terms of how many members attain the specified cut-off score deemed to constitute passing) for racial/ethnic groups have been noted. Therefore, the consequences of the use of such tests may have negative implications in terms of graduation rates as well as future employment and educational opportunities.

Based on the preceding discussion of reliability and validity, it appears that for most tests, these concepts may be viewed to some extent as context-specific. The context in this case refers to racial/ethnic group membership and other cultural factors. That is, one must not assume that because a particular measure is reliable and valid in one cultural context with a particular racial/ethnic group, these statistical properties will then generalize to other populations.

IMPLICATIONS SURROUNDING THE USE OF PERSONALITY AND COGNITIVE ABILITY TESTS IN RELATION TO CULTURALLY DIVERSE POPULATIONS

It is beyond the scope of this brief chapter to cover all of the cultural implications involved in the use of particular cognitive and personality tests with diverse racial/ethnic populations. Instead, this section highlights research findings for some of the most popular instruments in psychological assessment as well as some of the newer, alternative assessment procedures. For more comprehensive discussions of various psychological instruments and alternative assessment procedures, the reader is referred to Dana (1999) and Suzuki, Ponterotto, and Meller (2001).

Personality Assessment

The three measures to be covered in this section are those that have withstood a great deal of criticism in the field. The Thematic Apperception Test and the Rorschach are two popular instruments that have been the mainstay of projective testing. Though the Rorschach has become a more objective test over the years with the development of the Exner Comprehensive System, many continue to use more subjective formats in interpretation. The MMPI is perhaps the most well-researched objective test of personality. These three measures are standards in the field of psychological evaluation of personality (Branch, this *Handbook,* this volume).

Though not a focus of this chapter, it is important to note special considerations when examining the subjectivity and psychometric integrity (i.e., validity and reliability) of these projective tests. The more subjective the test, the more interpretation may be colored by the cultural perspective of the test developer and/or examiner. This interpretation may be at odds with the view being expressed by the examinee and may lead to overdiagnosis of pathological conditions. It should be noted that objectivity of a scoring system is tied in part to low level of interpretation on the part of the examiner at the scoring level. Objectivity is created by reducing or eliminating the amount of subjective interpretation on the part of the examiner (i.e., of the directions and scoring of the response). Interrater reliability estimates are assessed in part by clear directions and items with specific acceptable responses leading to ease in scoring. Therefore, a scoring system can be considered objective if there are clear methods and procedures in place that facilitate a high degree of interrater (i.e., interscorer) reliability.

Researchers have argued about the reliability and validity of projective tests such as the Rorschach, with conflicting opinions depending on how one interpreted the results (Hiller, Rosenthal, Bornstein, Berry, & Brunell-Neuleib, 1999; Vigilone, 1999; Wood, Nezworski, & Stejskal, 1996). The reliability and validity of projective measures is not as easily quantified as for other psychological instruments (i.e., aptitude and achievement tests). Reliabilities are often based on interrater judgments of an individual's responses to ambiguous stimuli. Determining the validity of projective measures is usually more difficult because the ambiguous nature of many of the projective tasks do not readily lend themselves to content validity or construct validity studies. Therefore, validity is often measured by criterion-based correlation studies with other instruments assumed to assess the same construct. For example, interpretations of Rorschach responses might be correlated with answers to MMPI scales. In addition, projective measures may be used to determine particular aspects of a diagnosis (e.g., rule out paranoia or psychosis). Although they may not be the most reliable tools for diagnosing conditions, projective tests can still provide many psychologists with useful clinical information about the individuals they serve. However, this information is best understood in light of the individual's culture and life circumstances.

Narrative Assessment

One of the most popular methods of personality assessment has been the incorporation of storytelling. The Thematic Apperception Test (TAT; Murray, 1943) is the most popular narrative assessment tool in use today. The TAT consists of 20 picture cards; individual test takers are asked to tell a story about the picture, including what happened before, what happened after, what happens at the end, and what the characters are thinking and feeling. In the absence of an objective system of scoring or analysis, the interpretation of themes derived rests on the often subjective impressions of the evaluator. Thus, indiscriminate use of the TAT has been criticized by a number of scholars in terms of its application to different racial/ethnic group members (GoPaul-McNicol & Armour-Thomas, 2002). Questions may also be raised with respect to the use of this measure with individuals of any ethnicity whose experiences are different from the mainstream group on which the test is based.

Due to concerns regarding the TAT's use with diverse populations, a need was identified for more culturally appropriate story cards with objective scoring frameworks (Dana, 1999). In 1987, Guiseppe Costantino published the TEMAS, "the only omnibus personality measure that offers nonminority and minority norms for four groups (African American, Puerto Rican, other Hispanic, and White)" (Costantino, Flanagan, & Malgady, 2001, p. 222). The TEMAS story cards pull for personality functions (i.e., interpersonal relations, aggression, anxiety, depression, achievement motivation, delay for gratification, self-concept, sexual identity, moral judgment, and reality testing), affective functions, and cognitive functions (e.g., reaction time, total time, fluency, omissions, transformations). An objective scoring system is provided in the test manual. However, the authors stress that this should not "preclude interpretation according to the clinical judgment and theoretical orientation of the examiner as well" (p. 222).

Rorschach

The Rorschach (1921) inkblot test was developed as a projective personality assessment tool. When it was first introduced, no objective scoring system was provided. Over the years, a number of scoring systems were constructed, including those by Klopfer and Kelley (1942) and Beck (1944). Many of these scoring systems were integrated in the Comprehensive System developed by Exner (1993):

> The Rorschach Comprehensive system is proposed as a culture-free assessment method for several reasons. First, the test stimuli (the inkblots) are sufficiently ambiguous to eliminate most cultural bias. . . . Taking the Rorschach is a novel experience for nearly everyone regardless of culture. . . . Also, the Rorschach inkblots are sufficiently ambiguous to avoid having any stimulus properties that may be biased for or against any culture. That is, it is unlikely that any of the blot configurations look very much like any culture-specific object. (Ritzler, 2001, p. 238)

In his review of the Comprehensive System, Ritzler (2001) provides data on non-patient adults from 12 countries. The data "reveals that there is remarkable consistency across countries on all variables in that very few of the means in each (scoring) category are separated by more than one standard deviation" (p. 240). Ritzler concludes that studies examining the impact of language and acculturation "have supported the multicultural rigor of the Comprehensive System so far" (p. 249). He does, however, report that more work needs to be done to develop appropriate norms for interpretation of the Rorschach Comprehensive System with individuals from diverse racial/ethnic groups. Determining racial/ethnic norms for the Rorschach would provide clinicians with needed interpretive information regarding the impact of cultural factors on performance in this measure. Although these norms would not eliminate cultural bias, they could lead to more culturally sensitive interpretations of the Rorschach variables.

The Minnesota Multiphasic Personality Inventory-2 (MMPI-2)

The MMPI-2 (Butcher, Dahlstrom, Graham, Tellegen, & Kaemmer, 1989) and its predecessor, the MMPI, are the most popular personality instruments available in the United States (Hall & Phung, 2001). One major reference on the MMPI-2 states the following with respect to racial/ethnic considerations:

> All the ethnic group samples fall very near the general normative sample mean on the MMPI-2 validity and standard scales. These data indicate that the MMPI-2 norms apply equally well regardless of ethnic group background and that no special interpretive considerations need to be made with regard to race. (Butcher & Williams, 2000, p. 191)

This conclusion is based on the ethnic group membership of the MMPI-2 normative samples for adult males and females, which included 2,117 Whites, 314 Blacks,

77 Native Americans, 73 Hispanics, and 19 Asians (Butcher & Williams, 2000). The small numbers of racially/ethnically marginalized group members is a clear limitation, and the conclusion may be overstated.

In a meta-analytic review of 31 years of MMPI/MMPI-2 research, Hall, Bansal, and Lopez (1999) point out the complexities of comparing the different MMPI/MMPI-2 subscales by racial/ethnic grouping (i.e., African American, Latino American) and diagnosis. Based on their findings, they note that

> none of the aggregate effect sizes suggests substantive differences from either a statistical or clinical perspective. The MMPI and MMPI-2 apparently do not unfairly portray African Americans and Latinos as pathological. Effect sizes across studies generally did not vary as a function of sociodemographic variables, research setting, or use of the MMPI versus MMPI-2. (p. 186)

This seems to support the statements by Butcher and Williams (2000) cited earlier. However, in their concluding discussion, Hall, Bansal, and Lopez state that more research is needed to examine potential race/ethnic differences. Information regarding within-group variability and psychopathology was often missing from the studies included in their meta-analysis. They note that the emphasis on between-group differences has led to neglect in examining potentially significant within-group factors such as generational status, language fluency, level of acculturation, ethnic identity, perceived racially and ethnically marginalized status, and discrimination in relation to the MMPI/MMPI-2 (see also, Branch, this *Handbook,* this volume).

Cognitive Assessment

Racial/ethnic group differences on cognitive ability tests have led to the greatest controversy. For example, in the academic community, a number of scholars have formed hypotheses about the meaning of racial/ethnic group differences in intelligence (e.g., Suzuki & Valencia, 1997). As noted throughout this chapter, a number of controversies, court cases, and accusations of bias, cultural loading, and equivalence have focused on the use of intelligence test measures with racial/ethnic and marginalized groups. In this section, we provide highlights of reviews on two of the most popular intelligence measures: the Wechsler Intelligence Scale for Children-III and the Stanford-Binet (fourth edition).

Wechsler Intelligence Scale for Children-III (WISC-III)

The WISC-III is considered by many to be the most widely used cognitive ability test in North America (e.g., Wilson & Reschly, 1996). David Wechsler, the original developer of the Wechsler scales, was concerned about the conclusions that might be made based on differential performance by diverse racial/ethnic groups. He

> viewed the differences in mean scores not as indicators of lower intelligence among certain groups but as indicators of differences in how our society and how variations in social, economic, political, and medical opportunities have an impact on intellectual abilities. (cited in Prifitera, Weiss, & Saklofske, 1998, p. 11)

Reports indicate that the WISC-III predicts achievement equally well for African American, Hispanic, and White children (Prifitera et al., 1998). Racial/ethnic group differences in overall IQ are reported from the standardization samples. These differences in intelligence test scores are decreased but not eliminated when comparison samples are matched on socioeconomic status, parental education, sex, age, region of the country, and number of parents living at home. Based on their re-view, Prifitera et al. (1998) conclude:

> The view that minorities have lower abilities is clearly wrong. IQ score differences between young African-American and White children and Hispanic and White samples with only gross matches on SES are much less than a standard deviation, and the index scores are even smaller. What would the difference be if even more refined variables had been con-trolled for, such as household income, home environment (e.g., parental time spent with children), per-pupil school spending, medical and nutritional history, and exposure to tox-ins? (p. 15)

Thus, the issue of racial/ethnic group differences on the WISC-III has not been fully addressed with respect to the multitude of factors that may be impacting test perfor-mance given that racial/ethnic group differences in IQ are still evident despite find-ings supporting the validity and reliability of the WISC-III with diverse samples. The test authors continue to suggest that with increased attention to other variables impacting intelligence, these group differences will most likely be decreased and perhaps even disappear.

Stanford-Binet Fourth Edition (SB-IV)

The SB-IV is the second most popular individualized cognitive measure currently used in school settings (Wilson & Reschly, 1996). Racial/ethnic group differences in area scores (i.e., Abstract/Visual Reasoning, Quantitative Reasoning, Short-Term Memory, Verbal Reasoning) are reported in the test manual (Thorndike, Hagen, & Sattler, 1986). It should be noted that the SB-IV test manual is one of the few that provides mean scores by racial/ethnic group and age. Many test guides do not provide this information directly. The test authors (Thorndike et al., 1986) report that these distinct patterns of scores are found consistently across all age groups:

> Hispanics had higher mean scores in Abstract/Visual Reasoning, Quantitative Reasoning, and Short-Term Memory than in Verbal Reasoning. Hispanic examinees at all ages had their highest mean score in Abstract/Visual Reasoning and Quantitative Reasoning. . . . In two of the three age groups, Asian examinees also had higher mean scores in Abstract/Visual Rea-soning and Quantitative Reasoning than in Short-Term Memory. The black examinees had their highest scores in Short-Term Memory. (p. 37)

Definitive explanations for these obtained profiles are often missing from these de-scriptions. Some have hypothesized that particular strengths noted in the subtest profiles may reflect culturally reinforced ability areas (Vernon, Jackson, & Mes-sick, 1988). For example, Asian cultures are often described as emphasizing non-verbal forms of ability (Iwakaki & Vernon, 1988). Others have indicated that the different profiles may be artifacts of the ways abilities are being measured (e.g., Helms, 1992). Thus, as noted earlier, concerns with respect to cultural bias, cultural loading, and issues of equivalence continue to be evident with respect to current measures.

Challenges continue to be raised with respect to the use of particular instruments with members of marginalized racial and ethnic groups. It appears clear that more work is needed to understand the implications of these group differences so that examiners can be provided with more definitive guidelines in terms of test selection, use of alternative scoring methods, comparisons to sociocultural or specific racial/ethnic norms, and so on. However, on an individual client level, a greater understanding of appropriate assessment techniques and procedures enables clinicians to use measures in more culturally sensitive and appropriate ways. For example, the Biocultural Model of Intelligence (Armour-Thomas & GoPaul-McNicol, 1998) provides a framework for understanding cultural and biological influences on intellectual behavior. In addition, the assessment system derived from this model highlights important practices (e.g., testing the limits, examining multiple intelligences, medical history, acculturation) that can be used in the process of evaluation to ensure more culturally sensitive measurement of ability areas, taking into consideration the unique context of each individual being tested.

CONCLUSIONS

Testing in racial-cultural psychology has evolved over time, with greater sophistication in development strategies and alternative assessment procedures. The most popular instruments continue to be studied with respect to racial/ethnic group differences, yet little has been provided to explain what these differences mean and how they should be interpreted.

In addition, despite acknowledgment of the importance of increased sensitivity to the subtle cultural nuances that may impact test performance, limitations still exist with available measures. Many tests appear to still emphasize an etic (universal) focus that assumes that psychological constructs exist universally and are not subject to different interpretations based on cultural context. Meanwhile, sociocultural measures, those developed from an emic (culture-specific) perspective, such as the TEMAS, remain few in number.

A number of alternative assessment tests and methods have been developed over the years. However, they generally have not unseated the most popular classic measures, including those mentioned in this chapter. To establish validity, newer tests are often compared to the old standards. Thus, new tests are not unique but share many characteristics with older measures. However, there are some new procedures that appear promising. Practices such as the Biocultural Model of Intelligence (Armour-Thomas & GoPaul-McNicol, 1998) can be effective in promoting better delivery of psychological services to individuals of diverse racial/ethnic background. At the same time, it rests with the academic community to ensure adequate training in the area of the multicultural use of psychological instruments. As Kaufman (1994) has noted, the examiner must be better than the instruments he or she uses.

This chapter discussed the importance of understanding the cultural context of the evaluation process and psychometric issues related to reliability, validity, and test development procedures. Given the limitations found in the use of any instrument with members of diverse racial/ethnic backgrounds, the ultimate meaningfulness of a particular test score or assessment procedure is dependent on an accurate and sensitive interpretation of the results.

REFERENCES

American Council on Education. (1997). *Yearbook of School Law: A narrative topical summary of decisions the higher courts in all states of the United States of America in cases involving school law, as reported during the preceding year.* Washington, DC: Author.

Armour-Thomas, E., & GoPaul-McNicol, S. (1998). *Assessing intelligence: Applying the bio-cultural model.* Thousand Oaks, CA: Sage.

Aronson, J. (2002). Stereotype threat: Contending and coping with unnerving expectations. In J. Aronson (Ed.), *Improving academic achievement: Impact of psychological factors on education* (pp. 281–304). New York: Academic Press.

Beck, S. (1944). *Rorschach's test: I. Basic processes.* Philadelphia: Grune & Stratton.

Butcher, J. N., Dahlstrom, W. G., Graham, J. R., Tellegen, A., & Kaemmer, B. (1989). *MMPI-2: Manual for administration and scoring.* Minneapolis: University of Minnesota Press.

Butcher, J. N., & Williams, C. L. (2000). *Essentials of MMPI-2 and MMPI-IA interpretation* (2nd ed.). Minneapolis: University of Minnesota Press.

Cohen, R. J., & Swerdlik, M. E. (1999). *Psychological testing and assessment: An introduction to tests and measurement* (4th ed.). Mountain View, CA: Mayfield.

Costantino, G. (1987). *Picture cards: The TEMAS (Tell-Me-A-Story) Test.* Los Angeles: Western Psychological Services.

Costantino, G., Flanagan, R., & Malgady, R. G. (2001). Narrative assessments: TAT, CAT, and TEMAS. In L. A. Suzuki, J. G. Ponterotto, & P. J. Meller (Eds.), *Handbook of multicultural assessment* (2nd ed., pp. 217–236). San Francisco: Jossey Bass.

Dahlstrom, W. (1986). Ethnic status and personality measurement. In W. G. Dahlstrom, D. Lachar, & L. E. Dahlstrom (Eds.), *MMPI patterns of American minorities* (pp. 3–23). Minneapolis: University of Minnesota Press.

Dana, R. H. (Ed.). (1999). *Handbook of cross-cultural and multicultural personality assessment.* Mahwah, NJ: Erlbaum.

Exner, J. (1993). *The Rorschach: A comprehensive system* (Vol. 1, 3rd ed.). Asheville, NC: Rorschach Workshops.

Geisinger, K. F. (1998). Psychometric issues in test interpretation. In J. Sandoval, C. L. Frisby, K. F. Geisinger, J. D. Scheuneman, & J. R. Grenier (Eds.), *Test interpretation and diversity: Achieving equity in assessment* (pp. 17–30). Washington, DC: American Psychological Association.

GoPaul-McNicol, S., & Armour-Thomas, E. (2002). *Assessment and culture: Psychological tests with minority populations.* San Diego, CA: Academic Press.

Hall, G. C. N., Bansal, A., & Lopez, I. R. (1999). Ethnicity and psychopathology: A meta-analytic review of 31 years of comparative MMPI/MMPI-2 research. *Psychological Assessment, 11*(2), 186–197.

Hall, G. C. N., & Phung, A. H. (2001). Minnesota Multiphasic Personality Inventory and Millon Multiaxial Inventory. In L. A. Suzuki, J. G. Ponterotto, & P. J. Meller (Eds.), *Handbook of multicultural assessment: Clinical, psychological, and educational applications* (2nd ed.). San Francisco: Jossey Bass.

Helms, J. E. (1992). Why is there no study of cultural equivalence in standardized cognitive ability testing? *American Psychologist, 47,* 1083–1101.

Helms, J. E. (1997). The triple quandary of race, culture, and social class in standardized cognitive ability testing. In D. P. Flanagan, J. L. Genshaft, & P. O. Harrison (Eds.), *Contemporary intellectual assessment: Theories, tests and issues* (pp. 517–532). New York: Guilford Press.

Helms, J. E. (in press). Challenging some misuses of reliability as reflected in evaluations of the White Racial Identity Attitude Scale. In R. T. Carter (Ed.), *Handbook of racial-cultural psychology and counseling: Theory and research* (Vol. 1, pp. 360–390). Hoboken, NJ: Wiley.

Hiller, J. B., Rosenthal, R., Bornstein, R. F., Berry, D. T. R., & Brunell-Neuleib, S. (1999). A comparative meta-analysis of Rorschach and MMPI validity. *Psychological Assessment, 11*(3), 278–296.

Iwakaki, S., & Vernon, P. E. (1988). Japanese abilities and achievements. In S. H. Irvine & J. W. Berry (Eds.), *Human abilities in cultural context* (pp. 358–384). New York: Cambridge University Press.

Kaufman, A. S. (1994). *Intelligent testing with the WISC-III.* New York: Wiley.

Kaufman, A. S., & Kaufman, N. L. (1983). *Kaufman Assessment Battery for Children.* Circle Pines, MN: American Guidance Service.

Kaufman, A. S., & Kaufman, N. L. (1990). *Kaufman Brief Intelligence Test.* Circle Pines, MN: American Guidance Service.

Klopfer, B., & Kelley, D. (1942). *The Rorschach technique.* Yonkers, NY: World Books.

Murray, H. A. (1943). *The Thematic Appreception Test.* Cambridge, MA: Harvard University Press.

Poortinga, Y. H. (1983). Psychometric approaches to intergroup comparison: The problem of equivalence. In S. H. Irvine & J. W. Berry (Eds.), *Human assessment and cultural factors* (pp. 237–258). New York: Plenum Press.

Prifitera, A., Weiss, L. G., & Saklofske, D. H. (1998). The WISC-III in context. In A. Prifitera & D. H. Saklofske (Eds.), *WISC-III clinical use and interpretation: Scientist-practitioner perspectives* (pp. 1–38). New York: Academic Press.

Reynolds, C. R. (1982). The problem of bias in psychological assessment. In C. R. Reynolds & T. B. Gutkin (Eds.), *The handbook of school psychology* (pp. 178–208). New York: Wiley.

Ritzler, B. A. (2001). Multicultural usage of the Rorschach. In L. A. Suzuki, J. G. Ponterotto, & P. J. Meller (Eds.), *The handbook of multicultural assessment* (2nd ed., pp. 237–252). San Francisco: Jossey-Bass.

Roid, G. H., & Miller, L. J. (1997). *Leiter International Performance Scale—revised.* Wood Dale, IL: Stoelting.

Rorschach, H. (1942). *Psychodiagnostik* (Hans Huber Verlag, Trans.). Bern, Switzerland: Bircher. (Original work published 1921)

Sattler, J. M. (1992). *Assessment of children* (3rd ed. rev. and updated). San Diego, CA: Author.

Steele, C. M., & Aronson, J. (1998). Stereotype threat and the test performance of academically successful African Americans. In C. Jenck & M. Phillips (Eds.), *The Black White test score gap* (pp. 401–427). Washington, DC: Brookings Institution.

Sternberg, R. J., & Kaufman, J. C. (1998). Human abilities. *Annual Review of Psychology, 49,* 479–502.

Suzuki, L. A., & Kugler, J. F. (2001). Multicultural assessment. In E. R. Welfel & R. E. Ingersoll (Eds.), *The mental health desk reference* (pp. 279–291). New York: Wiley.

Suzuki, L. A., Ponterotto, J. G., & Meller, P. J. (Eds.). (2001). *Handbook of multicultural assessment* (2nd ed.). San Francisco: Jossey-Bass.

Suzuki, L. A., & Valencia, R. (1997). Race/ethnicity and measured intelligence: Educational implications. *American Psychologist, 52*(10), 1103–1114.

Suzuki, L. A., Varniak, D. A., & Kugler, J. F. (1996). Intellectual assessment across cultures. In L. A. Suzuki, P. J. Meller, & J. G. Ponteroto (Eds.), *Handbook of multicultural assessment: Clinical, psychological and educational applications* (pp. 141–178). San Francisco: Jossey-Bass.

Takushi, R., & Uomoto, J. M. (2001). The clinical interview from a multicultural perspective. In L. A. Suzuki, J. G. Ponterotto, & P. J. Meller (Eds.), *The handbook of multicultural assessment* (2nd ed., pp. 47–66). San Francisco: Jossey-Bass.

Thorndike, R. L., Hagen, E. P., & Sattler, J. M. (1986). *Technical manual for the Stanford-Binet Intelligence Scale* (4th ed.). Itasca, IL: Riverside.

Trimble, J. E. (in press). An inquiry into the measurement of ethnic and racial identity. In R. T. Carter (Ed.), *Handbook of racial-cultural psychology and counseling: Theory and research* (Vol. 1, pp. 320–359). Hoboken, NJ: Wiley.

Valencia, R. R., & Suzuki, L. A. (2001). *Intelligence testing and minority students: Foundations, performance factors, and assessment issues.* Thousand Oaks, CA: Sage.

Van de Vijver, F. J. R., & Poortinga, Y. H. (1997). Towards an integrated analysis of bias in cross-cultural assessment. *European Journal of Psychological Assessment, 13,* 29–37.

Vernon, P. A., Jackson, D. N., & Messick, S. (1988). Cultural influence on patterns of abilities in North America. In S. H. Irvine & J. W. Berry (Eds.), *Human abilities in cultural context* (pp. 208–231). New York: Cambridge University Press.

Viglione, D. J. (1999). A review of recent research addressing the utility of the Rorschach. *Psychological Assessment, 11*(3), 278–296.

Wechsler, D. (1991). *Manual for the Wechsler Intelligence Scale for Children* (3rd ed.). New York: Psychological Corporation.

Wilson, M. S., & Reschly, D. J. (1996). Assessment in school psychology training and practice. *School Psychology Review, 25,* 9–23.

Wood, J. M., Nezworski, M. T., & Stejskal, W. J. (1996). The comprehensive system for the Rorschach: A critical examination. *Psychological Science, 7*(1), 3–10, 14–17.

CHAPTER 19

Racial-Cultural Issues in Clinical Assessment

Curtis W. Branch

Psychology is unique among the behavioral and social sciences. It attends to many variations in behavior by focusing on normative processes, that is, developmental psychology, and corrective actions for deviant behavior. Because of the breadth of issues covered under the branches of psychology that are akin to mental health (i.e., clinical psychology, counseling psychology, forensic psychology), they are sometimes linked with medical intervention models and the diagnosis and amelioration of psychiatric problems. One of the skills that psychologists bring to the task of diagnosing and treating psychiatric problems is psychological assessment, also called clinical assessment (Buckley & Frankin, this *Handbook,* this volume).

The strategies and approaches that psychologists have employed when interacting with diverse racial and cultural groups have a long and checkered history. Major changes in attempting to be sensitive to racial, ethnic, and cultural groups, hereafter referred to as people of Color, have been enacted by psychologists over the past 25 years. I review that history and highlight new advances in the area of clinical assessment, focusing on issues of race and culture.

In this chapter, four objectives are proposed. First, basic assumptions inherent in the lore of clinical assessment and their historic roots are reviewed. Second, the literature on specific instruments and its utility with people of Color is critiqued. Structured personality instruments, projective techniques, and structured interview protocols are explored. Third, a summary of the psychology community's strategies and approaches for evaluating people of Color is articulated. Fourth, a perspective of new directions is highlighted.

Throughout this chapter, the term *people of Color* refers to the collective category of individuals who are ethnic minorities. The term *ethnic minorities* is used only when the author whose work is being discussed includes this term. *Clinical assessment* refers to the use of standardized psychological tests, projective techniques, and clinical interviews. The emphasis in this chapter is on personality assessment. Issues of intelligence and educational performance are not discussed. Draguns's (1975) idea that there are three tasks/challenges of personality assessment (individual differences, constitutional consistencies, organization of characteristics and processes within individuals) is the operational definition of personality assessment employed here (Suzuki, Kugler, & Aguiar, this *Handbook,* this volume).

Before embarking on a discussion of how psychology has dealt with the issues of race and cultural matters in the clinical evaluation process, I think it is necessary to revisit some fundamental assumptions on which clinical evaluation rests. The assumptions presented in this chapter are so widely accepted that they are rarely questioned or even articulated.

BASIC ASSUMPTIONS

The process of clinical assessment is complex and involves multiple variables that interact simultaneously. I have chosen to highlight a few assumptions concerning the evaluator, the client, the evaluation process itself, and the interaction between the evaluator and the client. The person completing the clinical evaluation is assumed to be competent (Newland, 1973; Schafer, 1954). Clients are assumed to be motivated to do a good job during the assessment process (Schafer, 1954; Suzuki et al., this *Handbook,* this volume). The client's skills are usually assumed to be sufficient to express what he or she is thinking and feeling in a manner that is intelligible to the evaluator (Schafer, 1954). Instruments selected for use in the clinical assessment are assumed to be reliable and valid for the population with which they are being used. The behavior sample that is acquired during the evaluation is judged to be sufficient to justify the conclusions reached by the evaluator. The client's behavior during the assessment is assumed to be predictive of his or her behavior in the real world (Bellak & Bellak, 1952; Morgan & Murray, 1935; Schafer, 1954; Suzuki et al., this *Handbook,* this volume; Trimble, this *Handbook,* Volume One).

Concerning the Evaluator

It is generally assumed that the person completing a clinical evaluation is competent and skillful. In most states, the expectation of clinician competence is backed by statutory regulations governing who is qualified to complete professional clinical evaluations. With few exceptions, licensure is based on the examination of academic training and professional experience. In principle, such statutes provide protection from charlatans and inadequately trained clinicians.

Several decades ago, Schafer (1954) suggested that the tester brings a set of needs and problems to the testing situation (e.g., that of his or her professional situation, role in the testing relationship, own personality) that may adversely impact the outcome. Other scholars (Dana, 2000; Draguns, 1996) have also commented on the evaluator's level of knowledge of the unique racial and cultural history of clients and how they affect performance during a clinical evaluation. The task then requires the clinician to be conversant in social and developmental factors that may have impacted the client's development, including matters of race and culture. Perhaps it is an impossible task to really understand each person's unique life experiences, but a competent evaluator has an ethical responsibility to show a basic sense of understanding of variations in human growth and development that may occur as a result of racial and cultural variations (American Psychological Association, 2002).

Concerning the Client

The client is motivated to make a good impression during the assessment process. This assumption presumes that clients have a level of investment in the assessment process that will cause them to be cooperative and fully disclosing. Historically, this assumption can be traced to the early psychological writings of Schafer (1954) and Morgan and Murray (1935).

Lindzey (1952) reports that there are certain assumptions basic to the interpretation of projective techniques (e.g., Thematic Apperception Test). Specifically, Lindzey notes that in completing or structuring an incomplete or unstructured situation, the individual may reveal his or her own strivings, dispositions, and conflicts. Lindzey adds a note of caution to this assumption by further noting that the storyteller's dispositions, strivings, and conflicts are sometime represented indirectly or symbolically. Other early scholars-clinicians interested in projective techniques advanced a similar set of assumptions (McClelland, Atkinson, Clark, & Lowell, 1953; Z. Piotrowski, 1950; White, 1951). Z. Piotrowski (1950) notes that "the stories may not reflect genuine drives but superficial and stereotyped attitudes developed by the testee in order to hide his specific personality traits" (p. 16). Lasaga (1951) agreed with Piotrowski and called the patient's attempt to disguise conflicts a process of symbolic substitution.

Another common assumption in clinical assessment situations is that the client has sufficient exposure to psychological evaluation procedures to understand the ramifications of his or her behavior during the evaluation sessions. Clinicians often assume that the client understands that anything said in the session will be used as part of the deliberations, possibly resulting in conclusions that are not in his or her best interest.

The belief that people convey information about themselves based on what they say, what they do not say, and how they communicate such information when presented with a new or neutral stimulus is traceable to psychoanalytic tenets (Morgan & Murray, 1935; Phillips & Smith, 1953; Schafer, 1954). By now, the belief that when confronted with a neutral situation clients will necessarily project their authentic feelings onto the situation is tacitly accepted by many clinicians of various theoretical persuasions.

It is assumed that the client's skills are sufficient to adequately express what he or she is thinking and feeling. It is also widely assumed that the clinician is able to understand what the client is saying or knows enough to ask for clarifications when needed. These assumptions deserve to be converted into empirical research questions.

Concerning the Instruments and Procedures

Frequently, the type of responses elicited by standardized instruments are assumed to be sufficient to understand the life experiences of all people. What people say they would do is believed to be predictive of what they will do in real situations, an assumption of congruence between the real world and fantasy. This is the central foundation on which psychological assessment procedures rest. Asking clients about hypothetical situations does offer some insights into how they are able to cognitively respond to the situation. Questions of a hypothetical nature also provide the evaluator with a glimpse of what the client holds as an intellectual repertoire for responses. Frequently, hypothetical situations do not factor issues of race and ethnicity into the equation, a person's phenomenology as it relates to the real-world occurrence of such events, or the environmental contingencies that may be at work if the client encountered such an experience in real-world conditions.

In clinical assessment situations, clients are asked how they might respond to a situation or what they think might be happening in a picture. In the former situation, the racial and cultural identity of the adjacent actors is usually not mentioned. Many people have had different kinds of experiences when dealing with people unlike themselves. The assessment setting often does not explore such information.

Concerning Evaluator-Client Interactions

The tester/evaluator is acknowledged as a human being who brings personal issues to the assessment session (Schafer, 1954). The tester's issues are exacerbated by the relationship with the person who is being evaluated

> by the additional responsibilities he assumes and gratifications he seeks because of his personality make-up, and by the behavior of the patient and the particular conflicts in the tester this behavior stimulates. (p. 7)

Gitelson (1952) and Berman (1949) suggest that it is meaningless to attempt to set up an ideal (i.e., completely impartial) psychotherapy or evaluation session. Rather, they point out that the likelihood of countertransference should be recognized and embraced. Countertransference occurs when the evaluator has a negative and illogical reaction to the client. Fromm-Reichman (1950) observes that therapists seek gratifications and securities through their job and their relationship with patients. The same, Schafer (1954) asserts, can be said of the tester/evaluator.

Bellak (1986) assumes that evaluation sessions are also likely to be tempered by the phenomenon of transference. In this context, transference refers to "that part of the emotional relationship of the patient to his psychoanalyst which is predicated upon earlier feelings toward other significant figures" (p. 33). Transference implies that the patient transfers to the analyst (evaluator/tester) feelings that have been learned in other relationships (Liu & Pope-Davis, this *Handbook,* this volume).

The overarching assumption is that the interaction between the evaluator and the client is likely to reflect dynamics that have their origins in places and relationships that predate the evaluation session(s).

BASIC ASSUMPTIONS REVISITED: CONSIDERING ISSUES OF RACE AND CULTURE

The previous assumptions date back to an earlier period in the history of psychology. Since they were originally articulated some of the assumptions have been addressed directly by different constituencies in the psychological community. Specifically, the reality of racial and cultural differences among consumers of psychological services has been addressed at the level of policy guidelines that have profound implications for the competency level of clinicians. The formation of organizations (i.e., Association of Black Psychologists, Asian American Human Services Association,

Hispanic Psychological Association) devoted to the improvement of psychological services to different racial and cultural groups has also expanded the scope of scholarship relative to different groups.

Concerning the Evaluator

The American Psychological Association (APA) has provided concrete leadership in addressing the issue of competence of evaluators in assessing racial and cultural subgroup individuals by issuing several statements and guidelines that affirm the reality of racial and cultural differences. The APA statements not only affirm the reality of the subgroups of individuals but also speak to the need for clinicians to be sensitive and competent when dealing with such constituents.

The Vail Conference (Korman, 1974) states very directly that students in training for clinical practice areas should receive training and exposure to issues of diversity and cultural differences. Professional organizations concerned with the assessment of clients have outlined standards for the ethical use of tests in educational and psychological settings (American Educational Research Association, American Psychological Association, and National Council on Measurement in Education, 1999). In addition, APA has offered guidance for the use of standardized tests with racial and cultural groups:

> Psychologists use assessment instruments whose validity and reliability have been established for use with members of the population tested. When such validity and reliability has not been established, psychologists describe the strengths and limitations of tests and interpretation. (American Psychological Association, 2002, p. 1071)

More recently, APA adopted the Multicultural Guidelines in 2003 as a way of strongly encouraging psychologists to learn to effectively respond to issues of race and culture. All of these acts speak to legislative and policy positions. Whether and how the wisdom of the acts will infuse the academic endeavors of training programs and the practice standards of clinicians remains to be seen. Suzuki, Ponterotto, and Meller (2001) are optimistic about the movement in the direction of positive changes that now embrace cultural and racial differences as a reality of life. They point out that most counseling psychology programs now have at least one course devoted entirely to issues of race and culture, and many other programs have thoroughly integrated consideration of these issues into their curriculum. Scholars and clinicians have also focused on issues of race and cultural differences in completing psychological assessments (Ponterotto & Austin, this *Handbook,* this volume).

Concerning the Client

The development of racial and cultural identity theories in the past 25 years has impacted the clinical assessment enterprise, including the dynamics of clients being evaluated. The developmental phases through which many people of Color evolve have been subjected to research investigations by several scholars (Atkinson, Morten, & Sue, 1998; Cross, 1971; Helms, 1984) and are now being used as the basis for the development of new research paradigms (see Constantine et al., this *Handbook,* this volume; Constantine & Wilton, this *Handbook,* this volume). Cuellar (2000) notes that level of acculturation is a significant moderator of personality and psychological assessment. Notions of color-blind and completely objective assessment of people with varied and rich life courses are being discarded. Instead, the unique experiences that clients have are considered to be cardinal to understanding them and their way of being in the world. Avoidance of race- and culture-related issues is seen as antithetical to appropriate professional behavior.

The elevation of race and culture, one's own and that of others, to positions of prominence in the thinking of clinicians, I believe, helps to create a more inclusive lens for understanding clients. Various racial/ethnic and cultural groups have distinct histories that affect members of those groups differently (Cross, 1991); that is, not all members of a group will have the same phenomenology. To be effective, clinicians are required to be sensitive to the many faces of race and culture that may exist within a single group. Changes in client population has created new demands for clinicians to become conversant with multicultural issues in their approaches to assessment and psychotherapy (Ota Wang, this *Handbook,* this volume).

The belief in a client's propensity for projecting his or her inner psychological life onto a neutral object in a testing situation (e.g., inkblot) is further complicated when the issues of race and culture are added to the proceedings. For example, many clients of Color feel that the mental health establishment does not respect or appreciate them as human beings (D. Sue & Torino, this *Handbook,* this volume; Thompson, this *Handbook,* this volume). Entry into such a system for the purpose of an evaluation is likely to conjure up images of being misconstrued or even abused, harking back to negative experiences in the larger society. With such apprehensions, the client may reluctantly agree to the assessment while being in a state of perceived helplessness or duress.

Limited facility with the English language often interferes with many bilingual clients telling their story in a way that the clinician can fully understand. The risk of misrepresentation also operates among clients who use street vernacular in their daily verbal communications. If the clinician is not conversant in the client's language or dialect, there is a high probability that the client will not be heard accurately. The combination of unusual articulation of ideas plus anxiety about the whole assessment experience may result in an unreliable and inaccurate image of the client. Frequently, the fault is attributed to the client. Statements like "The client did not express himself clearly" and "The client was evasive in sharing information about herself" further serve to mask the fact that the client was being very clear but that the clinician did not understand what was being said (Faubert & Locke, this *Handbook,* this volume).

Concerning the Instruments and Procedures

The psychology community appears to have accepted race and culture as facts of life. In the area of clinical assessment and psychotherapy, several major volumes on multiculturalism have been published in the past 25 years (Dana, 2000; Pedersen, Draguns, Lonner, & Trimble, 1989; Sodowsky & Impara, 1996; Suzuki, Ponterotto, & Meller, 2001).

New strategies for assessing clients of Color are being advanced by scholars at a very rapid rate. Old theoretical positions of culture/race blindness and neutrality are being abandoned in favor of positions that acknowledge the primacy of race and culture. Lonner and Adamoulos (1997) note that personality and culture are inextricably intertwined. Several measures of racial and cultural identity have been developed and are being used by clinicians with varying degrees of success. The cultural self is highlighted in many assessments (see Helms, this *Handbook,* this volume; Trimble, this *Handbook,* this volume).

The revolution has even found its way into academic training settings, where sensitivity to racial and cultural differences is reflected in multicultural courses. The APA's (2003) adoption of the Multicultural Guidelines is an example of organizational and policy change in the direction of valuing cultural inclusiveness. Lopez (2000) describes his approach to integrating issues of race and culture into core courses on psychological assessment. All of the foregoing changes herald the beginning of a new era. The clinical assessment functions performed by psychologists are not being abandoned but are moving in the direction of acquiring a new identity themselves.

Many people of Color have had very painful experiences with people outside of their cultural reference group. Therefore, it cannot be assumed that what they say they would do in response to hypothetical situations may not be true, if the racial and ethnic identity of the other characters is not mentioned (i.e., in ambiguous cards).

Concerning Evaluator-Client Interactions

I believe most of the dynamics related to issues of culture and race that have been attributed to psychotherapy relationships also apply to psychodiagnostic relationships. Therefore, I believe that many of the findings originally posited in discussions of psychotherapy and counseling are relevant to clinical assessment.

Helms (1984) states that there is a difference of self-presentation in relationships between clinician and clients based on race. The clinician is perceived to be more powerful than the client; because of this, his or her racial identity has the potential to exert more power than the client's. Helms identifies four types of relationships (parallel, crossed, progressive, regressive) that are created by the interaction of the patient's and the therapist's racial identity statuses. Carter (1995) cautions:

> To understand the complexity of race in the therapeutic process it is necessary to extend traditional formulations of race and construct psychologically grounded theory where race is an important aspect of identity and worldview. (p. 74)

Porter (2000) indicates that because many people of Color have deferential attitudes toward doctors and other professionals, the dynamics of these relationships (e.g., client-doctor) may be characterized by transference reactions. More recently, Sommers-Flanagan and Sommers-Flanagan (2003) report that transference and countertranference reactions are likely to occur in clinical assessment dyads that are interracial.

The literature on assessment and psychotherapy appears to affirm the early basic assumption that clinician and client both bring their own issues to the assessment sessions. When the issues are racial and cultural in nature they probably will not get addressed openly and honestly, owing in part, I think, to the highly charged history that is associated with race, racism, and racial ideations in this country.

Over the past 25 years several scholars have commented on the impact of race and culture on psychotherapy and clinical assessment relationships and outcomes (Aponte & Clifford, 1995; Carter & Pieterse, this *Handbook,* this volume; Dana, 1995; Griffin, 1977; Lindsey, 1998; Parham & Helms, 1981; Ridley, 1995; Sodowsky & Impara, 1996).

CLINICAL ASSESSMENT INSTRUMENTS

A host of instruments are available to psychologists for purposes of evaluating personality. Rather than attempt to discuss most of those instruments, I focus here on the following: Minnesota Multiphasic Personality Inventories (MMPI, MMPI-2, and MMPI-A), Rorschach Inkblot Test, Thematic Apperception Test, and clinical interviews (Suzuki et al., this *Handbook,* this volume).

Minnesota Multiphasic Personality Inventories

The original version of the MMPI was published in 1943 (Hathaway & McKinley, 1940). It was not subjected to any major revisions until approximately 50 years later. The revision program resulted in the current version of the test intended for use with adults (MMPI-2) and the version intended for use with adolescents (MMPI-A). In its original format, the test was intended to be used in treatment settings for the purpose of routine diagnostic assessment. Over the years the test has come to be one of the most widely used psychological tests. It has routinely been used for a plethora of purposes in diverse settings, including psychiatric treatment proceedings.

The original test was standardized on 724 individuals who were visiting relatives or friends at the University of Minnesota Hospitals. All of the persons in the normative sample were White and residents of small towns or rural areas, mean age about 35 (Graham, 2000). After its introduction for professional use, the MMPI gained widespread popularity and was even translated into several languages. In the 1960s, concern was expressed that the test was outdated, used archaic language, and generally was not in touch with much of the audience with which it was being utilized. Concerns were also raised about the test's utility with clinical and nonclinical samples.

A study by Colligan, Osborne, and Offord (1980) demonstrated that there were problems with the test that could be attributed to historical effects. Colligan et al. collected data from normal persons in the areas where the original test data had been collected. The researchers found that there was a stronger pattern of endorsing items in the scored direction than had been reported by Hathaway and McKinley (1940). The tendency of clients to endorse items in the scored direction was interpreted by Colligan et al. as evidence that the normalized scores were appropriate for use with all subjects. Their conclusions were met with different results and conclusions by Hsu (1984) and Graham and Lilly (1986).

Gynther and his colleagues (Gynther & Green, 1980) and Greene (1987) raised questions concerning the use of the MMPI with Blacks. Gynther and Green reported that the differences in results with Black versus White test takers meant that normal Blacks were more likely than normal Whites to be incorrectly identified as abnormal. Dahlstrom, Lachar, and Dahlstrom (1986) countered by noting that when Black and

White groups were comparable in age, education, and other demographic character-istics, the differences were smaller and often not significant. An accuracy test was proposed by Pritchard and Rosenblatt (1980) as the only meaningful way of analyz-ing racial differences on the MMPI. Little progress was made on that front because of a general lack of consensus about what constitutes an accuracy test (Greene, 1987; Pritchard & Rosenblatt, 1980). Dahlstrom and his colleagues addressed the issue of racial disparity in profile performance between Blacks and Whites by suggesting:

> The best procedure was to accept the pattern of MMPI scores that results from the use of the standard profile sheet and, when the profile is markedly deviant, to take special pains to explore in detail the subjects' life circumstances to understand as fully as possible the na-ture and degree of their problems and demands and the adequacy of their efforts in dealing with them. (Graham, 1990, p. 191)

Perhaps the greatest complaint about the MMPI was the absence of racial and cultural diversity in the normative sample. The fact that people of Color were ex-cluded from the normative sample became a major point of contention among schol-ars and clinicians and spawned a large literature.

Walters, Greene, and Jeffrey (1984) investigated the influence of race (Blacks versus Whites) on MMPI performance. They discovered that the test failed to show differences across race when alcoholism status was controlled. They also found that the MMPI was useful in identifying White alcoholics but not Black alcoholics. Beck, McRae, Heinrichs, and Sneider (1990) examined the MMPI for racial and sexual dif-ferences. Their results, based on 11,571 males and 9,289 females, were interpreted by the authors as evidence that sex- and race-specific scoring methods were needed. Other researchers have weighed in on both sides of the debate concerning the bias of the MMPI and the need for race-specific norms; some are in favor of race-specific norms (Gynther, 1972; Gynther & Green, 1980); and others are against such special-ized norms (Dahlstrom, Lachar, & Dahlstrom, 1986; Greene, 1978, 1980; Holcomb, Adams, & Ponder, 1984). Gynther (1972), one of the strongest advocates for race-specific MMPI norms, summarized the controversy succinctly in a statement on the research:

> Definitive answers to the racial bias question may be difficult to reach due to the unlikeli-hood of finding the unbiased criteria required to test the accuracy of inferences about racial subgroups from the MMPI. (p. 878)

Timbrook and Graham (1994) explored African American and White differences on the MMPI-2 by analyzing the data of men (75 African American, 725 White) and women (65 African American, 743 White). All of the subjects were part of the MMPI restandardization sample. Gender differences were small and were attrib-uted to demographic characteristics. When the differences were controlled, fewer MMPI-2 scale differences were found. No significant racial group differences were found in terms of clinical profile types (e.g., elevated clinical scale scores). Bryan (1990) argued that the differences in MMPI-2 results should be subjective features of the assessment, like the race of the examiner, level of subjects' racial identity, and cultural influences. He specifically suggested that race (of examiner, of client) may explain Black people's differential responses to psychological evaluations. Sturmer and Gerstein (1997) reviewed 20 years of research exploring the possibility of racial bias in MMPI findings and concluded that the data were contradictory and not conclusive. In addition, they reasoned that it was inappropriate to compare the profiles of Black clients to a normative sample that was all White. The debate regarding the utility of the MMPI and MMPI-2 with Black subjects continues.

The issue of racial bias on the MMPI focused primarily on Black-White differences. Very little of the dialogue was extended to include other racial and ethnic groups. A multiracial normative sample was utilized for the revised version of the test (MMPI-2). People of Color were included in the normative sample in the same proportions as they appear in the U.S. census. Butcher and Williams (1998) assumed that the inclusion of ethnic minorities would end the controversy surrounding the racial/ethnic biases of the test. The expansion of the normative sample, however, did not end the discussion about the cross-racial and cross-ethnic utility of the test. In fact, it may have sparked even more discussion, evidenced in part by the large number of cross-cultural comparative studies using the test and the expansion of the dialogue to include racial and ethnic groups other than Blacks. In a review of the literature comparing Hispanics and Whites, Greene (1987) highlighted several studies that showed differences in their patterns of responding to the test. He concluded, however, that there was no pattern to the differences on the test between Hispanic and White subjects. The argument continues.

Some researchers have used misguided logic in extrapolating findings from Black samples to try to explain the pattern of responses of other cultural groups. For example, Graham (2000) asserts:

> Given data concerning the meaning of MMPI-2 scores of African Americans the expectation would be to find more similarities than differences in the meaning of MMPI-2 scores for Native Americans and Caucasians. (p. 229)

Recent guidebooks for the use of the MMPI-2 (Graham, 2000; Greene, 2000) have devoted a considerable amount of energy to explaining racial/ethnic differences. In each instance, the greatest coverage is of African Americans, always juxtaposed against White (Caucasian) subjects. Graham summarizes his presentation by noting that differences between African Americans and Caucasians are small when groups are compared on variables such as age and socioeconomic status. When differences are found, he reports, they tend to be associated with relevant extratest characteristics and probably should not be attributed to test bias (p. 223). Greene also presents an extensive review of Black-White comparative studies. The results of Greene's meta-analysis are interpreted as indicating that there are no significant differences between the performance of Blacks and Whites on the MMPI that can be attributed to racial factors.

The literature on Hispanics and the MMPI/MMPI-2 offers another variation on the theme of racial differences. There are few studies of Hispanics, and most of these are compared to Whites. They show a pattern of mixed results. Some of the studies indicate that there are significant differences in how Hispanics and Whites perform on the MMPI; other studies show no significant differences between the two groups. Whitworth and Unterbrink (1995) compared Hispanic Americans and Whites. Their results indicated that Hispanics scored higher than the White subjects on two of the three validity scales. There was a similar difference on the basic clinical scales, where Hispanics scored higher on 4 of the 10 scales. Whites scored higher on the Correction scale. Hispanics scored higher on 13 of 15 content scales. Whitworth and Unterbrink concluded that their results do not invalidate the use of the MMPI-2 with Hispanics. According to Whitworth and Unterbrink, there is no evidence to support separate Hispanic norms. Another study by Whitworth and McBlaine (1993) found no significant differences between Blacks and Hispanics (i.e., comparing MMPI and MMPI-2 profiles).

The issue of racial differences in MMPI (MMPI-2) performance has a long history. Attempts to resolve the observed differences, using different cultural and racial groups as the basis of comparison, have come in the form of single studies and large meta-analyses. Hall and his colleagues (Hall, Bansal, & Lopez, 1999) completed a meta-analysis of 25 comparative studies. They found aggregate effect sizes that suggest higher scores for some ethnic minority groups than European Americans on some scales and lower scores on others. In the context of their work, ethnic minority means African American and Latino American. The researchers concluded that the MMPI and MMPI-2 do not unfairly portray African Americans or Latinos as pathological. They do, however, believe that research focusing on within-ethnic-group psychopathology should continue. The within-group psychopathology issue has been studied by a few researchers who have focused on Latino populations.

Scott, Butcher, Young, and Gomez (2002) sampled the potential applications on the adolescent version of the MMPI (e.g., MMPI-A) by studying various Spanish-speaking adolescents in several countries. Their sample consisted of 385 participants, ages 14 to 18, in Colombia, Mexico, Peru, Spain, and the United States. A high degree of similarity was found in the results obtained on the basic content and supplementary scales. The U.S. sample was used as the implicit norm. The researchers note that there were no significant deviations from the norms observed among the U.S. participants. Some slight but statistically insignificant differences were observed among the males on the Faking, Hypochondriasis, and Masculinity-Femininity scales in Peru and Colombia. Female subjects deviated slightly from the U.S. sample on Scales Paranoia and Schizophrenia. Overall, the results were interpreted as evidence that the Hispanic MMPI-A is appropriate for adaptation in countries other than the United States.

A similar study focusing on Hispanic youth was conducted by Gumbiner (1998), with slightly different outcomes and interpretations. Gumbiner used the MMPI-A to study 30 Hispanic adolescents between the ages of 14 and 18. Elevated T scores on several scales for the females and lower than normal mean scale scores for females were found. Gumbiner concluded that the test underpathologized females. Another major finding of the study was that the males scored higher on the Immaturity scale than the females.

Negy, Leal-Puente, Trainor, and Carlson (1997) explored how 120 Mexican American adolescents, ages 13 to 18, performed on the MMPI-A, a short demographic questionnaire, and a five-item version of the Acculturation Rating Scale for Mexican

Americans. Results of the study suggest that there were minimal differences on the validity, clinical, and content scales between the experimental sample and the normative sample on whom the test is based. Level of acculturation and socioeconomic status were identified as significant contributors in test performance. The more acculturated and high-SES individuals scored more like the normative sample than the less acculturated and economically poorer individuals.

The adult literature concerning the utility and validity of the MMPI-2 with Spanish-speaking participants has also produced some interesting findings. Two studies in particular are of special significance. Cabiya et al. (2000) examined the validity of Spanish translations of the MMPI-2. Participants in their research were from Puerto Rico ($n = 290$), Mexico ($n = 1,920$), and the United State ($n = 28$). No significant differences were found on the mean scale scores earned by each subgroup of participants; the observed differences were all reported to be within 1 standard deviation. The authors perceive these findings to be significant because three different versions of the MMPI-2 were utilized.

Velasquez and his colleagues (Velasquez et al., 2000) report on a similar body of research. They report the findings of two separate studies that seem to confirm the comparability and usefulness of the English-language version of the MMPI-2 and the *Version Hispana*. In the first study, Velasquez et al. used two administrations of the MMPI-2, one in English and the other in Spanish, with 57 undergraduates. The second study compared the results of administrations of translated versions of the MMPI-2. Twenty-seven participants were involved in the second study. No significant score differences were found. Test-retest reliability was utilized. The rate of reliability of results was found to be higher among the participants who completed the English and Spanish versions of the test than those who completed only one version of the test. Despite their enthusiasm about the consistency of the results, the authors offer several cautionary notes, including the need for more within-group (i.e., persons in the Latino community) research and more research with clinical populations.

McNulty, Graham, Ben-Porath, and Stein (1997) commented on the latter point a few years earlier. They compared African American and Caucasian mental health center clients in an attempt to understand the clinical utility of the MMPI-2. They correlated mean scores for 123 African American and 561 Caucasian clients with conceptually related therapist ratings for the two groups. Several differences were noted. African American men scored significantly higher on the Lie and Fears content scales than did their Caucasian counterparts. African American women scored higher than their Caucasian counterparts on Hypomania. Caucasian women scored higher on the Low Self-Esteem content scale. No significant differences were noted when the MMPI-2 and patient rating forms were correlated. This pattern of inconsistent results was interpreted by the authors as evidence that there is no bias in the MMPI-2 but that the mean score differences represent real differences in levels of psychopathology.

Efforts to carefully delineate the impact of cultural factors and their influence on MMPI/MMPI-2 profiles have been explored most extensively throughout the Hispanic/Latino diaspora, with adult and adolescent clinical and nonclinical populations. Results have varied.

Mendoza-Newman, Greene, and Velasquez (2000) also offers research findings that are at variance with the canon of no significant difference between the MMPI-2 profiles of Hispanics and Caucasion normative groups. Mendoza-Newman et al. studied 65 Mexican American adolescents in the San Francisco Bay Area by using the MMPI-A, a demographic questionnaire, and the Acculturation Rating Scale for Mexican Americans II (ARSMA-II; Cuellar, Arnold, & Moldanado, 1995). They report that there was no relationship between acculturation or SES as individual variables and Lie Scale and Masculinity-Femininity (Scale 5). Surprisingly, there was a significant negative correlation between the combination of acculturation and SES and Lie Scale. There was no relationship between those variables and Masculinity-Femininity. Other scholars like Velasquez et al. (1998) moved away from comparing ethnic groups with Whites. Their study focused on comparisons of Hispanics and other ethnic minorities and Allen (1998) highlights understanding level of acculturation when examining Native Americans.

The MMPI-2 research data on Asian Americans is very limited. Graham (2000) points out that few Asian Americans ($n = 19$) were included in the normative sample for the MMPI-2. Okazaki (1998) notes that Asians/Asian Americans are also represented in a limited way in the literature on cultural competence assessment best practices. The limited coverage of Asians, Okazaki asserts, has made it difficult to set a research agenda for cultural competency in assessment (Suzuki et al., this *Handbook,* this volume).

The MMPI-2 has been shown to be of clinical utility when assessing clients of Color. Arguments about the test being biased have been subjected to a variety of statistical and clinical test. Some scholars (Cuellar, 2000; Lindsey, 1998) continue to call for race- and culture-specific norms as a way to eliminate the problems of test insensitivity when administered to people of Color. Draguns (1996) takes a more moderate approach: "The conclusion is still justified that the MMPI is a usable, but imperfect, tool of appraisal within the multicultural American setting, especially for the limited purpose for which it was originally designed (i.e., diagnostic aid)" (p. 69).

Rorschach Inkblot Test

The Rorschach Inkblot Test also has a long history. Since the test was introduced by Hermann von Rorschach it has been widely used for diagnostic purposes. French and Levitt (1992) estimate that the Rorschach is a widely used clinical instrument, competing closely with the MMPI-2 and Wechsler scales. Despite its popularity, the test has been the object of considerable criticism, based on the belief of many clinicians and researchers that the procedure by which it is administered, the stimuli, and the interpretive systems are culturally biased. Research to establish the efficacy and clinical utility of the Rorschach with diverse cultural groups has been sparse in comparison with the MMPI/MMPI-2 literature. Nevertheless, the issue of culture and test performance has been discussed.

Surprisingly, however, there has been little progress in showing that the test has widespread utility with multiple racial and cultural groups. Several years ago, Frank (1993) started to address this issue by reviewing studies that detail the performance of African Americans on the Rorschach. He observed that the historical tendency has been to compare the performance of African Americans against that of White Americans. Frank questioned why that pattern was the research paradigm of choice for so many researchers, including ethnic minority scholars. To date, his question has no substantive reply and the practice of installing White Americans as the implicit standard against which everyone else's Rorschach performance is compared continues without interruption (Carter, this *Handbook,* this volume).

Presley, Smith, Hilsenroth, and Exner (2001) were interested in the clinical utility of the Rorschach with African Americans. White Americans and African Americans were compared by Presley et al. A matched (i.e., age, sex, education, and SES) group of 44 subjects from each group was drawn from the Exner Comprehensive System. It was found that the African American participants offered fewer cooperative movement responses than their White counterparts. Presley et al. interpret the finding as possibly suggesting that:

> African Americans do not anticipate cooperative interactions with others as a routine event. This may reflect a shared feeling among African Americans that most members of our society are less likely to be sensitive to or responsive to their need relative to others.

No other significant differences between the groups were found. This latter finding led to a conclusion that the Rorschach does have a high degree of clinical utility for African Americans.

Bachran (2002) explored the issue of clinical utility of the Rorschach with Latinos. Specifically, Bachran examined the Popular response because it is highly analogous to basic perception. One hundred fifty self-identified Latinos were tested. Results from Bachran's sample were compared to those found in the Exner normative test data. The age groupings for participants were 13, 14, 15, 16, and 17+. All of the groups examined by Bachran differed significantly from Exner's published normative data. An additional comparison was made between Bachran's 17+ age group and Exner's norms for adult depressives, character disorders, and schizophrenics. Again, there were striking differences between the two samples. Bachran interpreted this pattern of consistent differences between her sample and the Exner sample as evidence that there is a need for new norms for Latinos.

Bachran (2002), but not Presley et al. (2001), assumes that the ethnic identity of the participants alone is sufficient to explain possible variation in test response pattern (Juby & Concepción, this *Handbook,* Volume One; Trimble, this *Handbook,* Volume One). Other demographic variables, such as educational level, level of acculturation, and life circumstances, are not explicitly addressed.

Cruz, Brier, and Reznikoff (1997) extended the question of moderator variables as contributors to Rorschach performance to include learning disability status. They studied 44 ethnic minority participants (ages 12 to 16). The form level responses of their participants were no different from those reported in previous studies conducted with White middle-class children. Cruz, Brier, and Reznikoff think the age, ethnicity, and lower SES level of their participants do not adversely impact the form level responses. Rather, they think it is the participant's learning disability status that explains the lower form level response, in their study and others, than is found among respondents without learning disabilities in Exner's normative data.

The dissimilarity of results and conclusions between these two studies highlight a significant point. What is the basis of conclusions about variance in test result differences? Presley and his colleagues (2001) attributed their outcomes to demographic variables (i.e., age, SES, sex, education).

The Rorschach and its utility with people of Color continues to be debated. Unfortunately, most of the studies affirming appropriateness of the test have relied on the overworked model of comparing the responses of people of Color to those of White Americans. Within-group comparisons would permit researchers to test the consistency of Cross's (1991) observation that all people with a shared historical legacy do not necessarily see the world in the same way or develop a common strategy for responding to social issues and obstacles. Researchers who use aggregate data to interpret individuals' response patterns on the Rorschach are seriously limited in their understanding of individual differences and the global concept of racial and cultural diversity. Perhaps a strategy of comparing responses of healthy and adjudicated pathological individuals in a specific racial/cultural group would offer more explanatory power than the models currently operating on the basic assumption of cultural homogeneity.

Other Structured Personality Inventories

The Thematic Apperception Test (TAT) was created in 1943 by Morgan and Murray as a technique to facilitate the process of self-revelation by the client during the early stages of therapy (Constantino, Flanagan, & Malgady, 2001, p. 217). Since its creation the test has experienced widespread popularity in the United States (Piotrowski, Sherry, & Keller, 1985; Watkins, Campbell, Nieberding, & Hallmark, 1995), despite the fact that it does not have an objective scoring system (Constantino et al., 2001).

In its original version, the TAT consists of 30 cards depicting characters in a variety of social situations. The clinical assumption associated with the TAT was that the cards would stimulate the client to tell a story about the scene depicted and in the process reveal something of the client's inner life (i.e., motivations, drives, values, and conflicts). Over the years, other variations on the TAT have appeared. The Children's Apperception Test (CAT; Bellak & Bellak, 1952), depicting animals instead of human figures in the pictures, and the Senior Apperception Technique, depicting older adults, are direct descendants of the Morgan and Murray (1943) work.

Modifications and cultural variations on the TAT have occurred in the past 50 years. The Thompson Modification (T-TAT; Thompson, 1949) utilizes redrawn Murray pictures. Thompson assumed that Black clients would feel more comfortable with Black characters in the stimulus cards and relate more directly with them. The anticipated result was that Black clients would engage in deeper levels of self-disclosure if they were presented with Black stimulus characters. Williams (1972) developed the Themes Concerning Blacks (TCB), also based on the assumption of greater utility of Black stimulus cards with Black clients. Dana (2000) thinks the TCB "may be used provisionally in preference to the T-TAT because of the culture-specific nature of the TCB cards but cautions that more research is needed on the scoring categories" (p. 67).

There is a paucity of literature from the past 15 years on the utility of the TAT with people of Color. Two studies of the TAT focus on issues of race and culture. Monopoli and Altworth (2000) examine the process of acculturation by using TAT protocols with Native Americans. Four themes consistent across two levels of acculturation were found. The authors note that social pressures and economic hardships, pervasively present throughout the Native American diaspora, explain their results. Hibbard et al. (2000) found that acculturation level and level of English-language proficiency were not significant factors in their study of 60 Asian Americans and 83 White students. Hibbard et al. used the Defensive Mechanism Manual (DMM; Cramer, 1991) to code TAT stories. Surprisingly, the DMM scales predicted defenses among Asian Americans at a higher rate than it did among Whites. According to the authors, "Desirable criteria were overpredicted for Asians (Asian Americans) whereas undesirable ones were overpredicted for Whites" (p. 351).

Dana (1990) thinks the MMPI/MMPI-2 and its lesser-known offsprings, 16PF and California Personality Inventory, have all consistently failed to convey a comprehensive picture of the person being evaluated. In particular, Dana notes, the tests have failed to evaluate their subjects on the dimensions of social and cultural self. In that sense, they could be perceived as biased: "The self is a product of culture and epoch" (1990, p. 20). Acculturation and racial/ethnic identity are two critical issues that influence an individual's cultural self. Dana (1990) cautions readers against assuming that acculturation and self-definition are simple and linear processes. Rather, he notes, they represent complex processes that may express themselves in a variety of ways (e.g., language skills, social values, social behaviors) (Suzuki et al., this *Handbook,* this volume). Other scholars have also indicated that acculturation can be a bi- and trilevel process (Mendoza, 1984; Mendoza & Martinez, 1981; Olmeda, 1979; Ramirez, 1984; Wong-Riegler & Quintana, 1987).

Likewise, racial identity (i.e., one's perceived sense of psychological identification with one or more racial groups) has also been articulated as a vitally important component of self (Helms, 1985, 1990, this *Handbook,* Volume One). Traditional assessment instruments have not made consistent or significant efforts to integrate concepts of the cultural self into an understanding of the client's psychological profile. Clinical interviews provide an opportunity for clinicians to obtain information about a client that is not elicited by standardized tests.

Clinical Interviews

The clinical interview is designed to gather information from the client that will assist the evaluating clinician in developing a comprehensive profile of the client and in answering the questions that are the basis of the referral. Clinical interviews can be completed at any phase of the assessment process (i.e., beginning, middle, or end). They can also be used to gather new information or to provide elaboration on information obtained from other sources. In many ways, the clinical interview is the most demanding and important component of the clinical assessment. Interview format, length, and focus may vary according to the purpose for which it is being used. Interviews provide clinicians with an opportunity to interact with the client in a spontaneous manner and to assess the client's verbal and cognitive skills in an ongoing dialogue. Three issues related to the clinical interview are briefly discussed here: level of structure, cultural match between clinician and client, and language.

Interviews can vary in level of structure from highly structured to minimally structured. Highly structured interviews often come in the form of prepackaged questions that greatly resemble personality inventories. Examples of structured interviews are the Diagnostic Interview Schedule for Children (DISC-IV; Shaffer, 1999) and the

Child Adolescent Schedule (CAS; Hodges, 1985). The DISC and CAS both have a high level of reliability and validity as clinical instruments, but neither specifically addresses questions related to issues of race and culture that may help to explain the client's pattern of symptomatology. Rather, the DISC-IV and CAS appear to operate from the assumption that the client's behavior is the result of factors that can be understood simply by applying traditional wisdom and predictive models.

Semistructured interviews are less rigid in their approach to understanding the client. They provide clients with an opportunity to express their own feelings about what is important, relative to the stated reasons for the evaluation. The chance that a client will share some part of his or her cultural belief system is greater with a semistructured interview than with a highly structured interview schedule. Such verbalizations, however, are not likely to enter into the discussion with the evaluator unless clients feel comfortable that they can add new issues, or variations on previously discussed issues, to the conversation with the clinician. The literature suggests that such levels of comfort are likely to occur when there is a perceived good match between the client and the clinician (Cokley, this *Handbook,* this volume; Sattler, 1998).

Interviews that are low in structure, sometimes called unstructured, are probably more akin to what most clinicians identify as clinical interviews. Despite being called unstructured, they do have an agenda: understanding the client's world and the factors that have contributed to the client's current situation. In many ways, interviews low in structure are the most challenging because they require active and sustained attention on the part of the client and the clinician.

Structured and semistructured interviews are often characterized as being impersonal because they do not directly ask about the client's specific and unique life experiences. Unfortunately, the literature has not addressed the question of whether the different levels of interviewing are differentially effective in eliciting information from racially and culturally different groups of client. Again, one of the assumptions of many structured interview schedules is that there is a cultural equivalence to concepts discussed in the instruments (Trimble, this *Handbook,* Volume One). Based on the assumption of equivalence, some instruments are translated into other languages without any conceptual adjustments. What has been done to make interview schedules useful across racial and cultural lines? What has been done to address the questions of racial/ethnic congruence of clinician and client and how that affects the outcome of clinical assessments?

LOOKING TO THE FUTURE

> *With managed care, the field of assessment is rapidly moving away from the historically prominent instruments, MMPI, Rorschach, TAT. Functional assessment, structured interviews, rating scales, etc. are on the rise. At the same time, there are developments in cultural assessment, scales of ethnic identification, acculturation, etc.*
>
> —J. Draguns, Personal communication, December 18, 2003

Several measures have been developed for the purpose of assessing the cultural self as a way of obtaining a more complete psychological profile of individuals. Padilla's

Acculturation Scale (Padilla, 1980), the Racial Identity Attitude Scale (Helms, 1986), the Suinn-Lew Acculturation Scale (Suinn, Richard-Figuero, Lew, & Vigil, 1987), the Na-Mea-Hawaii Acculturation Scale (Rezentes, 1993), ARSMA-II (Cuellar et al., 1995), and Tell-Me-A-Story (TEMAS; Constantino, Malgady, & Rogler, 1988) are examples of cultural self-assessment instruments that are currently in use (see also Helms, this *Handbook,* Volume One; Trimble, this *Handbook,* Volume One; Richardson, this *Handbook,* this volume; Suzuki et al., this *Handbook,* this volume). The introduction of instruments for assessment of the cultural self is hailed as a major step forward. There are limitations, however, associated with the premise of some of the instruments (see Draguns, 1995). Information from these types of instruments adds an important element to psychological test profiles, especially profiles of individuals who identify themselves as a person of Color. Lopez (2000) reports that self cultural data can be used to augment and, in some instances, make more intelligible data obtained by traditional assessment instruments.

Clinical assessments are intended to provide comprehensive appraisals of clients. Structured personality inventories are but one source of clinical data. They are limited in that they can provide only information within the scope of the test and the theory that undergirds the test. Additional sources of information can also be incorporated into the assessment process, including personal statements of the client, developmental history of the client, clinical interviews, and cultural self-assessment inventory.

CONCLUSIONS

The clinical practice and research literature on clinical assessment is filled with many assumptions. Issues related to cultural diversity are addressed in a variety of ways. In some instances, cultural variance among consumers (i.e., clients) and practitioners (i.e., clinicians) are completely ignored. The belief appears to be that all people are the same. Conversely, some literature notes that issues unique to persons for whom cultural identity (e.g., racial, ethnic) is paramount should be considered in the assessment process. The latter position has resulted in scholars noting that level of acculturation, language preference, and choice of instruments should be closely monitored.

Assumptions concerning the clinical evaluation process are so pervasive that they are rarely questioned. One big assumption has been that the absence of statistical difference in scores between racial and ethnic groups means that there is no difference. The tests on which no differences are found (e.g., MMPI-2, 16PF) are judged by some to show no bias. That is a limited perspective. Bias can also take the form of a test's failing to include critical items that are important to one group. This appears to be the case with the structured psychological inventories discussed in this chapter. The cultural self is ignored by the MMPI-2, 16PF, and California Inventory. Is one to assume that the authors of those tests believe that the cultural self is unimportant? Or, is one to assume that the creators of the tests do not acknowledge the existence of a cultural self?

The voluminous literature relating to cultural differences on the MMPI and MMPI-2 seems to operate on the assumption of cultural homogeneity. In an attempt to make the test more universal in its appeal, ethnic minority persons were included in the recent restandardization, in roughly the same proportions that they appear in the 1980 U.S. census. What is accomplished by this statistical balancing? Several things are accomplished, but none are as profound as they are assumed to be. First, the new standardization sample is able to establish that a test can produce a cluster of items that are answered similarly by most respondents. Second, the new standardization sample continues to assume that there is a high degree of homogeneity among ethnic minority persons. Having data about a small subset of minority persons does not explain the variance that may exist in another small sample. It is interesting to note that the level of acculturation of the ethnic minorities included in the standardization process is not considered, or at least it is not reported.

Some very promising efforts are being made in the area of assessment in the form of creating culturally sensitive instruments. There is a long history of this type of activity. TEMAS is a good example of researchers building on old assumptions and then directly addressing issues of race and culture. The research on TEMAS confirms its utility with people of Color and offers statistical evidence to support the reliability and validity of the test (Suzuki et al., this *Handbook,* this volume).

Traditional assessment procedures, however, continue to be used. Modification of a process by simply adapting the stimuli overcomes some of the problems inherent in the original process but does not overcome others. Perhaps new directions can articulate new stimuli as well as new methods for assessing clients, methods that are less wedded to old assumptions. The intensity of efforts in this regard is very promising! The proliferation of new material, rethinking of positions on race and culture that move beyond recycling of old assumptions may lead to new and novel creations. Perhaps in the near future we will have not only new wine but also new bottles in which to store it!

REFERENCES

Allen, J. (1998). Personality assessment with American Indians and Alaska Natives: Instrument considerations and service delivery style. *Journal of Personality Assessment, 70*(1), 17–42.

American Educational Research Association, American Psychological Association, and National Council on Measurement in Education. (1999). *Standards for educational and psychological testing.* Washington, DC: American Psychological Association.

American Psychological Association. (2002). Ethical principles of psychologists and code of conduct. *American Psychologist, 57*(12), 1060–1073.

American Psychological Association. (2003). Guidelines on multicultural education, training, research, practice, and organizational change for psychologists. *American Psychologist, 58*(5), 377–402.

Aponte, J., & Clifford, J. (1995). Education and training issues for intervention with ethnic groups. In J. F. Aponte, R. Young Rivers, & J. Wohl (Eds.), *Psychological interventions and cultural diversity* (2nd ed., pp. 283–300). Boston: Allyn & Bacon.

Atkinson, D. R., Morten, G., & Sue, D. W. (Eds.). (1998). *Counseling American minorities* (5th ed.). Boston: McGraw-Hill.

Bachran, M. (2002). Latinos' perception of the Rorschach inkblots: An examinations of the popular response. In E. Davis-Russell (Ed.), *The California School of Professional Psychology handbook of multicultural education, research, intervention and training* (pp. 151–161). San Francisco: Jossey-Bass.

Beck, N., McRae, C., Heinrichs, T., & Sneider, L. (1990). Replicated item level factor structure of the MMPI: Racial and sexual differences. *Journal of Clinical Psychology, 45*(4), 553–560.

Bellak, L. (1986). *The T.A.T., C.A.T., and S.A.T. in clinical use* (4th ed.). Boston: Allyn & Bacon.

Bellak, L., & Bellak, S. (1952). *The C.A.T.—H.—A human modification.* Larchmont, NY: C.P.S.

Berman, L. (1949). Countertransference and attitudes of the analyst in the therapeutic process. *Psychiatry, 12,* 159–166.

Bryan, P. (1990). Psychological assessment of Black Americans. *Psychotherapy in Private Practice, 7*(3), 141–154.

Butcher, J., & Williams, C. (1998). *Essentials of MMPI-2 and MMPI-A interpretation.* Minneapolis: University of Minnesota Press.

Cabiya, J., Lucio, E., Chavira, D., Castellanos, J., Gomez, F., & Velasquez, R. (2000). MMPI-2 scores of Puerto Rican, Mexican, and U.S. Latino students: A research note. *Psychological Reports, 87*(1), 266–268.

Carter, R. T., & Pieterse, A. L. (in press). Race: A social and psychological analysis of the term and its meaning. In R. T. Carter (Ed.), *Handbook of racial-cultural psychology and counseling: Theory and research* (Vol. 1, pp. 41–63). Hoboken, NJ: Wiley.

Colligan, R., Osborne, D., & Offord, K. (1980). Linear transformation and the interpretation of MMPI T scores. *Journal of Clinical Psychology, 36,* 162–165.

Constantine, M. G., Watt, S. K., Gainor, K. A., & Warren, A. K. (in press). The influence of Cross's initial black racial identity theory on other cultural identity conceptualizations. In R. T. Carter (Ed.), *Handbook of racial-cultural psychology and counseling: Theory and research* (Vol. 1, pp. 94–114). Hoboken, NJ: Wiley.

Constantine, M. G., & Wilton, L. (in press). The role of racial and cultural constructs in history of the multicultural counseling movement. In R. T. Carter (Ed.), *Handbook of racial-cultural psychology and counseling: Theory and research* (Vol. 1, pp. 64–77). Hoboken, NJ: Wiley.

Constantino, G., Flanagan, R., & Malgady, R. (2001). Narrative assessments: TAT, CAT, and TEMAS. In L. Suzuki, J. Ponterotto, & P. Meller (Eds.), *Handbook of multicultural assessment* (2nd ed., pp. 217–236). San Francisco: Jossey-Bass.

Constantino, G., Malgady, R., & Rogler, L. (1988). *TEMAS (Tell-Me-A-Story) manual.* Los Angeles: Western Psychological Services.

Cross, W. E., Jr. (1971). The Negro-to-Black conversion experience: Toward a psychology of Black Liberation. *Black World, 20,* 13–27.

Cross, W. E., Jr. (1991). *Shades of Black: Diversity in African-American identity.* Philadelphia: Temple University Press.

Cruz, E., Brier, N., & Reznikoff, M. (1997). An examination of the relationship between form level rating on the Rorschach and learning disability status. *Journal of Psychology, 131*(2), 167–174.

Cuellar, I. (2000). Acculturation as a moderator variable of personality and personality assessment. In R. Dana (Ed.), *Handbook of cross-cultural and multicultural assessment* (pp. 113–131). Mahwah, NJ: Erlbaum.

Cuellar, I., Arnold, B., & Moldanado, R. (1995). The Acculturation Rating Scale for Mexican Americans—II (ARSMA-II): A revision of the original ARSMA scale. *Hispanic Journal of Behavioral Sciences, 17*(3), 275–304.

Dahlstrom, W., Lachar, D., & Dahlstrom, L. (1986). *MMPI patterns of American minorities.* Minneapolis: University of Minnesota Press.

Dana, R. (1990). Cross-cultural and multi-ethnic assessment. In J. Butcher & C. Spielberger (Eds.), *Advances in personality assessment* (Vol. 8, pp. 1–26). Hillsdale, NJ: Erlbaum.

Dana, R. (1995). Culturally competent MMPI assessment of Hispanic populations. *Hispanic Journal of Behavioral Sciences, 17,* 305–319.

Dana, R. (2000). Psychological assessment in the diagnosis and treatment of ethnic group members. In J. Aponte & J. Wohl (Eds.), *Psychological intervention and cultural diversity* (2nd ed., pp. 69–89). Boston: Allyn & Bacon.

Draguns, J. (1975). Assessment of personality. In C. N. Cofer & H. E. Fitzgerald (Eds.), *Psychology: A programmed modular approach* (pp. 517–538). Homewood, IL: General Learning Press.

Draguns, J. (1996). Multicultural and cross-cultural assessment of psychological disorder: Dilemmas and decisions. In G. R. Sodowsky & J. Impara (Eds.), *Buros-Nebraska Symposium on Measurement and Testing: Vol. 9. Multicultural assessment in counseling and clinical psychology* (pp. 37–76). Lincoln, NE: Buros Institute of Mental Measurements.

Frank, G. (1993). The use of the Rorschach with Hispanic Americans. *Psychological Reports, 72*(1), 276–278.

French, J., & Levitt, E. (1992). Projective testing of children. In C. E. Walker & M. Roberts (Eds.), *Handbook of clinical child psychology* (2nd ed., pp. 149–162). New York: Wiley.

Fromm-Reichman, F. (1950). *Principles of intensive psychotherapy.* Chicago: University of Chicago Press.

Gitelson, M. (1952). The emotional position of the analyst in the psychoanalytic situation. *International Journal of Psychoanalysis, 33,* 1–10.

Graham, J. (1990). *MMPI-2: Assessing personality and psychopathology.* New York: Oxford University Press.

Graham, J. (2000). *MMPI-2: Assessing personality and psychopathology* (3rd ed.). New York: Oxford University Press.

Graham, J., & Lilly, R. (1986). *Linear T scores versus normalized T scores: An empirical study.* Paper presented at the 21st Annual Symposium on Recent Developments in the Use of the MMPI, Clearwater Beach, FL.

Greene, R. (1987). Ethnicity and MMPI performance: A review. *Journal of Consulting and Clinical Psychology, 55,* 497–512.

Greene, R. (2000). *The MMPI-2: An interpretive manual* (2nd ed.). New York: Grune & Stratton.

Griffin, M. (1977). The influence of race on the psychotherapeutic relationship. *Psychiatry, 40,* 27–40.

Gumbiner, J. (1998). MMPI-A profiles of Hispanic adolescents. *Psychological Reports, 82*(2), 659–672.

Gynther, M. (1972). White norms and Black MMPIs: A prescription for discrimination. *Psychological Bulletin, 78,* 386–402.

Gynther, M., & Green, S. (1980). Accuracy may make a difference, but does a difference make for accuracy? A response to Pritchard and Rosenblatt. *Journal of Consulting and Clinical Psychology, 48,* 268–272.

Hall, G., Bansal, A., & Lopez, I. (1999). Ethnicity and psychopathology: A meta-analytic review of 31 years of MMPI/MMPI-2 research. *Psychological Assessment, 11*(2), 186–197.

Hathaway, S., & McKinley, J. (1940). A multiphasic personality schedule (Minnesota): I. Construction of the schedule. *Journal of Psychology, 10,* 249–254.

Helms, J. E. (1984). Toward an explanation of the influence of race in the counseling process: A Black-White model. *Counseling Psychologist, 33*(1), 62–64.

Helms, J. E. (1985). Cultural identity in the treatment process. In P. Pederson (Ed.), *Handbook of cross-cultural counseling and therapy* (pp. 239–245). Westport, CT: Greenwood Press.

Helms, J. E. (Ed.). (1990). *Black and White racial identity: Theory, research, and practice.* Westport, CT: Greenwood Press.

Helms, J. E. (in press). Challenging some misuses of reliability as reflected in evaluations of the White Racial Identity Attitude Scale. In R. T. Carter (Ed.), *Handbook of racial-cultural psychology and counseling: Theory and research* (Vol. 1, pp. 360–390). Hoboken, NJ: Wiley.

Hibbard, S., Tang, P., Latko, R., Park, J., Munn, S., Bolz, S., et al. (2000). Differential validity of the Defense Mechanism Manual for the TAT between Asian Americans and Whites. *Journal of Personality Assessment, Volume, 75*(3), 351–372.

Holcomb, W., Adams, N., & Ponder, H. (1984). Are separate Black and White MMPI norms needed? An IQ-controlled comparison of murderers. *Journal of Clinical Psychology, 40*(1), 189–193.

Hsu, L. (1984). MMPI T scores: Linear versus normalized. *Journal of Consulting and Clinical Psychology, 52,* 821–823.

Juby, H. L., & Concepción, W. R. (in press). Ethnicity: The term and its meaning. In R. T. Carter (Ed.), *Handbook of racial-cultural psychology and counseling: Theory and research* (Vol. 1, pp. 26–40). Hoboken, NJ: Wiley.

Korman, M. (1974). National conference on levels and patterns of professional training in psychology: The major themes. *American Psychologist, 29*(6), 441–449.

Lasaga, J. (1951). In E. S. Shneidman (Ed.), *Thematic test analysis.* New York: Grune & Stratton.

Lindsey, M. (1998). Culturally competent assessment of African American clients. *Journal of Personality Assessment, 70,* 43–53.

Lindzey, G. (1952). TAT: Assumptions and related empirical evidence. *Psychological Bulletin, 49,* 1–25.

Lonner, W. J., & Adamopoulos, J. (1997). Culture as antecedent to behavior. In J. W. Berry, Y. H. Poortinga, & J. Pandley (Eds.), *Handbook of cross-cultural psychology* (2nd ed., Vol. 1, pp. 43–83). Boston: Allyn & Bacon.

Lopez, S. (2000). Teaching culturally informed psychological assessment. In R. Dana (Ed.), *Handbook of cross-cultural and multicultural personality assessment* (pp. 669–689). Mahwah, NJ: Erlbaum.

McClelland, D., Atkinson, J., Clark, R., & Lowell, E. (1953). *The achievement motive.* New York: Appleton-Century-Crofts.

McNulty, J., Graham, J., Ben-Porath, Y., & Stein, L. (1997). Comparative validity of MMPI-2 scores of African American and Caucasian mental health center clients. *Psychological Assessment, 9,* 464–470.

Mendoza, R. (1984). Acculturation and sociocultural variability. In J. L. Martinez, Jr. & R. H. Mendoza (Eds.), *Chicano psychology* (pp. 61–75). Orlando, FL: Academic Press.

Mendoza, M., Greene, R., & Velasquez, R. (2000). Acculturation, SES, and the MMPI-A. Paper presented at the 108th Annual American Psychological Association Convention, August 6, 2000. Washington, DC.

Mendoza, R., & Martinez, J. (1981). The measurement of acculturation. In A. Baron, Jr. (Ed.), *Explorations in Chicano psychology* (pp. 71–82). New York: Holt, Rinehart and Winston.

Monopoli, J., & Altworth, L. (2000). The use of Thematic Apperception Test in the study of Native American psychological characteristics: A review and archival study of Navaho men. *Genetic, Social, and General Psychology Monographs, 126*(1), 43–78.

Morgan, C., & Murray, H. (1935). A method for investigating phantasies: The Thematic Apperception Test. *Archives of Neurology and Psychiatry, 34,* 289–306.

Negy, C., Leal-Puente, L., Trainor, D., & Carlson, R. (1997). Mexican American adolescents' performance on the MMPI-A. *Journal of Personality Assessment, 69*(1), 205–214.

Newland, T. (1973). Assumptions underlying psychological testing. *Journal of School Psychology, 11*(4), 316–322.

Olmedo, E. (1979). Acculturation: A psychometric perspective. *American Psychologist, 34,* 1061–1070.

Padilla, A. (1980). The role of cultural awareness and ethnic loyalty in acculturation. In A. M. Padilla (Ed.), *Acculturation: Theory, models and some new findings.* Boulder, CO: Westview Press.

Parham, T., & Helms, J. (1981). The influence of Black students' racial identity attitudes on preference of counselor's race. *Journal of Counseling Psychology, 28,* 250–257.

Pedersen, P., Draguns, J., Lonner, R., & Trimble, W. (1989). *Counseling across cultures.* Honolulu, HI: University of Hawaii Press.

Phillips, L., & Smith, J. (1953). *Rorschach interpretations: Advanced techniques.* New York: Grune & Stratton.

Piotrowski, C., Sherry, D., & Keller, J. (1985). Psychodiagnostic test usage: A survey of the Society of Personality Assessment. *Journal of Personality Assessment, 49,* 115–119.

Piotrowski, Z. (1950). A new evaluation of the Thematic Apperception Test. *Psychoanalytic Review, 1,* 101–127.

Porter, R. (2000). Understanding and treating ethnic minority youth. In J. Aponte & J. Wohl (Eds.), *Psychological intervention and cultural diversity* (pp. 167–182). Boston: Allyn & Bacon.

Presley, G., Smith, C., Hilsenroth, M., & Exner, J. (2001). Clinical utility of the Rorschach with African Americans. *Journal of Personality Assessment, 77*(3), 491–507.

Pritchard, D., & Rosenblatt, A. (1980). Racial bias in the MMPI: A methodological review. *Journal of Consulting and Clinical Psychology, 48,* 263–267.

Ramirez, M., III, (1984). Assessing and understanding biculturalism—multiculturalism in Mexican American adults. In J. L. Martinez, Jr. & R. H. Mendoza (Eds.), *Chicano psychology* (pp. 77–94). Orlando, FL: Academic Press.

Rezentes, W. (1993). Na-Mea-Hawaii: A Hawaiian Acculturation Scale. *Psychological Reports, 73*(2), 383–393.

Ridley, C. (1995). *Overcoming unintentional racism in counseling and theory: A practitioner's guide to intentional intervention.* Thousand Oaks, CA: Sage.

Schafer, R. (1954). *Psychoanalytic interpretation in Rorschach testing.* New York: Grune & Stratton.

Scott, R., Butcher, J., Young, T., & Gomez, N. (2002). The Hispanic MMPI-A across five countries. *Journal of Clinical Psychology, 58*(4), 407–417.

Shaffer, D. (1999). *Diagnostic assessment in child and adolescent psychopathology.* New York: Guilford Press.

Sodowsky, G., & Impara, J. (Eds.). (1996). *Buros-Nebraska Symposium on Measurement and Testing: Multicultural assessment in counseling and clinical psychology* (Vol. 9). Lincoln, NE: Buros Institute of Mental Measurements.

Sommers-Flannagan, J., & Sommers-Flannagan, R. (2003). *Clinical interviewing* (3rd ed.). Hoboken, NJ: Wiley.

Sturmer, P., & Gerstein, L. (1997). MMPI profiles of Black Americans: Is there a bias? *Journal of Mental Health Counseling, 19*(2), 114–129.

Suinn, R., Richard-Figuero, K., Lew, S., & Vigil, S. (1987). The Suinn-Lew Asian Self-Identity Acculturation Scale: An initial report. *Educational and Psychological Measurement, 47,* 401–407.

Suzuki, L., Ponterotto, J., & Meller, P. (2001). Multicultural assessment: Trends and directions revisited. In L. Suzuki, J. Ponterotto, & P. Meller (Eds.), *Handbook of multicultural assessment* (2nd ed., pp. 569–574). San Francisco: Jossey-Bass.

Thompson, C. (1949). The Thompson modification of the thematic apperception test. *Journal of Projective Techniques, 17,* 469–478.

Timbrook, R., & Graham, J. (1994). Ethnic differences on the MMPI-2? *Psychological Assessment, 6*(3), 212–217.

Trimble, J. E. (in press). An inquiry into the measurement of ethnic and racial identity. In R. T. Carter (Ed.), *Handbook of racial-cultural psychology and counseling: Theory and research* (Vol. 1, pp. 320–359). Hoboken, NJ: Wiley.

Velasquez, R., Chavira, D., Karle, H., Callahan, W., Garcia, J., & Castellanos, J. (1998). Assessing bilingual and monolingual Latino students with translations of the MMPI-2: Initial data. *Cultural Diversity and Ethnic Minority Psychology, 6*(1), 65–72.

Walters, G., Greene, R., & Jeffrey, T. (1984). Discriminating between alcoholic and nonalcoholic blacks and whites on the MMPI. *Journal of Personality Assessment, 48,* 486–488.

Watkins, C., Campbell, V., Nieberg, R., & Hallmark, R. (1995). Contemporary practice of professional assessment by psychologists. *Professional Psychology: Research and Practice, 26,* 54–60.

White, R. (1951). In E. S. Shneidman (Ed.), *Thematic test analysis* (p. 188). New York: Grune & Stratton.

Whitworth, R., & McBlaine, D. (1993). Comparison of the MMPI and MMPI-2 administered to Anglo- and Hispanic-American university students. *Journal of Personality Assessment, 61*(1), 19–27.

Whitworth, R., & Unterbrink, C. (1995). Comparison of MMPI-2 clinical and content scales administered to Hispanic and Anglo-Americans. *Hispanic Journal of Behavioral Sciences, 16*(3), 255–264.

Williams, R. (1972). *Themes concerning Blacks.* St. Louis, MO: Author.

Wong-Riegler, D., & Quintana, D. (1987). Comparative acculturation of Southeast Asian and Hispanic immigrants and sojourners. *Journal of Cross-Cultural Psychology, 18,* 345–362.

CHAPTER 20

Racial-Cultural Practice: An Integrative Approach to White Racial Identity Assessment

Tina Q. Richardson and Eric E. Frey

Although race is a salient dimension on which all people in the United States are categorized, there is only a small body of theoretical literature concerning White Americans' perceptions of themselves as White and the implications of their racial group perceptions for intergroup interactions. Even more lacking in the literature are tools that provide objective and qualitative methods of assessing White identity. Kincheloe (1999) indicated that scholars are more equipped to explain privilege than to define the meaning of being White and how it is intertwined with politics and economic cycles and influenced by demographic changes. In counseling psychology and other domains of applied social sciences, theorists and researchers (Claney & Parker, 1989; Helms, 1990, 1995, 2001, this *Handbook,* Volume One; Rowe, Bennett, & Atkinson, 1994) have proposed models by which White people's racial self-perceptions might be investigated. White racial identity models can provide a means of understanding intrapersonal dynamics, interpersonal relationships, and issues of power and power differences between White and non-White people (Kincheloe, 1999).

Racial identity theory may have even greater potential for explaining intrapersonal and interpersonal dynamics if integrated with "mainstream" psychological theories and assessment (Richardson & Silvestri, 1999). The counseling profession has acknowledged that culture and worldview (e.g., racial identity) are an integral part of its theory and practice (Carter, this *Handbook,* this volume; Leong & Wagner, 1994; Richardson & Molinero, 1996; Sue, 1991; D. Sue & Torino, this *Handbook,* this volume). This idea occurred, at least in part, because of the realization that intraracial and interracial interpersonal dynamics affect the counseling process (Cook, 1994). Research on racial identity explains some of the complexities in such counseling relationships (Carter, 1990a; Helms, 1995; Helms & Carter, 1991; Liu & Pope-Davis, this *Handbook,* this volume; Ponterotto, Rieger, Barrett, & Sparks, 1994; Richardson & Helms, 1994). For example, racial identity theory explains why some counselors view clients solely in terms of their intrapsychic difficulties and overlook race and culture as possible external, systemic forces that affect clients. Thus, it is important to have effective methods to assess perceptions, affect, and behaviors that are associated with White identity. While some objective measures of White racial identity exist (Helms, 1990, 1995, this *Handbook,* Volume One; Pope-Davis, Vandiver, & Stone, 1999), we propose a qualitative approach for assessing White racial identity that emphasizes beliefs, affects, and behaviors that are related to race and racial group membership.

White racial identity models seem to offer the fullest perspective on the influences of intragroup perceptions on intergroup relations. White racial identity refers to a sense of group or collective identity based on one's perception that one shares a common White racial heritage with other Whites (Helms, 1990, this *Handbook,* Volume One). Helms's model of racial identity (1990, 1992) describes a variety of ways in which Whites may choose to identify with other Whites as a membership group, develop racial and cultural identities, and realize that sociopolitical implications result from their racial group membership. She describes six sequentially evolving ego statuses that differ in level of cognitive complexity with regard to racial identity. The first three statuses of identity (phase 1 identities) are associated with varying degrees of abandoning racism, whereas phase 2 identities (the last three statuses) reflect development toward a healthy nonracist identity. The statuses briefly summarized are as follows (Carter & Pieterse, this *Handbook,* Volume One; Helms, 1990, 1992, 1996, this *Handbook,* Volume One; Sue & Sue, 1999, 2003):

1. Contact is characterized by satisfaction with racial status quo and obliviousness regarding racism and one's participation in it.

2. Disintegration is characterized by a feeling of disorientation and anxiety caused by unresolved racial moral dilemmas that force one to choose between one's own racial group and humanity. As a result, one becomes increasingly aware of one's own Whiteness and experiences feelings of guilt, depression, helplessness, or anxiety.

3. Reintegration is best defined as the idealization of one's socioracial group and the denigration of and intolerance for other racial groups. This often leads to a feeling of entitlement regarding one's own racial group.

4. Pseudo-Independence is characterized by an intellectual commitment to one's own socioracial group and deceptive tolerance of other groups. This may lead to the reshaping of reality and selective perception.

5. Immersion/Emersion is best described as the search for an understanding of the personal meaning of racism and the ways that one benefits from it and a redefinition of whiteness.

6. Autonomy is characterized by an informed positive socioracial group commitment, the use of internal standards for self-definition, and the capacity to relinquish the privileges of racism. This may lead one to avoid options to participate in racial oppression.

Although Helms's (1990) model of White racial identity development postulates unique cognitive, affective, and behavioral correlates associated with each status, only attitudinal measures have been used to assess White racial identity (Claney & Parker, 1989; Helms, 1990). Helms's White Racial Identity Attitudes Scale (WRIAS) that assesses the six statuses has received the most empirical validation (e.g., Behrens, 1997; Helms, 1990, this *Handbook,* Volume One; Helms & Carter, 1990; Pope-Davis et al., 1999; Tokar & Swanson, 1991).

Rowe et al. (1994) also proposed a model of White racial consciousness that describes and predicts Whites' attitudes toward each other and other racial groups. White racial consciousness is defined as the characteristic attitudes held by a person regarding the significance of being White and what that implies in relation to those who do not share that membership. According to Rowe et al., the development and change of attitude is based on temporal and environmental influences but not necessarily on a developmental process. The focus of attitude change is on critical incidences that precipitate the occurrence of cognitive dissonance. The seven types of attitudes in the model are grouped into either an unachieved or an achieved status. There are three unachieved statuses which require no exploration or commitment to racial issues: (1) Avoidant reflects a lack of consideration of racial issues for self or others; (2) dependent refers to a superficial perspective on race based on the beliefs of significant others; and (3) dissonant reflects an uncertain position about race and racial issues. The four achieved identities result from exploration of racial issues and a commitment to beliefs. Achieved statuses are the (4) dominative type, which reflects strong ethnocentric views of one's own group; (5) conflictive type, which opposes both overt discrimination and overt systems designed to eliminate discrimination; (6) reactive type, which acknowledges racial discrimination and the privilege it affords Whites; and (7) integrative type, which values racial/cultural pluralism and integrates Whiteness in that value. Choney and Behrens (1996) developed the Oklahoma Racial Attitudes Scale (ORAS-P) to assess Rowe et al.'s (1994) model of White consciousness; the model has been validated in other research as well (Pope-Davis et al., 1999).

However, reliance on attitudinal measurement of racial identity, as is the case with Helms's (1990) and Choney and Behrens's (1996) scales, does not allow one to fully understand the complex process of White racial identity development (Ponterotto & Wise, 1987). According to Tokar and Swanson (1991), the degree of congruence between attitudinal and nonattitudinal components of identity development (e.g., observable communication patterns; affective states or feelings associated with cross-racial interactions) needs to be investigated. In addition, both Helms and Ponterotto and Wise indicated that future research may require the development of new instrumentation and innovative methodologies.

Additionally, Pope-Davis et al.'s (1999) psychometric examination indicates that neither the WRIAS (Helms & Carter, 1990) nor the ORAS-P (Choney & Behrens, 1996) fully measures the multidimensional construct of White identity as characterized by their respective models. The results of the factor analysis indicated that both the WRIAS and ORAS-P are best characterized by four constructs: (1) degree of racial comfort, (2) attitudes toward racial equality, (3) attitudes of racial curiosity, and (4) unachieved racial attitudes. However, neither of the scales measures all four of the constructs (i.e., both measure three of the four constructs). Given that the WRIAS was intended to measure five types of attitudes and the ORAS-P was supposed to measure seven, both seem to operate from limited dimensions (see also Helms, this *Handbook,* Volume One).

Strategies that assess the multidimensional nature of racial identity are needed to expand the limited focus of the WRIAS and ORAS-P. An alternative means of assessing racial identity must take into consideration the complexities of White racial identity development (e.g., the interplay between attitudes and behaviors). Structured (i.e., attitudinal) measures of racial identity development might work well in structured research or assessment situations, but to generalize racial identity to broader contexts, it seems necessary to have more flexible assessment techniques than existing attitude scales.

Richardson and Helms (1993) developed a projective measure that reflects the multidimensional complexity of White racial consciousness issues and generalizes to a wider range of social contexts than attitudinal measures. The White Racial Identity Reactions System (WRIRS; Richardson & Helms, 1993) uses an open-ended response format and provides the opportunity to respond to stimulus items on a variety of levels (i.e., affective, behavioral, and cognitive). The measure contributes to a more holistic method of assessing White racial identity in that the multidimensional levels of identity that are not captured in attitudinal scales are possible. In addition, the assessment of relationships are possible regarding White racial identity and interpersonal behaviors in a broad range of race-salient social contexts, such as interracial interactions, perceptions, and communications, as suggested by White racial identity theory.

PROJECTIVE MEASUREMENT OF WHITE RACIAL IDENTITY

The WRIRS, a projective measure, consists of 26 open-ended items that require written responses. The measure was designed to provide a semiprojective means of assessing White racial identity as described by Helms (1990, 1996). The projective measure provides a means of examining relevant affect, behaviors, and cognitions regarding White racial identity development. The items that constitute the scale are intended to elicit reactions concerning respondents' (1) awareness of their Whiteness (e.g., My race . . .); (2) manner of viewing themselves racially (e.g., I think of myself as . . .); (3) race-related cultural values (e.g., My racial background . . .); and (4) awareness of sociopolitical implications resulting from being White (e.g., Social class and race . . .).

The racial reaction categories based on Helms's (1990, 1996) theory of racial identity were used to develop the classification system to score the responses to the WRIRS. The participants are asked to provide three to four sentences for each sentence stem regarding beliefs, feelings, behaviors, and specific racial conflicts experienced. Each of 26 responses to stimulus items on the WRIRS are assigned to one of six racial mutually exclusive identity categories. A miscellaneous category exists in the event that a response does not clearly fit into any of the six categories. Each response is assigned to only one category, as indicated by a score of 1. Thus, the score for each category can potentially range from 0 to 26 for each participant. High scores or frequencies on a category indicate that a participant has a number of reactions that reflect a particular type of racial identity. The categories with the highest frequencies are indicative of a racial identity profile that can be used to understand how that individual thinks, feels, and behaves as a racial being.

Reliability of the reaction categories was established through interrater agreement (Richardson & Helms, 1993). Kappa coefficients for the seven categories were as follows: Contact = .82, Disintegration = .94, Reintegration = .73, Pseudo-Independence = .78, Immersion-Emersion = .90, Autonomy = .69, and Miscellaneous = .69. Pearson correlation coefficients were computed using the White racial identity attitude scale (Helms & Carter, 1990) as the criteria to determine convergent and divergent validity of the reactions measure. Intermeasure convergent validity was indicated by significant relationships between similarly named scales, Reintegration ($r(98) = .47$, $p \leq .001$) and Autonomy ($r(98) = .25$, $p \leq .01$) attitudes. Some significant relationships also involved sequential statuses of identity as proposed by the White identity model, whereas others involved parallel statuses. For example, significant sequential relationships exist between the Reintegration category and both the Disintegration scale ($r(98) = .46$, $p \leq .001$) and the Pseudo-Independent scale ($r(98) = -.28$, $p \leq .01$).

Several significant relationships between the reaction categories and scales provide support for divergent validity. The Disintegration scale was negatively related to Immersion ($r(98) = -.31$, $p = .001$) and Autonomy ($r(98) = -.29$, $p = .01$) reaction categories. The Reintegration scale was negatively related to Immersion ($r(98) = -.27$, $p = .01$) and Autonomy ($r(98) = -.26$, $p = .01$) reaction categories. Also, both the Pseudo-Independent and Autonomy scales were negatively related to the Reintegration category ($r(98) = -.28$, $p = .01$) and ($r(98) = -.39$, $p = .001$), respectively. Disintegration attitudes were significantly related to Reintegration reactions ($r(98) = .46$, $p = .001$) such that the higher one's Disintegration attitudes, the more likely one was rated to have expressed Reintegration reactions.

In addition, racial identity reaction categories predicted perceptions of racial dissimilarity. The overall regression model was significant ($R^2 = .25$, $F(6, 93) = 5.20$, $p = .0001$). Thus, when one's Reintegration reactions were frequent, Blacks and Whites were perceived to be dissimilar, and when Immersion reactions were frequent, Blacks and Whites were perceived to be more similar. Intergroup contact was predicted by racial identity reactions ($R^2 = .13$, $F(6, 93) = 2.35$, $p = .04$). Racial identity reactions also predicted intergroup anxiety ($R^2 = .25$, $F(6, 93) = 5.22$, $p = .0001$). Likewise, White racial identity reactions contributed to the predicted racial dissimilarity, intergroup contact, and intergroup anxiety beyond what was predicted by White racial identity attitudes (Richardson & Helms, 1993).

In summary, the results of the correlational analyses provided some support for both convergent and discriminant validity. The combination of racial identity reactions significantly predicted racial dissimilarity, intergroup contact, and intergroup anxiety.

APPLICATION OF THE PROJECTIVE MEASURE OF IDENTITY

According to racial identity theory (Helms, 1990; Rowe et al., 1994), each of the White identity statuses has its own unique effect on racial perceptions, behaviors, and emotions. However, the respective attitudinal scales (Carter & Helms, 1990;

Choney & Behrens, 1996) do not measure relevant behavioral and affective components of White identity. Additionally, the self-report attitudinal scales are quite susceptible to socially desirable responding, that is, political correctness and inflated identity profiles. The WRIRS can be used to circumvent some of these issues. For example, in a clinical setting, the WRIRS can help therapist and client explore attitudinal, affective, and behavioral tendencies that serve as the foundation of racial identity worldview where beliefs influence presenting concerns or relationship dynamics. The following cases provide illustrations.

—————————————————————— **Case 1** ——————————————————————

Sarah is a widowed, 52-year-old White female. She and her husband raised their three children in the suburbs of a major East Coast city. The children have graduated from college and started their adult lives. Sarah has always thought of herself as nonracist and quite liberal in her attitudes toward all people. She and her husband made a concerted effort to instill the same values in their children. However, she reports that her life has been turned upside down by her oldest son, who recently married an African American and is expecting her first grandchild.

Sarah indicates that her daughter-in-law is a nice person, well educated, and a credit to her race. However, she is terrified by her son's decision to bring a Black child into this world. She is angry with her son and does not want to have anything to do with this child. She indicates that she was looking forward to being a grandmother but would be embarrassed to go out in public with her son's family because she knows what everyone thinks. She indicates that she has Black friends and does not have any problems with them.

Sarah reported that one of her goals is to deal with her anger toward her son because he created problems for her grandchild. She would also like to understand why her son accuses her of being a racist because she taught him that being a racist is wrong.

———

If Sarah's racial identity is assessed via an attitudinal scale, she might have a racial identity profile that indicates a phase 2 identity status in Helms's model (1990, 1996). However, if her identity statuses are measured using an assessment strategy that takes into consideration the multidimensional aspects of attitudes, behaviors, and affect, a more accurate assessment of her racial identity status may be obtained. Accurate assessment is necessary in this case, as in most others, because neither therapist nor client can engage in the identity development process without a full understanding of the client's intrapersonal or interpersonal dynamics.

If the client is supported in the belief that her worldview is a liberal one, either through limitations created by attitudinal assessment or the therapist's one-dimensional conceptual understanding of race, the therapeutic process will be undermined. The client needs help understanding her concept of Whiteness in terms of the sociopolitical implications and how her concept undermines her family relations. In addition, she needs help dealing with anger and her son's accusations so that she may fully achieve a nonracist White racial identity.

The therapist can use the WRIRS to determine the combination of Sarah's White identity reactions and provide an accurate assessment of racial conflicts in her current identity status. The WRIRS will allow combination of the client's less developmentally sophisticated levels of racial attitudes, behaviors, and feelings (i.e., Contact, Disintegration, and Reintegration) that are theorized to be indicative of tendencies toward "racist" characteristics to be better understood. In the case of Sarah, a profile of her attitudes, affect, and behavior regarding race is not aligned. The WRIRS will allow the client to see the discrepancies in how her beliefs about the principles of equality do not correspond with her emotional experiences about people of Color and the types of relationships (i.e., feelings of love and affection) she believes are appropriate. Further, her behavior does not correspond with beliefs about equality. For example, Sarah is unwilling to be seen in public with her grandchild, who is an African American baby. It is through the integration of these dimensions that she may be able to understand her son's accusations.

On the other hand, racial identity attitudes, behaviors, and feelings reflective of more advanced levels of racial identity development (e.g., Immersion-Emersion, Autonomy) would also be identified. In turn, counseling interventions can incorporate the necessary strategies to help the client confront conflicts and integrate components of the desired identity. Whether the client's identity development occurs as a result of temporal and environmental influences (Rowe et al., 1993) or some other developmental processes, the WRIRS can be used to assist the change process.

APPLYING THE WHITE RACIAL IDENTITY REACTION SYSTEM

The WRIRS is a 26-item questionnaire that requires participants to qualitatively respond to sentence stems. The stems were designed to prompt each participant to reflect on his or her beliefs, feelings, and behaviors regarding differences between socioracial groups. For example, the sentence stem "I believe people of different racial backgrounds are . . ." prompts the participant to reflect on his or her beliefs regarding race. To prompt the participant to reflect on feelings regarding racial differences, the sentence stem "I feel emotionally close to people who are . . ." is designed to help participants think about their emotions regarding people from different socioracial groups. To assess behaviors, the sentence stem "If someone tried to talk to me about racial issues, I . . ." is an example of how the WRIRS determines the participant's behavior that might occur in situations related to socioracial differences.

Table 20.1 illustrates a summary of Sarah's responses on the WRIRS regarding her beliefs, feelings, and behaviors related to socioracial group differences. The results can yield a composite score that represents all three processes. In the case of Sarah, she provided responses that ultimately revealed that she is currently in the Disintegration status regarding her racial identity.

Figure 20.1 illustrates Sarah's reaction categories based on her reported beliefs, feelings, and behaviors. She appears to be in the Disintegration status regarding her beliefs because she is aware that there is a conflict with her son that is based on racial differences but she does not understand why her son is upset. Table 20.1 summarizes Sarah's beliefs that reflect her Disintegration status. It seems that Sarah is caught in a racial moral dilemma because she feels she must choose between her own socioracial group and her African American daughter-in-law.

Table 20.1   The Beliefs, Affect, and Behaviors That Sarah Indicated on the WRIRS

Step 1: Participant Responses to Sentence Stems	*Step 2: Reaction Categories*
Sample Sentence Stems and Responses	
Most White people believe ...	
All people were created equal.	
Everyone deserves a right to a happy life but people of Color are not willing to work hard enough.	Disintegration
Differences between groups are due to work ethics and determination.	
Regarding race, I was taught to believe ...	
Don't judge a book by its cover.	
There are some people of Color who are just as helpful as Whites.	
We have very little in common with most people of Color.	
Sample Sentence Stems and Responses	
The people of Color that I have the closest relationship with are ...	Contact
A colleague at work who does not cause me any problems.	
A neighboring Black family, whom I do not visit, seem very nice and do not cause problems.	
I see other people of Color in passing on a frequent basis.	
Sample Sentence Stems and Responses	
Around people of Color I feel ...	
I can exchange pleasantries with a neighbor and other people of Color, but no further contact.	Contact
Like securing my belongings (i.e., wallet or bags) when people of Color, especially males, are nearby, and I avoid places where they live.	Disintegration
The types of relationships that I have with people of Color are generally ...	Passive Reintegration
At work, and I attend church activities with Black families.	
The specific behaviors that demonstrate my racial beliefs are ...	
My son says I am rejecting and critical of my daughter-in-law and refuse to be seen in public with a Black grandchild. But I don't agree. I am only upset at what he's done and I have crying spells because of what my son has done to the family.	
Step 3:	
Determine the primary racial identity reaction categories associated with the responses	Disintegration and Contact

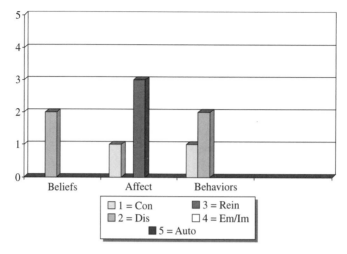

Figure 20.1   Sarah's reaction categories.

Sarah's responses regarding feelings on the WRIRS indicate that she is currently between the Contact and Reintegration status of her racial development. Her responses regarding feelings in Table 20.1 indicate that she fluctuates between acceptance of socially imposed rules regarding race (i.e., Contact) to the denigration of other racial groups and the idealization of her own socioracial group (i.e., Reintegration). According to her responses, Sarah does not appear to have strong emotionally engaged relationships with people of Color.

The behaviors reported by Sarah on the WRIRS indicate that she is currently between the Contact and Disintegration statuses of her racial identity development. Sarah indicated that she does associate with people of Color, which is consistent with obliviousness in the Contact status, but she has some awareness that there is a conflict related to racial differences. She is upset about the conflict, but she still does not fully understand why there is a problem. Table 20.1 illustrates her behaviors, which range from obliviousness regarding racism (i.e., Contact) to disorientation and confusion that is related to her racial moral dilemma regarding socioracial group commitment.

—————————————————————— **Case 2** ——————————————————————

Hope is a preschool teacher and has worked with children from different races and economic backgrounds for a number of years. She has always received recognition for doing a very good job with the children and they adore her. Because children are her passion, she was very disturbed by a parent who had serious concerns about how she organized show-and-tell one day. Hope's account of the incident to the therapist was the following. On the day in question, she greeted the children at the door when they entered the classroom. One of the mothers helped her African American son off with his coat and proceeded to hang it up. Hope noticed that the little boy was wearing an African print shirt with beautiful embroidery around the neckline of the garment. As the child greeted her, he was tugging on the bottom of the shirt. Assuming that he wanted to take it off, she told him to remove the shirt and hang it up until later, when he could wear it for the class at show-and-tell. The child obliged.

The next day, the child's mother asked to speak with Hope in private and informed the teacher of her displeasure at the suggestion that her son's "ethnic" clothes should be removed and worn for show-and-tell. Hope had no idea why the parent was upset but was very apologetic because she never intended to cause any harm or be insensitive. She was only trying to be helpful, prevent him from getting it dirty at play time, dress him like the other children, and ensure that he had something for show-and-tell.

Again, the therapist can use the WRIRS assessment procedure to help the client understand some of the subtle aspects of her racial identity and how it influences her interpersonally and professionally. Because the response format used on the WRIRS to assess racial consciousness is open-ended, as the client elaborates on various issues related to race, an accurate assessment of racial dynamics in the client's current identity can be obtained. If the client is supported in the belief that her worldview is a liberal one, through the therapist's limitations created by one-dimensional attitude assessment, the client's development and the therapeutic process will be undermined. The client needs help understanding how her concept of Whiteness as the social standard of judgment resulted in the objectification of at least one child's culture in the classroom. Although her intentions may have been positive, her actions made the child and manifestations of his culture (i.e., clothing) entertainment for the rest of the class in a manner that neither this child nor his clothes were intended to be.

In addition, Hope needs help integrating her attitudes, behaviors, and feelings so that she may fully achieve a nonracist White racial identity and enhance professional competence. Given the nature of her presenting concerns, I believe that she asked the therapist for help with both of these issues in the only manner that her current racial identity status would allow her to do.

Figure 20.2 indicates Hope's reaction categories based on her reported beliefs, feelings, and behaviors. She appears to be in the Contact status regarding her beliefs because she appears unwilling to recognize the inequality associated with race. Hope believes that everyone is equal and that race should not matter. This is indicative of the Contact status because she fails to realize that racism exists. Table 20.2 summarizes Hope's beliefs that she provided on the WRIRS.

The responses that Hope provided on the WRIRS reveal that she is between the Contact and Disintegration statuses regarding her feelings. This was determined because she was angry and offended that the child's mother made an issue about the clothing but did not fully understand why there was a problem. She also indicated that she feels indifferent toward people of Color and has few meaningful relationships with them. Hope is between the Contact and Disintegration statuses because she is aware of the conflict related to race, but she does not fully understand why there is a problem and still maintains her contact feelings regarding people of Color. Table 20.2 summarizes the feelings that Hope has regarding people of Color and the level of intensity of those feelings.

The behaviors that Hope provided for the sentence stems on the WRIRS indicate that she is currently in the Contact status for behavior. Hope teaches all of her children the same way because she believes there are no differences among them.

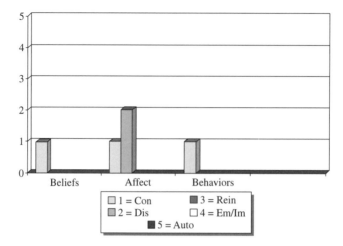

Figure 20.2   Hope's reaction categories.

She also volunteers at the soup kitchen because she wants to feel that she is willing to help people in need. Her behaviors reveal a low level of awareness that is consistent with the Contact status. Table 20.2 provides a summary of the behaviors that Hope provided on the WRIRS.

CONCLUSIONS

The WRIRS profile will allow better understanding of the combination of the client's less developmentally sophisticated and often subtle racial identity reactions (i.e., Contact, Disintegration, and Psuedo-Independence), which are theorized to be indicative of tendencies toward "racist" characteristics. Racial identity attitudes, behaviors, and feelings, reflective of more advanced levels of racial identity development (e.g., Immersion-Emersion, Autonomy) will also be identified. In turn, counseling interventions can incorporate the necessary strategies to help the client confront conflicts and integrate components of the desired identity. Whether the client's identity development occurs as a result of temporal and environmental influences (Rowe et al., 1994) or some other developmental processes, the WRIRS can be used to assist the change process.

Additional research is needed to examine the WRIRS with respect to various relevant variables. Research has indicated that White racial identity attitudes are related to (1) Whites' perceived comfort with Blacks (Claney & Parker, 1989), (2) cultural values (Carter & Helms, 1987), and (3) symbolic racism (Carter, 1990b), and (4) differentially related to several NEO personality constructs and aversive racism (Silvestri & Richardson, 2001). However, research regarding the relationship between reaction categories and counseling processes or personality constructs is almost nonexistent. Be that as it may, the WRIRS measure might be the better assessment strategy in circumstances where more accurate identity profiles are needed that include the interplay of cognitive, behavioral, and affective components of racial identity compared to attitudinal and socially desirable self-perceptions of respondents. However, when economics or other constraints prohibit

Table 20.2   The Beliefs, Affect, and Behaviors That Hope Indicated on the WRIRS

Step 1: Participant Responses to Sentence Stems	*Step 2: Reaction Categories*
Sample Sentence Stems and Responses	
I belief people of Color are ...	Contact
The same regardless of ethnicity.	
Have the same opportunities regardless of race.	
Regarding race, I was taught to believe ...	
Race is unimportant to children.	
Parents cause the problems about race.	
All kids need to learn the culture of the school.	
Sample Sentence Stems and Responses	
Around people of Color, I feel ...	
Affection for all children regardless of race or ethnicity.	Disintegration
Angry when a person of Color makes an issue out of nothing.	
Anger toward anyone who limits a child's potential.	Contact
Indifference toward people of Color in my neighborhood.	
The types of relationships that I have with people of Color are generally ...	
Positive, including people from different backgrounds.	
Good but not close or meaningful with people of Color.	
Sample Sentence Stems and Responses	
The specific behaviors that demonstrate my racial beliefs are ...	
I teach the same content with the same style regardless of who the student is.	Contact
I volunteer at soup kitchens for the holidays.	
Step 3:	
Determine the primary racial identity reaction categories associated with the responses	Contact Status

use of the reactions measure either alone or together with the attitudinal measure, it might be better to administer the attitudinal measure. The projective strategy for assessing racial identity development provides a means of minimizing or eliminating social desirability effects on participants' responses. Like attitudinal measures of racial identity, projective measures present stimuli in a manner that may make it more difficult for respondents to provide socially desirable responses. To the extent that the stimulus items are valid, projective measures may provide a nonintrusive means of measuring a broad range of racial identity constructs.

In addition to suggesting that racial identity reactions may enhance the understanding of White racial identity development, the relationships between racial identity and intergroup relations suggest that similar measures may prove useful in addressing issues of race relations on, for instance, college campuses. Current trends suggest that race-related issues and incidents are increasing on college and university campuses. Future research could potentially delineate developmental racial identity issues that characterize White college populations. Such research could serve as the basis for developing effective intervention strategies to improve intergroup relations and foster racial harmony on college campuses.

REFERENCES

Behrens, J. T. (1997). Does the white racial identity attitude scale measure racial identity. *Journal of Counseling Psychology, 44,* 3–12.

Carter, R. T. (1990a). Does race or racial identity attitudes influence the counseling process in Black and White dyads. In J. E. Helms (Ed.), *Black and White racial identity: Theory, research, and practice* (pp. 183–208). Westwood, CT: Greenwood Press.

Carter, R. T. (1990b). The relationship between racism and racial identity among White Americans: An exploratory investigation. *Journal of Counseling and Development, 69,* 46–50.

Carter, R. T., & Helms, J. E. (1987). The relationship of Black value-orientations to racial identity attitudes. *Measurement and Evaluation in Counseling and Development, 19,* 185–195.

Carter, R. T., & Helms, J. E. (1990). White racial identity attitudes and cultural values. In J. E. Helms (Ed.), *Black and White racial identity: Theory, research, and practice* (pp. 105–118). Westport, CT: Greenwood Press.

Carter, R. T., & Pieterse, A. L. (in press). Race: A social and psychological analysis of the term and its meaning. In R. T. Carter (Ed.), *Handbook of racial-cultural psychology and counseling: Theory and research* (Vol. 1, pp. 41–63). Hoboken, NJ: Wiley.

Choney, S. K., & Behrens, J. T. (1996). Development of the Oklahoma Racial Attitudes Scale-Preliminary Form (ORAS-P). In G R. Sodowsky & J. Impara (Eds.), *Multicultural assessment in counseling and clinical psychology* (pp. 225–240). Lincoln, NE: Buros Institute of Mental Measurements.

Claney, D., & Parker, W. M. (1989). Assessing White racial consciousness and perceived comfort with Black individuals: A preliminary study. *Journal of Counseling and Development, 4*(67), 449–451.

Cook, D. A. (1994). Racial identity in supervision. *Counselor Education and Supervision, 34,* 132–141.

Helms, J. E. (1990). *Black and White racial identity: Theory, research and practice.* Westport, CI: Greenwood Press.

Helms, J. E. (1992). Why is there no study of cultural equivalence in standardized cognitive ability testing? *American Psychologist, 47,* 1083–1101.

Helms, J. E. (1995). An update of Helms's White and people of Color racial identity models. In J. G. Ponterotto, J. M. Casas, L. A. Suzuki, & C. M. Alexander (Eds.), *Handbook of multicultural counseling* (pp. 181–198). Thousand Oaks, CA: Sage.

Helms, J. E. (1996). Toward a methodology for measuring and assessing racial as distinguished from ethnic identity. In G. R. Sodowsky & J. C. Impara (Eds.), *Multicultural assessment in counseling and clinical psychology* (pp. 157–158). Lincoln, NE: Burrows Institute.

Helms, J. E. (2001). Toward a methodology for measuring and assessing racial as distinguished from ethnic identity. In G. R. Sodowsky & J. C. Impara (Eds.), *Multicultural assessment in counseling and clinical psychology* (2nd ed., pp. 157–158). Lincoln, NE: Burrows Institute.

Helms, J. E. (in press). Challenging some misuses of reliability as reflected in evaluations of the White racial identity attitude Scale. In R. T. Carter (Ed.), *Handbook of racial-cultural psychology and counseling: Theory and research* (Vol. 1, pp. 360–390). Hoboken, NJ: Wiley.

Helms, J. E., & Carter, R. T. (1990). Development of the White racial identity attitude inventory. In J. E. Helms (Ed.), *Black and White racial identity: Theory research and practice* (pp. 67–80). Westport, CT: Greenwood Press.

Helms, J. E., & Carter, R. T. (1991). Relationships of White and Black racial identity attitudes and demographic similarity to counselor preference. *Journal of Counseling Psychology, 38,* 446–457.

Kincheloe, J. L. (1999). The struggle to define and reinvent whiteness: A pedagogical analysis. *College Literature, 26,* 162–194.

Leong, F. T. L., & Wagner, N. S. (1994). Supervision: What do we know? What do we need to know? *Counselor Education and Supervision, 34,* 117–131.

Ponterotto, J. G., Rieger, B. P., Barrett, A., & Sparks, R. (1994). Assessing multicultural counseling competence: A review of instrumentation. *Journal of Counseling and Development, 72,* 316–322.

Ponterotto, J. G., & Wise, S. L. (1987). Construct validity of the racial identity attitude scale. *Journal of Counseling Psychology, 34,* 218–223.

Pope-Davis, D. B., Vandiver, B. J., & Stone, G. L. (1999). White racial identity attitude development: A psychometric examination of two instruments. *Journal of Counseling Psychology, 46,* 70–79.

Richardson, T. Q., & Helms, J. E. (1993). *Using White racial identity reaction categories to predict intergroup characteristics.* Unpublished manuscript.

Richardson, T. Q., & Helms, J. E. (1994). The relationship of Black males' racial identity attitudes to perceptions of parallel counseling dyads. *Journal of Counseling and Development, 73,* 172–177.

Richardson, T. Q., & Molinero, K. L. (1996). White counselor self-awareness: A prerequisite for developing multicultural competence. *Journal of Counseling and Development, 74,* 238–242.

Richardson, T. Q., & Silvestri, T. J. (1999). White identity formation: A developmental process. In R. H. Sheets & E. Hollins (Eds.), *Racial-ethnic identity and human development: Implications for schooling* (pp. 49–66). Mahwah, NJ: Erlbaum.

Rowe, W., Bennett, S. K., & Atkinson, D. R. (1994). White racial identity models: A critique and alternative proposal. *Counseling Psychologist, 19,* 76–102.

Silvestri, T. J., & Richardson, T. Q. (2001). White racial identity statuses and NEO personality constructs: An exploratory analysis. *Journal of Counseling and Development, 79,* 68–76.

Sue, D. W. (1991). A model for cultural diversity training. *Journal of Counseling and Development, 70,* 99–105.

Sue, D. W., & Sue, D. (1999). *Counseling the culturally different: Theory and practice* (3rd ed., p. 143). New York: Wiley.

Sue, D. W., & Sue, D. (2003). *Counseling the culturally diverse: Theory and practice* (4th ed.). Hoboken, NJ: Wiley.

Tokar, D. M., & Swanson, J. L. (1991). An investigation of the validity of Helms (1984) model of White racial identity development. *Journal of Counseling Psychology, 38,* 296–301.

CHAPTER 21

Skills and Methods for Group Work with Racially and Ethnically Diverse Clients

Donna E. Hurdle

Culturally competent practice in the human services is frequently defined as using specialized treatment methods for particular racial and ethnic groups. Many texts provide counseling strategies tailored to the needs of specific racial and ethnic groups in both general (Green, 1999; Lum, 2000) and specialized areas of practice, such as family therapy (Alderfer, this *Handbook,* this volume; Goldenberg & Goldenberg, 1998; McGoldrick, Giordano, & Pearce, 1996). Some authors believe that providing services in ways that are culturally acceptable to client groups will enhance their participation, power, and engagement in services (Green, 1999). Such a culturally specific approach enables clinicians to incorporate indigenous values, practices, and problem-solving methods into the counseling or therapy methodology. A significant body of literature has developed that details therapeutic methods for working with specific racial and ethnic groups (e.g., Hurdle, 2002; Marsiglia, Cross, & Mitchell-Enos, 1998). While a culturally specific approach can be very successful, many human service practitioners work in settings serving clients from a variety of racial and ethnic backgrounds. Group work, in particular, often involves clients of different ages, races, ethnicities, and socioeconomic status. Therefore, the development of group work methods and interventions that can work effectively with racially and ethnically diverse members is critically important (McRae & Short, this *Handbook,* this volume).

Despite efforts by many institutions (education, religious denominations, legislative and judicial branches of government) over the past few decades, the multicultural society of the United States continues to stereotype, discriminate, and oppress specific racial, cultural, and religious groups as well as persons with differing sexual orientation, ability levels, and other nonnormative characteristics. The media frequently focus attention on acts of harassment and violation to or by members of diverse groups, which paradoxically serves to strength the cultural divide despite calls for tolerance and embracing difference. While practitioners in the helping professions work diligently to address their own bias and increase their cultural knowledge, clients bring to treatment their biases and stereotypes toward people who are similar and different. Group work, unique among the therapeutic modalities, places together clients with wide-ranging differences for the purpose of personal change.

Bringing together such diverse clients can be extremely challenging for practitioners, who must enable group members to embrace diversity as a means to develop the cohesion necessary for effective therapeutic work. Foundation texts in group psychotherapy rarely address this issue or provide appropriate intervention methods for achieving such cohesion (Yalom, 1995).

To develop competency in group work practice with clients from diverse racial and ethnic groups, it is necessary to look at three specific areas: the effects of racial and ethnic differences on group dynamics, the effects on leadership skills, and intervention strategies to productively integrate and embrace diversity in groups. Each of these areas is explored in this chapter and suggestions are given to improve group work practice and promote effective interpersonal growth in clients.

ISSUES RELATED TO RACE AND ETHNICITY IN GROUP DYNAMICS

Predictable patterns of interaction occur in groups that are commonly called "group dynamics." The constellation of individuals in a group will influence the dynamics that develop, and their racial and ethnic characteristics are a significant determinant of the interpersonal issues that occur. Particular concerns arise from stereotyping, power issues, and communication, which need individual discussion.

Stereotyping and Bias

Most, if not all, countries in the world have a history of racism and inappropriate treatment of certain groups of citizens. The legacy of such past and present practices is the development of prejudice, stereotypes, and bias about specific racial and ethnic groups by citizens. The specific forms of such prejudice and bias differ by country and by racial and ethnic group. However, it is a certainty that individuals will develop attitudes about persons who are racially or ethnically different from themselves, depending on their experiences, family background, and history in particular geographic areas. When individuals from different racial and ethnic backgrounds come together in a therapeutic group, there is a tendency to project one's cultural stereotypes and prejudices onto other group members. The prior relationships of group members with persons of different racial and ethnic groups will have ranged from positive to conflictual to nonexistent; this also influences their behavior in group. In addition, all group members will be influenced by the prevalent ethnic and racial stereotypes and biases that exist in the society in which they live (McRae & Short, this *Handbook,* this volume; Miller & Donner, 2000). There is great potential for problematic interpersonal relationships among racially and ethnically different clients due to inaccurate perceptions of others as well as difficulty distinguishing individuals from group stereotypes. Persons in the same racial group may vary considerably due to country of origin, tribe or clan affiliation, history of acculturation, cultural identification, and other factors. The "etic-emic conflict," referring to the characterization of individual qualities as either universal (etic) or group-specific (emic), is a dynamic with which helping professionals as well as clients will struggle (Lopez et al., 1989). Inaccuracies in perception must be handled carefully but openly in the group setting to preserve and honor cultures, and also to clarify individual qualities and intentions.

Yalom's (1995) theory of group dynamics indicates that members will interact with other group members as they interact with people in their social spheres, thus creating a "social microcosm" (p. 28) within the group. Clients will play out the roles and relationships of their world with other group members, making evident their interpersonal skills and deficits. Client behaviors will naturally include their typical behaviors toward persons who are different from themselves, thus illustrating their biases and stereotypes. These interactions will give group leaders an opportunity to discuss issues of stereotyping and bias, as well as to assist individual members in becoming aware of their negative and inappropriate views. While an open discussion of biased or prejudiced thoughts and feelings will be uncomfortable for all members, including leaders, the result will often be a positive learning experience for all and will develop cohesion in the group.

Power and Control

All societies apportion power differentially to persons of Color; therefore, a further dynamic in the social microcosm of group work will frequently be differences in power and privilege among group members. European American members, by virtue of their majority status, may take liberties in speaking first or more frequently or taking on informal leadership roles. Group leaders must be sensitive to issues of power in a group, particularly as this may parallel the lack of power many people of Color experience in their everyday life. Leaders will need to handle power issues sensitively and may need to either encourage or derail the efforts of individual group members depending on their effect on the group. Leaders may also wish to include various types of empowerment strategies in group activities to deliberately address the issue of power held by individuals of different racial and ethnic groups.

In forming a group, choices are made about membership that can enhance or impede the development of the group and its dynamics. If possible, the selection of multiple members from the same racial or ethnic group is preferable to a single person in order to reduce isolation and build support. Additionally, intergroup variation will be apparent during discussions of racial and ethnic differences and cultural mores and characteristics. A further concern regarding a group with unequal numbers of persons from specific racial or ethnic groups is the potential for subgrouping and domination by whatever group has more members (Davis, Galinsky, & Schopler, 1995; McRae & Short, this *Handbook,* this volume). Even in groups with equal numbers of racial and ethnic clients, European American clients may perceive a loss of control by lacking dominance in numbers. Issues of control and power are consistently intertwined in cross-cultural relationships and may impact the group process by enhancing or subduing the voice of members from different racial and ethnic backgrounds.

Communication Issues

Individual communication patterns often reflect cultural norms related to racial and ethnic group membership; this affects both verbal and nonverbal behavior patterns. For example, communication patterns of Native Americans often include limited verbalization, lack of eye contact, and limited sharing of personal information, while Asian clients may nod their head to indicate attentiveness rather than agreement (Lum, 2000). Differences also exist in needs for personal space, with American norms typically involving greater physical distance than the interpersonal distance used by persons from "contact" cultures in Latin American or Middle Eastern countries (Cormier & Cormier, 1998). Culturally based communication styles may lead to misinterpretation, anger, or anxiety for persons not familiar with these verbal and nonverbal practices. Problems in communication can therefore occur for both group leaders and members and will need to be addressed (Johnson, this *Handbook,* Volume One).

Group leaders are typically trained in interviewing skills that involve direct eye contact, frequent questions of a personal nature, probing, confrontation, and interpretation (Cormier & Cormier, 1998). Many persons of Color will have difficulty with such an assertive form of inquiry, and may perceive such a leadership style as rude or inappropriate. Many textbooks and group counseling courses typically suggest learning about culturally based communication styles, but this can be difficult to implement when leading a group with 8 to 10 members (or more) who may all come from different racial/ethnic groups. Perhaps the most salient message to helping professionals is to closely observe the communication patterns of culturally diverse clients in a group and then to mirror preferential modes of eye gaze and pacing of verbalization; consideration should also be given to bringing up this topic for discussion in the group.

Beyond the structural forms of communication (verbalizations, paralinguistics, proxemics) is the content. While counselors typically have a high expectation for client sharing of personal information, personal disclosure is antithetical to the cultural norms of many racial and ethnic groups (Sue & Torino, this *Handbook,* this volume). If a group has members who are reluctant to divulge personal information, sessions may be superficial and clients may be reluctant to share personal stories and life events. This may create difficulties in achieving the purpose of most group work, which is typically personal self-awareness and problem solving; however, this may not be as much of an issue in educational groups. For individuals from some racial and ethnic groups in which sharing personal information is shameful, a growth group may be an extremely difficult situation. The way to move through such an impasse is to have an open discussion of the purpose and methods of group work, as well as the cultural norms of members for privacy and personal sharing. Through this discussion, some accommodation or strategy can evolve, such as a plan to use a narrative format that involves client sharing of life stories with each other. Many cultures embrace storytelling as a method of teaching and building connection with strangers, so this may be a comfortable format for group members from many cultural backgrounds. Metaphor (including fables, myths, and parables) has been suggested as a way to discuss sensitive material with clients of Color (Zuniga, 1992). When myths or stories from a client's own culture are used, this method can provide a way of indirectly discussing problems by focusing on an external protagonist rather than the client's personal issues. For Latino clients, *dichos* or folk sayings are another way of explaining or framing issues, problems, or concerns in a cultural context that can be very useful (Zuniga, 1992).

Relationship Issues

Yalom (1995) suggested that therapy groups recapitulate the dynamics of a client's family of origin through the competition of peers (analogous to siblings) for the attention of the leaders (acting in a "parental" role). Using this conceptualization, persons with issues of competition or antagonism toward siblings or feelings of dependence on or defiance toward parents can gradually work through these issues in the supportive context of a therapy group. Yalom's comments refer explicitly to dynamics within nuclear families, which is the family background of most European American clients. How, then, does this theoretical framework apply to the person of Color whose upbringing reflects a more communal kinship system? One might hypothesize that growing up in extended family systems would enable persons from various cultural and racial/ethnic traditions to share more easily with others, and this may be the case when a sufficient level of intimacy develops in a group. However, strong kinship systems often develop clear boundaries from other such groups within a culture so that this background might conversely make sharing with nonrelated others more difficult. Group leaders will need to be sensitive to these dynamics and may choose to encourage members to discuss family norms and relationship boundaries in the group. Leaders can then pose questions as to whether these patterns may be influencing members' interpersonal behavior in the group (Liu & Pope-Davis, this *Handbook,* this volume).

Additionally, culturally based family relationship patterns may explain why group members respond differently to family roles, whether this is deference to elders, as is common in Asian and Native American families, or absence of male parents, which is often true in African American families. In some cultures, such as those in Middle Eastern countries, the continuing dependence of individuals on their family is expected into adulthood, and very distinct and traditional gender roles exist (Nobles & Sciarra, 2000). Whatever the family pattern for individual group members of Color, the impact of their background on how they behave in a group and their relationship with the leaders should be considered through the process described previously. Leaders should also be aware that stage theories of human development (such as that of Erikson, 1950) identify independence as an ultimate developmental goal; however, this developmental course has been questioned for women (Surrey, 1991) and may not be appropriate for persons from certain racial and ethnic groups. Relationship norms within a group member's culture should be explored as a way to understand a client's compliance with or deviation from familial expectations and development of relationships with others.

Leadership Skills

Developing multicultural leadership skills begins with personal awareness of one's own cultural background and then incorporates an in-depth knowledge of other racial and ethnic groups (Carter, this *Handbook,* this volume). This is consistent with frameworks for cultural competence in the helping professions, which also focus on self-awareness of the cultural context in which one was raised and identification of the resulting bias and stereotypes (Lum, 1999). This personal awareness must be coupled with an in-depth knowledge of various cultural groups, including their history, family patterns, interpersonal communication styles, issues of assimilation, and patterns of oppression. Human service workers must develop appropriate counseling skills for work with a diverse client population, including assessment, treatment planning, and various therapeutic methods (Wallace, this *Handbook,* this volume). Some professional associations, such as the American Association for Counseling and Development, have identified specific multicultural counseling competencies (Lum, 1999).

Beyond developing basic skills in cultural competence, helping professionals must be able to make accurate assessments of clients including understanding their cultural background and its impact on their interpersonal qualities and presenting problems (Suzuki, Kugler, & Aguiar, this *Handbook,* this volume). When considering an individual as a potential group member, his or her feelings toward members of various racial and ethnic groups should be ascertained. Strong negative affect toward specific cultures may preclude placement in a group with individuals from this background. Careful selection of specific individuals for groups may mitigate potential problems and diminish some of the potential cultural issues in group dynamics.

Consideration of the racial and ethnic background of the leader(s) in comparison to the group members is also important. There is some evidence that when given a choice, persons of Color prefer a leader from the same ethnic or racial background (Toseland & Rivas, 2001). If a human service organization matches group clients with ethnically and racially similar leaders, this may enable the leaders to more clearly understand cultural issues and possibly reduce language barriers. However, with the volume of clients needing services in many counseling agencies, the selection of homogeneous groups with leaders of similar culture will not be feasible. Davis et al. (1995) have developed a framework for leadership of multicultural groups that emphasizes three components: recognition of group racial dynamics and leader self-awareness, anticipating how racial issues may impact the group, and problem-solving issues related to race, ethnicity, or culture as they occur. This model includes leadership skills in composing groups, modifying attending skills to the culture of members, discussing racial and ethnic differences in groups, encouraging norms of tolerance and respect, and using culturally sensitive interventions. Leaders must encourage members to discuss racial and cultural issues and must be willing to "stop the action and confront directly when there is a problem between persons of different races" (Davis et al., 1995, p. 163). Using structured problem-solving exercises and providing clarity about group rules will give members guidelines about how to interact with others in a helpful manner.

CULTURALLY COMPETENT INTERVENTION STRATEGIES

Beyond leadership skills in handling the group process, which includes an ongoing discussion of culturally relevant issues, there is a need for interventions that are appropriate and helpful for groups whose members come from different racial/ethnic groups. While many standard interventions, such as cognitive-behavioral approaches, may be useful, leaders should also be aware that these methods are based on a framework of Western psychology that may be antithetical to some cultures. Separating cognitive and emotional processes may not make sense to persons from cultures with a more integrated view of the mind, body, and spirit. Methods of traditional healing that have been adapted by mental health professionals for specific racial and ethnic groups often integrate changing cognitions with resolution of relationship issues and the use of prayer (Hurdle, 2002). Cultural definitions of health and wellness, as well as the help-seeking behaviors of different racial and ethnic groups should also be considered in designing group interventions.

Empowerment

Freire (1970) was perhaps the first to use group work to educate members and simultaneously create awareness about their social conditions; this process then led to social action efforts to improve their situation. Working in South America, he taught literacy to uneducated persons by using a dialogical process in which themes and concepts were deconstructed and social awareness or "conscientization" developed. Freire inspired the development of both critical pedagogies and empowerment practices that have been used in many social sciences. Incorporating an empowerment focus into group counseling may include using power analysis strategies to raise awareness and teaching skills in problem solving, assertiveness, and self-advocacy (Gutierrez, 1990). Power analysis strategies enable clients to identify the individuals or institutions that have control over decisions and processes that affect their life situation. Such an exercise may then lead to an awareness of specific skills that may assist them in achieving their personal goals, such as using assertiveness skills to more effectively handle bureaucratic decision makers (Vera, Buhin, Montgomery, & Shin, this *Handbook,* this volume).

The Freirian practice of codification, using a visual image (such as a photo), a poem, some music, or a skit to capture themes or issues for group reflection, can also be implemented as a metaphor to assist clients in conceptualizing barriers to progress or achievement (Lee, 1994). A relevant example is a "wall of barriers" in which clients identify what the bricks represent (oppression, lack of opportunity, etc.) and pantomime pulling them down or destroying them (Lee, 1994). These techniques can be combined with focused group discussion that moves the content away from individual problems to an awareness of the impact of social forces that contribute to the problems, such as poverty and discrimination (Carter, Forsyth, Mazulla, & Williams, this *Handbook,* this volume. This discussion can naturally lead to social activism, encouraging member activity in community efforts or even group activist initiatives.

Culturally Based Interventions

Many ethnic cultures have a long tradition of solving problems and promoting harmony and interpersonal relationships through indigenous ceremonial healing processes. Some have been adapted by helping professionals for use in therapeutic work with clients of this culture. The advantage of using traditional methods of healing and problem resolution for a particular cultural group is that there is a match with the values, traditions, and worldview of the clients. Ho'oponopono is an indigenous Hawaiian family-based method of resolving conflict, originally performed by traditional healers but now used by elders within families and social workers in therapeutic work (Hurdle, 2002). This problem-solving method incorporates spirituality through the use of an opening and closing prayer and has specific stages in which the problem is identified and the repercussions on family members are identified (Shook, 1985; D. Sue & Torino, this *Handbook,* this volume). In subsequent steps, the parties ask forgiveness of each other, the conflict and hurt is then released, and the process is summarized with an affirmation of family strength. The process ends with a meal and a celebration. Although this is typically used as a method of family therapy, ho'oponopono has been adapted for use in groups in adolescent residential treatment centers (Shook, 1985). This is an example of an indigenous healing method which may work best with indigenous Hawaiians, but it has also been used effectively in multicultural groups (Shook, 1985).

As many cultures share similar holistic values, spiritual traditions, and extended family/kinship systems, traditional healing methods from one culture may be useful in a group with persons of different racial/ethnic heritage. To incorporate a spiritual focus, members may rotate offering an opening or closing prayer for the group, perhaps in their native language. Holistic frameworks such as the medicine wheel may also be a useful concept to introduce into the group as a way of discussing the interconnection of people and their community. Group members can also be invited to share their culturally-based methods of resolving problems and promoting harmony and wellness.

Other ways of incorporating cultural elements into group work are to use traditional arts and crafts, music, and ceremonial activities. For example, groups for Native American youth have used activities such as making masks and dream-catchers, visioning, and making dream pots to assist teens in identifying future goals and current issues (Marsiglia et al., 1998). Playing flute music and burning herbs was also used in this group to connect with the clients' culture and use cultural identity as a way to identify personal strengths. Creative arts therapies, such as art therapy, dance therapy, and music therapy, are also suggested as therapeutic methods as they are typically part of Native American religion and spirituality (Dufrene & Coleman, 1994). Storytelling can be effectively integrated with music and crafts to teach and reinforce positive health behaviors, as shown by research with Native American adolescents (Weaver, 1999).

Using interventions that incorporate cultural traditions and practices in group counseling will often enrich the group process and ensure its relevance to client cultural values and beliefs. Using a blend of arts and crafts from different cultures can enhance a group member's awareness and appreciation for the unique strengths and traditions of different cultural backgrounds. Additionally, participatory and nonverbal techniques may be more comfortable for ethnic group members whose cultural traditions proscribe intense verbalization.

CONCLUSION

Counseling groups with racially and ethnically diverse members can be both challenging and enriching for the group members and its leaders. Leaders of such groups must become skilled in the identification of the complex culturally related issues that may arise, and then learn how to address them. As cultural issues will probably not be the focus of the group, these elements must be integrated with other types of therapeutic work, such as anger management or parenting skills. The group dynamics that develop in groups with culturally diverse members will be different from those in more homogeneous groups, and group leaders must develop skills that are specifically suited to this type of practice (Hurdle, 1990). Leaders should also develop a repertoire of intervention skills that can incorporate cultural elements or transcultural themes in order to facilitate exploration of the impact of culture on individuals and the group as a whole. Culturally sensitive intervention skills will embrace and celebrate cultural differences, while providing opportunities for personal growth. Skills and methods for group work with clients from different racial and ethnic groups are an important addition to the skill base of all helping professionals providing group counseling services (McRae & Short, this *Handbook,* this volume).

REFERENCES

Cormier, S., & Cormier, B. (1998). *Interviewing strategies for helpers: Fundamental skills and cognitive behavioral interventions.* Pacific Grove, CA: Brooks/Cole.

Davis, L., Galinsky, M., & Schopler, J. (1995). RAP: A framework for leadership of multiracial groups. *Social Work, 49*(2), 155–165.

Dufrene, P. M., & Coleman, V. D. (1994). Art and healing for Native American Indians. *Journal of Multicultural Counseling and Development, 22,* 145–152.

Erikson, E. (1950). *Childhood and society.* New York: Norton.

Freire, P. (1970). *Pedagogy of the oppressed.* New York: Continuum.

Goldenberg, H., & Goldenberg, I. (1998). *Counseling today's families* (3rd ed.). Pacific Grove, CA: Brooks/Cole.

Green, J. W. (1999). *Cultural awareness in the human services: A multi-ethnic approach* (3rd ed.). Boston: Allyn & Bacon.

Gutierrez, L. M. (1990). Working with women of Color: An empowerment perspective. *Social Work, 35*(2), 149–153.

Hurdle, D. E. (1990). The ethnic group experience. *Social Work with Groups, 13*(4), 59–69.

Hurdle, D. E. (2002). Native Hawaiian traditional healing: Culturally-based interventions for social work practice. *Social Work, 47*(2), 183–192.

Lee, J. A. B. (1994). *The empowerment approach to social work practice.* New York: Columbia University Press.

Lopez, S. R., Grover, K. P., Holland, D., Johnson, M. J., Kain, C. D., Kanel, K., et al. (1989). Development of culturally sensitive psychotherapists. *Professional Psychology: Research and Practice, 20*(6), 1–8.

Lum, D. (1999). *Culturally competent practice: A framework for growth and acton.* Pacific Grove, CA: Brooks/Cole.

Lum, D. (2000). *Social work practice and people of Color* (4th ed.). Belmont, CA: Brooks Cole/Wadsworth.

Marsiglia, F. F., Cross, S., & Mitchell-Enos, V. (1998). Culturally-grounded group work with adolescent American Indian students. *Social Work with Groups, 21*(1/2), 89–102.

McGoldrick, M., Giordano, J., & Pearce, J. K. (1996). *Ethnicity and family therapy* (2nd ed.). New York: Guilford Press.

Miller, J., & Donner, S. (2000). More than just talk: The use of racial dialogues to combat racism. *Social Work with Groups, 23*(1), 31–53.

Nobles, A. Y., & Sciarra, D. T. (2000). Cultural determinants in the treatment of Arab Americans: A primer for mainstream therapists. *American Journal of Orthopsychiatry, 70,* 182–191.

Shook, E. V. (1985). *Ho'oponopono: Contemporary uses of a Hawaiian problem-solving process.* Honolulu: University of Hawaii Press.

Surrey, J. L. (1991). The "self-in-relation": A theory of women's development. In J. V. Jordan, A. G. Kaplan, J. B. Miller, I. P. Stiver, & J. L. Surrey (Eds.), *Women's growth in connection: Writings from the Stone Center.* New York: Guilford Press.

Toseland, R. W., & Rivas, R. F. (2001). *An introduction to group work practice* (4th ed.). Boston: Allyn & Bacon.

Weaver, H. N. (1999). Health concerns for Native American youth: A culturally grounded approach to health promotion. *Journal of Human Behavior in the Social Environment, 2*(1/2), 127–143.

Yalom, I. D. (1995). *Theory and practice of group psychotherapy* (4th ed.). New York: Basic Books.

Zuniga, M. E. (1992). Using metaphors in therapy: *Dichos* and Latino clients. *Social Work, 37,* 55–60.

CHAPTER 22

Family Counseling and Psychotherapy in Racial-Cultural Psychology: Case Applications

Anita Jones Thomas

The family is arguably the most important context for examining the role and influence of cultural factors on an individual's functioning, lifestyle, values, beliefs, and behaviors. The family serves as the primary socializing agent for children and transmits cultural values and norms. Racial-cultural factors influence the concept of families and define membership (nuclear, immediate, extended), communication patterns, roles for members, and rules for affective experiences, conflict resolution, and relationships with others (Alderfer, this *Handbook,* this volume; McGoldrick & Giordano, 1996). Racial-cultural factors also influence boundaries, levels of intimacy, and adjustment to stressors and life changes (McGill, 1992; McGoldrick, Giordano, & Pearce, 1996; Preli & Bernard, 1993). Effective clinicians must examine the role and influence of racial-cultural factors on families in treatment (Alderfer, this *Handbook,* this volume; Gushue, 1993; Johnson, 1995; Thomas, 1998). Clinicians must be sensitive to the specific role of cultural factors of their clients as well as intragroup differences. Behaviors that often seem or feel idiosyncratic to the family usually extend from the family's unique relationship to their cultural heritage and experiences with the dominant culture. It is critical, therefore, that therapists carefully assess the role of racial-cultural factors and select the appropriate culturally sensitive treatment interventions.

This chapter briefly reviews important racial-cultural factors for families and individuals and the influence of these factors on family functioning and dynamics. There are three primary areas that therapists must address. First, therapists must understand the influence of culture on the identity development of each family member and the system (Ota Wang, this *Handbook,* this volume; Wallace, this *Handbook,* this volume). Second, family therapists must understand the racial and cultural socialization process for families (Bowser, this *Handbook,* Volume One; Yeh & Hunter, this *Handbook,* Volume One). Third, therapists must understand the influence of racial-cultural factors on child-rearing practices and other tasks of families. The chapter also presents issues for the conceptualization, assessment, and intervention of culturally diverse families. Clinical cases are discussed to demonstrate culturally sensitive treatment.

RACIAL-CULTURAL FRAMEWORK IN FAMILY THERAPY/COUNSELING

Family therapists need to explore the influence of racial-cultural factors on family functioning. Race as a construct has been based on visual phenotypic differences in skin color, facial features, and hair, and has sociopolitical connotations, which leads to oppression and discrimination in this country. Racial affiliation often determines values, beliefs, behaviors, and lifestyle for individuals, as well as worldview orientation (McGoldrick & Giordano, 1996; Sue & Sue, 2003). The influence of other cultural factors may also be filtered through race; for example, race often defines gender role expectations. Social class, immigration patterns, and spiritual beliefs often determine intragroup differences in racial groups (Carter, this *Handbook,* Volume One).

Race and racial-cultural factors influence roles, functioning, and belief systems. For example, African American families value the extended family and have flexible family roles, and Asian American and Latino families value the extended family and greatly respect elders. White or European Americans value the nuclear family and emotional restraint and stress the importance of achievement and the work ethic (Boyd-Franklin, 1989, 2003; Sue & Sue, 2003). Racial-cultural factors also influence identity development of the family and individual members, so identifying racial or cultural identity is an important component in both conceptualization and assessment of clients' issues and concerns. Racial identity evolves from socialization experiences within the family, peers, and society and psychological and sociopolitical attitudes toward race (Helms, 1995, 2001; Thompson, this *Handbook,* this volume). Individuals progress through stages of low salience and awareness of race to integration of values and beliefs prescribed by race, according to most racial identity models (Atkinson, 2003; Vandiver, Fhagen-Smith, Cokley, Cross, & Worrell, 2001). Family members may differ in racial identity, leading to conflict within families (Gushue, 1993). For example, African American parents in an immersion status may encourage their children to express anger at Whites.

Racial identity is developed through socialization, and family therapists should understand the socialization process in families. Socialization includes the preparation of children for accepting adult roles and responsibilities in society through the teaching and learning of conventional beliefs, values, and patterns of behavior (Boykin & Toms, 1985). It includes the transmission of values, beliefs, and ideas about lifestyles and is derived from cultural knowledge of adult tasks and the competencies needed for adequate functioning in society (Harrison, Wilson, Pine, Chon, & Buriel, 1990). Parents and extended family members also serve as the primary agent for transmitting racial values to their children through both overt and covert means (Johnson, 1995; Preli & Bernard, 1993). Families transmit positive and negative messages about their particular cultural group as well as other cultural groups (Preli & Bernard, 1993). The majority of the research on cultural socialization has occurred for African American families (Sanders Thompson, 1994; Stevenson, 1995; Thomas & Speight, 1999). Racial socialization of African Americans has been defined as the process of helping children integrate a sense of self in a hostile environment, or to be physically and emotionally healthy in an environment of extreme stress, and occurs through both explicit and implicit methods (Greene, 1992; Stevenson, 1995). Family therapists should explore the impact of cultural or racial socialization, as a positive sense of racial or cultural identity is important for self-concept (Alderfer, this *Handbook,* this volume).

Finally, family therapists must understand the influence of culture on family functioning. The culture of a family affects individual behaviors, child-rearing practices, which includes discipline styles, and the importance of achievement and education. Parenting styles and child-rearing practices differ according to the racial-cultural factors and ethnic background. Cultural groups select child-rearing practices that reflect the culture, its history, and values in order to maximize survival and promote competence and success (Forehand & Kotchick, 1996; Yeh & Hunter, this *Handbook,* Volume One). Parenting goals also differ according to racial-cultural factors, particularly the extent to which families integrate with the mainstream or maintain traditional values (Bowser, this *Handbook,* Volume One; Garcia Coll, Meyer, & Brillon, 1995).

Family therapists need to assess cultural factors, particularly as these relate to the presenting problem, diagnosis, and functioning of the family. Assessment helps counselors to understand how representative the family is of their cultural group, to determine intragroup differences, and to identify potential resources and family strengths (Anderson, 1991; Gushue, 1993; Thomas, 1998). This assessment is important even if cultural dimensions seem unrelated to the presenting complaint. This may occur when working with White families, who may not readily consider the importance of cultural factors. Often, family members do not identify the role that racial-cultural factors have on the problem. Members may be at different stage levels of racial-cultural identity, and the differences in identity and acculturation levels may lead to various values in families (Kohatsu, this *Handbook,* Volume One). These differences in values often lead to differences in expectations and behaviors that may contribute to the presenting problem and the selection of diverse solutions. When assessing cultural differences, many families begin to better understand the relationship of culture, which leads to more efficient and effective resolution of the problems. Additionally, understanding the cultural context may determine the appropriateness of behaviors and whether symptoms are culturally sanctioned. Therapists have recognized the importance of assessing cultural variables when working with families (Canino & Spurlock, 1994; McGoldrick et al., 1996; Thomas, 1998).

There are a variety of methods for addressing culture in sessions with families, including direct questions related to the family's cultural background (Montalvo & Gutierrez, 1983; Paniagua, 1996; Ross & Phipps, 1986), culturally appropriate questions (Paniagua, 1996), and multicultural genograms or family maps (Gushue, 1993; Hardy & Laszloffy, 1995; McGoldrick, 1993; Preli & Bernard, 1993; Thomas,1998). The multicultural genogram, a diagram developed from an extensive family history interview, enhances communication in families, helps families to explore and share cultural backgrounds and traditions, improves cultural socialization, and helps therapists to determine the impact of culture on family roles and functioning (Alderfer, this *Handbook,* this volume; Thomas, 1998).

Therapists also need to consider culture when selecting treatment strategies. Counselors can use their understanding of cultural factors while developing hypotheses about the family. At other times, family therapists may need to incorporate a psychoeducational approach with families, or select theoretical orientations or interventions that suit the cultural factors. Family counselors should always remember that family theories and approaches were developed in a particular social and cultural context and may have limited effectiveness outside of these contexts. For example, a Bowenian (Kerr & Bowen, 1988) approach that focuses on independence, autonomy, and reason may be more appropriate for racial groups that value independence but inappropriate for racial groups with a collective social orientation (Thompson, this *Handbook,* this volume).

Cases Studies

The following case studies illustrate culturally sensitive treatment of families. An African American female therapist in an outpatient setting treated the families in the cases. The therapist follows multicultural counseling theory (Sue, Ivey, & Pedersen, 1996; Pedersen, this *Handbook,* Volume One), a comprehensive framework that encourages therapists to select interventions that reflect the cultural identity, values, and lifestyle of the client from a variety of theoretical orientations.

Case 1

Marcia, an 8-year-old African American girl, was referred to counseling by her school. First, although she performed above grade level on standardized tests, she was receiving failing grades in school and performed poorly in the classroom. She would often seem distracted when taking tests or completing assignments in the classroom. Teachers reported, however, that she would excel when they worked with her individually; her current teacher suspected emotional roots to her problems. Second, the school indicated that Marcia has poor peer relationships. Marcia does not have close friends, often eats alone in the cafeteria, and does not participate in group activities. Marcia did have one close friend during kindergarten, but that student relocated at the end of the school year. Marcia does relate well to teachers, although teachers report that she is alternately clingy or withdrawn and distant. Third, the school was concerned with the family dynamics. Neither of Marcia's parents seemed to be interested in becoming more involved with Marcia's education as neither parent was regularly available to attend parent-teacher conferences. When a parent did attend, it was usually Marc, Marcia's father. No administrator or school personnel could remember meeting Elizabeth, Marcia's mother.

Marcia was accompanied to the initial session by her father, Marc, and her younger brother, Mario, age 5. Marc indicated that his wife could not attend the session and that she would probably not be involved with the therapy due to her busy schedule. Elizabeth worked full-time as an assistant to a pharmacist, and she was studying at night to become a physician. Although Marc agreed that family therapy would be optimal, he did not believe he could convince his wife to attend. Marc indicated that the family was most concerned with Marcia's underachievement and withdrawn behavior and that there were no concerns with Mario. Mario seemed to be adjusting well to kindergarten and was making friends.

As the entire family was not available for the first session, the session was used to assess Marcia and she was seen individually. Marcia's behavior was consistent with the teachers' reports. She established rapport easily with the therapist, who invited her to play during the session. She responded well to questions and easily shared information and seemed to thrive on the attention from the therapist. When asked about her relationship with her mother, Marcia began to cry. She stated that she felt her mother did not like her and did not like to be around her. She felt this was because she was a "bad girl" and was born at the wrong time. She also thought that her mother's family did not like her because of the way she looked. She ended her time by stating that she "would try harder" to make her mother happy. The session ended by encouraging Marc to persuade Elizabeth to attend the next session.

Elizabeth attended the next session, stating that she believed it would be her only session due to her busy schedule, expressing her displeasure at having to attend. The session was spent gathering historical information, exploring family dynamics and family communication patterns, and discussing the presenting problems. Marc, a light-skinned African American, is an only child raised in a traditional nuclear family. Marc was the first to attend college in his family. He currently works as a consultant to a Fortune 500 company. When asked, Marc could not determine the role of culture in his life except for gender role expectations. He had expected that he would marry and have a traditional family with a wife who served primarily as a wife and mother. Elizabeth, a dark-skinned African American woman, was the middle of three daughters. When asked about culture, Elizabeth stated that she was constantly aware of the influence of culture in her life. Elizabeth was raised in a predominantly Caucasian environment, and she was teased by her peers for her skin color and hair, had few friends, and rarely dated. Her two sisters had lighter complexions, they were not teased as frequently, and Elizabeth often felt that her mother favored them because of it. Elizabeth was raised by "strong Black women," including her mother and her grandmother, who worked outside of the home while taking care of the family and the household, including cousins, family friends, and sometimes children from church. Her mother and grandmother presented messages to her that as an African American woman she needed to be strong and independent. She always assumed that she would have a dual-career marriage with flexible gender roles.

Elizabeth and Marc met in college during their senior year. Elizabeth was immediately attracted to Marc's light complexion and looks, but felt that he would not be interested in her due to her dark complexion. Marc was attracted to Elizabeth's independence and self-confidence. The two began dating and were married two months after graduation. Elizabeth had been a premed major and began medical school immediately after graduation. Marc began business school upon graduation and started his job upon completion of his MBA. Elizabeth became pregnant during her third year of medical school. She was diagnosed as having postpartum depression and was medicated. Elizabeth's mother was supportive during the pregnancy. However, she was disappointed that Marcia did not share her "father's good skin coloring," and Elizabeth felt that she pulled away from the family at that point. When the therapist commented that African American families often internalize the caste system from slavery based on skin color, Elizabeth agreed that her family probably struggled with this issue.

Both Marc and Elizabeth agreed that culture contributed to the problems that Marcia faced. First, Elizabeth agreed that Marcia did not have close relationships with extended family, particularly with her grandmother, due to skin color issues. Elizabeth indicated that she did not rely on her mother because she felt that Marcia had been rejected as a child. Elizabeth's mother would make comments such as "At least the child doesn't have a wide nose and dark skin" and "Her hair may be thick but it does have some length." The family agreed that Marcia could benefit from having a female role model to provide nurturing, as Elizabeth was so busy, and agreed to make this a treatment goal. Second, although the family lived in an integrated community, there were few African Americans with whom Marcia could develop relationships. Marcia stated that she did feel differently from her peers and thought that no one liked her due to the way that she looked. The family did not spend much time talking about race or cultural issues at home. They did not belong to a predominantly African American church or social organization that would help the children to learn about their culture and heritage. The family agreed that the second and third treatment goals would be to help Marcia improve her peer relations and to learn more about her culture. Elizabeth agreed to help with homework assignments, although she did not agree to continue her participation in treatment.

Treatment consisted of a combination of individual and family therapy to meet the three goals for the family. The family was encouraged to engage in a more formal racial socialization process with Marcia (Greene, 1992). The family was asked to attend Afrocentric cultural activities, including attending culturally oriented plays, musicals, and concerts. Marc and Elizabeth were asked to think of messages that they wanted to provide to the children regarding racial pride, racial heritage, and cross-cultural relationships. The therapist was concerned with the lack of female role models and nurturing for Marcia. In an effort to provide nurturing and to increase her exposure to her culture, individual sessions incorporated bibliotherapy using African American children's literature, primarily biographies and stories of heroes and role models. Marcia would sit and listen as the therapist read stories, and would draw pictures of her favorite scenes or moments from the stories. As a way to improve the interactions and communication with Marcia and Elizabeth, Elizabeth was encouraged to read African American stories with Marcia as a bedtime ritual (Satir, 1967). This became a special time for them, and both were able to share more personal issues in their lives. Elizabeth was also encouraged to develop a time to share with Mario.

Two solution-focused interventions were made to address Marcia's peer relationships (Weakland, Fisch, Watzlawick, & Bodin, 1981). The family had not made arrangements when she was younger for play dates for Marcia and had not networked with other parents in the neighborhood. First, it was suggested that the parents place Marcia in Girl Scouts or other activities where she could develop relationships. Marc inquired at the school and found a troop that met after school. Marcia joined the Scout troop and developed friendships with three girls in her classroom. Next, Marc was encouraged to meet the girls' parents and to develop times for play outside of the Scout meetings. As the relationships developed, the girls began to include Marcia in activities in the classroom and began to eat lunch with her. Although the parents were pleased with Marcia's new friendships, both Marc and Elizabeth agreed that they wanted Marcia to have exposure to other African American children. The family agreed that Marcia and Mario would attend church and Sunday school with their grandmother. Marcia developed friendships with two of the girls in the Sunday school class and invited them for her first sleepover.

Finally, Marc and Elizabeth were encouraged to meet with Marcia's teacher and administrators at the school. Many of Marcia's academic difficulties improved as her relationship with her mother and peers improved. The teacher reported that Marcia was more cheerful in class and displayed less clingy behavior. The parents were urged to become aware of the curriculum in the classroom to make certain that it was culturally relevant. Marc agreed to work with the school in preparing a program for Black history month. When treatment ended, Marcia's grades had improved, she had closer friendships, and the family reported higher levels of intimacy and connection.

Case 2

David was a 14-year-old who was entering therapy due to difficulties with school. He was constantly fighting with peers and was disruptive in the classroom. David would tease other students who gave incorrect responses or laugh at others. He would blurt out answers without being called on and become belligerent with teachers when reprimanded. During free periods, he would attempt to interact with peers only around academic or intellectual issues. When he was in the first grade, he was tested for a gifted program. The school psychologist found that he had an IQ of 145 and recommended that he be promoted to the third grade. His parents reluctantly agreed after David indicated his desire to learn more at school. He was placed in a college preparatory program on entering high school. David had few difficulties with peers until he reached seventh grade, where he continued to excel in his schoolwork. He reported that he "gets in trouble at school" because he is bored and no one is his "intellectual equal."

David's parents indicated great concerns with his school performance and wondered if they had made a mistake in promoting him one grade level due to what they labeled his "immature" behavior. David's father, Anil, was an immigrant from India, and his mother, Beth, was a Caucasian from England. The parents had met in London when Anil was doing some work as a consultant to an engineering firm. Beth worked as a freelance photographer and had pictures published in major news magazines. David had an older sister, Indira, who was 17 years old and a senior in high school. Indira was busy selecting a college and reported no problems at school or home. Her parents indicated that Indira was very popular at school; she had been selected for the homecoming team, sang with the school choir, and had been on the honor roll since her freshmen year. Indira felt that David was not liked due to his arrogance at school. According to his parents, David met all developmental milestones on a timely basis. He began to read when he was 3, and he expressed curiosity and interest in learning at an early age. David also displayed behavioral difficulties in the home. He often argued with his sister and mother. David called his mother "stupid" and said that if she were intelligent, she would have a better career. Although David would follow Anil's directives, he frequently ignored his mother.

During the first session, the parents indicated that the focus of treatment should be on David's inappropriate behavior at school and at home with his mother.

When asked about cultural issues, the family indicated that they had experienced many issues. When Anil and Beth first decided to date, they were certain that their family would be open to the interracial relationship. However, both sets of parents expressed disappointment in the relationship and discouraged them from continuing to date. Beth felt that her parents were concerned that she would move to India and they would not be able to visit. Anil was considerably older than Beth; he was 38 and she was 22 when they first met. His parents had attempted to arrange a marriage for him when he was 19, but he convinced them to postpone the marriage because he wanted to attend college and pursue a career in another country. Beth and Anil felt that the initial disapproval from their parents placed a strain on their relationship. Beth worried that Anil would regret not marrying a woman from India and that she may not be his ideal mate. Anil admitted that he was concerned about Beth's level of autonomy and independence. They became frustrated while dating when trying to discuss the influence of culture on their relationship and decided that their personalities were compatible enough to overcome cultural difficulties. Both Beth and Anil stated that this was probably a poor way of coping, but they are glad that they chose to stay together. They reported that the families seemed to fully come together when Beth announced her pregnancy.

Anil and Beth decided to immigrate shortly after Indira was born. Beth and Anil decided to move to the United States to be closer to Beth's parents after her father's company transferred them here. Although they reported having little difficulty adjusting to migrating to this country, they were concerned that Indira would have some difficulties as she was biracial. When David was born, they chose to give him an American name to minimize teasing by peers. The family was asked to discuss their connection and affiliation to their culture. Anil stated that he felt proud of his Indian heritage, and he participates in cultural organizations to maintain connections with people from his homeland. The family had little contact with Anil's family, as most still lived in India. Anil would take a trip once a year to visit his family but did not take his wife or children due to the expense of travel. Although his family communicated through letters and e-mails, the children indicated that they did not feel close to their Indian grandparents or aunts and uncles. Indira would like to visit India with her father, but she assumed that this would occur when she was older and could work to fund her travel. David indicated that he was not interested in visiting. Beth indicated comfort with her English heritage but struggled at times with being identified as White and seen as an oppressor. When David was born, many people assumed that she was an au pair that had been hired by the family to watch David, as both he and his sister had primarily Indian features and skin tone. She felt frustrated and hurt in explaining that they were her children. Beth tried to participate in activities with Anil and said that she was concerned that the children be proud of their Indian heritage. Indira indicated that she was proud of both her English and Indian heritage, but she associated more with her Indian heritage and assumed that her friends related to her more from that perspective. When asked about specific values that she adhered to, Indira endorsed respect for elders and authority.

She is most bothered about David's behavior toward his mother because it seems so disrespectful.

David became upset with the question and stated loudly that he has no cultural issues because he was born here, and that his identity is "100% American." David stated that many of the kids at school assume that because he is Indian he is really good at math, and that many of the teachers assume that he is going to be an engineer like his father. David's favorite subject was English, in fact, and he wanted to pursue a career as a writer or journalist. Although he is proud of his intellect, David wished that everyone could just recognize his brilliance as a part of him as opposed to because he is Asian. David also felt that he had never been accepted fully by his peers; he had never been invited to parties and was often last to be selected for teams when he was younger. "They just said, 'This Asian kid can't play,' so they never picked me." It was clear that much of David's difficult peer relationships occurred due to racial differences. David compensated for this rejection by focusing on his one identified strength, his intellect, to the exclusion of other personality traits. David was asked to develop a list of hobbies or interests to bring to the next session as a way to help select appropriate extracurricular activities.

The family was asked about the cultural socialization process for the children (Greene, 1992). Anil and Beth stated that they had been so concerned about making sure that the children fit in that they may not have socialized them to their culture. Indira participated in many of the school's cultural activities, but David always declined, saying that he preferred to read or conduct a science experiment. It was recommended to the family that they include David in more activities and that they expose both children to more of their British heritage. David felt proud of his father's career as an engineer because it was seen as an intellectual vocation and his father had completed a master's degree in engineering. Beth's career as a photojournalist was seen as less intellectual by David, so he devalued her work. It was suggested that Beth and David together take various culturally oriented photographs as a way to increase his respect for her profession and for his cultural background.

Anil and Beth were asked to discuss whether culture influenced child-rearing practices. Anil stated that he believed in being firm with the children, clearly stating expectations for behaviors and not allowing for inappropriate behavior. He also felt that David had certain responsibilities as a male child, including academic achievement. Anil stressed education and achievement with David and was pleased with his accomplishments. Anil also did not feel that chores were important for the children. Beth disagreed, as she felt that chores were important to teach both David and Indira responsibility and good stewardship. She developed a list of chores for both children to complete each week. Indira usually complied because she wanted to help around the house. David, however, would not complete chores he did not like. Beth was not able to impose consequences for David, and Anil did not help her to enforce the rules. Beth confessed that she was not consistent with consequences, however, because she wanted the children to be independent and learn to take responsibility for themselves. David probably ignored her when she was trying to enforce rules due to her lack of consistency. Anil and Beth were asked to discuss their goals for the children and their perspectives on child rearing in order to determine age-appropriate enforceable rules. They were then encouraged to develop rules for the household that would help both children to learn responsibility and develop independence (Minuchin & Fishman, 1981).

After six weeks, the family reported changes in David. David had developed a list of interests, which included drama and music. He had always wanted to join the drama club because of his love for Shakespeare and literature, but was afraid he would be rejected by his peers. When he expressed this interest, Beth began to read scenes with him to prepare him for an audition. David joined the club and was beginning to develop friendships with some of the other students. His teachers reported that he seemed more tolerant of others and did not call students names as frequently. Anil arranged for David to begin tutoring others at their church, also as a way to promote peer relationships. David and Beth's relationship also seemed to improve. Beth and Anil decided that each child would complete two chores each week and that the chores would be posted on the refrigerator, allowing each child to complete his or her tasks when convenient. Anil took more responsibility for enforcing consequences with David, allowing Beth to function in a more nurturing role. Finally, David's cultural identity began to change. He attended many of the cultural activities with the family. Beth's parents were excited that the children wanted to be more exposed to their cultural heritage, and they began to spend time with the children explaining their genealogical history. By the end of treatment, David declared that he was an Indian English American and that he might write a play about his history someday.

Case 3

The Sanders family entered treatment due to acting-out behaviors of the oldest daughter, Sharon, age 14. Sharon had started several small fires in the family home, was truant at school, and was failing most of her courses. The Sanders family consisted of Sherry, the mother, age 42; her husband, Dave, age 36; Sharon; and Nicole, her sister, age 8. Sherry divorced Tom, the girls' father, when Sharon was 9, and married Dave one year later. Sherry worked as an account manager in a Fortune 500 company, and Dave was an engineer in the same company. The family reported that adjusting to the marriage had been difficult, and that Sharon and Dave still have a conflictual relationship. Sherry and Dave admitted to marital difficulties, including difficulties with communication, intimacy and affection, and disciplining the children. Sherry indicated that she has a permissive style of childrearing, believing that children need to have some parameters but they need the freedom to experiment with behaviors and make choices. Dave believed that Sherry was too lax with the children and that they needed firmer limits. Dave also felt that Sherry underminded his discipline with the girls, implicitly giving them permission to disregard him. Sharon and Nicole also had intense sibling rivalry, with physical altercations often begun by Sharon.

Sharon had a history of acting-out behaviors. Tom had been abusive to Sherry when they were married, and although the children had not been abused, they had witnessed the domestic violence. Sharon set her first fire when she was 3 years old; Sherry punished her, but dismissed the behavior as curiosity. When Sharon was 9, shortly after the divorce, a fire in the kitchen destroyed the family home. Sherry suspected that the fire may have been started by Sharon, but she had no proof of this and the fire was deemed accidental by investigators. Since the family moved in with Dave, Sharon had started five fires. Sharon also had long-standing difficulties with school performance. Her elementary school teachers had recommended screening for learning disabilities, but Sherry refused, believing that Sharon would mature on her own and begin to improve her performance. When the school threatened to retain Sharon in the fourth grade, Sherry decided to place her in a private school.

In the initial session, Sharon blamed all of her problems on her relationship with Dave. She stated that she only set fires in the home when she felt frustrated and that her mother was favoring Dave. She claimed that the fires were only set in garbage cans and that she knew how to extinguish them before they burned out of control. Sharon also stated that she would be able to pull her grades up before the end of the school year, and that although she had come close to failing, she never had because she always knew what to do. Sharon also stated that she only fought with Nicole because Nicole was Dave's favorite. Dave grew angrier as Sharon told her version of the problems, and confessed that he was angry at both Sharon's behavior and Sherry's permissiveness. The family agreed that the fire setting was the first problem that needed to be addressed, followed by Sharon's school attendance and performance.

When asked if culture influenced the presenting problem or family functioning, the family appeared confused, and replied that they were not aware of the role of culture. The therapist decided to consider the family's cultural factors when assessing family functioning and selecting treatment strategies without an explicit discussion. Because the family was a White, middle-class family, the therapist hypothesized that they valued the nuclear family unit, individualism, separation and independence, hard work, and achievement. The emphasis on independence and achievement would be punctuated by the belief in individual control, personal power, and an internal locus of control. It was also hypothesized that the family was future-oriented and that the children would be expected to be successful in school and in their chosen career. Finally, it was hypothesized that the family would prefer a direct communication style but with controlled or restrained emotions. As these were only hypotheses about the culture, the therapist was careful to confirm them with the family before selecting interventions.

The first concern to be addressed with the family was the discipline styles of Sherry and Dave. It was clear that both expected the children to be independent, to find and develop their own interests, and to be successful. The therapist asked both parents to discuss their visions of the future for the girls. Sherry stated that she felt that both girls would find careers that suited their personalities, and that although she hoped they would be financially independent, she wanted them to be happy and fulfilled. Dave agreed that he pictured the girls being successful and competent in the future, and that they should be allowed to choose their own destiny. However, he also felt that it was important for them to have a well-rounded background and foundation so that they would be able to make choices in the future. His fear was that Sharon was not developing a strong academic foundation that would allow her to pursue college and select a challenging career. Both parents agreed that Sharon had the capacity to monitor her behavior and to make appropriate choices, including attending all of her classes and completing homework assignments. These statements seemed to confirm cultural beliefs in independence, internal locus of control, and the value of achievement. The therapist disclosed her feedback and hypotheses to the family, and they readily agreed to the highlighted values. Then the therapist suggested that although the parents had the same goals, the differences in the discipline styles hindered the growth and development of Sharon that they were trying to promote. It was suggested that the parents build from their commonalities and set clear and concrete rules for Sharon and Nicole. The structural family approach (Minuchin & Fishman, 1981) was used to select techniques, as it was suitable for the emphasis on the nuclear family unit and restoring the structure and hierarchy of the family by empowering the parents. Sherry and Dave were asked to develop a list of rules for the children and to select consequences that both would agree to enforce. They were also told that because of her level of independence and autonomy, Sharon would rebel against the rules and the united front, and that she may escalate her behavior or try to split the parents. It was emphasized that they needed to begin with rules that they could both enforce. The parents were also instructed to check Sharon for matches or lighters each day when she came home from school and to check her room daily.

During the following session, Sherry and Dave discussed the rules developed for the children. Sherry indicated that it was a difficult task because they were not able to easily develop consequences with which they both felt comfortable. They finally decided that both girls needed to do their homework immediately after coming home from school and that Sherry would check the homework after dinner. Sharon would also bring home a homework sheet to be signed by each teacher to verify her attendance in school. If she skipped school, she would be grounded for one day for each day missed. Sherry would handle the discipline with Dave's support. Nicole would lose phone privileges as her consequence. The family indicated that Sharon did not set fires during the week. They were encouraged to continue the daily monitoring for matches and lighters and agreed to use the same consequence if they were found.

The family was recommended to have an assessment for a learning disorder for Sharon. Because the family's cultural values emphasized achievement and hard work, it was suggested that if a learning disorder did exist, treating it would help to promote learning for Sharon and to eliminate frustration for her and the family. Sherry reluctantly agreed to the assessment, and it was discovered that Sharon was mildly dyslexic. Tutoring sessions were established for Sharon, and her grades began to improve.

As treatment progressed, Sharon became more compliant with family rules, eliminated her fire starting, and decreased fights with her sister. However, the marital tension between Sherry and Dave began to escalate. They were given a referral for a couples counselor and were encouraged to follow up with family therapy if difficulties reemerged (see also, Miehls, this *Handbook,* this volume).

CONCLUSION

The cases illustrate the importance of exploring racial-cultural factors in family therapy. First, therapists must explore the racial or cultural identity of family members, particularly as members may differ in both their salience of racial issues and their identity status. As children and adolescents develop their identity, they will need guidance from their parents on interpreting experiences with the dominant culture. As demonstrated in the first case, therapists must also understand the racial identity of parents. Elizabeth had issues with her racial identity due to internalized negative messages from the dominant culture. This negative identity was influencing her parenting style and relationship with her children. Family therapists must explore identity with parents and examine its relationship to the presenting problem. This is important as the racial identity of parents may influence the racial socialization process of families (Thomas & Speight, 1999).

Second, family therapists must explore the racial socialization process. Families need to examine messages that are transmitted to children about both the dominant and the traditional culture, as this influences identity development. Parents need to be encouraged to engage in the racial socialization process, teaching children about their heritage and history, racial pride, and values and beliefs from their culture. Greene (1992) outlines interventions to promote the racial socialization process in family therapy. Parents should be encouraged to include extended family members in the socialization process and to include children in cultural activities and events. Parents also need to be persuaded to become involved in school systems to promote and enhance cultural sensitivity. The first two cases demonstrated the importance of encouraging the racial socialization process.

Finally, family therapists need to explore the influence of culture on child-rearing practices and beliefs. Parents are responsible for raising children to become healthy, successful, and competent adults, and culture often determines the values and beliefs that successful adults have. The second and third cases illustrate the importance of examining child-rearing beliefs and practices. In case 2, the parents had two differing values for the children, which allowed the child to engage in inappropriate behaviors. Case 3 illustrates how members may have similar cultural values but differences in child-rearing practices, which led to difficulties with functioning. Family therapists also need to examine discipline practices, as some behaviors that are culturally sanctioned may seem inappropriate to the dominant culture and child welfare agencies. Counselors may need to advocate for their families with child welfare and social agencies so that culturally sensitive treatment may consistently be provided.

REFERENCES

Anderson, J. D. (1991). Group work with families: A multicultural perspective. *Social Work with Groups, 13,* 85–101.

Atkinson, D. R. (2003). *Counseling American minorities* (6th ed.). Boston: McGraw-Hill.

Bowser, B. P. (in press). The role of solialization in cultural learning: What does the research say? In R. T. Carter (Ed.), *Handbook of racial-cultural psychology and counseling: Theory and research* (Vol. 1, pp. 184–206). Hoboken, NJ: Wiley.

Boyd-Franklin, N. (1989). *Black families in therapy: A multi-system approach.* New York: Guilford Press.

Boyd-Franklin, N. (2003). *Black families in therapy: The African American experience* (2nd ed.). New York: Guilford Press.

Boykin, A. W., & Toms, F. D. (1985). Black child socialization: A conceptual framework. In H. P. McAdoo & J. L. McAdoo (Eds.), *Black children: Social, educational, and parental environments* (pp. 33–51). Newbury Park, CA: Sage.

Canino, I. A., & Spurlock, J. (1994). *Culturally diverse children and adolescents: Assessment, diagnosis, and treatment.* New York: Guilford Press.

Carter, R. T. (in press). Uprooting inequity and disparities in counseling and psychology: An introduction. In R. T. Carter (Ed.), *Handbook of racial-cultural psychology and counseling: Theory and research* (Vol. 1, pp. xv–xxviii). Hoboken, NJ: Wiley.

Forehand, R., & Kotchick, B. A. (1996). Cultural diversity: A wakeup for parent training. *Behavior Therapy, 27,* 187–206.

Gacia Coll, C. T. G., Meyer, E. C., & Brillon, L. (1995). Ethnic and minority parenting. In M. H. Bornstein (Ed.), *Handbook of parenting: Biology and ecology of parenting* (Vol. 2, pp. 189–209). Mahwah, NJ: Erlbaum.

Giordano, J., & McGoldrick, M. (1996). European families: An overview. In M. McGoldrick, J. Giordano, & J. K. Pearce (Eds.), *Ethnicity and family therapy* (2nd ed., pp. 427–441). New York: Guilford Press.

Greene, B. A. (1992). Racial socialization as a tool in psychotherapy with African American children. In L. A. Vargas & J. D. Koss-Chioino (Eds.), *Working with culture: Psychotherapeutic strategies with ethnic minority children and adolescents* (pp. 63–81). San Francisco: Jossey-Bass.

Gushue, G. V. (1993). Cultural-identity development and family assessment: An interaction model. *The Counseling Psychologist, 21,* 487–513.

Hardy, K. V., & Laszloffy, T. A. (1995). The cultural genogram: Key to training culturally competent family therapists. *Journal of Marital and Family Therapy, 21,* 227–237.

Harrison, A. O., Wilson, M. N., Pine, C. J., Chon, S. Q., & Buriel, R. (1990). Family ecologies of ethnic minority children. *Child Development, 61,* 347–362.

Helms, J. E. (1995). An update of Helms's White and people of Color racial identity models. In J. G. Ponterotto, J. M. Casas, L. A. Suzuki, & C. M. Alexander (Eds.), *Handbook of multicultural counseling* (pp. 181–198). Thousand Oaks, CA: Sage.

Helms, J. E. (2001). An update of Helms's White and people of Color racial identity models. In J. G. Ponterotto, J. M. Casas, L. A. Suzuki, & C. M. Alexander (Eds.), *Handbook of multicultural counseling* (2nd ed., pp. 181–198). Thousand Oaks, CA: Sage.

Johnson, A. C. (1995). Resiliency mechanisms in culturally diverse families. *Family Journal: Counseling and Therapy for Couples and Families, 3,* 316–324.

Kerr, M., & Bowen, M. (1988). *Family evaluation.* New York: Norton.

Kohatsu, E. L. (in press). Acculturation: Current and future directions. In R. T. Carter (Ed.), *Handbook of racial-cultural psychology and counseling: Theory and research* (Vol. 1, pp. 207–231). Hoboken, NJ: Wiley.

McGill, D. W. (1992). The cultural story in multicultural family therapy. *Families in Society, 73,* 339–349.

McGoldrick, M. (1993). Ethnicity, cultural diversity, and normality. In F. Walsh (Ed.), *Normal family process* (2nd ed., pp. 331–360). New York: Guilford Press.

McGoldrick, M., & Giordano, J. (1996). Overview: Ethnicity and family therapy. In M. McGoldrick, J. Giordano, & J. K. Pearce (Eds.), *Ethnicity and family therapy* (2nd ed., pp. 1–27). New York: Guilford Press.

McGoldrick, M., Giordano, J., & Pearce, J. K. (Eds.). (1996). *Ethnicity and family therapy* (2nd ed.). New York: Guilford Press.

Minuchin, S., & Fishman, C. (1981). *Family therapy techniques.* Cambridge, MA: Harvard University Press.

Montalvo, B., & Gutierrez, J. M. (1983). A perspective for the use of the cultural dimension in family therapy. In J. C. Hansen & C. J. Falicov (Eds.), *Cultural perspectives in family therapy: The family therapy collections* (pp. 15–32). Rockville, MD: Aspen.

Paniagua, F. A. (1996). Cross-cultural guidelines in family therapy. *Family Journal: Counseling and Therapy for Couples and Families, 4,* 127–138.

Pedersen, P. (in press). The importance of Cultural Psychology Theory for multicultural counselors. In R. T. Carter (Ed.), *Handbook of racial-cultural psychology and counseling: Theory and research* (Vol. 1, pp. 3–16). Hoboken, NJ: Wiley.

Preli, R., & Bernard, J. M. (1993). Making multiculturalism relevant for majority culture graduate students. *Journal of Marital and Family Therapy, 19,* 5–16.

Ross, J. L., & Phipps, E. J. (1986). Understanding the family in multiple cultural contexts: Avoiding therapeutic traps. *Contemporary Family Therapy, 8,* 255–263.

Sanders Thompson, V. L. (1994). Socialization to race and its relationship to racial identification among African Americans. *Journal of Black Psychology, 20,* 175–188.

Satir, V. M. (1967). *Conjoint family therapy.* Palo Alto, CA: Science and Behavior Books.

Stevenson, H. C. (1995). Relationship of adolescent perceptions of racial socialization to racial identity. *Journal of Black Psychology, 21,* 49–70.

Sue, D. W., Ivey, A. E., & Pedersen, P. B. (1996). *A theory of multicultural counseling and therapy.* Pacific Grove, CA: Brooks/Cole.

Sue, D. W., & Sue, D. (2003). *Counseling the culturally diverse: Theory and practice* (4th ed.). New York: Wiley.

Thomas, A. J. (1998). Understanding culture and worldview in family systems: Use of the multicultural genogram. *Family Journal: Counseling and Therapy for Couples and Families, 6,* 24–32.

Thomas, A. J., & Speight, S. L. (1999). Racial identity and racial socialization attitudes of African American parents. *Journal of Black Psychology, 25,* 152–170.

Vandiver, B. J., Fhagen-Smith, P. E., Cokley, K. O., Cross, W. E., & Worrell, F. C. (2001). Cross's nigrescence model: From theory to scale to theory. *Journal of Multicultural Counseling and Development, 29,* 174–200.

Weakland, J. H., Fisch, R., Watzlawick, P., & Bodin, A. M. (1981). Brief therapy: Focused problem resolution. In R. G. Green & J. L. Framo (Eds.), *Family therapy: Major contributions* (pp. 493–526). Madison, CT: International Universities Press.

Yeh, C. J., & Hunter, C. D. (in press). The socialization of self: Understanding shifting and multiple selves across cultures. In R. T. Carter (Ed.), *Handbook of racial-cultural psychology and counseling: Theory and research* (Vol. 1, pp. 78–93). Hoboken, NJ: Wiley.

CHAPTER 23

Couples Counseling and Psychotherapy in Racial-Cultural Psychology: Case Application

Dennis Miehls

Racially and culturally competent couples therapists must consider a number of factors as they complete a thorough biopsychosocial assessment of couple systems. Race and culture are powerful factors that influence identity, and as such, they are embedded in every therapeutic interaction. Wilkinson (1997) contends that race is the primary factor that influences the identity of individuals in the United States (Carter, this *Handbook,* Volume One). While assessing couple systems, I assume that race is the dominant factor that fundamentally shapes the therapeutic encounter. Wilkinson emphasizes this point:

> Racial differences in the U.S. and almost globally have always been and remain far more socially and politically potent than gender, ethnicity, or class, whether examined independently or separately. (p. 263)

Interventions that flow from the assessment are grounded in theory that integrates racial identity development and other aspects of cultural identity (Ota Wang, this *Handbook,* this volume; Thompson, this *Handbook,* this volume). To determine the racial identity status of each partner, the therapist assesses the readiness and ability of the partners to engage in dialogue about the racial and cultural backgrounds of each. The therapist needs to make clinical decisions that determine if and when issues of race are discussed in the therapy process (Thomas, this *Handbook,* this volume). Equally important, the therapist engages in a self-reflective process in which he or she is critically aware of his or her own racial and cultural identity development. In the couple relationship, tensions that arise out of racial-cultural differences can potentially be sites of growth for the couple system (e.g., Thomas, this *Handbook,* this volume). This chapter, then, examines sociocultural factors, such as ethnicity, socioeconomic class, and gender, that influence the assessment and treatment of couples. This chapter outlines assessment of racial-cultural identities; a thorough biopsychosocial assessment synthesizes concepts from object relations, attachment, intergenerational, trauma, and family theories (Alderfer, this *Handbook,* this volume; Wallace, this *Handbook,* this volume).

I first define key concepts and definitions related to racial-cultural couple counseling. Next, I elaborate key themes that inform a racial-cultural assessment of couples.

Finally, a clinical example is utilized to demonstrate how the resolution of key racial-cultural themes contributed to growth in the described couple system.

KEY CONCEPTS AND DEFINITIONS

Theorizing about culture and race carries traditions that are currently being challenged by a range of postmodern writers. As discussed by Laird (1998), Miehls (2001), and Rosenblum and Travis (1996), Western thinking has tended to organize constructs about difference as binary oppositions. Breaking free from essentialist thinking that positions anyone who is "different from me" as a devalued "other," postmodern writers suggest that it is more useful to consider that individuals are composed of multiple factors that shape their identities. Identity is fluid, with different parts of one's identity becoming salient at different times, depending on the context of the interaction (Laird, 1998; Ota Wang, this *Handbook,* this volume).

With the notion of multiple identities for both client and therapist in mind, the culturally competent practitioner allows for dissonance within the self (Dyche & Zayas, 2001; King Keenan, 2001; Miehls & Moffatt, 2000) that permits an openness to explore multiple meanings of behavior in an individual and in interactions with others. Dyche and Zayas (1995) encourage therapists to approach clients with an open stance that honors cultural difference. Carter (1995) argues that if the therapist understands how race-related issues influence the client, the "therapist can start to comprehend race's role in the client's intrapsychic and interpersonal relations" (p. 234). McGoldrick (1998) contends that developing

> cultural competence requires us to go beyond the dominant values and explore the complexity of culture and cultural identity . . . without accepting unquestionably our society's definitions of these culturally determined categories. (p. 8)

Pearlmutter (1996) claims that cultural competence implies that therapy will be intersubjective in nature; clients and therapists coconstruct the meaningful aspects of therapy (Aron, 1996; Benjamin, 1998; Bowles, 1999; McMahon, 1997; Miehls, 1999; Noonan, 1999; Thomson, this *Handbook,* this volume; Trop, 1997). Perez-Foster (1998) emphasizes that the recognition of clinician subjectivity and potential cultural countertransference "cannot be more vital than in the treatment of patients whose culture, race, or class markedly differs from that of the therapist" (p. 255).

Definition of Race

Once thought of as a biological demarcation, race is now considered a social construct that is situated in different historical locations (Carter & Pieterse, this *Handbook,* Volume One). Cornell and Hartman (1998) explain that race is a human group that is defined by another group who perceives common physical characteristics among those being observed:

> Determining which characteristics constitute the race—the selection of markers and therefore the construction of the racial category itself—is a choice human beings make. Neither markers nor categories are predetermined by any biological factors. (p. 24)

In postmodern thinking, "Race exists because we have created it as a meaningful category of difference between people" (Rosenbloom & Travis, 1996, p. 19).

Definition of Culture

Culture, as a construct, also has varied definitions (Johnson, this *Handbook,* Volume One). In this chapter, culture refers to a group's consensus about what meaning is attributed to a range of activities that will help them order their interactions. Cohen (1998) explains that culture "refers to the mostly unwritten rules and conventions of thought, communication, and behavior that people use so that they can interact in an orderly way" (p. 63). Biever, Bebele, and North (1998) describe culture as the sum of similar characteristics of a community that are conveyed through social interactions of members of the community (p. 321). Cohen (1998) noted that culture defines the rules of communication, including colloquial means of communication. In addition, roles and statuses of members of the community are defined through culture (Thompson, this *Handbook,* this volume). Cultures shape the way members perceive the world and the array of events. Cultures also influence how members understand or share their emotional worlds with each other.

With these working definitions of race and culture, let us now examine how individuals construct their racial identity development. Although the following models imply a sequential status approach to racial identity development, it is more accurate to think of the phases as building blocks to identity that are revisited during the life cycle. With each revisiting, the individual adds to the complexity of understanding of racial identity development.

RACIAL IDENTITY DEVELOPMENT

Cross (1991), Helms (1995, 2001), and Helms and Cook (1999) have all elaborated models of racial identity development. Racial identity development theories describe the transformative processes that people of Color and White individuals undergo to potentially achieve a sense of racial "maturity" or racial self-actualization. Tatum (1997) makes the point that "it is assumed that in a society where racial group membership is emphasized, the development of a racial identity will occur in some form in everyone" (p. 93). Although everyone experiences some form of racial identity development, there are different pathways to development for people of Color and Whites (Helms & Cook, 1999). Tatum (1992) points out the pathway of racial identity development is different as the privileges ascribed to Whites will naturally impact the process of their racial identity development (Helms, this *Handbook,* Volume One).

For people of Color, the sequence of development is as follows. Moving from a position that race does not matter, people of Color begin to recognize that they are part of a targeted group. Next, individuals often immerse themselves into their own culture; the person of Color experiences great pride in his or her racial identity during this period of development. During internalization, people of Color can move beyond the protective space of their own group and begin collaborative relationships with members of other oppressed groups. Finally, with integrated awareness (Helms & Cook, 1999) people of Color are able to take a proactive stance in which they transcend some issues of race (Cross, 1991). According to Helms and Cook (1999):

> The end goal of the maturational process is to acquire the latter status and be able to use it most of the time in coping with a racially complex world in which one's integrated and positive sense of self is frequently at risk. (p. 89)

White individuals are usually not initially aware of how their skin color privileges them; when they move from this ill-informed position, they often go into a state of disintegration (see Richarson & Frey, this *Handbook,* this volume). In this status, individuals begin to recognize the reality of inequity among racial groups. As anxiety rises, White individuals become reintegrated into and idealize White norms. There is little personal responsibility taken for racism at that point. Some move to a phase of pseudo-independence, in which there is a more deliberate period of self-reflection. Here, individuals begin to intellectually understand the disadvantages of people of Color, and stereotypes and myths are challenged. In the emersion phase, individuals seek out other White individuals with whom to share the new ideas, feelings, and behaviors associated with being less racist. During autonomy, Whites are able to forge alliances with people of Color. In addition, there is a "flexible analytic self-expression and responses to racial material" (Helms & Cook, 1999, p. 93) that characterize one's interactions with others.

As noted earlier, development is not linear and, Cooper and Lesser (1997) point out, racial identity statuses will be revisited at different points in time. Entering a new relationship, a new workplace, or a new community, for example, will necessitate a revisiting of earlier themes. Tatum (1997) describes development as spiral in form and the process of development as being similar to climbing a spiral staircase:

> As a person ascends a spiral staircase, she may stop and look down at a spot below. When she reaches the next level, she may look down and see the same spot, but the vantage point is not exactly the same. (p. 95)

A MULTICULTURAL LENS: COUPLE ASSESSMENT THEMES

Krohn (1998) suggests that many couples enter treatment at the time of a life cycle crisis. As such, the presenting concerns and issues will certainly be varied. However, it is important to ascertain a cultural assessment as one component of the larger biopsychosocial assessment of the couple. Regardless of the background of the individuals, it is important to have some assessment of the individuals' racial identity development (Alverez & Piper, this *Handbook,* this volume). Have the individuals grown up as members of an oppressed population? If so, how have they managed the ongoing insidious racial assaults that they have experienced? Are the partners from the same cultural background? If not, is one background more privileged in the couple system? Do you see any evidence of internalized racism? Does one partner enact racial dynamics for both partners? If the individuals have moved away from their cultural roots, is there survivor guilt? How do the couple's cultures intersect with each other?

It is important to recognize that regardless of the race of clients or clinician, the clinician's racial identity development will influence the intersubjective interaction of therapy. In other words, even when working with clients from a similar racial and cultural background, the response of the clinician is impacted by his or her own racial identity status. Similarly, one cannot presume common cultural knowledge and customs between clients and clinician, even if they or their ancestors originated in the same country or region of a country. It is important to assess if the clinician has examined his or her own racial identity status and cultural stereotypes. How do the clients' and clinician's racial identity statuses intersect and impact each other? In some clinical situations, the therapist may directly discuss the impact of culture and racial identity on the couple relationship. In other circumstances, and if the clients do not appear to have conscious awareness of their racial and cultural characteristics, open discussion is not always indicated or helpful. However, the therapist may guide interventions based on his or her assessment of the clients' racial and cultural identities (see Thomas, this *Handbook,* this volume).

Once the clinician has a firm sense of the racial identity status of the couple, it is useful to consider other aspects of culture. For example, have these individuals grown up in a Western culture that values independence? Or is the underlying value base related to ideas of collectivism (Bowser, this *Handbook,* Volume One; Falicov, 1998; Ho, 1990; Yeh & Hunter, this *Handbook,* Volume One)? If the couple relationship is embedded in a collectivistic network, the marital tie is not always given primacy over all other family relationships (Falicov, 1998). Therapists who have internalized Western values that privilege autonomy are cautioned not to pathologize those systems in which there are strong intergenerational and community connections. For example, Perez-Foster (1998) notes that in Hindu cultures, maturity is not related to separateness; rather, "selfhood . . . is viewed as a complex matrix of familial, individual, spiritual and social/hierarchical identifications" (p. 258).

In recognizing the potential for different values in terms of the partners' need for separation and connection, it is also important to assess the status of gender in the system (Goldner, 1989; McGoldrick, Anderson, & Walsh, 1989). Who holds the power in the system? Are women valued in the system? In what relationships are women valued? Is there a connection between mother and children that is afforded status? If so, how does this impact the couple system? What emphasis has been placed on education for women in this system? Are males privileged in terms of power, control of money, or education? How does the couple manage the division of labor? Is there a sharp demarcation of gender roles, or is there flexibility?

Have these individuals grown up in a culture that privileges heterosexuality? If so, how do gay/lesbian/bisexual or transgendered couples manage the homophobic responses of family members and the larger community? Is there internalized homophobia? Does this internalized homophobia get projected onto the partner? Are there particular cultural sanctions that exacerbate the difficulties of the gay or lesbian partnership (Constantine, Watt, Gainor, & Warren, this *Handbook,* Volume One; Greene & Boyd-Franklin, 1996; Liu & Chan, 1996; Morales, 1996)?

These broad cultural factors provide the overarching framework for a more specific assessment of each couple system. Dym and Glenn (1993) comment that each couple has to reconcile their relationship with that of the larger cultural narrative.

Couples judge themselves by the ideal standards that are imposed on everyone by the larger culture. Standards that underscore perfection and iconic status are popularized through the media. Each couple engages with the cultural narrative in different formats. Dym and Glenn (1993) comment: "Some follow it slavishly; others loosely; some rebel and defy; some try to change themselves in order to fit" (p. 28). Each family has either consciously or unconsciously made decisions about where they want to fit into the larger cultural narrative (Alderfer, this *Handbook,* this volume).

As the couple relationship evolves, is there support from each family of origin for the partnership? If not, what is the lack of support based on? How has the couple managed this dissension in their own family? As the couple system evolved, is there recognition of similar values in terms of holidays, rituals, traditions? If not, how have decisions been made during these times of difference? Has the couple been able to find ways to honor each person's traditions? What are the fundamental views of each around child rearing? In terms of these views, has the couple been influenced by other cultures? Does the couple share the same religious or spiritual beliefs? If not, is each background honored?

—————————————————————— **Case Study** ——————————————————————

Arif and Donna (the names of the couple have been altered, although the clinical process reflects the treatment issues) were referred to me by Donna's family physician. The physician reported that the couple was in a crisis. At that time, Donna was in the early stages of pregnancy and was being pressured by Arif to undergo genetic testing that would determine the gender of the fetus. Arif and Donna had two biological daughters. The partners are a racially mixed couple who were raised with different cultural values. Arif's parents immigrated to Canada when he was a small child. He is a dark-skinned East Indian Canadian who was assessed as fluidly moving between dissonance and internalization in his racial identity status. He was consciously aware of the influence of race in his relationships. He was making efforts to integrate complex information about race. He attended Canadian schools and is presently finishing a doctoral program at a publicly funded university. The family has always lived in a large urban center. Arif's parents, both Hindu, were born and raised in a large East Indian city. Arif presently described himself as agnostic in terms of religious affiliation.

Donna's grandparents immigrated to Canada. Her parents were both born in Canada and Donna was raised in a large urban center. She identifies as Caucasian. Her parents and brothers are blue-collar workers in a local factory. Donna was raised in a nonpracticing Roman Catholic household and she still identifies as Christian. She completed secondary school and worked as a retail sales clerk before marrying. She met Arif at a party given by mutual friends. After a brief courtship, the couple were engaged and married in a secular ceremony. Neither family supported the marriage, although in time, each family became somewhat more reconciled to the marriage. Donna has little contact with her family of origin. She had previously made a geographic move across the country to escape what she perceived as the domineering control of her mother. Arif's parents live one block away from the couple and are integrally involved with the couple's day-to-day activities. The two households usually have their evening meal together, and while the couple has blended some cultural traditions and experiences of the two backgrounds, Arif's parents have been influential in the couple's early relationship. In terms of racial identity status, Donna appeared to be in a pseudo-independence phase of development; she had attempted to challenge her stereotypes and was making efforts to be more open to others with cultural views and racial identities differing from hers.

In completing the cultural-racial assessment, I noted that the couple appeared to have a readiness to explore the meaning and impact of culture in the relationship. Each had sufficient ego strength to make this exploration. This couple was able to hold ambivalent feelings toward each other, even when angry, and the ambivalence did not threaten the relationship. Although the couple clearly did seem to be in a crisis, I assessed them as being strongly committed to the continuation of a long-term relationship; they clearly were proud parents, and they each looked forward to increased financial independence when Arif finished his doctoral program. At the time of the referral, the couple was financially dependent on Arif's parents. Donna worked a few part-time hours and her mother-in-law watched the two daughters when Donna worked. The couple shared many common interests and they described that they had a mutually satisfying sexual relationship. In fact, the couple described that they had been quite content before realizing that Donna was unexpectedly pregnant for the third time.

The Crisis

The couple had not been planning a third child at that time in their marriage. They planned to have one other child after Arif was firmly established in his career. Donna reported that Arif's mother was strongly encouraging Arif to direct Donna to undergo genetic testing. Arif's parents were suggesting that they did not want to support the couple's third child if female. They would, however, welcome a male grandchild into the system. Donna was ambivalent about being pregnant again, but she did not want to even consider the possibility of abortion of the fetus. Her physician had said that there were no observable risks to the child, as Donna was young, healthy, and had had two previous uneventful pregnancies. The couple's daughters were healthy, bright, and "lovable." At the time of the referral, the couple was in a gridlock. As mentioned, this couple had had a positive relationship until now, and this disagreement seemed to be equally distressing for them.

The Cultural Assessment

At the outset of the work, I was aware that my racial background might be a factor in the work with this interracial couple. When building the treatment alliance, I questioned Arif if he worried that I might "side with Donna," as she and I are both Caucasian. He told me that he had wondered if my race or cultural/religious beliefs might bias my interactions with them. However, he acknowledged that my raising the question about collusion eased some of his concerns (Liu & Pope-Davis, this *Handbook*, this volume). We agreed to revisit the issue of the cross-racial/cultural therapy if any of us detected any bias in my responses. So, with this framework, I proceeded to complete the biopsychosocial assessment.

I learned that the couple had previously made some adjustments to accommodate their cultural differences. At the beginning of the relationship, Arif's parents explicitly stated that they did not want their son to marry a White woman. Arif acknowledged that his parents had become more involved with his life when he announced that he was marrying Donna. Until then, he was following the culturally expected pathway of pursuing education as a means of solidifying his economic and professional status. He recognized that his father was powerful in the family system. He was not all that emotionally close to his father, although he and his mother did have a close bond. While his parents had openly expressed their disapproval of Donna, Arif remained true to his decision and chose to counter the family injunction. Arif and his parents had anticipated that biracial children would be marginalized in Canadian society; equally, they would not be completely accepted in the East Indian community. However, Arif's strong statement that he was committed to Donna propelled his mother to become more accepting of her. Eventually, his father also became immersed in the day-to-day activity of the two households.

Donna had insisted that the couple have their own living accommodations. Arif's parents thought that this was peculiar, but, again, Arif had maintained the couple boundary and respected Donna's wishes. Donna understood that she was somewhat devalued as a woman in Arif's family. She also grew to understand that her role with her mother-in-law was an important bond to nurture and she had indeed formed a close alliance with her. Arif's mother tutored Donna in the culinary and homemaking aspects of an Indian home. Donna expressed that she had also shown flexibility when her two daughters were born. To show respect for Arif and his parents, she had followed Hindu rituals of purification of the babies and child rearing. Although she would have liked more autonomy, she gave up some of her independence to live in a more communal, extended family. Donna was well aware that she had disappointed Arif and his parents when the couple's daughters had not been male children. Donna's geographic distance from her own family lessened the criticism of her own mother, but Donna was painfully aware that her family of origin was racist and that they looked down on Arif. When angry with Arif, Donna had to actively fight her own stereotypes of East Indian people. Her family had also shown little interest in her two children, and she continued to feel alienated from her family.

In the cultural assessment, I heard themes related to individualism versus collectivism. I heard that Donna's tendency to be more autonomous was part of Western culture. The two cultures have different views of the value of women. In Hindu families, the eldest son is the most powerful; he often stays emotionally distant from the father, and the mother-son relationship is close. The mother-in-law role is highly valued in the family system. Males are encouraged to pursue education as a way of maintaining and improving the family's economic (class) status. The clash between Christianity and Hinduism was also present. Though not a practicing Catholic, Donna opposed abortion. The couple was clearly polarized around this decision.

The Intervention

Initially, it was important for the partners to have an opportunity to express their views to me. While each clearly wanted me to agree with his or her position, I provided a neutral, value-free holding environment. This couple had a strong relationship history and had previously demonstrated their ability to honor each other's traditions. I articulated that I heard their abilities to respect difference in the past and I asked them what they thought made this circumstance different from previous disagreements.

Due to space limitations, I cannot fully elaborate the process of the therapy. However, what emerged was the couple's recognition that the polarization was being fueled by each partner's internal ambivalence around key individual issues. When each could own his or her own part of the conflict, they were able to move to a decision that was able to maintain a both/and stance (Biever et al., 1998). Each was able to once again reaffirm the commitment in the couple relationship and make a decision that was their choice and exempt from the influence of Arif's parents.

In the couple work, Arif came to understand that he was ambivalent about his family's privileging of him. While he recognized that he liked many of the benefits of being male in a Hindu tradition, he had increasingly found himself wanting to become more "Western." I questioned Arif about his own potential internalized racism. He felt that he was proud of being a Canadian Indian and that he was thus comfortable with his racial identity. However, his wish to become more Western meant that he wanted to be more actively involved with his children's lives; he did not want to be viewed only as an authoritative figure who had the power to make decisions. He acknowledged that he enjoyed the couple's relationships with other young families. He wanted to have an equitable partnership with Donna. He worried that his parents would criticize him for not giving his career his entire energy; he also worried that they would criticize him for totally turning his back on his culture. He did not want to discount his cultural background. Arif recognized that he had become focused on the idea of wanting a male child because he had been caught in a conflict in his own internal world. He understood that his desire to rid himself of any "feminine" traits, such as being a nurturing parent or partner, had become confused with his demand that the couple would value only a son. Arif had projected his wish for autonomy and independence onto Donna. He was able to acknowledge that he also wanted to blend the couple's traditions; he recognized that this would cause some tension between him and his parents, but he hoped that this would be a temporary adaptation to his increased independence. Arif expressed a wish that his biracial children could serve the function of bridging racial tensions in his family and community. I understood this statement as reflecting Arif's attempts to shift his racial identity status to a level of autonomy and integrated awareness.

While Donna initially held firm to the idea that she had compromised all that she could, she eventually was better able to understand her wish to exercise complete independence from Arif's family. She argued that she had previously welcomed her mother-in-law into the couple's home. Her mother-in-law had mentored her and she used this as proof of her willingness to be fluid in her cultural adaptation. Donna also said that she had allowed herself to be discredited as a woman and that she could no longer tolerate the expectations that she devote her life to Arif and her children. I encouraged Donna to consider her own ambivalence about mothers and mothering. She had made a geographic separation from her own domineering mother. Donna had not readily recognized that she had been enjoying the relationship with her mother-in-law; in fact, when prompted, she was able to articulate that she indeed enjoyed the attention that her mother-in-law had given. She often enjoyed being taken care of and given instruction in the craft of homemaking. Donna also acknowledged that she was fighting the ideal of the Western woman: a super mom who also has a successful profession. She recognized that she was ashamed of herself because she had not pursued education beyond a high school diploma. She became aware that her refusal to even consider abortion was partially based on the idea that this pregnancy would postpone her decision about further education. If she had another child, she would not have to immediately face her shame about her lack of advanced education and what that said about her sense of self. Like Arif, Donna worried that the couple's biracial children would face discrimination. Her family and some friends had challenged her privileged status as a White woman when they questioned why she had become so "East Indian."

The impasse was resolved when each recognized the symbolic meaning behind what was manifest as cultural differences. The life event of another pregnancy accelerated the dynamic issues that the couple likely would eventually have faced in the future. Arif was attempting to come to terms with his own wish to become more Western and White. He was struggling with his own status as a man of Color in a predominantly White professional world. Clearly engaged in a process of his own racial identity development, Arif shifted from some periods of dissonance to more integrated autonomy when he wished that his children's biracial status would bridge his and Donna's racial and cultural differences. Arif also needed to negotiate his stance with his parents. He did not wish to be distant and authoritative.

I encouraged Donna to consider her self-devaluation; she needed to recognize and deal with her lack of confidence about pursuing further education. In addition, she was able to own her ambivalence about being taken care of by her mother-in-law. She recognized that this did not mean that she had to lose her sense of self and independence. In terms of racial identity development, Donna continued to demonstrate attitudes that reflected her pseudo-independent status. She continued to be self-reflective about issues of race and culture and appeared open to others' ideas.

CONCLUSION

This chapter highlights cultural and racial identity themes that are important to assess when working with couples. It is important for the clinician to be aware of his or her own cultural biases and attitudes. With this self-awareness, the ability to conduct cross-cultural therapy is enhanced. I have also demonstrated that the assessment of cultural factors is embedded in a broader biopsychosocial assessment model. The couple would not have been able to utilize an insight-oriented approach in their therapy had they not demonstrated other developmental achievements. For example, in object relations terms, I assessed that each had attained a sense of object constancy. As noted previously, each could hold complex ambivalent images of the other, even when they were in conflict or frustrated. The couple could recognize the intergenerational patterns of their respective families of origin, and each was able to integrate insights about family dynamics that were being played out in this crisis. For example, Donna recognized that her wish for autonomy was partially determined by her troubled relationship with her controlling mother. Arif recognized the intergenerational cultural injunctions about male authority, for example, and directly challenged the repetition of this pattern in his relationships with his children. The clinical illustration demonstrates that the impasse was broken when, through insight-oriented work, each partner could recognize and own his or her unconscious conflict that was manifest in the couple's disagreement.

Racial identity statuses and cultural differences permeate the conscious and unconscious worlds of clients and therapists. As such, racial identity development and awareness of cultural difference facilitates sound interventions that flow from the biopsychosocial assessment. In this instance, the unplanned pregnancy was the catalyst that propelled the couple into a crisis. The interface of different cultural values and racial identities in the partnership led to disagreement and conflict that brought the couple into therapy. Using insight-oriented methods, the therapy assisted the couple to more fully examine their cultural differences and racial identities.

REFERENCES

Aron, L. (1996). *A meeting of the minds: Mutuality in psychoanalysis.* Hillsdale, NJ: Analtyic Press.

Benjamin, J. (1998). *The bonds of love: Psychoanalysis, feminism, and the problem of domination.* New York: Pantheon Books.

Biever, J., Bebele, M., & North, M. W. (1998). Therapy with intercultural couples: A postmodern approach. *Counseling Psychology Quarterly, 11*(2), 181–188.

Bowles, D. B. (1999). Intersubjectivity: Expanding our understanding of the worker-client relationship. *Smith College Studies in Social Work, 69*(2), 359–371.

Bowser, B. P. (in press). The role of solialization in cultural learning: What does the research say? In R. T. Carter (Ed.), *Handbook of racial-cultural psychology and counseling: Theory and research* (Vol. 1, pp. 184–206). Hoboken, NJ: Wiley.

Carter, R. T. (in press). Uprooting inequity and disparities in counseling and psychology: An introduction. In R. T. Carter (Ed.), *Handbook of racial-cultural psychology and counseling: Theory and research* (Vol. 1, pp. xv–xxviii). Hoboken, NJ: Wiley.

Carter, R. T., & Pieterse, A. L. (in press). Race: A social and psychological analysis of the term and its meaning. In R. T. Carter (Ed.), *Handbook of racial-cultural psychology and counseling: Theory and research* (Vol. 1, pp. 41–63). Hoboken, NJ: Wiley.

Cohen, M. (1998). *Culture of intolerance: Chauvinism, class, and racism in the United States.* New Haven, CT: Yale University Press.

Constantine, M. G., Watt, S. K., Gainor, K. A., & Warren, A. K. (in press). The influence of Cross's initial black racial identity theory on other cultural identity conceptualizations. In R. T. Carter (Ed.), *Handbook of racial-cultural psychology and counseling: Theory and research* (Vol. 1, pp. 94–114). Hoboken, NJ: Wiley.

Cooper, M., & Lesser, J. (1997). How race affects the helping process: A case of cross racial therapy. *Clinical Social Work Journal, 25*(3), 323–336.

Cornell, S., & Hartman, D. (1998). *Ethnicity and race: Making identities in a changing world* (pp. 15–38). Thousand Oaks, CA: Pine Forge Press.

Cross, W. (1991). *Shades of Black.* Philadelphia: Temple University Press.

Dyche, L., & Zayas, L. (1995). The value of curiosity and naivete for the cross-cultural psychotherapist. *Family Process, 34,* 389–399.

Dyche, L., & Zayas, L. (2001). Cross-cultural empathy and training the contemporary psychotherapist. *Clinical Social Work Journal, 29*(3), 245–258.

Dym, B., & Glenn, M. (1993). *Couples: Exploring and understanding the cycles of intimate relationships.* New York: Harper Perennial.

Falicov, C. (1998). The cultural meaning of family triangles. In M. McGoldrick (Ed.), *Re-visioning family therapy: Race, culture, and gender in clinical practice* (pp. 37–49). New York: Guilford Press.

Goldner, V. (1989). Generation and gender: Normative and covert hierarchies. In M. McGoldrick, C. Anderson, & F. Walsh (Eds.), *Women in families: A framework for family therapy* (pp. 42–60). New York: Norton.

Greene, B., & Boyd-Franklin, N. (1996). African American lesbians: Issues in couples therapy. In J. Laird & R. J. Green (Eds.), *Lesbians and gays in couples and families* (pp. 251–271). San Francisco: Jossey-Bass.

Helms, J. E. (1995). An update of Helms's White and people of Color racial identity models. In J. Ponterotto, J. Casas, L. Suzuki, & C. Alexander (Eds.), *Handbook of multicultural counseling* (pp. 181–198). Thousand Oaks, CA: Sage.

Helms, J. E. (2001). An update of Helms's White and people of Color racial identity models. In J. Ponterotto, J. Casas, L. Suzuki, & C. Alexander (Eds.), *Handbook of multicultural counseling* (2nd ed., pp. 181–198). Thousand Oaks, CA: Sage.

Helms, J. E. (in press). Challenging some misuses of reliability as reflected in evaluations of the White Racial Identity Attitude Scale. In R. T. Carter (Ed.), *Handbook of racial-cultural psychology and counseling: Theory and research* (Vol. 1, pp. 360–390). Hoboken, NJ: Wiley.

Helms, J. E., & Cook, D. (1999). *Models of racial oppression and sociorace: Using race and culture in counseling and psychotherapy* (pp. 69–100). Boston: Allyn & Bacon.

Ho, M. K. (1990). *Intermarried couples in therapy.* Springfield, IL: Charles C Thomas.

Johnson, S. D. (in press). Culture, context, and counseling. In R. T. Carter (Ed.), *Handbook of racial-cultural psychology and counseling: Theory and research* (Vol. 1, pp. 17–25). Hoboken, NJ: Wiley.

King Keenan, E. (2001). Using Foucault's "disciplinary power" and "resistance" in cross-cultural psychotherapy. *Clinical Social Work Journal, 29*(3), 211–228.

Krohn, J. (1998). Intercultural couples. In M. McGoldrick (Ed.), *Re-visioning family therapy: Race, culture, and gender in clinical practice* (pp. 295–308). New York: Guilford Press.

Laird, J. (1998). Theorizing culture: Narrative ideas and practice principles. In M. McGoldrick (Ed.), *Revisioning family therapy: Race, culture, and gender in clinical practice.* (pp. 20–36). New York: Guilford Press.

Liu, P., & Chan, C. (1996). Lesbian, gay, and bisexual Asian Americans and their families. In J. Laird & R. J. Green (Eds.), *Lesbians and gays in couples and families* (pp. 137–152). San Francisco: Jossey-Bass.

McGoldrick, M. (1998). Introduction: Re-visioning family therapy through a cultural lens. In M. McGoldrick (Ed.), *Re-visioning family therapy* (pp. 3–19). New York: Guilford Press.

McGoldrick, M., Anderson, C., & Walsh, F. (1989). Women in families and in family therapy. In M. McGoldrick, C. Anderson, & F. Walsh (Eds.), *Women in families: A framework for family therapy* (pp. 3–15). New York: Norton.

McMahon, M. (1997). Creating harmony out of dissonance: Applying theories of intersubjectivity to therapy with couples. *Journal of Analytic Social Work, 4*(3), 43–61.

Miehls, D. (1999). Couple therapy: An integration of object relations and intersubjective theory. *Smith College Studies in Social Work, 69*(2), 335–355.

Miehls, D. (2001). The interface of racial identity development with identity complexity in clinical social work student practitioners. *Clinical Social Work Journal, 29*(3), 229–244.

Miehls, D., & Moffatt, K. (2000). Constructing social work identity based on the reflexive self. *British Journal of Social Work, 30,* 339–348.

Morales, E. (1996). Gender roles among Latino gay and bisexual men: Implications for family and couple relationships. In J. Laird & R. J. Green (Eds.), *Lesbians and gays in couples and families* (pp. 272–297). San Francisco: Jossey-Bass.

Noonan, M. (1999). Difficult dyads: Understanding affective and relational components from an intersubjective perspective. *Smith College Studies in Social Work, 69*(2), 388–402.

Pearlmutter, L. (1996). Using culture and the intersubjective perspective as a resource: A case study of an African-American couple. *Clinical Social Work Journal, 24*(4), 389–402.

Perez-Foster, R. M. (1998). The clinician's cultural countertransference: The psychodynamics of culturally competent practice. *Clinical Social Work Journal, 26*(3), 253–270.

Rosenblum, K., & Travis, T. M. (1996). *The meaning of difference: American constructions of race, sex and gender, social class, and sexual orientation.* New York: McGraw-Hill.

Tatum, B. (1992). Talking about race, learning about racism: The application of racial identity development theory in the classroom. *Harvard Educational Review, 62*(1), 1–24.

Tatum, B. (1997). Racial identity development and relational theory: The case of Black women in White communities. In J. Jordan (Ed.), *Women's growth in diversity: More writings from the Stone Center* (pp. 91–106). New York: Guilford Press.

Trop, J. (1997). An intersubjective perspective of countertransference in couples therapy. In M. Solomon & J. Siegel (Eds.), *Countertransference and couple therapy* (pp. 99–109). New York: Norton.

Wilkinson, D. (1997). Reappraising the race, class, gender equation: A critical theoretical perspective. *Smith College Studies in Social Work, 67*(3). 261–276.

Yeh, C. J., & Hunter, C. D. (in press). The socialization of self: Understanding shifting and multiple selves across cultures. In R. T. Carter (Ed.), *Handbook of racial-cultural psychology and counseling: Theory and research* (Vol. 1, pp. 78–93). Hoboken, NJ: Wiley.

CHAPTER 24

Immigration and Transition: Implications of Racial-Cultural Counseling and Clinical Practice

Patrica Arredondo

> *The immigrants lived in crisis because they were uprooted. In transplanta-*
> *tion, while the roots were sundered, before the new were established, the*
> *immigrants existed in an extreme situation.*
>
> —Handlin, 1951, p. 6

PREMISES

- All clinical practice with immigrants must be grounded in contextual, racial-cultural, and sociopolitical frames of reference.

- Immigration introduces multiple life-changing experiences for immigrants and their families with differential consequences for mental well-being.

- To work effectively and ethically with immigrants, clinicians must draw on specific cultural and contextual models and competencies.

The purpose of this chapter is to examine how the pre- to postexperiences of immigration affect the transition and acculturation process of immigrants to the United States from a psychohistorical framework; examine conditions specific to immigrants' experiences, including acculturative stress (Aziz, 1999; Das & Kemp, 1997; Smart & Smart, 1995), cultural-racial harassment, loss and grief (Arredondo-Dowd, 1981; Kohatsu, this *Handbook,* Volume One), and role changes (Castex, 1997; Thompson, this *Handbook,* this volume); introduce relevant models for racial-cultural counseling; and provide competencies/guidelines for racial-cultural counseling with immigrants (Arredondo, 1998, 1999; Esquivel, 1998; Gates et al., 2000).

HISTORICAL AND POLITICAL CONSIDERATIONS

Immigration is and always has been a national and global phenomenon; however, international and cross-cultural migrations are unprecedented in their increase (Rogler, 1994). In the historical context of the United States, early literature about immigrants chronicles the entry of various European ethnic groups, leaving behind situations of distress and oppression in hopes of a better life across the ocean. Prior to 1880, immigrants arrived primarily from Northern European countries. From 1880 to 1920, newcomers arrived from Southern and Eastern Europe. These immigrants differed from many of their predecessors in having minimal to no formal education, agricultural backgrounds, and different/darker phenotype.

Historical accounts indicate that there were many critics of immigration, fueling feelings of xenophobia. Politicians, educators, and social scientists of the eighteenth and nineteenth centuries wrote about immigrants in less than favorable terms (Carter & Pieterse, this *Handbook,* Volume One; Cremin, 1961; Handlin, 1959; Tyack, 1967), although ironically, these same writers were only a generation or two removed from arrival to the colonies or to the new United States. Beginning in the 1880s, there were many anti-immigrant movements that parallel contemporary situations in this country. In 1880, the American Protective Association led the movement to have English designated the official language of the country and to restrict bilingual education in the schools. They also moved against Catholic schools because of their religious affiliation and their use of non-English languages in instruction (Leibowitz, 1974).

An immigration commission convened by Congress published a report in 1911 based on testing of immigrant children in public schools from 37 of the largest U.S. cities. The status "retarded" was used to categorize students. Based on testing, it was determined that birthplace, student age, father's ability to speak English, length of residence in the United States, and regularity of school attendance were contributing factors to one's retarded categorization (United States Immigration Commission, 1911). According to Arredondo-Dowd (1978), reports in the 41 volumes produced by the U.S. Immigration Commission (1911) characterized immigrants as "masses of uneducated, impoverished human liabilities" (p. 7). Some education and social policy writers admitted that immigrant students succeeded in spite of the barriers in the public schools, not necessarily with their assistance (Eisele, 1975; Greer, 1972).

Since the mid-1990s, legislation targeting immigrants has been enacted in Arizona, Texas, and California. The state of California has been very active in passing legislation relative to documented and undocumented immigrants. This legislation includes Proposition 203, a school bond prohibiting services to undocumented children; Proposition 227, antibilingual education legislation; and Proposition 107, a bill that denies public services, including health care, based on citizenship status. In Arizona, Proposition 109 introduced exclusionary practices, disproportionately affecting school-age immigrant children. Additionally, anti–affirmative action legislation in these states and others across the country continues, increasing barriers to higher education primarily for immigrants and students of Color.

Today's immigrants come primarily from non-European countries, with the majority of new entrants arriving from Mexico, the Philippines, Vietnam, China, and India (U.S. Census, 2000). In fact, it has been noted that the 1990s witnessed the second biggest wave of immigration since the 1880/1920 period. One of the differences between contemporary immigrants and those of the previous century is that they are primarily persons of Color and are moving in to small towns, not just big cities. Moreover, residents in many of the small towns are primarily of

European heritage and unfamiliar with non-English-speaking and culturally and racially different people (Ellis, Arredondo, & D'Andrea, 2000; Middleton, Arredondo, & D'Andrea, 2000).

CONDITIONS SPECIFIC TO IMMIGRANTS' EXPERIENCES

Whether the United States or another country is the destination point, immigrants have many similar experiences based on ethnic and racial minority identity and multiple changes and conditions that affect physical and mental well-being. This section outlines these conditions and links them to the discussion about implications for racial-cultural counseling.

Stressors emanate from personal/familial, economic, social, political, environmental, and unexpected occurrences. In Germany, neo-Nazi sympathizers have taken out their aggression on newcomers escaping ethnic cleansing in Bosnia and Albania, further traumatizing people who have been under threat because of their heritage. Immigrants to the United States, particularly from Mexico and Guatemala, continue to endure hostility and death threats along the Southwest border. Vigilante groups in Arizona have declared their right to shoot people on sight because they are entering the country illegally. Caribbean immigrants have experienced racial discrimination from Caucasians as well as persons of African descent (Carter, Forsyth, Mazulla, & Williams, this *Handbook,* this volume).

Another stressful situation faced by immigrants is separation of family members. It is not unusual for one parent, typically the father, to leave, or for both parents to set out without their children. The effects of these disruptions on the lives of immigrants, families, and entire ethnic groups will vary based on a number of contextual reasons, including racial climate, the political relationship between the United States and the sending country, the economics of the receiving country, and the locale (e.g., border town, large city with multiple immigrant groups, or small city with only one immigrant group).

Another distinction lies with documented and undocumented immigrants and refugees. The federal government usually accords refugee status to individuals fleeing life-threatening conditions. Cubans, Russian Jews, Vietnamese, and Cambodians are the most widely recognized groups in this category. With refugee status, these groups have been afforded a number of benefits in their resettlement process as well as protection from deportation. Undocumented immigrants, reportedly undercounted by 5 million in the 2000 census, however, are at high risk for deportation and other abuses by employers who may exploit their vulnerability. Groups in this undocumented immigrant category often are from Spanish-speaking and Asian countries. Films such as *El Norte* and *The Gatekeeper* capture the indignities and indentured servant status of undocumented immigrants.

Issues of immigration status arose in the 1980s with the flight of Haitians and Central Americans, particularly from El Salvador and Nicaragua. Both groups were experiencing various forms of political oppression because they were caught in the cross fire of their countries' civil wars. Yet, it was not until the early 1990s that the United States granted refugee status to Haitians and Central Americans. It has been stated that issues of race and culture prejudiced decisions against withholding refugee designation.

For helping professionals, this background information about politically based racial discrimination may be significant to understanding mistrust, anxiety, and other symptoms introduced by immigrants. Engaging clients, gathering relevant sociocultural-historical data, and culturally responsive-situational intervention planning require attention to all of these personal and contextual factors.

USING A HISTORICAL FRAMEWORK IN COUNSELING

To understand the immigrant in context requires various considerations. Erikson (1975) and Arredondo (2002) have discussed the psychohistorical approach as a means to understand an individual's current situation, historical realities, and emotional responses (Carter, this *Handbook,* this volume). In a discussion about identity-related themes for immigrant adults, Arredondo (1986) posited that the psychohistorical framework embodied three eras and prototypical behaviors. These eras are preimmigration (i.e., life conditions and rationale for leaving), immigration-specific (i.e., experiences incurred during the physical move), and postimmigration (i.e., life experiences in the new homeland and effects of these experiences based on preimmigration expectations). It is posited that events in the immigration-specific phase and the lack of realization of preimmigration goals in the postimmigration phase will predispose individuals to greater emotional distress.

Applying the Psychohistorical Approach

Following the three-phase, pre- to postimmigration model, varying lines of inquiry are proposed. Questions regarding preimmigration may include (1) What were the precipitants for leaving one's homeland? Were these precipitants economic, political, religious, cultural-racial, environmental (result of a natural disaster), or other? (2) Was the migration voluntary or involuntary? The move is often considered involuntary for children and adolescents and a female spouse. (3) Did one have familial or friendship contacts in the receiving town or city? (4) Was there a specific destination? Immigrants typically go where they know of employment opportunities and where there may be family members, friends from back home, or others of their cultural background. (5) Were there particular considerations regarding destination based on one's racial, cultural, gay/lesbian, and gender identity? Gays, lesbians, and transgendered individuals seek locations where there will be greater acceptance of who they are. Most immigrants are persons of Color or of ethnic/racial minority status. While their racial heritage and phenotype may not have been an issue in their homeland (particularly for those who were of the dominant group), they may not be fully aware that the United States is a race-based society (Alverez & Piper, this *Handbook,* this volume). Preimmigration expectations are likely to affect individuals' and families' acculturation processes, barriers or access to desirable goals, particularly employment, and reasons for seeking help.

For the migration-specific journey, possible questions are (1) What was one's mode of transportation for coming to the United States? Individuals from Mexico and Central America may not necessarily travel by air, whereas immigrants from the Philippines and China will likely depend on this mode of transportation, or travel by sea, and not as first-class passengers. (2) What were the conditions during this travel process? Some persons go through life-threatening or other oppressive circumstances during their journey. Some may be unaccompanied minors, without nuclear family members. Women traveling alone or with children often become victims of sexual abuse during the travel. Danger, estrangement, or aloneness will likely affect one's emotional state during the journey and thereafter. For undocumented entrants, life-threatening experiences have been reported (e.g., being shot at by southwestern landowners, crossing the desert without food or water, risking drowning because of inadequate boats, and nearly dying on transport ships).

The postimmigration period is the time during which individuals are likely to seek or be referred to counseling. The psychohistorical era framework allows for understanding how a process of major life change unfolds incrementally and then affects the transition and settlement tasks. There are a number of circumstances that may affect the emotional well-being of the immigrant during this postimmigration period, including contextual factors, such as racism and other forms of oppression; barriers in locating housing and employment; language differences; area of settlement (e.g., rural versus urban); isolation from family and a similar cultural group; and the realization of the barriers and enablers to one's preimmigration dreams and goals.

Another postimmigration reality is citizenship status. If one is undocumented because of illegal entry, one will experience different types of fears, pressures, and limitations in terms of employment, education, health care, and other services. Access to primary language and cultural resources also may be limited. Many immigrants have entered into rural areas of the country that are historically White (D'Andrea & Arredondo, 2000; Ellis et al., 2000); the arrival of non-English-speaking and culturally and phenotypically different residents can create challenges for school systems and other public agencies. Quite often, the economic and cultural benefits introduced by the newcomers are not immediately apparent because the residents may feel threatened by unfamiliar faces, languages, and lifestyle patterns. In some situations, xenophobia may persist, leading to interpersonal conflicts (D'Andrea & Arredondo, 2000).

CULTURAL-RACIAL HARASSMENT

Racism manifests in many forms for the unsuspecting immigrants. An example from Birmingham, Alabama, reports on the angry calls to a car dealership that had radio announcements in Spanish (Middleton et al., 2000). In other cases, children and families have been denied health care services because of their citizenship status, as has occurred in California as a result of Proposition 187.

Racial violence is another factor that overshadows the experiences of immigrants. In February 1999, four New York City police officers mistook documented Guinean immigrant Amadou Diallo for a rape suspect and, thinking that he was reaching for a gun, shot him 41 times. His brutal and tragic death made both the national and international press (Goldberg, 1999). Egregious incidents are ones that make the headlines. However, immigrants are surrounded by the daily stress of racism in many forms and situations, including racial profiling (Carter et al., this *Handbook,* this volume). Even when immigrants do not experience or report physical harm, there may be injury to their psychological and, by extension, physical health. Interdisciplinary research and narrative accounts provide data in support of the relationship between racism, health, and mental health (Jones, 1992; Ortiz, 1999).

Inevitably, there will be psychosocioemotional reactions during the transition process. To the unsuspecting immigrant, racial-cultural bias may be a contributing factor. In the next section, I discuss some of the symptoms of distress and how to better understand them as a consequence of the migration process through a cultural-racial lens and as coping behaviors.

NORMATIVE PRESENTING ISSUES FOR IMMIGRANTS AND REFUGEES

The mental health literature (Arredondo, 1986; Arredondo-Dowd, 1981; Bemak & Chung, 2002; Hong & Domokos-Cheng Ham, 2001; Smart & Smart, 1995; Uchison, 2003; Yeh, 2003) reports on different conditions that affect the mental well-being of immigrants and refugees. The ones receiving the greatest commentary are acculturative stress, loss and grief, adaptation and coping, and Posttraumatic Stress Disorder (PTSD). In addition to PTSD, "acculturation problem" is included as a V-code (V62-4) in the *Diagnostic and Statistical Manual of Mental Disorders (DSM-IV-TR)*. It can be posited that PTSD and acculturation problems, including acculturative stress and loss and grief, are both outcomes and precipitants of other symptoms, including alcohol and substance abuse, domestic violence, depression, and physical illness (Arredondo, Orjuela, & Moore, 1989; Bemak & Chung, 2002; Hong & Domokos-Cheng Ham, 2001; Santiago-Rivera, Arredondo, & Gallardo-Cooper, 2002). The proposed psychosocioemotional model specific to immigrants and refugees (Table 24.1) is designed to take into consideration various reasons that might bring individuals into counseling, some of the variables that give a context to the situation, and the possible issues that may manifest.

First and foremost, acculturation is a process of change with varying outcomes: separation from the new culture, assimilation, and bicultural integration (Berry, 1988). Acculturative stress has been described by numerous writers (Berry, 1988, 1998; Chun, Balls Organista, & Marin, 2002) as normative for all immigrant experiences. Smart and Smart (1995) indicate that acculturative stress has three components: lifelong duration, pervasiveness, and intensity. They point out that this form of stress manifests as a consequence of environmental and internal demands that bear down on the individual system. These stressors include social and cultural factors that become dominant forces in the process of immigration. In psychosocial terms, an immigrant's sense of belonging or fitting in will be more difficult because of language, socioeconomic, and racial-cultural differences. The question has been raised about the similarity of experiences of acculturative stress and adjustment for someone who is wealthy but differs from the mainstream culture by virtue

Table 24.1   Psychosocioemotional Model Specific to Immigrants and Refugees

Symptoms	Precipitants	Variables	Issues
Sadness/withdrawal/ depression, unprovoked crying, loss of appetite; suicidal gestures	Aloneness/isolation, separation from family	Age, geographic location, support system, religion, language	Job or school absence; unwillingness to join with family and friends as before; posttraumatic stress
Physical ailments that lead to disabling reactions	Racism on the job; working 2–3 jobs; downward employment mobility; economic crisis	Age, gender, length of time in the U.S.; language; group/family status	Nonmedical symptoms; helplessness; low self-esteem; identity crisis; posttraumatic stress
Anxiety/stress reactions; suicidal gestures	Guilt about leaving family members behind; living in a large, urban area, having come from a rural community; economic and family crises; migration and postmigration experiences	Role in the family; group status; religion; race and ethnicity; language; citizenship status; health status	Job or school absence; lack of useful coping mechanisms; posttraumatic stress; acculturative stress
Alcoholism	Aloneness/separation from family; economic crisis; sociocultural isolation	Age, gender, religion, citizenship status	Acculturative stress; job identity confusion or loss
Domestic violence	Economic crisis; intergenerational conflicts	Gender, religion, citizenship status	Loss of job because of legal problems

of language, ethnic, or racial differences. Because changes and loss occur for all immigrants and refugees, it can be conjectured that the benefits of affluence may serve as buffers or coping mechanisms but that affluence does not prevent cultural and racial discrimination or the emotional loss of homeland.

Pearlin, Lieberman, Menaghan, and Mullan (1981) discuss stress process models, concluding that immigration is the primary stressor and the acculturation process is the secondary stressor. This suggests that the act of immigration should be added to the Precipitant column and acculturation to the Variable column in Table 24.1. Either way, the practitioner would have to take into consideration both factors to make sense of the client's symptoms, presenting issues, and coping behavior.

Loss and grief have been discussed as an expectant process for all immigrants in their transition in a new country. Different theoretical stage models of culture shock (Oberg, 1972) and models of loss related to death (Bowlby, 1961; Kubler-Ross, 1970) have been introduced to understand the immigrant's experience. To discuss manifestations of loss and grief, Arredondo-Dowd (1981) proposed that the immigrant be viewed as the "survivor," with the homeland and those left behind as symbolic of the loss. Borrowing from Bowlby's model (1961) on attachment and loss and informed by her own work with immigrant adolescents and their families, Arredondo-Dowd outlined three phases of the grieving process:

1. Numbness, shock, and disbelief, with differential experiences for children and adults based on who made the decision to leave.

2. Pain, despair, and disorganization, with the use of defense mechanisms such as displacement, projection, and reaction formation in response to multiple stressors, including racism. "Survivor's guilt" is often an experience in phase 2.

3. Hopefulness, sense of rebeginning life in a new land, and acceptance of the new realities of life, though not necessarily "liking" all of them.

It is unclear how long the grieving process will take because different circumstances lead to the migration process and to the events that unfold in the new land for each immigrant.

The decision to stay and not return to one's homeland does not necessarily mean that an immigrant feels at home in the United States. Racism may, in fact, be part of individuals' daily lives, but they have no way to avoid or overtly combat it. In a longitudinal study with immigrants, it was found that immigrants from the Caribbean, all with visible African phenotype, chose to delay their application for citizenship; the same was not true for Russian Jewish refugees and immigrants from Tawain and Hong Kong (Arredondo, 1986).

Specific to refugees from Cambodia, Bemak and Chung (2002) indicate that preimmigration experiences and trauma predispose individuals to higher risks for mental distress. They cite that young men under 21 arriving without familial support are vulnerable. Trauma in the preimmigration period may result from loss of family members. For Cambodian refugee women, there may be heightened disorientation and adjustment difficulties because of low or no formal education and illiteracy.

─────────── **Case Conceptualization with Racial-Cultural Models** ───────────

Jean Louis is a 35-year-old immigrant from Haiti who came to the United States with his mother at age 15. He is married and the father of three young children. Jean Louis has a bachelor's degree in accounting. He was referred to counseling by his primary care physician, who indicated that he found no evidence of physical illness. Jean Louis had originally gone to his physician complaining about stomach upsets, work-related paralysis, and other depression-related symptoms (e.g., loss of appetite, sleeplessness, and job-related stress). An accountant, he told his counselor that he was terrified about a recent promotion he had been given, uncertain that he could meet the demands of the new role and functions. Since the promotion, he had overheard comments that he was promoted because of affirmative action and was not really qualified for the new position.

Iris found her way to the college counseling center after she talked to a friend. A biology major, she found herself continuously on the defensive in most of her White male-dominated classes on an Ivy League campus. Iris is a Mexican national (with U.S. citizenship) born in Mexico City but living in San Antonio, Texas, since age 10. San Antonio is home to thousands of families of Mexican heritage. In counseling, Iris reported that at first, the joking comments and references about her "kinky" hair and green eyes that did not seem to fit a "White girl" seemed harmless. However, she reported, she was getting tired of this form of attention: "It hurts." Her friends were quick to tell Iris that the comments were racist. "You are in a hostile environment," they pointed out. She reported that, although some of the comments were made in earshot of the instructor, he never intervened.

These are but two examples of presenting situations that introduce compounding dynamics, require an understanding of possible precipitants outlined in Table 24.1, and require interventions from racial-cultural perspectives. Each case is analyzed separately with references to Table 24.1 and models that can be applied in racial-cultural counseling.

MODELS FOR ANALYSIS OF ENVIRONMENTAL AND CONTEXTUAL STRESSORS

Three models are introduced and then discussed with reference to the two cases: the locus of control/locus of responsibility model (Sue, 1978), the dimensions of personal identity development model (Arredondo & Glauner, 1992), and the racial-cultural identity model (Atkinson, Morten, & Sue, 1998; Sue & Sue, 2003).

Locus of Control/Locus of Responsibility

Many immigrants are from cultural backgrounds that value collectivism, interdependent relationships, and interpersonal respect. Historically, immigrants have pursued economic betterment for themselves and their families, making a work identity and earning power core to their sense of self-efficacy (Arredondo, 1986). They possess what is described as high degrees of internal locus of control and internal locus of responsibility (IC/IR). They have charted their path by leaving their homeland and continuing their lives elsewhere. The same situation does not apply to refugees who typically have no control over circumstances that cause them to move. Their situation is termed external locus of control and internal locus of responsibility (EC/IR). The four dimensions of this model (Sue, 1978) provide a structure for understanding racism and oppression. Referring to the model, it can be posited that most immigrants will be in the EC/IR quadrant, meaning that they probably feel there is very little they can do to confront or change severe obstacles like prejudice and discrimination, but at the same time, they attribute their current status and life conditions to their own unique attributes (Sue & Sue, 1999, 2003). It is also quite possible that some immigrants, particularly women who may not have been employed prior to emigrating and who speak minimal English, experience external locus of control and external locus of responsibility (EC/ER). They may find themselves without a support network and entirely dependent on their husband and children. They may experience symptoms and precipitants of sadness, withdrawal, physical ailments, and anxiety, described in Table 24.1.

Jean Louis's symptoms of loss of appetite and sleep may be associated with the misattributions in the workplace about his abilities. It can be speculated that precipitants of racism on the job and, quite likely, avoidance by his peers and subordinates are contributing to a sense of helplessness, aloneness, frustration, and low self-esteem. Jean Louis is an immigrant who is being challenged because of his new responsibilities. Anxiety about a promotion or a new job is not unusual, but for Jean Louis, the anxiety is now heightened by others' hostility. This situation might describe him as having an EC/IR worldview. He cannot control the discriminatory remarks, but he is not acting helpless and is still assuming responsibility by meeting with a physician and a counselor.

A counselor working with Jean Louis needs to be cognizant of collectivistic thinking that motivates and pressures individuals to work on behalf of family who are with them or back home. The counselor also must recognize the client's achievement orientation: He is an immigrant with a college degree. Perhaps Jean Louis considers himself a high achiever and has not had to confront questions about his competence previously.

It is important to note that psychological well-being and maturity often have been measured by indicators of internal locus of control and autonomy, more reflective of an individualistic worldview. A culturally competent practitioner recognizes that the individualistic model of IC/IR, which posits that individuals have complete control and responsibility for their circumstances and lives, would not be an appropriate principle for developing an intervention with Jean Louis: He cannot control others' perceptions.

Iris has stepped into a new cultural environment, one very different from San Antonio, where she was a member of the cultural majority. She, too, may be in the EC/IR dimension, and perhaps EC/ER, believing that it is up to her professor to intervene. As with Jean Louis, Iris's counselor will have to be astute about racial harassment and the forms it may take in a college classroom.

Dimensions of Personal Identity Model

The dimensions of personal identity model (DPI) was originally developed to describe a holistic approach to understanding and planning interventions with immigrants (Arredondo et al., 1996). This is a contextual, psychohistorical model (Figure 24.1) that describes how A dimensions (e.g., age, gender, race, and sexual orientation) and the C dimension (e.g., historical and sociopolitical events) may affect an immigrant's B dimensions (e.g., educational and work opportunities). Although individuals cannot control the A and C dimensions, these still affect opportunities or choices one may or may not have in the B dimension.

Iris, the college student, cannot change her kinky hair, green eyes, or cultural group (A dimensions), the very attributes that are bringing her demeaning attention. Immigration (C dimension) introduced her to B dimensions such as the San Antonio geographic location and educational opportunities, but now another C dimension, forces of societal racial discrimination, may challenge her choice about the college she is attending. The DPI can also be useful in profiling the majority A dimensions in this college setting, pointing out to Iris that she is unique in this setting. Concomitantly, the counselor may become a sounding board as well as an advocate, consulting with the instructor with Iris's permission (Vera, Buhin, Montgomery, & Shin, this *Handbook,* this volume).

This model also applies readily to Jean Louis. His presenting issues of stress and loss of appetite are influenced by doubts of competence and a hostile environment.

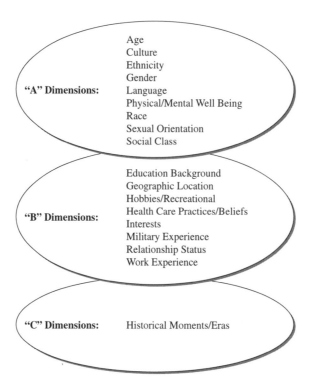

Figure 24.1   Dimensions of personal identity.

Although he is an immigrant, he has a college degree and what appears to be a respectable position. Because of these successes and others, he may not have previously considered how A and C dimensions have helped or hindered him. It may be that Jean Louis has previously minimized or ignored experiences with racial discrimination (Carter et al., this *Handbook,* this volume). The counselor could refer to the locus of control/locus of responsibility continuum as well as the DPI to plan supportive and clarifying counseling with Jean Louis.

Racial-Cultural Identity Model

Other models that might assist counseling from a racial-cultural perspective (Carter, 1995) include those of minority identity (MID) or racial cultural identity development (RCID; Atkinson et al., 1998; Helms, 1990) and others more specific to acculturation processes (Berry & Kim, 1988; Kohatsu, this *Handbook,* Volume One; Sanchez & Fernandez, 1993). The RCID posits five stages (conformity, dissonance and appreciating, resistance and immersion, introspection, and integrative awareness) and differing attitudes toward self, others of the same ethnic/racial minority group, members of other ethnic/racial minority groups, and members of the dominant cultural group (e.g., in the United States, persons of Euro-American heritage). It is important to know that most immigrants arrive with an intact sense of cultural identity (Arredondo, 1986). However, in a race-based society, different forms of racism manifest through verbal taunts, nonverbal microaggressions (ignoring a person), and racial profiling. Understandably, these experiences lead immigrants to begin to question their sense of cultural identity, self-esteem, and self-efficacy. The RCID model assists a counselor in hypothesizing about the stage of a particular client and individuals in that family. By so doing, the counselor can recognize the interplay between presenting issues and the contexts in which the individual resides, works, and tries to survive.

Jean Louis may come into therapy in the Dissonance stage (Atkinson et al., 1998), experiencing conflict about who he is now that he has been promoted and is experiencing others' negative behavior toward him. If he has been successful thus far in pursuing the "American dream," questions about his competence will raise concerns for him about self-esteem and work identity. Iris's friends are giving her feedback about environmental racism that may move her into the Resistance and Emergence stage of the RCID model. With this status, she is likely to develop negative opinions and feelings toward members of the dominant group, holding them responsible for the negative experiences of other students of Color.

APPLYING CULTURAL-RACIAL MODELS TO IMMIGRANTS IN CONTEXT

Because immigrants come to the United States principally for employment and economic reasons (C dimension and IC/IR behavior), the workplace as a hostile environment, emotionally and physically, cannot be overlooked. Immigrants, particularly those with limited English proficiency, often assume work in maintenance and service functions not only with low pay, but often where their language and culture are demeaned. They are subjected to verbal abuse from statements such as "Learn English" and "Why don't you people go back to where you came from?" These words demonstrate devaluation, but also an expectation that the immigrant is here to take the jobs of Americans.

In reality, most immigrants come to improve their economic situation and will take on almost any kind of work (EC/IR). Unfortunately, their outsider status based on racial, cultural, and linguistic differences (A dimensions) renders them incapable of defending their personhood, and on a daily basis they encounter race-based stress (Carter et al., this *Handbook,* this volume).

As has occurred historically, educational opportunities are sought by immigrant parents for their children, although access and outreach may not be easily forthcoming from the schools. Many parents express the expectation that the schools know what is best for their children (EC/ER), and they defer their authority to school officials. This expectation is based on the authoritative roles of teachers in countries such as China, the Philippines, and Mexico. For immigrants who have two or three jobs, it is nearly impossible to attend meetings during the normal school day. School officials often fail to see that the parents' sense of responsibility is compromised by the external circumstances of work obligations, driven by economics; teachers and counselors lament what they see as the lack of parents' interest and concern for their children's education. With this example, the conflict of two worldviews is evident: School personnel expect IC/IR behavior from parents who behave according to the EC/IR dimension.

THE IMMIGRANT AND MENTAL HEALTH FACILITIES

Reasons for underutilization of mental health services by ethnic/racial minorities has been reported for more than 40 years (Acosta & Evans, 1982; Pine, 1972; Sue & Sue, 2003; Surgeon General's Report, 2001). In this group of ethnic/racial minorities were immigrants. Typical barriers to use of services included location of the mental health facility, language barriers, concerns about trust and mistrust, and the lack of cultural sensitivity and competence of service providers and employees at mental health agencies. Additional impediments are impersonal, culturally and linguistically inappropriate intake forms, tests, and other interventions or practices that do not provide the service, comfort, or "cure" being sought. Even when newcomers genuinely seek assistance, if agencies are not prepared to provide counseling services that are racially-culturally based and in the language of the client (Faubert & Locke, this *Handbook,* this volume), it is likely that the problem of the revolving door will continue. Ineffective responses to requests for assistance with an urgent matter may contribute to additional emotional duress.

It behooves agencies to review their organizational policies, practices, and procedures to determine their relevance for immigrant clients and families (see Evans, Delphin, Simmons, Omar, & Tebes, this *Handbook,* this volume). Among the agencies that have made organizational adaptations, ethnic-specific agencies included immigrant community residents on advisory boards; these individuals became spokespersons for the agency or cultural brokers. Several mainstream agencies made presentations about recent immigrant and refugees from the church-based groups that were helping with the newcomers' settlement process. One agency sold its facility to move to a neighborhood where more immigrants could walk to offices and from which clinicians could easily move into the community. Another organization conducted a needs assessment to determine services in place that were and were not meeting the intended consumers; based on their findings, administrators were able to plan more strategically for the delivery of culturally-racially responsive services.

IMPLICATIONS FOR CULTURAL-RACIAL COUNSELING WITH IMMIGRANTS

Issues identified in Table 24.1 and in the previous discussion are simply starting points for conceptualizing approaches to culturally and racially responsible counseling and clinical practice with immigrants. Similar considerations can also be made for working with refugees. Neither presenting issues nor symptoms in Table 24.1 can be taken at face value, for to do so might lead to cultural-racial malpractice. The practitioner needs to take a holistic approach and consider all of the possible precipitants, variables, and contextual factors. The scenarios of Jean Louis and Iris underscore the importance of recognizing symptoms of acculturative stress and interpersonal/contextual dynamics that challenge racial identity and self-concept. Environmental factors may or may not be racially discriminatory; however, when the impact of these incidents renders the immigrant confused and self-doubting, analysis through the use of the locus of control/locus of responsibility model is essential.

The situations of Jean Louis and Iris also call for a counselor's knowledge of the DPI and the RCID models as they apply to immigrants in different life transitions. Situational, environmental stressors can predispose individuals to lose a sense of who they are and engender ethnic and work identity confusion. The culturally responsive therapist could refer to these two models to conceptualize a client's personal and cultural-racial identity status, thereby planning interventions with the client that are more appropriate and culturally synergistic (Miehles, this *Handbook,* this volume; Thomas, this *Handbook,* this volume).

COMPETENCIES FOR CULTURAL-RACIAL COUNSELING WITH IMMIGRANTS

The previous sections have identified multiple contextual and acculturation-based variables that may affect the emotional well-being and cultural-racial self-efficacy of immigrants. There has been particular attention to interacting variables and stressors that are often not visible or readily reported by an immigrant except perhaps through physical symptoms. The chapter concludes with recommended competencies for clinicians working with immigrants. These are based on an article entitled "Developing Successful Cross-Cultural Relationships with Immigrants and Refugees" (Arredondo, 1998) and follow the framework of the multicultural counseling competencies (Sue, Arredondo, & McDavis, 1992). This framework posits competencies in three domains: clinician's self-awareness, knowledge, and skills; clinician's awareness and knowledge regarding the client's worldview; and clinician's application of culturally responsive interventions (D. Sue & Torino, this *Handbook,* this volume).

Practitioner Awareness of Self

Culturally competent clinicians:

- Are aware of the history of immigration of their own families. They know how their ancestors "arrived" in the United States.
- Recognize their own perceptions and assumptions and biases about immigrants, including what they believe about immigrants as employees, as participants in educational and health care systems, and as future citizens of the United States (Arredondo, 1998).
- Recognize their own affective reactions (dis/comfort) when working with immigrants (e.g., their fear or sense of willingness to engage with individuals based on their country of origin).

Practitioner Knowledge about Immigrants' Worldview

Culturally competent clinicians are knowledgeable about:

- Pre- and postimmigration factors that affect immigrants' worldview and physical and emotional well-being.

- Presenting symptoms that may mask loss and grief, acculturative stress, cultural identity confusion, racism, and other forms of cultural oppression.
- Interacting variables that contribute to stress, including career/role dislocation, within-family cultural conflicts, citizenship status, and racism.
- The immediacy of immigrant issues that may require more pragmatic responses.

Practitioner Application of Appropriate Skills and Strategies

Culturally competent clinicians are able to:

- Draw on racial-cultural and immigrant-specific identity models to develop culturally responsive, situational interventions.
- Use psychohistorical assessment procedures that promote knowing the immigrant in context.
- Communicate in the primary language of the client.
- Direct clients to appropriate resources for collateral services.
- Assess the client's worldview through theories deemed helpful for immigrants, such as locus of control/locus of responsibility.
- Involve collateral resources as needed.
- Seek consultation from culturally appropriate sources.

REFERENCES

Acosta, F. X., & Evans, L. A. (1982). Effective psychotherapy for low-income and minority patients. In F. X. Acosta, J. Yamamoto, & L. A. Evans (Eds.), *Effective psychotherapy for low-income and minority patients* (pp. 51–82). New York: Plenum Press.

Arredondo-Dowd, P. M. (1978). *Psychological education and the foreign born adolescent.* Unpublished doctoral dissertation, Boston University.

Arredondo-Dowd, P. (1981). Personal loss and grief as a result of immigration. *Personnel and Guidance Journal, 59,* 376–378.

Arredondo, P. (1986). Immigration as an historical moment leading to an identity crisis. *Journal of Counseling and Human Services, 1,* 79–87.

Arredondo, P. (1998, December). Developing successful cross-cultural relationships with immigrants and refugees. *Counseling Today,* pp. 30–31.

Arredondo, P. (1999). Multicultural counseling competencies as tools to address oppression and racism. *Journal of Counseling and Development, 77,* 102–108.

Arredondo, P. (2002). Counseling individuals from specialized, marginalized and underserved groups. In P. Pedersen, J. G. Draguns, W. J. Lonner, & J. E. Trimble (Eds.), *Counseling across cultures* (5th ed., pp. 233–250). Thousand Oaks, CA: Sage.

Arredondo, P., & Glauner, T. (1992). *Dimensions of personal identity model.* Boston: Empowerment Workshops.

Arredondo, P., Orjuela, E., & Moore, L. (1989). Family therapy with Central American war refugee families. *Journal of Strategies and Systemic Therapies, 8,* 41–50.

Arredondo, P., Toporek, R., Brown, S. P., Jones, J., Locke, D. C., Sanchez, J., et al. (1996). Operationalization of the multicultural counseling competencies. *Journal of Multicultural Counseling and Development, 24,* 42–78.

Atkinson, D. R., Morten, G., & Sue, D. W. (1998). *Counseling American minorities: A cross-cultural perspective* (5th ed.). Boston: McGraw-Hill.

Atkinson, D. R., Morten, G., & Sue, D. W. (2002). *Counseling American minorities: A cross-cultural perspective* (6th ed.). Boston: McGraw-Hill.

Aziz, N. (1999). Cultural sensitization and clinical guidelines for mental health professionals working with Afghan immigrant/refugee women in the United States. *Dissertation Abstracts International, 60*(3), 1293B.

Bemak, F., & Chi-Ying Chung, R. (2002). Counseling and psychotherapy with refugees. In P. Pedersen, J. G. Draguns, W. J. Lonner, & J. E. Trimble (Eds.), *Counseling across cultures* (5th ed., pp. 209–232). Thousand Oaks, CA: Sage.

Berry, J. W. (1998). Acculturative Stress. In P. B. Organista & K. M. Chun (Eds.) et al. (1998). *Readings in ethnic psychology* (pp. 117–122). Florence, KY: Taylor & Francis/Routledge.

Berry, J. W., & Kim, U. (1988). Acculturation and mental health. In P. Dasen, J. W. Berry, & N. Sartorius (Eds.), *Health and cross cultural psychology* (pp. 207–236). London: Sage.

Bowlby, J. (1961). Separation anxiety: A critical review of the literature. *Journal of Child Psychology and Psychiatry, 1,* 251–269.

Carter, R. T. (1995). *The influence of race and racial identity in psychotherapy.* New York: Wiley.

Carter, R. T., & Pieterse, A. L. (in press). Race: A social and psychological analysis of the term and its meaning. In R. T. Carter (Ed.), *Handbook of racial-cultural psychology and counseling: Theory and research* (Vol. 1, pp. 41–63). Hoboken, NJ: Wiley.

Castex, G. M. (1997). Immigrant children in the United States. In N. K. Phillips & S. L. Ashenberg Straussner (Eds.), *Children in the urban environment: Linking social policy and clinical practice* (pp. 43–60). Springfield, IL: Charles C Thomas.

Chun, K. M., Balls Organista, P., & Marin, G. (Eds.). (2002). Washington, DC: American Psychological Association.

Cremin, L. A. (1961). *The transformation of the school.* New York: Alfred A. Knopf.

D'Andrea, M., & Arredondo, P. (2000, October). Cultural and linguistic diversity as a new community experience. *Counseling Today,* pp. 32, 34.

Das, A. K., & Kemp, S. F. (1997). Between two worlds: Counseling South Asian Americans. *Journal of Multicultural Counseling and Development, 25,* 23–33.

Eisele, J. C. (1975). John Dewey and the immigrants. *History of Education Quarterly, 15,* 67–85.

Ellis, C., Arredondo, P., & D'Andrea, M. (2000, November). How cultural diversity affects predominately white towns. *Counseling Today,* p. 25.

Erikson, E. H. (1975). *Life history and the historical moment.* New York: Norton.

Esquivel, G. B. (1998). Group interventions with culturally and linguistically diverse students. In K. C. Stoiber & T. R. Kratochwill (Eds.), *Handbook of group intervention for children and families* (pp. 252–267). Boston: Allyn & Bacon.

Gates, R. D., Arce de Esnaola, S., Kroupin, G., Stewart, C. C., van Dulmen, M., Xiong, B., et al. (2000). Diversity of new American families: Guidelines for therapists. In W. Nichols,

M. A. Pace-Nichols, D. S. Becvar, & A. Y. Napier (Eds.), *Handbook of family development and intervention* (pp. 299–322). New York: Wiley.

Goldberg, J. (1999, June 20). What cops talk about when they talk about race. *New York Times Magazine,* 51–57, 64, 85.

Greer, C. (1972). *The great school legend.* New York: Basic Books.

Handlin, O. (1951). *The uprooted.* Boston: Little, Brown.

Handlin, O. (1959). *Boston's immigrants.* Cambridge, MA: Harvard University Press.

Helms, J. E. (1990). *Black and White racial identity.* Westport, CT: Greenwood Press.

Hong, G. K., & Domokos-Cheng Ham, M. (2001). *Psychotherapy and counseling with Asian American clients.* Thousand Oaks, CA: Sage.

Jones, J. M. (1992). Understanding the mental health consequences of race: Contributions of basic social psychological processes. In D. N. Ruble, P. R. Costanzo, & M. E. Oliveri (Eds.), *The social psychology of mental health: Basic mechanisms and applications* (pp. 199–240). New York: Guilford Press.

Kohatsu, E. L. (in press). Acculturation: Current and future directions. In R. T. Carter (Ed.), *Handbook of racial-cultural psychology and counseling: Theory and research* (Vol. 1, pp. 207–231). Hoboken, NJ: Wiley.

Kubler-Ross, E. (1970). The care of the dying: Whose job is it? *Psychiatry in Medicine, 1,* 103–107.

Leibowitz, A. H. (1974, August). *Language as a means of social control: The United States experience.* Paper prepared for VIII World Congress of Sociology, University of Toronto, Juneau.

Middleton, R., Arredondo, P., & D'Andrea, M. (2000, December). The impact of Spanish-speaking newcomers in Alabama towns. *Counseling Today,* p. 24.

Oberg, K. (1972). Culture shock and the problems of adjustment to new cultural environments. In D. Hoapes (Ed.), *Readings in intercultural communications.* Pittsburgh, PA: Pittsburgh Intercultural Communications Network of the Regional Council for International Education.

Ortiz, S. O. (1999). You'd never know how racist I was, if you met me on the street. *Journal of Counseling and Development, 77,* 9–11.

Pearlin, L., Lieberman, M., Menaghan, E. G., & Mullan, J. T. (1981). The stress process. *Journal of Health Social Behavior, 19,* 337–356.

Pine, G. J. (1972). Counseling minority groups: A review of the literature. *Counseling and Values, 17,* 35–44.

Rogler, L. H. (1994). International migrations: A framework for directing research. *American Psychologist, 49,* 701–708.

Sanchez, J. I., & Fernandez, D. M. (1993). Acculturative stress among Hispanics: A bidimensional model of ethnic identification. *Journal of Applied Social Psychology, 23,* 654–668.

Santiago-Rivera, A., Arredondo, P., & Gallardo-Cooper, M. (2002). *Counseling Latinos y la familia: A practical guide.* Thousand Oaks, CA: Sage.

Smart, J. F., & Smart, D. W. (1995). Acculturative stress of Hispanics: Loss and challenge. *Journal of Counseling and Development, 73,* 390–396.

Sue, D. W. (1978). Eliminating cultural oppression in counseling: Toward a general theory. *Journal of Counseling Psychology, 25,* 419–428.

Sue, D. W., Arredondo, P., & McDavis, R. J. (1992). Multicultural competencies and standards: A call to the profession. *Journal of Counseling and Development, 70,* 477–486.

Sue, D. W., & Sue, D. (1999). *Counseling the culturally different: Theory and practice* (3rd ed.). New York: Wiley.

Sue, D. W., & Sue, D. (2003). *Counseling the Culturally diverse* (4th ed.). New York: Wiley.

Tyack, D. (1967). *Turning points in American educational history.* Waltham, MA: Blaisdell.

Uchison, J. (2003). Multiculturalism and immigrants. In G. Roysircar, D. Singh Sandhu, & V. E. Bibbins (Eds.), *Multicultural competencies: A guidebook of practices.* Alexandria, VA: Association for Multicultural Counseling and Development.

U.S. Census Bureau. (2001). Census 2000 current population reports. Washington, DC: Government Printing Office.

U.S. Department of Health and Human Services. (2001). *Mental health: Culture, race, and ethnicity—A supplement to Mental health: A report of the surgeon general.* Rockville, MD: U.S. Department of Health and Human Services, Substance Abuse and Mental Health Services Administration, Center for Mental Health Services.

United States Immigration Commission. (1911). *Reports of the immigration commission* (Vols. 1–41). Washington, DC: Government Printing Office.

Yeh, C. J. (2003). Age, acculturation, cultural adjustment, and mental health symptoms of Chinese, Korean, and Japanese immigrant youths. *Cultural Diversity and Ethnic Minority Psychology, 9,* 34–48.

CHAPTER 25

A Psychohistorical Analysis of the African American Bicultural Experience

Shawn O. Utsey, Rheeda L. Walker, Nancy Dessources, and Maria Bartolomeo

> *"Africa!" I repeated the word to myself, then paused as something strange and disturbing stirred slowly in the depths of me. I am African! I'm of African descent. . . . Yet I'd never seen Africa; I'd never really known any Africans; I'd hardly ever thought of Africa.*
>
> —Richard Wright, 1954, p. 3

The bicultural experience of Africans in America (i.e., African Americans) is unique, complex, and dissimilar to other racial/ethnic groups living in the United States. The term "bicultural" is used to describe the experience of individuals living in two distinct cultures (Bell, 1990; Fishman, 1989). Current models of biculturalism assume that the acquisition of a second culture is a voluntary process and results in the development of an expanded repertoire of cultural behaviors; new behaviors are typically adopted from the dominant cultural/social group (Bell, 1990; LaFromboise, Coleman, & Gorman, 1993; Rudmin, 2003). Given that Africans in America were forcibly removed from their indigenous culture and subjected to a systematic program of deracination and forced acculturation, traditional theories of biculturalism are limited in their application with this population. The goal of this chapter is to review the literature on current conceptualizations of biculturalism, examine the historical bicultural experience of Africans in America, and discuss mental health issues related to the African American bicultural experience.

The current chapter addresses the contemporary psychological issues related to the bicultural experience of African Americans through a historical lens. We begin with a review of the literature regarding traditional theories of biculturalism and their application to African Americans. Next, we examine the African origins of African American cultural beliefs, values, and behaviors. We also discuss the influence of the African slave trade, chattel slavery, and Jim Crow segregation on the bicultural identity development of African Americans and how it differs from that of other racial/ethnic groups who were not forcibly relocated to the United States. Finally, we examine the psychological issues related to biculturalism and the contemporary African American experience.

TRADITIONAL CONCEPTUALIZATIONS OF BICULTURALISM

Biculturalism has been described as the way people learn and practice both the dominant culture and their own indigenous culture at the same time (Bell, 1990; LaFromboise et al., 1993; Rashid, 1984). The assumption here is that an individual can participate and be competent in two or more cultures simultaneously (Mpofu & Watkins, 1997). This definition evolved from earlier theories of biculturalism that espoused a deficit model to characterize living in two cultures. These theorists (Park, 1928; Stonequist, 1937) described individuals who vacillated between two cultures as "marginal." According to Bell (1990), a marginal individual is

> one who lives on the boundaries of two distinct cultures, one being more powerful than the other, but who does not have the ancestry, belief system, or social skills to be fully a member of the dominant group. (p. 463)

A number of scholars have suggested that marginality leads to psychological and emotional conflict, lowered self-esteem, inferiority complexes, and identity confusion (see Bell, 1990; Park, 1950; Rudmin, 2003; Stonequist, 1961).

Many contemporary theorists have rejected the "marginal person syndrome" (Atkinson, Morten, & Sue, 1997; Bell, 1990; Rashid, 1984). In fact, some scholars assert that biculturalism has negative consequences only if the individual internalizes the conflict that results from negotiating two or more cultures (LaFromboise et al., 1993). In this case, the marginal person is said to feel caught between the values of two cultures, with minimal psychological commitment to neither, thus creating psychological distress. In contrast, Bell suggested that individuals who are bicultural have access to two cultures, each offering myriad unique rewards and resources. According to Bell, there is a hierarchical relationship between the two cultures, and although one group is considered dominant, individuals seek opportunities and resources from both cultures (Carter & Pieterse, this *Handbook,* Volume One).

LaFromboise and colleagues (1993) examined the psychological impact of biculturalism from a multidimensional perspective. They identified a number of mechanisms by which the individual acquires a second culture and achieves a bicultural orientation (i.e., assimilation, acculturation, alternation, multiculturalism, and fusion). Each mechanism differs in its explanation of the psychological processes associated with the acquisition of a second culture. Nevertheless, they address individual strategies for achieving competence in an alternative culture (see LaFromboise et al., 1993, for a full discussion of these mechanisms).

Some discussion of African American acculturation is warranted here, as it will be essential to later discussions of bicultural competence in this population. Literally speaking, acculturation is a move toward another culture (Berry, 1994). While some argue the relevance of acculturative phenomena for African Americans (see Joiner & Walker, 2002; Kohatsu, this *Handbook,* Volume One; Landrine & Klonoff, 1996), it has received little attention in the literature because "African American" is thought to describe a race and not a cultural group and because all remnants of African culture are said to have been destroyed during slavery (Akbar, 1984; Frazier, 1964). However, Landrine and Klonoff (1996) have proposed a model of African American acculturation that addresses why some African Americans acculturate to the majority or dominant culture.

According to Landrine and Klonoff (1996), African American acculturation is guided by four principles: the principle of return, the principle of fractionization and allopatricity, the principle of quality of contact, and the principle of ethnic socialization. The *principle of return* asserts that acculturation is a dynamic process in which the individual is likely to gravitate toward the culture of origin by the end of the life span; one is said to be motivated by age, children, and encounters with discrimination (Carter, Forsyth, Mazulla, & Williams, this *Handbook,* this volume). That is, as acculturated individuals grow older, they are likely to seek cultural roots due to feelings of nostalgia, a longing for communal ties, and pending mortality. Acculturated and bicultural parents may be motivated to expose their (acculturated) children to their culture of origin so that they are knowledgeable of the culture-specific beliefs, values, and practices (see Thomas, this *Handbook,* this volume). A final motivation for returning to the culture of origin is discrimination and racism, which forces the individual to reject the dominant culture.

The *principle of fractionization and allopatricity* emphasizes the individual's "split" from the culture of origin. Individuals who are said to be "marginal" and less involved in their cultural group are expected to experience fewer challenges while acculturating. According to the *principle of quality of contact,* the extent and nature of the contact between the individual and the dominant culture will impact the acculturative process. Thus, individuals who have positive and prolonged contact may experience rapid acculturation, whereas individuals who experience negative prolonged contact may experience failed acculturation. The *principle of ethnic socialization* adds another dimension to the acculturation outcome as the individual's perception of the dominant group (i.e., "They're all bad and not to be trusted" or "They're all good so I must prove to them that I'm not bad") also plays a role in the acculturation outcome. That is, individuals who believe the dominant group to be "all bad" are unlikely to assimilate to the dominant group. Individuals who have differing opinions of the dominant group will potentially have different outcomes.

Both Landrine and Klonoff (1996) and Anderson (1991) have noted that some African Americans experience "acculturative stress," the tension associated with moving toward the majority culture and away from the culture of origin. According to Anderson, threats to racial identity, cultural values, and patterns of living are particular stressors for African Americans that contribute to vulnerability for distress and compromised health. Anderson asserts that an understanding of core Afrocentric values will allow social scientists and others to examine acculturative (Eurocentric) influences that negatively impact African American people.

A PSYCHOHISTORY OF THE CULTURAL AND BICULTURAL DEVELOPMENT OF AFRICAN AMERICANS

The Africans who were enslaved and transported to the United States came from many regions of the African continent, but were primarily from the coastal areas in western and central Africa (Holloway, 1990). Although many cultures were represented among the enslaved, space limitations do not permit for a comprehensive review. Consequently, we discuss the common cultural elements found among the peoples of this region. For the sake of brevity, we review only the most salient features of these African cultures: worldview, religion, social organization, and art. Parham, White, and Ajamu (1999) and Asante (1990; Nobbs, 1998) highlight spirituality, interdependence, oral tradition, and present rather than future orientation as key themes that inform an African (and also African American) worldview.

The African worldview in its essence is a spiritual reality; it is grounded in the belief that a supernatural spirit-force governs the universe (Gyekye, 1996; Mbiti, 1990; Richards, 1985). To maintain harmony in the universe, rituals were performed to appease the spirit-force, acknowledge one's position in the universe, and maintain spiritual equilibrium (Coleman, 1997). According to Richards, the African worldview prescribed that all things in the universe were interrelated and interdependent. In the African context, the self was extended in time to include ancestors, the unborn, all things in nature, and the community (Myers, 1998). A universal ontological tenet of the African worldview was that the dead, having transitioned to the realm of ancestors, continued to have power over the lives of the living (Gyekye, 1996).

Religion was an integral part of all aspects of African life and is at the center of the African worldview (Gyekye, 1996; Mbiti, 1990; Richards, 1985). Religion informed Africans' understanding of all phenomena occurring in the universe. It was believed that one's thoughts, feelings, and actions were inspired by a religious/ spiritual worldview. In African societies, there was no distinction between the religious and nonreligious, the sacred and the secular, or the spiritual and the material (Gyekye, 1996; Mbiti, 1990). Religion was viewed as a communal activity and not something practiced by an individual (Mbiti, 1990). Given the communal nature of African religion, it served to reinforce the social cohesion, harmony, and cooperation among members of the community, thus having social relevance in the lives of African people (Gyekye, 1996).

The social organization underlying most African societies was primarily based on kinship relations (Yansane, 1990). In the African context, family was not simply the husband-wife-children triad but included both extended family and "fictive kin" (Hill, 1999; Yansane, 1985). Fictive kin were members of the extended family not related by blood or marriage, but who served important functions such as child rearing, resource procurement, and social and emotional support (Hill, 1999). The African ethos was fundamentally communal; thus, an individual's identity was solely in relation to that of the group or community. In African culture, interpersonal relationships among family, kin (i.e., extended family and fictive kin), siblings (clan), and other members of the community were highly valued (Myers, 1998). In African societies, elders were accorded a high degree of reverence and authority within the family, extended family, sib group, and community. Their authority was derived from the closeness of their relationship with the ancestors (Coleman, 1997; Herskovits, 1958).

Though regional differences existed, all African cultures found expression in the arts (Asante, 1990). Dance, music, art (e.g., wood carving, sculpture), and oral artistry (e.g., folklore, storytelling) were not just aesthetic expressions of African cultural life, but also served religious purposes and as recreational outlets and entertainment. African dances, for example, were performed for ritual, initiation, naming, birth, and marriage and ceremonies (Herskovits, 1958; Pasteur & Toldson, 1982). Art forms such as woodcarvings, sculptures, and textiles (e.g., kente cloth), like other African expressions of culture, were not created simply for art's sake, but derived meaning from their magical power and supernatural qualities (Bacquart, 1998). Similarly, African oral artistry, such as storytelling, proverbs, riddles, and folklore, was used to instruct, make a point, conduct rites, and as sanctions for social institutions, and not simply for amusement (Herskovits, 1958).

Slavery and the Disruption of African Cultural Life

The cultural disruption and social dislocation set off by the European slave trade was cataclysmic to African life. Though slavery had existed in Africa before the arrival of Europeans, it was a vastly different institution. Individuals captured in war, debtors, and persons found guilty of crimes could be enslaved in African societies (Manning, 1994). However, these individuals were often absorbed into that society and could someday rise out of servitude. Such individuals were not treated as chattel, and in many instances (excluding prisoners of war) were extended the same rights and privileges accorded other members of that society (Everett, 1991).

The middle passages entailed some of the most heinous acts of human cruelty in the history of the world. The initial capture and enslavement of Africans through warfare, slave raids, and kidnapping resulted in both physical and psychological trauma for the captives (Miller, 1994). The journey from the interior of the African continent to the coast was estimated at 500 miles and took anywhere from four to six months (Everett, 1991). Many of the enslaved died en route from disease, malnutrition, and exhaustion (Miller, 1994; Rodney, 1994; Semmes, 1996). Others committed suicide rather than face enslavement or being eaten by the White cannibals, as some feared (Everett, 1991; Miller, 1994). Ship captains packed 400 to 600 enslaved Africans, "spoon fashion," into the holds of ships to maximize profits (Cowley & Mannix, 1994). The men were shackled two together with leg and wrist irons. The women were forced to endure rape and other abuses from members of the captain's crew. Conditions in the ship's hold were unsanitary, and the captives were often forced to lay in their own excrement, urine, vomit, and blood (Everett, 1991; Semmes, 1996). The journey at sea lasted from five weeks to three months (Everett, 1991). In many instances, the mortality rate was as high as 40% (Miller, 1994).

Shortly after their arrival in the New World, those who had survived the horrors of the middle passage were sold in an open market or at a slave auction. The enslaved Africans were further traumatized as both men and women were forced to disrobe and were subjected to intrusive physical examinations by potential buyers (Everett, 1991; Semmes, 1996). Undoubtedly, the ultimate and most enduring trauma for the African captives occurred as a result of being sold away from family and kinship ties.

During the embarkation process, the enslaved Africans were certified as Christians; they received instruction in Catholicism and were forcibly baptized (Miller,

1994). Additionally, the process required each man, woman, and child to receive a brand on his or her chest or upper arm to indicate ownership by a particular government or shipping company (Everett, 1991; Miller, 1994). The embarkation process was likely the beginning of African acculturation and the development of Black culture in America.

Slavery and the Bicultural Identity Development of African Americans

The bicultural realty of African Americans is inextricably linked to the institution of chattel slavery, as African slaves were transformed into the "New World Negro" (Morgan, 1985). During slavery, there was a systematic process of deracination whereby the culture and cultural identity of the enslaved Africans was forcibly suppressed (Frazier, 1964; Pinkney, 1993). To survive, the enslaved Africans had to develop competencies in both the creolized African culture created by the amalgamation of the various west and central African subgroups living together on the plantations and the culture of the White slave master. Identification with the oppressor (and denial of self) was one coping strategy for managing psychological distress (Guthrie, 1998). The process of developing dual competencies set the course for African American bicultural identity development.

The enslaved Africans were forced to learn a new language, adopt a new religion, and incorporate an alien worldview diametrically opposed to their own (Anderson, 1991; Parham, White, & Ajamu, 1999; Pinkney, 1993; Semmes, 1996). There was a complete prohibition against the practice of indigenous African religions and rituals. In the rare case that enslaved Africans on the same plantation spoke the same African language, communication in the native tongue was prohibited (Stampp, 1956). Furthermore, the institution of chattel slavery did not allow for the interconnected social and family structures that had existed in Africa (Frazier, 1963; Herskovits, 1958; Pinkney, 1993). In fact, only informal efforts were made to recognize or preserve the family ties that existed on the plantation. Though it was expected that the newly enslaved African would eventually adapt to the plantation regimen, there was a formal system, known as the "seasoning period," in place to expedite this process.

The seasoning period, which lasted anywhere from two to four years, was aimed at "breaking in" newly imported Africans and familiarizing them with the plantation regimen (Frazier, 1963; Semmes, 1996). For the purpose of seasoning, the newly imported Africans were assigned in small groups to a veteran (seasoned) enslaved African who was responsible for their orientation to the plantation labor system (Semmes, 1996). The seasoning process was also intended to acquaint the newly arrived Africans with the plantation's code of conduct. In addition, the seasoned enslaved Africans were assigned the task of helping their charges acquire enough rudiments of the English language to enable them to understand the commands of the master and overseer (Frazier, 1963). Note that there was no formal system to teach English, and thus the language that evolved used English words juxtaposed with West African rules of grammar. Rudiments of this language can be observed in present-day Black English, Ebonics, and African American vernacular (Herskovits, 1958; Holloway, 1990).

The acculturation process for the enslaved African, in large part, was a multi-layered, multidimensional process influenced by many factors. Recall that the enslaved Africans were imported from many different parts of western and central Africa and represented many ethnic and tribal groups. The first level of acculturation was characterized by a melding of various African cultures into a creolized culture that gave the enslaved Africans a sense of connectedness (Holloway, 1990; Lovejoy, 1997). Next, they were forced to abandon their own culture and incorporate that of their oppressors. At the final juncture there was a melding of the creolized indigenous African culture with the culture of the oppressor and a fusing of cultural patterns created out of the enslaved Africans' need to survive under the brutal system of U.S. slavery (Pinkney, 1993).

There has been much heated debate regarding the retention of Africanisms in African American culture. Some social scientists have proposed that all remnants of African culture were lost under the brutality of slavery (Frazier, 1963; Kardiner & Ovesey, 1951). Others believe that there is a recognizable African influence on African American culture (Herskovits, 1958; Holloway, 1990; Pasteur & Toldson, 1982; Richards, 1985; Utsey, Bolden, & Brown, 2001).

Lovejoy (1997) presents two competing theories to explain the process of second-culture acquisition experienced by Africans during slavery. The *creolization* theory, according to Lovejoy, posits that because the enslaved Africans did not share a common culture, language, religious system, and social structure, it is unlikely that these elements had any influence on the evolution of African American culture. Essentially, this theory holds that a new culture evolved from the amalgamation of many diverse cultures. The *revisionist* theory proposes that African American culture has an African core (Lovejoy, 1997). Lovejoy posited that Africans were able to maintain cultural ties to their homeland via newly arrived slaves. Moreover, in spite of the fact that the Africans had no control over their physical condition (slavery), they remained agents of their own identities. Consequently, many enslaved Africans, despite systematic efforts to undermine their African identity (deracination), continued to regard themselves as African (Herskovits, 1958; Lovejoy, 1997). Whereas revisionist theory reflects a reformulation of African culture, creolization theory reflects the amalgamation of various African cultures with European culture, thus creating a new culture. The enslaved Africans and their descendents recreated social systems (kinship, extended family, fictive kin), religious practices (shouting, falling out, spirit possession, etc.), and cultural expression (music, food, naming patterns, oral tradition, etc.) from their firsthand knowledge and collective memory of African culture (Herskovits, 1958; Lovejoy, 1997). Hence, despite the Africans' status as chattel, the restrictive nature of slavery, and the systematic efforts of the Europeans to crush their African identity, they remained connected to their African past (Lovejoy, 1997; Pinkney, 1993).

In addition to Lovejoy (1997), Herskovits (1958) identified several other anthropological factors that influenced the acculturation process of African Americans during slavery. One factor was the amount of contact between slave and master. Contact or interaction between two or more cultures is a basic element of the acculturative process (i.e., developing competence in two cultures; Berry, 1994; Landrine & Klonoff, 1996). Hence, enslaved Africans who had more intimate contact with their White masters experienced the most direct route to adopting European cultural values and modes of behavior. The amount of personal contact with the slave master was determined by the size of the plantation, the ratio of enslaved Africans to Whites (master and family, overseers, etc.), and, most important, whether the individual was a house servant or a field hand (Herskovits, 1958).

Herskovits (1958) also noted that African American acculturation was facilitated by the unconscious, and sometimes conscious, identification of the enslaved with the values and customs of the White master. The power that the slave master wielded over the lives of the enslaved Africans was evidence enough that Whites' way of life was superior and certainly more desirable than that of a slave. The perception of superiority attributed to the White slave master, in addition to accelerating the adoption of European cultural values, may have convinced the enslaved Africans to discard their indigenous cultural values and beliefs (Herskovits, 1958; Stampp, 1956).

Ironically, in addition to these factors, the acculturative process among the enslaved Africans was likely enhanced by their West African cultural values. A practice among many West African cultures was that when one group conquered another, each group would adopt some of the cultural traditions of the other (Coleman, 1997; Herskovits, 1958). This practice reflected a philosophical framework that held that it was more prudent to accept an opposing point of view if there was no chance of prevailing against it (Herskovits, 1958).

Historians and other observers have erroneously attributed the enslaved Africans' adaptability to their wretched condition as acquiescing to the impossibility of ever escaping their situation. Lovejoy (1997) points out that the cultural pliability of the enslaved Africans allowed them to reinterpret their cultural and religious practices in the context of their oppression. On this subject, Blassingame (1979) stated, "In the process of acculturation, the slaves made European forms serve African functions" (pp. 20–21). For example, by adopting the surface-level (as opposed to deep-level) cultural practices of the White slaveholders, the enslaved Africans were able to mask their own indigenous cultural beliefs and behaviors and thereby continue their practice unmolested (Herskovits, 1958).

Cultural Alienation and the Bicultural Identity of African Americans

Got one mind for white folks to see, "Nother for what I know is me."

—Author unknown

Having examined the deracination, assimilation, and acculturation of Africans, we now further explore the bicultural experiences of the enslaved Africans as they tried to negotiate the unrelenting demands of plantation life under the brutal conditions of chattel slavery. It is here, we assert, that the *dilemma* of "double consciousness" described by Du Bois (1953) had its origins.

The bicultural experience of African Americans during slavery cannot be discussed using conventional definitions of biculturalism. The idea of being bicultural, in the traditional sense, presupposes that an individual is able to participate competently in two or more cultures simultaneously and that there is reciprocity between the cultures (Mpofu & Watkins, 1997). Under the strict and rigid control of chattel slavery, African Americans, for the most part, were not allowed to participate in the culture of the White slave owners with whom they shared the same geographic space. And there was certainly no reciprocity (Herskovits, 1958; Stampp, 1956).

In addition to the culture that developed from a fusion of indigenous African beliefs, values, and practices with Euro-American culture, a distinct culture developed out of the institution of chattel slavery. A "culture of chattel slavery" defined the relationships between and among its participants (enslaved Africans, slave masters, overseers, the slavocracy), dictated their behavior, and prescribed a value/belief system/worldview based on the superiority of Whites and the inferiority of the African. We posit that the bicultural experiences of enslaved Africans was in relation to developing competence in the culture of chattel slavery, while simultaneously maintaining their own unique culture (what would later come to be known as African American culture: Africanisms fused with aspects of Euro-American culture).

The culture of chattel slavery evolved out of the mechanics of an economic system that relied on the domination and exploitation of the enslaved Africans for the purpose of extracting their labor. The most basic feature of this culture was the unconditional submission of the enslaved to the will of the slave master and to Whites in general (Stampp, 1956). The unconditional submission of enslaved Africans was achieved through the slave masters' willingness to use whatever violence was necessary to establish and maintain strict discipline (Stampp, 1956). Other features of the culture of slavery included the enslaved Africans' mimicry of White ideals and behaviors, a disposition of subservience (usually exaggerated) toward Whites, and a theatrical display of stereotypical behaviors (e.g., Sambo, Clown, Trickster) said to reflect the enslaved Africans' happiness in bondage (Akbar, 1984). Others believe that the Sambo, Clown, and Trickster were in fact a form of resistance based on cunning and trickery designed to dupe the master into believing that the enslaved had willfully capitulated to the conditions of servitude (Allport, 1958; Wyatt-Brown, 1985).

Wyatt-Brown (1985) posited that the culture that developed out of the institution of chattel slavery allowed African Americans to acquire a posture of shamelessness in order to avoid experiencing the full effects of their degradation and debasement. She proposed three types of servility, each incorporating the concept of shame, to describe the coping mechanisms used by African Americans in an effort to buffer themselves from the reality of their condition. The first was *ritualized compliance* and was characterized by the ability of the individual to maintain his or her self-regard while carrying out the wishes of the slave master. A *socialization of subordination* was characteristic of those enslaved Africans who had assimilated into the culture of chattel slavery and came to accept their servitude as reflecting the natural social order. The third level of subordination was the *Sambo*. Samboism reflected a complete sense of shamelessness in the enslaved and was an effective guise that could be adopted or cast aside as needed (Wyatt-Brown, 1985).

Other coping mechanisms rooted in the culture of slavery included the Clown and the Trickster. According to Akbar (1984) and Allport (1958), clowning was a survival strategy used by some enslaved African Americans to entertain the slave master with the hope of gaining favor or special consideration. Clowning, according to Allport, was also used to control the violent and abusive master. The Clown would intentionally degrade himself by performing silly antics using exaggerated stereotypical "Negro" speech and behavior (e.g., laziness, stupidity). The Trickster, on the other hand, was the sly and cunning individual who would steal the master's goods or sabotage his equipment as an act of revenge for harsh treatment (Allport, 1958). A sense of pride resulted from having outsmarted the White slave master, and Tricksters enjoyed a special status in their community. Cunning and slyness was not limited to sabotage and stealing, but also included other types of pretense, all having survival implications for the enslaved African American.

According to Mpofu and Watkins (1997), bicultural competence represents a repertoire of situation-specific behaviors that allow for greater role flexibility. In the context of chattel slavery, the ability of African Americans to move between their own unique culture (i.e., Africanisms infused with Euro-American culture) and the culture of slavery reflected their bicultural competence. The ability of enslaved African Americans to be bicultural had implications for their well-being and survival. Given the harsh and brutal reality of slavery, the Sambo, Clown, and Trickster all reflected aspects of bicultural competence for the enslaved African American.

Carter G. Woodson (1933), the imminent African American historian, was among the first to address the impact of segregation on the bicultural experience of the "American Negro." Of particular concern for Blacks were the negative consequences of being "miseducated" under an educational system steeped in the assumptions of White supremacy. According to Woodson, the educated Negro was estranged from his brethren *because he seemed to willingly identify with his White oppressor.* He summarized the duality of the African American experience this way:

> He goes forth to play his part in life, but must be both social and bisocial at the same time. While he is a part of the body politic, he is in addition to this a member of a particular race to which he must restrict himself in all matters social. (p. 6)

The generalized alienation and psychological duality experienced by African Americans as a result of Jim Crow segregation was accurately captured by the following statement:

While being a good American, he must above all things be a "good Negro"; and to perform this definite function he must learn to stay in a "Negro's place." (Woodson, 1933, p. 6)

Twenty years later, Frantz Fanon (1967) addressed the duality of the Black experience in the widely acclaimed book *Black Skin, White Mask,* first published in 1952. According to Fanon, "The black man has two dimensions. One with his fellows, the other with the white man" (p. 17). He attributed this self-division in Black people to their subjugation and oppression under White domination. Fanon viewed the bicultural behavior of the oppressed African as constituting a psychic crisis and resulting in the inauthentic expression of the African self.

During Jim Crow segregation, African Americans had little access to Anglo-American culture for the purpose of developing bicultural competence. However, as indicated by Woodson (1933), African Americans still felt a desire to express their American identity in spite of being denied participation in the cultural and social life of the country. Bell (1990) discussed the complexity of African Americans adopting a bicultural lifestyle in negotiating the cultural and social institutions of a racist society. She noted that when one group, usually a socially subordinate group, is excluded from full participation in the culture of the socially dominant group, the former assumes a position of marginality. Clearly, in the case of Jim Crow segregation, the bicultural experiences of African Americans were at best marginal.

BICULTURAL IDENTITY AND THE PSYCHOLOGICAL FUNCTIONING OF AFRICAN AMERICANS

Fanon (1963) believed that adopting the cultural reality of the oppressor and abandoning one's own resulted in a profound sense of alienation for the oppressed. He proposed the following five aspects of alienation as a reaction to conditions of oppression: (1) alienation from the self—to be alienated from one's personal identity; (2) alienation from the significant other—estrangement from one's family or group; (3) alienation from the general other—characterized by violence between Blacks and Whites; (4) alienation from one's culture and history—estrangement from one's language and history; and (5) alienation from creative social praxis—denial and/or abdication of self-determination and socialized and organized activity, which is at the core of the realization of human potential.

Akbar (1984) proposed an Africentric classificatory system of mental disorders that result from bicultural adaptation and the assimilation of an alien worldview (i.e., European) for people of African descent. The first, *alien-self disorder,* is characterized by a conscious rejection of one's African reality, a denial of the reality of racism, and the active attempt of African Americans to emulate a European worldview/reality. Second, *anti-self disorder,* shares some characteristics with the alien-self disorder, but has the added element of covert and overt hostility toward all things African. The *self-destructive disorder,* on the other hand, reflects the ineffective and destructive attempts of African Americans to cope with the unnatural conditions of White supremacy and domination. Finally, *organic disorder* refers to the physiological and biochemical diseases having their etiology in the oppressive conditions typical for the victims of White supremacy (e.g., ecological racism, poor nutrition, substandard health care).

Kambon (1992) posited that African Americans who are alienated from their African self-consciousness experience *psychological/cultural misorientation.* Those prescribing to an individualistic orientation, expressing or exhibiting anti-African/ Black behavior, manifesting self-depreciating or self-destructive tendencies, or who are exploitative or hostile to other African Americans suffer from this Africentrically defined mental disorder. According to Kambon, African Americans can experience cultural misorientation with varying degrees of severity (i.e., minimal, moderate, or severe). For example, persons experiencing minimal cultural misorientation manifest a weak propensity toward a Eurocentric worldview. Individuals experiencing moderate cultural misorientation have a tendency to internalize Eurocentric cultural values, beliefs, attitudes, and behaviors, while at the same time manifesting some pro-Black cultural values, beliefs, attitudes, and behaviors. Severe cultural misorientation is characterized by a predominance of internalized Eurocentric cultural values, beliefs, attitudes, and behaviors. A most insidious feature of this degree of psychological/cultural misorientation is that individuals appear "normal" when viewed through the lens of a Eurocentric worldview (Kambon, 1992).

Research on Black career women indicated that adopting a bicultural orientation allowed mobility in both cultures (Bell, 1990). Such an orientation encouraged women to remain true to their community and cultural values while participating in predominantly White organizations and institutions. The bicultural orientation also allows individuals to reap the benefits that exist in both cultures. However, identity conflict is a potential consequence of a bicultural orientation. Bell noted that in order for Black women to be successful in the workplace they had to conform to the organization's culture, which tended to promote White male values and norms. Thus, climbing the corporate ladder may require one to set aside one's racial/ethnic and gender identity, possibly leading to psychological conflict.

In relation to education, African Americans have been found to experience a wide range of psychological distress, such as feelings of isolation, ambivalence, anxiety, and depression, in an effort to be successful in traditionally White school systems (Fordham, 1988). Mpofu and Watkins (1997) found that African American children and adolescents enrolled in primarily White schools demonstrated low self-esteem and low self-worth and experienced lower teacher expectations. The results suggested that there are psychological consequences associated with the conflict in values between the culture of the dominant society and that of the indigenous culture. Individuals in the study (Fordham, 1988) were challenged with reconciling the conflict between the values of individualism embedded in the American school system and the collectivist beliefs of their community.

Fordham (1988) suggested that African Americans experience conflict over achieving in school while remaining true to their ethnic identity. Central to her position is the notion of *fictive kinship,* which is a unique connection or mind-set representative of Black identity that is challenged when children enter the school system of the dominant culture. According to Fordham, Black students have two options: to maintain their affiliation with the Black community by recreating the indigenous culture in the school environment (which may lead to academic failure), or to assimilate into the school culture, which will increase their chances of succeeding in school; to do so, students begin to take on the attitudes, behaviors, and characteristics that are not generally attributed to being African American. This strategy serves to both rid students of the stigma attached to being Black and to help them achieve vertical mobility; however, it may lead to feelings of isolation and identity confusion.

In addition to the distress experienced from adapting to the educational system of the dominant culture, Fordham (1988) noted that African Americans face isolation from others in the Black community who view them suspiciously. Thus, their less successful peers might reject them (i.e., if they are high-achieving students) because they are perceived as taking on characteristics that are considered to be White. Boykin (1986) referred to the dilemma faced by individuals negotiating the multiple realities of African American life as the *triple quandary* phenomenon. He posited that African Americans must relate to the "minority" experience, the Black cultural experience, and the mainstream (White) cultural experience. Inevitably, attempting to negotiate these three realms of existence will result in psychological and emotional conflict.

In a study conducted by Mpofu and Watkins (1997), additional evidence was found that supports the potential of negative (psychological) consequences for adopting a bicultural identity. They found that African American students in predominantly White schools had more negative outcomes as a result of differences in cultural values. For example, the values of cooperation and sharing associated with the African American community and the values of individualism, competition, and achievement prevalent in the culture of the dominant White society were implicated in accounting for differences in achievement. It was found that Black students in classes taught by White teachers had significantly lower academic self-esteem than their White classmates. This was in part due to the fact that the Black students received less academic recognition from the teachers and were perceived as academically less competent than their White counterparts (Mpofu & Watkins, 1997). Furthermore, the Black students may have perceived their cultural values as incompatible with those of the school's culture.

Given the negative psychological outcomes that African American students potentially experience, Rashid (1984) emphasized the importance of promoting biculturalism during the early school years. He posited that by fostering a bicultural environment in early childhood programs, African American children are more likely to experience a smooth transition from the culture of the family unit to that of the dominant culture. For proper psychological growth to occur, early childhood programs must expose children to the history and culture of African Americans (Rashid, 1984). This early exposure is critical for African American children who will have to cope with racism and classism in today's society. Moreover, Rashid stated:

When children have developed the ability to survive and thrive within the context of their own culture as well as that of the broader society, a genuine appreciation for the variety of cultures that comprise America is the next step. (p. 15)

CONCLUSION

Explicit among the goals of this chapter has been to examine the unique bicultural experiences of African Americans. To accomplish this goal, we began the chapter by reviewing the traditional models of biculturalism, provided an introduction to African culture as the genesis of African American culture, and discussed the acculturation process (during slavery) that transformed Africans into African Americans. In addition, we discussed the bicultural behaviors developed as survival strategies to negotiate the brutal reality of slavery (e.g., Sambo, Trickster, Clown) as well as the duality (or double consciousness) of the Black experience during Jim Crow segregation. The chapter concluded with a discussion of contemporary issues (i.e., professional and educational) related to the bicultural experiences of African Americans.

The major thesis of this chapter is that current models of biculturalism are inadequate to describe the process of second-culture acquisition for African Americans. Not only is there a dearth of both theoretical and empirical literature on the topic, but what is available fails to take into account African Americans' experience during slavery and Jim Crow segregation and current forms of societal racism and oppression. What role does the continued reality of racism and oppression play in the contemporary bicultural experience of African Americans? It is our position that a new model delineating the psychology of the African American bicultural experience needs to be developed. This model must take into account the psychohistorical experiences of African Americans, including but not limited to the African genesis of African American culture, slavery, Jim Crow segregation, and modern forms of racism and oppression (Arredondo, this *Handbook,* this volume). Once a theoretical model is formulated, we anticipate that empirical studies testing the model and examining the process of second-culture acquisition among people of African descent will follow.

REFERENCES

Akbar, N. (1984). *Chains and images of psychological slavery.* Jersey City, NJ: New Mind Productions.

Allport, G. W. (1958). *The nature of prejudice.* New York: Doubleday/Anchor Books.

Anderson, L. P. (1991). Acculturative stress: A theory of relevance to Black Americans. *Clinical Psychology Review, 11,* 685–702.

Asante, K. W. (1990). Commonalities in African dance: An aesthetic foundation. In M. K. Asante & K. W. Asante (Eds.), *African culture* (pp. 72–82). Trenton, NJ: African World Press.

Atkinson, D. R., Morten, G., & Sue, D. W. (1997). *Counseling American minorities: A cross-cultural perspective* (pp. 24–30). New York: McGraw-Hill.

Bacquart, J. (1998). *The tribal arts of Africa.* New York: Thames and Hudson.

Bell, E. L. (1990). The bicultural life experience of career oriented black women. *Journal of Organizational Behavior, 11,* 459–477.

Berry, J. W. (1994). Acculturation and psychological adaptation: An overview. In A.-M. Bouvy, F. J. R. van de Vijver, P. Boski, & P. Schmitz (Eds.), *Journeys into cross-cultural psychology* (pp. 129–141). Lisse, the Netherlands: Swets & Zeitlinger.

Blassingame, J. (1979). *The slave community.* New York: Oxford University Press.

Boykin, A. W. (1986). The triple quandary and the schooling of Afro-American children. In U. Neisser (Ed.), *The school achievement of minority children* (pp. 57–91). Hillside, NJ: Erlbaum.

Carter, R. T., & Pieterse, A. L. (in press). Race: A social and psychological analysis of the term and its meaning. In R. T. Carter (Ed.), *Handbook of racial-cultural psychology and counseling: Theory and research* (Vol. 1, pp. 41–63). Hoboken, NJ: Wiley.

Colemen, W. (1997). West African roots of African American spirituality. *Peace Review, 9,* 533–539.

Cowley, M., & Mannix, D. P. (1994). The middle passage. In D. Northrup (Ed.), *The Atlantic slave trade* (pp. 99–112). Lexington, MA: Heath.

Du Bois, W. E. B. (1953). *Souls of Black folk.* New York: Blue Heron Press.

Everett, S. (1991). *History of slavery.* Seacaucus, NJ: Chartwell Books.

Fanon, F. (1967). *Black skin, white masks.* New York: Grove Weidenfeld.

Fishman, J. A. (1989). Bilingualism and biculturalism as individual and societal phenomena. *Journal of Multilingual and Multicultural Development, 1,* 3–15.

Fordham, S. (1988). Racelessness as a factor in factor in Black students' school success: Pragmatic strategy or pyrrhic victory. *Harvard Educational Review, 58,* 54–84.

Frazier, E. F. (1964). *The Negro church in America.* New York: Schocken Books.

Guthrie, R. V. (1998). *Even the rat was White: A historical view of psychology* (2nd ed.). Boston: Allyn and Bacon.

Gyekye, K. (1996). *African cultural values: An introduction.* Philadelphia: Sankofa.

Herskovits, M. J. (1958). *Myth of the Negro past.* Boston: Beacon Press.

Hill, R. B. (1999). *The strengths of African American families.* New York: University of America Press.

Holloway, J. E. (1990). The origins of African-American culture. In J. E. Holloway (Ed.), *Africanisms in American culture* (pp. 1–18). Bloomington: Indiana University Press.

Joiner, T. E., Jr., & Walker, R. L. (2002). General factorial construct validity of a measure of acculturative stress in African-Americans and Anglo-Americans. *Psychological Assessment, 14,* 462–466.

Kambon, K. K. K. (1992). *The African personality in America.* Tallahassee, FL: Nubian Nation Publication.

Kardiner, A., & Ovesey, L. (1951). *The mark of oppression.* New York: Norton.

Kohatsu, E. L. (in press). Acculturation: Current and future directions. In R. T. Carter (Ed.), *Handbook of racial-cultural psychology and counseling: Theory and research* (Vol. 1, pp. 207–231). Hoboken, NJ: Wiley.

LaFromboise, T., Coleman, H., & Gorman, J. (1993). Psychological impact of biculturalism: Evidence and theory. *Psychological Bulletin, 114,* 395–410.

Landrine, H., & Klonoff, E. A. (1996). *African American acculturation: Deconstructing race and reviving culture.* Thousand Oaks, CA: Sage.

Lovejoy, P. E. (1997). The African diaspora: Revisionist interpretations of ethnicity, culture, and religion under slavery. *Studies in the World History of Slavery, Abolition, and Emancipation, 2.*

Manning, P. (1994). Social and demographic transformations. In D. Northrup (Ed.), *The Atlantic slave trade* (pp. 148–160). Lexington, MA: Heath.

Mbiti, J. S. (1990). *African religions and philosophy* (2nd ed.). Oxford, England: Heineman Educational.

Miller, J. C. (1994). Deaths before the middle passage. In D. Northrup (Ed.), *The Atlantic slave trade* (pp. 120–132). Lexington, MA: Heath.

Morgan, J. C. (1985). *Slavery in the United States: Four views.* North Carolina: McFarland.

Mpofu, E., & Watkins, D. (1997). Self-concept and social acceptance in multiracial African schools: A test of the insulation, subjective culture, and bicultural competence hypotheses. *Cross-Cultural Research, 31,* 331–355.

Myers, L. J. (1998). The deep structure of culture: Relevance of traditional African culture in contemporary life. In J. D. (Ed.), *Afrocentric visions: Studies in culture and communication.* Thousand Oaks, CA: Sage.

Nobels, W. W. (1998). To be African or not to be: The question of identity or authenticity— some preliminary thoughts. In R. L. Jones (Ed.), *African American identity development.* Hampton, VA: Cobb & Henry.

Parham, T. A., White, J. L., & Ajamu, A. (1999). *The psychology of Blacks: An African centered perspective.* Upper Saddle River, NJ: Prentice-Hall.

Park, R. E. (1928). Human migration and the marginal man. *American Journal of Sociology, 33,* 881–893.

Pasteur, A. B., & Toldson, I. L. (1982). *Roots of soul: The psychology of Black expressiveness.* Garden City, NY: Anchor Press/Doubleday.

Pinkney, A. (1993). *Black Americans* (4th ed.). Englewood Cliffs, NJ: Prentice Hall.

Rashid, H. (1984). Promoting biculturalism in young African-American children. *Young Children, 39,* 13–23.

Richards, D. (1985). The implications of African-American spirituality. In M. K. Asante & K. W. Asante (Eds.), *African culture* (pp. 207–231). Trenton, NJ: African World Press.

Rodney, W. (1994). The unequal partnership between Africans and Europeans. In D. Northrup (Ed.), *The Atlantic slave trade* (pp. 135–147). Lexington, MA: Heath.

Rudmin, F. W. (2003). Critical history of the acculturation psychology of assimilation, separation, integration, and marginalization. *Review of General Psychology, 7,* 3–37.

Semmes, C. E. (1996). *Racism, health, and post-industrialism.* Westport, CT: Praeger.

Stampp, K. M. (1956). *The peculiar institution: Slavery in the ante-bellum south.* New York: Random House.

Stonequist, E. V. (1937). *The marginal man.* New York: Charles Scribner's Sons.

Stonequist, E. V. (1961). *The marginal man: A study in personality and culture conflict.* New York: Russell & Russell.

Utsey, S. O., Bolden, M. A., & Brown, A. L. (2001). Visions of revolution from the spirit of Franz Fanon: A psychology of liberation for conseling African Americans confronting societal racism and oppression. In J. Ponterotto, J. M. Casas, L. A. Suzuki, & C. M. Alexander (Eds.), *Handbook of multicultural counseling* (2nd ed., pp. 311–336). Thousand Oaks, CA: Sage.

Woodson, C. G. (1933). *Mis-education of the Negro.* Washington, DC: Associated Publishers.

Wyatt-Brown, B. (1985). The mask of obedience: Male slave psychology in the old south. *American Historical Review, 93,* 1228–1252.

Yansane, A. Y. (1990). Cultural, political, and economic universals in West Africa. In M. K. Asante & K. W. Asante (Eds.), *African culture* (pp. 39–68). Trenton, NJ: African World Press.

CHAPTER 26

White Racism and Mental Health: Treating the Individual Racist

James E. Dobbins and Judith H. Skillings

Racism impacts the lives of all Americans regardless of where they fall on the color line (Thompson, this *Handbook,* this volume). In social sciences literature, much has been written about the impact of racism on various racial groups (especially among groups who are termed people of Color). Conversely, the heart of this discussion focuses on the fact that the impact of racism on White Americans has been less well researched or discussed. Whites represent the predominant racial group in the United States; as such, their role in the perpetuation and reduction of racism is critical. What is less often considered is that while being in the role of a perpetrator, Whites are also harming themselves.

The international community of scholars has actively studied the causes, meaning, and effects of racism for over 50 years. A half century ago, the United Nations Educational, Scientific, and Cultural Organization (UNESCO, 1954) conducted a massive study of race as a biopsychosocial, legal, and historical issue. The general consensus of that study was that race and racism are complex terms that lack precise scientific definition. This is an observation that contemporary researchers have also found to be true, especially as it relates to mental health concerns (Carter, 1995; Carter & Pieterse, this *Handbook,* Volume One; Dobbins & Skillings, 1991; Thompson, Shin, & Stephens, this *Handbook,* Volume One). However, one of the major differences between contemporary and earlier investigations is that the initial studies addressed racism as a cultural and institutional problem, to the exclusion of considering the clinical aspects of the individual racist. In this chapter, we assert that there is a mental health concern for individuals who are the agents of cultural and institutional racist agendas.

We further advance the belief that racism has a negative impact on Whites as well as people of Color. The key to appreciating this insight is rooted in the observation that race and racism cannot be separated from the developmental aspects of our socialization or our routine social processes (Bowser, this *Handbook,* Volume One; Carter, 1995). Speaking of the United States, Carter states that race is one of the key determinants to personality development in a race-based culture. He further explains that race and racism significantly affect how we see ourselves and how we relate to others. In his inclusive model of race and psychotherapy, he explains how racial identity status is not based on biological aspects of race alone. Indeed, the catalytic elements in ethnocultural transactions are fundamentally integrated with how we perceive ourselves as racial beings, which in turn influences observable differences in relational processes.

Dobbins and Skillings (1991) assert that racial identity is a developmental process. It is influenced by cultural, institutional, and individual race-based ideas and traditions. It is not presumed that all race-based transactions are racist. Taylor, Wilson, and Dobbins (1972) discuss race-based enactments that they define as "racialistic." In a racialistic context, the individual can respond to race without a connotation of antipathy, rigid generalizations, or a xenophobic reaction. We acknowledge that not all transactions are racist, any more than all transactions of a Christian are Christ-like, nor are all interactions bizarre with a person who has schizophrenia. People can be something without acting on their beliefs or conditions at all times. On this premise, we assert that only Whites can be racist because, in a race-based society, the dominant racial group is the one that has the requisite institutional power to enforce and sanction racist practices. But not all Whites act racist at all times.

In framing our discussion, we have located our position on the often-debated notion that racism is a White person's problem. Our position is supported by a growing awareness of this reality among scholars from the social sciences and related fields (C. Bell, 2000; Cuomo & Hall, 1999; Nakayama & Martin, 1999). A statement by Bell emphasizes this proposition when he states that "people of Color can resist racism, but only White people can eliminate racism." Racism has an undeniable institutional foundation. It is not a sufficient criteria of racism that a person have racist ideas or behaves in a way that expresses xenophobic antipathy toward others. These behaviors as expressed by a Black man might convey something called "race hate," but it cannot be called racism. If that person was able to discriminate and have that behavior overlooked or sanctioned by Black and White members of the society, as well as supported by law and custom, then this would be the near equivalent to racism.

To illustrate how racism hurts Whites as well as people of Color, we draw attention to subtle and obvious aspects of racism that make racism a clinical concern. We rely on the assumption that White privilege and conferred dominance, when allowed to remain hidden from its hosts, constitute the primary clinical determinant of racism, that is, denial. Secondary to racial denial is the addictive use of behaviors that are invoked to maintain individual, institutional, and cultural forms of racism.

We acknowledge the arguments of those who eschew the issue of racism as a mental health concern. Some well-regarded scholars argue against the need for mental health interventions to change individual racist behavior and thinking (Thomas & Sillen, 1976; Wellman, 2000). Others take the position that racism represents a clear mental health issue for all parties involved (Delaney, 1991; Dobbins & Skillings, 2000; Fanon, 1967; Skillings & Dobbins, 1991; Taylor et al., 1972; Welsing, 1970; Williams, 1995).

In this chapter, we propose that a viable mental health perspective of individual racism can be illustrated without discounting the necessity for interventions at cultural and institutional levels. We discuss conceptual models of racism represented in the social science literature and map those findings onto clinical models of addictive and abusive behavior. In this sense, we see the clinical significance of individual racism as a clinical syndrome as it cross-references two or more diagnostic domains of nosology, that is, abuse and neglect, personality and addiction disorders (Dobbins & Skillings, 2000). This discussion further elaborates the clinical aspects of racism, which include diagnostic, etiological, and intervention considerations.

MODELS AND DYNAMICS OF RACISM

Historically, investigators have tended to view racism as an institutional problem. As the social interventions of the day directed scholars to a better understanding of some of the personal dynamics of racism, a prominent group of social psychologists turned their attention to racism as a manifestation of personality (Adorno, 1950; Allport, 1970; Rokeach, 1960). Hitler's anti-Semitic and overt racist agenda against Jews and people of Color resulted in intense scientific interest and study of what was believed to be a "racist personality type." These investigators most often used direct and obtrusive measurement of affect, sentiments, and attitudes or discriminatory behaviors in a kind of dichotomous paradigm, that is, "racism present" or "racism not present." However, researchers who studied racism by direct observation had produced inconclusive results (Crosby, Brombley, & Saxe, 1980). It was noted that significant findings were more consistently obtained when unobtrusive measures were used to evaluate the effects of race-related sentiments, verbal communications, and discriminatory behaviors. Crosby et al. stated that a broader conceptual net needed to be cast to obtain a clearer picture of the behaviors and attitudes that characterize the racist. We suggest that that net include a reformulation of what is measured as well as how it is measured. It is critical to look at the individual effects of racism, similar to how Du Bois (1969) likened the individual effects of racism on the Negro as a target of racism.

Du Bois illustrated that the Negro acquired a pervasive personality dimension associated with his adaptation to the effects of racism. His formulations were intended to inform sociological study, but a century later, they also have clinical applications. The salience of his formulations is found in his observation that at the hands of racism, the Negro manifests a psychological splitting that he called "dual consciousness" (Utsey, Walker, Dessources, & Bartolomeo, this *Handbook,* this volume). This splitting is a serious matter in regard to healthy identity development because the dual reactance to racism portends that there is a true self and a false or invented self that acts out the projections of the dominant culture in service to their anxieties about the Negro. At times, the weight of this dual consciousness results in severe pathology for the Black individual or for the group as a whole (Fanon, 1967). Critically, Du Bois did not make mention of the same sort of mental determinants for perpetrators of racism. However, more contemporary investigators are making such arguments (Dobbins & Skillings, 2000).

Half a century after Du Bois postulated the psychosocial dynamic of dual consciousness, Myrdal (1944) analyzed the White American double bind. His analysis drew scholarly attention to the gap between "deed and creed," that is, an openly segregated society with an egalitarian ethic. He framed the disparity and cognitive dissonance of the hypocrisy of the great White dilemma as the "the Negro Problem," which was a most costly projection for Blacks because it seemed to imply that the blame and solution for the problem should be placed on the victim. The clinical significance of Myrdal's work is the absence of psychosocial postulates that discuss or allude to the possibility of personality variables for Whites that represent the same kind of double bind that racism creates for Blacks.

Myrdal's strongest assertion was that Whites lacked sufficient moral stamina to make changes in the Blacks condition palatable to White society (Drake, 1990). Thus, there was no accountability called for at individual levels and a weak one even at institutional levels. Accountability and change interventions were left in the hands of the politicians, whom the dominant culture largely controlled. The very institutions created for the well-being of the dominant culture were given the challenge of developing mechanisms for socially engineering the uplift of the Black, which logically would require big government to legislate change in the source of its power. We have seen initiatives such as affirmative action come and go, largely at the will of the dominant culture; it seems obvious that social engineering is at best only a partial solution to racism.

The next cohort of studies was social and psychological in focus (Adorno, 1950; Allport, 1970; Bowser & Hunt, 1981, 1996; Rokeach, 1960). Allport, Adorno, and Rokeach were concerned with identifying significant personality characteristics and the social psychology of the racist. They relied on operational definitions of the racist as one who is a highly dogmatic, authoritarian, or racially prejudiced. One of the principal theses in their social psychological approach is that by nature or by nurture, the bigot reflects consistent personality traits that can be observed in attitudes, sentiments, affects, and overt discriminatory behaviors.

Given this emphasis on personality variables in the formation of racism, the next logical leap was to consider racism as a mental health issue. Several investigations have focused on possible comorbid links between personality development and racism. For example, Pettigrew (1981) provided an important bridge between personality traits and mental health conceptualizations. He conducted a comprehensive review of the literature on the mental health consequences of racism and found an inconsistent relationship between mental health and overtly racist attitudes or sentiments; he stated that no causal relationship was supported. However, he also stated that positive mental health was marked by self-awareness, potential actualization, integrated psychic functioning, operational internal controls, and perceptions of reality that have consensual validation and are seen as evidence of environmental competence or mastery. Critically, he further stated that highly prejudiced persons, in general, have less positive mental health as measured by these same factors.

On the basis of the Pettigrew (1981) report, we might be encouraged to believe that racism is reflective of a slightly diminished mental health profile. In Pettigrew's account, the relationship between racism and personality is not one that would be defined in pathological terms. If anything, it suggests that at worst, we might expect an adjustment disorder. We agree that individual racism has some elements associated with adjustment disorders, especially if the person is using racism as a displacement for other dysfunctional aspects of his or her life, such as marital problems, low self-esteem, or unassertiveness. But we also believe that there are more pathological aspects to the syndrome.

One of the perspectives that we take is that racism is a multidimensional construct with a multifaceted social etiology (Taylor et al., 1972; Thompson, Shin, & Stephens, this *Handbook,* Volume One). At its most benign, it is generated by social effect. People act racist when they don't believe they are because they desire to impress racists who are in positions of authority or power. At the most pathological end, people act racist in order to build themselves up because of their low self-concept and low self-esteem. This ego-defensive racist is most dangerous because his or her personality rests on proving racist dogma as the truth, in spite of consequences or data that speaks otherwise.

Speaking from a different perspective, specifically a developmental point of view, Dennis (1981) makes the observation that racism affects White children in deleterious ways. He lists five areas of concern for the White child: ignorance of other people, double social psychological consciousness, rigidity in group conformity, moral confusion, and social ambivalence, all of which have mental health etiological considerations. He states that racism engenders irritability, inhibits intellectual growth, and negates true democracy. We would add that these developmental roots support the double-bind and dual-consciousness hypotheses and represent a number of clinically significant precursors to problems in the person's ongoing psychological development and adjustment. Such early relationships should not be looked on lightly, as it is quite possible that these dynamics predispose the child to a White identity that is dependent on someone else's identity (Ota Wang, this *Handbook,* this volume). This is in part what Carter (1995) meant when he described the United States as a race-based society. Members of the dominant culture cannot be White and privileged unless someone else is not White and thus relatively unprivileged.

Dobbins and Skillings (2000) agree strongly with the idea of developmental aspects as stepping stones to the expression of racism. We further suggest that the White child will eventually experience cognitive dissonance that he or she is hard pressed to resolve except through rather detrimental intrapsychic defenses (Thompson, this *Handbook,* this volume). If Blacks and other people of Color are projected as inferior, how does the child reconcile the accomplishments of those people of Color who are prominent educators, politicians, artists, athletes, healers, and so on, and, more critically those that are their peers, teachers, and doctors? If Blacks are not inferior, how does the child reconcile the inaction of his or her parents in the face of the differential treatment of Blacks in the lunch line, in the media, in the bombing of Black churches, and other hate crimes (Skillings & Dobbins, 1991)?

We conclude that White children are taught to truncate their perception of certain contextual cues, and thus repress their feelings and awareness of self-in-context as a way of coping with the racial inequalities of U.S. society. The works of Du Bois and Myrdal can now be brought into sharper focus. A White person, as a dominant member of the Black-White racial dynamic, also has a true self and a false self. The false self is an idealized projection of racist privilege. The true self can be realized only if one is willing to abandon the falsely entitled self.

Helms (1984, 2005), Helms and Carter (1990), and Carter (1995) significantly clarify our understanding of how Whites move along a developmental sequence of mental statuses related to their racial identity development. The key to the developmental transformative process of racial awareness is sustained cross-racial exposure. Exposure promotes insight and social competence. Conversely, the key to the maintenance of racism is denial and the luxury to be able to avoid, fixate on, or regress in one's willingness to engage cross-racial experiences. Van den Berghe (1967) operationally defines this privilege as a form of institutional power. He makes clear that racism is organized by the ability to define and maintain rules of "social distance."

Aldefer (1994) defined racism as a form of institutional power that is operationalized as denial of privilege. Whites unequivocally have social power, which translates into individual benefits whether or not the White person activates them consciously. McIntosh (1988) illustrates 50 conceptual varieties of invisible privilege that routinely mitigate in service to Whites. The works of McIntosh and Aldefer draw attention to the broad range of psychological issues that demarcate racist behavior and punctuate the assertion that racism is largely the problem of persons who hold power to define culture and promulgate institutional rules.

Social distance and denial of privilege are two sides of the racism coin. We further draw the conclusion that the use of power in race relations is narcotizing and addictive because, without the denial of the incongruities, the reality of one's status in life may be too painful and threatening. Thus, the use of denial and schema of irrelevance operate as a narcotic in service to White privilege. That denial also establishes a model of racism as an addiction to power and privilege. Denial is commonly understood as the principal feature of any addiction that may be further diagnosed by patterns of abuse and dependence.

The addiction model applies to a lifestyle that seeks monocultural solutions while being insulated by a significant number of unearned entitlements of dominance in a multicultural world. The unwarranted assumption of the racist is to be able to consume more and more of the good things and honored positions in the world, which is accompanied by less and less conscious concern for the cost to nondominant others and a denial of the interrelatedness of self to others.

FRAMING RACISM AS AN ADDICTION

Wellman (1977) disagrees that racism is a mental illness. He and others assert that it is instead an evil. His central thesis is that White individuals are only seeking what they believe to be appropriate for their upward mobility; therefore, White racism does not involve conscious thought because it is accommodated by a natural process of competition for resources. We do not disagree. However, this is only a partial response to the problem. We posit further that people engaged in the process of the competition are too often already intoxicated on the sweet elixir of power of which those who drink freely are fearful that there is a limited quantity. A social aspect of the addiction is a mind-set that says "Because I can't drink it all," and "I only feel comfortable sharing with people who know how to drink like I do."

Debate continues over whether racism should be considered a mental illness (Dobbins & Skillings, 2000; Wellman, 2000). Critics of the view that it is not a mental health issue (Wellman, 2000) have suggested that because Whites do not report the guilt or remorse that we would expect in a healthy person who has done something unhealthy and because there are no reports of apparent discomfort at the individual level, no psychopathology exists. However, the lack of expressed guilt or remorse is a common defense when a person intrapsychically can't deal with his or her own aberrant behaviors. Such self-centeredness is commonly seen in addiction work, where the crack addict, for instance, will deny that she objects to trading sexual favors for crack or an alcoholic will deny that he regrets choosing alcohol in the face of an ultimatum from his spouse. The racist as an addict reflects a number of attitudinal and behavioral problems as well as thinking errors.

In a mental health context, the individual expression of racism can be mapped onto a set of behaviors and symptoms that parallel the *DSM-IV-TR* criteria for substance dependence, as illustrated by the following descriptions and examples:

1. Tolerance is the first indicator, as observed in an increasing frequency, duration, or intensity of the maladaptive behavior or reduced sensitivity to continued occurrences of a maladaptive behavior. Frequency, duration, and intensity may be exemplified by an individual who progresses from telling racist jokes at a local bar, to making specific racist threats while with his buddies at the bar, to actually carrying out the threat on a person of Color. An example of reduced sensitivity is marked by a school principal who originally is shocked when she overhears an ethnic slur on the playground but does nothing and ultimately becomes accustomed to hearing children call other children belittling racial names.

2. Withdrawal and isolation are aspects of privilege in that they are maladaptive behaviors that help a dominant culture person avoid uncomfortable or unfamiliar situations caused by exposure to experiences resulting from healthier affinitive behaviors. For example, a parent with conferred dominance (Whiteness) joins a multicultural parent group that has come together to address violence in the schools. The parent drops out because he doesn't feel comfortable with the Latina woman who is running the meeting. He sends his daughter to private school because he feels that the public school will have problems with violence because of the increased Latino population.

3. The compulsive use of maladaptive behavior often occurs in situations where the person would like to exhibit a healthier behavior. For example, a person laughs at an ethnic joke, even though she knows that ethnic jokes stimulate office peers to act out in other exclusionary ways.

4. There may be a persistent but unsuccessful desire (craving) to develop healthier affinitive behaviors. For example, a person who clearly wants to move into a multicultural world finds that the experience of talking about race and color make him or her too nervous and upset and abandons the desire.

5. A great deal of time, energy, and resources may be invested in maintaining these maladaptive behaviors.

6. Important social, occupational, or recreational activities are given up or reduced because of the maladaptive behavior. For example, a White father alienates his daughter and Black son-in-law because he is against mixed-race marriages.

7. The maladaptive behavior is continued despite negative consequences. For example, the White dean of a graduate school continues to disallow the Multicultural Affairs Committee to hold a Martin Luther King celebration despite feedback that his failure to do so is resented by many of his staff and will broadly affect his ratings among the faculty.

The severity of symptoms might range from routine use (e.g., failing to interrupt an ethnic joke), to abuse (e.g., denying due process to a person on the basis of Color), and ultimately to dependence (e.g., blaming and projecting one's self-inflicted unemployment problems on people of Color because the racist believes they are getting special consideration). Considering racism as an addiction also helps explain the persistence of this aberrant form of behavior in spite of half a century of institutional interventions designed to undo the social effects of "separate but equal" treatment. Racism at the individual level, like other addictions, is remarkably resilient, despite economic, social, legal, and political interventions.

Our schema of racist addiction loosely fits the *DSM-IV-TR* behavioral sciences nosology. However, the consideration of racism as a significant White mental health problem does not end with the social sciences. Indeed, the mental health debate has now moved beyond the boundaries of social science, as noted in the works of a contemporary cohort of investigators from the fields of communications and philosophy (Cuomo, Kim, & Hall, 1999; Nakayama & Martin, 1999). These investigators address a major etiological factor in noting that racism is about privilege and suppression of affect as communication. Via narrative and analysis of speech, they indicate that such suppression is a part of the everyday life of the individual White person and in so doing make clear that to apologize for racism is not antiracist rhetoric. To apologize is the equivalent of a drunk driver saying, "I am sorry that I ran over you. . . . I didn't know what I was doing." The apology may be sincere, but the disease is still untreated and, contrary to some critics, one should not be let off the hook on the basis that one was drunk while driving recklessly. Recovery principles (Narcotics Anonymous, 1988) call for the responsibility of the addict to clean up his or her "wreckage of the past" and to be fully accountable to the consequences of addictive behaviors.

Allowing that these mental health considerations are hard distinctions to make, let's return for a moment to the proposition that racism is a social evil. Under this assumption, racism should be dealt with by legislating compulsory affiliation and punishing violations of civil rights. We submit that such legislative agendas are necessary but not sufficient. They have not stopped White racism from its progression any more than we have stopped alcoholism. The horrific Jasper, Texas, murder of James Byrd happened because Mr. Byrd was a Black man and for no other reason. One might call this a hate crime, not a mental health problem. However, the APA's position paper on hate crimes states that:

> Most hate crimes are carried out by otherwise law abiding young people who see little wrong in their actions. Alcohol and drugs sometimes help fuel these crimes, but the main determinant appears to be personal prejudice, a situation that colors people's judgment, blinding the aggressors to the immorality of what they are doing. (American Psychological Association, 2003, p. 2)

So what would be the *DSM-IV-TR* diagnosis of the racism that surrounds the Jasper, Texas, lynching? Possibly a V code for abuse? We propose the diagnosis of a syndrome that includes physical abuse, psychological abuse, and abuse of an ideological substance called White supremacy and White privilege. The syndrome is based on the presence in this case of two or more of these elements but privilege is the basis of the syndrome.

We follow the supposition that these are law-abiding young White men who live in a race-based society that tells them that they are privileged. This is a privilege that their society accords them as White men (and does not accord Black men), which they falsely or correctly understood to be true. These young men committed this crime based on race beliefs fueled by faulty logic and grandiose entitlement.

If we look at this crime as a metaphor for addiction as well as psychological and physical abuse, we see the syndrome more completely. It is clear that these men had a dependence on something that could make them believe that they could do this heinous crime and not be held accountable (extreme denial). Their craving and tolerance for the substance (privilege) must have increased beyond their routine use and needs, representing a progression of their diseased thinking. It is possible that these young men were medicating their pain with alcohol or other mood- or mind-altering activities prior to the crime. These elixirs may have further diminished their ability to self-control. If so, whatever they were using to medicate proved to be inadequate for the pain and anxieties that they experienced. It should also be noted that if they used these remedies and substitutions regularly, at no time did it reduce their control so that it led them to kill a White person. It appears that they took too much of their mood- and mind-altering substance once too often, which released their inhibitions beyond tolerance and control, which fueled the killing as a totally self-centered act.

It is not known if they ever tried to cut back on their sense of entitlement, thus showing loss of control. They went to great lengths to use their drug of choice, and probably gave up other productive activities to use it, thus illustrating compulsion and preoccupation, which also led to the loss of control. The father of one of the defendants has apologized to the family of the deceased, but as of this writing, the perpetrators have not admitted to having a problem with racism, or admitted that they did anything wrong, illustrating their self-seeking denial. Thus, abstinence does not equal recovery. If given the same set of circumstances, could we be sure they would not try it again, but with more determination to avoid getting caught?

If this metaphor is at all logical or believable, it would constitute a syndrome of abuse and victimization and possibly a matter of unconscious motives over competition for shared resources (Wellman, 1977, 2000). Data on hate crimes tend to support the notion that most hate crimes are perpetrated against Blacks (American Psychological Association, 2003). The APA online report further stipulates that since pre-Depression times, hate crimes have not been influenced by economic downturn, contrary to Wellman's argument. The APA report goes on to state that hate crimes against property and person are intended to convey a message to a particular group of people that they are not welcome.

ETIOLOGICAL AND RECOVERY CONSIDERATIONS

Why is racism so resistant to extinction, unless it is somehow reinforced? Who has the power to reinforce it, and what maintains its pernicious manifestations in the individual? When examining racism as an addiction, it may be useful to consider the analogy of drunk driving. The pathological behavior is often ego dystonic to the perpetrator, who never intended to place at risk the lives of others when she set out for an evening of socialization. Innocent people are as likely to be the targets of the drinker's pathological behavior as the drinker herself. Despite legislation directing that people not drink and drive, the penalties are not effective deterrents due to the underlying addiction to the abused substance. Further, the alcoholic may well work with, worship with, and live with people who don't drink alcoholically, but that, in and of itself, is not going to change her behaviors if she is an alcoholic.

In the model of racism as an addiction to privilege and power, the addiction is maintained by the belief that one is "doing it the right way," "doing it as well as anybody else," or "only doing it to myself." In reality, either racists are actively exercising the power of the dominant culture or passively receiving that same power simply by doing nothing. Pursuing the analogy of an addiction to power leads us to examine thinking errors and behaviors that might be conceptualized as other kinds of opportunistic impulse control disorders.

At the earlier statuses of racial development there is a crucial awareness of "other" that is missing; this impedes impulse control and appropriate relational responses. Said differently, racism is sometimes accompanied by disorders in which individuals act out because, in addition to having a distorted self-concept or fractured self-esteem and unresolved frustration aggression issues, they also feel they have the power to act out in ways that nondominant members of the society cannot. We have already seen how this analogy parallels racism with addiction. We should now consider the epidemiological significance of how people succumb to the disorder and what the consequences are.

Members of dominant groups drink at the well of false entitlement from the moment of birth and, in time, become relatively addicted to its pleasures. The pleasures seem so simple, so basic, so necessary to one's well-being. Thus, the addiction is subtle, baffling, and powerful, resting on a self-centered core that is encapsulated in denial and the projection of blame (Narcotics Anonymous, 1988).

The critical role of denial in the etiology of racism becomes increasingly evident as the racist begins to flirt with the idea that some of his general problems in regard to relationships with self and others may be related to his attitudes and beliefs about others. If he has experienced severe consequences, such as the loss of a position or job because of these ideas or beliefs, the conditions are ripe for recovery from racism. The most ideal condition is when he sustains losses that no longer allow him to use social distance as a means to advance his standing in the world. However, as addiction specialists will attest, the more resistant to change the addict becomes, the more we suspect that secondary to underdeveloped healthy coping mechanisms is a profoundly impaired self-esteem. Such ragged self-esteem stems directly from being ego-defensively trapped in inauthentic choices, perhaps motivated by low self-worth or inaccurate self-concepts, and most concretely driven by a self-centered fear that draws the racist to choose a self-destructive course against rational values and alternatives.

In the metaphor of racism as addiction, the damage to the inner core is comparable whether it is purchasing heroin with the rent money or hiding one's Black boyfriend from one's White parents. We pay for our addictions with money but more so with psychological currency such as damaged self-esteem and restricted self-concept.

It is important to conceptualize the progression of the disorder and the process of change for the better or worse. For some, the disease progresses to pathological denial, but for others, their denial is broken when there are internal consequences such as extreme guilt and confusion over discriminatory behavior that conflicts with personal values. In recovery, we would distinguish those who have "high bottoms" from those who have "low bottoms." And those who accept no bottom go on to the bitter end: jails, institutions, and death. The high bottom might happen when a person has a firsthand experience that creates cognitive dissonance beyond her capacity to rationalize privilege or apply childhood lessons of irrelevance about nondominant persons and matters that pertain to them. The process of positive change moves the addict from denial to self-acceptance to active change of ideas, attitudes, and behaviors.

Such a process of change of ideas and attitudes are reflected in Helms's (1984, 2005) model of White identity development. Gushue and Carter (2000) stated that reliance on stereotypes is closely linked to an individual's developmental level of racial awareness. The Helms model is described in many studies and it is mentioned here to illustrate the accuracy of the Gushue and Carter statement. To refresh our memory of the names of each status, they are Contact, Disintegration, Reintegration, Pseudo-Independence, Immersion/Emersion, and Autonomy.

The process of developing White racial identity begins as the individual awakens to the fact that her view of the world has been overly simplified due to lack of a need for affiliation with people of Color (Contact). In deciding to make contact, the White individual experiences confusion, distress, and the disintegration of a familiar worldview (Disintegration). She then reestablishes an alternative worldview, which is accompanied by a great deal of anxiety and affect (Reintegration). As the individual gains experience with this new worldview, she may begin to go through the motions of being accountable for the ways that conferred dominance benefits her at the expense of others (Pseudo-Independence). With ongoing cross-racial interactions, study, and application (Immersion/Emersion), the individual ultimately will evolve a life-changing commitment to critically and honestly examine the role of racism in her life, her extended family, and culture (Autonomy).

The recovery from racism model implies that, in time, the individual arrives at a level of acceptance of self as an individual, operating in a White privileged system, and is willing to be accountable for his actions in racial contexts. But throughout the model, a willingness to stay engaged with people of Color—to "stay sober"—and struggle to not retreat behind the buffers of conferred dominance is the *sine qua non* of healing and change.

This model puts the change focus on maintaining engagement in the process of cross-racial interactions and experiencing responsibility and, if necessary, the consequences for racist interactions. The recovery focus stands in contrast to the assumption that if one changes the personality structure, the addiction will vanish. As long as there is a dominant culture there will be a need to make interventions on racism. Some legal scholars inform us that racism may be permanent (D. Bell, 1992). If the removal of racism were a simple matter of making people compassionate or different in their personalities, the millions of socially acceptable individuals who make racist comments would simply stop exhibiting racist behaviors. It should be clearly stated that social acceptability is not a functional equivalent for recovery (Narcotics Anonymous, 1988). In a chemical dependency framework, thinking that social position equals recovery is analogous to treating the symptom and not the problem. It is almost always through the pain and insight generated by removing the addict's drug of choice that the addict chooses to find a new way to cope and communicate in the world. For racism, the intervention is the same as in the disease model of drug addiction. It is only through having enough consequences that one will self-diagnosis as a racist and allow the psychological space for the recovery process to begin. One is still responsible for the wreckage to one's past; this is not a model that exonerates one from criminal or personal wrongs by using the excuse that "the disease made me do it."

TREATMENT AND REMEDIATION

The primary focus of this chapter has been the dynamics of racism at the individual level of White Americans. While we agree that modern racism has historical socioeconomic and political roots and is significantly perpetuated at systemic levels, we also believe that racism and its passive face, that is, White privilege, impacts each individual who functions in our society. Further, we assert that the nature of the impact of racism is a legitimate mental health issue that robs the one who holds a racist perspective of vitality, jobs, family resilience, and authenticity.

When therapists are confronted with values on the part of their clients with which they do not agree, they have essentially two choices: They can leave the belief intact or treat it as part of the clinical package. For example, most clinicians would agree that a person's preferred political party rarely represents legitimate material for clinical intervention, whether or not the clinician shares the client's political beliefs. The same is generally true of a client's spiritual beliefs, whether or not they parallel the clinician's cosmology. However, in contrast, if a client who is working on issues of depression reports that she is smoking marijuana on a daily basis, this should become a significant part of the clinician's treatment considerations.

When a depressed White male struggles with his self-concept because he lost a job to a person of Color, rather than commiserating with the down side of affirmative action the therapist might consider examining with the client what assumptions he has about how things are "supposed" to go for him. When a child uses a derogatory ethnic phrase, rather than ascribe it to the teen culture's nomenclature, the adult should, at a minimum, set a limit and preferably process what that form of name calling means to the child. Such actions could lead to a rich intervention about the child's personal lack of self-esteem and use of people of Color as a way to artificially defend against her own feelings of low self-worth. If a peer is making sweeping negative generalizations about people of Arab descent or Muslims, the listener needs to note this type of pathological information processing and look for an opportunity to call it to the peer's attention. In a client, more than likely, flawed information processing will be comorbid with anxiety, depressive, or AXIS II disorder.

As with other clients with a broad range of inaccurate cognitions, unpleasant emotions, or maladaptive behaviors, the form of any intervention with a racist client will depend on the therapist, the client, and the way in which the blind assumptions of White privilege are intertwined with the client's other psychopathology. Generally speaking, a deficit in the client's ability to perceive herself in context and the defenses put in place to protect this myopia will limit her mental health. Interventions that expand the client's capacity to tolerate an awareness of self in context and respond to that information will only increase the client's healthy functioning.

An intervention that is acceptable to many Whites is sensitivity training. It is acceptable because it allows them to delude themselves that they are actually addressing racism without an awareness that they have to become uncomfortable in their own skin before an active process of change has begun. A diversity workshop sometimes can increase awareness enough to promote a commitment to change that will be continued in other venues. We consider diversity training to be a psychoeducational prevention and not an intervention.

If racism were not a mental health disorder but simply the result of a lack of information, one-shot prevention experiences, such as diversity workshops, would have had significantly more impact than they have in fact produced. For example, racial profiling might be covered as part of the content of a workshop. Yet, despite its racist misuse and the loud public education to its abuses, profiling has become a legalized form of discrimination primarily directed toward people of Color. There is no appreciable support from the vast majority of White people to end a procedure that literally kills and psychologically damages an untold number of people of Color daily, yet they have the political capacity to end it. We assume it is lack of racial consciousness and protection of privilege that is at the core of the resistance.

We also assume that because lives are at stake, only an unusual amount of individual and institutional denial could support such a clear menace to the egalitarian fundamentals of the American social contract.

The important thing is that White people who go through such training still commit racist acts. Those who cannot benefit from information fast enough and are collecting consequences such as job reprimands and legal charges probably need more intensive treatment or support to maintain and build on any insights that might have been acquired from the training. Gushue and Carter (2000) speak to the observations of numerous scholars when they write, "The mere acquisition of information about diverse racial and ethnic groups is not enough to ensure cultural competence" (p. 207). They go on to posit that unless the distorted encoding system is impacted, the information processed by that encoding system will have little impact. This is consistent with Skillings and Dobbins's (1991) theory of racism as a disease in which they posit that the racist grows up with a schema of irrelevance about people of Color. The schema of irrelevance distorts information from and about people of Color in ways that insulate White Americans from the impact of the information.

Likewise, trying to work on racism alone is like an alcoholic trying to talk himself into a sober lifestyle while still surrounded by his drinking buddies. Who is there to help him be accountable for his negative behaviors, attitudes, and unconscious assumptions? By nature of belonging to a dominant group he is selectively insulated from feedback in the natural course of events. Any analysis that fails to take selectivity into account is a band-aid rather than an intervention designed to make us more connected to and competent in a multicultural world.

According to Marty (1999) and Aldefer (1994), a White person can begin the process of healing from racism by learning how to engage in antiracist dialogue. The process of becoming antiracist begins when the individual is able to state a truth or fact clearly and without equivocation about her racism, for example, "Yes, there is institutional racism in this organization because there are no people of Color on the board of directors and this is an inner-city agency. And yes, I complicitly support this racism by my silence." According to Marty, the antiracist must then stand by the truth without excuse or apology and also continue the dialogue by making sure that she is relational and conventional in the process. Making a clear, unconditional reference to the things one has done to offend another or a group is a way of "hitting bottom." It represents a first step in the process of recovery. Such admissions have been a key element for many alcoholics and drug addicts who find a way to recover from the problem of living life on life's terms. The healing process begins with internalized ownership and acceptance of the problem.

For Marty (1999), being relational means realizing that the dialogue cannot move forward unless one is able to explain how one intends to or can move beyond admission and apology to accountability. Being conventional means finding a way to do that so that one's actions are understood universally to be a change in racial polity. Ring (2000) provides discussion and illustration of what it means for a White man to have awareness of who is empowered to define the criteria for what accountability means as an antiracist (e.g., expressing a clear, measurable plan for what one intends to do to change the White power matrix).

Several people in the field have advocated for the use of self-help groups to provide guided orderly direction for persons who want or need to change the ways racism manifests within them. There are a variety of self-help group formats, each of which is useful to different people with different manifestations of the disease. Community dialogue models (Hope in the Cities, 2000) and Recovery from Racism workshop models (Katz, 1989; Williams, 1995) are increasingly used in contemporary practice, including cognitive-behavioral universal 12-step models (Peiser & Sandry, 2000), which claim to be appropriate for all addictions.

The approach we find most useful follows a 12-step model. Recovery, which is an ongoing program of change in ideas, attitudes, and behaviors, has been used by countless people to achieve a measure of change in problems with personal control (Narcotics Anonymous, 1988). There are those who bemoan the proliferation of 12-step program formats and state that the model has been generalized far beyond the very specific addictions it was designed to address. We do not propose that this is necessarily the essential treatment paradigm for racists seeking recovery. We suggest that the model has several extremely useful components that clinicians should consider.

First, it is necessary to break through the White person's denial that the disease of racism has not impacted her. It is vital that she be able to make some critical admissions that racism exists, at first to herself and at some later point to others. It is necessary to admit having racist thoughts and feelings whether or not she wishes to have such feelings. And that whether or not she wishes to belong to the power-holding group of White status in the United States, she does. In this sense, it is useful to admit we are powerless to change the fact that racism has impacted us and made us hosts to a disordered process in ways for which we did not consciously volunteer, but nonetheless find inescapable. The racist will need to embrace the reality that she can stop and lose the desire to behave in racist ways. Racism cannot be cured, but it can be arrested through the application of an honest admission, remaining open-minded about the need for suggested changes, and willingness to engage a prescribed set of steps to keep it arrested.

From a single admission, a watershed of healing becomes possible. It opens the path for the next step, which is to acknowledge that the toxic lifestyle of benefiting from another's loss is not working for self or others. We propose that essentially the same intervention process used by people who are in recovery from drugs is feasible for the racist. Recovery from racism is an ongoing program of change of ideas, attitudes, and behaviors. This is the type of program that is used for people who, no longer under the influence of mood- or mind-altering chemicals, learn to stop victimizing others and hurting themselves and ultimately find a new way of life (Narcotics Anonymous, 1988). We propose a recovery from racism framework that includes group discussion and working with persons who have longevity and experience changing their racist ideas, attitudes, and behaviors. Such a person, who might be called a sponsor, is necessary because deficits in self-honesty and open-mindedness, as well as a lack of accurate awareness of self in context, are very difficult to detect and repair in oneself.

An important caveat for implementing the recovery model of racism is that it is very difficult for people with White privilege to have the opportunity to step out of contexts where this privilege does not exist and to get honest about what they don't know about themselves. The goal of the modified 12-step program for racism is not to create a closed, White-only group that seeks only itself for feedback, but to create a safe context where authentic multicultural functioning can be enhanced. Toward this end, the leadership of such groups needs to build in a facilitative role for skilled professionals, including input from the perspective of at least one person of Color. In such cases, the person of Color would have to be clear that he is not taking the role of the menial who does the work for the dominant culture. He should also be experienced enough that guilt-invoking behaviors can be critically avoided and examined for latent hostility. Primarily, he can serve outside of the group as a listener and consultant to the individual who has the willingness to seek his input and suggestions.

In cases where the development of healthier coping styles has been critically compromised by low self-esteem, we anticipate a stronger dependence on lower-lever racial identity statuses according to the Helms and Carter (1990) model of identity development. Early stages of development rely heavily on the types of defenses that are correlated with lower statuses. We will likely observe a great deal of ego defensiveness triggered by the threat of accepting that one is incorrect in one's organizing principles. In such cases, individual therapy or counseling is probably indicated. Other reasons a client's racism might need to be dealt with in individual work includes the realization that the client may lack the motivation to go to an ongoing group, or there might not be such a group in the area. In such instances, addressing the ways the person's assumptions of false entitlement impact her psychopathology should be part of the individual's intervention plan.

Whatever the actual intervention style, clients' assumptions and related affect can be significantly impacted in the therapeutic context. For instance, cognitive techniques such as reframing, cognitive restructuring, and rational-emotive therapy can address beliefs regarding false entitlements. Universal 12-step programs, grief work, art therapy, visualization techniques, writing a life story, and a host of other techniques can help the individual work through his sense of loss and insecurity.

In a more traditional clinical approach, one might conduct an assessment of the racial attitudes and beliefs of the potential candidate. Using the Helms and Carter (1990) status model, an interpersonal or psychometric assessment of the client's location on the statuses of racial identity will prove helpful to guide intervention planning. For example, a clinician identifies that her White client is thinking of dropping out of school in part because he is unfamiliar with the context of being one of only five White freshmen in a class of 20 students. We would hope that the clinician will recognize this as Contact status and will state one of the clinical goals as keeping the client on a track to stay engaged in multicultural ways. If the clinician colludes with the client by encouraging him to transfer to a predominantly White setting, she is causing the client to miss this growth opportunity.

The F-scale, the White Racial Identity Attitude Scale, and other scales of racialism (Helms & Carter, 1990; Taylor et al., 1971) might also be used to better estimate the racialistic profiles of clients who need individualized behavioral plans. Treatment ought not be limited to people professing a desire for change. The underpinnings of racism include an addiction to power. An assumption of privilege and an expectation of entitlement are fostered in members of the dominant culture by forces that have little to do with individual choice or consciously chosen values. These same underpinnings of racism are also underlying issues in a vast array of already diagnosed psychopathologies. They correlate with symptoms such as suicidal depression when one is not being treated well and anxiety when one is not in control. To treat the symptoms and not the cause is like ignoring problem drinking or "dry drunk" behavior in a person who comes to therapy to work on marital dysfunction.

Behavioral interventions and homework can help the client begin to work on skill building around reducing the ways he colludes with the status quo. For example, role-playing and problem solving can be used to help an anxious client address introducing his Black girlfriend to his parents. Historically, clinicians have tended to focus on low self-esteem and poor assertiveness skills in such a client; they may well be missing the ways the client is compromising his values and his authenticity by buying into racist ideas and, in the process, feeling inauthentic and vulnerable.

Identifying the need to treat racism does not constitute the medicalization of a societal evil. Rather, we seek to provide additional tools with which to confront the contagion of false beliefs and false entitlements that distorts the reality of many U.S. citizens. No one can convince another that racism plays an integral part in his or her adjustment and that he or she would not be well advised to start weeding it out. The consequences of such behavior become the catalyst for change. What we can do is offer education, treatment, objective feedback, and consequences and refuse to cooperate with the diseased thinking. Self-diagnosis is ultimately required for someone to change. Once the diagnosis is made, however, self-help groups or individual therapeutic work can be indispensable to helping the person stay on track with his or her change process and commitment to refrain from the abuse of power, however the opportunity makes itself manifest.

CONCLUSION

This discussion concerned primarily the effects of racism on its agents. A significant number of Whites in the United States simply and clearly acknowledge that racism is inherent in most U.S. institutions, including the family, schools, churches, sports, and entertainment. However, what is most important is their unwillingness or inability to be accountable for how they plan to address inequities. A massive, deeply ingrained, defensive structure, at both individual and systemic levels, impedes the process at all levels and statuses of being. While we do not dispute that there are sociological contributors to the defense system, we assert that, once in place, these defenses take on clinical mental health significance at the individual level.

Racism is a disorder that manifests at individual levels based on institutional and cultural foundations. A key focus in our discussion has been the clinical significance of racism, including its passive face of White privilege, in limiting the development of White individuals. We introduced a paradigm that examined racism as an addiction to power and privilege, whereby members of the dominant culture suffer from problems of denial in regard to the irrelevance they ascribe to others and false entitlements that come to them by virtue of conferred dominance. Thus, they lose touch with an accurate sense of themselves in context, possibly leading to manifestations of depression, anxiety, aggression, and distortions of information processing as well as the more obvious and salient acting-out that is stereotypically associated with the behavior of bigots.

On the basis of the etiological and progressive aspects of racism presented here, it is essential that when an individual White person experiences internal conflicts or race-related consequences, the practitioner be ready to direct such persons to appropriate levels of support. Self-help groups and competent therapists are needed who can establish a course of ongoing intervention so that the individual can sustain antiracist behavior in an environment that will not promote relapse. Thus, the ultimate goal of recovery is to help the racist to stop victimizing, lose the willingness to continue in active or passive racist behaviors, and find a new way to live that does not foster collusion with White privilege.

REFERENCES

Adorno, T. W. (1950). *The authoritarian personality.* New York: Harper.

Aldefer, C. P. (1994). A White man's perspective on the unconscious process within black-White relations in the United states. In E. J. Trickett, R. J. Watts, & D. Brinman (Eds.), *Human diversity* (pp. 123–165). San Francisco: Jossey-Bass.

Allport, G. (1970). *The nature of prejudice.* Reading, MA: Addison-Wesley.

American Psychological Association. (2003). *Hate crimes today: An age-old foe in modern dress* (Public affairs: PsychNET). Washington, DC: APA Online.

Bell, C. (2000). *Keynote address: Race-related police violence.* Annual meeting of the American Orthopsychiatric Association, Audio Archives International, La Crescenta, CA.

Bell, D. (1992). *Faces at the bottom of the well: The permanence of racism.* New York: Basic Books.

Bowser, B. P. (in press). The role of socialization in cultural learning: What does the research say? In R. T. Carter (Ed.), *Handbook of racial-cultural psychology and counseling: Theory and research* (Vol. 1, pp. 184–206). Hoboken, NJ: Wiley.

Bowser, B. P., & Hunt, R. G. (1981). *Impact of racism on White Americans.* Beverly Hills, CA: Sage.

Bowser, B. P., & Hunt, R. G. (1996). *Impact of racism on White Americans.* (2nd ed). Beverly Hills, CA: Sage.

Carter, R. T. (1995). *The influence of race and racial identity in psychotherapy: Toward a racially inclusive model.* New York: Wiley.

Carter, R. T., & Pieterse, A. L. (in press). Race: A social and psychological analysis of the term and its meaning. In R. T. Carter (Ed.), *Handbook of racial-cultural psychology and counseling: Theory and research* (Vol. 1, pp. 41–63). Hoboken, NJ: Wiley.

Crosby, F., Brombley, S., & Saxe, L. (1980). Recent unobtrusive studies of Black and White discrimination and prejudice: A literature review. *Psychology Bulletin, 87,* 346–563.

Cuomo, C. J., & Hall, K. Q. (Eds.). (1999). *Whiteness: Feminist philosophical reflections.* Lanham, MD: Rowan and Littlefield.

Delaney, L. T. (1991). The other bodies in the river. In R. L. Jones (Ed.), *Black psychology.* New York: Harper & Row.

Dennis, R. M. (1981). Socialization and racism: The white experience. In B. P. Bowser & R. G. Hunt (Eds.), *Impacts of racism on White Americans.* Beverly Hills, CA: Sage.

Dobbins, J., & Skillings, J. (1991). The utility of race labeling: Conceptual tool for the social science practitioner. *Journal of Counseling and Development, 70,* 37–44.

Dobbins, J., & Skillings, J. (2000). Racism as a clinical syndrome [Special Section]. *American Journal of Orthopsychiatry, 70,* 14–27.

Drake, S. (1990). *Black folk here and there.* Los Angeles: UCLA CAAS.

Du Bois, W. E. B. (1969). *The souls of Black folks.* New York: New American Library.

Fanon, F. (1967). *Black skin, White masks.* New York: Grove Press.

Gushue, G., & Carter, R. (2000). White racial identity and social memory. *Journal of Counseling Psychology, 47*(2), 199–210.

Helms, J. E. (1984). Toward a theoretical explanation of the effects of race on counseling: A Black and White model. *Counseling Psychologist, 12,* 153–165.

Helms, J. E. (in press). Challenging some misuses of reliability as reflected in evaluations of the White Racial Identity Attitude Scale. In R. T. Carter (Ed.), *Handbook of racial-cultural psychology and counseling: Theory and research* (Vol. 1, pp. 360–390). Hoboken, NJ: Wiley.

Helms, J. E., & Carter, R. T. (1990). The development of the White Racial Identity Inventory. In J. E. Helms (Ed.), *Black and White racial identity attitudes: Theory, research and practice* (pp. 67–80). Westport, CT: Greenwood Press.

Hope in the Cities. (1990). *A call to community and a companion dialogue guide for communities to engage in the process of conversation and change.* Richmond, VA: National Office of Hope in the Cities.

Katz, J. (1989). *Contemporary classic resources for White group work in anti-racism.* Norman: University of Oklahoma Press.

Marty, D. (1999). White antiracist rhetoric as apologia: Wendell Berry's the hidden wound. In T. K. Nakayama & J. N. Martin (Eds.), *Whiteness: The communication of social identity.* Thousand Oaks, CA: Sage.

McIntosh, P. (1988). *White privilege and male privilege: A personal account of coming to see correspondences work in women's studies.* Wellesley, MA: Wellesley College, Centers for Women.

Myrdal, G. (1944). *An American dilemma: The Negro problem and modern democracy.* New York: Harper.

Nakayama, T. K., & Martin, J. N. (Eds.). (1999). *Whiteness: The communication of social identity.* Thousand Oaks, CA: Sage.

Narcotics Anonymous World Services Incorporated. (1988). *The narcotics anonymous basic text.* Van Nuys, CA: Author.

Peiser, K., & Sandry, M. (2000). *The universal 12-step program: How to overcome any addiction and win.* Holbrook, MA: Adams Media.

Pettigrew, T. (1981). The mental health impact. In B. P. Bowser & R. G. Hunt (Eds.), *Impact of racism on White Americans* (pp. 97–118). Beverly Hills, CA: Sage.

Ring, J. M. (2000). The long and winding road: Personal reflections of an anti-racism trainer [Special Section]. *American Journal of Psychiatry, 70,* 73–81.

Rokeach, M. (1960). *The open and closed mind—Investigations into the nature and belief systems and personality systems.* New York: Basic Books.

Skillings, J., & Dobbins, J. (1991). Racism as a disease: Etiology and treatment implications. *Journal of Counseling Development, 70,* 206–212.

Taylor, J., Wilson, M., & Dobbins, J. (1972). *Racialistic inventory.* Unpublished inventory, University of Pittsburgh.

Thomas, A., & Sillen, S. (1976). *Racism and psychiatry.* Seacaucus, NJ: Citadel Press.

Thompson, C. E., Shin, C. E., & Stephens, J. (in press). Race and research evidence. In R. T. Carter (Ed.), *Handbook of racial-cultural psychology and counseling: Theory and research* (Vol. 1, pp. 277–294). Hoboken, NJ: Wiley.

United Nations Educational and Scientific Organization. (UNESCO). (1954). *World Conference on Racism.* Paris.

Van den Berghe, P. (1967). *Race and racism.* New York: Wiley.

Wellman, D. T. (1977). *Portraits of White racism.* Cambridge, MA: Cambridge University Press.

Wellman, D. T. (2000). From evil to illness: Medical zing racism [Special Section]. *American Journal of Psychiatry, 70,* 28–32.

Welsing, F. C. (1970). *The Cress theory of Color confrontation and racism (White supremacy).* Washington, DC: C-R Publishers.

Williams, C. (1995). *Recovering from racism.* Detroit, MI: Institute for Racial Healing.

CHAPTER 27

Racial Discrimination and Race-Based Traumatic Stress: An Exploratory Investigation

Robert T. Carter, Jessica M. Forsyth, Silvia L. Mazzula, and Bryant Williams

Even after being freed from slavery, Blacks in particular and people of Color in general (Hispanics, Asians, Native Americans, and historically disenfranchised Americans) were denied the basic civil rights of access to and opportunity in most areas of life in the United States. Racial discrimination was part of the American way, and in most parts of the country it was legally sanctioned and thus an integral part of social traditions. As Jaynes and Williams (1989) noted, during this time, "most Black Americans [and other people of Color] could not work, live, shop [or] eat, where they chose" (p. 3).

The social and racial attitudes of Americans changed dramatically following the civil rights movement of the 1960s. The overt and hostile racial attitudes reflected in racial segregation and discrimination shifted as the system of legal segregation was dismantled. Nevertheless, based on 50 years of research on Black participation in American society, Jaynes and Williams (1989) noted, "The foremost conclusion is that race still matters greatly in the United States" (p. 155). Their report showed that even after changes in the explicit rule of racism by law, the notion that one's value and worth is determined by race remains a strong aspect of American behavior, despite Americans' proud endorsement of principles of equality and fairness.

Today, it can be hard to recognize racism and its manifestations because race-based experiences have been isolated and disconnected from a systematic set of policies and experiences associated with race. The meaning associated with race and racism has become dismantled and fragmented, and as a result, its institutional ramifications continue to be overlooked. For instance, the discourse on race in education and employment has been replaced by a discourse on affirmative action. Similarly, the use of terms like "racial profiling" and "racial bias" in reference to the practices of the police and the criminal justice system serves to separate these actions from the systematic beliefs and attitudes about members of particular racial groups that inform these policies. Individual and collective acts of racism are now primarily viewed as isolated acts of hate or bias (Dobbins & Skillings, this

Handbook, this volume). The focus on the actions and attitudes of groups and individuals who are perceived to be aberrations from the norm obfuscates the existence of systemic racism.

Regardless of the state and federal laws that prohibit discrimination on the basis of race, people of Color continue to experience racial discrimination (Arredondo, this *Handbook,* this volume). For instance, an article by Greenhouse (2003) in the *New York Times* reported a lawsuit filed by Asian and Hispanic job applicants against Abercrombie & Fitch (A&F). The applicants were informed that they could not fill sales positions because they did not have the "A&F look," which is White and upper middle class. An article in the *Philadelphia Inquirer* by Prichard (2003) reported that over the span of several days in September, administrators at Abington Memorial Hospital ordered African American employees at all levels (including physicians and nurses) to refrain from entering a patient's room after a man ordered that no Blacks assist his child's birth or his wife's care. In addition to these reports, in 2003 the Equal Employment Opportunity Commission (EEOC) received some 28,000 claims of racial discrimination in employment settings (EEOC Web page). Hence, discrimination seems still to be a part of life in the United States. The effects of discrimination on its targets are not adequately addressed, nor are they understood.

Our chapter explores the psychological and emotional effects of racism for people of Color through a phenomenologically based, qualitative investigation. It is our contention that a major contributing factor to the problem of treating and understanding race-related experiences is a failure to comprehend and document the psychological and emotional effects of racism on its targets, due in part to the vagueness associated with the term *racism.* Racism has become a broad and indistinct term with shifting meaning. Therefore, a second purpose of this chapter is to deconstruct racism through a differentiation between two types of racism and to argue for a distinction that does not currently exist in the literature.

Finally, we propose a new paradigm for understanding *race-related* stress, called *race-based* stress, that can be used to enhance clinical interventions with people of Color. We contend that targets of racism suffer physical and psychological harm in the form of stress and other symptoms as a consequence of chronic and persistent racism (Williams, Neighbors, & Jackson, 2003). To aid in understanding this phenomenon, we integrate existing psychological models and research on race and severe stress reactions. The proposed new paradigm will contribute to reducing mental health professionals' limited understanding and treatment options for race-related stress.

DECONSTRUCTING RACISM

Many of the laws against discrimination emanate from the passage of the Civil Rights Act in 1964. However, when those laws are translated into institutional and organizational policies and procedures designed to protect people from racial discrimination, they frequently lack clear guidelines on what constitutes *racial discrimination.* The same is not true for *sexual discrimination.* In most organizations, the policies and procedures designed to protect people from sexual discrimination and harassment are supported by specific descriptions of what constitutes sexual discrimination and harassment as well as clear guidelines for the steps needed in filing reports. In reference to the discrepancy between how racial and sexual discrimination are handled in the workplace, Feagin and McKinney (2003) noted:

> Although the idea of a "hostile work environment" originally extended from racial discrimination cases to sex discrimination cases, the courts have only occasionally accepted the kind of evidence to demonstrate a hostile racial climate that they accept to demonstrate a hostile sexual climate. (p. 204)

Perhaps the effects of racial discrimination are not as clear as sexual discrimination or are not well articulated in the mental health literature. Another possibility is that there are no clear race-specific diagnostic or assessment criteria to help mental health professionals assess how one has been impacted by the experience of racial discrimination. As a result, we feel it is necessary to unpack and deconstruct racism, as the term has become vague and associated with various meanings (J. Jones, 1997). We offer a new way to specify aspects of racism by distinguishing between racial discrimination and racial harassment. We hope the distinctions will (1) facilitate recognition by targets and others of the new and more modern forms of systematic, covert, subtle, and unconscious racism; (2) serve as a guide for mental health professionals' assessment of targets' experiences of racism; and (3) allow for a more accurate understanding of the perceptions, experiences, and reactions of the targets of racism. In unpacking racism, it might be possible for mental health practitioners to understand people's experiences and to help targets understand how they have been affected.

Carter and Helms (2002) introduced the notion of distinguishing between racial discrimination and racial harassment. According to their conceptualization, *racial discrimination* is a form of averse or avoidant racism. They define racial discrimination as behaviors, actions, policies, and strategies that have the intended or accidental effect of maintaining distance or minimizing contact between members of the dominant racial group and members of nondominant racial groups (Darity, 2003; Feagin & McKinney, 2003; Klonoff & Landrine, 1999). Racial discrimination may occur at the individual level (e.g., holding "secret" business meetings, not interacting with a person of Color), at the system or contextual level (e.g., race-based hiring or promotion, not showing homes or apartments to prospective buyers/renters), and at the policy level (e.g., use of tests for inclusion that unfairly advantage members of the dominant racial group, setting criteria that exclude members of particular racial groups).

Carter and Helms (2002) posit that *racial harassment,* although related to racial discrimination, is a distinct form of racism. They define racial harassment as a form of "dominative or hostile racism" that involves actions, strategies, and policies intended to communicate or make salient the target's subordinate or inferior status due to his or her membership in a nondominant racial group (Feagin & McKinney, 2003; J. Jones, 1997; Kovel, 1970). Racial harassment is often characterized by active race-based hostility, which might include the commission of or implied or actual institutional permission to commit flagrant acts of racism. For instance, being verbally or physically assaulted, profiled, or informed that one does not belong in a particular setting because of one's racial group membership would be considered forms of racial harassment. It might also occur as a form of pressure to "fall into line" with institutional racial policies as a condition of continued employment, education, or social participation (i.e., quid pro quo racial harassment).

The distinctions between racial harassment and racial discrimination are important for both legal and mental health professionals. Experiences with either type of racism may have different implications for targets; therefore, it is imperative that professionals who may be consulted regarding instances and experiences of discrimination and harassment be aware of these distinctions. Additionally, what is clear from the different definitions of racism as discrimination or harassment is that both types of racism can be stressors for their targets.

According to the literature, there are two primary ways to understand and identify extreme stress reactions. One way is to use the criteria of the current version of the *Diagnostic and Statistical Manual of Mental Disorders* (*DSM-IV-TR;* American Psychiatric Association, 2000), and the other is to use the concept of traumatic stress (Carlson, 1997), which does not fit the diagnostic criteria of Posttraumatic Stress Disorder (PTSD) or Acute Stress Disorder. Carlson has argued that many life events may produce stress reactions that are experienced by some as traumatic. Traumatic stress has gained recognition after an increase in the number of people suffering from severe stress that produces psychiatric and psychological symptoms. Some reactions to life events, such as war zone exposure, meet the criteria for diagnosis based on *DSM-IV-TR* guidelines. But many of the signs and symptoms associated with stressful life events do not meet the diagnostic criteria set forth in the *DSM-IV-TR.*

Herman (1992) and Carlson (1997) have argued that broader criteria be used in assessing severe stress. They argued for consideration of what some call *traumatic stress,* which is characterized by subjective perception of experiences as negative, sudden, and uncontrollable and that result in a range of symptoms and responses. Similarly, Norris (1992) has posited that a traumatic event can be defined as any event that is perceived or experienced by the individual as shocking enough to produce symptoms of intrusion, numbing, and arousal. Researchers have found that people who develop traumatic stress reactions share three core elements of symptoms that may be expressed through a range of modalities (e.g., affective, cognitive, behavioral; Carlson, 1997). According to Carlson, the common elements are (1) intrusion or reexperiencing, (2) arousal, and (3) avoidance or numbing. In addition, people are likely to have associated responses, such as loss of self-worth, and problems in interpersonal relationships (Norris, 1992). Norris's definition is presumably broader and therefore more applicable to the types of experiences associated with racial discrimination and harassment.

As a stressor, racism can produce severe stress reactions that might not be captured by the narrow criteria for PTSD or Acute Stress Disorder as outlined in the *DSM,* but might be better captured by models of traumatic stress. Therefore, we briefly review the literature on PTSD in an effort to understand how people of Color exhibit symptoms of stress. Moreover, we highlight the limitations involved in relying solely on the *DSM* to understand the stress reactions produced by exposure to racial discrimination or harassment.

PTSD IN VETERANS AND GENERAL POPULATIONS

With the increased recognition of PTSD in various areas of life, researchers (e.g., Kulka et al., 1990a; Norris, 1992) have investigated the incidence and prevalence of lifetime PTSD, as well as the possibility that exposure (within one year) to potentially stressful life events for citizens and war veterans might produce PTSD symptoms. Kulka et al. reported the results from the National Vietnam Veterans Readjustment Survey (NVVRS) conducted by the National Center for PTSD that studied veterans who were exposed to war zone combat. The survey found that 21% of Black, 28% of Hispanic, and 14% of White veterans had diagnosable PTSD as well as other psychological symptoms. Similarly, studies of the lifetime rates of PTSD among the American Indian population found that 45% of Southwest American Indian veterans, 57% of Northern Plains Indian veterans, and 38% of Native Hawaiian veterans were diagnosed with PTSD (McNeil, Porter, Zvolensky, Chaney, & Kee, 2000; Robin, Chester, Rasmussen, Jaranson, & Goldman, 1997). Thus, a significant number of war veterans experience PTSD as well as other psychological symptoms as a result of exposure to stressful life events.

Norris's (1992) review of the literature found that estimates of lifetime PTSD in the general population ranged from 5% in noncombat situations to 15% for veterans. Norris cited studies that reported lifetime rates of PTSD at 1%, while others reported the lifetime prevalence of PTSD in the general population was 9%. However, most researchers in Norris's review found that after exposure to a potentially traumatic event, only a small portion (1% to 5%) of people develop PTSD.

One objective of studies of veterans and epidemiological studies of trauma among the general population was to determine whether the definition or classification of a traumatic event could go beyond that provided by *DSM* criteria. Norris (1992) and Breslau (2001) found that in a general population sample, there were racial differences in response to stressful life events, and that perceived stress from exposure was highest for Blacks in general, and for Black men in particular. Norris argued that conflicting findings point to the need for specifying the racial-cultural context in which stress occurs. Regarding trauma assessment, she found that victims needed to exhibit three or more symptoms of the *DSM* criteria C (i.e., "inability to recall an important aspect of the trauma, markedly diminished interest or participation in significant activities, feeling of detachment or estrangement from others, restricted range of affect") to meet the criteria for PTSD (American Psychiatric Association, 2000, p. 468). She also noted that if the criteria were altered by using two rather than three symptoms, the rates for PTSD would double.

Several studies have considered the racial-cultural context in which stress occurs. For example, Loo et al. (2001) measured three types of race-related stress in Asian

American veterans. They found that 37% of the 300 participants in the study met the criteria for a diagnosis of PTSD. Loo et al. determined that race-related stressors were stronger predictors of PTSD symptoms than exposure to combat, suggesting that personal experiences of racism were potent risk factors for PTSD. Among Hispanic veterans, Ruef, Litz, and Schlenger (2000) reported that 29% of Mexicans, 28% of Puerto Ricans, and 22% of other ethnic group members met the criteria for a diagnosis of PTSD. Likewise, Kulka et al. (1990b) reported that Black and Hispanic veterans experience higher levels of PTSD than White veterans.

Studies of the effects of life events on people of Color found that in a Southwestern Indian community, the prevalence of lifetime PTSD was 22%, a rate higher than in the general population (Robin et al., 1997). In a study of Plains Indian adolescents, 61% reported having witnessed a traumatic event or having had a direct traumatic experience (M. Jones, Dauphinais, Sack, & Somervell, 1997). Of the group that reported a stressful experience, 50% reported experiencing one to three PTSD symptoms, and 17% reported more than six symptoms of PTSD. Yet overall, only 3% of the total sample met the criteria for a diagnosis of PTSD. Perilla, Norris, and Lavizzio's (2002) study of a racially diverse sample after Hurricane Hugo found that, in general, participants of Color had three times the rate of PTSD symptoms (24%) than was found in a national sample (8%). African Americans and Latinos were found to be more distressed than Whites, Latinos were more distressed than African Americans, and Spanish-speaking Latinos were more distressed than English-speaking Latinos. In summary, the reviews of the PTSD and traumatic stress literature show that some people exposed to potentially stressful life events develop psychological symptoms. The general rate of developing PTSD after exposure to a potentially stressful life event was between 5% and 10%. People of Color experienced higher rates of PTSD after exposure to stressful life events and their symptoms were more severe, even when the criteria for PTSD were not met. In addition, veterans of Color had higher rates of PTSD and other psychological symptoms of distress not explained by the specific exposure to combat trauma. The current literature suggests that when the racial-cultural context in which stressful life events occur is considered, people of Color in general have higher rates of extreme stress reactions or PTSD symptoms. However, the literature fails to capture how stress reactions, or harm incurred when race is a stressor, may contribute to people of Color's susceptibility to higher levels of PTSD or severe stress reactions. In addition, the current criteria for PTSD fail to address personal experiences of racism as potent risk factors.

The high rates of severe stress experienced by people of Color may be explained by exposure to race-related events in the form of racism. Researchers suggested that although Whites have greater exposure to stressful life events, their social status seems to buffer the impact of the life events that might produce stress for them (Norris, 1992). Furthermore, researchers contended that people of Color are confronted with hostility, neglect, and racism that may heighten the effects of stressful life events (Breslau, 2001). Therefore, the PTSD and stressful life events literature provides indirect evidence that racism in the form of discrimination and harassment might be a stressor. More direct evidence of race-related stress comes from studies of people's experiences with racism and the resulting stress reactions they report.

RACISM AS A STRESSOR

Our contention that racial discrimination and harassment can be experienced as stressors that may lead to psychological and emotional reactions has been investigated by several researchers (Clark, Anderson, Clark, & Williams, 1999; Ocampo, 2000). They demonstrated that the psychological and emotional reactions or impacts of racial discrimination may be similar to the experience of psychological trauma and stress associated with physical or psychological abuse, emotional and verbal assault, or rape (Dunbar, 2001).

In a study of discrimination and health, Guyll, Matthews, and Bromberger (2001) found that for Black women, blatant discrimination was not related to any reaction, but subtle discrimination was related to higher cardiac activity. Clark et al. (1999) pointed out:

> There is a tendency to discount reports of racism simply because they involve a subjective component. Such a tendency to discount perceptions of racism as stressful is inconsistent with the stress literature, which highlights the importance of the appraisal process. (p. 810)

Clark et al. highlight that the subjective experience of an event as stressful is important in assessing the responses to stress. Moreover, they report that perceptions of an event as racist impact psychological stress responses to these situations and has mental health outcomes. Thus, the fact that a person perceives an event associated with racism as stressful qualifies racism as a stressor. Furthermore, researchers in laboratory and naturalistic settings (e.g., Feagin & Sikes, 1994; Feagin, Vera, & Batur, 2001; Janoff-Bulman & Frieze, 1983; Nazroo, 2003; Noh & Kaspar, 2003; Williams et al., 2003) have shown that people of Color report such racial incidents as distressful.

Sanders Thompson (1996) found that one-third of her participants, who were Black, reported an experience with racism within the prior six months. As a result of these experiences, respondents reported subjective distress, accompanied by intrusive thoughts and avoidance behavior. Other investigators (Kessler, Mickelson, & Williams, 1999; Williams et al., 2003) have reported that psychological distress, generalized anxiety, and major depression were associated with the stress of acute and chronic discrimination. Klonoff and Landrine (1999) studied Blacks' experiences and appraisals of stress associated with racist events. They found that 96% of the participants reported an experience of racial discrimination in the prior year that left them feeling stressed.

In addition, studies show that racism as a chronic stressor may lead to various physiological problems (e.g., higher blood pressure) in addition to psychological stress reactions (Clark et al., 1999). In spite of the fact that we know people may be harmed by racism, and that people of Color experience these events as stressful, there still seems to be inadequate information for mental health professionals to use in assessing how someone was affected by racism. Moreover, studies of racial discrimination have several limitations that make it difficult to generalize the results to the experiences of people of Color. These limitations include the following: (1) Most of the studies focused exclusively on African American populations and therefore there is limited information on other groups of Color; (2) many of the studies were conducted in laboratory settings, which limits their external validity; (3) in some cases, the evidence from the research was indirect (i.e., high rates of PTSD to life events); and (4) few studies drew directly from participant descriptions of their encounters with discrimination and the accompanying effects.

RESEARCH REPORT

The purpose of the present exploratory study was to discover the types of racial discrimination people of Color continue to experience. We then sought to understand the types of emotional and psychological reactions produced by experiences of racial discrimination. We wanted to determine whether the reports of the psychological and emotional experiences were better captured by Carlson's (1997) model of traumatic stress or the *DSM-IV-TR* (American Psychiatric Association, 2000) criteria for PTSD, Acute Stress Disorder, or Adjustment Disorder.

Participants

A total of 352 individuals participated in the study. Of the 352 individuals, 262 completed the study in its entirety. Of the 262 completed responses, 29 (11%) reported that they *had not* had an encounter with racial discrimination, and 233 (89%) indicated that they *had* experienced racial discrimination. Because our primary interest in this study was to understand the psychological and emotional impact of racial discrimination, the participants who indicated that they had not experienced racial discrimination were excluded from further analysis. Of the 233 who indicated that they had experienced discrimination, 72% ($n = 167$) were female and 27% ($n = 63$) were male. The age range of the participants was as follows: Fewer than 3% of the participants were younger than 20 years old ($n = 6$); the majority, 39%, ranged in age from 21 to 30 years old ($n = 91$); 24% were between 31 and 40 ($n = 55$); 15% were between 41 and 50 ($n = 34$); and 19% were older than 50 ($n = 45$). The majority of the participants, 120, were Black (51%); 42 were Hispanic/Latino (18%), 34 were Asian (15%), 22 were biracial (10%), and 13 identified themselves as other (6%). Regarding educational levels, most of the participants, 115, had a graduate degree (49%), 41 had some graduate education beyond college (18%), 43 had a college degree (18%), 28 had some college education (12%), and fewer than 6 had a high school diploma or some high school education (3%).

Measures

There were 11 demographic questions asking respondents to report their age, gender, race, ethnicity, socioeconomic status, religion, place of birth, occupation, years in job, and education level.

On another questionnaire, participants were asked the following about their experiences with racial discrimination: (1) Have you had an experience of racial discrimination? (2) Was it once or more often? (3) When did it happen? (4) Where did it happen? (5) What happened? (6) Were there any lasting effects?

Procedures

The Web-based research design employed a phenomenologically based qualitative approach intended to investigate participants' experiences of racial discrimination. Participants were solicited by sending e-mail announcements to list-serves of various organizations throughout the country. The announcement requested that the information about the study be passed on to others; this request was intended to create a snowball sampling effect. The announcement provided the potential participants with the Web address where the study could be accessed. The first page of the Web-based study included a consent form which informed participants of their rights as participants, including the right to withdraw from the study at any time. Once the subjects agreed to participate, they were directed to the demographics questions, followed by the experiences of racial discrimination questions, and finally a debriefing form, which included resources for those participants who wanted further assistance with their experiences.

Data Analysis: Development of Themes

From the completed responses, the first author derived categories that captured the essence of the participants' narrative reports. Using phenomenological content-based coding procedures (Creswell, 2003), categories were developed that captured both the existing literature and respondents' reported experiences. To understand the types of racial discrimination that the participants reported, the primary investigator derived 10 categories from the participants' responses to the question "What happened?" For the question about whether the participants experienced any lasting effects, the primary investigator derived nine categories in an effort to capture the psychological and emotional effects they reported.

The 10 categories (see Table 27.1 for definitions and examples of category statements) for types of racial discrimination were as follows: (1) Verbal Assault (i.e., called a name, racial slurs, stereotype used in conversation, subject to racial jokes, false accusations); (2) Denied Access or Service (e.g., ignored, made to wait, not allowed in, told had less ability); (3) Hostile Work Environment (e.g., low performance evaluations; demeaned, not promoted; lower pay); (4) Violated Racial Rules (e.g., did not belong); (5) Profiled (e.g., followed in store, accused or suspected of theft, stopped by police); (6) Treated on Basis of Stereotype (e.g., should step aside, pay more for goods, achievements denigrated, denied personal accomplishments); (7) Physical Assaults (e.g., spat on, beaten, intimidated by police); (8) Own Group Discrimination (i.e., experienced hostility due to skin color, looks, speech, behavior); (9) Multiple Experiences (e.g., many acts of discrimination and harassment); and (10) Other Event.

Table 27.1   Categories of Racial Discrimination Events

	Category	Definition	Sample Statements
1	Verbal Assault	Called a name, racial slurs, stereotype used in conversation, subject to racial jokes, false accusations.	"I was walking down the school hallway and a white boy said where you going nigger." "I was directly told that 'niggers don't live in this area.'"
2	Denied Access or Service	Ignored, made to wait, not allowed in, told had less ability, advised not to go to college, told did not have ability to progress.	"Was told on the phone property was available, but when showed up it had 'just' been rented." "The waitress wouldn't serve me and ignored me asking for service and continued to serve every White person entering instead." "I, along with a Caucasian female friend, was looking for apartments in one of the Midwest states. When we went to rental offices the apartment managers/office managers would only speak to my friend—even when I was asking the questions."
3	Hostile Work Environment	Low performance evaluations, demeaned (ability, performance, qualification), not promoted, lower pay.	"I have two master's degrees. I worked at a social service agency conducting research. My boss was a White male who had not earned a bachelor's degree. Although I did high-quality work, he unjustifiably criticized me and demeaned me by pointing his finger in my face. He also accused me of incompetence and of making underhanded attempts to undermine him." "Coworkers kept referring to my work with ethnic minority issues as not being important." "My boss and supervisor spoke to me in a belligerent and condescending manner. And, my work was never good enough for either one of them."
4	Violated Racial Rules	Did not belong (school/job/social), thought to be foreigner (could not speak English), cross-racial dating.	"Walking down the street, hand-in-hand, we were harassed by a group of Black people who were hanging out. They yelled 'Sell-out! Look at that sista with a White man!'" "It was assumed that because I was an African American female I would be unable to do undercover work in certain all-White neighborhoods."
5	Profiled	Followed in store, accused or suspected of theft, stopped by police, searched.	"Followed by store security, stopped by police, had my pockets emptied by a store patron who lost his wallet, only for his daughter to find it in his bag." "The attendant seemed extra cautious as myself and a group of friends walked into the clothing store."

456

6	Treated on Basis of Stereotype	Should step aside, pay more for goods, achievements denigrated, denied personal accomplishments (school/work/social), failed to recognize ability, question qualifications.	"One of my professors was impressed with one of my papers and ability to express myself so well in English and was amazed that I speak English well. I said I was born in the United States, she gave me a blank look and said, 'Really, with your accent I thought you had just moved here.' My grade was a C+." "Counselor told me I did not need to go to college. I should stay home and have babies like the rest of my people."
7	Physical Assault	Spat on, beaten, intimidated by police or other authority person, arrested and charges dropped.	"Went to an all-White school. Was slapped by a priest and called a 'spic' in front of the whole class." "I was the only African American in the class of 60 and I was selected by my peers as 'The One Most Likely to Succeed.' The mother of one of my peers followed me to the ladies room and spit on me, saying 'Who do you think you are? . . . just a Black nigger bitch.'" "I was pulled over and told it was a survey happening with every five cars and it wasn't every five cars, as I observed (the lot was full of, as society would say, minorities). Then I started to be searched and spoken to in a manner that showed the cop was a prejudiced man. I ended up being held there for about two hours for no apparent reason except to be humiliated."
8	Own Group Discrimination	Experienced hostility due to skin color, looks, speech, behavior, and so on.	"Because of my lighter complexion, other Black students would tease me and call me half-breed and not associate with me. They did not consider me Black." "I am half Puerto Rican and half Mexican. I grew up in Texas, where the Chicana/o/Latina/o population is predominantly Mexican. Because I was half Puerto Rican and do not look completely Mexican. . . . I was not accepted by the other Hispanics at my school."
9	Multiple Experiences	Multiple acts of discrimination and harassment.	"At jobs I've often been the sole African-American in a department. I've had Caucasians group together to tell me a racial joke. I've had coworkers talk about my hometown in degrading ways. I've had Black speech imitated. In stores, I've been followed around and watched. At some social events, I've been treated as though I wasn't welcome."
10	Other Event	Events not captured by any other category.	"Disproportionate number of Black faculty and staff to those of the student body." "There seemed to be high number of Asian Americans hired that year."

The nine categories (see Table 27.2 for definitions and sample statements) that were generated for psychological or emotional effects were as follows: (1) Extreme Emotional Distress (e.g., upset, multiple emotions); (2) Hypervigilance or Arousal (e.g., more aware, recognized reality of racism, self-conscious); (3) Mild Emotional Distress (e.g., single mild emotion); (4) Avoidance (e.g., stayed away, more distant); (5) Intrusion (e.g., recurring memories, nightmares); (6) Distrust (e.g., unwilling to have cross-race relationships, will not believe what people say, think most are ignorant, aware of true feelings); (7) Lower Self-Worth (e.g., doubt about choices, lower self-esteem, hurt my performance or ability, created confusion); (8) Positive Outcome (e.g., stronger, more determined); and (9) Other (i.e., effects not captured in other categories).

Coding Categories

From the categories derived by the primary investigator, two researchers independently coded each participant's responses into the two sets of categories. They calculated the percentage of agreement for the coding and found that during the first round of coding, there was 68% agreement for the racial discrimination categories and 60% agreement for psychological and emotional effect categories. After discussion and clarification of the categories, participants' responses were independently recoded and the percentage of agreement recalculated. The second round of coding resulted in 83% agreement for the racial discrimination categories and 68% agreement for psychological and emotional effect categories. The coders then discussed their disagreements for both sets of categories and found their discrepancies to be minor. They then reached a 100% agreement through a process of consensus.

Types of Discrimination Reported

The most frequently reported experiences of racial discrimination (presented in order of frequency) were: Multiple Experiences (18% of respondents), Hostility in the Work Environment (17%), Verbal Assaults (14%), Denied Access or Service (12%), and Profiled (12%). Following these were: Treated on the Basis of a Stereotype (9%), Violated Racial Rules (8%), Other Events (4%), Physical Assaults (2%), and Own Group Discrimination (1%).

Types of Discrimination by Racial Group

The frequency of the types of discrimination reported was examined by race (Table 27.3). Blacks accounted for the largest proportion of those reporting Hostile Work Environment (65%), Verbal Assault (40%), being Profiled (50%), being made aware that they had Violated Racial Rules (60%), being Denied Access or Service (66%), and being Treated Based on a Stereotype (48%). Latinos accounted for the highest proportion of those reporting Physical Assaults (40%). After Blacks, Latinos made up the second highest proportion of those reporting being Profiled (29%), Denied Access (14%), Violated Racial Rules (17%), and Treated Based on Stereotype (29%). After Blacks, Asians accounted for the second largest proportion of those reporting Hostile Work Environment (13%) and Verbal Assault (25%). Blacks, Asians, and biracial people reported Physical Assault with equal frequency (20%).

Table 27.2 Categories of Psychological or Emotional Effects

	Category	Definition	Sample Statements
1	Extreme Emotional Distress	Upset, multiple emotions (sadness, anger, depression), shock, rage, physically ill.	"Recurring feelings of rage, sadness, helplessness, getting a cold after an incident of discrimination, recurrent memories of incidents." "Psychological stress, shame, daily anxiety, embarrassment, anger, resentment. Feeling stuck. Most hurtful is career immobility. I feel I can handle 'accidental discrimination,' harassment incidents, e.g., people calling names 'jap, nip, chink,' on the street. But it is very difficult for me to experience this daily discrimination and mistreatment by this person."
2	Hypervigilance/ Arousal	More aware, recognized reality of racism, self-conscious.	"I feel as if I need to protect myself constantly from the stares, the subtle non-verbal cues, and overt language that I'm the perpetual foreigner, the exotic doll from South Pacific. You're on constant alert and seek more fervently the company of other POC." "Self-conscious in unfamiliar surroundings . . . particularly where I am the only black." "Me being hypervigilant when people talk about my ethnicity, and/or my abilities to speak Spanish. I always question why people assume I don't speak Spanish."
3	Mild Emotional Distress	Single mild emotion (disappointed, frustrated, anxious, resentful).	"Firstly, I felt violated, i.e., they had no right to say something like that. But then angry." "Felt betrayed, did not want to continue working for this firm, dedication to assignment was weakened." "I was pissed off."
4	Avoidance	Stayed away, more distant, withdrew, didn't go back, work to dispel negative beliefs, could not sleep, could not remember.	"I'm overall pretty disinterested in relationships with White people. I went to an all-Black college so that I could live without White people for a while." "Well, before this I had a respect for policemen, I would put aside what my peers said and have my own judgment, but then, after this I no longer did. I avoid them at all costs and I don't enter that part of Route . . . unless I necessarily have to."
5	Intrusion	Recurring memories, nightmares, dreams, cannot forget, could not concentrate.	"Distraction for weeks because I was afraid it would happen again. Isolation because it was clear I wasn't welcome." "I can still see that smile and hear those words."

(continued)

459

Table 27.2 (*Continued*)

	Category	Definition	Sample Statements
6	Distrust	Unwilling to have cross-race relationships, will not believe what people say, think most are ignorant, aware of true feelings.	"I have difficulty in trusting supervisors outside my race." "I am distrustful of making purchases as a Black woman, because people treat me so differently than my White friends." "Hesitant to make friends in school."
7	Lower Self-Worth	Doubt about choices, lower self-esteem, hurt my performance or ability, created confusion.	"I felt less secure and I lacked confidence in myself. It took me until graduate school to feel comfortable raising my hand in my classes. I didn't think I was intelligent." "A sense of inferiority, that I somehow deserved the treatment I received." "Self-doubt in my ability, always looking over my shoulder, decided to give up my director position and work as an ordinary nurse again."
8	Positive Outcome	Stronger, more determined.	"After this experience I grew stronger in the knowledge that I must ALWAYS surround myself with POSITIVE mentors, family and friends. I must surround myself with dream boosters, not dream killers." "I took that same paper, gave it to my advisor and asked her to proofread my paper. After reading it over, her words were, 'This is an A.' I didn't pursue anything because I managed to prove to the other professor that she was wrong." "I was determined to be the best in everything that interested me. I respond in a positive manner to negative 'stuff.'"
9	Other	Effects not captured in other categories.	"Eventually, my son developed friendships with some neighborhood children. Some of these friendships still exist. My wife and I, however, lived in that community for more than 20 years without developing nothing more than casual or superficial relationships with any of our neighbors."

Table 27.3 Frequency of Reports of Harassment and Discrimination by Race

Race	Harassment					Discrimination				
	HWE (%) $n = 40$	VA (%) $n = 32$	PRO (%) $n = 28$	VRR (%) $n = 18$	PA (%) $n = 5$	DAS (%) $n = 29$	STE (%) $n = 21$	OD (%) $n = 3$	ME (%) $n = 42$	OTH (%) $n = 10$
Black	65	40	50	60	20	66	66	NA	52	20
Latino	10	9	29	17	40	14	14	33	21	20
Asian	13	25	7	11	20	10	10	NA	17	10
Biracial	7	17	11	NA	20	7	7	33	9	10
Other	5	9	3	11	NA	NA	NA	33	NA	30

DAS = Denied Access or Service; HWE = Hostile Work Environment; ME = Muliple Events; OD = Own Group Discrimination; OTH = Other Events; PA = Physical Assault; PRO = Profiled; STE = Treated Based on Stereotype; VA = Verbal Assault; VRR = Violated Racial Rules.

Blacks and Asians did not report Own Group Discrimination. These findings suggest that there are some differences between racial group members in terms of their exposure to certain types of racism.

Types of Racism: Discrimination and Harassment

Based on Carter and Helms's (2002) definition of racial discrimination as aversive racism, and of racial harassment as hostile or dominative racism, Denied Access, Stereotyped, and Own Group Discrimination were categorized as examples of racial discrimination. Hostile Work Environment, Verbal Assaults, Profiled, Violated Racial Rules, and Physical Assaults were categorized as examples of racial harassment. Due to the complexity of the various events coded as Multiple Experiences or Other Events, these experiences could not be accurately defined as either discrimination or harassment and were therefore excluded from this portion of the analysis.

Our analysis of the types of racism reported by the respondents as a group revealed that 54% of the reported incidents were experiences of racial harassment, and 23% were experiences of racial discrimination.[1] Furthermore, of the four most frequently reported events (excluding Multiple Experiences), three were incidents of racial harassment. These findings suggest that across all races, experiences of racial harassment appear to be more frequent than experiences of racial discrimination.

Single or Repeated Events of Discrimination or Harassment

Our analysis indicated that across all types of discrimination and harassment, including Multiple Experiences and Other Events, the majority of respondents characterized the reported incidents as recurring events (64%), 34% of the respondents characterized the incidents as single events, and 2% did not specify the frequency of the events. Multiple Experiences, Hostile Work Environment, being Profiled, being Treated on the Basis of Stereotypes, Violated Racial Rules, Other Events, and Own Group Discrimination tended to be described more often as recurring events. Verbal and Physical Assaults and being Denied Access were described more frequently as single incidents. These findings suggest that when racial discrimination or harassment is experienced, it is more often than not a repeated event. Additionally, the findings indicate that experiences of racial harassment, in particular, were more frequently described as recurring events.

Location of Experiences of Discrimination

The type of discrimination and harassment the participants reported was found to vary by location. Overall, incidents of racial discrimination and harassment occurred most often at work (21%), in multiple locations (21%), and at school (19%). The sample reported incidents that occurred at social events (13%), in other locations (11%), in residential areas (8%), and in stores or shopping areas (7%) somewhat less frequently.

---

[1] The remaining 23% of reported incidents were either Multiple Experiences or Other Events.

In nearly all locations, incidents of harassment were reported more often than were incidents of discrimination. At work, in shopping areas, in residential areas, and at school, harassment was reported more frequently than discrimination. At work, 88% of the encounters reported were experiences of racial harassment, including Hostility (78%), Verbal Assault (6%), and Violated Racial Rules (2%). In contrast, 6% of the reported experiences at work were discrimination. In stores, 74% of the events reported were racial harassment, including Profiled (64%), Verbal Assaults (7%), and Violated Racial Rules (3%); 23% of reported experiences in stores were discrimination. In residential areas, 47% of the reported events were harassment, including Verbal Assaults (21%), Violated Racial Rules (16%), Physical Assaults (5%), and being Profiled (5%); 21% of the reported incidents were discrimination. At school, 43% of the events reported were incidents of harassment, including Verbal Assaults (18%), Violated Racial Rules (16%), Physical Assault (7%), and Hostility at work (3%); 34% of reported incidents were experiences of discrimination. At social events and in multiple settings, incidents of harassment and discrimination were reported with equal frequency: At social events, both were reported 47% of the time; in multiple settings, harassment and discrimination were reported 20% of the time each. In all cases, Multiple Experiences and Other Events accounted for the remaining percentage of reported events.

When the types of discrimination reported were analyzed by the settings in which they occurred, five out of the nine different types of discrimination occurred most frequently at school. Among these experiences were Verbal Assaults, Violated Racial Rules, Physical Assaults (harassment), and Own Group Discrimination and Stereotype (discrimination). In addition, when compared to the proportion reported across all locations (2%), Physical Assaults occurred three times more often at school (7%). The findings suggest that experiences of discrimination and harassment are quite common in organizational settings (work and school), with harassment accounting for a large proportion of these events.

Psychological and Emotional Effects of Racial Discrimination

Overall, 74% ($n = 173$) of respondents who reported incidents of racial discrimination had experienced psychological and emotional effects, 24% ($n = 55$) were not affected by their experiences, and 2% ($n = 5$) did not respond to this question. Across all types of discrimination reported, respondents who had experienced racial harassment were more likely to report experiencing lasting psychological and emotional effects (between 75% and 94%, depending on the particular event), whereas those who had experienced racial discrimination were generally less likely to report psychological and emotional effects (between 48% and 67%; Table 27.4).

We examined the frequencies for psychological and emotional effects in a number of ways. First, we analyzed reports of effects across all types of discrimination (or events). Across all events and all racial groups, Extreme Emotional Distress (EED; reported by 36% of respondents) was the most commonly reported psychological and emotional effect, followed by Mild Emotional Distress (MED; 16%) and Hypervigilance or Arousal (HYP; 15%). Lower Self-Worth (LSW), Avoidance

Table 27.4   Reports of Psychological and Emotional Effects (Yes or No) by Type of Discrimination or Harassment

		Harassment					Discrimination		
Effects	Overall $n = 233$	HWE (%) $n = 40$	VA (%) $n = 32$	PRO (%) $n = 28$	VRR (%) $n = 18$	PA (%) $n = 5$	DAS (%) $n = 29$	STE (%) $n = 21$	OD (%) $n = 3$
Yes	74	83	75	75	94	80	48	67	67
No	24	17	25	25	6	20	52	33	33

DAS = Denied Access or Service; HWE = Hostile Work Environment; OD = Own Group Discrimination; PA = Physical Assault; PRO = Profiled; STE = Treated Based on Stereotype; VA = Verbal Assault; VRR = Violated Racial Rules.

(AV), and Distrust (DIS) were reported with almost equal frequency, at 9%, 8%, and 8%, respectively. Positive Outcome (PO; 3%), Intrusion (INT; 2%), and Other (3%) were reported much less often.

Second, we analyzed the frequencies for psychological and emotional effects across all events by racial group (Table 27.5). Overall, when examined across all types of discrimination and harassment, Blacks and Latinos tended to report similar types of effects, and biracial people and Asians were more similar to one another. Blacks and Latinos tended to report Extreme Emotional Distress, followed by Hypervigilance. Blacks and Latinos differed in their third most frequently reported effects, with Blacks reporting Moderate Emotional Distress and Latinos reporting Lower Self-Worth. Among Asians, Moderate Emotional Distress was the second most commonly reported emotional effect. Biracial people reported Moderate Emotional Distress at the same rate that they reported Extreme Emotional Distress.

Although Extreme Emotional Distress was the most frequently reported effect for all racial groups, reports among Asians and Latinos were particularly high. For Asians, 56% of the effects they reported were Extreme Emotional Distress, and for

Table 27.5   Frequency of Reports of Emotional and Psychological Effects by Race

	Race				
Emotional Effects	Black (%) $n = 85$	Latino (%) $n = 35$	Asian (%) $n = 25$	Biracial (%) $n = 15$	Other (%) $n = 12$
EED	30	43	56	27	34
MED	15	3	28	27	17
HYP	18	20	4	13	8
LSW	7	14	8	7	8
AV	11	9	NA	7	8
DIS	9	6	NA	13	17
PO	3.3	3	4	NA	NA
INT	3.3	3	NA	NA	NA
OTH	3.3	NA	NA	7	8

AV = Avoidance; DIS = Distrust; EED = Extreme Emotional Distress; HYP = Hypervigilance; INT = Intrusion; LSW = Lower Self-Worth; MED = Moderate Emotional Distress; OTH = Other; PO = Positive Outcome.

Latinos the frequency was 43%. Blacks and biracial people reported Extreme Emotional Distress at rates of 30% and 27%, respectively. These findings suggest that there are variations in how members of different racial groups are affected by discrimination and harassment. While all racial groups experience Extreme Emotional Distress as a result of racial harassment and discrimination, Asians and Latinos may experience Extreme Emotional Distress with more frequency than other groups. Blacks and Latinos tend to experience more Hypervigilance, and Asians and biracial people tend to experience more Moderate Emotional Distress.

Third, we examined psychological and emotional effects as a function of the type of racial discrimination or harassment experienced (Table 27.6). For most types of racial discrimination and harassment, Extreme and Mild Emotional Distress were the most frequently reported effects. Exceptions were Violated Racial Rules (29% LSW, 24% EED), Denied Access or Service (36% HYP, 21% EED), and Own Group Discrimination (50% HYP, 50% AV).

Among cases of racial harassment, those who reported Verbal Assault and being Profiled tended to experience Moderate Emotional Distress and Extreme Emotional Distress at similar rates. The majority of those respondents who reported Hostile Work Environment and Physical Assault tended to report Extreme Emotional Distress (55% to 60%). Those who reported Violated Racial Rules tended to report experiencing Lower Self-Worth (29%) and Extreme Emotional Distress (24%) at similar rates. Among cases of racial discrimination, those who reported being Denied Access and Own Group Discrimination tended to experience Hypervigilance most frequently (36% and 50%). These findings suggest that targets of racial harassment may experience Extreme Emotional Distress more frequently than do targets of racial discrimination, and that Hypervigilance may be a more common response to racial discrimination.

Fourth, we examined differences in how racial group members experienced psychological and emotional effects as a function of the type of racial discrimination and harassment they reported. Of those respondents who reported Extreme Emotional Distress in a Hostile Work Environment, the majority were either Black (56%) or Asian (28%). Among those reporting psychological and emotional effects as a result of Verbal Assault, Asians were the most frequent reporters of Moderate (43%) and Extreme Emotional Distress (50%), and Blacks were the most frequent reporters of Hypervigilance (60%). Among those who reported emotional effects when made aware that they had Violated Racial Rules, only Blacks (80%) and Asians (20%) reported experiencing Lower Self-Worth.

Among those who reported being Profiled or Denied Access or Service, only Blacks and Latinos reported experiencing psychological and emotional effects. The most frequently reported effects for Denied Access were Hypervigilance (36%), Extreme Emotional Distress (21%), and Lower Self-Worth (14%). Those who reported being Profiled were most likely to experience Moderate Emotional Distress (24%), Extreme Emotional Distress (19%), Hypervigilance (19%), and Avoidance (19%). When Profiled, Blacks were three times more likely than Latinos to report experiencing Avoidance, and were the only ones to report Moderate Emotional Distress. Latinos who were Profiled were three times more likely than Blacks to report

Table 27.6 Frequency of Reports of Emotional and Psychological Effects by Type of Discrimination or Harassment

Emotional Effects	Overall $n=173$	Harassment					Discrimination				
		HWE (%) $n=33$	VA (%) $n=24$	PRO (%) $n=21$	VRR (%) $n=17$	PA (%) $n=4$	DAS (%) $n=14$	STE (%) $n=14$	OD (%) $n=2$	ME (%) $n=36$	OTH (%) $n=8$
EED	36	55	25	19	24	60	21	29	NA	50	25
MED	16	6	29	24	6	NA	7	21	NA	19	25
HYP	15	9	21	19	12	NA	36	14	50	11	NA
LSW	9	9	8	NA	29	NA	14	14	NA	6	NA
AV	8	9	8	19	6	40	NA	NA	50	8	NA
DIS	8	9	4	14	18	NA	7	7	NA	NA	25
PO	3	NA	NA	NA	NA	NA	7	14	NA	NA	12.5
INT	2	3	NA	NA	NA	NA	7	NA	NA	3	NA
OTH	3	NA	NA	5	6	NA	NA	NA	NA	3	12.5

Emotional and psychological effects: AV = Avoidance; DIS = Distrust; EED = Extreme Emotional Distress; HYP = Hypervigilance; INT = Intrusion; LSW = Lower Self-Worth; MED = Moderate Emotional Distress; OTH = Other; PO = Positive Outcome.
Type of event: DAS = Denied Access or Service; HWE = Hostile Work Environment; ME = Muliple Events; OD = Own Group Discrimination; OTH = Other; PA = Physical Assault; PRO = Profiled; STE = Treated Based on Stereotype; VA = Verbal Assault; VRR = Violated Racial Rules.

466

Hypervigilance. In contrast, Blacks who were Denied Access were four times more likely to report Hypervigilance than Latinos, and both groups were equally likely to report experiencing Lower Self-Worth. For both types of events, Blacks were between two and three times more likely than Latinos to experience Extreme Emotional Distress. Among those reporting Physical Assault, 75% reported experiencing Extreme Emotional Distress, and 25% reported Avoidance. Latinos accounted for 67% of those who reported Extreme Emotional Distress, with members of "other" racial groups accounting for the remaining 33%. All of those reporting Avoidance in response to experiences of Physical Abuse were Black.

These findings suggest that there are differences in the way that particular types of discrimination and harassment affect members of racial groups. Blacks and Asians tended to be more deeply psychologically and emotionally affected by incidents of Verbal Assault, Hostile Work Environment, Violated Racial Rules, and Treated Based on Stereotype. Blacks and Latinos were more likely to be targets of and to be psychologically and emotionally affected by being Denied Access and being Profiled, but they tended to experience Hypervigilance and Avoidance differently depending on the type of event. Finally, Latinos reported Physical Assaults at a greater rate than other groups and tended to be more deeply emotionally affected by these incidents than members of other racial groups.

Discussion

The primary objectives of the present study were to discover the types of racism people of Color continue to encounter and where those encounters take place, and to determine whether being a target of racism is associated with lasting emotional and psychological reactions. Additionally, we sought to determine whether the psychological and emotional reactions to experiences of racial discrimination and harassment are best captured by *DSM-IV-TR* criteria for PTSD or Acute Stress, or by Carlson's (1997) description of how to assess traumatic stress reactions. Our secondary objectives were to examine whether the types of experiences reported as well as the types of effects incurred differ by racial group members, whether the psychological and emotional effects differ by the type of racism encountered, and whether there are any differences between the incidence of racial discrimination and the incidence of harassment.

The overwhelming majority of our respondents (89%) indicated that they had an experience with racial discrimination. Of those who did encounter discrimination, approximately 75% reported some lasting emotional and psychological effect. Moreover, although African Americans have been historically the most visible target for overt and covert acts of racism, they were not the only racial group to report such experiences. We found that Latinos, Asians, and biracial people also reported experiences with racism.

For most of the participants, encounters with racial discrimination were not isolated events; rather, many encounters were recurring, thus potentially chronic experiences. It is also important to highlight that racial discrimination occurred in many aspects of the participants' lives, including work, school, and social situations as well as where they live and shop. Both racial discrimination and harassment seemed to occur more often, and with greater lasting psychological and emotional impact, at work and at school.

In most locations, with the exception of social events, racial harassment was reported more frequently than racial discrimination. This was particularly true in the work environment, where nearly 90% of the reported experiences were incidents of harassment. Similarly, racial harassment occurred more frequently than discrimination in residential and shopping areas and at school. Furthermore, physical assaults were reported more than twice as often at schools than in all other settings. These findings suggest that incidents of racial harassment and discrimination are in fact occurring quite frequently in institutional settings.

The results revealed differences between racial groups with respect to exposure to certain types of discrimination and harassment. We found that Blacks reported more workplace hostility, verbal assaults, violations of racial rules, and stereotyping and were profiled more often than the other racial groups. Latinos reported more physical attacks and experiences with being profiled and stereotyped than Asian or biracial groups, and Asians encountered more hostility at work and verbal attacks.

We also found variation in how members of different racial groups were affected by experiences of discrimination and harassment. Blacks and Latinos tended to report more similar effects, and Asians tended to be more similar to biracial people. Asians and Latinos tended to report Extreme Emotional Distress with greater frequency than other groups. Blacks and Latinos tended to be more likely to report Hypervigilance than other groups, and Asians and biracial people were more likely to report Mild Emotional Distress.

Across all racial groups, those who experienced harassment were more likely to report lasting emotional and psychological effects than were those who had experienced discrimination. In addition, Extreme Emotional Distress was most commonly associated with experiences of harassment, whereas those respondents exposed to discrimination tended to react with Hypervigilance. These results suggest that there may be a number of differences between experiences of racial harassment and experiences of racial discrimination, primarily with respect to the types of lasting emotional and psychological effects they elicit. These apparent differences support the contention that deconstructing the way that racism (i.e., racial discrimination) is presently defined could offer a more complex understanding of targets' emotional responses and experiences.

Overall, the results of this investigation supported our contention that people of Color continue to be subjected to experiences of racism, and that these incidents are experienced as stressors that might rise to the level of being traumatic. We found that, in general, nearly all of the emotional and psychological effects reported by respondents seemed to be consistent with Carlson's (1997) model of traumatic stress, and that a smaller proportion also fit the narrower criteria for PTSD or Acute Stress. Additionally, the results revealed that there are apparent differences between the types of experiences that constitute racial harassment and racial discrimination and that they result in different effects. This latter finding provided support for Carter and Helms's (2002) proposal to deconstruct and redefine racism into harassment and discrimination.

We think that the frequency with which the participants in this study reported extreme distress and other psychological and emotional reactions suggests that the lasting psychological and emotional effects associated with racial discrimination and harassment are both acute and chronic. Though it is clear the effects reported by the participants are experienced as traumatic, it remains uncertain whether those reported effects would be best captured by the *DSM-IV-TR* categories of PTSD or Acute Stress Disorder or Carlson's (1997) model of traumatic stress. In the next section, we examine the events and effects reported by the participants in the context of both the *DSM-IV-TR* and Carlson's model in an effort to determine which would be a more effective tool for assessing and diagnosing the impact of racial discrimination and harassment.

RACE-BASED TRAUMATIC STRESS: PSYCHOLOGICAL ISSUES

For the first time, the current edition of the *DSM-IV-TR* (American Psychiatric Association, 2000) makes reference to potential cultural factors that can influence the exhibition of symptoms. However, these factors are limited to a list of international cultural syndromes and confined to an appendix. In its current form, the *DSM-IV-TR* offers little guidance on how to understand the unique experiences of Americans of Color (i.e., African American, Latino, Asian, and Native Americans), which include but is not limited to the experience of being a target of racism. For instance, in the *DSM-IV-TR*'s list of the numerous psychosocial and environmental problems that are presented as potential causes of an Adjustment Disorder, there is no reference to racism (Scurfield & Mackey, 2001). Discrimination is mentioned once; however, its referent is not specified (i.e., national origin, religion, sex, or race; American Psychiatric Association, 2000, p. 31). Presumably, the experience of racism and its associated effects could potentially fall under the category of an Adjustment Disorder; however, the *DSM-IV-TR*'s lack of an adequate description of the race-based experiences increases the likelihood that clinicians using the manual will minimize or overlook the impact of race-related experiences.

Although it appears that race-based stress may share some of the symptoms of PTSD and Acute Stress Disorder as outlined in the *DSM-IV-TR,* such as hypervigilance and avoidance, overall the etiologies and symptom manifestations are incongruent. In regard to etiology, the main area of difference lies in the types of experiences that qualify as having the potential to illicit the symptoms of PTSD. The *DSM-IV-TR* criterion A for PTSD and Acute Stress Disorder explicitly states, "The person experienced, witnessed, or was confronted with an event or events that involved actual or threatened death or serious injury, or a threat to the physical integrity of self or others" (American Psychiatric Association, 2000, p. 467). If we consider the experiences reported by the participants in this study, only those who reported being targets of an actual or threatened physical assault could be considered for the diagnosis of PTSD or Acute Stress Disorder, regardless of whether the resulting symptom manifestation was congruent. It is important to note that the vast majority (98%) of the participants did not experience an actual or threatened physical assault. In contrast, Carlson's (1997) model for traumatic stress posits that for an experience to qualify as having the potential to produce a traumatic stress reaction it needs to have been perceived as negative, to have been sudden in its occurrence, and to have been uncontrollable by the target. The participants in our study perceived their experiences of discrimination and harassment as extremely negative and out of their control, and from their descriptions we surmised that they were experienced as sudden. Additionally, racial discrimination and harassment may be experienced indirectly or by use of symbols or coded language (Feagin & McKinney, 2003), which Carlson's model considers a legitimate experience to produce traumatic stress reactions. Using the rubric of Carlson's model, each type of racial discrimination and harassment reported by the participants qualifies as having the potential to produce a traumatic stress reaction.

As noted, the symptom manifestations of PTSD and Acute Stress Disorder and race-based stress overlap in regard to the reexperiencing, avoidance of stimuli associated with the trauma, and increased arousal or vigilance. However, the criteria for PTSD and Acute Stress Disorder have strict rules regarding the number of symptoms in each category that clients need to exhibit before they qualify to meet the criteria for the diagnosis. Again, there is a danger that the use of these strict criteria will result in the minimization of the impact of racial discrimination or harassment on targets simply because they failed to manifest a specific number of symptoms. Additionally, the criteria for the diagnoses do not take into consideration the client's subjective appraisal of the traumatic experience, which research demonstrates has a significant impact on the resulting effects.

In addition to these trepidations about the usefulness of the *DSM-IV-TR* (American Psychiatric Association, 2000) for assessing the impact of racial discrimination or harassment, we are concerned about labeling the effects of racial discrimination or harassment a disorder (Carter, 2004). Even in the event that an individual's experience of racial discrimination or harassment and resulting effects were congruent with the etiology and symptom manifestation of PTSD or Acute Stress Disorder, we do not believe that it is necessarily helpful to locate the problem within the individual. Locating the problem of racism within the targets could lead to treatment strategies that focus exclusively on the person's symptoms, while ignoring his or her lived situational reality of racism, which in fact exists outside of the person. The notion of a disorder can encourage clinicians to make dispositional attributions, which, in the case of the effects of racial discrimination and harassment, is essentially labeling racism as a people of Color problem. We concur with Dobbins and Skillings (this *Handbook,* this volume), who contend that racism is not a problem created by people of Color, rather it was created and enacted by White people and White-identified people of Color. Their distinction accurately locates the cause of the effects of racial discrimination and harassment in the person's environment, thereby lessening the chances that individuals seeking help will blame themselves.

Some clinical scholars have proposed that the *DSM-IV-TR* include what can be considered a nonpathological diagnostic category (e.g., Turner, Lukoff, Barnhouse, & Lu, 1995). Currently, these scholars have limited their conceptualizations of this category to religious and spiritual problems. However, if it was expanded to consider the types of experiences reported by the participants in this study, the category could prove to be useful, as it may solve the problems inherent in conceptualizing the effects of racial discrimination and harassment as a disorder, which implies pathology. However, the combination of the aforementioned problems regarding the use of the current *DSM-IV-TR* as a diagnostic tool for categorizing the effect of racism (i.e., racial discrimination and harassment) renders Carlson's (1997) model potentially more useful. As noted, the way Carlson's model defines what constitutes a traumatic event is more congruent with the descriptions of racial discrimination and harassment offered by the participants in this study. Based on Carlson's model, most of the lasting emotional and psychological effects reported by this sample, with the exception of Positive Outcome, Mild distress, and Other, would qualify as symptoms of traumatic stress reactions. This suggests that racism is indeed experienced as a stressor. Additionally, Carlson's model takes into consideration the person-environment interaction in the production of psychological distress to a greater extent than do the diagnostic categories of the *DSM-IV-TR,* which tend to locate the cause of the problem within the person. We, therefore, suggest that rather than attempting to use the *DSM-IV-TR* to diagnose the psychological and emotional effects of racism (i.e., racial discrimination and harassment), it might be more accurate to borrow the conceptual frame of Carlson's model and consider the effects reported by these participants as manifestations of what we would call *race-based traumatic stress.*

CLINICAL IMPLICATIONS

As discussed previously, it is important to distinguish between the two forms of treatment that derive from racism and contribute to hostile racial environments, discrimination and harassment. Our study suggests that both lead to psychological distress. Discrimination as "aversive racism" operates to maintain distance from the undesirable group members. Thus, racial discrimination helps dominant racial group members engage in racism without overtly appearing to do so; consequently, it is difficult to detect because other feasible reasons can be used to explain people's behavior. Racial harassment or "dominative or hostile racism" as we have defined it is the mechanism used to communicate one's subordinate or inferior status due to one's race or nondominant group membership (Kovel, 1970). These messages may be communicated in hostile work settings as messages about violations of racial rules, or as behavior that is based on stereotypes or by being profiled.

The utility of distinguishing between racial discrimination and harassment was supported by our findings, in that the two types of experiences resulted in different types of lasting emotional effects. According to the participants' self-reports, racial harassment results in more severe and longer-lasting psychological and emotional effects than does racial discrimination. The relationship between racial harassment and emotional reactions was not examined directly, so it must be viewed with caution. However, the frequency with which participants reported extreme emotional distress in response to racial harassment highlights the importance of conducting future research, which should employ qualitative and quantitative methods to determine whether or not our observation is accurate.

As noted, the study found that a large portion of our sample attributed their experiences of lasting psychological and emotional distress to experience/s of racism in the form of racial discrimination and racial harassment. However, a portion of the participants indicated that even though they had experienced racial harassment or discrimination, they denied that it had lasting impact on them. Similarly, another group of participants denied ever having an experience of racial discrimination or harassment. These findings indicate that some people of Color are spared the indignity of racism. Another possibility is that the psychological distress that a person of Color thinks is happening because of personal issues or other factors might actually be unrecognized race-based stress induced by racial discrimination or harassment. Because racism has become so subtle, chronic, and pervasive, people may fail to attribute their distress to race-related experiences. Additionally, the error in their attribution as to what caused their distress may be made in an effort to cope with the ongoing experience of racism in their lives.

Our findings support the importance of not treating members of any racial group as monolithic or psychologically similar simply because they are members of the same racial group (Carter & Gesmer, 1997; Thompson & Carter, 1997). The results of this study indicated that despite the fact that we may believe that all people of Color are exposed to some form of racism by virtue of having lived in this country, 11% of the participants denied having an experience of discrimination. Similarly, participants from the same racial group did not experience identical psychological and emotional effects even when exposed to some type of discrimination or harassment. As our results demonstrate, not all Black participants responded in the same way to a hostile work environment and not all Latinos reacted uniformly to physical assaults. One way to understand the within-group variation is to consider the impact of racial identity (i.e., an individual's psychological orientation to his or her racial group membership) on the perception of racist events. In their studies examining perceptions of incidents of racial discrimination and of institutional racism, Watts and Carter (1991) and Sellers and Shelton (2003) have found that Black people's perception of discrimination varied as a function of their racial identity. Thus, it is important to consider the racial identity status of the target in an assessment of racial trauma or race-based traumatic stress. Similarly, according to Helms's (1990) White racial identity theory, the racial identity ego statuses of Whites involved in mental health service provision or those seeking help should be considered as they are likely to influence the degree to which Whites will consider racism as a potential stressor for himself or herself or others. White service providers who have not developed a mature racial identity ego status will be limited in their capacity to understand, much less accurately assess, race-based traumatic stress (Carter, 1995; Carter, Helms, & Juby, 2003).

STUDY LIMITATIONS

As with any research, our study has several limitations that must be considered. First, because the study was descriptive or qualitative in nature, the results do not establish that a causal relationship exists between the reported incidents of racial discrimination and harassment and psychological/emotional effects. Similarly, the data collected from participants were entirely self-report as well as retrospective, and therefore are potentially subject to personal biases and distortions. The sample size was small for some of the racial groups (e.g., biracial and Asians), so it is especially important to be cautious in generalizing the findings for those groups. Another factor was that the respondents tended to be well educated, and thus the types and frequencies of the experiences and psychological effects they reported may not be similar in a sample of people of Color with less education. Because the study was Web-based, we had no control over who participated or over the quality of the information provided. Therefore, our findings should be replicated with more diverse samples using direct data collection methods.

Nevertheless, there are a few indications that our findings, with the limitations noted, may reveal important information about the respondents' encounters with racism and the effects of those experiences. First, a recently published study comparing Web-based research with traditional methods of data collection found that several concerns regarding Web-based studies were unfounded (see Gosling, Vazire, Srivastava, & John, 2004). Second, our findings seem to be consistent with previously published investigations of PTSD in the general population as well as studies examining the impact of racial discrimination. Third, we think that the Web-based approach to data collection allows for a certain degree of anonymity not available in direct data collection and therefore might free people to share their experiences with more comfort and ease. Thus, despite the aforementioned limitations, we have confidence that the findings of our study serve to advance our knowledge about racism and its effects.

CONCLUSION

We have presented a new paradigm for understanding race-based traumatic stress that involves unpacking racism and distinguishing between racial discrimination and harassment. The results of our exploratory investigation support the contention of numerous scholars who claim that racial discrimination and harassment can result in race-related stress reactions (Sanders Thompson, 1996; Utsey, Chae, Brown, & Kelly, 2002). Our findings suggest that clear and consistent definitions of racial discrimination and harassment can improve our understanding of the impact of racism on people's lives. Separating racial harassment from racial discrimination appears to have been a crucial distinction, because racial harassment, according to our study, seems to have resulted in more severe lasting psychological and emotional reactions than did discrimination. We hope this understanding will increase the effectiveness of both legal and psychological services designed to assist people suffering from the results of such experiences. Additionally, the findings support the need for clear policies and procedures for filing complaints of racial harassment and discrimination in organizations and institutions.

Given the frequency with which the participants reported experiences of racial discrimination and harassment across numerous settings, it would serve mental health professionals to recognize the reality of the effects of race-based stress in their assessment of clients. This reality includes the possibility that experiences of racial discrimination and harassment are sufficient to result in severe psychological and emotional distress, and that they may compound the stress experienced in other areas of one's life. Because the effects of race-based traumatic stress appear to fall outside of our current systems of assessment and diagnosis, scholars need to develop assessment strategies, diagnostic criteria, and treatment models that are specifically designed to assess and assist people in coping with the effects of race-based traumatic stress. To more adequately understand race-based traumatic stress, it is necessary to employ a system-focused perspective that considers the person in a racial-cultural and historical context that is interactive and mutually influencing. At the same time, we should not ignore the psychological variability in how individuals can identify with their race. Considering that there is considerable effort in our society to deny the presence of racism, to keep its targets silent, and to ignore its effects, we believe that the results of this investigation demonstrate that it is imperative that the psychological and emotional experience of racism no longer be overlooked or minimized.

REFERENCES

American Psychiatric Association. (2000). *Diagnostic and statistical manual of mental disorders* (4th ed., text rev.). Washington, DC: Author.

Breslau, N. (2001). The epidemiology of posttraumatic stress disorder: What is the extent of the problem? *Journal of Clinical Psychiatry, 62*(17), 16–22.

Carlson, E. B. (1997). *Trauma assessments: Clinician's guide.* New York: Guilford Press.

Carter, R. T. (1995). *The influence of race and racial identity: Toward a racially inclusive model.* New York: Wiley.

Carter, R. T. (2004, February). Does racism cause psychological and emotional injury? Paper presented at the annual Winter Roundtable Conference on Cultural Psychology and Education. Helms lecture. Teachers College University, New York, NY.

Carter, R. T., & Gesmer, E. (1997). Applying racial identity theory to the legal system: A case of family law. In C. Thompson & R. T. Carter (Eds.), *Racial identity theory: Applications to individual, group, and organizational interventions* (pp. 219–236). Mahwah, NJ: Erlbaum.

Carter, R. T., & Helms, J. E. (2002, September). *Racial discrimination and harassment: A race based traumatic stress disorder.* Paper presented at the American College of Forensic Examiners Conference, Orlando, FL.

Carter, R. T., Helms, J. E., & Juby, H. (2003). The relationship between racism and racial identity profiles. *Journal of Multicultural Counseling and Development, 30,* 19–29.

Clark, R., Anderson, N., Clark, V., & Williams, D. (1999). Racism as a stressor for African Americans: A bio-psychosocial model. *American Psychologist, 54,* 805–816.

Creswell, J. W. (2003). *Qualitative inquiry and research design: Choosing among five traditions.* Thousand Oaks, CA: Sage.

Darity, W. A. (2003). Employment discrimination, segregation, and health. *American Journal of Public Health, 93*(2), 226–231.

Dobbins, J. E., & Skillings, J. H. (this volume). White racism and mental health: Treating the individual racist. In R. T. Carter (Ed.), *Handbook of racial-cultural counseling and psychology: Training and practice.* New York: Wiley.

Dunbar, E. (2001). Counseling practices to ameliorate the effects on discrimination and hate events: Toward a systematic approach to assessment and intervention. *Counseling Psychologist, 29*, 279–307.

Feagin, J. R., & McKinney, K. D. (2003). *The many costs of racism*. Lanham, MD: Rowman & Littlefield.

Feagin, J. R., & Sikes, M. P. (1994). *Living with racism: The Black middle-class experience*. Boston: Beacon Press.

Feagin, J. R., Vera, H., & Batur, P. (2001). *White racism* (2nd ed.). New York: Routledge Press.

Gosling, S. D., Vazire, S., Srivastava, S., & John, O. P. (2004). Should we trust web-based studies? A comparative analysis of six preconceptions about internet questionnaires. *American Psychologist, 59*(2), 93–104.

Greenhouse, S. (2003). Clothing chain accused of discrimination. *New York Times* (June 17).

Guyll, M., Matthews, K. A., & Bromberger, J. T. (2001). Discrimination and unfair treatment: Relationship to cardiovascular reactivity among African American and European American women. *Health Psychology, 20*(5), 315–325.

Helms, J. E. (Ed.). (1990). *Black and White racial identity: Theory, research, and practice*. Westport, CT: Greenwood.

Herman, J. H. (1992). *Trauma and recovery*. New York: Basic Books.

Janoff-Bulman, R., & Frieze, I. H. (1983). A theoretical perspective for understanding reactions to victimization. *Journal of Social Issues, 39*, 1–17.

Jaynes, G. D., & Williams, R. M. (1989). *A common destiny: Blacks and American society*. Washington, DC: National Academy Press.

Jones, J. M. (1997). *Prejudice and racism* (2nd ed.). New York: McGraw-Hill.

Jones, M. C., Dauphinais, P., Sack, W. H., & Somervell, P. D. (1997). Trauma-related symptomology among American Indian adolescents. *Journal of Traumatic Stress, 10*(2), 163–173.

Kessler, R. C., Mickelson, K. D., & Williams, D. R. (1999). The prevalence, distribution, and mental health correlates of perceived discrimination in the United States. *Journal of Health and Social Behavior, 40*, 208–230.

Klonoff, E., & Landrine, H. (1999). Cross validation of the schedule of racist events. *Journal of Black Psychology, 25*, 231–254.

Kovel, J. (1970). *White racism: A psychohistory*. New York: Pantheon Books.

Kulka, R. A., Schlenger, W. E., Fairbank, J. A., Hough, R. L., Jordan, B. K., Marmar, C. R., et al. (1990a). *The national Vietnam veterans readjustment study: Tables of findings and technical appendices*. New York: Brunner/Mazel.

Kulka, R. A., Schlenger, W. E., Fairbank, J. A., Hough, R. L., Jordan, B. K., Marmar, C. R., et al. (1990b). Trauma and the Vietnam War generation. Report of findings from the National Vietnam Veterans Readjustment Study. New York: Brunner/Mazel.

Loo, C. M., Fairbank, J. A., Scurfield, R. M., Ruch, L. O., King, D. W., Adams, L. J., et al. (2001). Measuring exposure of racism: Development and validation of a race-related stressor scale (RRSS) or Asian American Vietnam veterans. *Psychological Assessment, 13*(4), 503–520.

McNeil, D. W., Porter, C. A., Zvolensky, M. L., Chaney, J. M., & Kee, M. (2000). Assessment of culturally related anxiety in American Indians and Alaska natives. *Behavior Therapy, 31*, 301–325.

Nazroo, J. Y. (2003). The structure of ethnic inequalities in health: Economic position, racial discrimination, and racism. *American Journal of Public Health, 93*(2), 222–284.

Noh, S., & Kaspar, V. (2003). Perceived discrimination and depression: Moderating effects of coping, acculturation, and ethnic support. *American Journal of Public Health, 93*(2), 232–238.

Norris, F. H. (1992). Epidemiology of trauma frequency and impact of different potentially traumatic events on different demographic groups. *Journal of Consulting and Clinical Psychology, 60*(3), 409–418.

Ocampo, C. (2000). Psychophysiology and racism. *American Psychologist, 55,* 1164–1165.

Perilla, J. L., Norris, F. H., & Lavizzio, E. A. (2002). Ethnicity, culture, and disaster response: Identifying and explaining ethnic differences in PTSD six months after hurricane Andrew. *Journal of Social and Clinical Psychology, 21*(1), 20–45.

Prichard, O. (2003). *Why a local hospital gave in to a racist demand.* Retrieved March 17, 2004, from http://www.philly.com/mld/inquirer/news/local/6919504.htm.

Robin, R. W., Chester, B., Rasmussen, J. K., Jaranson, J. M., & Goldman, D. (1997). Prevalence and characteristics of trauma and posttraumatic stress disorder in a southwestern American Indian community. *American Journal of Psychiatry, 154*(11), 1582–1588.

Ruef, A. M., Litz, B. T., & Schlenger, W. E. (2000). Hispanic ethnicity and risk for combat-related posttraumatic stress disorder. *Cultural Diversity and Ethnic Minority Psychology, 6*(3), 235–251.

Sanders Thompson, V. L. (1996). Perceived experiences of racism as stressful life events. *Community Mental Health Journal, 32,* 223–233.

Scurfield, R. M., & Mackey, D. W. (2001). Racism, trauma and positive aspects of exposure to race-related experiences: Assessment and treatment implications. *Journal of Ethnic and Cultural Diversity in Social Work, 10*(1), 23–47.

Sellers, R. M., & Shelton, N. J. (2003). The role of racial identity in perceived racial discrimination. *Journal of Personality and Social Psychology, 84*(5), 1079–1092.

Thompson, C. E., & Carter, R. T. (1997). *Racial identity theory: Applications to individual, group, and organizational interventions.* Mahwah, NJ: Erlbaum.

Turner, R. P., Lukoff, D., Barnhouse, R. T., & Lu, F. G. (1995). Religious or spiritual problem: A culturally sensitive diagnostic category in the *DSM-IV. Journal of Nervous and Mental Diseases, 183*(7), 435–444.

U.S. Equal Employment Opportunity Commission. *Race-based charges: FY 1992-FY 2003.* Retrieved March 18, 2004, from http://www.eeoc.gov/stats.race.html.

U.S. Equal Employment Opportunity Commission. *Race/color discrimination.* Retrieved March 18, 2004, from http://www.eeoc.gov/stats.race.html.

Utsey, S. O., Chae, M. H., Brown, C. F., & Kelly, D. (2002). Effect of ethnic group membership on ethnic identity, race-related stress, and quality of life. *Cultural Diversity and Ethnic Minority Psychology, 8*(4), 366–377.

Watts, R. J., & Carter, R. T. (1991). Psychological aspects of racism in organizations. *Group and Organization Studies, 16*(3), 328–344.

Williams, D. R., Neighbors, H. W., & Jackson, J. S. (2003). Racial/ethnic discrimination and health: Findings from community studies. *American Journal of Public Health, 93*(2), 200–208.

CHAPTER 28

Enhancing Therapeutic Interventions with People of Color: Integrating Outreach, Advocacy, and Prevention

Elizabeth M. Vera, Larisa Buhin, Gloria Montgomery, and Richard Shin

The effective delivery of psychological services to racial and ethnic people has been an increasing priority of the field of psychology over the past decade (Atkinson, Morten, & Sue, 1993; Atkinson, Thompson, & Grant, 1993; Fouad & Brown, 2000; Sue & Sue, 1999, 2003). While the literature on service delivery to people of Color is continuously evolving, there is a general consensus that effective interventions with such populations requires efforts beyond the status quo of traditional therapy models. For example, the multicultural counseling competencies (Sue, Arredondo, & McDavis, 1997; Sue & Torino, this *Handbook,* this volume) represent the culmination of various recommendations on how counseling professionals can be more effective (e.g., through knowledge, beliefs, and skills) with clients of Color.

In addition to having knowledge, beliefs, and skills, it is important for counselors to be flexible with their professional roles in order to be culturally responsive to their clients (Arredondo, this *Handbook,* this volume; Atkinson, Morten et al., 1993; Lewis, Lewis, Daniels, & D'Andrea, 1998; Vera & Speight, 2003). Koss-Chioino and Vargas (1992) argued that cultural responsiveness requires mental health professionals to do more than be "sensitive" to cultural diversity: It requires us to assess the cultural variables of the client (e.g., race, ethnicity, socioeconomic factors) and provide services that are appropriate to the needs of that individual. Often, when our clients are members of historically underserved racial and ethnic groups, it may be necessary to enhance our therapeutic efforts with services that assist the client outside of the context of therapy. For example, if a client resides in a community where there is exposure to environmental dangers such as community violence or drug problems, it may be necessary to treat not just the problem that brings the individual to counseling, but also to anticipate psychological issues that may arise in the future. As such, a counselor might engage in preventive interventions for not only the client, but for his or her immediate family as well. Alternatively, a racial and/or ethnic client may be involved in relationships with other systems such as a school or legal system. Often, bureaucratic problems prevent clients from successfully maneuvering through or benefiting from such systems. When systemic problems affect the mental health of our clients, it may be appropriate that we engage in some form of advocacy that facilitates their interactions with relevant organizations or systems. Finally, many racial and ethnic families live in communities that are vastly under-resourced when it comes to the services of physicians and mental health professionals (Evans, Delphin, Simmons, Omar, & Tebes, this *Handbook,* this volume). To reach members of the community who may be in the most need of our services, we may engage in outreach services that allow us to maximize our visibility in the community. This chapter outlines the ways psychologists and other mental health specialists can integrate outreach, advocacy, and prevention into their therapeutic work with culturally diverse clients.

EXISTING MODELS

Atkinson and his colleagues (Atkinson, Thompson, et al., 1993) proposed a three-dimensional model that articulates ways we can enhance our practice with racial and ethnic clients via role flexibility. The three dimensions of the model are locus of problem etiology, levels of client acculturation, and goals of counseling. A consideration of the three factors determines in what capacity a counselor can best respond to a client. For example, if an acculturated client were suffering from a sleep disorder, traditional therapy in a traditional counseling setting (e.g., a hospital, clinic) might be appropriate. Relaxation techniques or medication might bring the client symptom relief. However, if a recent immigrant client was illegally fired from her job, a counselor's response might be very different. In this case, the client may be trying to avoid a financial crisis that would leave her and her children homeless. As such, the counselor might be of most help by helping the client activate services that provide emergency aid and by identifying free legal assistance to protect the client's rights.

According to the three-dimensional model (Atkinson, Thompson, et al., 1993), a counselor adjusts his or her role to the needs of the client. In essence, the planes and intersections of the three dimensions create eight major roles for counselors working with culturally diverse clients: advisor, advocate, self-help group facilitator, facilitator of indigenous support and healing systems, consultant, change agent, counselor, and psychotherapist (Chen, this *Handbook,* this volume; Thomas, this *Handbook,* this volume). Because of our training, most mental health professionals are familiar with the last two roles. However, all of the roles embrace the traditional emphases of counseling as envisioned by Krumboltz (1966): facilitating clients' decision-making processes, prevention, and remediation of problems.

Lewis et al. (1998) presented another model of service delivery that outlines ways counselors can enhance the lives of their clients. They emphasize many of the direct client service roles outlined in Atkinson, Thompson, et al.'s (1993) model (counselor, outreach) and identify indirect client service roles such as consulting and working to influence public policy. Lewis et al. describe other roles that are targeted at the community in general rather than a particular client. These roles include advocate, psychoeducator, and collaborating with community leaders (e.g., ministers, folk healers) (Thomas, this *Handbook,* this volume). The needs of the client determine which services are utilized and, consequently, which roles are most beneficial. Several of these roles (facilitator of indigenous support, consultant, advocate) require professionals to be familiar with and active in the communities in which their clients reside (D. Sue & Torino, this *Handbook,* this volume). However, many counselors may not be accustomed to establishing community ties. Therefore, we focus on the process of engaging in outreach in the next section.

OUTREACH

Outreach can be broadly defined as a larger-scale, direct service approach to psychological service provision that takes place in the context of a community designed to address an existing or anticipated obstacle to psychological growth and well-being (Ibrahim & Cameron, this *Handbook,* Volume One; Lewis et al., 1998). As the word implies, outreach work requires professionals to leave the confines of an office, hospital, or agency environment and make contacts with clients in their natural environment. The kinds of contacts made via outreach can vary. In some cases, they involve developing traditional therapeutic relationships. Home-based therapy is one example of outreach utilized when transportation or session attendance may be problematic. Aside from being more convenient for clients, home-based therapy can be useful when the counselor wants to observe how clients interact in their home setting. However, home-based therapy is often initiated after a client has been referred to a counseling agency. In many cases, clients never find their way to a counselor's office, even if the need for counseling exists. This can happen for a variety of reasons, both cultural and pragmatic.

For example, in some racial and ethnic communities, seeking therapy is perceived as an admission of weakness or a violation of cultural norms regarding seeking help from "outsiders." Problems may be addressed more informally (e.g., within the family, through prayer) or by seeking advice from culturally sanctioned individuals (e.g., talking with a minister or folk healer; Broman, 1987; Taylor, Hardison, & Chatters, 1996). Other reasons such clients, particularly recent immigrants, may not patronize counseling agencies are lack of awareness of available services and distrust of the community mental health center, hospital, or university. In some cases, counseling agencies may not be accessible to clients. Inaccessibility may be geographic, as is the case in many impoverished neighborhoods where basic health care services are not present. Inaccessibility may also be due to institutional barriers. Counseling services may not be culturally "user-friendly," especially to racial and ethnic groups for whom English is a second language (or English is not spoken) (Faubert & Locke, this *Handbook,* this volume).

Culturally responsive professionals must use all available resources to seek out individuals from racial/ethnic groups who may not be aware of the services that are available to them. For instance, an early study conducted by Szapocznik, Lasaga, Perry, and Solomon (1979) found that the use of mass media was a highly effective method for engaging Hispanic elders in need of mental health services into treatment. Once clients are connected to services, one cannot assume that clients are not motivated for treatment simply because they miss an appointment or are reluctant to commit to a specific time that is convenient for the counselor (D. Sue & Torino, this *Handbook,* this volume. Gottheil, Sterling, and Weinstein (1997) evaluated the efficacy of an outreach strategy designed to engage a group of predominantly

African American outpatients who did not keep their initial treatment appointment. In an effort to engage clients in treatment, the investigators simply contacted the prospective clients via telephone to reschedule their appointments. The researchers found that a significant number of the individuals they contacted attended their rescheduled intake session.

In addition to being more proactive about basic outreach activities, such as making follow-up calls and rescheduling appointments, counselors may also design more comprehensive community outreach programs. To reach out to underserved communities, three essential steps must be followed: relationship building, collaborative efforts, and needs assessment (Lerner, 1995). While relationship building is the starting point for any psychological work, the relationships made through outreach often are established via collaboration and needs assessment. The three components of outreach work are equally important to the design of an intervention, its implementation, and evaluation. When professionals initially attempt to offer services (e.g., a parenting workshop, facilitation of support groups), it is critical to affiliate with a trusted member (e.g., a minister, school principal, or community activist) or credible establishment in the community (e.g., a church, school, community recreation center). As outsiders, we often have to work very hard to establish our credibility in the community in ways that differ from traditional counseling work (Ibrahim & Cameron, this *Handbook,* Volume One).

Members of the majority culture and universities are typically strangers to non-White communities. It is naïve to expect that as strangers, we will be greeted with open arms at first sight. Underserved racial and ethnic groups have historically been used and abused by outside researchers and professionals, often in the name of scientific progress (i.e., data harvesting) that fails to benefit the community (Ibrahim & Cameron, this *Handbook,* Volume One; Reiss & Price, 1996). Building a trusting relationship typically means that counselors have to rely on personal integrity, not professional training and credentials, as proof of trustworthiness. Ongoing commitment and permanence in the community also cannot be undervalued (Lerner, 1995). Ongoing collaboration means that as professionals, we avoid "one-shot" interventions in favor of establishing a long-term presence in which we exhibit the flexibility to accommodate the changing needs of the community, even when they fall outside the original design of the intervention.

While conversation and collaboration are the processes through which we establish relationships and assess needs, we must be able to modify our ideas to fit the realities of the community. Our perspective as professionals may illuminate some sense of what may be beneficial to a particular community. However, it is essential that our own ideas, hypotheses, and prejudices do not cloud important community goals. In an ideal collaborative relationship, both parties bring valuable expertise to the table.

Lerner (1995) advocated that developing appropriate outreach initiatives is enhanced by thinking contextually about the causes of and solutions to community problems, including as many community voices as possible, and incorporating evaluation as an ongoing part of any intervention. Through collaborative processes of information gathering, program development, and continual feedback, the likelihood that outreach programs are supported by the community will be increased. Paying insufficient attention to collaboration could result in decreased relevance and success of outreach work (Reiss & Price, 1996). Whitmore (1998) echoed such a philosophy by arguing that stakeholder participation in program evaluation increases the relevance, ownership, and utilization of research in the community. She referred to such research as "transformative participatory evaluation research," which may be particularly relevant to working with racial/ethnic communities of Color because the democratization of social change is at the core of transformative research. Although some have argued that the science of research becomes "less objective" with such an approach, Prilleltensky (1997) argued that because no research is "value-free," the values that guide our work should include social justice, liberation, and community empowerment (Trimble, this *Handbook,* Volume One).

Now that the general principles of outreach work have been presented, we may consider an example of engaging in outreach. A local university would like to collaborate with a neighborhood middle school (fifth to eighth grades) in designing interventions to enhance retention and discourage school dropout. The school has a primarily Latino population and there has been a long-standing problem of too many eighth-graders failing to successfully transition to high school. Following the successful establishment of preliminary ties with the school administration, we would attempt to identify the key groups likely to be interested in or affected by the program (stakeholders). In this example, we would include students, their parents, and teachers. To assess the needs of the community accurately and to establish a collaborative connection, we would conduct focus groups with stakeholders from each of the identified strata. The focus groups would be aimed at identifying circumstances that disrupt transitions to high school and resources that facilitate academic persistence. Questions about hopes, worries, problems, or concerns would generally encourage discussion of both positive and negative school transition issues with school-age children, their parents, and teachers.

Data gathered from the focus groups would be summarized, then presented back to the community to ensure the validity of the process and clarify any miscommunications. If the stakeholders agree with the accuracy of the needs assessment, we can begin designing interventions collaboratively (e.g., asking students what type of activities they enjoy, asking parents and teachers for feedback about content) and tailoring our methods to the racial, cultural, and sociopolitical context of the community. The particular characteristics of the community (racial and ethnic composition, primary language, location, available resources, etc.) as well as general developmental considerations would guide the choice of materials and activities. The more accurately the outreach program represents the members of the community, the more successful the program will be. However, we would also establish methods of evaluation that are meaningful to the community (both short term and long term) that would allow us to determine whether the program has made a difference. Long-term goals might be an increase in the percentage of students graduating high school. Short-term goals might be to improve attitudes toward school, to improve parent-teacher communication, and to increase the number of school services (e.g., bilingual tutors, afterschool homework clubs) that help youth who exhibit early signs of trouble.

Obstacles encountered in engaging in outreach work in this example can come in the form of constituent needs requiring changes in program content or process. For instance, if an event in the community, such as an act of random violence, occurred during the course of the intervention, the program counselors may be asked to help the students by interrupting the curriculum and offering crisis management. Alternatively, the school may be unable to provide a continuous stream of time in which to offer the interventions due to other obligations, such as state-mandated testing periods, or special events (e.g., graduation practices). In such situations, modifications would need to be made in the interest of maintaining positive, long-term ties with the constituent groups.

It is clear that many racial/ethnic communities would benefit from professionals who are actively designing and implementing outreach programs. However, there will always be a limit to the number of communities that we can work with directly. Therefore, another important outreach activity involves psychologists training other mental health professionals and educators who have access to working with racial/ethnic people in need. The Virginia Youth Violence Project is an excellent example of how the field of psychology can have a significant impact on the crucial issue of youth violence in American schools and communities. The goal of this study was to maximize the impact of educators and human service professionals to disseminate antiviolence programs to youth in the community. Violence prevention training programs and outreach courses were delivered to educators and human services professionals working with aggressive and at-risk youth to provide participants with the knowledge and skills to develop violence reduction programs in the community. The program's success was evaluated by tracking the follow-up activities of the participants regarding the development and implementation of violence reduction projects. Over 60 school- and community-based violence reduction programs were identified that involved more than 8,700 youth participants throughout the state of Virginia (Sheras, Cornell, & Bostain, 1996). This study demonstrated the breadth of impact that is possible when psychologists work to train community members and advocate outreach efforts for racial and ethnic communities that are disproportionately affected by social problems such as violence.

In summary, outreach is critically important in working with historically underserved populations. People of Color face unique challenges living in the midst of racism and other forms of oppression (poverty, sexism; Black & Krishnakumar, 1998; Fouad & Brown, 2000). In the aforementioned example, students may be in greater need of a dropout prevention outreach program because racism and classism have contributed to poorer quality public schools or a perception that people of Color do not benefit from formal education in the same way that majority individuals do (i.e., receiving high-paying jobs, occupational advancement opportunities). In general, oppression such as racism, sexism, and classism leads to health disparities and overexposure to stressors that compromise the well-being of ethnic and racial people in the United States. Systemic oppression and resulting mental health challenges typically contribute both directly and indirectly to the underutilization of psychological services in such communities. Outreach efforts can be one way we actively eliminate barriers that have excluded people of Color from making contact and having positive experiences with mental health professionals. When we are successful at casting a larger net into the community, we extend a hand to clients who may not typically seek out our services.

ADVOCACY

Even though some of the more formal models of service delivery roles for counselors have been published in recent years, conversations on expanding the traditional role of psychologists began to surface as early as 1975, when Gottlieb urged practitioners to play an active role in advancing the rights of their clients. He proposed the addition of an "advocate professional" model to supplement the traditional scientist-professional model. Gottlieb's declaration was in response to the landmark case in 1971, when a federal judge in Alabama ruled that residents of state mental institutions have a constitutional right to treatment and rehabilitation (Gottlieb, 1975). Soon after this case, the American Psychological Association (APA) began to strongly encourage psychologists to take action against institutions and agencies that were having a negative impact on the lives of their clients. While advocacy is still not considered to be a fundamental activity of most counselors, its function is at the core of our profession (McCluskie & Ingersoll, 2001).

Advocacy has traditionally been defined as the act of speaking up for people whose rights may be in jeopardy (Lewis et al., 1998). Advocacy can be encouraged so that clients intervene on their own behalf or so that another concerned person, such as a counselor, intervenes. Advocacy activities range from those as simple as making a phone call on someone's behalf to taking legal steps to ensure that a client's rights are not being violated (McCluskie & Ingersoll, 2001). There are both similarities and differences between client advocacy and counseling services. The goals in each arena may be consistent even though the methods vary.

D. Brown (1988) indicated that counseling is typically associated with the process of directly assisting clients to mobilize their personal resources so that they can more effectively function in their environment. Through advocacy, counselors can also work to intervene in the environment, which will indirectly empower clients. Intervention can be directed at the microenvironmental level (i.e., family, school) or at the macroenvironmental level (i.e., community, society) to make these systems more responsive to the needs of clients. As Lewis et al. (1998) wrote, the two basic purposes for providing advocacy services to clients is to increase clients' sense of personal power and to facilitate environmental changes that reflect greater responsiveness to their personal needs. Regardless of the specific objective (e.g., client self-empowerment, public policy change), advocacy entails intervening with some organizational body or system (or an individual representing either) as a means of exercising clients' rights or highlighting injustices that negatively affect a client's well-being. In this way, advocacy work is closely related to social justice issues (Vera & Speight, 2003).

The current concern regarding the appropriateness of advocacy roles for psychologists has resulted from our increasing attention to environmental stressors that negatively affect clients' lives (Atkinson, Thompson, et al., 1993; Carter, Forsyth,

Mazzula, & Williams, this *Handbook,* this volume), especially in the case of people of Color. Although there is consensus that the loci of many problems faced by racial and ethnic communities are external (e.g., underemployment, racism, discrimination), there is still considerable disagreement over whether counselors should intervene in their clients' lives outside the realm of the traditional therapeutic relationship. Often, such actions are interpreted as overly intrusive or tantamount to forcing an agenda on a client. However, if the agenda involves an active protest of social inequities, advocacy might be viewed as appropriate for professionals with a commitment to social justice when working with racial and ethnic clients (Carter et al., this *Handbook,* this volume).

Smith (1985), Sue (1995), and others have argued that the traditional training of most psychologists has focused too much on helping clients adjust to or cope with the aftermath of negative forces such as racism instead of engaging in activities that are aimed at eliminating such forces (Carter, this *Handbook,* this volume). The de-emphasis on political activism may be because psychology has traditionally attempted to be politically neutral (L. Brown, 1997). Lewis et al. (1998) suggested that a clinician's work with racial and ethnic clients should include helping clients to become agents of change in the community. It can be an incredibly empowering experience for clients to affiliate with other community members to facilitate changes in schools, business organizations, and community agencies. Ultimately, such social changes may result in improved well-being and fewer health disparities through the reduction of community stressors. As an example, imagine a client who presents with symptoms of anxiety exacerbated by chronic fears about the safety of his children in a neighborhood plagued by community violence. While treatment options would likely focus on (1) symptom reduction and/or (2) exploring ways the client could relocate to a safer community, a counselor could also encourage the client to participate with other parents in acts aimed at changing public policy (e.g., an organized march against gangs in the neighborhood, participating in meetings with police and other public officials). Furthermore, a counselor functioning in an advocate role could take on the responsibility of organizing such events that would benefit the community as a whole and ultimately enhance the psychological well-being of its members.

There are instances in which a counselor may have to take a more direct role in advocating when a client lacks the skills to advocate for himself or herself and the urgency of the situation requires immediate action. It could be that a client is being ignored or mistreated by a caseworker or is intimidated by some formal process such as a multidisciplinary staffing in a school system. Some members of racial and ethnic groups, especially those who have recently immigrated to the United States, may lack the English-speaking skills, knowledge of health systems, and economic resources to confront barriers raised by social service agencies, legal institutions, and employment agencies (Arredondo, this *Handbook,* this volume; Atkinson, Thompson, et al., 1993). In cases where systemic barriers contribute to mental health problems, it may be appropriate for mental health professionals to intervene because of their professional status in society and their familiarity with the laws and regulations of this country.

There are some who caution against the use of advocacy efforts, arguing that such interventions actually prevent clients from feeling empowered (because the clinician is doing what the clients should be learning to do for themselves). Additionally, there is a concern that advocacy work can overemphasize the importance of external factors in clients' lives. For example, Parham and McDavis (1987) pointed out that by focusing on external factors alone, we suggest that clients lack the mental fortitude to deal effectively with adverse conditions in society. An alternative position, however, is that advocacy can be an important additional tool that can help in minimizing external stressors that affect racial and ethnic clients. In fact, the goal of advocacy is ultimately self-empowerment of the client. Thus, if a counselor attends a school hearing or legal procedure with a client who feels intimidated by the system, the counselor can help to make sure that the client understands what decisions are being made and also can help the client protect her rights during the proceedings. Whether the counselor directly participates in the procedure or encourages the client to intervene on her own behalf, the counselor's actions model the assertiveness skills the client may be working on developing.

Researchers have found evidence to suggest that advocating for clients at multiple levels can be more effective than traditional approaches to client treatment. For instance, Emshoff and Blakely (1983) evaluated the effectiveness of two intervention strategies designed to divert delinquent youth from further court processing. The researcher randomly assigned a group of 73 adolescents who had committed serious misdemeanors or nonserious felonies to receive services focused exclusively on the family (Family condition), to receive advocacy interventions and other services in a wide range of domains frequently assessed as being critical to adolescent behavior and development (e.g., school, peers, and employment; Multifocus condition), or to a Control condition (where the youth received court treatment as usual). The youngsters in the Multifocus group showed a significantly greater decrease in the frequency and seriousness of court and police contacts, reported fewer delinquent behaviors, and performed better in school than participants in the other groups.

In some cases, neither the counselor nor the client may be qualified or feel able to advocate in a particular situation. Rather than feeling disempowered, counselors can help clients form networks with groups who engage in advocacy work (e.g., legal defense funds; Lewis et al., 1998). These groups are composed of citizens working to improve the lives of other citizens who are unable to perform activities critical to daily living (Wolfensberger & Zauha, 1973). Clients may not be aware of the advocacy groups that exist in their communities, which is why counselors need to be knowledgeable about social services that are available in the community. With such knowledge, it is possible to directly recruit the services of a citizen advocacy group (e.g., groups that advocate for the educational rights of special education children) when necessary. Connections with these various resources would be excellent sources of support for clients who feel isolated and disconnected from their communities.

Finally, professional psychologists and counselors working with people of Color have firsthand knowledge of the mental and physical health consequences of living in a racist society (Ota Wang, this *Handbook,* this volume). Thus, it behooves us morally and ethically to be involved in every way we can outside of our professional responsibilities (i.e., as citizens) to advocate for policies and programs that reduce poverty, racism, and discrimination and improve education. Lessening such stressors will enhance the well-being of our clients and promote social justice in our society.

PREVENTION

The theme of prevention is a natural extension of the topics addressed throughout this chapter because it is closely linked to the goals of advocacy and the philosophy of outreach efforts. It has been stated that to enhance our work with people of Color in particular, mental health professionals need to explore varying roles and strategies that provide optimal effectiveness for clients. Preventive interventions fit well into the frameworks presented by Atkinson, Thompson, et al. (1993) and Lewis et al. (1998) for working with racial and ethnic communities.

A number of problems, such as drug abuse, violence, school dropout, and unemployment, are overrepresented in communities of Color. The reasons for this are multiple, but are undoubtedly tied to the stressors associated with experiencing racism and oppression (Carter et al., this *Handbook,* this volume; McWhirter, McWhirter, McWhirter, & McWhirter, 1998). Prevention programs in communities of Color are quite simply some of the best ways we have of reducing the future incidence of psychological disorders. It is much more sensible, more economical, and less time-consuming to provide programs to youth that attempt to prevent drug use and possible addiction, for example, than it is to provide rehabilitation services once addiction has occurred (Lewis et al., 1998). Preventing particular disorders before they occur also leads to a decrease in associated problems. For instance, drug addiction can be related to theft, child abuse and neglect, family difficulties, homelessness, and more. Prevention interventions not only decrease the identified problem within the community, but may also eliminate the development of related difficulties that occur as a result of these problems. Two meta-analyses (Tobler, 2000; Wilson, Gottfredson, & Najaka, 2001) provide strong evidence to support the effectiveness of school-based prevention programs in reducing or preventing crime, substance use, dropout/nonattendance, and other conduct problems among adolescent youth. Indeed, prevention has been a historical emphasis of psychology embedded in such goals as (1) to identify and promote skills and talents and (2) to help all people lead more satisfying lives. The two goals have been too often overshadowed by psychology's third and apparently overarching objective: to "cure" established problems and mental disorders (Seligman, 1998; Thompson, this *Handbook,* this volume). Due in part to the remedial culture of mainstream society, especially when it comes to health issues, not enough attention has been given to research and practice that exemplifies health promotion and optimal life fulfillment. However, when considering the alarming levels of particular psychological disorders and health disparities present in many racial and ethnic communities, it is urgent that concentrated efforts be made to minimize the need for remediation in the future (Carter, this *Handbook,* Volume One).

Prevention is traditionally divided into three levels: primary, secondary, and tertiary (Munoz, Mrazek, & Haggerty, 1996; Vera & Reese, 2000). Interventions at the tertiary level involve reducing the incidence of problems and precluding further distress for those individuals and groups who have experienced dysfunction. Psychotherapy is often synonymous with tertiary prevention. Secondary prevention strategies are centered on populations who are at risk for the development of future problems but who have not yet shown signs of impairment. The purpose of such programs is to detect possible problem areas early on and to impede their progress. Finally, primary prevention programs are geared toward groups who have not been affected by a particular problem. The focus here is on promoting competence and resilience to prevent dysfunction before it occurs and to foster continued positive development (Black & Krishnakumar, 1998; Vera & Reese, 2000).

Positive development involves highlighting preexisting skills and talents and increasing competence. It uses a strength-building perspective to cultivate protective factors (i.e., factors that reduce risk) and positive aspects of an individual, group, or community. For example, teaching communication skills to youth and families equips them with alternatives for interpersonal interaction that may not only result in better relationships, but prevent the need to rely on aggression and violence in times of conflict. In many cases, the etiology of problem behavior and poor decision making (e.g., premature sexual involvement, drug experimentation, and other delinquent behavior) is not uniquely attributable to environmental stress, family dysfunction, or intrapersonal disturbance. But the combination of these factors can result in suboptimal developmental life paths (Larson, 2000). Prevention efforts that focus on skill building, goal direction, and internal motivation help to prepare individuals to become more productive and conscientious adults, regardless of what risk factors may exist in the environment.

As mentioned before, the utilization of mental health services with ethnic/racial groups tends to vary depending on such factors as the availability of services and cultural beliefs regarding counseling. For those clients who do participate in counseling in more traditional settings, such as community mental health clinics, hospitals, or university counseling centers, preventive interventions can easily be integrated into our work. For example, a client may be referred for services due to drug or alcohol addiction. Therapy for this individual would perhaps involve keeping the client sober, examining issues or stressors that may have contributed to the use of drugs, and also preventing relapses (i.e., tertiary prevention). Additionally, the counselor may bring the client's children into sessions so that information and refusal skills involving drugs and alcohol can be presented, as children of chemically dependent parents are at higher risk for having substance abuse problems themselves. Such psychoeducational intervention activities represent secondary prevention efforts.

Another common way preventive interventions are delivered, especially in the case of primary prevention, is through group-based programs located in schools, clinics, or community recreation centers. Primary prevention is sometimes more difficult to integrate into therapy because of the lack of any presenting problem. However, a therapist may choose to engage in primary prevention through an affiliation and collaborative relationship with other community organizations. For example, developing and implementing a study skills/time management program to reduce the risk of dropout for first-generation college students is a primary prevention approach. Delivering a violence reduction program in an elementary school setting is another example.

Sometimes local agencies/organizations may wish to contract with psychologists to deliver psychoeducational intervention services. At other times, we may engage in these activities as part of our regular job (e.g., in college counseling centers or community mental health clinics). In either case, we can commit our time and energy to larger-scale interventions that attempt to build on existing strengths and maximize clients' potential. Larger-scale interventions may be of particular relevance for racial and ethnic individuals who live in psychologically toxic environments (i.e., amid racism, poverty, and oppression). Rather than wait for these stressors to take their toll on a person, we can work in ways that help clients to transcend these realities (Carter et al., this *Handbook,* this volume).

Proactive intervention is not a novel concept in the profession of counseling and psychology. However, job analysis studies have found that prevention is much less likely to be the focus of our work than is remediation (Osipow & Fitzgerald, 1986). Remediation is emphasized by our third-party payment systems (e.g., HMOs, insurance companies), and given that many practitioners rely on such payment for income, there is systemic complicity in rewarding a remedial focus. Unfortunately, as Albee (2000) suggested, this reliance on remedial interventions will do nothing to stop the emergence of new disorders.

Integrating prevention efforts in therapy may not be the only way psychologists and counselors can engage in proactive efforts on behalf of client populations. While many prevention programs rely on direct interventions with client populations, there are also indirect approaches to prevention that attack problems at their environmental core. These approaches in many cases resemble advocacy efforts. For example, environment-centered prevention approaches attempt to change important contexts of the client's life such as family, peer groups, or community. Some professionals who engage in alcohol and drug prevention work advocate involving individuals in activities that seek to modify community norms regarding substance use. Examples include designing media campaigns or advocating for the availability of recreational options for youth that do not involve drugs (e.g., midnight basketball leagues, alcohol-free dance parties on weekend evenings). Often, these more systemically based, environment-centered primary prevention programs allow therapists to intervene in community contexts that may be exacerbating or perpetuating problems with people of Color. Systemic-based intervention is critical because systemic problems such as poverty, inadequate housing, and discrimination cannot be prevented with crisis-oriented, client-directed programs (Evans et al., this *Handbook,* this volume; McWhirter et al., 1998).

Whether we use preventive approaches to supplement the work we do in the context of counseling or we create new contexts of service delivery with marginalized communities of Color (e.g., through outreach), the long-term benefits of prevention work should not be underestimated.

CONCLUSION

We have highlighted some ways our work as counselors can be enhanced by integrating approaches such as outreach, advocacy, and prevention. The most important point is: Being culturally responsive in our work with people of Color and other underserved racial and ethnic people requires us to think in innovative, socially responsible ways. Although some nontraditional approaches might not be emphasized in traditional professional psychology training programs, they all are consistent with the overarching goals of the field of counseling, which should legitimize their place in our professional lives.

In particular, when it comes to promoting the mental health of racial and ethnic clients, we must be constantly aware of how oppression operates in our society. Among other serious problems, oppression results in overexposure to negative life stressors, a lack of access to basic physical and mental health services, and the overrepresentation of particular mental health problems in African American, Latino, Asian American, and Native American communities. Because our clients are forced to live with additional systemic burdens, we must be prepared to use additional strategies on their behalf. Engaging in outreach allows us to help greater numbers of individuals in need, especially those who may not seek out services independently. Advocacy gives us an avenue in which to fight against policies and practices detrimental to our clients' quality of life. Prevention allows us to actively work to minimize the emergence of future problems. In combination with counseling and therapy, these activities add to the arsenal of skills we have. By having as many tools as possible, we are in a more advantageous position to improve the mental health of our clients.

REFERENCES

Albee, G. W. (2000). Commentary on prevention and counseling psychology. *Counseling Psychologist, 28,* 845–853.

Atkinson, D. R., Morten, G., & Sue, D. W. (1993). *Counseling American minorities: A cross-cultural perspective* (4th ed.). Madison, WI: Brown & Benchmark.

Atkinson, D. R., Thompson, C. E., & Grant, S. K. (1993). A three-dimensional model for counseling racial-ethnic minorities. *Counseling Psychologist, 21,* 257–277.

Black, M. M., & Krishnakumar, A. (1998). Children in low-income, urban settings: Interventions to promote mental health and well-being. *American Psychologist, 53,* 635–646.

Broman, C. L. (1987). Race differences in professional help seeking. *American Journal of Community Psychology, 15*(4), 473–489.

Brown, D. (1988). Empowerment through advocacy. In D. J. Kurpius & D. Brown (Eds.), *Handbook of consultation: An intervention for advocacy and outreach* (pp. 5–17). Alexandria, VA: Association for Counselor Education and Supervision.

Brown, L. S. (1997). The private practice of subversion: Psychology as tikkun olam. *American Psychologist, 52,* 449–462.

Carter, R. T. (in press). Uprooting inequity and disparities in counseling and psychology: An introduction. In R. T. Carter (Ed.), *Handbook of racial-cultural psychology and counseling: Theory and research* (Vol. 1, pp. xv–xxviii). Hoboken, NJ: Wiley.

Emshoff, J. G., & Blakely, C. H. (1983). The diversion of delinquent youth: Family focused intervention. *Children and Youth Services Review, 5*(4), 343–356.

Fouad, N. A., & Brown, M. T. (2000). Role of race and social class in development: Implications for counseling psychology. In S. D. Brown & R. W. Lent (Eds.), *Handbook of counseling psychology* (3rd ed.). New York: Wiley.

Gottheil, E., Sterling, R. C., & Weinstein, S. P. (1997). Outreach engagement efforts: Are they worth the effort? *American Journal of Drug and Alcohol Abuse, 23*(1), 61–66.

Gottlieb, S. C. (1975). Psychology and the "treatment rights movement." *Professional Psychology, 6*(3), 243–251.

Ibrahim, F. A., & Cameron, S. C. (in press). Racial-cultural ethical issues in research. In R. T. Carter (Ed.), *Handbook of racial-cultural psychology and counseling: Theory and research* (Vol. 1, pp. 391–413). Hoboken, NJ: Wiley.

Koss-Chioino, J. D., & Vargas, L. A. (1992). Through the cultural looking glass: A model for understanding culturally responsive psychotherapies. In L. A. Vargas & J. D. Koss-Chioino (Eds.), *Working with culture: Psychotherapeutic interventions with ethnic minority children and adolescents.* San Francisco: Jossey-Bass.

Krumboltz, J. D. (1966). Behavioral goals for counseling. *Journal of Counseling Psychology, 13,* 153–159.

Larson, R. W. (2000). Toward a psychology of positive youth development. *American Psychologist, 55,* 170–183.

Lerner, R. M. (1995). *America's youth in crisis: Challenges and options for programs and policies.* Thousand Oaks, CA: Sage.

Lewis, J. A., Lewis, M. D., Daniels, J. A., & D'Andrea, M. J. (1998). *Community counseling: Empowerment strategies for a diverse society* (2nd ed.). Pacific Grove, CA: Brooks/Cole.

McCluskie, K. C., & Ingersoll, R. E. (2001). *Becoming a 21st century agency counselor.* Belmont, CA: Brooks/Cole.

McWhirter, J. J., McWhirter, B. T., McWhirter, A. M., & McWhirter, E. H. (1998). *At risk youth: A comprehensive response.* Belmont, CA: Brooks/Cole.

Munoz, R. F., Mrazek, P. J., & Haggerty, R. J. (1996). Institute of medicine report on prevention of mental disorders: Summary and commentary. *American Psychologist, 51,* 1116–1122.

Osipow, S. L., & Fitzgerald, L. (1986, May). An occupational analysis of counseling psychology: How special is the specialty? *American Psychologist, 41*(5), 535–544.

Parham, T. A., & McDavis, R. J. (1987). Black men, and endangered species: Who's really pulling the trigger? *Journal of Counseling and Development, 66,* 24–27.

Prilleltensky, I. (1997). Values, assumptions, and practices: Assessing the moral implications of psychological discourse and action. *American Psychologist, 52,* 517–535.

Reiss, D., & Price, R. H. (1996). National research agenda for prevention research: The National Institute of Mental Health Report. *American Psychologist, 51,* 1109–1115.

Seligman, M. E. P. (January, 1998). Building human strength: Psychology's forgotten mission. *APA Monitor, 29.*

Sheras, P. L., Cornell, D. G., & Bostain, D. S. (1996). The Virginia youth violence project: Transmitting psychological knowledge on youth violence to schools and communities. *Professional Psychology—Research and Practice, 27*(4), 401–406.

Smith, E. M. J. (1985). Ethnic minorities: Life stress, social support, and mental health issues. *Counseling Psychologist, 13,* 537–579.

Sue, D. W. (1995). Multicultural organizational development: Implications for the counseling profession. In J. G. Ponterotto, J. M. Casas, L. A. Suzuki, & C. M. Alexander (Eds.), *Handbook of multicultural counseling.* Thousand Oaks, CA: Sage.

Sue, D. W., Arredondo, P., & McDavis, R. (1997). Multicultural counseling competencies and standards: A call to the profession. *Journal of Counseling and Development, 70,* 477–486.

Sue, D. W., & Sue, D. (1999). *Counseling the culturally different* (3rd ed.). New York: Wiley.

Sue, D. W., & Sue, D. (2003). *Counseling the culturally diverse* (4th ed.). New York: Wiley.

Szapocznik, J., Lasaga, J., Perry, P. R., & Solomon, J. R. (1979). Outreach in the delivery of mental health services to Hispanic elders. *Hispanic Journal of Behavioral Sciences, 1*(1), 21–40.

Taylor, R. J., Hardison, C. B., & Chatters, L. M. (1996). Kin and nonkin as sources of informal assistance. In H. W. Neighbors & J. S. Jackson (Eds.), *Mental health in Black America* (pp. 130–145). Thousand Oaks, CA: Sage.

Tobler, N. S. (2000). Lessons learned. *Journal of Primary Prevention, 20*(4), 261–274.

Trimble, J. E. (in press). An inquiry into the measurement of ethnic and racial identity. In R. T. Carter (Ed.), *Handbook of racial-cultural psychology and counseling: Theory and research* (Vol. 1, pp. 320–359). Hoboken, NJ: Wiley.

Vera, E. M., & Reese, L. E. (2000). Prevention interventions with school-age youth. In S. D. Brown & R. W. Lent (Eds.), *Handbook of counseling psychology* (pp. 411–434). New York: Wiley.

Vera, E. M., & Speight, S. L. (2003). Multicultural competence, social justice, and counseling psychology: Expanding our roles. *Counseling Psychologist, 31,* 253–272.

Whitmore, E. (1998). *Understanding and practicing participatory evaluation.* San Francisco: Jossey-Bass.

Wilson, D. B., Gottfredson, D. C., & Najaka, S. S. (2001). School-based prevention of problem behaviors: A meta-analysis. *Journal of Quantitative Criminology, 17*(3), 247–272.

Wolfensberger, W., & Zauha, H. (1973). *Citizen advocacy and protective services for the impaired and handicapped.* Toronto, Ontario, Canada: National Institute on Mental Retardation.

CHAPTER 29

Developing a Framework for Culturally Competent Systems of Care

Arthur C. Evans Jr., Miriam Delphin, Reginald Simmons,
Gihan Omar, and Jacob Tebes

Recognition of the central role of culture, race, and ethnicity in health and healing is not novel. For decades researchers have explored the influence of culture on personality formation, symptom expression, help-seeking attitudes and behaviors, health and illness models, and treatment process and outcomes (Abromowitz & Murray, 1983; Adebimpe, 1981; Alarcon, Foulks, & Vakkur, 1998; Baker & Bell, 1999; Delphin & Rollock, 1995; Draguns, this *Handbook,* Volume One; Gardner, 1971; Griffith & Gonzales, 1996; Pedersen, this *Handbook,* Volume One). Although significant progress has been made in understanding the relationship between culture and health, behavioral health policymakers and researchers continue to be challenged by the need to develop large systems of care that meet the needs of individuals from diverse racial-cultural backgrounds. The success of these efforts is critical given that, by the year 2050, people of Color will constitute nearly 50% of the national population (U.S. Department of Health and Human Services [DHHS], 2001). If effective services are to be provided, significant advances are needed in creating systems of care able to render services to individuals from diverse racial-cultural backgrounds (Vera, Buhin, Montgomery, & Shin, this *Handbook,* this volume).

Since the late 1970s, issues of culture in the effective delivery of behavioral health services have received considerable attention in the mental health research, practice, and policy arenas. The multicultural counseling and therapy movement of the early 1980s pioneered an emphasis on tailoring treatments to the culture of the individual client so as to ensure their cultural relevance and sensitivity (Carney & Kahn, 1984; Constantino, Malady, & Rogler, 1986; Constantine, Watt, Gainor, & Warren, this *Handbook,* Volume One). Such efforts were subsequently supplemented by an understanding that organizations, and the providers who serve diverse clients, must reorient practices and policies to take into account racial-cultural diversity (Cross, Bazron, Dennis, & Issacs, 1989; DHHS-OMH, 2001b). Similar developments were also taking place at the policy level, as evidenced by the emphasis in the Child and Adolescent Service System Project of the need to ensure that services be culturally competent in comprehensive systems of care for children and families (Friedman, 1986; Knitzer, 1984). The emphasis on culture in the provision of mental health services was also evident in several federal reports, such as *Healthy People 2000* (DHHS, 2000) and the U.S. surgeon general's report on *Mental Health: Culture, Race and Ethnicity* (DHHS, 2001). *Healthy People 2000* called for substantial health improvements for people of Color in the United States, thus advancing the need for further research. The report by the surgeon general described striking disparities in access, availability, and quality of mental health services between White and non-White populations (Carter, this *Handbook,* Volume One). Further, the surgeon general noted that "culture counts" and, as a result of treatment inequities among Whites and non-Whites, not all Americans share equally in the hope of recovery from mental illness. Among recommendations such as integrating mental health with primary care, ensuring language access, and extending health insurance to the uninsured as a means of addressing health disparities, it was recommended that providers and organizations develop (and evaluate for effectiveness) culturally and linguistically appropriate mental health services designed to meet the needs of people of Color.

Yet, despite the considerable attention given to cultural competence over the past two decades, progress in advancing theory, research, and practice remains slow (C. Ridley, Baker, & Hill, 2001). For the most part, cultural competence research has emphasized individual and, perhaps, organizational models and applications of the concept; less attention has been given to systems-level conceptualizations and approaches (Hanley, 1998). This chapter is an attempt to address systems-level cultural competence through the presentation of practices and policies enacted by the Connecticut Department of Mental Health and Addiction Services (DMHAS). After providing a brief overview of cultural competence research, we (1) provide a rationale for examining cultural competence from a systems perspective, (2) present a practical approach to developing a culturally competent system of care using the Connecticut DMHAS as a case example, and (3) discuss next steps and directions for cultural competence policy, research, and practice at the system level.

We define "cultural competence" as effective service delivery to people from various cultural backgrounds that is mindful of their cultural values, norms, and customs and is consistent with best practice approaches (Carter, this *Handbook,* this volume). While an approach may not be effective with every individual, culturally competent care is demonstrably effective for the cultural group(s) for which it is designed. We define "systems of care" as complex, interrelated sets of people and organizations focused on the delivery of health care services to a defined set of individuals. Such systems typically serve thousands of people, employ hundreds of practitioners, and are often governed by a complex set of local, state, federal, and credentialing organization policies and regulations. Furthermore, many rules may be unspoken, such as traditions and "political" considerations. People receiving treatment in systems of care must often rely on multiple organizations and myriad rules to obtain the services they need to fully recover from their health care condition.

OVERVIEW OF CULTURAL COMPETENCE RESEARCH

A comprehensive review of cultural competence research is beyond the scope of this chapter. (For comprehensive reviews, see Constantine & Ladany, 2001; Fuertes &

Gretchen, 2001; Ponterotto, Fuertes, & Chen, 2000; R. Ridley, Mendoza, & Kanitz, 1994.) R. Ridley, Mendoza, Kanitz, Angermeier, and Zenk (1994), however, we offer a brief overview of individual, organizational, and system approaches to cultural competence to provide a context for the practitioner-, program-, and policy-level interventions described later that illustrate our implementation of a culturally competent approach in a state-wide system of care.

Over the past two decades, numerous definitions and models of cultural competence have been proposed, many of which address different dimensions of the construct. As Ridley, Mendoza, Kanitz, Angermeier, et al. (1994) noted, terms such as cultural sensitivity, cross-cultural competence, cross-cultural expertise, cross-cultural effectiveness, cultural responsiveness, cultural awareness, and culturally skilled have all been used to describe aspects of what is believed to be essential for the provision of culturally responsive services or care. In this chapter, we use the terms "cultural competence" and "racial-cultural competence" interchangeably unless a given literature utilizes other specific terminology.

Among the conceptualizations of cultural competence that have received perhaps the greatest degree of consensus in the field has been the work of Sue and colleagues (Sue, Arredondo, & McDavis, 1992; Sue et al., 1982, 1998). Sue et al. (1992) proposed a set of cultural competency guidelines that have been adopted as standard by six divisions of the American Counseling Association and two divisions of the American Psychological Association. These competency standards are based on a 3 × 3 matrix (counselor characteristics × competency domain) whereby characteristics of a culturally skilled counselor are cross-classified with the primary domains of cultural competence, creating a total of nine competency areas. Culturally skilled counselor characteristics include (1) counselor awareness of own assumptions, values, and biases; (2) counselor understanding of the worldview of the culturally different client; and (3) ability to develop culturally appropriate intervention strategies and techniques. Cultural competency domains include (1) attitudes and beliefs, (2) knowledge, and (3) skills (D. Sue & Torino, this *Handbook,* this volume). As part of Sue et al.'s (1992) model, for each of the nine cultural competency areas, a number of specific explanatory guidelines are presented to create a total of 31 recommended standard guidelines for the delivery of culturally competent services.

Though the Sue et al. (1992) standard guidelines have been accepted in the field, general critiques of cultural competency models and guidelines have included questions regarding their specific behavioral indicators as well as outcomes to expect when they have been successfully carried out (Iwamasa, Larrabee, & Merritt, 2000; C. Ridley, Baker, et al., 2001). Recognizing the need for further clarification of the Sue et al. cultural competency guidelines, the Professional Standards and Certification Committee of the Association for Multicultural Counseling and Development expanded the guidelines by adding operational definitions of diversity and multiculturalism and by adding explanatory statements that further operationalize each of the 31 standard guidelines (Arredondo et al., 1996). Thus, for the guideline that pertains to a counselor's awareness of his or her own cultural assumptions, values, and biases in the attitudes and beliefs domain, the cultural competency explanatory statement indicates that a culturally skilled counselor:

> Can identify at least five features of culture of origin and explain how these features affect their relationship with culturally different clients. (Arredondo et al., 1996, p. 59)

The expanded guidelines added the following statements pertaining to counselors:

> Can identify implications of such statements as internalized oppression, institutional racism, privilege, and the historical and current political climate regarding immigration, poverty and welfare (public assistance). (p. 65)

and

> Can identify and communicate possible alternatives that would reduce or eliminate existing barriers within their institution and within local, state, and national decision making bodies. (p. 69)

The standard guidelines and the related explanatory statements have been helpful in operationalizing cultural competence. However, with only a few exceptions (Sue, Ivey, & Pedersen, 1996), the field has not focused on theory in fostering an understanding of cultural competence. In an early attempt to supply a theory, R. Ridley et al. (1994) developed an information-processing perceptual schema approach to defining cultural competence. The authors focused on cultural sensitivity, defining it as "the ability of counselors to acquire, develop and actively use an accurate perceptual schema in the course of multicultural counseling" (p. 130). Cultural information that might constitute a schema could include, but not be limited to, a client's racial identity, self-perception in the family, acculturation level, and natural support systems and natural coping styles. In addition, for each type of cultural information, counselors are believed to have a generic framework that can be used in perceiving a client. Ridley et al.'s framework was to be individualized and made more specific with idiographic data obtained through interactions with the client. Idiographic data could "include spoken language, nonverbal behaviors, cognitions, emotions, physiological responses, sensations, spirituality, and the vast interaction among and between these" (p. 130). Skills believed to assist counselors in this task include continuous counselor self-processing, using cultural schemata flexibly, and actively selecting and attending to cultural stimuli.

Although most cultural competency research has focused on the individual level of analysis, Cross et al. (1989) provide an organizational analysis of cultural competence. These authors define cultural competence as a set of congruent behaviors, attitudes, and policies that come together in a system or agency or among professionals and enable that system, agency, or professionals to work effectively in situations that cross racial-cultural boundaries. For instance, Cross et al. also propose a five-stage continuum model of multicultural organizational development created specifically for health care organizations. At the most negative end of the continuum is cultural destructiveness; agencies defined as culturally destructive have policies and practices that are actively destructive to non-dominant cultures and individuals of different cultures. Next on the continuum is cultural incapacity; this describes agencies that, although not purposefully destructive, do not have the capacity to deal effectively with people of Color and their communities. Culturally incapacitated agencies may perpetuate societal biases and beliefs in racial inferiority. The next stage along the continuum is cultural blindness; agencies at this stage attempt to be unbiased in their approach by maintaining that race and culture make no difference in service provision and thus use a dominant culture approach with all clients. Next are culturally precompetent agencies, which make attempts at becoming more multicultural but continue to have difficulty addressing the specific needs of diverse clients. Next are agencies with basic cultural competence skills in areas such as awareness and acceptance of difference; culturally accepting organizations recognize their strengths and limitations in working with racial-cultural populations and staff. Finally, culturally proficient agencies incorporate concepts of cultural competency into relevant policies, practices, and overall agency climate.

The Cross et al. (1989) continuum model of cultural competence has been a valuable contribution to the field. However, a limitation of the model is that it does not address the steps necessary for an organization to advance from one stage to another on the continuum. In summarizing key research, Sue et al. (1998) provide some guidance in this regard. The authors developed a list of six characteristics essential to the provision of culturally competent care or education, noting that a culturally competent organization:

1. *Values diversity:* Culturally competent organizations recognize, value, and respect the varying cultural values, beliefs, worldviews, and communication styles of staff and clients from different cultural backgrounds. Additionally, within-group cultural differences are acknowledged and appreciated.

2. *Possesses the capacity for cultural self-assessment or cultural auditing:* Organizations, often with the help of outside consultants, assess their services for effectiveness, cognizant of the fact that service provision is inevitably a cross-cultural enterprise in which larger service system values interact with the beliefs and attitudes of clients from varying racial-cultural backgrounds.

3. *Clarifies its vision:* Staff have an awareness of the organization's training and educational goals overall and with respect to multiculturalism.

4. *Understands the dynamics of difference:* Staff and administrators have an awareness of the "dynamics that can occur when two or more cultural groups confront stereotypes, political, and power differences and the histories of misinterpretation and misjudgment that combine in expressions of racism, sexism, or other forms of discrimination" (Sue et al., 1998, p. 108).

5. *Institutionalizes its cultural knowledge:* On an ongoing basis, organizations provide opportunities for staff to acquire, share, and discuss cultural knowledge. Such opportunities could include scheduling regular case presentations and discussions that highlight key cross-cultural issues, organizing speaker series with invited presentations from representatives from key culturally related community groups, or hiring consultants to provide ongoing cultural competence training and education.

6. *Adapts to diversity:* Organizations will adapt to the changing needs of the populations to whom they provide services. Adaptation may include designing new programs as particular needs are identified, incorporating traditional

healing practices or folk healers in the treatment process, or, where possible, inviting key family members to participate in the treatment process as a means of enhancing engagement.

In response to numerous efforts to outline organizational practices needed for the provision of culturally competent services, and in an attempt to move toward national consensus, the U.S. Department of Health and Human Services Office of Minority Health formed a national advisory board charged with the task of developing a set of standards necessary for assuring cultural competence in health care (DHHS-OMH, 2001a). The standards were developed to provide guidance in the delivery of culturally and linguistically appropriate services (CLAS) and were based on a comprehensive review of linguistic and cultural competence tools, policy documents, internal institutional guidelines, state and federal laws and regulations, certification standards, accrediting guidelines, and relevant research addressing outcomes in relation to cultural and linguistic health care services. The U.S. DHHS-OMH is currently in the process of developing a step-by-step practical guide to assist organizations in implementing the CLAS standards. Table 29.1 summarizes the recommendations of the OMH to health care organizations and providers that form the basis for the standards.

System-level conceptualizations of cultural competence are extremely scarce in the literature. However, Sue (2001), in his most recent conceptualization of the construct, discussed the need for more large-scale and system-level approaches to implementing cultural competence. He notes that intervening at the individual level, to the neglect of organizational or systems levels, is likely to hinder broad-based change. He proposes a $3 \times 4 \times 5$ multidimensional conceptual framework for organizing the primary dimensions of cultural competence, whereby (1) Dimension 1 represents race- and culture-specific attributes of cultural competence (African American, Asian American, Latino American, Native American, European American); (2) Dimension 2 represents the components of cultural competence (knowledge, skills, and awareness of attitudes/beliefs); and (3) Dimension 3 represents the foci of cultural competence (individual, professional, organizational, societal). Strengths of the Sue (2001) model include its broad-based conceptualization of the construct and recommendations to use systematic and multilevel interventions when possible as a general means of enhancing cross-cultural work. Further, with its focus on four different domains of cultural competence, the model integrates well previous research that has generally addressed multilevel analysis using separate models. A limitation of the Sue model is its lack of development of the systemic-level focus of cultural competence, perhaps because of the paucity of research in this area. Further, as noted by Reynolds (2001), an additional limitation of the Sue model is that with its complexity, difficulties may arise in concrete and practical applications of the model's various dimensions.

Our review summarized key approaches to conceptualizing cultural competence at the individual, organizational, and service system levels. Although research on systems-level cultural competence has progressed over the past two decades, translating models and definitions into practice continues to be a challenge for practitioners, researchers, and policymakers. A practical example of implementing cultural competence at the systems level is presented to provide a framework for bringing about systems-level change in promoting culturally competent systems of

Table 29.1   Recommended Standards for Culturally and Linguistically Appropriate Health Care Services

1 Promote and support the attitudes, behaviors, knowledge, and skills necessary for staff to work respectfully and effectively with clients and each other in a culturally diverse work environment.

2 Have a comprehensive management strategy to address culturally and linguistically appropriate services, including strategic goals, plans, policies, procedures, and designated staff responsible for implementation.

3 Utilize formal mechanisms for community and consumer involvement in the design and execution of service delivery, including planning, policymaking, operations, evaluation, training, and, as appropriate, treatment planning.

4 Develop and implement a strategy to recruit, retain, and promote qualified, diverse, and culturally competent administrative, clinical, and support staff who are trained and qualified to address the needs of the racial and ethnic communities being served.

5 Require and arrange for ongoing education and training for administrative, clinical, and support staff in culturally and linguistically competent services.

6 Provide all staff with limited English proficiency access to bilingual staff or interpretation services.

7 Provide oral and written notices, including translated signage at key points of contact, to clients in their primary language informing them of their right to receive no-cost interpreter services.

8 Translate and make available signage and commonly used written client educational material and other materials for members of the predominant language groups in service areas.

9 Ensure that interpreters and bilingual staff can demonstrate bilingual proficiency and receive training that includes the skills and ethics of interpreting, and knowledge in both languages of the terms and concepts relevant to clinical and nonclinical encounters. Family or friends are not considered adequate substitutes because they usually lack these abilities.

10 Ensure that client's primary spoken language and self-identified race/ethnicity are included in the health care organization's management information system as well as any client records used by provider staff.

11 Use a variety of methods to collect and utilize accurate demographic, cultural, epidemiological, and clinical outcomes data for racial and ethnic groups in the service area, and become informed about the ethnic/cultural needs, resources, and assets of the surrounding community.

12 Undertake ongoing organizational self-assessment of cultural and linguistic competence and integrate measures of access, satisfaction, quality, and outcomes for CLAS into other organizational internal audits and performance improvement programs.

13 Develop structures and procedures to address cross-cultural ethical and legal conflicts in health care delivery and complaints or grievances by clients and staff about unfair, culturally insensitive, or discriminatory treatment, or difficulty in accessing services, or denial of services.

14 Prepare an annual progress report documenting the organization's progress with implementing CLAS standards, including information programs, staffing, and resources.

care. Our example is based on work done in Connecticut DMHAS, the single state agency responsible for the delivery of safety net mental health and addiction services to Connecticut's adult citizens. Services are provided both directly by the Department and through contracts with private providers through grants-in-aid and fee-for-service arrangements. The Department funds several hundred providers and serves over 60,000 people annually. The Department is a provider of services, a payor for services, and an administrator responsible for ensuring the integrity of a comprehensive continuum of care for adults receiving care in the public sector. Complex systems of care present unique challenges to those attempting to ensure effective service delivery across different racial-cultural groups.

A SYSTEMS FRAMEWORK FOR CULTURAL COMPETENCY

The public behavioral health system is crucial to the provision of services for members of different cultural groups (DHHS, 1999; Snowden, 1999). It is the safety net provider for those who often do not have the finances or insurance to receive services elsewhere. It is also the provider of services for people who have severe mental health or substance use disorders. Taxpayers and governments will continue to bear the brunt of the failure of behavioral health care systems to adequately engage and retain clients from various racial-cultural groups through increased medical costs stemming from revolving-door emergency room admissions, homelessness, and costs associated with incarceration of behaviorally disordered individuals (Snowden, 2001). In Connecticut, the total alcohol and other drug abuse costs for residents is estimated to be $3.75 billion annually, or approximately $1,100 for each man, woman, and child in the state. These costs include, but are not limited to, medical care, lost productivity due to illness or injury and premature death, motor vehicle accidents and fatalities, police enforcement, incarceration of offenders, victims of crime, AIDS, and fetal alcohol syndrome (DMHAS, 1999). In contrast, efforts to adequately engage clients can increase the likelihood that many will become productive members of society. The common focus of addressing how cultural competence can inform clinical intervention at the practitioner level is important, but neglects the role of public behavioral health care system policies and practices.

Although much has been written about the need to better serve members of different racial-cultural groups, much of the literature has focused on the therapeutic relationship and how clinicians should improve their skills to become more effective in working cross-culturally. Relatively little has been written about program design, and there is a significant dearth of information about how systems should be designed to be responsive to the needs of culturally diverse groups. The lack of attention to systems of care is particularly troubling when one considers that what practitioners can do is often constrained by programmatic and other policy considerations. For example, clinicians may develop skills that allow them to be more effective in the therapeutic relationship, but to the extent that there are program or organizational policies that do not support culturally competent approaches, their increased clinical skill may not result in improved clinical outcomes. An example is a program that failed to establish protocols for the smooth transition of clients to the next lower level of care. The clinician may do an excellent job of engaging the person, but because the person did not get a timely referral to a lower level of care, she relapses and ends up in an acute care setting. Program design and policies must support culturally competent care to achieve the desired clinical outcomes. Likewise, for those responsible for a system of care, like the Connecticut DMHAS system, which involves hundreds or perhaps thousands of practitioners, an individually oriented approach alone is not practical. One must have a way of conceptualizing the system that informs broad policy direction, system design, and system management.

We describe a framework for developing a culturally competent system of care. The framework posits that effective therapeutic relationships are necessary but not sufficient for culturally competent systems. Race and culture are used as a frame of reference for understanding group differences—in this case, clinical outcomes. We describe a strategy for developing a culturally competent system of care. At the heart of our strategy is a definition of cultural competence that is objective, measurable, and easy to articulate to large and diverse audiences. In the framework described here, cultural competency is viewed in light of major health disparities between people of Color and Whites that are well documented in the health care literature.

Although there has been increasing attention to the issue of health disparities in the physical health community, relatively little attention has been paid to health disparities in the behavioral health care arena. As mentioned previously, a notable exception is the surgeon general's report (U.S. DHHS, 2001), which clearly identifies health disparities in mental health treatment. The surgeon general notes that although the prevalence of many disorders for racial-cultural groups is comparable to the White population, because of issues of access and responsive treatment, behavioral health outcomes are poor (Carter, this *Handbook,* this volume). Among the disparities specified are that minorities (1) have less access to, and availability of, mental health services; (2) are less likely to receive needed mental health services; (3) once in treatment, often receive a poorer quality of mental health care; and (4) are underrepresented in mental health research. Identifying and understanding these disparities can offer guidance on how culturally competent systems of care can be developed. Ensuring equality in access, utilization, and outcomes of mental health care becomes the framework for developing a culturally competent system. Such attention to broad system indicators and strategies for intervention is a departure from strategies that focus exclusively on clinician knowledge, skills, and attitudes or even on ensuring culturally competent programs.

In developing culturally competent systems, one is presented with several challenges. The first is communicating what is meant by a culturally competent system to a large and diverse group of people. A system of care includes highly trained clinicians from various disciplines, program administrators, nonclinical staff, advocates, recovering people, clients, and policymakers. All of these individuals affect how a behavioral health care system operates. All of them have a role in how effective that system is in serving people from various racial-cultural groups. Therefore, a framework must be adopted that can easily, clearly, and concisely communicate to them what the goals are in developing a culturally competent system. A second issue is that interventions must be developed that are cost-effective and can be implemented across different racial-cultural groups. This is particularly true for public sector providers, who generally operate with small budgetary margins. Third, policies must be evaluated and modified to achieve one's goal. This requires an ability to evaluate policies from some objective framework. Health disparities are useful here in that one can develop clear, measurable goals. For example, well-documented disparities in access might lead to a change in policy that promotes access in certain geographic areas. Whether policy change is effective is an empirical question subject to objective evaluation.

Another challenge in developing culturally competent systems of care is identifying an appropriate strategy for system change. The Connecticut DMHAS adopted internal and external approaches. The internal approaches were organizational development activities that enhanced agency staff's ability to provide culturally competent services and to ensure that the DMHAS service system was effective for people from various cultural backgrounds. The internal strategies were based on the belief that to promulgate a culturally competent system, staff that had overall responsibility for managing and monitoring the system had to have the requisite knowledge, skills, and attitudes with regard to providing services to people from different racial-cultural groups. External approaches were those activities done with organizations outside of the agency designed to ensure access and effective services for people from various cultural backgrounds. The external strategy was based on the notion that specific changes needed to occur within the system to achieve the goal of better outcomes for people from different racial-cultural groups. These external strategies happened at multiple levels and from multiple perspectives.

The various levels that were targeted included the practitioner, programmatic, and policy levels. DMHAS embraced a multiple perspective strategy as well. Specifically, both culturally specific and transcultural approaches were utilized. Culturally specific approaches are those interventions that take into account the unique characteristics of a cultural group and are optimized to work with people from that group. For example, a culturally specific program for Latinos might be a program in which services are delivered in Spanish and address issues unique to Latinos from the local community. Transcultural approaches, on the other hand, are good clinical practices that apply across different cultural groups. For example, family involvement in treatment has been found to be correlated with positive clinical outcomes for persons with severe mental illness. Similarly, many who have written about culturally competent approaches have identified family involvement as an important ingredient in good clinical care. Thus, promoting family involvement in treatment is an important strategy for effective service delivery to people from a variety of cultural backgrounds.

We believe that both approaches are necessary for large-scale systems change. Next, we give concrete examples of how racially and culturally specific approaches and transcultural approaches were implemented.

AN EXAMPLE OF A MULTILEVEL APPROACH TO CULTURAL COMPETENCE: CONNECTICUT DMHAS

DMHAS is the public sector behavioral health system for adults in Connecticut. It averages $560 million a year in operating expenses and is the safety net provider for the underinsured and uninsured adults with psychiatric and/or substance use problems. It has the responsibility of designing, financing, and delivering services that are accessible and quality-driven to an underserved population. The agency consists of 3,600 employees, two inpatient psychiatric hospitals, and 15 Local Mental Health Authorities (LMHA) that allow for coverage of the entire state. The LMHAs provide a broad range of services: outpatient, residential, vocational, emergency crisis, case management, and psychosocial rehabilitation. Moreover, 250 private, nonprofit providers are contract-funded to provider community-based services for DMHAS clients.

In 2000, the overall racial composition of Connecticut DMHAS clients was 61% White, 20% Black, 18% Latino, and 1% other. Whites are underrepresented and Blacks and Latinos are overrepresented in the client population, as indicated by the total state population of each racial-cultural group: 82% Whites, 9% Blacks, and 9.4% Latinos, as determined by the 2000 U.S. census. Moreover, there exists racial variation in client population across the five regions of the state. For example, in the southwestern region, Blacks and Latinos constitute 30% and 25% of the client population, respectively, while in the eastern region, these groups constitute only 12% and 9%, respectively.

Over the past several years, Connecticut DMHAS has initiated efforts to make cultural competence pervasive throughout the system so as to inform practice, programming, and policy. The DMHAS cultural competence initiative is intended to advance its mission of being a behavioral health care system that can effectively promote recovery for all of its clients. The Connecticut DMHAS has chosen a multilevel approach to infusing cultural competence in its system of care, targeting interventions at the practitioner, program, and policy levels. At the practitioner and program level, some interventions are designed to foster culturally competent practice for all clients, while others are specifically designed to engage clients from particular racial-cultural groups who have a lower rate of utilizing traditional community-based behavioral health care services. Both types of interventions are described next.

Practitioner Level

Practitioners are program staff, such as therapists, case managers, and nurses, who work directly with clients and are responsible for implementing the clinical and/or program intervention. The DMHAS Office of Multicultural Affairs has developed and implemented a comprehensive, 16-module training on cultural competence designed for practitioners that occurs two days a week over a seven-month period. All state-operated and contracted providers are notified of training dates and requested to send their practitioners. In 2001–2002, representatives from approximately 25 agencies attended each session. This training advanced both the culturally specific and transcultural approaches. The training focused on specific knowledge of the major racial-cultural groups and also promoted an approach to increase providers' understanding of the impact of race and culture on behavioral health disorders and treatment, thus enhancing their ability to work across various cultural groups.

A culturally specific approach to infusing cultural competence at the practitioner level involved the hiring and training of peer-engagement specialists in 1999. Peer-engagement specialists, currently called recovery managers, were former substance abusers recruited and trained to find frequent users of intensive substance-abuse services such as inpatient detoxification and engage them in recovery-oriented care. Peer-engagement specialists were highly respected and credible in both the drug-using and mainstream community, were visible, had been sober for a number of years, were bilingual, and knew the culture of the drug-using population. They worked mostly to engage same-race individuals in the inner-city areas of Connecticut who were suffering from addictions that were the same or similar to those they themselves had once suffered. The use of peer-engagement specialists significantly increased the engagement of chronic substance-abusing individuals in treatment. Such specialists now exist in every region of Connecticut.

Program Level

Within Connecticut DMHAS, efforts to infuse cultural competence at the program level were facilitated by requiring all providers of behavioral health care to develop plans for increasing cultural competence in their programs as a condition to receive continued funding. The DMHAS initiative was guided by a manual entitled *Multicultural Behavioral Healthcare: Best Standard Practices and Implementation Guidelines* (DMHAS, 2001) developed by OMA and disseminated to the entire provider community. With the aid of the Multicultural Training and Research Institute of Temple University, the manual names and defines best practices for an agency to be culturally competent in the following eight dimensions: (1) service access, (2) conduct of culturally appropriate assessments, (3) treatment/rehabilitation planning, (4) availability of bilingual staff and materials that are in the preferred language of the client, (5) assessing quality of life, (6) case management, (7) discharge planning and service linkage, and (8) availability and accessibility of culturally compatible recovery, self-help groups, and natural supports.

In August 2001, DMHAS launched a three-pronged approach to encourage providers to adopt the culturally competent practices outlined in the manual. First, providers were required to assess their cultural competence by rating their programs on eight dimensions (see Appendix). Second, providers were then asked to use the assessment of their program to identify program strengths and needs and to prioritize goals and objectives to be addressed in their cultural competence plan. Each plan emphasized addressing client access, engagement, and retention. Third, the plans were then submitted for review to the regional team leader for each provider. Upon receipt, the Office of Multicultural Affairs staff reviewed and rated plans and approved recommendations for improving or implementing each plan. DMHAS currently contracts with 136 providers, 131 of which have implemented approved plans. The final step of encouraging providers to adopt culturally competent practices involved development of policy that established accountability standards for ensuring that objectives stated in the plans are actively pursued.

A second approach to promoting culturally competent programming involved development of culturally specific programs designed for use with clients from specific cultural groups who have either not entered treatment previously or, upon entry, have not remained in treatment. Seven such programs exist for Latino, African American, and Asian clients dealing with a range of clinical issues, including substance abuse, HIV/AIDS, and linking substance-using clients recently released from incarceration to community-based treatment. Although these programs are unique, they share several common features. First, they utilize outreach workers and therapists who are bicultural and, in some cases, bilingual. For example, the Latino Outreach Initiative uses outreach workers who are bilingual and know the culture of the respective community. The result has been a substantial increase in numbers of clients engaging in treatment who traditionally were difficult to reach. Second, culturally specific programs engage clients in the community instead of waiting for potential clients to walk into a clinic. It is not uncommon for members of certain cultural groups to avoid mental health facilities due to mistrust, lack of faith in the utility of mental health services, and shame or stigma that may have ensued from pursuing mental health treatment (DHHS, 1999). The surgeon general (DHHS, 1999) notes that best practices in culturally competent care may also involve interacting with clients in their home or other community setting to increase the likelihood of engagement in treatment. For example, the outreach workers of the Latino Outreach Initiative do not wait for clients to come to them but instead go to known locations where potential clients may buy or use drugs in order to engage them in treatment, or to community locales where substance-using Latino men are known to congregate. Another example of a culturally specific program developed by DMHAS seeks to engage women in preventative behavioral health services; outreach workers approach potential clients in shopping malls. Third, and finally, all culturally specific programs provide services in a manner that takes into account the whole person. A holistic approach addresses all areas of a client's life that may facilitate recovery, such as providing employment support or aid to secure vocational, educational, or health care services.

Simultaneous with the Department's efforts to provide culturally specific programs, it initiated an effort to increase the level of evidence-based practice that was occurring in the field, that is, strategies that increased the use of empirically supported treatment. The evidence-based practice initiative included articulating the importance of providing high-quality services and measuring outcomes. Also, the Department emphasized recovery-oriented approaches that focused treatment on assisting people to achieve their highest level of independent functioning. The evidence-based practice and recovery strategies are examples of transcultural approaches. They raise the bar on service delivery overall and promote effective service delivery regardless of the cultural background of those being served.

Policy Level

Policy changes also have been used as a vehicle for developing an infrastructure that supports adoption of cultural competence into the overall philosophy and mission of DMHAS. One such change involved altering the program monitoring procedure to include assessment of a provider's implementation of its cultural competence plans. The monitoring procedure was accompanied by policy that facilitated adoption of new language into the contracts of all state-funded providers that holds them accountable for development and implementation of their cultural competence plans.

The program monitoring system is a two-day comprehensive process that includes focus groups with clients, interviews with the agency director and staff, and a review of recordkeeping practices. The monitor completes a checklist that rates the agency on the eight dimensions of cultural competence described previously, and also assesses whether cultural competence plans have been implemented. If plans have not been developed or implemented, DMHAS noncompliance procedures are enacted, which ultimately can result in withheld funding. This builds in accountability to encourage systemwide adoption of culturally competent behavioral health practices. Policy development has also been used to influence adoption and use of information systems to understand the racial-cultural composition of DMHAS clients and document disparities in care. In examining the system as a whole, we have been able to document disparities in (1) the successful transition from acute care to rehabilitative care, (2) inpatient psychiatric hospitalization rates, and (3) use of community-based services designed to promote recovery. Such data have provided evidence to policymakers and providers that disparities do exist in the treatment system that merit attention. Furthermore, racial-cultural disparities found highlight the cost of not providing effective care. The result has been the integration of cultural competence into the overall philosophy and mission of the service system.

Such data also allow us to determine the racial-cultural composition of a provider's service area and compare that information with a provider's client composition. DMHAS is in the process of developing a mechanism by which such information is disseminated to the provider. If disparities exist, the provider will be requested to develop strategies to address the disparities with assistance from the Office of Multicultural Affairs if needed. The regional monitor will then assess the degree to which the strategies have been implemented during the monitoring process. Moreover, the information systems will be used to monitor reduction in disparities and client outcomes after adoption of strategies.

The policy strategies related to monitoring represent both culturally specific and transcultural approaches. Data are used to look at how specific cultural groups are fairing in the system, but the overall approach to using data to monitor and manage the system is one that has benefits across all cultural groups being served in the system.

CONCLUSIONS AND FUTURE DIRECTIONS: SUSTAINING CULTURAL COMPETENCE IN A SYSTEM OF CARE

The case study presented here is representative of the growing and evolving nature of cultural competence as it continues to move past the individual level into organizational and statewide policy efforts. However, according to Cross et al. (1989), cross-cultural competence does not occur solely in a one-day training, by reading a book, or by bringing in consultants. Rather, it depends on the development of knowledge and skills and ongoing self-evaluation of progress.

In our example, Connecticut DMHAS has implemented strategies at the practitioner, program, and policy levels to implement a framework that promotes a comprehensive culturally competent system of care. These include implementation of a cultural competency training program for service providers and incorporation of peer-engagement specialists at the practitioner level. At the program level, cultural competency plans were developed in 131 agencies and programmatic services were implemented that addressed the needs of specific cultural and racial groups. Finally, at the policy level, a major focus of improvement was program monitoring, which concentrated on individual agency implementation of cultural competency plans.

Despite some of our successes, we believe it is imperative to identify areas for continuous quality improvement to ensure cultural competence within DMHAS. We describe our next steps for sustaining systems-level cultural competence through a quality improvement process. Areas of focus are as follows: (1) explore how DMHAS and its contracted agencies and organizations view culture and cultural competency; (2) continue to reduce behavioral health disparities in access to care and treatment among racial-cultural groups, such as including more programs to meet the needs of racial-cultural groups; (3) conduct research on accessing evidence-based outcomes of racially-culturally specific as well as universal approaches to service provision; (4) develop and refine measures that assess cultural competence at the individual and organizational levels, including conducting research to assess the validity and reliability of existing measures; (5) develop a method of checks and balances to measure the fidelity of interventions to promote cultural competence, such as more work toward systematizing approaches to tracking/monitoring systems-level cultural competency changes; (6) develop a model to assist other service systems to increase cultural competence across all levels; (7) be creative in providing organizations with incentives for implementing their cultural competency plans and for demonstrating a reduction in classic health disparities cited in the literature; (8) obtain feedback from programs and consumers on what works in promoting cultural competence and what areas need improvement; and (9) continue to hold organizations accountable through ongoing policy development.

APPENDIX

MULTICULTURALLY COMPETENT SERVICE SYSTEM ASSESSMENT GUIDE

Instructions

Rate your organization on each item in Sections I through VIII using the following scale:

1	2	3	4	5
Not at all		**To a moderate degree**		**To a great degree**

Suggested Rating Interpretations:

#1 and #2:   **"Priority Concerns"**

#3:   **"Needs Improvement"**

#4 and #5:   **"Adequate"**

I. Agency Demographic Data (Assessment)

A Culturally Competent Agency uses basic demographic information to assess and determine the cultural and linguistic needs of the service area.

_____   Have you identified the demographic composition of the program's service area (from recent census data, local planning documents, statement of need, etc.) which should include ethnicity, race, and primary language spoken as reported by the individuals?

_____ Have you identified the demographic composition of the persons served?

_____ Have you identified the staff composition (ethnicity, race, language capabilities) in relation to the demographic composition of your service area?

_____ Have you compared the demographic composition of the staff with the client demographics?

II. Policies, Procedures and Governance

A Culturally Competent Agency has a board of directors, advisory committee or a policy making group that is proportionally representative of the staff, client/consumers, and community.

_____ Has your organization appointed executives, managers, and administrators who take responsibility for, and have authority over, the development, implementation, and monitoring of the Cultural Competence Plan?

_____ Has your organization's director appointed a standing committee to advise management on matters pertaining to multicultural services?

_____ Does your organization have a mission statement that commits to cultural competence and reflects compliance with all federal and state statutes, as well as any current *Connecticut Commission on Human Rights and Opportunities* nondiscriminatory policies and affirmative action policies?

_____ Does your organization have culturally appropriate policies and procedures communicated orally and/or written in the principle language of the client/consumer to address confidentiality, individual patient rights and grievance procedures, medication fact sheets, legal assistance, and so forth as needed and appropriately?

III. Services/Programs

A Culturally Competent Agency offers services that are culturally competent and in a language that ensures client/consumer comprehension.

A. Linguistic and Communication Support:

_____ Has the program arranged to provide materials and services in the language(s) of limited English-speaking clients/consumers (e.g., bilingual staff, in-house interpreters, or a contract with outside interpreter agency and/or telephone interpreters)?

_____ Do medical records indicate the preferred language of service recipients?

_____ Is there a protocol to handle client/consumer/family complaints in languages other than English?

_____ Are the forms that clients/consumers sign in their preferred language?

_____ Are the persons answering the telephones, during and after-hours, able to communicate in the language of the speakers?

_____ Does the organization provide information about programs, policies, covered services, and procedures for accessing and utilizing services in the primary language(s) of clients/consumers and families?

_____ Does the organization have signs regarding language assistance posted at key locations?

_____ Are there special protocols for addressing language issues at the emergency room, treatment rooms, intake, and so forth?

_____ Are cultural and linguistic supports available for clients/consumers throughout different service offerings along the service continuum?

B. Treatment/Rehabilitation Planning

_____ Does the program consider the client/consumer's culture, ethnicity and language in treatment planning (assessment of needs, diagnosis, interventions, discharge planning, etc.)?

_____ Does the program involve clients/consumers and family members in all phases of treatment, assessment, and discharge planning?

_____ Has the organization identified community resources (community councils, ethnic/cultural social entities, spiritual leaders, faith communities, voluntary associations, etc.), that can exchange information and services with staff, clients/consumers, and family members?

_____ Have you identified natural community healers, spiritual healers, clergy, and so forth, when appropriate, in the development and/or implementation of the service plan?

_____ Have you identified natural supports (relatives, traditional healers, spiritual resources, etc.) for purposes of reintegrating the individual into the community?

_____ Have you used community resources and natural supports to re-integrate the individual into the community?

C. Cultural Assessments

_____ Is the client/consumer's culture/ethnicity taken into account when formulating a diagnosis or assessment?

_____ Are culturally relevant assessment tools utilized to augment the assessment/diagnosis process?

_____ Is the client/consumer's level of acculturation identified, described, and incorporated as part of a cultural assessment?

_____ Is the client/consumer's ethnicity/culture identified, described, and incorporated as part of a cultural assessment?

D. Cultural Accommodations

_____ Are culturally appropriate, educative approaches, such as films, slide presentations, or video tapes utilized for preparation and orientation of client/consumer family members to your program?

_____ Does your program incorporate aspects of each client/consumer's ethnic/cultural heritage into the design of specialized interventions or services?

_____ Does your program have ethnic/culture-specific group formats available for engagement, treatment, and/or rehabilitation?

_____ Is there provider collaboration with natural community healers, spiritual healers, clergy, and so forth, where appropriate, in the development and/or implementation of the service plan?

E. Program Accessibility

_____ Do persons from different cultural and linguistic backgrounds have timely and convenient access to your services?

_____ Are services located close to the neighborhoods where persons from different cultures and linguistic backgrounds reside?

_____ Are your services readily accessible by public transportation?

_____ Do your programs provide needed supports to families of clients/consumers, for example, meeting rooms for extended families, child support, drop-in services, and so forth?

_____ Do you have services available during evenings and weekends?

IV. Care Management

_____ Does the level and length of care meet the needs for clients/consumers from different cultural backgrounds?

_____ Is the type of care for clients/consumers from different backgrounds consistently and effectively managed according to their identified cultural needs?

_____ Is the management of the services for people from different groups compatible with their ethnic/cultural background?

V. Continuity of Care

_____ Do you have letters of agreement with culturally oriented community services and organizations?

_____ Do you have integrated, planned, transitional arrangements between one service modality and another?

_____ Do you have arrangements, financial or otherwise, for securing concrete services needed by clients/consumers (e.g., housing, income, employment, medical, dental, and other emergency personal support needs)?

VI. Human Resources Development

A culturally competent agency implements staff training and development in cultural competence at all levels and across all disciplines, for leadership and

governing entities, as well as for management, supervisory, treatment, and support staff.

_____ Are the principles of cultural competence (e.g., cultural awareness, language training skills, training in working with diverse populations) included in staff orientation and ongoing training programs?

_____ Is the program making use of other programs or organizations that specialize in serving persons with diverse cultural and linguistic background as a resource for staff education and training?

_____ Is the program maximizing recruitment and retention efforts for staff who reflect the cultural and linguistic diversity of populations needing services?

_____ Have the staff's training needs in cultural competence been assessed?

_____ Have staff attended training programs on cultural competence in the past two years?

Describe: _____

_____

_____

VII. Quality Monitoring and Improvement

A culturally competent agency has a quality monitoring and improvement program that ensures access to culturally competent care.

_____ Does the Quality Improvement (QI) Plan address the cultural/ethnic and language needs?

_____ Are clients/consumers and families asked whether ethnicity/culture and language are appropriately addressed in order to receive culturally competent services in the organization?

_____ Does the organization maintain copies of minutes, recommendations, and accomplishments of its multicultural advisory committee?

_____ Is there a process for continually monitoring, evaluating, and rewarding the cultural competence of staff?

VIII. Information/Management System

_____ Does the organization monitor, survey, or otherwise access, the QI utilization patterns, Against Medical Advice (A.M.A.) rates, and so forth, based on the culture/ethnicity and language?

_____ Are client/consumer satisfaction surveys available in different languages in proportion to the demographic data?

_____ Are there data collection systems developed and maintained to track clients/consumers by demographics, utilization and outcomes across levels of care, transfers, referrals, re-admissions, and so forth?

REFERENCES

Abromowitz, S. I., & Murray, J. (1983). Race effects in psychotherapy. In J. Murray & P. R. Abramson (Eds.), *Bias in psychotherapy* (pp. 215–255). New York: Praeger.

Adebimpe, V. (1981). Overview: White norms and psychiatric diagnosis of Black patients. *American Journal of Psychiatry, 138,* 279–285.

Alarcon, R. D., Foulks, E. F., & Vakkur, M. (1998). *Personality disorders and culture: Clinical and conceptual interactions.* New York: Wiley.

Arredondo, P., Toporek, R., Brown, S. P., Jones, J., Locke, D. C., Sanchez, J., et al. (1996). Operationalization of the multicultural counseling competencies. *Journal of Multicultural Counseling and Development, 24,* 42–78.

Baker, F., & Bell, C. (1999). Issues in the psychiatric treatment of African Americans. *Psychiatric Services, 50*(3), 363–368.

Carney, C. G., & Kahn, K. B. (1984). Building competencies for effective cross-cultural counseling: A developmental view. *Counseling Psychologist, 12*(1), 111–119.

Carter, R. T. (in press). Uprooting inequity and disparities in counseling and psychology: An introduction. In R. T. Carter (Ed.), H*andbook of racial-cultural psychology and counseling: Theory and research* (Vol. 1, pp. xv–xxviii). Hoboken, NJ: Wiley.

Connecticut Department of Mental Health and Addiction Services. (1999). *FFY 2000 Substance Abuse Prevention and Treatment Block Grant Allocation Plan.* Presented to Connecticut General Assembly, September 1999, Hartford, CT.

Connecticut Department of Mental Health and Addiction Services. (2001). *Multicultural Behavioral Healthcare: Best Standard Practices & Implementation Guidelines.* Hartford: Author.

Constantine, M., & Ladany, N. (2001). New visions for defining and assessing multicultural counseling competence. In J. Ponterotto, J. M. Casas, L. Suzuki, & C. Alexander (Eds.), *Handbook of multicultural counseling* (pp. 482–498). Thousand Oaks, CA: Sage.

Constantine, M. G., Watt, S. K., Gainor, K. A., & Warren, A. K. (in press). The influence of Cross's initial black racial identity theory on other cultural identity conceptualizations. In R. T. Carter (Ed.), H*andbook of racial-cultural psychology and counseling: Theory and research* (Vol. 1, pp. 94–114). Hoboken, NJ: Wiley.

Constantino, G., Malady, R., & Rogler, L. (1986). Cuento therapy: A culturally sensitive modality for Puerto Rican children. *Journal of Counseling and Clinical Psychology, 54,* 639–645.

Cross, T., Bazron, B., Dennis, K., & Issacs, M. (1989). *Toward developing a culturally competent system of care.* Washington, DC: Georgetown University Child Development Center, CASSP Technical Assistance Center.

Delphin, M. E., & Rollock, D. (1995). University alienation and African American ethnic identity as predictors of attitudes towards, knowledge about and likely use of psychological services. *Journal of College Student Development, 36*(4), 337–346.

Draguns, J. G. (in press). Cultural psychology: Its early roots and present status. In R. T. Carter (Ed.), H*andbook of racial-cultural psychology and counseling: Theory and research* (Vol. 1, pp. 163–183). Hoboken, NJ: Wiley.

Friedman, R. M. (1986). Major issues in mental health services for children. *Administration in Mental Health, 14,* 6–13.

Fuertes, J., & Gretchen, D. (2001). Emerging theories of multicultural counseling. In J. Ponterotto, J. M. Casas, L. Suzuki, & C. Alexander (Eds.), *Handbook of multicultural counseling* (2nd ed., pp. 509–541). Thousand Oaks, CA: Sage.

Gardner, L. H. (1971). The therapeutic relationship under varying conditions of race. *Psychotherapy: Theory, Research and Practice, 8,* 78–87.

Griffith, E. H., & Gonzalez, C. A. (1996). Essentials of cultural psychiatry. In R. E. Hales & S. C. Yudofsky (Eds.), *The American Psychiatric Press synopsis of psychiatry* (pp. 1283–1306). Washington, DC: American Psychiatric Press.

Hanley, J. (1998). Applying cultural competence principles within a state mental health system. In M. Hernandez & M. Isaacs (Eds.), *Promoting cultural competence in children's mental health services* (pp. 17–19). Baltimore: Brooks.

Iwamasa, G. Y., Larrabee, A. L., & Merritt, R. D. (2000). Are personality disorder criteria ethnically biased? A card-sort analysis. *Cultural Diversity and Ethnic Minority Psychology, 6*(3), 284–296.

Knitzer, J. (1984). Mental health services to children and adolescents: A national view of public policies. *American Psychologist, 39,* 905–911.

Pedersen, P. (in press). The importance of Cultural Psychology Theory for multicultural counselors. In R. T. Carter (Ed.), *Handbook of racial-cultural psychology and counseling: Theory and research* (Vol. 1, pp. 3–16). Hoboken, NJ: Wiley.

Ponterotto, J. G., Fuertes, J. N., & Chen, E. C. (2000). Models of multicultural counseling. In S. D. Brown & R. W. Lent (Eds.), *Handbook of counseling psychology* (3rd ed., pp. 639–669). New York: Wiley.

Reynolds, A. (2001). Multidimensional cultural competence: Providing tools for transforming psychology. *Counseling Psychologist, 29*(6), 833–841.

Ridley, C., Baker, D. M., & Hill, C. (2001). Critical issues concerning cultural competence. *Counseling Psychologist, 26*(9), 822–832.

Ridley, C. R., Mendoza, D., & Kanitz, B. (1994). Multicultural training: reexamination, operationalization and integration. *Counseling Psychologist, 22*(2), 227–289.

Ridley, C. R., Mendoza, D., Kanitz, B., Angermeier, L., & Zenk, R. (1994). Cultural sensitivity in multicultural counseling: a perceptual schema model. *Journal of Counseling Psychology, 41*(2), 125–136.

Snowden, L. R. (1999). Psychiatric inpatient care and ethnic minority populations. In J. M. Herrera, W. B. Lawson, & J. J. Sramek (Eds.), *Cross cultural psychiatry* (pp. 783–813). New York: Wiley.

Snowden, L. R. (2001). Barriers to effective mental health services for African-Americans. *Mental Health Services Research, 13,* 181–188.

Sue, D. W. (2001). Multidimensional facets of cultural competence. *Counseling Psychologist, 29*(6), 790–821.

Sue, D. W., Arredondo, P., & McDavis, R. J. (1992). Multicultural counseling competencies and standards: A call to the profession. *Journal of Counseling and Development, 70,* 477–486.

Sue, D. W., Bernier, Y., Durran, A., Feinberg, L., Pederson, P. B., Smith, E. J., et al. (1982). Position paper: Cross-cultural counseling competencies. *Counseling Psychologist, 10,* 45–52.

Sue, D. W., Carter, R., Casas, J. M., Fouad, N., Ivey, A. E., Jensen, M., et al. (1998). *Multicultural counseling competencies: Individual and organizational development.* Thousand Oaks, CA: Sage.

Sue, D. W., Ivey, A. E., & Pedersen, P. B. (1996). *A theory of multicultural counseling and therapy.* Pacific Grove, CA: Brooks/Cole.

U.S. Department of Health and Human Services. (1999). *Mental health: A report of the Surgeon General.* Rockville, MD: Author.

U.S. Department of Health and Human Services. (2000). *Healthy people 2000: National health promotion and disease prevention objectives* (Department of Health and Human Services Publication No. 91-5050212). Washington, DC: U.S. Government Printing Office.

U.S. Department of Health and Human Services. (2001). *Mental health: Culture, race and ethnicity, a supplement to mental health: A report of the Surgeon General.* Rockville, MD: Author.

U.S. Department of Health and Human Services, Office of Minority Health. (2001a). *A practical guide for implementing the recommended national standards for culturally and linguistically appropriate services in healthcare.* Retrieved February 9, 2002 from http://www.omhrc.gov/clas/guide3a.asp.

U.S. Department of Health and Human Services, Office of Minority Health. (2001b). *Assuring cultural competence in health care: Recommendations for national standards and an outcome focused research agenda.* Retrieved August 25, 2001 from http://www.omhrc.gov/clas/cultural1a.htm.

CHAPTER 30

An Ethical Code for Racial-Cultural Practice: Filling Gaps and Confronting Contradictions in Existing Ethical Guidelines

Leon D. Caldwell and Dolores D. Tarver

Since its initial publication in 1953, the American Psychological Association's (APA) Ethical Principles of Psychologists and Code of Conduct, popularly referred to as the Ethics Code, has been the standard by which the practice of its members are held accountable. As with most professional organizations providing mental health services (e.g., American Counseling Association), counseling interventions (American Association of Marriage and Family Therapy), or human services (e.g., National Association of Social Workers), ethical codes are intended to maintain a standard of care that protects the public welfare. Since the writing of this manuscript, APA updated the Ethics Code (December 2002) effective June 2003. The purpose of this chapter is to (1) present an overview of the 2002 Ethics Code, (2) review limitations of the 1992 Ethics Code, (3) evaluate the efforts of the 2002 Code to address previous limitations, and (4) offer recommendations for a racial and cultural ethical code. The authors stipulate that an ethical code for racial-cultural practice must confront the existing shortcomings and limitations of existing codes.

The ethical code of any organization is a good starting point for understanding that organization's implicit and explicit cultural frame. Numerous authors have critically examined the ethical codes of mental health professional organizations and their relationship to and impact on racially and culturally diverse groups (e.g., Caldwell, in preparation; Casas, Ponterotto, & Gutierrez, 1986; Casas & Thompson, 1991; Ibrahim & Arredondo, 1986; LaFromboise & Foster, 1989; Pedersen, 1989, 1995; Pedersen & Marsella, 1982; Ridley, Liddle, Hill, & Li, 2001). These critiques found the 1992 professional Ethics Code to be individualistic, masculine-focused, confined to middle-class values, culturally encapsulating, and too narrow, promoting the values, norms, and expectations of a Eurocentric male ethos. Thus, the Code's universal applicability with an increasingly racially and culturally diverse population is in question (Kambon, 1998; LaFromboise & Foster, 1989; Pedersen,

1997). We believe that professional standards should be adopted for the 2002 Code that protect diverse approaches to healing and helping.

OVERVIEW OF THE 2002 ETHICS CODE

The APA Ethics Code consists of an introduction, a preamble, five general principles, and specific ethical standards. The introduction describes the intent, organization, procedural considerations, and scope of application of the Code. The preamble and general principles are aspirational goals intended to guide psychologists toward the highest ideals of psychology, and the ethical standards set forth enforceable rules for conduct as psychologists (APA, 2002). Essentially, the broadly written Ethics Code is the governing rule for the practice of psychology.

The general principles are organized into five categories: (1) beneficence and nonmaleficence, (2) fidelity and responsibility, (3) integrity, (4) justice, and (5) respect for people's rights and dignity (APA, 2002). The general principles offer broad guidelines for the ethical behavior of psychologists under the overarching theme of protecting the public. Psychologists and counselors are to practice within the scope of their education, training, and experience. Psychologists have a responsibility to be aware of cultural, individual, and role differences and to abstain from exploitative professional relationships (Corey, Corey, & Callanan, 1998).

The ethical standards are organized into 10 categories: (1) resolving ethical issues, (2) competence, (3) human relations, (4) privacy and confidentiality, (5) advertising and other public statements, (6) recordkeeping and fees, (7) education and training, (8) research and publication, (9) assessment, and (10) therapy.

Prior to 1953, APA and its members participated in research, training, and practice that overtly exploited and systematically abused non-White, non-European, low-income populations. As a result of the mental health field's historical substandard treatment of underserved and underrepresented populations (Thomas & Sillen, 1972), racially and culturally diverse individuals have developed various levels of "cultural mistrust" (Terrell & Terrell, 1981) and "healthy paranoia" (Ridley et al., 2001). Despite the evolution of the Ethics Code, there is evidence that even today, members of APA continue to engage in exploitative racial-cultural practices, such as the use of inappropriate assessments (Suzuki, Kugler, Aguiar, this *Handbook,* this volume), providing culturally incompetent services and supervision (Chen, this *Handbook,* this volume), and the use of fallacious statistical procedures resulting in inflated, inaccurate, and often overgeneralized results. It makes one wonder if the current Code is any more capable of protecting a demographically diverse population than the original Code written in 1953. The question remains: Are current professional codes adequate for racial-cultural practice?

COMPARISON OF THE 1992 AND 2002 ETHICS CODE

In creating the Ethics Code to govern competent practice of psychologists, APA set forth principles and standards for addressing cultural differences. Though it provided broad guidelines intended to promote cultural competency, the 1992 Ethics

Code needed to be modified to promote more enforceable rules of racial-cultural practice (LaFromboise, Foster, & James, 1996). For example, Ethical Standard 2.01b reads as follows:

> Where scientific or professional knowledge in the discipline of psychology establishes that an understanding of factors associated with age, gender, gender identity, race, ethnicity, culture, national origin, religion, sexual orientation, disability, language, or socioeconomic status is essential for effective implementation of their services or research, psychologists have or obtain the training, experience, consultation, or supervision necessary to ensure the competence of their services or they make appropriate referrals, except as provided in Standard 2.02, Providing services in emergencies. (APA, 2002)

The 1992 Standard 1.08 was updated to include gender identity and culture. The phrase "is essential for effective implementation of their services or research" was also added. One of the criticisms of the 1992 standard was the implicit assumptions of the language used. "Where," at the beginning of the standard, connoted that instances may exist in which the factors (age, gender, race, ethnicity, etc.) should not be considered. The language used in the 2002 revision, though updated to include gender identity and culture, still reflects the assumption that clients and participants are homogeneous.

One of the more controversial ethical standards impacting racial-cultural practice is that governing multiple relationships (3.05a): Psychologists are to "refrain" from engaging in social or other nonprofessional contacts with those individuals with whom they interact in a professional capacity. The 1992 standard may have had the most explicit influence on utilization rates of culturally diverse populations because it is unrealistic for psychologists and psychologists-in-training to expect that historically oppressed and marginalized groups will benefit from the socially detached, objective observer-therapist model. Psychologists need to form a therapeutic alliance with clients that is culturally relevant to the client (D. Sue & Torino, this *Handbook,* this volume; Thompson, this *Handbook,* this volume). Consequently, the counseling relationship may take on different facets for various clients. Sue (1997), using Asian cultures as an example, stated that some Asian clients believe that self-disclosure is most appropriately discussed with an intimate acquaintance (relative or friend). Thus, a psychologist may have to interact with the entire family system to establish rapport and trust.

Formerly Standard 1.17, Ethical Standard 3.05a has been modified to more clearly acknowledge that in many communities and situations, social and nonprofessional contacts may be unavoidable, and multiple relationships should be assessed for harm to the client (APA, 2002). Standard 3.05a now explicitly states that "multiple relationships that would not reasonably be expected to cause impairment or risk exploitation or harm are not unethical." This addition reflects APA's investment in a more culturally relevant Ethics Code and is a positive step toward addressing the limitations of a rigid ethical standard. For example, Sue (1997, pp. 108–109) offered a set of guidelines for racial-cultural practice when dual relationships are unavoidable:

- Personal and professional integrity must be the guiding force behind a decision to enter a dual relationship or maintain one. Consider the client's welfare/therapeutic benefit and not personal agenda.

- Be thoroughly knowledgeable about your profession's code of ethics and the spirit in which it was developed.

- Be educated and knowledgeable about cultural and community standards of practice.

- If dual relationships are uncomfortable or contain too many risks, it is your responsibility to make this clear to the client and to offer referrals to other helping sources.

- In all situations when a dual relationship is unavoidable and engaged, it is necessary that consultation be sought.

Similarly, in providing an African-centered perspective on dual relationships, Parham (1997) cautioned against prohibitions that are rigidly applied due to fear of loss of objectivity, projecting inappropriate dependency, and power differentials that lead to exploitation. Alternatively, he suggested that nonexploitative dual relationships, particularly in racial-cultural practice, may be therapeutically beneficial, even a prerequisite for clients engaging in psychological services (Vera, Buhin, Montgomery, & Shin, this *Handbook,* this volume).

The changes in the standard governing multiple relationships address many of the limitations cited in the 1992 Code. However, we suggest the addition of a section addressing the benefits of therapeutic, nonexploitative dual relationships as well as a section distinquishing serving in multiple roles from engaging in a multiple relationship.

The need for the Code to address providing culturally competent training and supervision was another criticism of previous versions of the Code. The 1992 Ethics Code did very little to direct a psychologist or a psychologist-in-training in the provision of ethically competent service delivery in a racial-cultural context. APA did not promote cultural competence in training programs through the Ethics Code. The 1992 standard stated that training programs should seek to ensure that programs are competently designed, provide the "proper experiences, and meet the requirements for licensure, certification, or other goals for which claims are made by the program" (6.01). Standard 7.01 was updated in the 2002 version of the Code to add that training programs take "reasonable steps" to ensure that the programs are designed to provide "appropriate knowledge." Such vague language still doesn't provide explicit guidelines for programs to follow. In the introduction and applicability section, the modifiers "reasonably," "appropriate," and "potentially" indicate that the language in the Ethics Code was chosen to help psychologists make decisions regarding their professional behavior. The Code is intended to provide general guidelines and does not by itself determine legally enforceable rules for an ethical violation; there are no obligations to ensure that training programs provide culturally competent training or that students are culturally competent. We suggest the addition of an explicit rule declaring that training programs not in compliance with multicultural education requirements are committing an ethical violation, and thus are ineligible to receive accreditation from professional organizations (Carter, this *Handbook,* this volume).

The lack of specific guidelines regarding multicultural competence may partly stem from the position that reaching multicultural counseling competency is aspirational at best. However, training programs that do not adequately prepare psychologists for the integration and infusion of racial-cultural factors in understanding ethical dilemmas render their graduates culturally incompetent. Although full accreditation currently requires an ethics course and a multicultural course in the curriculum, there may be few courses that integrate multicultural concepts with ethical decision making. An overwhelming majority of training programs offer scant practica or field placements with racial-cultural practice experiences. The completion of a few multicultural courses does not provide the type of training necessary for counselors to become multiculturally competent (Arredondo & Arciniega, 2001; D'Andrea, Daniels, & Heck, 1991; Jacob & Greggo, 2001; Rooney, Flores, & Mercier, 1998). Cross-cultural contact, multicultural supervision and mentorship, and the presence of culturally diverse faculty and staff have been cited in the literature as beneficial components of multicultural competency training (Arredondo & Arciniega, 2001; Diaz-Lazaro & Cohen, 2001; Neville et al., 1996; Ponterotto & Austin, this *Handbook,* this volume; Rooney et al., 1998; Steward, 1998). And yet, Standard 7.01 does not explicitly mandate promoting multicultural counseling competency.

Another standard under scrutiny in the 1992 Ethics Code is 6.21, governing the reporting of research results. Now 8.10a in the 2002 Code, this standard mandates that researchers "do not fabricate data" (the phrase "or falsify results in their publications" was omitted in the 2002 version). Also, Standard 9 of the 2002 Ethics Code addresses assessment explicitly. Subsection 9.02b states:

> Psychologists use assessment instruments whose validity and reliability have been established for use with members of the population tested. When such validity or reliability has not been established, psychologists describe the strengths and limitations of test results and interpretation.

Implicit in the previous versions of the Ethics Code was the assumption that assessment instruments were appropriately normed on diverse racial and cultural groups and that samples used in research are culturally and racially representative (Branch, this *Handbook,* this volume; Pedersen, 1989; Suzuki et al., this *Handbook,* this volume). By specifying assessment requirements, Standard 9.02b makes great strides in the direction of culturally competent research. However, the Code remains ambiguous about prohibiting research used to promote classism and racism (Ibrahim & Cameron, this *Handbook,* Volume One). Again, we suggest more explicit language when describing unethical research. Also, how long will researchers continue simply to cite limitations instead of making changes to existing instruments until they meet ethical standards? Until inaccurate research procedures are no longer allowed and explicitly stated as ethical violations, assessments will continue to be limited with respect to racially and culturally diverse groups.

Regarding multicultural counseling competency, in the 1990 version of the APA codes, there were only five specific references to race, ethnicity, and national origin (McGinn, Flowers, & Rubin, 1993; Pedersen, 1989). The 1992 Ethics Code included only two references more than the previous version (APA, 1990). Critics of the 1992 Code posited that the lack of specific multicultural references allowed psychologists to develop a personal set of cross-cultural rules that compromise the very intent of the Professional Code of Ethics (Cayleff, 1986; LaFromboise et al., 1996; Pedersen & Marsella, 1982; Ridley, et al., 2001). Mabe and Rollin (1986, pp. 294–295) in Ridley et al. (2001) identified prominent limitations of the 1992 Ethics Code:

1. There are some issues that cannot be handled in the context of the code.
2. There are some difficulties with enforcing the code, or at least the public may believe that enforcement committees are not tough enough on their peers.
3. There is often no way to systematically bring the interests of the client, patient, or research participant into the code construction process.
4. There are parallel forums in which the issues in the code may be addressed, with the results sometimes at odds with the findings of the code (e.g., in the courts).
5. There are possible conflicts associated with codes: between two codes, between practitioner's values and code requirements, between the code and ordinary morality, between the code and institutional practice, and between requirements within a single code.
6. There is a limited range of topics covered in the code, and because a code approach is usually reactive to issues already developed elsewhere, the requirement of consensus prevents the code from addressing new issues and problems at the "cutting edge."

The 2002 Code does a better job of addressing conflicts with differences between the Code and legal mandates in the introduction and applicability section. The language of the Ethics Code has been clarified in an effort to minimize potential conflict between individual standards, and additions have been made to reflect a multicultural society. Yet, even with these improvements, gaps and contradictions continue to exist. The terminology used in the Code is still general and vague (e.g., "appropriate," "necessary"); explicit, enforceable rules need to be added.

CONFRONTING ASSUMPTIONS IN THE ETHICS CODE

In addition to the previously mentioned limits on operationalizing the 2002 Ethics Code in general practice, there is another set of limitations that hinder racial-cultural practice. At their core, all codes of ethics contain philosophical assumptions. Many multicultural scholars scrutinized the utility of previous versions of the APA Ethics Code for racial-cultural practice on the basis of an erroneously universal assumption of a Western Eurocentric worldview (e.g., Casas et al., 1986; Casas & Thompson, 1991; Cayleff, 1986; Kambon, 1998, LaFromboise & Foster, 1989; Pedersen & Marsella, 1982; Ponterotto, Casas, Suzuki, & Alexander, 1995, 2001).

Lerman and Potter (1990, pp. 6–7) critiqued the 1990 Ethics Code, calling attention to the legalistic and medical models from which the Code is derived. They enumerated six major concerns:

1. Most codes are reactive rather than proactive.
2. Behavior is described in "good-bad" dichotomies and fails to recognize the full complexities of interpersonal relationships.

   The dichotomous nature of ethical principles does not lead to an understanding of the contexts or circumstances that lead to violations and how they can be prevented.
3. Most codes have usually ignored the special circumstances of underserved and underrepresented populations.
4. Procedures for redress and grievances are paternalistic toward consumers.
5. The complaint procedures have frequently been developed to legally protect the profession rather than out of compassion for the client.
6. The codes have been added to in a piecemeal fashion, without further examination of the values, premises, and assumptions from which they were formulated.

With the development of the 2002 Ethics Code, some of those implicit assumptions were addressed. The language now reflects APA's attempt to incorporate a worldview consistent with that of racially and ethnically diverse populations. However, if practitioners generically apply the Ethics Code to all populations, they may still find themselves practicing unethically (Ridley et al., 2001).

Table 30.1   Cross-Cultural Philosophical Principles Translated into Practice

Principle	Racial-Cultural Translation
Altruism	Focuses psychological interventions and research from the abstract theory to the resolution of real psychosocial problems.
Responsibility	Focuses the relevance of actions and community involvement. It requires a deliberate reciprocal counseling relationship.
Justice	Focuses on the quality of fairness. Psychologists are intolerant of exploitation and oppression by one group over any other group.
Caring	Psychologists promote trust and personal investment in helping culturally different clients regardless of the consequences.

Source: From *Handbook of Racial/Ethnic Minority Counseling Research,* by J. C. Ponterotto and J. M. Casas, 1991, Springfield, IL: Charles C. Thomas.

RECOMMENDATIONS FOR A RACIAL-ETHICAL CODE

Recommendations have been made to explicitly interject multicultural philosophies and practices in the Ethics Code through specific references in the principles and standards (McGinn et al., 1994; Pedersen, 1995, 1997; Sue, Arredondo, & McDavis, 1992). Ponterotto et al. (1995, 2001), in their critique of the philosophical premises of the 1992 Ethics Code, proposed four ethical principles that translated into ethical practice in a racial-cultural context (see Table 30.1). To fill gaps and confront contradictions in the existing Ethics Code, stronger, more explicit guidelines are needed in such areas as training standards, accreditation and licensure, competence, professional relationships, client welfare, and assessment techniques (McGinn et al., 1994).

Professional Guidelines

Adopted as policy in August 2003, the Guidelines on Multicultural Education, Training, Research, Practice, and Organizational Change for Psychologists serve as tools for providing services in a multicultural society. The Board of Ethnic Minority Affairs of the APA drafted the Guidelines for Providers of Psychological Services to Ethnic, Linguistic, and Culturally Diverse Populations (APA, 1992). Although unenforceable, these guidelines specifically address the need for psychologists to be aware of their own cultural background, biases, values, and attitudes in both practice and research.

In the practice of rehabilitation counseling, McGinn et al. (1994) suggested that future revisions of the Code of Professional Ethics for Rehabilitation Counselors explicitly address the profession's responsibility and expectations for providing culturally competent services. Similarly, the authors believe the APA Ethics Code should offer specific guidelines for delivering culturally relevant and competent services.

Lerman and Potter (1990) stated that although the 1992 Ethics Code prohibited sexual and dual relationships, the Code did not mention the potential harm of the opposite behaviors: distant, uninvolved therapist-client relationships. An alternative set of guidelines for racial-cultural practice that allows practitioners freedom to forge strong, therapeutic relationships is needed. According to the authors, the Feminist Therapy Ethical Code (1987) is guided by the underlying principle to protect the well-being of clients. That Code's authors acknowledge that it is a living document that is continually in the process of change. Organized into five sections, the Feminist Code offers some guidelines that may also be applicable to racial-cultural practice:

I. Cultural Diversities and Oppressions
II. Power Differentials
III. Overlapping Relationships
IV. Therapist Accountability
V. Social Change

Arguably, feminist therapy has had limited applicability for racial-cultural practice. However, the Feminist Code serves as an exemplar for racial-cultural practitioners to fill gaps and resolve contradictions in the APA Ethical Code.

Multicultural Counseling

Ibrahim and Arredondo (1986, p. 351) proposed the following set of ethical standards for cross-cultural counseling preparation, practice, assessment, and research:

Counseling Practice

Standard 1: Counselors need to incorporate into their practice knowledge of the client's general cultural system and specific worldview.

Standard 2: Counselors need to recognize, assess, and accept their own worldviews, cultural contexts, and biases.

Assessment

Standard 1: Counselors need to appraise the client as a cultural entity before any other assessment strategy is undertaken. Understanding the client as a cultural entity implies an understanding of the client's philosophy of life, beliefs, values, and assumptions in the context of his or her primary and secondary cultures and in the context of the larger societal system.

Standard 2: Counselors need to use multisource, multilevel, and multimethod approaches to assess the capabilities, potentials, and limitations of the client.

Counselor Preparation

Standard 1: Counselor preparation programs, in their policies, procedures, and curricula, recognize and respond to the cultural diversity among students, faculty, and clients.

Standard 2: Counselor educators are prepared to teach and to supervise competently about cross-cultural factors in counseling practice.

Research

Standard 1: Research studies recognize and address such cultural factors as ethnicity, race, gender, lifestyle, and social class.

Standard 2: Research methodology is culturally appropriate to the group and topic under study.

Illustrations Using a Racial and Cultural Code

The scenarios below are fictional illustrations of real ethical issues that may confront practitioners. We acknowledge that there are numerous responses to ethical problems and offer the following as merely examples of ethical behavior that in some cases are appropriate for ethnically/culturally responsive practices.

——————————————— **Scenario 1** ———————————————

Rosita is a 26-year-old Latina client who is being seen by Dr. Universal, a 33-year-old Caucasian female. Due to the small size of the community, Dr. Universal is the only psychologist specializing in Latino research and practice. Rosita, who does not want to come to Dr. Universal's office for fear that her family will find out that she is seeking psychological services, invites Dr. Universal to come to a play with her at a university located outside of town. After reading Standard 3.05a regarding multiple relationships, Dr. Universal decides that she will not go to the play because she does not want to engage in social relationships with her clients. She informs Rosita that she will not be able to attend the play because she provides a professional service to Latino clients and therefore cannot be involved socially with them.

Scenarios similar to this describe a common struggle, especially for novice counselors. A conservative interpretation of the guidelines governing multiple relationships (3.05a) would render Dr. Universal culturally offensive, while an accurate reading provides clear guidelines. Relationships that would not reasonably be expected to cause impairment, risk, or harm are not unethical (APA, 2002). In a racial-cultural context, or even more accurately, within the boundaries of the counselor role, psychologists often have to step outside the comforts of their office and bring their services to clients. Psychologists, especially those in small communities, may have multiple roles: as counselor, advocate, researcher, and teacher. Dr. Universal could have explained the limits of confidentiality of the public setting and explained her role as psychologist and advocate and attended the play without violating the Ethics Code.

--------------------------------- **Scenario 2** ---------------------------------

First Born is a Native American 30-year-old male who is seeking Dr. Universal's services for difficulties adjusting to a new city. First is currently employed making minimum wage and living in a low-income housing apartment complex. Even with the sliding-scale option offered at the Counseling Center, First is unable to afford the psychological services fees. In lieu of cash payment, he offers to provide workshops on Native American spirituality at no cost to Counseling Center staff. Usually, the Center provides payment for these services, which would adequately cover the cost of First Born's sessions. However, Dr. Universal, after reading APA Standard 6.05, decides that engaging in a "bartering arrangement would be exploitative" of the counseling relationship.

In Scenario 2, Dr. Universal again makes a hasty decision out of fear of violating the Ethics Code. As with multiple relationships, avoiding exploitative relationships is the key to ethical behavior of practitioners. The Center usually pays for spirituality workshops, so First and the staff could easily negotiate what appropriate compensation for the workshops would be. That amount could be placed into an account and used to cover First's counseling sessions. Thus, the bartering relationship would not pose any risk for exploitation as long as fees and charges were assessed up front. First, who is financially strained, would be able to receive psychological services and provide a service to the staff, which may present opportunities for him to provide other services on the university campus and in the community. Thus, he would also have an opportunity to meet people and get adjusted to the new city, which is why he sought counseling in the first place.

--------------------------------- **Scenario 3** ---------------------------------

Multi Racial is a 45-year-old male of Japanese, African American, and European decent. He is seeking the services of Dr. Culturally Competent, a 30-year-old

African American male, for career counseling. Multi served as an FBI agent for 25 years and now wants to explore some educational fields, perhaps as a professor of forensic psychology. Dr. Competent, believing that he can easily relate to African American clients, processes the case with some other colleagues. They discuss the value of exploring all of Multi's racial and cultural heritage and not focusing primarily on his African decent. Dr. Competent also explores with colleagues his concerns that Multi is older than he and has been in the workforce for over 20 years; Dr. Competent just received his doctorate last year, so Multi might be somewhat skeptical of Dr. Competent's ability to provide career counseling.

Dr. Competent prepares a battery of career inventories to help explore Multi's interest, only to find that Multi has had bad experiences with assessments in the past. In accordance with Ethical Standard 9 governing the appropriate use of evaluation and assessments, Dr. Competent explores Multi's past assessment experiences as well as the limitations of assessments. He also validates Multi's hesitation to use assessments by sharing experiences of how he has seen unqualified individuals improperly interpret results and use instruments for purposes other than those for which they were intended. Dr. Competent discusses some of the historical misuses of assessments with underserved populations and explores Multi's goals for career counseling as well as how cultural, social, and economic factors could impact his career options.

They also discuss the process of transition from the FBI after 25 years to looking for a new career. Dr. Competent then explores Multi's views on receiving career counseling from someone who has only been in the workforce for a year. After mapping out the information Multi wants to obtain and providing him with information on populations the assessment had been used with, Dr. Competent gives Multi the option of choosing one of the assessments while Dr. Competent chooses another one. Multi appreciates the collaborative nature of the assessment and feels more comfortable with the assessment process as well as with Dr. Competent's skills.

This scenario illustrates some of the suggestions provided for developing a racial-cultural code. Dr. Competent was able to address the client's needs by exploring not only the cultural values and history of the client, but also by realizing how his own biases and values might impact the session. Evaluating the Ethics Code through a cultural lens, the counselor was able to address Multi's reluctance to take assessments. Dr. Competent functioned not only as counselor, but also as educator and advocate (Vera et al., this *Handbook,* this volume).

SUMMARY

There seems to be an overabundance of ethics training models that rely on didactic instruction by Code familiarity (i.e., review of the Ethics Code) and ethical dilemma resolution. There should be more training models that integrate ethics knowledge, client's cultural awareness, and trainee ethical decision-making strategies. Racial-cultural ethical codes promote ethically sound decision making in the context of racial-cultural practice that allows for the incorporation of personal values, psychological needs, and therapeutic dynamics (Hill, Glaser, & Harden, 1995).

These scenarios, though oversimplified, provide support for the argument that the Ethics Code needs to mandate that psychologists be culturally competent and that there be consequences for training programs that fail to provide culturally competent training components. The Code also needs to provide more specific guidelines for working with racial and ethnic minorities.

The approaches to addressing the limitations of the Ethics Code for racial-cultural practice have been varied. In their critique of the Ethics Code, some authors have suggested that the philosophical premise of the Code needs to be revised. In other instances, authors have suggested that the insertion of key phrases and explicit terminology would make the Ethics Code more useful in racial-cultural practice. Whatever the method of addressing the flaws and contradictions of the current Code, new models must be philosophically inclusive of diverse worldviews. Practitioners of psychology and counseling should be guided toward racial-cultural competence by their professional organizations, not just their personal priorities. Standardizing a level of care for racial-cultural practice, through both professional aspirations and enforceable mandates, will truly allow the spirit of the Ethics Code—protection of public welfare—to be realized for racial-cultural practices (Ridley & Mollen, this *Handbook*, this volume).

Since the writing of this manuscript, a joint project of APA Divisions 17 (Counseling Psychology) and 45 (Society for the Study of Ethnic Minority Issues), the Guidelines on Multicultural Education, Training, Research, Practice, and Organization for Psychologists, was adopted as policy by APA. Because of its newness, it is difficult to determine if this organizational policy will have an impact on filling gaps and resolving contradictions in racial-cultural practice. The guidelines represent a slow ascension toward recognizing the limits and possibility of providing psychological services to racially and culturally diverse populations. Of course, future studies are needed to investigate the implementation and utility of this new policy.

REFERENCES

American Psychological Association. (1990). Ethical principles of psychologists. *American Psychologist, 45,* 390–395.

American Psychological Association. (1992). Ethical principles of psychologists and code of conduct. *American Psychologist, 47,* 1597–1611.

American Psychological Association. (2002, October 8). *Ethical principles of psychologists and code of conduct.* Retrieved June 4, 2003, from http://www.apa.org Ethics Code 2002 doc.

American Psychological Association. (2003). Guidelines on multicultural education, training, research, practice, and organizational change for psychologists. *American Psychologist, 58,* 377–402.

American Psychological Association, Office of Ethnic Minority Affairs. (1991). *Guidelines for providers of psychological services to ethnic, linguistic, and culturally diverse populations* (pp. 464–481). Washington, DC: American Psychological Association.

Arredondo, P., & Arciniega, G. M. (2001). Strategies and techniques for counselor training based on the multicultural counseling competencies. *Journal of Multicultural Counseling and Development, 29,* 263–273.

Caldwell, L. D. (in preparation). *The influence of culture on the ethical decision-making process: Towards a cultural integrative paradigm shift.* Manuscript in preparation.

Casas, J. M., Ponterotto, J. G., & Gutierrez, J. M. (1986). An ethical indictment of counseling research and training: The cross-cultural perspective. *Journal of Counseling and Development, 64,* 347–349.

Casas, J. M., & Thompson, C. E. (1991). Ethical principles and standards: A racial-ethnic minority research perspective. *Counseling and Values, 35,* 186–195.

Cayleff, S. E. (1986). Ethical issues in counseling gender, race, and culturally distinct groups. *Journal of Counseling and Development, 64,* 345–352.

Corey, G., Corey, M. S., & Callanan, P. (1998). *Issues and ethics in the helping professions* (5th ed.). Pacific Grove, CA: Brooks/Cole.

D'Andrea, M., Daniels, J., & Heck, R. (1991). Evaluating the impact of multicultural counseling training. *Journal of Counseling and Development, 70,* 143–150.

Diaz-Lazaro, C. M., & Cohen, B. B. (2001). Cross-cultural contact in counseling training. *Journal of Multicultural Counseling and Development, 29,* 41–56.

Hill, M., Glaser, K., & Harden, J. (1995). A feminist model for ethical decision-making. In E. J. Rave & C. C. Larsen (Eds.), *Ethical decision-making in therapy: Feminist perspectives* (pp. 18–37). New York: Guilford Press.

Ibrahim, F. A., & Arredondo, P. M. (1986). Ethical standards for cross-cultural counseling: Counselor preparation, practice, assessment, and research. *Journal of Counseling and Development, 64,* 349–353.

Ibrahim, F. A., & Cameron, S. C. (in press). Racial-cultural ethical issues in research. In R. T. Carter (Ed.), H*andbook of racial-cultural psychology and counseling: Theory and research* (Vol. 1, pp. 391–413). Hoboken, NJ: Wiley.

Jacob, E. J., & Greggo, J. W. (2001). Using counselor training and collaborative programming strategies in working with intergenerational students. *Journal of Multicultural Counseling and Development, 77,* 294–302.

Kambon, K. K. K. (1998). *African/Black psychology in the American context: An African-centered approach.* Tallahassee, FL: Nubian Nation.

LaFromboise, T. D., & Foster, S. (1989). Ethics in multicultural counseling. In P. B. Pedersen & J. G. Draguns (Eds.), *Counseling across cultures* (3rd ed., pp. 115–136). Thousand Oaks, CA: Sage.

LaFromboise, T. D., Foster, S., & James, A. (1996). Ethics in multicultural counseling. In P. B. Pedersen, J. G. Draguns, W. J. Lonner, & J. E. Trimble (Eds.), *Counseling across cultures* (pp. 47–62). Thousand Oaks, CA: Sage.

Lerman, H., & Potter, N. (1990). The contribution of feminism to ethics in psychotherapy. In H. Lerman & N. Porter (Eds.), *Feminist ethics in psychotherapy.* New York: Springer.

Mabe, A. R., & Rollin, S. A. (1986). The role of a code of ethical standards in counseling. *Journal of Counseling and Development, 64,* 294–297.

McGinn, F., Flowers, C. R., & Rubin, S. E. (1994). In quest of an explicit multicultural emphasis in ethical standards for rehabilitation counselors. *Rehabilitation Education, 7,* 261–268.

Neville, H. A., Heppner, M. J., Louie, C. E., Thompson, C. E., Brooks, L., & Baker, C. E. (1996). The impact of multicultural training on white racial identity attitudes and therapy competencies. *Professional Psychology: Research and Practice, 27,* 83–89.

Parham, T. (1997). An African-centered view of dual relationships. In B. Herlihy & G. Corey (Eds.), *Boundary issues in counseling: Multiple roles and responsibilities* (pp. 109–111). Alexandria, VA: American Counseling Association.

Pedersen, P. B. (1989). Developing multicultural ethical guidelines for psychology. *International Journal of Psychology, 24,* 643–652.

Pedersen, P. B. (1995). Culture-centered ethical guidelines for counselors. In J. G. Ponterotto, J. M. Casas, L. A. Suzuki, & C. M. Alexander (Eds.), *Handbook of multicultural counseling* (pp. 34–49). Thousand Oaks, CA: Sage.

Pedersen, P. B. (1997). The cultural context of American Counseling Association code of ethics. *Journal of Counseling and Development, 76,* 23–28.

Pedersen, P. B., & Marsella, A. J. (1982). The ethical crisis for cross-cultural counseling and therapy. *Professional Psychology, 13,* 492–500.

Ponterotto, J. G., Casas, I. M., Suzuki, L. A., & Alexander, C. M. (Eds.). (1995). *Handbook of multicultural counseling.* Thousand Oaks, CA: Sage.

Ponterotto, J. G., Casas, I. M., Suzuki, L. A., & Alexander, C. M. (Eds.). (2001). *Handbook of multicultural counseling* (2nd ed.). Thousand Oaks, CA: Sage.

Ridley, C. R., Liddle, M. C., Hill, C., & Li, L. C. (2001). Ethical decision making in multicultural counseling. In J. G. Ponterotto, J. M. Casas, L. A. Suzuki, & C. M. Alexander (Eds.), *Handbook of multicultural counseling* (pp. 165–188). Thousand Oaks, CA: Sage.

Rooney, S. C., Flores, L. Y., & Mercier, C. A. (1998). Making multicultural education effective for everyone. *Counseling Psychologist, 26,* 22–32.

Steward, R. J. (1998). Connecting counselor self-efficacy and supervision self-efficacy: The continued search for counseling competence. *Counseling Psychologist, 26,* 285–294.

Sue, D. W. (1997). Multiple perspectives on multiple relationships. In B. Herlihy & G. Corey (Eds.), *Boundary issues in counseling: Multiple roles and responsibilities* (pp. 106–109). Alexandria, VA: American Counseling Association.

Sue, D. W., Arredondo, P., & McDavis, R. J. (1992). Multicultural counseling competencies and standards: A call to the profession. *Journal of Multicultural Counseling and Development, 20,* 64–88.

Terrell, F., & Terrell, S. (1981). An inventory to measure cultural mistrust among Blacks. *The Western Journal of Black Studies, 5,* 180–184.

Thomas, A., & Sillen, S. (1972). *Racism and psychiatry.* New York: Brunner-Mazel.

CHAPTER 31

Racial-Cultural Training and Practice Moving from Rhetoric to Reality: Summary and Conclusion

Robert T. Carter, Bryant Williams, and Alex Pieterse

Psychology is an integral aspect of the academic, health, and professional landscape of American society and as such is largely influenced and shaped by the social context of its time. In response to the social movements of the 1960s, which advocated for greater focus on civil rights, equality, and the recognition of marginalized peoples, professional psychology and counseling has increasingly, albeit slowly, highlighted the role of racial and cultural variables in the domains of scholarship, research, training, and practice. The slow pace of change might be due to psychology and counseling's legacy of racial-cultural oppression in combination with the field's desire to maintain the status quo. The establishment of such professional bodies as the Association of Black Psychologists, the Association of Multicultural Counseling and Development, the Asian American Psychological Association, the National Latino Psychological Association, and the Society for the Psychological Study of Ethnic Minority Issues–Division 45 of American Psychological Association (APA), are representative of the resistance of mainstream psychological and some counseling organizations to incorporating the views and experiences of people of Color. At the same time, the development of these organizations also represents in tangible ways how psychologists, counselors, and other mental health professionals have responded to Wrenn's (1962) call for counseling and the mental health field to move beyond "cultural encapsulation."

Another manifestation of the shift away from cultural encapsulation was the APA's publication of Multicultural Guidelines (2003) in the *American Psychologist,* which represented over 25 years of activism, dialogue, negotiation, and scholarship, largely undertaken by people of Color, to secure a more relevant and ethical approach to dealing with race and culture, especially in the area of applied psychology. However, the fact that the Multicultural Guidelines are only offered as suggestions and are in no way binding indicates that more work is to be done. The monumental task of creating the Multicultural Guidelines was frequently undertaken in the face of vocal criticism and institutional resistance (Sue et al., 1998), yet the researchers, scholars, and practitioners involved persevered and were not deterred from their objective. The publication of the guidelines (APA, 2003) represents an important step forward in psychology's attempt to become more inclusive of all of the people the discipline claims to serve. Additionally, the Multicultural Guidelines are indicative of psychology's struggle to gain a more accurate understanding of the full range of human experience as well as create and adopt service orientations and practices that are not racist or oppressive.

Another concrete manifestation of the struggle to move psychology and counseling forward as a science and applied discipline is the group of works contained in this volume, *The Handbook of Racial-Cultural Psychology and Counseling: Training and Practice.* The contributors to the present volume have offered the field a rich source of practical approaches designed to push the field beyond the rhetoric of racial-cultural issues to the reality of integrating and acknowledging race and culture in every facet of training and practice in applied psychology and counseling. In highlighting the ongoing needs of the field, the *Handbook* contributors have underscored the critical need for psychology and counseling to overcome their historical legacy and become accountable for their failures in regard to their mission to serve all people, thereby adopting theories, training modalities, and practices that meet the needs of people from all racial and cultural backgrounds (Department of Health and Human Services [DHHS], 2001). The collective works also note that although some change has occurred, there is still a long road ahead. As some of the volume's contributors have emphasized, the task of bringing race and culture to the center of psychological theory and practice is still in its nascent phases (Alvarez & Piper, this *Handbook,* this volume; Carter, this *Handbook,* this volume; Cokley, this *Handbook,* this volume; Thompson, this *Handbook,* this volume; Utsey et al., this *Handbook,* this volume). Perhaps the most pressing issue facing us concerns how to translate the growing body of racial-cultural scholarship and research into structural and systemic changes in mental health training and practice. The changes that the authors and other mental health professionals advocate for, and with which we concur, are not simply alterations to the façade of psychology, but deep constitutive changes that would allow for a paradigmatic shift in the practice and application of counseling, psychotherapy, and other forms of psychological and health interventions.

These chapters provide concrete suggestions for how to go about implementing many changes in how we train psychologists and provide services to individuals, families, groups, and organizations. The following summary highlights several themes that have emerged from our reading of the chapters in this volume, which we hope will serve to organize the vast amount of information provided in the *Handbook.* The themes include the ongoing need to use a racial-cultural context for understanding the human experience; the importance of practitioners and educators taking a self-reflective stance with regard to race and culture; concrete recommendations for how to bridge the gap between training and practice in racial-cultural psychology and counseling; and finally, overcoming systemic and structural barriers to racial-cultural competency.

THE RACIAL-CULTURAL CONTEXT OF THE HUMAN EXPERIENCE: AN ONGOING NEED

American society has, from its inception, been racially and culturally diverse. Racial and cultural differences have been treated by the dominant group as deviance, deprivation, and, even worse, inferiority. Because Whites have remained a numerical majority, they have held the power to define reality and so these notions were rarely challenged. Yet, as many of the contributors have noted, the demographics of U.S. society are rapidly changing, and people of Color will soon emerge as the numerical majority (e.g., Sue & Torino, this *Handbook,* this volume). Sue and Torino suggest that racial-cultural competence is therefore superordinate to the ability of psychologists and mental health professionals to attend to the needs of nondominant racial/ethnic groups. Highlighting research that indicates the underutilization of mental health services and an increased rate of premature termination by people of Color undergoing counseling, Sue and Torino (this *Handbook,* this volume), Faubert and Locke (this *Handbook,* this volume), and Carter (this *Handbook,* this volume) believe that the Eurocentric worldview that counseling and psychotherapy is built on presents an impediment to mental health professionals' efforts to be more relevant to the lives of individuals and communities they intend to serve. Furthermore, Cokley (this *Handbook,* this volume) charges, "If clinical work in psychology is to remain relevant in the lives of all people, it must recognize that the constructs of race and ethnicity should not be viewed as merely demographic characteristics" (p. 260).

The importance of race and culture as psychological and social constructs that directly influence all aspects of human development and experience is a reality that has yet to become an integral aspect of theory building and psychotherapeutic intervention. In emphasizing the need for a shift in training approaches, Ota Wang (this *Handbook,* this volume) and Wallace (this *Handbook,* this volume) remind us that psychological theory has real effects on real people's lives. Ota Wang states, "Limited and insular theories and training models coupled with inexperienced professionals have perpetuated inequities and have continued disparities in educational achievement, mental health, and general well-being of" many people (p. 80). If indeed "racial and cultural factors are an integral part of daily life" (McRae & Short, this *Handbook,* this volume), then the structures of domination and oppression that have been cultivated and sustained in American society need to be incorporated in the understanding of interpersonal processes, as highlighted by Carter (this *Handbook,* this volume) and Thompson (this *Handbook,* this volume). While Alderfer (this *Handbook,* this volume), Carter (this *Handbook,* this volume), and Ponterotto and Austin (this *Handbook,* this volume) document an encouraging shift in the quantity and type of racial-cultural training, it is evident from their chapters that the majority of counselor training programs still do not adhere to nor have they implemented an integrated approach to racial-cultural training.

In the area of postdoctoral training, the focus on race and culture is even more sporadic. Ridley and Mollen (this *Handbook,* this volume) indicate that a psychologist can easily undergo advanced postdoctoral training without any exposure to issues pertaining to the development of racial-cultural competence. In making racial-cultural competence superordinate to general counselor or mental health professional competence, Ridley and Mollen advocate for a standardized approach to postdoctoral training that would include racial-cultural competence as part of state licensure and continuing education. Additionally, Ridley and Mollen emphasize the need for a top-down approach, that is, for institutional administrators to be more proactive in the formation of comprehensive postdoctoral training models for racial-cultural inclusion.

SELF-REFLECTION AS A CONSTANT FOR RACIAL-CULTURAL COMPETENCE

Carter (this *Handbook,* this volume), Ota Wang (this *Handbook,* this volume), Chen (this *Handbook,* this volume), Liu and Pope-Davis (this *Handbook,* this volume), Wallace (this *Handbook,* this volume), and Reynolds (this *Handbook,* this volume) draw attention to the role of personal examination in racial-cultural competence. Carter advocates for the appreciation of racial and cultural socialization processes as important aspects of an individual's personality. Furthermore, he argues that psychologists and counselors can appreciate the significance of race and culture in the lives of their clients only if they have been able to acknowledge and understand the impact of racial-cultural factors in their own lives. The imperative for practitioners to engage in an authentic and genuine exploration of personal biases, worldviews, and cultural assumptions that shape our day-to-day interactions is a prerequisite to understanding how racial-cultural factors in turn shape the interactions in therapeutic service provision. The importance of this type of self-examination is underscored by both Chen and Reynolds in their discussions of various aspects of the supervisory relationship. It is now a distinct possibility that some recent trainees could emerge from their initial training with a greater appreciation and understanding of racial-cultural factors than their supervisors. The contributions of Chen and Reynolds dovetail with the work of other scholars who have recently addressed the dilemmas that accompany this dynamic (Helms & Cook, 1999).

BRIDGING THE GAP BETWEEN TRAINING AND PRACTICE IN RACIAL-CULTURAL PSYCHOLOGY AND COUNSELING

As the *Handbook* contributors note, one of the problems still facing racial-cultural psychology and counseling is the gap between training and practice. The chapters on assessment and diagnosis, offered by Buckley and Franklin (this *Handbook,* this volume), Suzuki, Kugler, and Aguiar (this *Handbook,* this volume), Richardson and Frey (this *Handbook,* this volume), and Branch (this *Handbook,* this volume), highlight that although mental health trainees may be instructed to consider the influence of race and culture on psychological process in their educational programs, the tools they are given to assess and diagnosis their clients once they begin practicing are so riddled with Eurocentric biases that they preclude the possibility of adequately attending to the reality of race and culture in their clients'/patients' lives. For example, the *DSM-IV-TR,* which is the tool used to diagnosis clients in most practice settings, continues to relegate cultural syndromes to an appendix (Buckley & Franklin, this *Handbook,* this volume). This reflects the fact that the influence of race and culture is not considered to be a priority, or even a consideration, when clinicians are assigning a diagnosis (see Carter, Forsyth, Mazzula, & Williams, this *Handbook,* this volume). Similarly, the established practices and procedures and even the psychological tests themselves that are used in psychological assessment are inherently Eurocentric in nature (Branch, this *Handbook,* this volume; Suzuki et al., this *Handbook,* this volume). Therefore, the structure of the testing situation (evaluator and client interactions) and the actual format of the tests (time limitations, bonus points for speed) inhibit even well-trained clinicians from practicing in a racially-culturally competent fashion.

Despite the ongoing gaps that exist between training and practice, the authors of the *Handbook* provide recommendations for how to translate what is learned in training programs to applied settings (e.g., Ihle-Helledy et al., this *Handbook,* this volume). In Hurdle's (this *Handbook,* this volume) chapter on group work, she suggests that in the initial group meeting, rather than request that clients speak about themselves personally, storytelling can be used to build rapport among strangers. She posits that many cultures utilize metaphors as a means of referring to sensitive issues, which allows group members to focus on "an external protagonist rather than the client's personal issues" (p. 357). The gap between training and practice is also addressed in the context of couples and family counseling in Thomas's (this *Handbook,* this volume) and Miehls's (this *Handbook,* this volume) chapters. Both authors provide case studies in which racial-cultural psychological theory is applied to assist clients in dealing with racial identity issues, generational conflicts, and racial dynamics in therapy. Thomas describes the process of addressing race and culture directly in working with a White family who, like many Whites, deny the relevance of their race and culture. In her chapter on immigration, Arredondo (this *Handbook,* this volume) recommends incorporating a psychohistorical perspective by taking into consideration a client's pre- to postimmigration experiences. Like that of Alvarez and Piper (this *Handbook,* this volume), her model is exemplary of bridging the gap between training and practice because she provides concrete suggestions for the questions that can be used to assess the impact of immigration on a client's current functioning as well as differentiate its influence from other clinical syndromes.

These and the other authors' chapters have outlined some of the steps necessary to move from rhetoric about race and culture to the reality of changing the way psychologists, psychiatrists, social workers, and counselors practice. Building on the work that has been done answering the question of why racial-cultural competence is needed, the *Handbook* scholars answer the more crucial question of how. Because these scholars have offered concrete suggestions for how to improve the delivery of mental health services, the field no longer has the excuse that these ideas regarding racial and cultural competence are well and good, but can they really be translated in a way that actually informs practice?

OVERCOMING SYSTEMIC AND STRUCTURAL BARRIERS TO RACIAL-CULTURAL COMPETENCY

As our contributors highlight, one of the major factors that inhibits the implementation of racially-culturally competent practices are the systemic and structural barriers that exist in the counseling centers, clinics, and hospital settings where mental health professionals practice. As racial-cultural researchers, scholars, and practitioners struggled to bring to the fore the notion that psychological processes occur in the context of race and culture, they were often met with overt resistance to their suggestions that policy and procedural changes needed to take place if a real transformation was to occur. The resistance to the inclusion of a racial and cultural framework in the field's theoretical models and intervention strategies is a manifestation of the ongoing racism that exists at the level of institutions and social and political policy.

Dobbins and Skillings's (this *Handbook,* this volume) chapter on White racism suggests that one reason these institutional and sociopolitical barriers are perpetuated is that racism is perceived as a problem for people of Color. This conceptual mistake or, perhaps more accurate, evasion maintains institutional racist structures and policies by "blaming the victim" (Carter, this *Handbook,* this volume; Ryan, 1976). Dobbins and Skillings posit that in reality, racism is a "White person's problem," and they cite scholars who emphasize "that 'people of Color can resist racism, but only White people can eliminate racism'" (p. 428). They also note that White privilege is a type of addiction to institutional power, by which the dominant culture can perpetuate the status quo through the hording of the authority to define reality by keeping the sociopolitical and institutional policies, rules, and structures intact. Their recommendations for overcoming the institutional barriers lie in conceptualizing racism as an addiction or an abuse of power that White people have. Subsequently, Dobbins and Skillings contend that racism has a detrimental effect on White people (Bowser & Hunt, 1996). This approach shifts the focus away from people of Color and holds individual White people responsible for combating racism. They propose a step-by-step treatment model to assist Whites in their recovery from the addiction to power based on racism. Dobbins and Skillings's work is important because it holds the institutions accountable for the perpetuation of racism by focusing on the individuals that actually commit the acts of racism. Similarly, Carter et al. (this *Handbook,* this volume) show how people who are the targets of racism are psychologically and emotional effected. Thus, these scholars demonstrate the mental health cost to both the targets and the perpetrators of racist institutional policies and procedures.

Another strategy for overcoming the barriers to racial-cultural competency is proposed in Vera, Buhin, Montgomery, and Shin's (this *Handbook,* this volume) chapter on outreach, advocacy, and prevention for people of Color. Vera et al. note that the systems that are designed to assist people of Color are often built on racist and oppressive ideologies, which can result in further harm to those who seek help. Additionally, the traditional services offered by many clinics often are not designed to adequately meet the needs of all of the people who are in need of services. As a result, if clinicians are to offer effective services, they must move beyond the traditional helping roles based on White American cultural patterns and participate in client advocacy and outreach. These roles require that the clinician offer concrete assistance such as referrals for legal or financial services or offering the client "home-based therapy" outside of the hospital or clinic. Vera and colleagues' recommendations can potentially help to overcome the sociopolitical and institutional barriers to racial-cultural competence through transforming the definitions of the types of activities that constitute help. Expanding the roles of mental health professionals may make mental health services more available and more appealing to a wider range of people and may reduce the well-documented disparities that exist in mental health services (DHHS, 2001).

Evans, Delphin, Simmons, Omar, and Tebes's chapter (this *Handbook,* this volume) addresses the systemic barriers to racial-cultural competence through outlining the changes to the policies and practices that are currently being enacted by the State of Connecticut's Department of Mental Health and Addiction Services (DMHAS). The chapter is unique and inspiring: What they outline is not hypothetical; rather, it is actually currently being implemented. In the chapter, Evans and colleagues outline the specific strategies that were adopted to transform the DMHAS into an entity that is capable of delivering racially-culturally competent care designed to reduce racial disparities in behavioral health access and outcome. This involved the implementation of strategic modifications to their organization on two levels: internal, or changs in the institution's policies and procedures, and external, involving activities outside of the organization "designed to ensure access and effective services for people from various cultural backgrounds" (p. 501). Evans and his colleagues' work at DMHAS is commendable and provides an excellent example of how to move from the dialogue about the importance of racial-cultural competence to the reality of changing how services are implemented. Their work highlights the importance of focusing on the level of competence possessed by institutions and organizations as well as the individuals within them.

Recommendations for overcoming the systemic and structural barriers to racial-cultural competence are also outlined in Caldwell and Tarver's (this *Handbook,* this volume) chapter on ethics. They note that the current Ethical Code of APA can inhibit our development of racial-cultural competence. They call for specific changes to the ethical codes developed by the profession to eliminate contradictions with the leading racial-cultural scholars regarding the development of racial-cultural competency. Their chapter is noteworthy because it deals specifically with the institutional barriers that exist within the profession of psychology.

CONCLUSION

The chapters that constitute this volume provide substantial evidence that race and culture together form the context in which the human experience occurs. The models, frameworks, illustrations, and suggestions offered by the *Handbook* authors represent an important and necessary ingredient in the ongoing attempt to make racial-cultural factors more central in the training and practice of psychologists. Collectively, the contributors have claimed that without thorough training in how race and cultural impact psychological processes, mental health professionals will be at a loss to provide effective services. We are, therefore, hopeful that this volume will serve as a useful bridge as the field moves closer to the reality of racial-cultural integration and thereby allow psychology, counseling, and other helping professions to become more consistent with the lived experiences of their consumers.

REFERENCES

American Psychological Association. (2003). Guidelines on multicultural education, training, research, practice, and organizational change for psychologists. *American Psychologist, 58,* 377–402.

Bowser, B. P., & Hunt, R. G. (1996). *Impacts of racism on White Americans* (2nd ed.). Thousand Oaks, CA: Sage.

Helms, J., & Cook, D. (1999). *Using Race and Culture in Counseling and Psychotherapy.* Boston: Allyn & Bacon.

Ryan, W. (1976). *Blaming the victim.* New York: Vintage Books.

Sue, D. W., Carter, R. T., Casas, J. M., Fouad, N. A., Ivey, A. E., Jensen, M., et al. (1998). *Multicultural counseling competencies: Individual and organizational development.* Thousand Oaks, CA: Sage.

U.S. Department of Health and Human Service. (2001). *Mental health: Culture, race, and ethnicity—A supplement to Mental health: A report of the Surgeon General.* Rockville, MD: U.S. Department of Health and Human Services, Substance Abuse and Mental Health Services Administration, Center for Mental Health Services.

Wren, G. (1962). The culturally encapsulated counselor. *Harvard Educational Review, 32,* 444–459.

Author Index

Subject Index